SONDHEIM AND LLOYD-WEBBER

The Great Songwriters Series

Noel and Cole: *The Sophisticates*

The Wordsmiths: *Oscar Hammerstein 2nd* and *Alan Jay Lerner*

Sondheim and Lloyd-Webber: *The New Musical*

Other Books

Play It Again, Sam—By Ear (*A Piano Method*)

The Paderewski Memoirs (*Editor*)

The Inn and Us (*with Anne Edwards*)

Songwriting: *A Complete Guide to the Craft*

The Musical: *From the Inside Out*

SONDHEIM AND LLOYD-WEBBER

The New Musical

STEPHEN CITRON

Chatto & Windus
LONDON

Published by Chatto & Windus 2001

First published in the USA in 2001 by
Oxford University Press

2 4 6 8 10 9 7 5 3 1

First published in Great Britain in 2001 by
Chatto & Windus
Random House, 20 Vauxhall Bridge Road, London SW1V 2SA

Random House Australia (Pty) Limited
20 Alfred Street, Milsons Point, Sydney,
New South Wales 2061, Australia

Random House New Zealand Limited
18 Poland Road, Glenfield,
Auckland 10, New Zealand

Random House (Pty) Limited
Endulini, 5A Jubilee Road, Parktown 2193, South Africa

The Random House Group Limited Reg. No. 954009
www.randomhouse.co.uk

A CIP catalogue record for this book is available from the British Library

ISBN 1 85619 273 3

Papers used by Random House are natural,
recyclable products made from wood grown in sustainable forests.
The manufacturing processes conform to the environmental
regulations of the country of origin

Printed and bound in Great Britain by
Biddles Ltd, Guildford

For
THOMAS Z. SHEPARD
whose music and recordings
have enriched the lives
of so many,
and whose enduring friendship
is my own special dividend

Acknowledgments

Few will disagree that in the latter half of the twentieth century the direction of musical theater in the United States and England was steered by Stephen Sondheim and Andrew Lloyd-Webber. To each of these colossi my most profound thanks for reading through the manuscript and making suggestions for change or accuracy. Don Black, who has worked on many projects with Andrew Lloyd-Webber, is a superb lyricist and a dear friend who has also been most helpful. Thanks too to other creative musical experts who have contributed ideas and information—Charles Strouse, Jerry Bock, Richard Maltby Jr., Jerry Herman—and to those who have worked with Stephen Sondheim—the late Flora Roberts and Paul McKibbins, who cleared rights at Rilting Music, and David Robinson, Paul's opposite member at The Really Useful Group.

For an informative interview on workshopping a musical I thank composer-lyricist Susan Burkenhead, and for their discussions of orchestration and orchestral balance my thanks go to Luther Henderson, Mark Dorrell, Don Pippin, Jonathan Tunick, and Paul Gemigniani. My thanks also go to Julia McKenzie, a superb Mrs. Lovett in the Royal National Theater's *Sweeney Todd*, who gave me a most interesting take on interpreting the role. Thanks to Sally Ann Howes, who made the role of Desirée her own in the New York City Opera's production of *A Little Night Music* and also gave me insight into my personal favorite Sondheim musical.

My gratitude to Louise Gold, who gave me an interesting interview on the London revisions to *Assassins;* to Myra Sands, who brought insight into her role in *Jesus Christ Superstar* and shared her thoughts with me; and to Susanna Fellowes, who did the same after starring in Lloyd-Webber's *Aspects of Love*. Thanks to David Kernan, Ned Sherrin, and Millicent Martin, each of whom told me about his or her involvement with the creation of *Side by Side by Sondheim*.

I came to know Michael Kerker, who runs the ASCAP Workshop, through my longtime friend Madeline Gilford, whose encyclopedic knowledge of what's the news on the Rialto is truly astounding. Michael put me in touch with many of the young writers who we both felt will be steering musicals in the future. I interviewed several and thank Douglas Bernstein, Dennis Markell, Brad Ross, and Joe Keenan for sharing their candid ideas and playing me their fresh and original scores.

Sheridan Morley and Ruth Leon are both splendid chroniclers of the theater in general and musicals in particular. For their treasured friendship and for the interviews with musical personalities they shared with me, I am grateful.

For an informative interview concerning Andrew Lloyd-Webber's extensive collection of pre-Raphaelite paintings I am indebted to Jason Rosenfeld, the Tate Gallery's lecturer and authority on the subject.

Certainly a book of this scope needs a great deal of technical assistance, and I am fortunate enough to have had a double measure—Christopher Sinclair-Stevenson in London, who believed in this series from the outset, and his counterpart in New York, Sheldon Meyer, editor emeritus of Oxford University Press, who stood behind the book even when its publication was delayed. Both men have read and reread the manuscript, always offering helpful suggestions, and to them goes my deep thanks. Others at OUP who were helpful are Andrew Albanese, Woody Gilmartin, Susan Day, Penelope Ander-son, and Charles Sterne, Joellyn Ausanka goes far beyond her official title of production editor, as she has that rare combination of talents: an eagle's eye for spotting inconsistencies in the text, a superb sense of grammar, and, best of all, a fine-tuned musical background. She went over the manuscript twice: before Stephen Sondheim and Andrew Lloyd-Webber commented on the text as well as after. For her collaboration, a deep bow. At the New Milford Library, Carl DiMillia facilitated my research, and at the Library of Congress, Elizabeth Auman, Ray White, Mark Horowitz, Charles Sens, Stephen Soderberg, and Walter Zvonchenko did the same. Marty Jacobs at the Museum of the City of New York gets my thanks for his help with the pictures.

David Van Eysen talked to me about Westminster School, where Andrew Lloyd-Webber spent his early years, and Gouverneur Cadwallader, Lawrence Nusbaum, Barbara Obarski, Kingdon Swain, and Lt. Col. Calvin Fenton gave me much help in researching Stephen Sondheim's school years.

David LeVine, former Executive Director of The Dramatists Guild, gave me much advice about musicals during his time there when Stephen Sondheim was also an officer. Mitchell Douglas is a literary agent by profession and a man of the theater by inclination. Besides supplying me with rare Sondheim and Lloyd-Webber recordings and videos, he gave me new insights into musicals in general. Thomas Z. Shepard is not only the book's dedicatee, but a dear friend and a superb musician who is responsible for the finest cast albums of musicals of the century. Because he has produced albums devoted to both the protagonists of this book, his formal and informal interviews were full of information and ideas.

I should also like to thank the following for their help in various capacities. They are listed below in alphabetical order:

Dr. Leo Altschul, Milton Babbitt, Christine Baranski, Marion Bell, David Brown, Lila Burkeman, Sally Carr, Andrea Chapin, Irene Clark, Bert Fink, Joan Fisher, Ian Marshall Fisher, Margaret Gardner, Susan Granger, Benny Green, James Hammerstein, William Hammerstein, Roberta Hansen, Sheldon Harnick, Kitty Carlisle Hart, Jim Henney, Mary Vann Hughes, Evan Hunter, Maurice Keller, Louise Kerz, William Kinsolving, Larry Kramer, Arthur Laurents, Richard Lawrence, Jerome Lawrence, Julian Lloyd Webber, Alice Hammerstein Mathias, Delphine Marcus, Elizabeth Markowitz, Ruth Mitchell, Dick Moore, Tarquin Olivier, Robert Osborne, Jane Powell, Dory Previn, Hal Prince, Douglas Rae, Rex Reed, Chita Rivera, Paul Salsini, Jonathan Schwartz, Robert Shanks, Rose Tobias Shaw, Leonard Soloway, Faith Stewart-Gordon, Mark Steyn, Jerry Stiller, Haila Stoddard, Dr. Joseph Sumo, K. T. Sullivan, Ion Trewin, Simon Trewin, Rick Ulfick, Caroline Underwood, and Betty Walberg.

To my son, Alexander Citron, a fine musician who becomes more of a colleague with each passing year, many thanks for preparing the voluminous musical and lyrical examples in this text.

Finally, and most important, to my wife, Anne Edwards, who has always taken time away from the book she was working on to listen to a Sondheim or Lloyd-Webber gem I had excitedly just discovered or to read and reread my latest chapter and make cogent and constructive suggestions, my deep gratitude and deepest abiding love.

Beverly Hills, California   S. C.
March 2001

Contents

SONDHEIM AND LLOYD-WEBBER

The New Musical

CHANGES IN MUSICAL THEATER evolve so slowly that one is reminded of an old garment district story. A mass-producing Seventh Avenue dress manufacturer who was queried by his designer about the line for the coming season answered enigmatically, "I want it should be the same—only different."

So it is with Broadway and the West End. The ever-spiraling costs of producing an evening of song and dance have always made producers wary of change. In the past, when changes occurred, they came slowly enough not to alienate the tourists on holiday, the couple on a night out away from baby bottles and diapers, or the tired businessmen, all of whom, along with the dedicated theatergoer, are the main support of the box office.

Yet one only has to set fine and successful shows like *No, No, Nanette, Anything Goes, Babes in Arms, Girl Crazy, Hit the Deck, Roberta, On Your Toes, Cabin in the Sky, Gentlemen Prefer Blondes, Oliver, Guys and Dolls, Bells Are Ringing, Finian's Rainbow,* or *Brigadoon* next to the musicals of the current era to be aware that (apart from revivals where the producer plays safe) the theater has moved on. If we look carefully we will see that it has done a total about-face. Musicals like *A Chorus Line, Baby, Hair, Grease, La Cage aux Folles, Jesus Christ Superstar, Starlight Express, Tommy, Cats, Blood Brothers, Falsettos, Sweeney Todd, Miss Saigon, Kiss of the Spider Woman, Into the Woods, Beauty and the Beast,* and *Passion*—and certainly *Rent, Bring in 'da Noise, Bring in 'da Funk Contact, Jekyll and Hyde, The Lion King, Aida, The Full Monty,* and *Parade*—could never have been produced in an era earlier than the one in which they were actually presented.

The appearance of these kinds of *new* musicals was due to several things that happened so gradually that the theatergoing public was hardly aware of them. Cumulatively, over the last thirty years they brought about the 180-degree change that separates the earlier listed group from the current one. They represent (1) a rapprochement between popular music and theater music; (2) the tremendous advancement of stagecraft technology; (3) a reassessment of morality; and (4) the realization among the producing faculty, especially as costs rose, of the many advantages of workshopping, touring, and previewing to sculpt the raw materials of a production into a professional show.

Most of this transformation is due to the public's redefinition of what they have come to expect from an evening of musical theater and the willingness of librettists, lyricists, composers, choreographers, set and costume designers, and even sound engineers to let them have that experience. (That does not imply that it has been a mindless sell-out. The musical of the current generation has gone in several directions: of oversized theatricality as represented by Andrew Lloyd-Webber or Claude-Michel Schönberg and Alain Boublil; of intellectual stimulation as exemplified by Stephen Sondheim and perhaps William Finn, John La Chiusa, and Adam Guetell; of revivals, because the American musical theater did produce some masterpieces that, like opera, are constantly in need of dusting off and reconception; and, in a belated attempt to entice younger audiences, of rock and pop retrospective.)

To examine the phenomena that brought about these changes, one must understand a bit about the musical's evolution, and to do that it will be necessary to reassess the shows of the era between the '20s and the '60s and compare the musicals of those decades with those today.

It was a time when plot was secondary. Diversion was the byword in the earlier days, while songs that moved the plot forward were barely tolerated. Audiences accustomed to operetta's lack of realism had come to expect simplistic stories in musical comedy; they knew these bits of dialogue were inserted only to give the performers and audience a respite between musical numbers. If a song was good and its creators believed in it, they had no qualms about writing a few lines to make it fit into several succeeding shows until it found its audience. "The Man I Love," perhaps the Gershwins' most splendid song, was in and out of three shows before it settled down in *Strike Up the Band*. "Bill," by Wodehouse and Kern, suffered the indignity of having been ejected from as many musicals— once even having been sung by a panhandler to his last dollar bill.

The restless public of the Jazz Age made the '20s to '40s the heyday of the revue. Intimate or topical, these entertainments dispensed entirely with believable plot in favor of songs, dances, and sketches. The form was not a total waste, however, for it often spawned new talent and introduced many of the songs we think of as standards today.

Popular music, songs written outside the theater to be performed on radio or in the movies, was marching along beside theatrical offerings and was not so different from the tunes that emerged from Broadway. The man on the street could not tell which songs that made the Lucky Strike Hit Parade (equivalent to today's Top 40) had their roots in the musical stage. Nor did he care. If you asked him which of the triumvirate of composer, lyricist, or librettist was the least important to a musical's success; assuming he knew what the word "librettist" meant; he would certainly point to the one who writes the story as being low man on the totem pole.

"Hit" was the byword. Even the most altruistic producers were not above interpolating works of other composers into their shows as insurance that the familiarity would generate a flurry at the box office. Over the vociferous objection of Rodgers and Hart, who were well known then, Florenz Ziegfeld slapped them in the face by interpolating Irving Berlin's megahit "Blue Skies" into their score for *Betsy*. When Cole Porter's songs for *The Greenwich Village Follies* did not catch on after the first few performances, producer Raymond Hitchcock replaced them one by one until nothing remained of Porter's excellent score.

All this searching for the hit song led composers and lyricists to direct their art not toward character development but toward the goal of having as many hits per show as possible. Rodgers and Hart's *Babes in Arms* produced five memorable standards, "My Funny Valentine," "The Lady Is a Tramp," "Where or When," "Johnny One-Note," and "I Wish I Were in Love Again," as well as the minor miracles "Way Out West on West End Avenue" and the title song. Cole Porter's *Anything Goes* did not lag far behind, with "I Get a Kick Out of You," "All Through the Night," "You're the Top," "Blow, Gabriel, Blow,"[1] "Be Like the Bluebird," and its title song. In both shows, megahits overcame their dreadfully contrived librettos.

Jule Styne once remembered "when we could walk into a record company and say, 'Here it is: So-and-so will record this number and so-and-so will do that one.' And you had eight singles before the show opened."

Change came rapidly and drastically as the growth of television spelled the demise of the revue, which was far more appropriate to the cabaret and thus found an ideal medium on the small screen rather than a cavernous theater. Well-known performers could now be invited into one's living room for a no-charge evening at home. Eventually these mostly one-person extravaganzas dried

---

[1] To illustrate how little importance was paid to the validity of story one might recall that "Blow, Gabriel, Blow," a clear candidate for hit status, was written long before *Anything Goes* was conceived. When Ethel Merman, whose clarion voice was ideal to "sell" the song, was cast in the leading role of high-living Reno Sweeney, it was decided that the only way she could get away with blasting out a number with biblical references would be to make her a former gospel singer. It made no sense, but it generated a memorable musical moment.

up as well. Nowadays, a single song sung by a celebrity on a late night talk show
is more than enough to satisfy an impatient public.

Stephen Sondheim recalls "going to *Hello, Dolly!* when the title song was
already a hit. The feeling the audience had was of welcoming an old friend.
That doesn't happen any more. Today some of the biggest hit shows don't have
any hit songs." (Or they have only one, as *Cats*'s "Memory," *Evita*'s "Don't Cry
for Me Argentina," *Les Misérables*' "On My Own," and Sondheim's almost accidental hit from *A Little Night Music*, "Send in the Clowns.")

With hit songs gone, the musical stage soon began to adapt to telling a story
in believable terms rather than building up its number of hummable songs. That
change from as-many-hits-as-possible to songs that elucidated a character soon
became the goal. Perhaps Sheldon Harnick's remembrance of a conversation he
had with Marvin Hamlisch best illustrates the current thinking about hits, at
least on Broadway:

> He [Marvin Hamlisch] had never done a show, and he was working with the very
> gifted lyric writer and composer Ed Kleban [on *A Chorus Line*]. They articulated
> the fact that they had a choice; they could have tried to write songs which might
> have had a chance in the commercial record market; or they could let Michael
> Bennett steer them in very specific directions toward songs which would probably
> be limited to their use in the show. They made the wise decision that they couldn't
> be in better hands than Michael's. They listened to him and they wrote numbers
> which served the show exclusively. They made the decision right at the top not to
> worry about what songs might be recorded but instead to ask themselves what is
> the situation. What would these characters say? What's going to be effective on
> stage? How can we serve the *show*? Only the last song, "What I Did for Love," was
> an attempt to go for that hit. The show itself is an extraordinary knitting together
> of all theater elements. I can't help feeling that Hamlisch and Kleban made abso-
> lutely the right decision.

But if *A Chorus Line* has only one genuine song hit, "What I Did for Love,"
that song has a contemporary feel to it and is just as much at home in the soft
rock interpretation it generally gets offstage. So too are the songs of Andrew
Lloyd-Webber; however, those of Stephen Sondheim, depending heavily on
their lyrical content, seem more comfortable when extracted from the plot and
placed in the theatrical or cabaret setting they are usually given.

With the growth of rhythm and blues which receives its cumulative effect
from repetition, the clever line, the sensitive lyric—always underplayed in the
musicals—became redundant. Rock and country, too, took a divergent path that
only occasionally (in shows like *The Wiz, Hair,* or *Tommy*) led to the theater.

Propelled by Andrew Lloyd-Webber's superhit songs, the presence of a super-
force like the Disney Organization, which has taken over a segment of Broadway,
and Barbra Streisand's successful Broadway albums, a potpourri that does not

exactly fall into the category of show music but which I would rather call a recording extravaganza, there seems to be a reaching out, a glimmer of hope— especially because of hits like *Rent*, *Aida*, and *Jekyll and Hyde*—that however temporary the rapprochement is, musicals and popular music are once again looking to shake hands.

The second area of great change in the musical theater came in technology. One must also think of those earlier shows to realize the differences in the *new* musical.

In the earliest years of this century, although the technology in most theaters was unwieldy and slow, certain houses were noted for their spectacular display. Among the largest was the Hippodrome on Sixth Avenue, known since the beginning of the century for its extravaganzas. On its gigantic stage, capable of holding a thousand people, Billy Rose presented his enormous production of Rodgers and Hart's *Jumbo*. The Center Theater, across from the Radio City Music Hall, was also built for lavish productions. In one of the grander moments in *The Great Waltz*, a Viennese café is transformed into a sumptuous ballroom before the audience's eyes. The entire orchestra of fifty is raised from the pit below the stage and ensconced in a balcony at the rear of the set.

But as the depression of the '30s deepened and it was realized the movies were not going to go away, these big theaters, profitable only in the evening, and with their costly mechanical contrivances needing scores of stagehands, were torn down to make room for office buildings.

By the '40s, the musical had become smaller, brighter, and more intimate. It also developed a technical formula. De rigueur it began with a lavish number for the full company.[2] Ensuing small scenes were often played in one (stage front) while the next set was being flown in and anchored. A traveler, a curtain that moved across the stage, or a drop hid all the activity behind. For aesthetic balance, slow numbers alternated with fast ones, and solos were followed by ensembles with formulaic regularity. The last scene of the first act and the first of the second were usually the most opulent, and those few theatergoers who kept to their seats during the intermission could hear the carpenters industriously hammering the second act sets into place.

But sooner than they imagined, in the '30s, producers realized that musicals could not survive even if their oversized theaters were pulled down. Musicals would have to face the competition from movies. Having been offered enormous fees for their scores for movies, Broadway's composers and lyricists shuttled back and forth between the coasts. Soon stars of the caliber of Al Jolson, Maurice

[2] In 1943 *Oklahoma!*'s opening, with a lone cowboy singing a capella about what a beautiful mornin' it was, was considered sheer folly by the producing fraternity.

Chevalier, and Grace Moore alternated appearances in New York with their movie making. Some, such as Fred Astaire, Bob Hope, and Cary Grant, who had made a name on Broadway, opted to stay permanently in the land of perpetual sunshine.

Hollywood began developing its own stable of musical stars: Judy Garland, Alan Jones, Jeanette MacDonald, June Allyson, Van Johnson, Jane Powell, and, later, Leslie Caron. It was helpful but not essential that movie musical luminaries be able to sing. Rita Hayworth, Leslie Caron, and Audrey Hepburn would all have others dub in their sound tracks.

The public too took the lavishness of cinema for granted, always realizing that the musical stage was no match for a dozen chorines singing while apparently standing on an airplane wing and flying down to Rio. They understood that those beauties were not insouciantly floating several thousand feet in the air, but that a photographed landscape was moving behind them and a wind machine was whirring gently enough in front of them to ripple their dresses but not to ruffle their hair much. It became clear to all that a Busby Berkeley extravaganza can only be possible if the audience was privileged enough to see it through the camera's eye.

Eventually Broadway and the West End realized it was a losing battle and understood that musicals and cinema[3] were different arts. Musicals finally accepted the limitations of the stage and began counting on, as Noël Coward says, "their flesh and blood quality."

They had always known they weren't privileged to burn up the set (even an obsolete one, as Selznick did when filming *Gone With the Wind*). Another would be needed for tomorrow's matinee. Nor could musicals make miniatures to photograph and later enlarge as Hollywood so frequently does. Any desired technical upheaval on stage had to be stylized. Designers began using their imaginations to make a fanciful suggestion of a car or a train. Animals as in *Man of La Mancha* or *Camelot* or *The Lion King* are far more amusing if made of wire or papiermâché.[4] Any changes must be worked into the production as part of the atmosphere or permanent stage illusion.

How then to justify the chutzpa of a producer who requests the theater prac-

---

[3] Perhaps the prime example of this realization is Bob Fosse's cinema version of *Cabaret* as differentiated from Hal Prince's stage version. Each is brilliant, valid, and eminently suitable to its medium.

[4] Although *Annie* and *Beauty and the Beast* do use animals, musicals generally prefer to stylize them, keeping costs down while avoiding risks. The last preview of *Funny Girl* was near disastrous because (according to John Patrick) Barbra Streisand was unable to control the pair of Russian wolfhounds that led her on stage. The dogs were not used at the premiere. Worse was the opening night fiasco of a musicalization of the *Three Musketeers*. A nervous horse defecated on stage during the first act, and the unfortunate cast had to play around the pile until the curtain was able to be brought down.

tically be torn down and reassembled as was necessary in the restaging of a succès d'estime but box-office flop like *Candide?* Hal Prince's vision, which saw Voltaire's picaresque tale as a basic treatise on the human circus, insisted his production be played out on multiple stages or rings. It called for the venue to be turned into a big-top, complete with sideshows.[5] Luckily it paid off and is responsible for a trend.

This kind of thinking opened new routes for the musical. It did not need hundreds of extras like Hollywood demanded for its gigantic productions. The rethinking of technology brought on a theater that spins, giving the audience the view they might get while walking through a back alley. It happens nightly and twice on Tuesdays at the West End's New London Theatre, where *Cats* has been holding out for almost twenty years.

These feats were precursors in the technical explosion that could run humans impersonating trains on tracks through the audience as was done in *Starlight Express* or enlarge the flyspace in both the Drury Lane and Broadway theaters to allow for the entrance of a helicopter in *Miss Saigon*. Perhaps the grandest tour de force of all these extravagant productions occurs in the second act of *Sunset Boulevard*. There, Norma Desmond, a former silent movie superstar, is celebrating New Year's Eve alone and unhappy in her huge and glittering mansion—the main setting for Act I. Slowly John Napier's enormous set rises high enough to reveal a cramped Hollywood apartment underneath, its denizens having a raucous good time. As the action shifts back to Norma's palazzo, the set descends while we are still aware of the whirling wriggling bodies in the set below. These and the technical miracles conceived for *Beauty and the Beast* and recently for *The Lion King* are not only a far advance from the inclusion of a swimming pool that kept audiences marveling at *Wish You Were Here*, a second-rate show of the early '50s, but are unique in that they are generic, part of the concept of the show.

In all of these cases one needs the assurance that the entertainment will not close in a week and leave theater owners, who invariably have a clause in their contracts that demand the house be returned to its original condition, with a bankrupt producer. *Cats*, *Starlight Express*, and *Sunset Boulevard* were guaranteed by Andrew Lloyd-Webber's previous success.

When I mentioned that one of the things that brought about the *new* musical was a reassessment of morality, I should have added that it is in the eye of the beholder. Of course, morality is subjective, for what is acceptable ethical conduct

---

[5] It must be allowed that Prince's restaging of the Hellman-Wilbur-Bernstein masterpiece was eminently successful at the Chelsea Theatre Center of Brooklyn before it was deemed wise to transfer it to Broadway. Additional lyrics for this improved version were commissioned from Stephen Sondheim.

for one may be looked on as immoral by another. The stage has always had its own code, which gave it far more freedom than movies. Yet when it came to the musicalization of a play or novel, the ha-ha song and dance aspect always took over. Musical prostitutes invariably had golden hearts. *Sweet Charity*, which was an adaptation of the Fellini film *Nights of Cabiria*, softened the realism of the original script just as *New Girl in Town* whitewashed O'Neill's searing dramatic play *Anna Christie*. Perhaps the worst offender was Rodgers and Hammerstein's script for *Pipe Dream*, which cleaned up the whores of John Steinbeck's *Cannery Row*.[6]

But the musical stage was still smarting from a preconception of what was acceptable. Hadn't the critics, with their references to morality, tried to sink Rodgers and Hart's imaginative *Pal Joey*, in which the "hero" and his older, married benefactor are a twosome? "One cannot draw sweet water from a foul well," was the way Brooks Atkinson put it in *The New York Times*. A double standard prevailed, and musical comedy meant just that: "music" and "comedy."

From the '40s on, and only very gradually, little inroads of discontent crept into sketches of revues, attacking the status quo. Although the majority, the hacks, played it safe, well-known librettists of the caliber of Arthur Laurents, Alan Jay Lerner, Moss Hart, and Oscar Hammerstein gradually became somewhat more daring with the topics they thought suitable for musicalizing. Hammerstein, who back in 1927 had introduced miscegenation into his script for *Show Boat*, held fast with his partner, Richard Rodgers, when in 1949 theater stalwarts asked them to remove "You've Got to Be Carefully Taught" from *South Pacific*. The song's message is that prejudice is learned, not inborn.

The list of shows below is arranged in somewhat chronological order beginning in the mid-'30s, and will serve as a kind of Baedeker of ideas not theretofore espoused in musicals. I suspect readers will have their own candidates for inclusion.

The Cradle Will Rock	Pro-unionism, speaking out for causes, anti-bossism
Lady in the Dark	Psychiatry, dreams, Freudianism, woman executive
Porgy and Bess	Cocaine (happy dust), unmarried man and woman living together, murder
Pins and Needles	Unionism

[6] Hammerstein's libretto is not totally at fault. Steinbeck wrote *Sweet Thursday*, his sequel to *Cannery Row*, with the intention that it would be set to music by R & H. Maybe the fault lay in casting Metropolitan Opera soprano Helen Traubel as a benevolent madam, or perhaps, as James Hammerstein has said, "They were simply the wrong guys for that kind of gutsy musical."

Bloomer Girl	Dolly Bloomer, feminist; birth and death in the Civil War ballet
Carousel	Wife abuse, attempted robbery, suicide
St. Louis Woman	Wife abuse, murder
The Medium and the Telephone; The Rape of Lucretia; The Saint of Bleecker Street; Street Scene	Opera on Broadway
South Pacific	Racial prejudice
Lost in the Stars	Fear in South Africa, racial prejudice, murder
The King and I	The hint of a love affair between the King of Siam and a nineteenth-century Englishwoman
The Threepenny Opera	Beggars, thievery, murder, extortion. A flop when first presented in the United States in 1933, a success the second time around in 1953.
The Pajama Game	Unionism again but this time mixed with woman's equality
West Side Story	Gang wars among youths, killing in anger, ethnic hate
Flower Drum Song	The generation gap, assimilation versus parochialism
Gypsy	Frustrated stage mother; ends with what Hammerstein called "watching a woman have a nervous breakdown"
Camelot	Cuckoldry, near immolation
How to Succeed in Business Without Really Trying	A spoof of the art of climbing the corporate ladder
I Can Get It for You Wholesale	A heel rises to the top and is eventually bankrupt and deserted by all the women he loves except his mother. Hard hitting, no punches pulled
Anyone Can Whistle	Political corruption, greed. Poses the enigma: who is crazy? Pretending to be another in order to lose inhibitions
Fiddler on the Roof	Family tradition, anti-semitism
On a Clear Day You Can See Forever	ESP

Mame	Prejudices of the middle class, snobbishness
Man of La Mancha	Spanish Inquisition, madness, gang rape
Cabaret	Promiscuity, the Nazis, betrayal, abortion
Your Own Thing	Cross dressing, gender confusion
Hair	Attacking everything the establishment stands for
Promises, Promises	Attempted suicide
1776	History retold
Applause	Theatrical venom, scene in a gay bar
Company	Ambivalence, desperation, seduction, tepidity of relationships
No Strings	White journalist falls in love with black model in Paris; difficulties of their situation and their eventual separation
Godspell; Jesus Christ Superstar	Biblical rock
Pippin	The quest for identity
Seesaw	A basically two-character opus in which the couple go separate ways at the end
Shenandoah	Dodging the draft
Chicago	Woman kills boyfriend, is acquitted, forms a successful night club act with another murderess
A Chorus Line	Life stories of would-be "gypsies" (dancers)
I Love My Wife	Wife swapping
Pacific Overtures	The opening of Japan, the rape of Japan
Baby	A concept musical: conception, impotence, parenting
The Rink	Mother and daughter interdependency, gang rape
The Knife	Sex-change operation
La Cage aux Folles	A gay couple, wholesome presentation of drag queens
Falsettos	A gay father, his lover, his wife, at the time of their son's Bar Mitzvah
Sandhog	Building a tunnel beneath the Hudson River

Nunsense	Spoof of Catholics and Catholicism
Kiss of the Spider Woman	Prison, torture, homosexuality, fantasy
Jelly's Last Jam	Denial of one's race
Miss Saigon	Prostitution, miscegenation, desertion, suicide
Assassins	Assassination, the false American dream
Passion	Obsession
Sunset Boulevard	Murder, selling out, older woman–young man, insanity
Rent	The East Village of today, drugs, transvestism, adaptation of Puccini opera to rock
Parade	Lynching of an innocent, falsely accused man
The Full Monty	Male striptease

Workshopping and previewing are the fourth influence on the new musical. Musicals formerly spent very little time fine-tuning themselves, but it is now the rare one that opens cold on a Broadway or London stage.

It was not always so. Open the show. Let it be hit or flop. If hit, go on to write the next one; if flop, salvage the best songs to insert in the next show. Prolificacy was the byword.[7]

A week in New Haven, two in Philadelphia or Boston was the limit throughout the '20s and most of the '30s. Reliving those days, one has the image of the composer and lyricist locked in a Taft Hotel room, frantically trying to come up with a new number to replace the one in the second act that was met with tepid applause last night. The librettist is holed up next door, the carpet littered with discarded pages while he is hysterically scribbling dialogue to replace a weak scene. The actors are coping as best they can after being handed one set of lyrics to be sung at the matinee while another is to be offered at the evening's performance. Or the song could be cut. Every audience saw a different show.

As the '30s gave way to the '40s and believable plots became essential, producers insisted their composers, lyricists, and librettists take their time. But it was an era of burgeoning theatrical offerings, and as the New York theater had to be reserved months (sometimes a season) in advance, no matter what, a show

---

[7] 1924, a banner year for the Gershwins, saw three new shows, *Sweet Little Devil*, *Primrose*, and *Lady, Be Good!*, in addition to a contribution to *George White's Scandals of 1924* and George Gershwin's acknowledged masterpiece, *Rhapsody in Blue*. In 1926 the team of Rodgers and Hart outdid them by presenting six new shows: *The Fifth Avenue Follies*, *The Girl Friend*, *The Garrick Gaieties*, *Lido Lady*, *Peggy-Ann*, and *Betsy*.

had to honor its booking and opening date.[8] Even the hint of a delayed opening smelled like the show was in trouble, and angels and ticket-buyers would fall away.

Soon it was considered better business to have a longer preview[9] period, to play while readying the show. This angered the critics—and rightly so. Restrained from writing their reviews before the production opened officially, they felt their readership was being bilked by a producer who should not be selling tickets to a show not yet ready to be seen. Many of them broke the rules, wrote critiques, and spilled the beans on shoddy productions. Eventually long preview periods were replaced by out-of-town tours. But even that could not give the group—composer, lyricist, librettist, choreographer; scenic, costume, lighting, and sound designers—a true picture of how the show would play on Broadway. They were frequently working on a constricted stage before an audience whose reactions might be light years behind those of the blasé first-nighters whose thumbs up or down would mean hit or flop.

The ideal solution would be the one Bertolt Brecht used. His method was to write the script, cast it, have the sets built, and get through the early rehearsals. Then he would dismiss the actors for six months while he went back to his studio and rewrote the entire play. He would throw everything away and start anew with Act One, Scene One.

In a way that is just what the burgeoning workshop process has accomplished. As theater on the West Coast began to become more vital, workshop theaters, generally state funded, began sprouting throughout the whole United States. Certain funded theaters like the Papermill Playhouse in New Jersey or the La Jolla in California specialize in big musicals. Others with fortunate endowments sprang up seemingly because of need—Playwrights Horizon, the National Music Theater Network, the Eugene O'Neill Theater Center, Mark Taper Forum, the Long Wharf, the Rosetta LeNoire Music Theater, and Goodspeed to mention just a few. Workshops have proliferated abroad as well. England's Chichester and Stratford festivals frequently provide the genesis for plays that will be polished until they can gleam on the West End.

---

[8] Agnes de Mille, who was hired to direct and choreograph Rodgers and Hammerstein's *Allegro*— their third collaboration after the smash hits of *Oklahoma!* and *Carousel*—told this writer, "There was no decent second act so I begged them to postpone the opening, saying 'you two probably won't have a flop, but imagine what a masterpiece you could create in a few more months.' They were committed to presenting a show every two years and didn't listen to me." *Allegro* had a run of 315 Broadway performances and closed in the red.
[9] To bolster the sale of an "as yet uncritiqued show," preview tickets used to be offered at reduced prices. Previews now cost the same as regular performances, although tickets for previews (except for a sure-fire hit) are generally available at half-price ticket booths in both London and New York.

Lee Adams combines the terms "workshopping" and "showcasing" and defines them according to his own Webster's as "a method of trying out new theatrical material without the huge cost of a full-scale production."

When and where did all this start? The idea seems to have been born in 1961, when, after having written A Funny Thing Happened on the Way to the Forum, Stephen Sondheim, Larry Gelbart, and Burt Shevelove asked Jerome Robbins to direct it. Although he liked the idea, the script, and the songs, Robbins asked for a reading with professional actors before he committed himself to the project, and producer Hal Prince obliged. Although movement was important in that show, eventually Robbins bowed out, and luckily the master of farce, George Abbott, finally directed the show. The experience was so valuable that Prince repeated it with every Sondheim musical after that. It was not very expensive (in those days the actors received no more than twenty-five dollars for the reading), and, Sondheim said, "We learned a lot about what was right and what was wrong."

In the musicals he has created since working with Harold Prince, Sondheim continues this process with collaborators James Lapine and John Weidman. As he recalled at a meeting of the Dramatists Guild:

> About four months before rehearsal date, no matter how much is written—even if it's just one act and five songs—we get a professional group together, and I play the songs and the actors read the script. Afterwards we discuss what is good and bad, and then we do the same thing about six weeks later. Now there are eight songs and an act and a half. And we do it a third time. . . . We keep doing it anywhere from two to four times before the rehearsals begin, and as a result we are always in much better shape when we open than most shows are.

Sondheim does those readings in New York, while Andrew Lloyd-Webber follows a not dissimilar pattern, established years ago when he was preparing Cats, of presenting his unpolished ideas before a seasoned group of theater people at his country estate in Sydmonton. Susannah Fellowes, who starred in the first performances of Aspects of Love in the country, remembered:

> The estate is glorious. It's a stately home and on the grounds you have this, I think, sixteenth-century chapel which has been desanctified and converted into a theater . . . It's nice because the atmosphere is electric. Andrew invites everybody who's anybody in the theater—all the people he's worked with in the past and hopes to work with in the future—people of great wealth and position and authority. Afterwards he listens to what they have to say about the work. He considers their collective advice very seriously before proceeding further with the project.

Both the Sondheim and Lloyd-Webber methods are examples of a preparatory idea devised by a commercial producer, but in recent years, with the spiraling expenditure of preparing a show, a solution simply had to be found, and the workshop, a sort of open-ended rehearsal period, was ideal. The workshop version of *Dreamgirls*, which was developed by director-choreographer Michael Bennett, cost $150,000, a sum infinitely more logical than the $3.5 million bill for its Broadway mounting. *Baby* and *Nine*, both interesting conceptual musicals and both Tony winners, came up through the workshop process.

These days producers unable to support the costs of readying a musical have had to rely on support coming from a non-profit theater producer. Then they are forced to give away part of their share to these organizations. *Kiss of the Spider Woman* and *Jelly's Last Jam* each had a decade's odyssey full of rewrites before reaching their hit status on Broadway. Susan Birkenhead, lyricist of *Jelly's Last Jam*, recalled her experiences with the heavily funded Mark Taper Forum:

"Luther Henderson, the arranger-composer-orchestrator, was the only one who was involved from the beginning. There were other writers . . . a script by August Wilson, one by Ken Cavender. Nothing worked until they found George Wolfe. He called me late one night (we were working on a Duke Ellington show, *Sweetie Pie*) and said, 'I've figured out a way to do this show. You know, Jelly Roll Morton was a racist, but who he is, is in his music." And we talked about an artist not being in a vacuum but being a sum of all his parts.

"Then we had three workshops in Los Angeles. We opened in April 1992 at Mark Taper Forum. They provided rehearsal space, two stage managers, rehearsal pianist and their company of actors. We had a two-week workshop of the first act, after two weeks, a walk-through with scripts in hand. This was before an invited audience of seventy-five. A lot of movie people. Very smart. A question and answer period after.

"Then we went back to work in New York, armed with what we had learned from that. Endless rewriting. *Jelly* was the kind of show that I'd say was half created on its feet. But there were certain things that were in those two very first workshops that remained throughout the show . . .

"In New York we finished large parts of the second act and then we came together several months later to do a workshop of it. Very little remains of that. And then a few months later we did get a third workshop—this time putting the two acts together. Then we did a production there. A full main stage, million dollar production, and it was a huge hit, breaking box office records. Still it was a very different show from the one you saw in New York. We did another workshop and Gregory [Hines, their star] did not want to do it, but then with no tap dancing in the show we felt that Jelly's character was still a little too angry, and there were still things that needed to be worked on.

"When Gregory Hines came back we did another, because now we had to put tap back into the show. That was at 890 Broadway [Michael Bennett's old workshop building]. We did a six-week workshop culminating in performances for investors, and there was a lot of excitement, so of course that was it. During that workshop it was decided that instead of using percussion we would use tap as the percussion instrument. That number opened up a whole new look of the show for us. It was no longer just the rhythm of the streets, but it became that link between African rhythm and the music that was in Jelly which became physicalized. Then we went into rehearsal."

When asked if much was changed in rehearsal, Birkenhead answered, "Absolutely! It kept growing. We rewrote the second act in previews. I really think the difference between shows that survive and shows that die is the willingness of the creative staff to take the blinders off and say 'this really needs to be fixed here.' It's very hard to fix during previews because you don't want it to look messy in front of an audience, and you finally get things up to a performance level and then have to tear it apart. You're so scared you get sick to your stomach, but then you have to say, it will be better by next Tuesday."

Workshopping has made audiences come to expect polished theatrical experiences on opening nights. But it must be remembered that it is only one of the aspects of the current musical theater that have made it such a viable art. Small wonder, then, that with these huge changes in the manner of readying musicals, as well as contemporizing their very conceptual essences, they have become more polished and therefore more appealing to the public at large—a public accustomed through television to rejecting anything that smacks of amateurism. Audiences will accept a local theater group's mistakes at a musical, even an original that costs but a few dollars a ticket, but at Broadway's inflated prices nothing less than true professionalism is tolerated. And who can blame them? Workshopping leads to musicals that run with almost computerized polish. That is why a growing number, especially of the younger audience, unaccustomed to the improvised, the hypeless, or the unexpected, has come to think of the musical as their entertainment of choice when they think of attending the theater.

Although they frequently overlap, today's audiences for musicals seem to have split into several camps. There are those who want the poplike show-sound, as exemplified by *Blood Brothers*, *Tommy*, *Leader of the Pack*, *Bring on 'da Noise*, *The Buddy Holly Story*, or *Rent*. The recent success of this kind of musical and the fascinating *Smokey Joe's Cafe* often makes one deplore Broadway's snobbishness in not having provided an atmosphere in the past for more musicals like them. Many critics feel that musical theater has been ruled by crusty old gentlemen who offer the public the same old formulas. The public, in turn, resents the fact that for the last three decades it has been fed a diet of the same old revivals instead of new works by Lieber and Stoller, Randy Newman, Jimmy Webb, and their like.

But although rock, soul, metal, hip-hop, rap, reggae, and country have dominated popular music almost exclusively, they have not invaded the mainstream musical theater except tangentially. The guarantee of success, that is, playing it safe, is still in the remountings, generally conceived or produced by an older generation. And there are plenty of theatergoers who want to relive the past in revivals such as *Carousel*, *Show Boat*, *Guys and Dolls*, *Crazy for You*, *Kiss Me, Kate*, or *The King and I*.

But vastly more popular with the majority are the oversized, larger-than-life, over-the-top romantic epics as exemplified by *The Phantom of the Opera*, *Les Misérables*, *Miss Saigon*, or *Sunset Boulevard*. There is also an audience, if less substantial, for musical plays on the opposite side of the spectrum, those who are taken with the eclecticism and intellectuality of works like *Lolita, My Love*, *Pacific Overtures*, *Falsettos*, or *Passion*.

It is curious that aficionados of these last two kinds of musicals are in violent opposition, so much so that members of either camp refuse to attend perform-ances of the other persuasion. One might generalize and call the latter group the cerebralists, the cultists, and the academics and the former the sentimen-talists and romantics. Of course their chief gurus are Stephen Sondheim and Andrew Lloyd-Webber. These two men have dominated the *new* musical theater for almost two generations. And it looks as if their oeuvre will direct the course of the art well into the new millennium.

Early Sondheim

O N M A R C H 2 2, 1 9 3 0,[1] the day Stephen Sondheim was born, the *New York Times* headline screamed: UNEMPLOYMENT HERE WORST SINCE 1914. This was only the backlash of the calamity that had begun six months earlier when the Stock Exchange closed in a frenzy of selling. The drastic financial times this crisis ushered in came to be known as The Great Depression, and by the time 1929 eased its way into the '30s, the hardship it forebode had filtered down to almost every American. This debacle in the United States triggered repercussions in Germany, Japan, and Great Britain, whose shaky economies would not begin to pull away from their doldrums until rearmament began, half a decade later.

If the world was in such a calamitous financial climate, imagine the state of world theater—always "the fabulous invalid," for besides being considered a luxury, the stage had to suffer further problems. Straight plays and musicals in particular were deeply buffeted by the advent of the new "all-talking, all-singing" movies. This new cinema technology could not have been perfected at a less propitious time for Broadway, whose plays and operettas were struggling to keep afloat.

Quality musicals such as Nöel Coward's romantic *Bitter Sweet*, a huge success in Britain, were not able to weather the hard times. Even a critical success like Kern and Hammerstein's *Sweet Adeline* was unable to play out the season. Only a few plotless shows like Cole Porter's *Wake Up and Dream*, Earl Carroll's *Sketchbook*, and Lew Leslie's *International Revue* were able to survive. Luckily an ad placed by Irving Berlin created enough interest in the witty songs Cole Porter

---

[1] Sondheim shares a birthday with his only rival in the area of the powerfully influential in contemporary musical theater: Andrew Lloyd-Webber. The latter came into the world on March 22, 1948. Perhaps it is the most interesting musical coincidence since the shared birthdays of Jerome Kern, January 27, 1885, and Mozart, who was born on the same day 129 years earlier.

had written for *Fifty Million Frenchmen* to turn it from flop to hit, while the critics' glowing reviews did the same for the most innovative new musical of the season—the Gershwins' and George S. Kaufman's *Strike Up the Band*. This show single-handedly lifted the spirits and set America humming "I've Got a Crush on You," "The Man I Love," and the title song. Except for those sparkling entertainments the season was dismal indeed—and curtailed. From over fifty productions just two years before, in 1929–30, the musical offerings had shrunk to only thirty new shows.

But bleak times had little adverse effect in the household of Herbert Sondheim, his wife, Janet (née Fox and nicknamed "Foxy"), and their only offspring, Stephen Joshua. Herbert Sondheim Incorporated, his Seventh Avenue dress manufacturing firm, was flourishing nicely. Now the clothes he and his wife, his chief designer, created moved into a cheaper line. The rich may no longer have been able to afford transatlantic voyages, but they still needed to wear smart clothes.

Throughout those years the Sondheims maintained a rather elegant apartment in one of the most fashionable skyscrapers fringing Central Park. The San Remo, on Manhattan's Upper West Side, was and still is a very récherché address. Foxy Sondheim frequently entertained the dress buyers who made their semiannual pilgrimage to Gotham for selection of fall and spring apparel. Herbert himself was an amateur pianist, adept at playing by ear.[2] "He was a natural musician and a terrific fellow—wonderful, wonderful," his son recalled.

After placing a healthy order with the firm, the out-of-towners were frequently treated to a Broadway musical followed by an at-home supper. Herbert usually went to the grand piano and entertained by playing all the songs from the show they had just attended.

Sometimes he would also play for his young son who, years later, would remember "sitting on the piano bench and my father putting my small hand on his little finger—because he always played the melody with the top note." Herbert Sondheim usually played in what is called "inverted style." This translates to a rather sophisticated manner, with full right hand chords twisted around so the melody, played by the little finger, comes out on top. In this style the left hand generally plays octaves.

By the time he was four, besides being able to read books and stories on his

---

[2] The mature Sondheim has stated that he is not an improvising pianist. Rather than play by ear, he much prefers reading or memorizing a written arrangement. There is no doubt that without the obligation to be impelled forward by the rhythm of the song, the performer can work out an "ideal" harmonization which is often missing in "ear" players' renditions. Harmony, which is elusive, instinctual, and variable to most of them, is vital to Sondheim. "Harmony is the most important element in music," he has said. "It gives it its character."

own, Stephen began picking out melodies without his father's guiding his hand. His mother boasted about his musical gifts, crowing to a reporter from *Newsweek* after her son had become successful that "Aaron Copland said he obviously had tremendous talent." The mature Sondheim denies his mother's braggadocio, saying, "she never met him." But whether Copland was merely making chit-chat or the boast was a product of Foxy's imagination, it was obvious that Stephen was an extremely musical and literate child.

His parents enrolled him at age six in first grade at The Ethical Culture School, which has a reputation for fostering classic education. He was far ahead of his classmates, for by then he was able to read the *New York Times*. His vocabulary and diction at this early age were vastly superior to that of the other boys in his grade, but being the smartest kid in the class brought him shame rather than pride, and Sondheim was to recollect that his desire to conform made him "purposely drop my g's because I spoke English so well."

As the Depression eased and money began to flow more freely, Herbert Sondheim's business grew and called for both parents to spend more and more time away from their apartment. Stephen was shunted away and cared for by a series of nannies and cooks, "whomever they could hire," he was to say bitterly. But that autumn, 1936, his father took him to the theater, and he never forgot his first musical, *The White Horse Inn*, an opulent production of a German operetta that was packing the cavernous Center Theatre nightly. His parents probably attended more sophisticated fare, such as Cole Porter's *Red, Hot and Blue!*, Noël Coward's *Tonight at 8:30*, and Rodgers and Hart's *Babes in Arms*, which were the reigning hits that season.

This was the time that he first began really to study piano. Gifted, he made rapid progress but was reluctant to practice. He was later to attribute the reason to a resentment at being forced to entertain at his mother's cocktail parties. "My father would come home, my mother would come home from work and I would play 'Flight of the Bumble Bee' and everybody said 'Isn't he wonderful?' " But the interest didn't last very long. "I got tired of being dragged out for company and because of it quit lessons entirely."

During the ensuing years Stephen was aware of the eroding feelings and the growing hostility between his parents. From his own point of view, he appreciated the easygoing quality of his father and resented many of the things his mother stood for. As an adult he was to remonstrate with her, saying that "she had a set of values that even at that age I knew were suspect in that she liked celebrities and money a lot."

But Herbert was the musician, giving and generous, who sparked Stephen's interest in theater. He can still remember his father's taking him to a musical when he was nine. "The curtain went up and revealed a piano. A butler took a duster and brushed it up, tinkling the keys. I thought that was thrilling." What he did not know was that the musical, *Very Warm for May*, would have libretto and lyrics by Oscar Hammerstein, who would shortly come to be a surrogate father to him. He was also not aware that the show's hit song, "All the Things You Are," would be one he would analyze in depth as a student, later expounding on its unique harmonic and melodic structure to his own students.

"As for his parents, he claimed they had a marriage of convenience because they were both in the same business," his friend Gouverneur Cadwallader told this writer. "And when they got married they agreed theirs was no great love affair. 'If one of us meets somebody else, we can get a quiet divorce.' Steve claimed that his mother, over a period of time, fell in love with his father and his father was unaware of it. Then when his father met someone else and wanted a divorce, his mother was very upset. She did not let on that she was upset but maintained that a bargain is a bargain and that's what they had agreed to." Cadwallader added that he never knew whether this was a romanticized story on Sondheim's part, "or the truth, perhaps as he saw it."

When Sondheim was ten his parents did go through a bitter divorce. His mother was given custody of Stephen, but the boy was allowed weekly visits with his father. Foxy warned her son she was having him followed whenever he went to visit his father and told him that if he ever saw Herbert's new wife, the former Alicia Babé, she would have his father thrown in jail. He never got over it, and although he has written scathingly about his hatred of his mother, he still harbors resentment for his father. One wonders if this is not the reason why he is so attracted to themes of injustice and revenge (*Pacific Overtures, Sweeney Todd, Into the Woods, Assassins*).

If Sondheim gravitated toward his father, he also seems to have inherited his pessimism. He recalled that "we lived very nicely, on Central Park West, but at the back of the building. After my father remarried he moved to Fifth Avenue, still at the back of the building. He always looked at the black side, imagined the worst that could happen. Eventually my stepmother and I forced him to retire and I'm sorry to say I think it killed him—he missed the worry."

But Sondheim's bête noire was certainly his mother. "I had a difficult childhood," he told Michiko Kakutani in a 1994 *New York Times* interview, "because my mother was a genuinely monstrous woman, and my father, whom I liked a lot, left me in the dragon's lair. I can't blame him—but I blame him."

Even when Sondheim was in his forties and had had extensive psychological help, the hurts his mother inflicted on him remained unhealed. "She was going to the hospital to have a pacemaker put in," he told Kakutani, "and said 'mother's going in for open heart surgery, and usually at that time parents write their children a letter.' I said 'It's a pacemaker,' but she wrote me a letter, hand-delivered, because she thought she was going to die. And she wanted to make sure I got it. She said 'the night before I undergo open heart surgery . . . the only regret I have in life is giving you birth.' "

"We all think our parents are suffering from misplaced love or possessiveness or whatever," was Sondheim's comment on the above, "but she didn't want me on earth. And I realized why: she had a career and she didn't want a child. In a way, her letter was a good thing for me . . . so I wrote her a letter saying 'I finally understand.' "

For his early grammar school education he attended the Ethical Culture School; later he was transferred to their Fieldston campus in Riverdale, a bus ride away. Now because of the divorce the youngster was taken out of those familiar environments and enrolled in the New York Military Academy in Cornwall-on-Hudson. Although the discipline might have seemed strict, Sondheim reveled in the structure and orderliness of life there. He began to study the organ because "they had the second largest manual organ in the state. I just loved all the buttons. I played things like 'To a Wild Rose' standing up since my feet couldn't hit the pedals."

At that time, boys, especially young boys not aiming for a career in the army, who were enrolled in military academies were generally from homes in which divorced parents were in a quandary as to what to do with the child, or else they were spoiled children whose parents believed they needed disciplining. The cadets were only given leave during major holidays and summer recess, which seemed a perfect solution to Herbert Sondheim's new-found relationship and Foxy's preoccupation with the reestablishment of her career.

Although the majority of the Academy's young cadets were teenagers, at that time New York Military Academy had nearly forty boys of grammar school age, mostly from broken homes. All these boys were domiciled in a special house. Bard House was far more homelike than the main barracks where the older boys dwelt, but discipline there was still maintained.

For Stephen, life at the Academy was a total change from what he had known. His day began with a reveille bugle at 6:30. After inspection for the neatness of his clothes closet, bureau drawers, and uniform, he joined the others hurrying to first mess. Classes began at 7:45 and lasted until 12:45. All the instructors (except for the music teacher and nurses) were male and invariably dressed in full uniform. Once the afternoon drill was out of the way, there were the obligatory sports—football and baseball. In his early days at the academy, Sondheim went out for the football squad and became the manager of the Academy's junior baseball team, but later he somehow managed to get to the library or the organ room while his classmates were outside on the field. (His roommate, Lawrence Nusbaum Jr., vividly recalled that "when the Bard Hall group was dispatched to play, Stephen was granted special permission to take organ lessons at the Academy chapel.") Five nights a week, after the evening mess there was study hall. Once more the bugle was sounded for recall. Cadets then hurried back to their rooms for final toothbrush inspection and taps, followed by "lights out" at nine.

Entering as a sixth grader in the autumn of 1940 Stephen did fantastically well in his studies, so well that by February 1941 he was listed as "honor cadet." This distinction, besides announcing that he had attained superior grades, allowed him to wear a silver star on each side of his uniform collar. He was so bright, his roommate recalled, that he did the *New York Times* crossword puzzle daily. Sondheim, who was always interested in puzzles and word games, was to develop a magic act and even at this early age performed his show for family and friends. Lawrence, who was in awe of him, perceived Sondheim's magic act to be far more than a childish showing off. Steve was able to do "complex tricks."

Students at the Academy considered Sondheim the "brains of the class." His roommate remembered that Steve "was taking calculus while we, fifth graders, were studying arithmetic." The next year his academic record was even more outstanding, so much so that by midterm he was transferred, "skipped" from seventh to eighth grade. Homework assignments became more demanding once he joined the "big cadets." Classes for these older boys were held in the massive Academic Building, and boys here were not mollycoddled.

According to Sondheim, one afternoon in the summer of 1941,[3] after Stephen had completed his first year at the Academy, Dorothy Hammerstein came to visit and brought along her ten-year-old son, Jimmy. Foxy, who was now a freelance interior designer, got on well with Dorothy, who ran her own decorating business. As two career women, they had much in common.

James, tall for his age, super bright, and quick with words, was just the kind of companion Steve was looking for. A hot game of Monopoly sealed an instant friendship. It was agreed that Foxy and son should come down the following weekend to be guests at the Hammerstein farm in Bucks County, Pennsylvania. James was scheduled to return to his habitual summer camp (which he hated) instead of passing an "unstructured" summer, but once the boys got together James was granted a reprieve.

"Steve came out one weekend and then he too was going to go back to camp. We had such a good time that we never were sent to camp. We just stayed there for the whole summer," James remembered in an interview with this writer. "He sort of became one of the family that summer. We got along so terrifically

---

[3] Although Sondheim as well as most of his biographers have written of the Hammerstein meeting as having taken place in 1941, James Hammerstein believes otherwise. In a recent interview he told this writer, "We moved out there in '42 and he came out to Bucks County when he was twelve and I was eleven. The biographers are totally wrong."

because we both loved games. And also he was a city kid, and I remember what delight he had when I taught him how to ride a bicycle—he had never ridden one. We used to go on twenty-five, thirty-mile rides. In those days you could do that and stop at a farm and ask for water and they'd say, 'there's the pump out there—and a tin cup. Use it.' And nobody worried about you when you were gone all day. That's what you were supposed to do when you were a kid— it's not the same now."

In 1942, when Stephen was twelve, his mother decided to rent a farm near the Hammersteins' Bucks County property and to commute to New York for business. By then the area had become a mecca for successful artists, poets, novelists, playwrights, and musicians. Many writers and theater people had summer homes there. Chief among them were the Moss Harts, the George S. Kaufmans, and playwright Howard Lindsay and his wife, actress Dorothy Stickney. Alexander Woollcott's comment, on seeing Hart's farm was, "It's just as God would have done, if he had the money." Foxy tried to know these celebrities, but it was probably the proximity of the Hammersteins' nearby farm that influenced her decision.

Oscar Hammerstein was well known as a distinguished lyricist-librettist, but by the summer of 1942 his career was in a tailspin. In spite of past triumphs like *Show Boat, Rose-Marie, The Desert Song,* and *Music in the Air,* the word on the street was "Hammerstein? Why, he can't write his hat!" The modern musical seemed to have passed him by. Four of the movies for which he had provided the lyrics had been junked while the two that were released were flops. All his recent musicals—*Gentlemen Unafraid, Very Warm for May,* and *Sunny River*— had been failures.

A few months before he came to know young Sondheim, Hammerstein had developed an idea to write an adaptation of Bizet's *Carmen,* which he thought might have promise. He appreciated the lack of stress working for the first time in his life on a project without deadline afforded him. Here was a project at which he could work at his own pace and did not have to bow to the whims of a composer. It was tonic. By July he had finished *Carmen Jones* and had sent the script off to Max Gordon, who promised to produce it but couldn't say when. Gordon's stalling was no great trauma for him; between the income from Dorothy's decorating business and royalties from past successes, the Hammersteins were able to maintain their affluent lifestyle, which included a Manhattan apartment and the Bucks County gentleman's farm. The delay gave Oscar Hammerstein the leisure to reassess his waning career. It also gave him time to enjoy his family, to play chess or checkers with Jimmy and Steve, or to walk briskly (the Hammersteins never strolled) about his seventy-two acres with his beloved Dorothy and their Irish setters.

At the moment he had what he called only minor things on his agenda: a possible revival of *Show Boat*, a new song for the movie version of *Very Warm for May*, some necessary changes for a new staging of *Music in the Air*, and a promise he had made to the Theatre Guild that he would have another look at Lynn Riggs's play, *Green Grow the Lilacs*.

Always a disciplined worker, no matter how little or how much the pressure, he stuck to a workaday schedule. When he was involved in creative work he closed the door to his study, which was above the large central room, and while he paced the floor, humming, as he conjured up a lyric, all activity in the house was silenced. During those hours young James and Steve were restrained from noisy games or their favorite indoor sport—playing the piano.

"The real bone of contention between Steve and me was that there was only one piano and we both liked to play a lot. We used to race for it and get quite physical," James recalled. "It was a games house. Word games and chess and bridge and checkers," he continued, adding that his father was also included in the playing. "And outside there was croquet and tennis—we didn't have a tennis court that first year. A local farmer had one, and he let us use it. Stevie (I call him Stevie to this day—his secretary says "What?") loved the outdoor as well as the indoor games."

Sondheim remembered those days with Jimmy, especially playing golf "because the Hammersteins lived right next to a golf course. Jimmy and I would sneak out on the course and play three holes where we couldn't be seen by the pros."

Once he opened his office door and came downstairs to join the family, Hammerstein was never preoccupied or gloomy, despite the knowledge that his career was at its nadir. As the United States had entered the war the previous winter and rationing was now the rule of the day, he felt his family would be secure at Highland Farm. Knowing they could raise ample food from the land, he stocked his barns with enough livestock to remain self-sufficient should the conflict come to American shores. That was, after all, one of the main reasons he bought the property in 1940. Bill and Alice, his two grown children from his previous marriage, and Susan, Dorothy's daughter, used to come to the farm occasionally, but now that Bill was in the service and Alice was off at college, Hammerstein contented himself with the squeals of the two rambunctious boys and relished the challenges and joy these competitive preteenagers brought into his life.

Bucks County is not too far off the beaten track between New York and Philadelphia, and theatrical friends en route to the favorite tryout city of Philadelphia would often stop by to visit at Highland Farm. One evening Richard Rodgers, who was attending a tryout of a friend's musical, drove in from Philadelphia and confided to Hammerstein the troubles he had had in getting his current hit show, *By Jupiter*, to the stage.

Rodgers recounted how his collaborator Lorenz Hart's drinking problem and frequent disappearances for days at a time had nearly scuttled the show. With tears in his eyes he told Oscar how, while they were writing the musical, he had committed Larry to Doctor's Hospital to keep him away from his usual haunts and had taken the room next door so they could write the last songs ostensibly undisturbed—but actually so that he could keep an eye on his collaborator. Rodgers, who lived from show to show, was never happy until he had mapped out his next project.

That night he mentioned to Hammerstein that he had promised the Theatre Guild to look at *Green Grow the Lilacs* and wondered if Oscar knew the play. Hammerstein told him he knew Lynn Riggs's folk-play very well and had even tried to interest Jerome Kern in collaborating on an adaptation with him, but Kern had turned it down, saying the third act was weak.

Even though *Lilacs* as presented by the Guild had been a flop, both men were convinced that there was much unexplored freshness and beauty in the play, and Rodgers ventured that it would be a wonderful project for them if they ever decided to work together as they had done many years ago.[4] Still, Rodgers honored his commitment to Hart, and for his part, Hammerstein would do no more than promise that if Larry's alcoholism stymied their new show, Oscar would be "waiting in the wings to help out."

As it turned out that autumn, Hart was not interested in working on *Green Grow the Lilacs*, which he called "a horse opera," and so, after much negotiation, many misgivings, and much heartbreak, the team of Rodgers and Hart, which had produced twenty-six musicals, was essentially dissolved. Hart and Rodgers worked together again on a revival of their evergreen success, *A Connecticut Yankee*, but shortly after the opening of this musical Hart's alcoholism overcame him once more and led to his untimely death. By then the new partnership of Rodgers and Hammerstein had been cemented.

Sondheim left the military academy that auspicious autumn of 1942 and matriculated at the George School, a Friends establishment about thirteen miles away in Newtown, Pennsylvania. Gouverneur Cadwallader was to enroll a year later and James Hammerstein the year after that. Both students remember that by the time he graduated from the school, Sondheim was a social lion on the campus with a large circle of friends.

The school offered a liberal curriculum specializing in the classics. But its rules were strict. In those days 98 percent of the enrollment were live-in students, often with divorced parents (not unlike those at the military academy).

---

[4] Hammerstein had contributed lyrics to music written by Robert Lippman and others to several of the Columbia University Varsity Shows for which Richard Rodgers had written most of the music from 1919 through 1922. He had even directed one: *You'll Never Know* in 1921. Later, he wrote three fledgling lyrics for a Rodgers score. "Weaknesses" and "Can It" were duds, but "There's Always Room for One More" in *Up Stage and Down* showed some promise.

They were permitted to leave the campus only one weekend a semester, "so that meant on Saturday night," Dean John Talbot, who was known on campus as "Uncle Jack," remembered, "we had to provide either an outside speaker or a movie. The dramatic director and I, between us, presented about eight plays a year. Incredible for a high school to do that many plays."

"Steve reveled in the heady theatrical atmosphere from his first years," continued Talbot in an interview with this author. "In the fall of '43 I was directing *Mr. Pim Passes By* by A. A. Milne. We used to rehearse in our small assembly room after supper from 7:15 to 9:15, which was study hour. I was rehearsing this play and I noticed a small boy, obviously a freshman, in the back of the room every night. Finally I went up to him and asked, 'You're a freshman?' And he said 'yes.' I said, 'Well, this is study hour and you should be on your books. I realize you come here because you enjoy watching the play but you should be studying.'" Talbot recalled Sondheim's answering that there was no cause to worry, he was well up on his lessons. "He was an excellent student indeed," continued Talbot, "and, as a matter of fact, in his senior year when the Latin teacher took sick Steve taught the senior Latin class brilliantly for two weeks."

During the four years Sondheim was to remain at the George School until his graduation and entrance into Williams College, rather than spending his holidays with his own parents in New York, he could more often be found at Highland Farm. Steve, Gouv, and Jimmy all boarded at the school during the winter and spring terms, but whenever there was an extended holiday—even a summer vacation—Sondheim chose Dorothy and Oscar Hammerstein as surrogate parents, and they in turn accepted him as a member of their extended family.

Like Sondheim, Gouverneur Cadwallader was extremely gifted in mathematics, and since his own parents lived only a few miles away from the Hammersteins, he was frequently enlisted as a fourth at bridge on weekends or during summer holiday. The foursome—Stephen, Jimmy, Gouverneur, and Oscar—played "hot and heavy, often until midnight."

"I remember that there seemed to be a rapport between Oscar and Steve on the occasions when we played bridge," Gouverneur recalled. "As for myself, I was embarrassed by being in the presence of so celebrated a man as Oscar Hammerstein, and felt a bit ill at ease. The first time we played Steve was calling him 'Ockie' [a nickname created when Hammerstein's baby brother, Reggie, had trouble pronouncing "Oscar"] and Jimmy was calling him 'Dad,' and I was calling him "Mr. Hammerstein." The thirteen-year-old would occasionally get excited at the bridge table and call Oscar "Dad" or "Ockie" and remembered that "he was very pleasant and turned to me and said, 'Would you feel more comfortable calling me "Mr. Ockie?"'" It put me at ease."

If Stephen spent as much time playing games and absorbing theater at the

Hammersteins' as he could during those four years, his mother, in turn, spent as little time in the country as possible. Sometimes, when Foxy was "in residence," he and James would bicycle over to her house, only seven miles away, but after a few disastrous luncheons James let Stephen go off and then return to the fold when he got ready.

"If his mother said 'come visit me,' he could do that and be gone again before she noticed," James recalled. "A seven-mile ride for a kid with a bike is nothing, but having a meal at his house with just the three of us was like [*Who's Afraid of*] *Virginia Woolf*—the play." James was to remember that "Steve and Foxy would go after each other in a way that would make Virginia Woolf blush. They were snide, they would dig at their weak points. There were no holds barred. It was the nastiest relationship I've ever known between a mother and a son. And yet it was intellectual in that they were both able to keep their minds working as they got at each other. It was a piece of work. He didn't want to stay there . . . he was at our house all the time."

One afternoon during the summer of his junior year at George School Sondheim met Mary Rodgers, the daughter of Hammerstein's collaborator. A year younger than Steve, Mary was something of a whiz kid herself, and to break the ice (since he did not introduce himself), she challenged him to a game of chess. "He beat me three times in a row, very handily and a little snottily, and I thought, I'm dealing with heavy-duty brains here."

Mary confided that although Sondheim was "a real slob, I found him immensely attractive—and then when he sat down and played Gershwin I fell madly in love with him." But there was more than admiration that brought the teenagers together. Dorothy Rodgers was by all accounts a difficult, crazy-clean, and unbending woman—quite the opposite of her counterpart in the R & H team, warm and gracious Dorothy Hammerstein. Life with the Rodgerses was rigid enough for Mary to say, "It was my fantasy that my parents would die and I would be adopted by the Hammersteins." In a way, Steve already had been adopted by them, so now the youngsters could talk about how much they resented their parents. No wonder he only went to visit his mother on demand.

Drawn as he was to the world of the theater, a world that opened its doors to fantasy, Sondheim and his adopted family left the Seventh Avenue garment trade, the world of disposable fashion design—even the necessity to make money—far behind. As Martin Gottfried wrote of those impressionable teen years spent with the irrepressible Hammersteins in Bucks County: "He would live not with ordinary citizens but among creatures who dwelt in theaters and spoke a language of opening numbers, ensemble turns, and comedy routines. In this alien land, blockbuster hits and showstoppers were life's important things. [It was a] world where creativity and laughter were matters of everyday life."

And what a time for musicals it was, those four years that Sondheim passed between the George School, New York, and the Hammersteins. The very next spring Oscar Hammerstein and Richard Rodgers were to revolutionize the musical with their version of *Green Grow the Lilacs*. Renamed *Away We Go* and eventually *Oklahoma!*, it was to make history and to elevate "musical comedy" to "musical play." Now, almost sixty years later, it is thought of as "folk operetta." But no matter what slot *Oklahoma!* is put into, this seminal show was also a thoroughly American product that would command respect from the rest of the world.

Among the show's many innovations was its dispensing with the obligatory opening ensemble in favor of the lone cowboy hero singing about "what a beautiful mornin' " it was and having a villain who was both attractive and psychologically intriguing. Perhaps the show's greatest contribution to the development of the musical was its classically inspired dancing—the addition of ballet either to flesh out characters or to continue the story. This inspiration was Agnes de Mille's, and her style was to catch on and dominate most serious musicals for the next decade. With *Oklahoma!* dance became a generic part of the musical, not just a diversion.

But *Oklahoma!* dug deeper, and its honesty did more than merely destroy theatrical convention. It talked about the individual's responsibility to the group without once getting up on a soapbox. Beyond that, it was the first of the R & H musicals to leave audiences glowing with feeling (and message) while giving them a good time.

Yet the reader must not come away with the impression that the success of *Oklahoma!* is to be attributed only to its sweeping landmark changes. The world and theatergoers in particular were ready. It was wartime, and that particularly American quality, the this-is-the-way-of-life-we're-fighting-to-keep of this musical made all the European-type operettas seem overblown and nonessential. Bawdy girlie reviews, the former staples of Broadway, now seemed a tawdry throwback to outdated vaudeville. Yes, this show had undressed chorus girls, but they were in the "French Postcard" ballet, a dream sequence that whitewashed the sex with a heady dose of psychology.

Wholesome is the appropriate word. This show was perfect for American GIs headed overseas to take a girl to, or to see solo, to bolster their patriotism before they shipped out. Then too there was the fresh and unknown apple-cheeked American cast: Alfred Drake, Joan Roberts, and Celeste Holm. Last, *Oklahoma!* became a hit of such fantastic proportions and became so newsworthy that everyone, even in the hinterlands, would journey to New York and come back with stories of how they had wangled tickets to this "miracle." Before *Hello, Dolly!*, *My Fair Lady*, or *Cats* had theatergoers lined up around the block, *Oklahoma!* spread the news that Broadway musicals could be a healthy investment for both "angels" and audiences.

Oklahoma! opened the gates to such experimentally intelligent and solid Broadway innovations as *One Touch of Venus*, a Kurt Weill–Ogden Nash fantasy, and *Bloomer Girl*, a Civil War story with a stunning score by "Yip" Harburg and Harold Arlen. Two years after the debut of *Oklahoma!*, Rodgers and Hammerstein hit pay dirt again with another adaptation. They took *Liliom*, a dark story, one that involved wife-beating, robbery, and suicide, transferred the setting to the coast of Maine, and created *Carousel*, another purely American masterpiece.

Sondheim never forgot that Oscar Hammerstein himself took him to a preview of *Carousel*, a "serious musical" yet a success from its earliest performances. During wartime and the postwar years when Sondheim was attending the George School, there were, of course, other successful musicals, musicals that set out merely to entertain. Cole Porter's *Something for the Boys*, *Mexican Hayride*, and *Seven Lively Arts* supplied their share of amusement with little care about plot construction. Irving Berlin wrote arguably his best score in *Annie Get Your Gun*. New talent was having its day, with the sophisticated team of Lerner and Loewe making its debut with a succès d'estime, *The Day Before Spring*. But perhaps the freshest musical of those years would be *On the Town*, which introduced Betty Comden, Adolph Green, Jerome Robbins, and Leonard Bernstein to theatergoers. Sondheim's first great success would be *West Side Story*, written almost a dozen years later in collaboration with the latter two artists.

Theater and things theatrical had by this time become a way of life for Sondheim—although he has stated it was to emulate Hammerstein. Later in life he was to refer to him as "a man of limited talent but infinite soul."[5] James Hammerstein disputes Sondheim's often quoted words—"had my father been a geologist, he would have followed that profession"—as being simplistic, but there is no doubt that Stephen's life revolved around Oscar. Yet it is equally patent that Sondheim was headed toward a life in the theater and would have followed such a career even without Hammerstein's help.

Stephen was involved in every play George School mounted during his years there and could be dashingly dramatic even when he left the campus. Gouverneur Cadwallader remembered the weekend they spent in New York that commenced with a visit to Herbert Sondheim's apartment.

> Steve was sort of a practical joker. When we first went up to his father's apartment—he lived on the twelfth or fourteenth floor [actually, Herbert Sondheim lived on the tenth] of some big apartment building, I remember that when we were

[5] Taking the other side of the coin, Sondheim referred to Richard Rodgers, with whom he wrote *Do I Hear a Waltz?*, as "a man of infinite talent—and limited soul." In 1998, Sondheim said that the often repeated quote about his views on Rodgers's and Hammerstein's respective talents and souls was in response to a reporter's asking, "Why do you think Rodgers and Hammerstein make a good team?"

walking across the lobby, Steve saw several people in the elevator and he deliberately pushed a button for the fifth floor instead of the higher one where we were
going. And then in a very agitated voice he said, "Gouv, I don't know what to do,
but that actress we saw in the movie last week—well, I came back to my apartment
and there she was lying on the floor with her throat cut. Oh, here's our floor. Let's
get off." He had enough acting ability to stun these people and they must have
looked in the newspapers for the next two or three days for news of the murder in
their house.

In the autumn of his senior year, at the age of fifteen, he played in Edna St.
Vincent Millay's *Aria da Capo* and the farce *Incognito*. He had perhaps his best
role the following January as the lead in Noël Coward's *Blithe Spirit*. Now he
also found time to practice the piano diligently, performing frequently for his
classmates. He even considered becoming a concert pianist until he got rattled
during a performance of Chopin's "Polonaise-Fantasie" and forgot the middle
section. Regaining his composure and repeating the first section, he says his
audience was oblivious to the switch, but it was enough to make him renounce
his dreams of the concert stage. After that he took his piano playing more
jokingly. One of his classmates remembered a school recital at which he improvised a sonorous group of chords leading up to a climax on a G7 chord and
then left the stage while his audience waited for a chord of resolution. But by
that time his classmates were already mightily convinced of his mastery of the
keyboard and knowledge of the fundamentals of music.

He talked excitedly about the Greek modes to any of the students who would
listen—seemingly to spread his newfound information. This was material he had
dug out himself, for he was miles ahead of the school's music department. But
he was not involved exclusively in serious music, although *The Caravan*, the
school yearbook, of which he somehow found time to become editor-in-chief,
nicknamed him "George School's own Rachmaninoff." The school had a prize-
winning mathematics team, whose leaders were Sondheim and Cadwallader. "I
was probably the only person at George School who could keep up with Sondheim in mathematics, and I do remember one instance of the first time I recognized how really brilliant Steve was."

Cadwallader recalled a complicated mathematical puzzle wherein the solver
was required to find the smallest integer that fit specific conditions—knowing
that with paper and pencil he could, in time, answer the question. "And Steve
got sort of a dreamy look in his eye and solved the problem intuitively." He
added, "I was just astounded—because I always considered myself the brightest
person I ever knew, until I met Steve. Steve was the first person I recognized
as being a real genius. And that's when I knew that I wasn't."

Because he was a natural actor and performer, Sondheim had continued and
augmented his magic act. Now he reveled in putting on a quite polished show

whose climax was an escape from a straitjacket. Sondheim put Gouverneur into the jacket and terrified his classmate. "I was unable to get out, but eventually Steve undid the thing. Then he showed me that it was a *trick jacket* and that when *he* got into it he could get out easily."[6]

Later in the year, on the urging of Oscar Hammerstein, Sondheim organized a group that would put on the school's first original musical comedy, *By George*, a thinly disguised version of life on campus, with the teachers' names changed by one vowel or consonant.

Arthur Henrie, who played the romantic lead, remembered that "each person in the show memorized the music, and the only script we were given was the part when our character was on stage."

Dean Talbot admitted that the plot was not memorable, but he appreciated "the music, all by Steve and the lyrics which were mostly by him. One of the songs was 'I'll Meet You at the Doughnut.' Now the doughnut was in the center of the main hall. It was a circular couch around a post where the students used to gather. The songs were so successful that the kids kept singing them long after the performances were over."

Perhaps because all of his classmates were singing his songs that spring, Stephen Sondheim may have believed himself to be the next innovator of the Broadway musical, and he asked Oscar Hammerstein to read the script of *By George*.

"I was arrogant enough to say to him 'will you read it as if it was a musical that just crossed your desk as a producer,' because he and Richard Rodgers produced shows as well," he told an audience at a lecture on songwriting. " 'Pretend you don't know me.'" He said 'okay' and I went home that night with visions of being the first fifteen-year-old [Sondheim was actually sixteen at the time] to have a show on Broadway—because I knew he was going to love it. He called me the next day and I came back to see him, and he said, 'Now you really want me to treat this as if it was by somebody I don't know?' And I said, 'Yes please.' And he said, 'Well, in that case it's the worst thing I've ever read in my life.'

"And he must have seen my lower lip tremble or something, because he followed it up by saying, 'I didn't say it wasn't talented. I said it was terrible. And if you want to know why it's terrible, I'll tell you why.' And he started

---

[6] The mature Sondheim was to lose his interest in magic shows, but he didn't lose his penchant for puzzles and games. Throughout the '50s and '60s (often in collaboration with Anthony Perkins) he organized the most fiendishly clever scavenger hunts. Although he still collects antique games, he feels he has outgrown that period. "But puzzles," he says, "that's a whole other matter. The fitting together of notes, the fitting together of words have by their very nature a puzzle aspect." Sondheim introduced the enigmatic Cryptic Puzzles that stumped readers of *New York* magazine and continued to contribute them for a year and a half.

with the first stage direction and he went through the piece for one afternoon, really treating it seriously—it was a seminar on this piece, as if it was *Long Day's Journey into Night*. Detail by detail, and in the course of that afternoon he told me how to structure songs, how to build them, with a beginning, a development, and an ending. He taught me about character, how to introduce character, what relates a song to a character, stage techniques and so forth. It was four hours of the most packed information. At the risk of hyperbole, I dare say I learned more in that afternoon than most people learn about songwriting in a lifetime, not that I could write songs, but I knew all about them. And I remember almost everything."

And what did Hammerstein tell his avid young student that spring afternoon? He impressed on him that the rules of lyric writing have to do with intelligibility—the way the words sit on the music—and differentiated among dramatic intelligibility, theatrical intelligibility, and verbal intelligibility. Among other basic principles of lyric writing, Hammerstein talked of communicating with an audience. Criticizing a lyric, he told him that "it's better to be funny than clever. You know, cleverness is fun for other clever people—but to be funny has to do with attitude, situation, character."

Sondheim recalled Hammerstein's words on that afternoon to an avid group of would-be songwriters during a lecture he gave in 1971 at New York's "92nd Street Y." He then read the assemblage a lyric from *By George* so that "any of the budding songwriters in the audience don't have to feel embarrassed. This is the first lyric I ever wrote—it isn't so bad, it's just excruciatingly dull." The concept of the lyric, called "The Reason Why," was puzzlement at the end of a love relationship. The song ends with:

If it's finished and we're through	I'll think of you as just a passer-by.
Then there's nothing else to do.	But beneath my casual smile
So any time we meet	I'll be wond'ring all the while
While walking down the street,	The reason why.

"We finally got to the title," Sondheim announced laughingly to his audience. "And that was one of the first things he explained to me, what a title was supposed to be, what a refrain was supposed to be, and why you come back to a refrain to help structure a song."

Of course, throughout this lecture the mature Sondheim was denigrating himself in order to show budding lyricists how amateurish his early lyrics were. Yet, Hammerstein's comments aside, *By George* was received by faculty and students with great enthusiasm. Coming at the end of Sondheim's four-year stint, it was a fitting finale to a brilliant record at George School. His academic history alone gave Sondheim the option of being accepted at any college of his choice. He chose Williams College in Williamstown, Massachusetts, a small university then committed to an all-male enrollment numbering slightly over a thousand students. The school had only a two-man music department, both members of which were respected by their colleagues yet not celebrated teachers. But the intimacy of the campus and the school's reputation for quality education were paramount in his mind as Sondheim—only sixteen, a full year younger than the age at which most freshmen enter college—went off to live in Williamstown for the next four years.

Sondheim in Williamstown

WILLIAMSTOWN, IN WESTERN MASSACHUSETTS, with its mostly white colonial architecture, is picturesque to the point of New England cliché. Williams College, which sits on the town's highest elevation, at the center of the town's historic buildings, dominates the village. Nestled in the rolling Berkshire hills, between the intellectual capitals of Stockbridge and Bennington, with its wide, tree-lined streets and spired churches, Williamstown promises an old-world serenity. Offering frequent lectures, recitals, theatrical performances, and concerts, Williamstown seemed a perfect venue for a young man with an IQ in the genius range who might be in search of a liberal classical education.

A part of what is known as "the little Ivy League," Williams College maintains one of the highest educational standards in the nation. Dean Baxter, in welcoming the 350 freshmen who comprised the Class of 1950, mentioned the "nine shadowy figures who lurked behind each man"—the nine applicants who were not admitted for every man who was.

Although Sondheim has said that he went to Williamstown and to Williams with an open mind, undecided whether he would major in English, mathematics, or music, he was already determined to carry out the plan Oscar Hammerstein had laid down for him that fateful summer afternoon. The huge assignment, learning the entire craft of writing a musical, was to take him through four years of college and well beyond. Hammerstein had asked his young pupil to adapt and write libretto, music, and lyrics for four entire musicals.

For the first one Hammerstein asked him to take a play that he admired and turn it into a musical. Sondheim chose *Beggar on Horseback* by George S. Kaufman and Marc Connelly. With true professional acumen Sondheim obtained the authors' permission to adapt their hit comedy and put it on for a run of three performances at Williams's Adams Memorial Theatre during Sondheim's sophomore year. Next, Hammerstein suggested his eager student take a play he liked but didn't think was very good, which might be improved by the addition of music.

For that one Sondheim chose *High Tor* by Maxwell Anderson. In this case he was unable to get Anderson's permission to put it on at the college because the playwright himself intended to fashion a libretto to be musicalized by Kurt Weill. Anderson, himself a fine lyricist, had collaborated with Weill on *Knickerbocker Holiday*, which produced the unforgettable "September Song." But both Anderson and Weill got embroiled in other projects, and they never got around to the play.

And it was just as well, for it is impossible to see how even these artists could have succeeded with this mishmash of a drama. *High Tor*, despite having won a Pulitzer Prize, is a confused quasi-poetic play with diverse themes. Its message-laden plot involves ecology, escaped bank robbers, noncompromise, and political corruption. All these themes are spouted by cardboard characters (often in non-rhyming verse), while a group of specters from the past return to inhabit a desolate mountain top.

Still, Sondheim was not to be dismayed. "I did it and that taught me something about playwriting—how to structure something. How to take out fat and how to make points," Sondheim recalled at a lecture at New York's 92nd Street Y.

"Then Oscar said, 'For your third effort take something that's nondramatic . . . a novel, a short story, something like that.' So I landed on *Mary Poppins*, and I spent about a year doing a musical of Mary Poppins, and that's when I first encountered the real difficulties of playwriting, and that's one of the reasons I'm not a playwright. It was an attempt to structure a group of short stories and make a piece out of them—and it was very hard and I wasn't able accomplish it.

"And then he said, 'For your fourth show do an original.' So right after I got out of college, I wrote an original musical." [It was called *Climb High*.] The first act was ninety-nine pages and the second act was some sixty-odd. Oscar had recently given me a copy of *South Pacific* to read, and the *entire show* was ninety pages long. So when I sent it to him I got it back with a circle around the ninety-nine with just a 'wow!' written on it."

Preoccupied over the next four years with writing his four "assigned" musicals, Sondheim was not aware that he was also building a strong technique of musical construction as well as a "trunkful" of songs. All these would serve as his portfolio when, after college, he sought to fly out on his own without Oscar's embracing arm.

Sondheim entered eagerly into college life. During his first year he joined

Beta Theta Pi[1] fraternity, not because he wanted to be part of an exclusive club but simply because Williams offered only rudimentary dining facilities. But he was on campus only a few weeks when, similar to his activities at George School, he began to involve himself in the literary and theatrical activities the school offered. He was hardly settled into university life when he acted as part of the three-man Chorus in Sophocles' *Antigone*. He decided to become a music major and was soon so deeply interested in it that he knew theater in some form must be his life's work.

"I took an elective in music during my freshman year," Sondheim said. "The teacher, Robert Barrow, was so sensational that if he had taught geology I would probably have become a geologist."[2] Most of the students at Williams College avoided Barrow's classes because he was considered factual and dry in his teaching of harmony and theory. Barrow looked at music as a craft and taught his students to make their music as dispassionately as a carpenter makes a table. In truth, basic theory and counterpoint with its plethora of rules is not unlike fitting the pieces of a complicated puzzle together—an assignment that would mightily please the teenage Sondheim.

"I thought he was wonderful," Sondheim added, "*because* he was very dry. Barrow made me realize that all my romantic views of art were nonsense. I had

---

[1] Stephen Birmingham, who would become a distinguished chronicler of life amid the wealthy and megawealthy, was among the other twenty-four Beta Theta Pi pledges that year.

[2] Although Sondheim made a similar comment about following the profession of his mentor Oscar Hammerstein, he has never been glib about the "art" of teaching. In his sixties, after he received SMU's Meadows Award for Excellence in the Arts, he recalled some of his early teachers. "I tend to get very teary when I think about how my life was changed by teachers. . . . First, there was Lucille Pollack, my Latin teacher in high school, who just loved language. I had skipped a grade where the basics of grammar were taught, so I really didn't know quite what a noun or adverb or verb was, and here I was taking first year Latin. She was using words like that, and I went to her for help and she spent the afternoon with me, and by the end of the afternoon (I was good in language and precocious), I was ready almost for the second half of the year in Latin. I not only learned English grammar, but I learned Latin in that afternoon. The passion with which she threw the ball to me made me catch it. And the same thing happened with the music teacher [Barrow] in college because I was going to major in English. In both those cases it was the passion of the teacher that got across, and I think that's what you have to do. You have to hook the listener's imagination with the force of your own feeling. It can't be just an intellectual process. What's ironic is that it *is* an intellectual process, but it's got to come from the gut. And if it does, and if you believe in it, and if you care about the subject, and about the conveying of information, that's what I mean when I say 'art is teaching.' Art is caring about conveying a view of the world. It's conveying information, only not information you can put into a notebook, but it's conveying something.

"Society suffers so badly, particularly in this country, from rigid ways of thinking. Obviously I think in terms of art, because it's so hard to persuade people to leave their prejudices at the door. A preconception is death, and I think if I taught that's what I would constantly teach."

always thought an angel came down and sat on your shoulder and whispered in your ear, 'dah-dah-dah-DUM' [the opening motif of Beethoven's Fifth Symphony]. It never occurred to me that art was something worked out. And suddenly it was the skies opening up. . . . He taught me to first learn the technique and then put the notes down on paper."

Although Sondheim immersed himself in Barrow's music program, he still found time for theater and played a role in *Trade Name*, a play by Peggy Lamson, as well as the important part of Henry in Thornton Wilder's *The Skin of Our Teeth*. In May he was Garth in Maxwell Anderson's *Winterset*. Throughout what must have been an enormously busy spring, Sondheim worked on *The Purple Cow*, the college's literary magazine, which published three of his longish stories. One was an interior monologue whose theme was escape from the mundane, another a pastiche on the hard-boiled detective written under the pseudonym of Hashell Dammit, but the third, titled "The Brass Goddess," was a bitter diatribe outlining a daughter's dependently hateful relationship with her mother.

Hardly disguising his own point of view by changing the sex of the narrator and calling her Ellen, Sondheim's prose refused to pull punches and even went so far as to use "Foxy" for the name of the mother in the story. Sondheim has Foxy die at the story's end, although it must be added that the protagonist suffers remorse. Parallels abound:

> Why couldn't she have gone to live with Dad? . . . Dad was kind and understanding and not the least nervous or superficial. Dad with a new wife and child. . . . And she knew only too well why. Mother had won custody of her and was getting alimony. Mother was always complaining how little it was, but Ellen knew the extravagance with which she lived. . . . The dress business. . . . The cheapest, most hypocritical business in the world. Mother loved it although she professed not to . . .
>
> "Why can't I live with my father? He loves me. You hate me, you spend your life trying to make me as miserable as you can. Why don't you stop trying to climb the social ladder?"

This story would only have worsened the relationship between mother and son, had his mother read it, but according to Sondheim, she never did. At the end of the college term Stephen moved back with his father because he did not want to live with his mother.

After such a active academic year, one would assume a slowdown, but actually Stephen experienced a speed-up when he had his true baptism into the professional theater.

Oscar Hammerstein was preparing his and Richard Rodgers's third musical, this time an original, *Allegro*. Announced for a mid-October opening, by summer it was nowhere near ready. In spite of that, Oscar and Dick adamantly decided to stick to the original theater booking and open at the prearranged time. This meant furious rewriting and a doubled-up rehearsal schedule. When rehearsals began Sondheim was hired as a gofer, sent out to get coffee and Danish, but sometimes helping with retyping. With his strong interest in music having been compounded by Robert Barrow's musical course, and his daily presence in the Broadway theatrical area, he would certainly have been aware during that theatrical summer of the new spirit that had suddenly enveloped the musical.

Beggar's Holiday, Street Scene, Finian's Rainbow, and *Brigadoon* had all opened in a three-month period in the middle of the 1946–47 season, during which Hammerstein was writing *Allegro. Beggar's Holiday,* a fresh treatment of *The Threepenny Opera* with a magnificent new score by Duke Ellington and cynical lyrics by John Latouche,[3] and *Street Scene,* a somewhat operatic treatment of Elmer Rice's 1929 hit play with lyrics by Langston Hughes and music by Kurt Weill, were not successful at the box office. Both shows were artisticly ambitious, and that old truism—the higher the aspiration, the more difficult its perfect realization—was proved once again. Critics who held the shows in high regard were unable to communicate to their readers that although they considered the shows imperfect, the public should come to see them for the unusual qualities they *did* possess. But the two later arrivals, *Finian's Rainbow* and *Brigadoon,* needed little help from the critical fraternity. They gave the public fresh and original books that made fantasy a popular alternative from the mostly R & H inspired rage for Americana.

Before he returned to Williamstown in September, Sondheim traveled with the *Allegro* company and sat in on the previews in New Haven. In that way he became closer to what is perhaps the most personal of all of Hammerstein's libretti (and one that so never satisfied him that he was tinkering with and revising it until his death in 1960). The readying of *Allegro,* the first professional show Sondheim would be able to look at first hand, had to make an enormous effect on Sondheim's artistic viewpoints.

"I was concerned when I wrote *Allegro,*" Hammerstein wrote, "about men who are good at anything and are diverted from the field of their expertise by a kind of strange informal conspiracy that goes on. People start asking them to join committees, and the first thing you know they are no longer writing or practicing medicine or law. They are committee chairmen, they are speech makers, they are dinner attenders."

Sondheim empathized with his mentor-adviser: "He was so successful, he had so many responsibilities," he reported, "that they cut into his artistic life." In-

---

[3] John Latouche (1917–56) wrote lyrics to Vernon Duke's music for *Cabin in the Sky, Banjo Eyes,* and *The Lady Comes Across.* Besides supplying libretto and lyrics for Ellington's *Beggar's Holiday,* he worked with Jerome Moross on *Ballet Ballads* and *The Golden Apple.* Because of his sensitive, literate lyrics, some critics have considered him a precursor of Sondheim.

deed, Oscar, always keen to champion humanitarian responsibilities, had been an organizer of the Anti-Nazi League in the '30s, was a member of the War Writers' Board from its inception until after World War II, and recently had been elected president of the Author's League.

"He accepted these responsibilities because he felt they were worth attending to. But at the same time he found himself farther away from his profession," Sondheim continued. "He transformed that into the story of a young doctor who comes to the big city at the behest of his upwardly mobile wife. Oscar turns the doctor into a politician who ends up laying cornerstones at hospitals."[4]

Sondheim got to see at first hand just how deeply an artist can become caught up in the Doctor-Joseph-Taylor-Jr. syndrome. Heavily occupied with the R & H schedule as producers and committed to a fixed opening night, Hammerstein could not conceive of delaying the premiere. Nor, with all his extraneous activities, could he seem to find time to sit back and take a critical look at what he and Rodgers had created. At last, with a deadline upon them, Oscar rallied to help his overworked director, Agnes de Mille, by directing the book scenes himself. It must be admitted that the vogue for ballet-in-musical had passed, and Oscar, looking back on what was to be his most personal show, always felt de Mille was not up to the task of directing the entire production. She had passed her peak, and although she was to continue to choreograph-direct, only her choreographic efforts were successful.

Although *Allegro* was a financial failure, it has since been called a succès d'estime, and contemporary historians have been kinder to the show than critics were in 1947. They often cite *Allegro* as the first concept musical, or a show written around a theme. With no character standing out, none being given more than one song, one comes away with the "idea" that Joe's particular story is secondary to the concept that success corrupts. Flawed though *Allegro* may have been, it opened the door to a splendid new way of writing for musical theater. Plot became secondary to philosophy. Besides *Company*, whose idea is the dissection of marriage and which would be credited as the next concept musical, shows like *Baby*, which is concerned with approaching parenthood, *Starlight Express* (an experiment concerning trains), *Sunday in the Park with George* (how

---

[4] The compromise of ideals is not an innovative theatrical idea. As the basic theme of *Allegro* it bears a close musical kinship with Sondheim's *Merrily We Roll Along* (1981). But adjusting one's artistic sights is a theme of other Sondheim work, notably *Sunday in the Park with George*. There are more parallels in the particular case of *Allegro* and *Merrily*. Both were written when Hammerstein and Sondheim were in their early fifties, and both were failures. Their creators became so enmeshed in the *manner* of telling the story (with chorus and oblique point of view of the former or back-to-front storytelling of the latter) that their largely unpleasant protagonists, Dr. Joseph Taylor Jr. and composer Franklin Shepherd, remain cardboard characters who create very little empathy with their audiences.

an artist rearranges reality), and A *Chorus Line*, whose concept is auditioning, would have been impossible had *Allegro* not led the way.

Allegro was a blow to Rodgers and Hammerstein's no-flop record, and it hurt Oscar far more than the money lost on a theatrical venture into unchartered territory. *Allegro* was his last attempt to expand the musical theater, to nudge in a new direction the form he had tried all his life to develop. Had they been younger or had *Allegro* been somewhat more successful, Oscar and Dick would certainly have been daring again. For Hammerstein and Rodgers it remains their only attempt to revolutionize the musical. Henceforth for the rest of their collaborative years they would play safe.

By the time *Allegro* opened in October 1947, Stephen was back in Williamstown, entering his sophomore year. From the beginning he was wrapped up in a demanding project: writing music and lyrics and collaborating with Josiah Horton on the book for the first Williams College musical. Called *Phinney's Rainbow* (after the new Broadway hit *Finian's Rainbow* and with a sweeping bow to Williams's president, James Phinney Baxter), it was given four performances in April and May.

This take-off of life on a prep school campus turned out to be far more sophisticated but not unlike what Sondheim had written for George School. Contrary to other acting plays put on at Williams, *Phinney's* was performed with the male students playing the parts of all the females, à la Princeton's Triangle Club, Harvard's Hasty Pudding Club, or Yale's Whiffenpoofs. With the men dressed up as cleaning women, the hit of the evening was the raucous "Q-Ladies' Waltz."

The plot, concerning a group of students who revolt at the school's compulsory physical education program and come up with their own idea, "Strength Through Sex," was certainly sophomoric. But the show was able to enlist a cast of fifty-two, about fifteen of whom dressed as charwomen or pin-ups. Sondheim wrote a full score of eighteen numbers, three of which, "Phinney's Rainbow," "Still Got My Heart," and "How Do I Know?," were eventually published by BMI.

Of the three, "How Do I Know?," a waltz, is the most interesting. Beginning with the I–VI–II–V harmonic scheme, the same chord pattern thousands have used against the melody of "Heart and Soul," Sondheim soon departs into more interesting harmonic territory. Of course, there is very little hint in this melody of the iconoclastic Sondheim to come, but perhaps the only utterly corny moment in the song is its climax on a forced V^7 chord. But to his credit, one must say that it is a thoroughly professional sounding number.

The lyric, especially the last lines, which are quoted below, gives us a rather amusing picture of the feelings a young swain's rejection engenders. Sondheim says that "it's not a serious lyric, but a satire on all the question songs, " 'How

Deep Is the Ocean?" etc." The frequent use of "know" and "no" are confusing to the ear, part of the joke. It is the same kind of joke the mature Sondheim's unfavorite lyricist, Lorenz Hart, frequently used.

. . . You said "goodbye"	But how will I know
When I said "hello"	When I know that you said "no."
And I asked you then,	I just don't know.
And you said I would know.	

The very act of presenting *Phinney's Rainbow*, a musical, at the staid Adams Memorial Theatre, where, as Sondheim says, "their idea of student plays was *Oedipus* in the Fitzgerald translation," was to loosen the theatrical rules at Williams a bit and even raise some money for the theater. Throughout the spring, with the success of his revue still ringing in his ears, Sondheim was able to go back to his acting, playing the role of the young murderer, Dan,[5] in the thriller *Night Must Fall*. His performance garnered the best reviews of his brief acting career.

"Sondheim gave a vivid and credible characterization in the difficult role of the murderous Dan," the reviewer for *The Williams Record* began. "For the first time on the Adams Memorial Theatre stage, he gave rein to the high talents which have previously been confined. Here at last is an actor who knows how to use his whole body dramatically. His gestures, movements and even the angles of his body anticipated, participated in and completed his vocal presentation of the character. His hands were never idle or awkward, but beautifully expressive at all times. He was acting every minute he was on the stage and acting very well."

Because Oscar Hammerstein, who readied a new show every two years, had just begun to work on *South Pacific*, Sondheim chose not to take a regular theatrical gofer job that summer. Instead with three classmates, he took an auto trip across the country, during much of which time he began work on the first of the major projects Oscar had assigned, *Beggar on Horseback*, which he renamed *All That Glitters*. In this case, per Hammerstein's instructions, he would dispense with a collaborator and adapt the book himself.

Sondheim worked simultaneously to finish his musical comedy without letting go of his studies. He had developed a way of writing his songs, he told a classmate, wherein he began with "a refrain line, fitting this to a musical motif, and then completing the lyrics."

By December, his show was far enough along for him to take time away from the thirteen songs he needed to complete his musical to become a "triple-

---

[5] Dominick Dunne, who was later to become a best-selling novelist, was Sondheim's schoolmate and understudy.

threat"—directing, composing, and acting in a single evening. He was the assistant director of Tennessee Williams's two-character curtain raiser, *Auto-Da-Fe*. This was followed by *Spreading the News*, a short play by the Edwardian Lady Gregory, to which Sondheim contributed the incidental music. The main feature of the evening was Clifford Odets's hard-hitting play, *Waiting for Lefty*. Robert Scott Taylor, writing in the *Williams Record*, praised the performance of Dominick Dunne as Dr. Benjamin. Taylor did not care much for Odets's agitprop play but raved about Sondheim "for his skillful handling of the climax of the play. Without Sondheim's sensitive understanding of voice," he continued, "the play would be pretty ragged. As it is, he brings it together much better, at various moments in the performance, than one has any right to think is possible (despite the fact that Sondheim's lines approach the ridiculous) and if all is not entirely well that ends well, this evening in the theater is considerably improved."

But if Sondheim tossed off his acting roles with great aplomb, he worked hard throughout that winter on his musical. *Beggar on Horseback*, which was not an original Kaufman and Connelly idea but an adaptation of a play by Paul Apel, is a strange fantasy play to musicalize. Yet it is obvious to anyone who knows the play just why Sondheim chose to adapt it.

It is a "dream" play, an honorable descendant of *Alice in Wonderland*, mostly comprising a mad nightmare whose climax bears a similarity to that of another early Sondheim oeuvre, *Anyone Can Whistle*. But far more than that, *Beggar on Horseback* is largely a diatribe, now (and even more so in 1949) outdated, on the uselessness of sham and material prosperity. As such, although a comedy, Sondheim's first musical has much of the same message as his long story, "The Brass Goddess."

The plot revolves around Neil, the protagonist, a serious composer, making his living teaching and arranging jazz or pop. He loves the girl who lives across the hall but is dazzled by and will wed one of his wealthy students. One can almost hear the voice of Herbert Sondheim or Foxy quizzing their son in what would become the prologue:

> CADY (the future father-in-law): Making a lot of money out of your music?
> NEIL: With music you don't make a lot of money.
> CADY: Now what I like is a good lively tune, something with some snap to it. I understand you go in for highbrow music.

Cady could easily be the prototype for the producer in *Merrily We Roll Along* who asks for tunes "you can hum."

Eventually, in a long dream sequence that comprises most of the play and musical, after the composer marries her for her money, his wife tears up his symphony. Then Neil kills her and her family. Musical comedy? Yes, indeed.

And even in this jejune work we see foreshadowings of the macabre humor that would surface in "A Little Priest" from *Sweeney Todd* or "Every Day a Little Death" from *A Little Night Music*.

As for the adaptation, Sondheim's musical stuck closely to the original play except for his substitution of a "Chess Ballet" instead of the second-act pantomime. But that ballet, although an innovative idea, was executed so amateurishly that it only slowed the action to a snail's pace. (In the Kaufman–Connelly play, a prince and princess, married to each other, disguise themselves and have a clandestine affair. Taking place in their bedroom the next morning, the pantomime speaks volumes about the state of the characters in the play.)

All That Glitters was heavily advertised and well attended. The critic for the *Williams Record* found the songs "second-rate," complaining (just as the characters in the play had) that he wanted tunes "he could whistle and didn't get them." To rub further salt in Sondheim's wounds, the critic found some of the songs similar to those in *Allegro*. Indeed, Oscar had had great input into *All That Glitters* and at least twice in recent months had gone over the entire musical with Sondheim. During one of their times together, according to Hammerstein's daughter Alice, she and Sondheim had even collaborated on one of the songs, "Drink to Zee Moon."[6]

It was a blow to Stephen that Hammerstein could not be present at any of the performances, but in true theatrical tradition the lyricist-librettist and his partner were working around the clock in Boston at the other end of the state to fix the few faults still remaining in their megahit *South Pacific*, then in previews.

"The compulsory drive in my case wasn't toward success," Sondheim was to reflect later. "I think I wanted to please Oscar. I wanted him to be proud of me . . . I wanted my father to be proud of me too, but that wouldn't have been enough, because Oscar was my teacher."

But if Sondheim was disappointed that his mentor missed his debut musical—his first for which he had adapted a story—he had to have been heartened that, contrary to its usual policy, *Variety* sent a reporter up to Massachusetts to cover *All That Glitters*. The showbiz bible wrote that the score had been "composed as an integral part of the play, and Stephen Sondheim displays great potential ability as a lyricist-composer." More than that, BMI, always on the look-out for budding songsmiths they could enlist, published five of the songs from the show. Those, plus the three they had in print from *Phinney's Rainbow*, gave Sondheim

---

[6] The phoney French used in this lyric is in the same spirit as that in "Come Play Wiz Me" which Sondheim would use to better advantage as an inhibition breaker in *Anyone Can Whistle*. Perhaps, more important, the song is intended to be a "quasi-French-type pop song" and as such would be Sondheim's first entrance into pastiche.

the start of a minicatalogue. If Sondheim never fulfilled his fantasy of "being the first fifteen-year-old to have a show on Broadway," he could at least take heart having been one of the first nineteen-year-olds to have come this far.

Too ambitious to spend his nineteenth summer lolling at the farm in Bucks County, Sondheim, who was now living with his father, took a hiatus in the considerable job of writing his next (unproduced) musical, *High Tor*,[7] and immersed himself in splendid theater for those months. Not only did he see Oscar Hammerstein's reigning hit *South Pacific*, he remembers going to *Kiss Me, Kate* with his father and reveling in the clever Cole Porter score. But *Kiss Me, Kate* was not the only intellectually stimulating musical on Broadway that summer. Alan Jay Lerner and Kurt Weill had collaborated on a quasi-concept musical called *Love Life*, and although it hardly moved the theater ahead, one could not overlook the natural sophistication to be found in a vaudevillelike musical that took the same protagonists into different generations. Frank Loesser's *Where's Charley?* and the revue *Lend an Ear* were also smash hits.

But there was more. With so many playwrights having so many postwar themes to exploit, the nonmusical theater was bursting its seams. In that season alone one could see *Death of a Salesman; Anne of the Thousand Days; The Madwoman of Chaillot; Detective Story; Edward, My Son; Life with Mother; Goodbye, My Fancy; The Silver Whistle;* and *Light Up the Sky.*

On Sondheim's return for his last year at Williams he continued to work on *High Tor*. He has spoken very little of his disappointment when he was denied permission to present the completed musical, merely saying that he kept the songs and ideas and gratefully "learned from the experience."

In February 1950 he portrayed Cassius in the Cap and Bells production of *Julius Caesar*. The initially laudatory reviewer found his performance vis-à-vis Brutus in the scene in which the latter discovers Portia's death "the finest in the play. There was a wonderful feeling there, too unusual in amateur productions as though these people were actually and importantly responding to each other."

But then the critique continued: "Sondheim was inclined at times to slightly overplay his part. His gestures were a few too many, even for Cassius, and there was a certain tone of voice—a desperate kind of pleading—which he used too often particularly with Casca until it finally could no longer be believed."

This somewhat carping review spelled the last of Sondheim's theatrical performances at Williams; indeed, except as a lark, he would never again appear

---

[7] Sondheim's musicalization of the Maxwell Anderson play has never been produced, but another musical version of the play eventually was presented on television. Starring Bing Crosby and Julie Andrews, it had book and lyrics by Anderson and music by Arthur Schwartz.

in an acting role. For the rest of his time at college he would content himself with supplying the creative. His only contribution to the 1950 college revue was an original song called "No Sad Songs for Me," the title borrowed from a tear-jerking movie that starred Margaret Sullavan.

Sondheim graduated magna cum laude and was a shoe-in to garner the prestigious Hutchinson Prize,[8] a $3000 cash award, renewable for a second year with no strings attached, for further musical study. He left Williamstown with copies of all his stories and sketches plus an incomplete novel, *Bequest*, a dark work about a composer who goes mad. More important, his suitcase also contained the scores of *Phinney's Rainbow*, *All That Glitters*, *High Tor*, and his unfinished version of *Mary Poppins*. He knew exactly what he would do with the prize money. He was going to apply it to study composition. Now all he needed to do was to find the right teacher.

[8] William Finn, composer-lyricist of the respected Broadway musical *Falsettos*, graduated from Williams, class of 1974. He too won the Hutchinson Prize.

Early Lloyd-Webber

WHEN *OKLAHOMA!* REVOLUTIONIZED the musical in wartime America, it made all the other musicals playing on Broadway or the West End seem old hat. Welcomed by a public embroiled in rationing, deprivation, and the great conflict, its sunniness coupled with record-breaking box office success soon became front page theatrical news.

After the war, in 1947, a company composed largely of Yanks at last appeared at the Theatre Royal Drury Lane in London to perform this most acclaimed hit. They were greeted as if they were a liberating army, for up until then the British musical theater (which had formerly kept pace with Broadway) seemed as if it might be singing and especially dancing in a time warp.

Besides *Oklahoma!*, in recent seasons Broadway's theatergoers had been treated to blockbuster hits, while the Drury Lane and other large London musical houses, where most American musicals would be seen thenceforth, had been saddled with Noël Coward's backward look at operetta, *Pacific 1860*. But because the war had so drastically severed transatlantic communication, the British, who had as healthy an interest in musicals as the Americans did, were forced to content themselves with only reading about the tremendous success of these lighthearted musicals.

Of course, all this was to change, quickly, as the country got back on its feet. Still it would be many years before the English would be able to compete with the Americans in *creating* musicals. But gradually their thirst for hit American blockbusters was slaked because producers of successful Broadway musicals developed the habit of sending a company abroad once they had a bona fide hit and the show was well into a long run.

Yet no matter how they tried, nobody in the British Isles could create musicals. Except for the musicals of Novello and Coward and Vivian Ellis's superhit, *Bless the Bride*, along with occasional revivals of bygone favorites—most of which were attended by what the British call "pensioners" and the Yanks call "seniors"—the new British musical was stymied. Luckily a few intimate revues like *Cage Me a Peacock* and *Oranges and Lemons* were staged, or the British would have had to be content only with musical imports that came from the other side of the Atlantic.

And come they did. Big, fresh, and brassy: *Song of Norway, Oklahoma!, Annie Get Your Gun,* and *Finian's Rainbow* in 1947; *High Button Shoes* in 1948; *Brigadoon* and *Lute Song* in 1949; and *Carousel* in 1950.

Into this world of the American musical, one almost might say the world of imported Rodgers and Hammerstein, Andrew Lloyd-Webber[1] was born on March 22, 1948.

If young Sondheim's household was one of elegant, upper-middle-class Jewish propriety, the world of his confederate in the domination of the twentieth century musical worldwide was at the other end of the spectrum. It might be described as a universe of bohemianism. "Bohemianism is far too mild a word," corrects Julian Lloyd Webber, Andrew's younger brother. "Chaotic would be a better term."

Andrew and Julian's father, William, had been a prodigy, giving organ concerts at ten. But prodigies grow up, and unless they are phenomonally gifted (which William was not) their careers vanish. As a teenager in the 1920s, in order to earn extra money he provided the organ background to silent movies, improvising heavily from cue sheets. Eventually as the talkies replaced the silents, and this avenue was closed to him, he applied for and was appointed teacher of theory at his alma mater, the Royal College of Music.

Fired by his instructorship (eventually professorship) of theory and harmony, he then sought and attained the post of organist at the nearby All Saints Margaret Street Church and began to write sacred songs. Yet he was always bitter

---

[1] Speaking at a Dramatists Guild seminar, Andrew Lloyd-Webber stated that his "name should be simply Webber." As for the origin of the double barreled name: Andrew Lloyd-Webber's father, William Southcombe Lloyd Webber, the son of a plumber with theatrical aspirations, used the name of W. S. Webber until his enrollment in the Royal College of Music when he was seventeen. In that year, another organ student, William George Webber, who signed himself as W. G. Webber, matriculated at the school, and so, to avoid a mix-up and not wanting to employ the awkward Southcombe in his name, he brought his middle name into service, and called himself William S. Lloyd Webber, or W. S. Lloyd Webber. He liked the sound of the compound name, and so when his sons were born he had them baptized Andrew Lloyd Webber and Julian Lloyd Webber. Today the press and public alike invariably refer to the composer and his cellist brother as "Lloyd Webber," although one should assume from the foregoing that they should be known by their patronymic, "Webber."

When Andrew Lloyd-Webber was given a knighthood and entitled to enter the House of Lords he received the right (as did all the members of that body) to hyphenate his name, and he picked up his option. Therefore, throughout this book we have included the hyphen in his name.

about not having an outstanding career and thought of himself as a composer manqué.

It was while he was teaching at the Royal College that he met Jean Hermione Johnstone. She was attracted to his dark enigmatic eyes—deep set and long lashed, below thick ebony brows. Always darting, they reminded her of cat's eyes, in that they missed no trick. These were set into his rounded face with swarthy complexion atop a solid, almost chunky frame.

Jean, too, was very musical from an early age. Although close to her family she was, like her mother, Molly, a very determined person. Molly, half Scottish and independent, had divorced her husband and come to London in the 1920s soon after her only son had drowned. Interviewed fifty years after the tragedy, Jean still remembered her favorite sibling's death as "the worst thing that's ever happened to me."

Molly settled in Kensington with her two daughters at 10 Harrington Road, near the South Kensington Underground Station, an area of faintly shabby chic, where large flats could be had at cheap prices. Jean was only two years old at the time, and her older sister, Viola (who eventually managed a minor career as an actress on the London stage but whose personality was eminently theatrical), was seven.

From time to time Molly left the genteel South Ken area to travel into London's poorer areas. She believed in what the mature Andrew called "the Victorian ethic of charitable help for the less fortunate. My grandmother was a founding member of something called the Christian Communist Party." Molly was unable to interest Viola in her "do-gooder" work but found a willing subject in Jean, who usually accompanied her on these forays into London's bleak slums.

Once Jean met William, all of her energy and interest was directed toward him, and she went after him. First, playing the violin, she joined the school orchestra he led; then, in 1941, when William's church choir was evacuated to the countryside during the battle of Britain, and he brought his students from the Royal College of Music to sing in his church, Jean volunteered to join the group because by this time her crush had developed into a deep attraction.

After three years of dating, they were married in October 1942. As it was wartime, William was conscripted into the Royal Army Pay Corps in Chelsea but returned nightly to the top floor of Molly's house in South Ken, where they set up housekeeping. Beyond the musicality and bohemianism, a stranger entering their household would be struck by their collection of cats. Jean regarded pedigreed cats as one of nature's miracles. Like talented music students, they were to be protected, nurtured, and cared for.

Around the time of Andrew's birth in 1948 William wrote *Aurora*,[2] which,

---

[2] It was recorded in 1986 as filler for the performance of Andrew's *Variations*.

although never published, did attain a hearing on the BBC in 1951. This short tone poem in sonata allegro[3] form shows a very little originality, although it must be allowed that the orchestration is thoroughly professional. *Aurora* is an eclectic score in which it is obvious that William was emulating his gods, Edward Elgar, Eric Coates, even Richard Rodgers and Giacomo Puccini. But he lacked their strength, drama, and, above all, their originality. Perhaps it was because his own personality and his abilities were so undefined that he vacillated between the popular and accessible serious music. This made him unsuccessful in both areas.

So unsure of the worth of his music was he that he never showed anyone his work. Long after their father died his two sons, Andrew and Julian, discovered his music. "Apart from two cello pieces," Julian remembered, "I hadn't heard one note of it until he died." He recalled how his father would get quite drunk and shut himself away and play his private recordings. Stationed outside the door, Andrew and Julian could hear their father weeping.

As William Lloyd Webber grew older he came no closer to understanding himself or his career. "I think he almost despised himself because he hadn't got Andrew's drive," said Jean late in her life. "He used to get very upset when people talked to him of the pride he must be feeling in his sons. Indeed, he was very proud of them, but these seemingly harmless remarks drove him almost mad. He thought they were inferring that *he* hadn't done anything with his music, but his sons had."

"I think my father was afraid of being subjected to scrutiny," Julian told a reporter for the *Independent* in 1993, adding, "he could not have withstood the criticism and of course he paid the price for that, because it made him thoroughly miserable."

Lloyd Webber's failures made him negative about his own children's accomplishments. He was so bitter about his own plodding career he tried to discourage his sons from going into music. Even when Andrew became a successful and respected composer he told him sourly, "If you ever write a tune as good as 'Some Enchanted Evening' I'll tell you." But he never did.

Andrew took after his father physically and emotionally. A difficult child, wailing, shrieking, and yelling so much that he shattered the peace of his largely residential neighborhood, he was, according to his father, "a mass of energy who wanted to go around screaming the whole time. He wouldn't go to sleep at night."

"The only thing that might calm him down," Jean added, "was 'The Wedding Samba' and other Latin records of bandleader Edmundo Ros. We would play this all night if necessary."

---

[3] See Glossary, p. 423.

When Andrew was three he came down with appendicitis and was rushed to the University College Hospital. The child screamed so loudly that the doctors decided immediately to operate and found that his appendix had burst. He (and his mother) stayed four days in the hospital but were forced to move nightly because the child's screaming got them evicted from every room. During the days, fortunately for the other patients, little Andrew was somewhat becalmed by the picture books of ancient castles his mother brought him. They were to begin his lifelong interest in classical architecture.

His brother, who was born on April 14, 1951, was quite the opposite, both physically and temperamentally, of his older sibling. Julian, oval of face, was to grow tall, whereas Andrew, like his father, was to remain round-faced with beetle brows and attain medium height. Where Andrew was explosive and complaining—his father's son—Julian was calm, assured, patient, and determined—like Jean.

When his mother, who needed the money, decided to leave baby Julian at home with Grandma Molly and take Andrew, three and a half, along to her piano teaching at Wetherby School, the child simply could not be made to sit still. Jean thought that contact with other children would make her boisterous son conform. But she was wrong. Although he himself was a noisy child, to say the least, he could not seem to stand the racket the other children made and at the school would cover his ears to protect himself.

Wetherby was a private school for the affluent and genteel, and Jean's position there was a godsend for the family. Not only did it provide enough money for a more comfortable lifestyle, but its varied program at least kept a boisterous, complaining Andrew occupied.

Jean worked long hours, arriving at the school at 8:00 A.M., teaching a full day, then going from neighborhood to neighborhood by bicycle to visit her private pupils, sometimes not arriving home until ten in the evening. Even then she was not averse to giving a piano lesson to an interested student at that hour. Molly looked after the boys, put them to bed, and saw to their needs. "I was closer to my grandmother," a mature Andrew was to confide, "than I was to either of my parents."

Julian resented the manner in which Andrew would get what he wanted. He would "have tantrums. If he couldn't get his way over something he would wear people down, and eventually make people give in. . . . My grandmother was the one who used to give in to Andrew all the time. . . . He would say 'where are my socks?' and he'd start getting quite agitated, and she would run around and try to find his socks or put together a pair."

Julian feels that the tantrums, anxieties, and obsessiveness are still part of his brother's personality. "That's one of the secrets of his success. . . . He wants to sit in at every rehearsal of his shows, and afterwards he'll be phoning up Trevor Nunn, [the director] to talk about what needs changing."

Although both brothers in maturity have written of their childhood, it is Julian who described the early days so well in his book, *Travels with My Cello.*

> Harrington Court, the large, run-down, late Victorian, red brick block of flats was chiefly memorable for the astonishing ear blowing volume of musical decibel which seemed to burst forth from every room most of the day and night, [including] my father's electric organ, mother's piano, grandmother's deafening (she was deaf) television, elder brother's astounding piano and French horn, and my own scrapings on the cello and blowings on the trumpet.

With well-known English forbearance, Carleton Hobbs, the BBC radio voice of Sherlock Holmes and the neighbor who lived below, complained only twice of the cacophony coming from above: once when Julian emptied a bag of bricks on the floor and again when Andrew's pedal stomping shattered his ceiling.

Today one might diagnose young Andrew Lloyd-Webber as a hyperactive child; back in those days, although his father nicknamed him "Bumper" because he was always rushing around and colliding with the furniture, he was merely considered "full of energy." One wonders whether Andrew's involvement in music, coupled with his noisy habits, was another cry for attention. He showed little aptitude for horn or piano, nor did he display much dexterity on either instrument. Chiefly interested in using the keyboard to create his own tunes, he practiced dutifully if not inspiredly, although his father tried to get his son more interested in music by loudly playing gramophone records of the latest American shows at full volume. Help in the musical-theatrical field came from Aunt Vi, now married to a doctor and retired from the stage, who would come by and occasionally take her favorite nephew along to a musical.

And what a time for the American musical in Britain it was. The year 1951 brought in Cole Porter's *Kiss Me, Kate*, which was especially cherished by the English because of its roots in Shakespeare's *Taming of the Shrew*. Later that year, London saw *South Pacific* (whose movie version a ten-year-old Andrew Lloyd-Webber would sit through a dozen times). The next year brought Irving Berlin's brassy hit *Call Me Madam* and the long-awaited British premiere of George Gershwin and DuBose Heyward's *Porgy and Bess*. The following year, 1953, outdid the prior half decade in that it brought a bonanza of American musicals that swamped the British theater. *Paint Your Wagon*, *Guys and Dolls*, *The King and I*, and *Wish You Were Here* all opened to great acclaim. In the face of this deluge of hits and holdovers like *Carousel* that were still running, the native producers could only offer Ivor Novello's tepid copy of the American backstage classic *42nd Street* with the unfortunate title of *Gay's the Word* and a "small is beautiful" musicalization of the life of Samuel Pepys. Finally, as if to save the British musical stage from total ignominy, two important British entrants arrived in 1953. *Salad Days* by Dorothy Reynolds and Julian Slade was a tale of two college graduates who encounter a tramp with a magic piano capable of making all who hear it break into dance. In spite of mixed reviews, the show remained at the Vaudeville Theatre, brightening the West End for five and a half years, setting a record that would not be broken until *Oliver!* overtook it a decade later. The other show, *The Boy Friend*, with book, words, and music by Sandy Wilson, fell somewhere between camp and nostalgia. It was a charmer that soon crossed the Atlantic to great enthusiasm. In its American incarnation it brought Broadway one of the musical theater's most incandescent luminaries, Julie Andrews.

Undeniably, *The Boy Friend* was beguiling and refreshing, but it was a back-ward look for the burgeoning '50s, a time when the American musical was invading new areas in a headlong rush. Broadway had a good creative start, with its burnished golden assets like Irving Berlin, Frank Loesser, Rodgers and Hammerstein, Harold Arlen, Cole Porter, and Arthur Schwartz still near their peaks, while works by newer composers and lyricists like Lerner and Loewe, Jule Styne, Jerry Herman, Comden and Green, Leonard Bernstein, Adler and Ross, Sheldon Harnick, and Jerry Bock were beginning to be heard.

One could easily counter the continental sentiment of *The Boy Friend* (1954) with a wholly Broadway fable like *Guys and Dolls* (1950). Based on well-known beloved Damon Runyon characters, the show possessed such a daring score that it created a cohesion, a oneness with its book that was to become the hallmark of the American musical for decades to come.

The next year, 1951, Rodgers and Hammerstein outdid themselves in this department by creating *The King and I*, another fresh and daring idea. By this time Jerome Robbins had taken over Agnes de Mille's mantle as number one Broadway choreographer.

It was the rise of television that made the musical theater take a nosedive for the next few seasons. There were, of course, the noble attempts that same year— *A Tree Grows in Brooklyn*, *Flahooley*, and *Paint Your Wagon*—but there was a feeling that Broadway was marking time. The area seemed to be waiting for the next blockbusters to come—and they did not disappoint. *Wonderful Town*, *Can-Can*, and *Kismet* (all 1953) and *By the Beautiful Sea*, *The Pajama Game*, *Peter Pan*, and *Fanny* (all 1954), although not exactly groundbreaking examples of the genre of sensible book and singable songs, showed that by 1955 Broadway had fine-tuned itself and would no longer suffer competition from the "idiot box" that was soon to find a permanent place in the world's living rooms.

Buried among these largely successful but not truly outstanding shows was a little gem that was produced on the fringes of Greenwich Village. *The Golden Apple* was a fresh retelling of the myths of *The Iliad* and *The Odyssey* moved to turn-of-the-century America. Ulysses is returning from the Spanish-American War at the time of a rural county fair. Helen, the sheriff's wife, falls in love with traveling salesman Paris and runs off with him.

The show had a literate book with charming songs by Jerome Moross and John Latouche.[4] More important, because the show cost only $75,000 to mount, it seemed as if the talented creators were thumbing their noses at Broadway, where production costs were soaring. To make matters worse for the Main Stem, *The Golden Apple* won the coveted Critics' Circle Prize and became the first off-Broadway show to move uptown. Unfortunately the show lost its steam in the transfer and closed shortly thereafter, but it was to start a trend. Shows that succeeded in modest surroundings, like *Ain't Misbehavin'*, *Hair*, *A Chorus Line*, or *Rent*, would go on to a long life in larger theaters on Broadway.

When musical theater buffs get together to talk about the sad demise of *The Golden Apple* they invariably mention *House of Flowers*, another radiant musical, which may have been dragged down by Truman Capote's outlandishly poetic book and lyrics. It opened at the end of 1954, the same year as *The Golden Apple*. This was a big, expensive show, very Broadway, which was beloved by the critics, but with a largely unknown black cast it had a curtailed run and lost a pot of money to boot. Musical aficionados remind anyone who will listen that the show was gifted with a combination of Oliver Messel's poetically imaginative costumes and sets and with Harold Arlen's luminous score. The show included "A Sleeping Bee" (which was included on Barbra Streisand's very first solo album), the tender "I Never Has Seen Snow," and "Two Ladies in de Shade of de Banana Tree," in addition to the title song. The failure of *House of Flowers* in spite of its many excellences proved once again that the musical had progressed beyond the point at which excellence of music, lyrics, dancing, costume, or decor could keep a show afloat. It needed a believable libretto. Without that no show could survive. Hammerstein had made us believe what we saw on stage, but he had also sounded the death knell for shows whose only raison d'être was "entertainment."

That axiom would be further tested in March of 1956 when the musical theater would reach its apogee, strangely enough with an American adaptation of a British play, Lerner and Loewe's *My Fair Lady*. Music historian Gerald Bordman says that "it unquestionably represented the glorious fruition of the contemporary school of musical plays with its aim of cohesiveness and tonal integrity." It was a massive hit of the kind that can only be compared to

[4] See p. 40n.

Oklahoma! and *South Pacific*. Its close to three thousand performances on Broadway, a six-year run in London's West End, and frequent revivals attest to *My Fair Lady*'s imperishability.

The original cast recording of the show turned out to be a bonanza for Columbia Records, chalking up the greatest sales worldwide since *Oklahoma!* and *South Pacific*. In a curious note, the British producer Binkie Beaumont insisted that the American recording be withheld from the British public until after the London premiere, which made the disc a much-desired item on the black market. Once it arrived in Britain legally it was played everywhere, especially at Harrington Court Road, where it was heard incessantly. This melodic score soon became familiar to William, Andrew, and even little Julian Lloyd Webber.

But by then Andrew's interest in listening to recordings had waned, and he began to pay attention to historic buildings. At the age of seven, he made up his mind as to what his calling in life would be. He wanted to be an inspector, nay, since even in childhood he never thought small, "Chief Inspector of Ancient Monuments in Britain." To this end he badgered the family into taking holidays where they could visit castles with crumbling walls and the piles of ancient ruins that dot the English landscape.

Jean expected her son to expand his interest in ancient buildings and eventually to choose this as his profession. She taught gifted children every day, and, although Andrew played acceptably the miniature violin on which she taught him, she observed no special talent. He managed to do a bit better on the piano but stopped practicing once he had mastered the pieces she assigned. Then he would begin to paraphrase them. "He was very good at making up his own tunes," was the best she could offer in an interview late in her life. According to Jean, "making up tunes" was not making music.

His mother would have preferred that he study history, for which she always felt he had an aptitude. Accordingly she groomed him, once he finished Wetherby, for Westminster Under School. Jean envisioned Andrew's historical aptitude as a stepping-stone to the great Westminster School, one of the six top public schools (private in American parlance) in England. Gradually she relaxed her demands that Andrew practice his music, as Julian, by contrast, became the performer of the two and could generally be found practicing on his miniature cello. Sometimes the boys would get together for a violin and cello duet.

William Lloyd Webber enjoyed seeing his sons make music together and had them enrolled in the Royal College of Music's Junior Department. A performance of Haydn's *Military Symphony* was being prepared, and because both boys would need to prove proficiency on another instrument, he let them choose their instruments for inclusion in this concert. They chose percussion—Andrew on cymbals and Julian on the bass drum. Poor Carleton Hobbs, rehearsing in the flat below them his forthcoming lines for Sherlock Holmes, must have had a time of it, for the boys did most of their practicing at home.

Jean increased her insistence that Andrew maintain his academic standard, for she knew that he needed to attain superior grades to enter Westminster on scholarship. Without discounted tuition the school would be beyond their means.

But Jean didn't count on the influence that was to be exerted upon him by his Aunt Vi. After attending a performance of My Fair Lady, the teenager decided to combine his love of ancient buildings, long-gone panoply, parental approval, mastery over his kid brother, and control—all this could be had by involving himself in the theater. With the support of his aunt he self-centeredly involved everyone in the building of a toy theater.

This was to be no cardboard trinket, but an operative miniature house built of bricks and wood. Andrew remembered it as being several feet wide. It had a florid proscenium arch, flyspace, and wings where characters could stand poised, ready for their entrances. The backdrop was colored paper, and there was a curtain and "travelers" made of fabric borrowed from samplebooks. There was even a revolving stage made from a discarded phonograph's turntable.

Andrew Lloyd-Webber soon was to become a theatrical producer. Now he peopled the shows (for which he wrote his own music or adapted the music of others) with a stageful of toy soldiers and a complete marching band in the pit. He would move the leading characters around from scene to scene.

"He was a perfectionist, the same as he is now," recalls his brother, Julian, who was quickly forced into a theatrical apprenticeship. The programs and the cast list were all neatly typed out. "He'd play the music at the piano and I would operate the toy soldiers. Everything had to be right or Andrew would be furious. Sometimes I'd move to the back of the room and handle the torch [flashlight], and the family and all the cats in the house would come and watch these extravaganzas." "Friends too," Jean added deprecatingly, "would sometimes be subjected to these plays although normally it was just us."

Andrew had sketched his first tunes on paper when he was seven and from time to time had gone beyond mere improvisation of his melodies. Now that he was eleven, he collected a sheaf of the best ones he used in his home theatrical performances, wrote them out, and called the work The Toy Theatre, arranged as a suite of six piano pieces. He labeled it "Opus 1."

William came to his rescue by correcting his son's musical orthography. Then he sent a copy of the manuscript to the well-known British pedagogic magazine Music Teacher, accompanied by the following rather patronizing letter:

I have been rather amused at the efforts of my own boy, Andrew, to find his own harmonies for the tunes he composes on his play-room piano. He makes up various "incidental pieces" for plays which he "produces" in his play-room theatre: it is all quite spontaneous, and this branch of his music making is deliberately left "self-taught" at the moment. In the six pieces he has composed, the tunes and the harmonies are all his own: and all I have done is do the slight editing which is obviously necessary to make them acceptable to players.

In publishing the pieces, the editor of *Music Teacher* added a footnote stating that the magazine believed that the pieces "which are clearly a product of a gifted child of one of our most distinguished musicians will be enjoyed because of their natural and spontaneous qualities."

The pieces themselves are negligible, reminiscent of the childhood etudes all children are forced to practice and which Andrew Lloyd-Webber often twisted around to create a modicum of originality. One of them, consisting of a descending scale line followed by a skippy line, was remembered and used more than thirty years later as the basis of *Aspects of Love*'s "Chanson d'Enfance." With a French lyric added by Don Black and Charles Hart, this naive melody plays while the romance's young lovers journey cinematically through the production's "idyllic local scenery."

As a published composer, now Andrew became increasingly the family star, and using his clout to pursue his burgeoning interest in history, he could direct the family excursions more and more frequently. After they returned from each jaunt Andrew wrote amazingly mature monographs on the subject. These he typed up neatly and illustrated with postcards and photographs clipped from travel magazines. He gave his essays the imposing title of *Ancient Monuments in the Home Counties*. Under the title he printed "First edition, November 1959 and Second edition, (revised) February, 1960. By Andrew Lloyd-Webber[5] (Also Author of Ancient Monuments in England and Wales, and Our Monastic Heritage, (not yet in print) 8 Volumes."

He never completed the grandiose eight volumes he planned, but by the time he was thirteen he had written a treatise he called *Roman Ruins in England and Wales* and another, *The Welsh Border Castles*. He made several copies of each, put prices on them and sold them, to family and friends. Although his first wife, Sarah Hugill, said (after their divorce) she found the selling of his homemade books "cheeky," most of his relatives were struck with the youth's sense of entrepreneurship. The books were Andrew's own precursors of desktop publishing.

If he was too old to stamp his feet to something he objected to, he was not too young to get up on a soapbox to complain about the state of repair of sacred monuments. Here are some excerpts from a letter he wrote to the Minister of Works:

Dear Sir:
    I am very concerned about the state of ancient monuments which are not under the care of the Ministry of Works.

[5] In several of the youthful monographs and letters, Andrew chose to hyphenate his last name.

I have been making a tour of the buildings on the Welsh border, and in the course of this, two or three horrible examples of decaying buildings were visited.

The first was Usk Castle. This is covered with ivy and plants to the extent that one can hardly make out the periods of construction . . .

An even worse example can be seen at Clun. . . . The castle hove is owned by the parish council and it is in a terrible state . . .

The last is at Whittington in Shropshire, which, I understand has been offered to you for preservation, but due to lack of finances you are hesitating to accept. This is the most terrible state of affairs and surely something can be done about it.

Yours sincerely,
Andrew Lloyd-Webber [sic]
(Aged 13)

Jean, who never thought much of Andrew's prospects in music, heartily endorsed her son's passion for historical monuments and to that end urged him to augment his knowledge of the past. Besides, at about this time she had a burgeoning musical genius to supervise. His name was John Lill, future winner of the prestigious Tchaikovsky International Piano Competition, then seventeen and for some unfathomable reason deeply interested in nine-year-old Julian. Julian remembered that he was

the star student at Junior college and took an interest in me and it wasn't long before I asked him to come home and meet my parents. We took to him at once and he would amuse us with his party trick which was to look at a piece of music, then go straight to the piano and play it from memory. My mother, in particular, took a lot of interest in John who seemed to become almost like another son to her.

In short order, Lill, who came from a poor family in London's East End, was invited to spend a night or two each week and join the musical assemblage at Harrington Court. His father, who worked in a wire factory, had incurred debts from which he was unable to free himself; his mother had taken on "three vicious factory jobs" in order to hold the family together and to pay for his musical education. No sooner had Lill come to stay with them than William Lloyd Webber began giving him composition lessons. It was as though his own son, Andrew, was too willful, wanting fiercely to make his own way, so Lill became the surrogate who could take direction.

One cannot help but see a similarity in the Webbers' welcoming a precocious talent like Lill into their family to the Hammersteins' opening their home to Sondheim. Sondheim's carte blanche into his parents' life fostered resentments in James Hammerstein, who felt his friend had usurped some of his father's attention that rightly should have been directed at him; so did Andrew harbor resentment at Lill's proficiency in an art that stood at the peak of his mother's esteem.

It was important for Andrew Lloyd-Webber to prove himself to his mother, because Jean devoted so much of her energy to seeking out other people's talented children, whom she would encourage. It was noble work, but her generosity left her mark on her two sons. "There were moments when we felt that nobody was really interested in us," says Andrew. "It always seemed to be in the other people," he added, certainly meaning Lill.

Andrew was torn because his father now saw an echo of his own compositional eclecticism and pulled him to follow music, never insisting it be in the classic tradition, but rather believing Andrew's real gift lay in the popular field. But Jean's influence was stronger, and following his mother's dictum, he applied for admission to Westminster. It must be added that Andrew Lloyd-Webber, torn between following a career of historian and one in the theater, had already evolved a plan that would appease both parents: "I knew it had to be the theater with architecture and history in second place," he confessed.

Westminster was known for both academic excellence and what its housemasters called the "cultivation of a certain kind of individualism in its students." Former student David Van Eysen feels "Westminster students were—and still are—distinguishable from students at other schools by their style of dress, insouciant demeanor and by their sense of intellectual value."

The urge to please his parents, however great, was not nearly as strong as the urge to be accepted by his peers. Perhaps because Andrew wanted so desperately to conform and be like his classmates, he developed a working knowledge of the music of his own era. "I was a bit young for Elvis, but I sort of caught the tail-end of him," he was to report. Yet even though he admired the Beatles and the harmony of the Everly Brothers, he was pretty much of an outsider in this area. Trapped between two stools or actually between two schools, "it was pretty natural for me to hear Rock and Roll alongside Prokofiev." But one can see from the music he admired at the time that it was neither the elemental rhythmic propulsion of rock nor the angular melodic line and nontraditional harmony of Prokofiev that appealed greatly to his aesthetic. Rather it was the strongly melodic Broadway ballad, or perhaps its sentimentality, that attracted him most.

"My ideal, really, was Richard Rodgers," he was to admit, "and then, subsequently, it grew into musicals in general by all the best writers and composers. I remember I was able to play some of their tunes on the French horn which I was rather better at than the violin.

"I suppose I was being influenced to compose my own tunes in roughly their style. Though I must say that, when I think back to those days, I remember almost nothing to do with music at all. It was prep, prep, prep, and being made to learn this and that."

The prepping paid off, and Andrew Lloyd-Webber was allowed to enter Westminster, where he would be one of the seventy Rigaud House's day students.

Fortunately his tuition didn't cause a family hardship, for it was covered by a small inheritance Molly had come into. Once he was there his academic record was not outstanding, but he was literate and musical enough to impress Rigaud's headmaster, Frank Klivington, with his manner at the piano. But Klivington found Andrew "a rather nervous boy who was very determined about where he was going and also where he was *not* going."

Klivington, an aficionado of Gilbert and Sullivan, wanted to raise the literary standard of the house, and in 1960 he persuaded his sixteen-year-old head boy, Robin Barrow, rather a facile rhymer, to devise new, topical lyrics for productions of *The Mikado* and *HMS Pinafore*.

Later that year, the budding lyricist, dissatisfied with being a mere parodist, began looking for a tunesmith with whom he might tackle an original musical. He lit on the new day boy who was a specialist in medieval architecture and played the piano rather facilely.

Barrow's need was a godsend for Lloyd-Webber, who says that "by then most of the people of my vintage were trying to be Beatles, while I found it almost impossible to write music which didn't have a theatrical basis on which to do it. I still find it hard if there isn't a theatrical raison d'être." In this he is like Stephen Sondheim, who has stated that he has neither the gift nor the interest in creating songs that have no place in the theater.

"I underestimated him," Barrow admitted. "I saw myself as an accomplished lyric writer and Andrew as a useful piano-player." Already wedded to the concept he achieved in mature shows like *Aspects of Love* or *The Phantom of the Opera*, Andrew wanted their show, *Cinderella*, to incorporate a single theme that kept returning, but Barrow, three years his senior, overruled him. Although he was vetoed on the leitmotif idea, nevertheless he and Barrow turned out a satirical pantomime that they titled, provocatively, *Cinderella Up the Beanstalk*[6] *(and Most Everywhere Else!)*. Some of the songs, mawkish and sentimental by turns, were "Foolish Tears," "Greater Men Than I," and "I Continually Reflect on My Present State of Mind."

Andrew Lloyd-Webber's nervousness meant that he constantly gave a childish appearance to Barrow. More importantly, he tried desperately to be "shag," which in Westminster parlance meant "the art of achieving a natural superiority without really trying."

The next year, which would be Barrow's last at the Underschool, Lloyd-Webber and Barrow concocted a libretto that spoofed everyone from Zeus to Socrates (with a lot of James Bond thrown in along the way). So mercurial was

---

[6] In scheme and plotting the admixture of fairy tales and fantasy in this musical was a precursor of and not unlike the reinvented fables James Lapine would create in his 1987 collaboration with Stephen Sondheim, *Into the Woods*.

the plot that four titles were chosen: *Utter Chaos, No Jeans for Venus, Socrates Swings,* and *Lovers and Friends.*

The best-received songs in the new revue were a juvenile, "Too Young to Understand," and another on a similar theme, "Too Shy." This revue was not totally original in that many of the songs had been heard before in *Cinderella.* To appease the audience, the young collaborators inserted the following note in the program: "They are all Barrow-Webber compositions so you may have heard them before under different titles." Recycling, like thematic unity, would be a lifelong habit of Andrew Lloyd-Webber. But in that musical frugality he was not unlike Jule Styne or even Richard Rodgers, who, if a tune didn't work in a given situation, would squirrel it away and bring it out in a more favorable setting.

The next year, just days before his fourteenth birthday (the final cut-off for applications), Jean persuaded a reluctant Andrew to fill out the forms and write a paper on history so he might apply for Westminster. His essay on Victorian architecture won him the coveted Challenge Scholarship, which paid the full tuition of £400 per year. Considering that William was only earning £3000 per annum, it was a godsend for the Lloyd Webbers.

Now that Andrew was a scholar, it was obligatory that he board at the school, and he was not permitted to leave Westminster except on weekends, which he looked forward to eagerly. According to one of his classmates, all the boarders sneaked out even during the week for an adventure into Piccadilly Circus or Carnaby Street—where the action was.

Even at home, life was more exciting now, for the moment he had moved out, Jean had offered his room to John Lill, and the budding pianist had accepted, indeed welcomed, moving into this bohemian accommodation. For the past two years, Lill had often spent the night with the Lloyd Webbers, especially when he had classes or rehearsal early the next morning at the nearby Royal College of Music.

Living at Harrington Court, Lill frequently accompanied Julian, now a diligent burgeoning cellist, who was also headed for a recital career. For his part, Andrew was able to put aside his resentment toward the young interloper into his mother's affection, for as both young men matured, their interests diverged, Lloyd-Webber's into theater and pop, Lill's toward the concert platform. Assured of his parents' love, Andrew's main concern was to rise above plodding through the highly competitive atmosphere of Westminster.

Life at school was enough of a care. One of his classmates reported that even in music, his best subject, "at Westminster, where the tradition was certainly classical music, he didn't fit in." Try as he might, all the music he wrote was out of sync with all around him. For the teachers it was too pop oriented; to the other students his ballad-like melodies, strongly evocative of *The Sound of*

Music or *South Pacific*, seemed old hat. His music came nowhere near the clean Mersey sound that by now had flooded Britain.

Younger than his classmates, shy and solitary, and terrible at sports, Andrew Lloyd-Webber was hardly the ideal entrant in the British public school tradition. Almost immediately he was excused from team sports, because Jean came down to the school and bluntly told the headmasters that "he needn't waste his time with sports, when it was perfectly obvious that he was no good at them and would never need them later in life." She insisted that he could spend his time far more profitably in music. He was not, however, excused from the routine of the compulsory military corps, although he is reported to have been Westminster's most inept cadet. "It was the thing I loathed the most," he was to state. "I was nearly thrown out of it, which would have been something of a feat— the only person ever to be thrown out of something that was compulsory!"

Andrew, who was always fiercely self-promotional, had, at thirteen, sent some of his ideas for a fledgling musical comedy—songs (with lyrics by a friend of his Aunt Vi) and a hint of the plot—to an agent, who got it to one of Britain's top agencies, the Noel Gay Organization. After the fortunes the papers announced that were being made by signing young talent at the *very* beginnings of their careers, it was not uncommon for respected agencies to sign youths with even the slimmest talents.

Since the early '60s and the phenomenal success of the Beatles, agents and impresarios had become aware that much money was to be made by catering to the major record buyers—the teen-age market. Now, worldwide, the important rock artists were coming from Britain, although it had not been so in the beginning.

British music had begun an about-face due to three major infusions from the United States. The first, a fad called "skiffle," a form of American washboard and tin-can band music, gripped England in 1956. Anyone who had an old metal washboard and a chest could play it. The song that started it all, "Rock Island Line," was sung in a high-pitched wail by a young Lonnie Donegan. It soon became a teenage anthem.

The second was a movie about American juvenile delinquents called *Blackboard Jungle*. Based on a hard-hitting novel by Evan Hunter, not only did the movie romanticize teen rebellion in general, but the pervasive song "Rock Around the Clock" was unlike anything ever heard before in Great Britain. Sung by a plump and balding middle-aged man named Bill Haley, there was a driving quality to the music that most teenagers found narcotic.

The third and most powerful influence was the musical and physical embodiment of rock and roll, a teenager like the majority of his fans, Elvis Presley. Before the year was out he would make two top-grossing movies, cut two number one albums, and place an unbelievable *seventeen* songs on national charts.

Young Brits had copied and adopted the American sound, refined it, and cornered the record market. Soon it seemed every small town had a major group, some of whom like Gerry and the Pacemakers, The Dave Clark Five, The Who, The Kinks, and the Rolling Stones, were to become well known.

Andrew Lloyd-Webber was not so fortunate. His contract with the Gay Organization expired after two years and nothing came of it, but in 1963 his song "Make Believe Love" was recorded (though never released), as part of a new contract. This came about because Andrew had sent a demo of the song, as musicians say, "over the transom" to Decca Records. It had come into the hands of Charles Blackwell, who was a client and friend of the well-known British publisher of Arlington Books, Desmond Elliott. Elliott, who was also a theatrical and literary agent, felt the song was close enough to the main stream to be acceptable and its young creator "groomable" and signed Andrew to a contract to be represented by his firm. The song eventually got the fifteen-year-old composer an exclusive contract with Southern Music.

For a composer, having an agent, even as powerful a one as Elliot, may be a source of pride but it is no panacea. Unless he wants to write only symphonic music, he needs a capable lyricist. To Andrew, his minicareer, hardly begun, was at a standstill. Now in his last year at Westminster, asked to write a revue, he felt even more keenly the pinch of being lyricless. Whatever the worth of the products he and Barrow had turned out—songs with titles as sophomoric as "I Continually Reflect on My Present State of Mind"—working with Barrow was better than working alone.

At last he hit on an idea of producing a variety show, enlisting various home-grown pop groups, among them The High Fives, The Witnesses, and The Trekkers. And, of course, Andrew could perform his own songs—those that did already have lyrics—on the program.

The show, which debuted on June 30, 1964, was essentially Lloyd-Webber's farewell to Westminster. Called *Play the Fool*, its novelty was a departure for stuffy Westminster, and it was hailed as a great success. Several of the groups it introduced were signed to record contracts. The last page of its program, which included laudatory remarks from the heads of the school to the young producer, also contained a quote from Lloyd-Webber as to his plans for the future, which read: "I expect I'll give up writing 'pop' soon. Then I'll devote myself to composing for the musical theatre."

Having made a fruitless search for talent at Westminster, and having heard that Oxford was home to the country's avant-garde poets, Andrew sensed it was time to move on. True to his resolve, by December he had applied for and, with a paper on Victorian architecture, won the Exhibition Scholarship to Magdalen College, Oxford.

Unlike Sondheim when he headed to Williamstown, Andrew Lloyd-Webber knew what he wanted to make his life's work. He also knew he was so ungifted with words that no amount of reading or study would ever make him capable of writing lyrics to his own songs. Thus he was convinced that his career could not take off unless he could work with an imaginative—hopefully poetic—lyricist.

Tim Rice, an intellectual with an encyclopedic knowledge of pop music, was in a similar boat. He had written both music and words to some songs and had even had one recorded. But in his heart of hearts he too knew his failings. He knew he was not a composer.

While he was following every lead in order to meet a suitable one, he had developed an idea for a book that would list the world's top hit singles, a sort of compendium that was not unlike what would come to be called *The Guinness Book of Popular Hits*. Now he wangled an introduction to publisher Desmond Elliott. That afternoon Elliott turned thumbs down on the book but was interested to hear about Tim's ambitions as a lyricist.

He immediately thought of putting him together with his client, the Westminster whiz kid who was capable of writing any kind of song. "Get in touch with him," Elliott said, jotting down the Lloyd Webbers' address. "Maybe something will come of it."

Sondheim—Words Only

IN 1963, HIS LAST YEAR at Westminster, none of his contemporaries thought of Andrew Lloyd-Webber as a lyricist, notwithstanding the fact that he had written words *and* music for his first recorded song, "Make Believe Love." Conversely, in the same year the public at large pegged Stephen Sondheim as a lyricist, not a composer, because he had had such stunning success in that capacity with *West Side Story*.[1]

The first hint to the British that Sondheim was capable of turning out lyrics *and* music came that very year when *A Funny Thing Happened on the Way to the Forum* was first presented in London. As its music was not greatly successful, it did not change the public's conception of Sondheim as a brilliant lyricist but a so-so composer. His lyrics for *West Side Story* and *Gypsy* had so impressed the British critics—notoriously in awe of brilliant wordsmiths—that it was to take him years to be accepted as a composer for the theater, one capable of writing lyrics as well as music—a total songsmith.

Yet from his college days on, he saw himself as a composer.

The $3000 Hutchinson Prize enabled him to follow that path. He planned to apply it to further study but was not interested in going to a conservatory. He simply wanted to understand "how music works."

His choice as a teacher, Milton Babbitt, was, on first glance, an odd one to lead him along that path, to explain how music works. Babbitt is primarily known as a composer of atonal music, but he had been classically trained and, like Sondheim, is an eclectic who, once he has solved a problem, believes in moving on.

---

[1] The film version of *West Side Story* opened abroad in 1961 to great acclaim, although here, as in the stage version, Sondheim's contribution was largely overlooked by the critics. The truncated film version of *Gypsy*, starring Rosalind Russell, was released two years later. Strangely, the original theater version did not play the West End until Angela Lansbury re-created the role especially for the London stage in 1973.

By the time Sondheim first came to know his mentor, Babbitt had already wiped his hands of traditional tonal music. Then, in an era in which many composers were still embracing the atonal and twelve-tone school, Babbitt began experimenting with electronic synthesizers—a novelty in those days. Nor was he ever in search of commercial success or musical acceptance.[2]

He was, as Sondheim stated, "in the avant-garde of the avant-garde," adding that "his work was so inaccessible he is a true composer's composer." Yet the academic community must have seen merit in Babbitt's music, for by that time he had been appointed associate professor of music by Princeton University.

Babbitt was also a frustrated songwriter. At the time Sondheim came to his studio in New York City's Chelsea area for the first of his all-afternoon lessons, Babbitt was preparing a show he hoped would star Mary Martin as Helen of Troy.

Beyond their interest in musical theater, they had a lot in common, for Babbitt too was a skilled mathematician, with a gift, nay a passion, for the orderliness and mathematical basis of the relationships of notes. He could agree with Sondheim's assertion that "an octave is not just two C's; there's an eight there. It's almost subconscious. If you study music you must be aware of these things. It's a language . . . almost computerese."

Babbitt knew Sondheim was chiefly interested in writing for the musical stage, not the operatic stage. (Opera is anathema to Sondheim; he has voiced his low regard for the form on more than one occasion, because he feels that opera is concerned with the singer while musical theater is interested in the song.) To that end, before tackling the analysis of a Beethoven sonata or a Mozart symphony, separating movements, analyzing harmony and instrumentation, or going into species counterpoint, teacher and pupil would spend an hour analyzing the best, and only the best, in popular music.

Sondheim never forgot Babbitt's penetrating analysis of Jerome Kern's masterful song "All the Things You Are," and he even passed on an explanation of its unique harmonic complexities to his students when he gave a seminar on musical theater at Oxford almost forty years later.

But lest the reader assume Sondheim was running the show and could direct his course of instruction as he chose, one must add that Milton Babbitt filled in the advanced areas that were not beyond Williams professor Robert Barrow's ken, but beyond his course of study. Sondheim learned about orchestration,

---

[2] Since 1958 Babbitt has been inexorably associated with an essay misnamed "Who Cares If You Listen?," which was published in *High Fidelity* magazine. The composer's original title for the speech he gave to his colleagues, which was reprinted in the magazine, was "The Composer as Specialist." Babbitt (who won a Pulitzer Prize for Music in 1982) remains chagrined that his words were published under so provocative and misleading a title.

thematic development, the use of dissonance, harmonic rhythm, and complex counterpoint. Babbitt was a stickler when it came to understanding what makes an interesting composition—its organization, its development, its total structure.

For his part, Babbitt found Sondheim "terribly bright and ambitious. He could have been good as any sort of composer, but there was no question that Broadway was where he wanted to be." He was also able to analyze the reasons he believed Sondheim would achieve his ambitious goals. Citing the social pressure, Sondheim's sophistication, his strong sense of loyalty to principles, his many theatrical contacts (helpful in securing performances of his work), and his lack of financial urgency, "he was simply going to make it. It was perfectly obvious that he had grown up in a society of celebrities and he wanted to become a fellow celebrity," Babbitt concluded.

Why wouldn't Sondheim have theatrical connections? After having spent so much time with the Hammersteins and knowing Richard Rodgers, he and the composer's daughter Mary worked as apprentices at the Westport Playhouse the first summer after his graduation. They not only learned about summer stock that year but cemented their social and songwriting friendship. According to biographer Meryle Secrest, he had been introduced to Harold Prince by Mary Rodgers on the opening night of *South Pacific*. Sondheim says it was the Hammersteins who made the introduction. But no matter who made the presentation, now both young men met frequently and talked incessantly about the future of the theater and their place in it. From his college days onward Sondheim also developed an enduring friendship with Burt Shevelove, who was to co-author the book of *A Funny Thing* a few years down the road.

He could lament with these buddies about much of the tired hack work that the musical theater of the '50s had ushered in. Irving Berlin, Rodgers and Hammerstein, Harold Arlen, Arthur Schwartz, and Howard Dietz were all well into middle age and complacency. Indeed, the deplorable season 1951–52 was the nadir for the musical. Only nine new musicals were offered, the fewest since well back in the nineteenth century, and, except for *Paint Your Wagon*, not a hit among them.

Sondheim was champing at the bit and Babbitt knew it. In some ways his apprenticeship with Babbitt was as important as his years under Hammerstein's aegis. "One was theater," he told Samuel Freedman in a *New York Times* interview, "the other music. What I was learning from Milton was basic grammar—sophisticated grammar, but grammar. It was a language, whereas what I learned from Oscar was what to do with language. They are twin pillars, but it's like one is red and one is white. I learned from Milton the means of holding an ear over a period of time, how you keep someone listening for forty-five minutes so that at the end they feel they've heard a piece. And that's not what I learned from Hammerstein."

In the two years they were to work together Sondheim produced a concerto for two pianos, but in his "other" area he continued to work on the last of his "Hammerstein projects," the fourth, the original musical.

"Composing was my indulgence," Sondheim was to say. He was living with his father and Alicia on Fifth Avenue and 82nd Street and was sleeping on a cot in their dining room. He liked his father's Knabe grand piano and wrote and tried out most of the songs from his show *Climb High* on it. But not being pressed for money—he had the substantial Hutchinson prize money—he dawdled about, polishing and finally finishing the show.

Both Oscar Hammerstein and Dorothy remained very close to their surrogate son, and he continued to visit them in New York and at the Bucks County farm. But after Sondheim had completed his second year of study with Babbitt, they knew he was ready to move on. Besides, his father and Alicia made it clear that they wanted their dining room back.

Always trying to help his career, the Hammersteins brought him along one evening to a dinner party at the home of Donald and Pat Klopfer. Donald was the publisher who co-founded Random House, and it was at that party Sondheim met George Oppenheimer, then a screenwriter and later a critic. Oppenheimer needed an assistant to help him write the twenty-nine segments of the series of *Topper*[3] scripts for which he was contracted, and Oscar, knowing that Sondheim needed a job, asked him to show Oppenheimer some of his work. He liked what he saw of Sondheim's literary output, and a few weeks later the twenty-three-year-old was off to the West Coast, where he and Oppenheimer fulfilled the commitment. Sondheim turned out about ten shows alone, they collaborated on another ten, and Oppenheimer completed the rest.

It was quite a feat, and although Martin Gottfried has described Sondheim "as a composer first, a lyricist by knack, and a librettist only when necessary," it is amusing to think that his first professional earnings came from yet another area—writing television scripts.

Sondheim has said he was grateful for the solvency writing the *Topper* episodes allowed him as well as the experience of telling a story in four chapters, totaling twenty-two and one-half minutes, each chapter followed by a commercial. Certainly the discipline of ending each segment with a "teaser" is marvelous training for anyone intending to write musical theater.

---

[3] *Topper*, originally a 1937 movie starring Constance Bennett, Cary Grant, and Roland Young, is the story of two obstreperous ghosts who return to bedevil and dominate the life of their former banker (Young). Adapted from a novel by Thorne Smith, the film was so successful that it spawned several sequels. The enormously popular television series it engendered starred Anne Jeffreys and Robert Sterling and ran from October 1953 until May 1957. Reruns can still be seen on late-night TV.

His time in California also allowed him to finally wrap up *Climb High*. The show's title comes from a maxim inscribed on a pillar at Sondheim's college dormitory: Climb High, Climb Far / Your Goal, The Sky / Your Aim, The Star. The musical concerned an undergraduate who comes to New York intending to be an actor. As per his assignment from Hammerstein, Sondheim wrote the libretto and score and sent it off to Oscar for a comment.

Hammerstein's comment that the script was too long has been mentioned before, but even though Sondheim realized his scenario needed cutting, he knew the songs it contained had some merit and played them for many of the show-biz friends he had cultivated. One of these was Lemuel Ayers, whom Sondheim had met when they were both ushering at a mutual friend's wedding.

Ayers, one of the country's best set designers (*Oklahoma!*, *Bloomer Girl*), had recently added producing to his dossier (*Kiss Me, Kate*, *Out of This World*). He had a property called *Front Porch in Flatbush*, about a group of kids in Brooklyn in 1928 who all invest in the stock market. The play was written by two Hollywood screenwriters, twin brothers Julius and Philip Epstein, who won an Academy Award for *Casablanca*. Ayers had first approached Frank Loesser to musicalize this, thinking of Loesser's *Guys and Dolls*, especially since this story was very "New York," but Loesser was busy with *The Most Happy Fella* and turned it down.

"So Lem heard some of my stuff from these four apprentice musicals," Sondheim was to say, "and hired me on spec [he paid Sondheim $100 for each song] to write three songs which he and Julie [Epstein, the co-librettist] liked, and we then went into supposed production of this show which was then retitled *Saturday Night*. It was the first professional work I'd done, I was prepared to do professional work because of what Oscar had made me go through."

During the course of the first backer's audition Sondheim found himself in a now humorous, but then embarrassing predicament. He was scheduled to play *and* sing the entire score, and he came to the Ayers' apartment early to warm up at the piano. To his alarm he noticed that the zipper on his fly was broken. He beckoned to his by now close friend Mary Rodgers, who had come to lend moral support, and asked her to taxi to his father's apartment and bring back his "dress" suit. Telling her it was in the hall closet that contained only coats, she found the suit, which she recognized because of "a dead carnation in the lapel." Sondheim had been an usher at a friend's wedding several months earlier, and as Mary said, was "very casual and unconcerned about his clothes."

Rodgers, mission completed, got back to the Ayers apartment just in time for Sondheim to slip into the suit and proceed with the audition. Unfortunately that audition "didn't raise a cent," so Ayers decided to use performers like Arte Johnson, Jack Cassidy, Alice Ghostley, and, several auditions later, Joel Grey.

Sondheim remembered that there were about seven more auditions, but "Lem died and the show never got anywhere. The rights passed to his widow and she couldn't raise the needed money, and so it just lay in the trunk,[4] but that was my portfolio."

Saturday Night was no better, and not much worse, than many of the musicals that were being done in the early '50s. Martin Gottfried in *Sondheim* says the scenes work "to conclude with a musical number of one kind or another. The common wisdom," he continues, "at the time was that a musical's script should be a complete play, coherent without the songs, and that is probably the best that could be said about this one." But Sondheim disagrees, and maintains that the songs "make large patches of dialogue unnecessary." He must certainly have felt so because, according to critic Peter Marks, in its latest incarnation Sondheim "served as editor and slashed Julius Epstein's book" to a workable length.

According to theater historian Gerald Bordman, "The early 1950s was a time of lowering of standards . . . to an abysmal state." Most of the better Broadway musicals of those years were either one-man or one-woman shows (Beatrice Lillie, Victor Borge, Ethel Waters) or else they had a slight book that gave wide latitude to a star like Phil Silvers or Nancy Walker to do their "shtick" to draw in the customers. It was a time when the revue, expanded from the cabaret— *Bagels and Yox, The Borscht Capades, New Faces, Two's Company*—proliferated. Later in the decade, the majority of shows were strongly plotted.

As for the score of *Saturday Night*, the most that can be said of Sondheim's eclectic songs is that they are thoroughly professional and eminently singable. Although the story is supposed to take place in 1928, there is, apart from a few ricky-tick syncopations here and there, very little that suggests the buoyant Charleston era. Except for the title song, which does have a naive quality, most of the rather sophisticated lyrics sound like they are coming from the mouths of Manhattanites rather than from denizens of Brooklyn. "In the Movies," a long number about the disappointment a young woman gets in reality as opposed to

---

[4] There was an attempt to revive *Saturday Night* in 1959, after *Gypsy* opened on Broadway, Jule Styne announced that he would present it in a production by Bob Fosse. Once into auditions, however, Sondheim realized it was already too late to go back to its juvenile style and the production was abandoned again. But in late 1997 the Bridewell Theatre Company in London presented the show for a limited run. A CD recording of this production was released in September 1998.

In May 1999, the Pegasus Players, a tiny Chicago troupe to which Sondheim entrusted the material, presented the show with two new songs. Peter Marks, writing in the *New York Times*, noted that "the show is no mere peek at messy, fraying pages from Mr. Sondheim's discard pile . . . [but] is a musical comedy of beguiling innocence that hints at a composer's promise in every downy-smooth and stylish number."

Then early in 2000, Second Stage Theater produced the show for a limited run off-Broadway and included two more songs that had been omitted from the Bridewell Production. Critics found "a sweet innocence" in the work, while Sondheim called it "his baby picture."

the experiences she sees in the cinema, tries terribly hard for cleverness. One gets rhymes like "Stella Dallas's" and "callouses." But its melodies are pure show tunes, attesting to Sondheim's mastery of the ABAC form. His melodies have all the swagger, singability, and Broadway pizzazz of the kind of show tune we would identify with Jerry Herman a decade later.

Most of the lyrics, which are heavily Lorenz Hart-ish as seen through the eyes of Cole Porter, are too clever by half. Because of this many of the numbers sound like cabaret turns. For example, "Love's a Bond," replete with references to the stock market, ends with a predictable, "though love is common, still and all it's preferred," and never travels far beyond its Wall Street references. But its verse, which is far more interesting than its refrain, is certainly clever.

I'm smart as a fox,	I like to invest
With bonds and with stocks	But I won't be a great financier.
I've cornered wheat, alfalfa, and rye.	No, the stock I like
But now I'm tired of	Is free and clear.
That hue and cry.	And I'll be blue chip
Consolidated love is all I'll buy.	If you chip
When put to the test	In with me, my dear . . .

Perhaps the most interesting song in *Saturday Night* is its simplest ballad. "All for You" is the kind of song that Sondheim writes effortlessly. Its vamp reminds me of a song to come, "Losing My Mind," from *Follies*. Both songs share the vacant first beat of the bar so reminiscent of Rodgers when he was working with Hart. The motif, which employs wide skips, is not new, but in its final few bars, reaching up to the skip of a major seventh, we get more than a hint of the emotionality Sondheim would show in later works.

The song's lyric is artless and pure. One feels Hammerstein over his pupil's shoulder, advising him that "honest is better than clever." But in the A2 and release, a glimmer of ambivalence—that a loving relationship might include anger, a snake in the garden, a concept that Hammerstein's love songs would never have allowed—shows through. It presages the Sondheim of "Sorry-Grateful," "Every Day a Little Death," or "Good Thing Going."

I'm all for you,	If I get mad
Whatever happens,	When I think you're wrong,
My dreams are yours to share.	Maybe I am wrong
Sometimes it's true,	Too.
My words are bitter,	But good or bad,
But that's because I care.	Ev'rything I do
	Is all for love of you.

Looking over the score and libretto of *Saturday Night* one can see that had the show been produced as planned in 1955, without the book revisions, additional songs, and new orchestrations that were done in 1999, it might not have lasted more than a few performances, but still the score stands head and shoulders above the maiden efforts of even acknowledged geniuses like Rodgers, Porter, or Coward.

The production's collapse before the musical was even on its feet was a crushing blow to Sondheim, yet auditioning for members of the theatrical community was to pay off for him. One of the people who listened to his score was playwright Arthur Laurents, who would become the librettist of *West Side Story*.

The odyssey of *West Side Story* began in 1948, when Jerome Robbins first conceived the idea, although the show did not reach Broadway until almost a decade later. Robbins's idea for a serious musical, a modernization of the tragic conflicts in *Romeo and Juliet*, was engendered when he was asked by his friend Montgomery Clift for help in playing the role of Romeo in a fresh way. It was the search for the contemporary that made him think of moving the locale to the East Side of New York. The tragic implications of two young people who fall in love despite antagonism from each of their peer groups was not new, even with Shakespeare[5] His idea centered on the antagonism of the Italian Catholics who lived in tenement slums near their wealthier Jewish neighbors. Robbins set the conflict in spring, at a time when Passover and Easter fall on the same date. The time slot was to be contemporary. In 1949 he came to Leonard Bernstein with the idea.

Aiming to repeat the success he and Bernstein had had with *On the Town* (also an original idea of his), he envisioned the same collaborators, Betty Comden and Adolph Green as lyricists, Oliver Smith for scenery.[6] Needing a serious librettist, he approached Arthur Laurents, who had never written a musical but

---

[5] The story of Romeo and Juliet, which involves parental disapproval, the eventual love affair of the young lovers, and their death, has its origins in *Pyramis and Thisbe*, a well-known tale from Greek mythology. The plot as we know it first surfaced in 1530, when Luigi da Porto published his version as a long poem. Matteo Bandello took the tragedy and wrote it in Italian as a *nouvelle* in 1554. Less than a decade later, Arthur Brooke translated Bandello's poem into English, and it became widely known as *The Tragicall Historye of Romeus and Juliet*. Shakespeare certainly used this long poem written in heroic couplets as his guide when he published his play in 1597.

[6] In 1944 Oliver Smith designed the set for the Bernstein-Robbins ballet *Fancy Free*, which provided the source material for *On the Town*, which he coproduced as well as designed. Other shows for which he did the sets that made him one of the most sought-after designers on Broadway were *Beggar's Holiday* (1944); *Brigadoon* (1946); *High Button Shoes* and *Look, Ma, I'm Dancin'* (1947); *Miss Liberty* and *Gentlemen Prefer Blondes* (1949); *Paint Your Wagon* (1951); *Carnival in Flanders* (1953); *My Fair Lady* and *Candide* (1956). After *West Side Story* he continued to be one of the most active designers, with additional glittering scenic successes such as *Flower Drum Song* (1958); *Destry Rides Again* and *The Sound of Music* (1959); *The Unsinkable Molly Brown* and *Camelot* (1960); *Hello, Dolly!* (1964); *On a Clear Day You Can See Forever* (1965); *Gigi* (1973); *Carmelina* (1979).

who had scripted two splendid straight plays, *Home of the Brave* and *The Time of the Cuckoo*.

Bernstein liked Laurents's qualifications and eagerly agreed to the other collaborators, by now old friends. Then he excitedly commenced a log of the project in which he wrote about telling a "tragic story in musical-comedy terms, using only musical-comedy techniques and never falling into the 'operatic' trap." A month later he defined the theme of the new work as prejudice rather than family feuding. As for the music, Bernstein intended it to be "serious, yet simple enough for all people to understand."

Although they didn't realize it, the show, as then outlined and called *East Side Story*, later *Gangway!*, was already old hat, reminding most producers of the long-running comedy of the '20s, *Abie's Irish Rose*, in reverse. In a more serious vein Robbins's concept was not unlike that of Sidney Kingsley's 1930s drama, *Dead End*, which had been a successful play and eventually a classic movie. Furthermore, by mid-century, most of the tenement slums of the Lower East Side of New York had been pulled down. Although all the collaborators liked the germ of the idea, Bernstein, Laurents, Robbins, and Smith became caught up in other ventures before working out the details of the script, and *East Side Story* was shelved. But the idea which everybody believed would be groundbreaking never was far from the minds of any of the collaborators.

In August 1955, taking a respite from his conducting duties at the Hollywood Bowl, Leonard Bernstein, was sunning himself at the pool of the Beverly Hills Hotel. Arthur Laurents, who had come west to adapt the scenario of his stage success, *The Time of the Cuckoo*, into *Summertime*, a film vehicle to star Katharine Hepburn, spotted him there.

During their talk, Laurents noticed on a nearby deck chair a copy of the *Los Angeles Times* whose headlines screamed stories of gang warfare in the Mexican neighborhoods of the city. Bernstein thought this the perfect solution to their "Romeo" project, to have the clashes and the prejudices occur between the Mexicans and the white Angelinos. Laurents opted for leaving the story in New York and having the conflict between the blacks and Puerto Rican immigrants. The central issue moved from religion to "turf." With the papers full of juvenile delinquency and gang fighting, the story seemed to take shape.

Laurents sketched out the plot, changing the blacks to whites of no particular ethnicity, and he and Bernstein called Jerry Robbins excitedly. "A second solemn pact has been sworn," Bernstein wrote in his log on September 6, 1955. "Jerry loves our gang idea. Here we go. God bless us."

Two weeks later, when Sondheim was attending the opening night party for the play *Island of Goats*, which his friend Burt Shevelove had directed, he spied Arthur Laurents and went over to talk with him. "I said 'what are you doing?'" Sondheim recalled, "and he said 'I'm about to begin on a musical of Romeo and

Juliet with Leonard Bernstein and Jerry Robbins,' " and I asked, just idly, " 'who's doing the lyrics?' " Sondheim's idle query was not provoked because he was looking for a job, for he thought of himself as a composer—in the lyric department he felt he was still a novice.

"I never thought of you," Laurents told Sondheim, "and I liked your lyrics very much. I didn't like your music very much"

"Arthur is nothing if not frank," Sondheim allowed. Then Laurents proposed that Sondheim meet Bernstein and play the score of *Saturday Night* for him.

Sondheim did not really like Laurents's rather left-handed offer but, like any young composer, eagerly wanted to meet one of the giants of the musical world. At the audition, Bernstein was enthusiastic about Sondheim's work and about working with someone far younger than himself on such a seriously contemporary theme. But he told him he could not be definite for at least a week because Comden and Green, with whom he had worked so smoothly on *On the Town* and *Wonderful Town*, were trying to get out of a Hollywood contract to do a movie for Gene Kelly. They had been given first option to supply the lyrics.

In reality, Bernstein wanted that week to think it over. He had considered himself capable of writing the lyrics for the new musical since he himself had written a few of the lyrics to *Candide*,[7] which he was still working on. But as conceived, the Romeo project looked like it was going to need more music— "ballet music, symphonic music, development music. More than I could possibly write if I were doing lyrics too," Bernstein remembered. Having already completed quite a few of the lyrics that went along with his score, the most he could offer Sondheim was the job of co-lyricist on the new play, now definitely titled *West Side Story*. Again he apologized, for he knew that Sondheim considered himself a composer-lyricist.

As it turned out Comden and Green could not get out of their Hollywood commitment, and Sondheim could have the job—if he wanted it. Once the audition had turned into a realistic offer of a contract, Sondheim went directly to Oscar Hammerstein. "He was my mentor all through my career until he died. And he said, 'I think it will be very valuable for you to work with professionals of this caliber—they are first rate in their fields. The project sounds exciting and you will learn a great deal that I couldn't teach you because it's practical experience. So I think you ought to do it.' "

They began to work, sometimes together, sometimes apart. After the show opened, Bernstein conceded that Sondheim's contribution "far exceeded even *my* expectations. What made him so valuable was that he was also a composer and I could explain musical problems to him and he'd understand immediately."

---

[7] According to Sondheim, at that time Bernstein had written only one that remained in the show, "I Am Easily Assimilated," and "there may be two that he wrote that were cut."

He found the collaboration a joy and after the end of the Philharmonic season took the time to note in his log: "Back to *Romeo*. From here on nothing shall disturb the project, whatever happens to interfere I shall cancel summarily. It's going too well to let it drop again."

Because of the uncompromising angriness of the subject, the hard-hitting unpleasant story, it was difficult to find a producer. Roger Stevens liked the idea but felt it was too risky to tackle alone. By that time Hal Prince had become a close friend of Sondheim's. He had been intrigued by some of the numbers from the dissonant, vital score that Sondheim had played for him without Bernstein's knowledge. When George Abbott, who had been approached by Robbins and Bernstein to act as producer of *West Side Story* turned thumbs down on the project, Sondheim suggested his friend Hal, then known as Broadway's *wunderkind*, as producer. Two years older than Sondheim, Prince had graduated from being George Abbott's employee to being the successful producer (along with Robert Griffith) of *The Pajama Game, Damn Yankees,* and now *New Girl in Town.* But Prince and Griffith declined an early version of *West Side Story.* Leland Hayward too refused to become involved in such an ugly show, which left two dead youths on stage at the end of Act One. Nor could Sondheim interest Rodgers and Hammerstein—by this time almost as well known as a team of producers as they were as creators—in the project.

At last the show was optioned by Cheryl Crawford in association with Roger Stevens, who had financed the show since its inception. Crawford had a splendid record of bringing forth daring quality musicals, starting with a revival of *Porgy and Bess* in 1942. She had produced *One Touch of Venus, Brigadoon, Love Life,* and *Paint Your Wagon* and had even brought Marc Blitzstein's opera *Regina* to Broadway in 1949.

Now casting began in earnest. Larry Kert, Carol Lawrence, Chita Rivera, Grover Dale, Tony Mordente, Martin Charnin, Lee Becker—unknowns, all at the outset of their careers—were chosen. The collaborators purposely avoided opting for well-known theater names. The show itself was to be the star. Arthur Laurents completed most of the plot and submitted his dialogue to Bernstein and Sondheim. In the true collaborative spirit he made no objection if the lyricist and composer "stole" his words to become part of their songs. After many conferences with Robbins, Bernstein discovered he had the lion's share of the work ahead of him as the show was to contain so much dancing and, contrary to common Broadway practice, he planned to take the onus on himself of writing these complete ballet scores *and orchestrating* them.[8]

---

[8] Few Broadway composers, with the exception of Bernstein, Kurt Weill, Meredith Willson, and Leroy Anderson, are able to orchestrate their work. (Sondheim sometimes gives clues to his orchestrator on his piano score as to what instrumentation he desires.) Because of the pressing

Sondheim had no temerity about suggesting inventive musical forms to Leonard Bernstein. After Bernstein first played the verse of "Something's Coming," Sondheim suggested the song would need more of a "Broadway feel, more like a show-tune. I said it needed a 2/4 feeling and he had written something in 3. I then took the verse and turned it into a 2/4." In its completed form, with its rising cello line over a constant I–V–I–V bass, the song creates the rumbling heartbeat of anticipation.

Then, on April 22, two months before *West Side Story* was to go into rehearsal, Crawford called all the collaborators together for a meeting in her office. She told them she felt the musical was taking a dramatic shape she did not approve of. The show she had optioned was supposed to explain *why* these delinquents were the way they were. She also objected that Laurents's script contained no "well known slang." Robbins maintained that the piece was a "poetic fantasy, not a sociological document," but Crawford was adamant.

She said she wanted Laurents and the other collaborators to reconsider the script to highlight the story's social significance. It was an impossible demand, tantamount to asking Shakespeare to find the underlying social reasons for the feuding Capulets and Montagues. At last Cheryl Crawford gave them an ultimatum. "You have to rewrite the whole thing," she stated flatly, "or else I won't produce it.[9]"

Robbins, Sondheim, Bernstein, and Smith each remember what happened next slightly differently, but they all recall rising up, "as though a conductor had cued us," and dazedly leaving Crawford's office. Leaving Smith behind, the trio walked to the Algonquin Hotel but were not admitted because Laurents was not wearing a tie. So they moved next door to the Iroquois, where they phoned Roger Stevens in London. Stevens told them not to despair but to keep working on the project.

That night Sondheim called his friend Hal Prince, who said he and Robert Griffith[10] would come down from Boston after the opening night of their (and

---

problem of creating new replacement songs when a show is in early rehearsal or preview, orchestration, the last element to be added, is generally left to a specialist. Usually the composer will not even create the ballet or dance music. This has long been the province of the dance arranger— in *West Side Story*'s case, according to Sondheim, "It was outlined by Betty Wallberg, the pianist for Jerry Robbins, and then reset by Lenny." Usually the dance arranger takes the composer's melodies and, working with the choreographer, fits the music to the dance steps. *West Side Story*'s stunning orchestration is the work of Sid Ramin and Irving Kostal. It was supervised by Bernstein.
[9] "Gee, Officer Krupke" was the score's only attempt at blatant social comment. The only comedy song in the show, because of its ironic lightheartedness it was the opposite of what Crawford wanted.
[10] Robert Griffith (1907–61), who had been George Abbott's stage manager since 1935, formed a partnership with Harold Prince in 1953. Together they produced *The Pajama Game* (1954), *Damn Yankees* (1955), and *New Girl in Town* (1957) before *West Side Story*.

Abbott's) new show, listen to a run-through of the Laurents-Bernstein-Sondheim material, and decide. The day after *New Girl in Town* opened, they gave the okay—over Abbott's strong objection—and began raising the $300,000 necessary to open *West Side Story*. For Prince it was an emancipation proclamation. His relationship with Abbott had not been unlike Sondheim's tie to Hammerstein, and, indeed, after *West Side Story* he too reached maturity.

The show went into rehearsal in June, and because of Jerome Robbins's careful directoral preparation and early repair of any major flaws, it was brought in in eight weeks, with very few changes in script or song. One amusing story of the pre-Broadway opening was told by Sondheim at a Dramatists Guild symposium. It is repeated here simply to prove the old chestnut about the show going on.

> When we got down to Washington there had been a mistake made—somebody hadn't gotten the right dimensions of the stage. When the bedroom set rolled off in the second act to make room for the dream ballet, which required a totally cleared, empty stage, about a third of it didn't roll off. The space at the National Theater was too small. I was afraid that we couldn't open, but Jerry said that we had fifteen hundred people coming Monday night, so we would just take a saw and saw it in half. He was affected more than anybody because, after all, this was the moment, the ballet toward which he was building the entire scene and music—and here it just didn't work at all. He was totally cool. They got a saw and sawed the set in half, and on opening night half the bedroom went off one way and half the other.

The show opened to great acclaim at the Broadway's Winter Garden Theater on September 26. All the critics noted the origin of the story, but few of them wrote of the contemporary parallels to be found in Laurents's version. *West Side Story* leaves us with a wise look at the problems of our times. Laurents's story used Shakespeare's tragedy as his template, but he took it farther into his world of the '50s. Contemporary society, the wars and ethnic antagonisms of today with their overt anger and violence, is the same as that in *West Side Story's* world.

All of this adds to *West Side Story's* complexity, which shows the tragedy of modern society in which the gulf between the generations and between authority and disobedience has become so deep that youngsters turn to violence with knives and eventually with guns. In Shakespeare, despite the patent hatred between the Montagues and Capulets, when the young quarrelers are ordered by a higher authority to lay down arms, they do so—however grudgingly. It is otherwise in *West Side Story*. Here the gangs not only fight against each other, they revolt against the adult world. They invariably overrule Officer Krupke or Sergeant Schrank, who are purposely portrayed as fools. They make fun of and call the law names as soon as these "heavies" are out of earshot.

Leonard Bernstein rehearses the "America" number with his "Puerto Rican" chorus, Chita Rivera (far left), and Carol Lawrence (far right), with a twenty-seven-year-old Sondheim filling in at the piano. Photo: Fred Fehl. © Museum of the City of New York.

Shakespeare's lovers foresee their misfortunes and follow their star-crossed fate in spite of it. Laurents's, on the contrary, foresee only the fulfillment of their love and accept without moralizing the bitter understanding that their love is a triumph over hate and violence and the differences of the generations.[11]

While they were writing the score, composer and lyricist did not always agree as to what makes a good lyric. "Lenny's idea of poetic lyrics was not mine," Sondheim was to reveal many years later, "and he tended to like purple prose. My idea of a poetic line is 'Maria, Maria, I just met a girl named Maria,' and his idea was the lyric of 'Tonight.'"

"Tonight" is probably the show's best-known ballad, yet in this writer's opinion, commercial enough to be inconsistent with the rest of the score. After the special run-through arranged so that Oscar could see the show, he found the song "not soaring enough" to cap the emotional balcony scene. Sondheim and the other collaborators, except Bernstein, agreed with Hammerstein, citing that

[11] Laurents overruled Robbins on the ending, which differs starkly from Shakespeare's in that Maria lives on. Laurents's rationale was that her death "just didn't work in contemporary terms."

"Tonight" had not been written for that scene but had been transported there from the quintet that comes before "The Rumble." That was, according to Sondheim, several weeks before the opening, but the duet still remained and by now has become a much loved section of the score.

The difference between a Bernstein lyric and one by Sondheim is clearly shown in the finale from the duet between Maria and Anita. The counterpointed voices each express the tug of personal emotions. With Anita trying to discredit Tony while Maria defends him and her love in this number, the section is very moving. The music was given lush, poetic images in its Bernstein version concentrating on the passion and fire of love. In the penultimate section, as rewritten by Sondheim, Maria convinces Anita to change from antagonist to confederate by singing of the overwhelming power of her love.

Although he could see his collaborator's point of view, Sondheim never accepted Bernstein's tempestuous lyrics. "The show is very conscious of what it is," he stated in 1994. "It's not a spontaneous piece and it's not supposed to be. Even the dialogue is highly stylized, very compressed and very unreal, and so in a sense that kind [Bernstein's] of lyric writing is acceptable; it's just that I don't like it."

The original melody of "One Hand, One Heart," which Bernstein had written for *Candide*, had only a dotted half note to each bar.

Sondheim realized he would have to set all the lyrics using one syllable words, which would make for a dragging, incomprehensible effect. "You cannot go 'Ne ver,'" he explained at a lecture, "because by the time you hit the 'v' the audience's ear has lost the 'ne' and they're asking 'what was that?' So I was stifled. Down in Washington, Lenny, after my endless kvetching, put in two little quarter notes so I could write 'Make of our hands'—not a great deal better but it has a little more freedom."[12]

Sondheim's favorite *West Side Story* lyrics are "Something's Coming" and "The Jet Song." He also appreciates the "Gee, Officer Krupke" number, not because it always brought down the house but because it was a genuine piece of humor that depended "not on cleverness, but on the kids' attitude. And that of course is what humor is about. Character is what humor is about," Sondheim was to add. But in looking over the score he found several lyrics he didn't care for. As is usual with composers of quality work, they were the most popularly successful ones in the score. The tone of "I Feel Pretty" is indeed overelegant, for, as Sondheim has quipped, with lines like "it's alarming how charming I feel," "this Puerto Rican girl, newly arrived in the United States, would not be unwelcome in Noël Coward's living room." Before they previewed in Washington Sondheim

---

[12] His newly found freedom notwithstanding, Sondheim's moving lyric—except for the words "only," "even," "begins," and "after"—sticks to words of one syllable throughout.

The second most famous balcony scene—Larry Kert and Carol Lawrence as Tony and Maria in West Side Story. Photo: Irving Carsten. © Museum of the City of New York.

rewrote the lyric for "I Feel Pretty," his collaborators outvoted him and the changes were not made.

Another lyric he was not particularly happy with was "America," with its "twenty-seven words to the square inch." In a lecture on lyric writing Sondheim deplored the last line of the first stanza: "I like to be in America / OK by me in America / Everything free in America / For a small fee in America." "The 'for a small fee' was my little zinger except that 'for' is accented, and when the line is sung fast nobody knew what it meant."

Despite Sondheim's self-denigration, he knew in the larger scheme he had written lyrics to character—and his collaborators knew it too. He also knew that he had written almost all the lyrics, scrapping or rewriting Bernstein's originals. So he was not surprised when during the Washington tryout Bernstein asked Sondheim if he wanted solo credit.

"That would be wonderful," Sondheim answered.

When Bernstein offered him the total lyricist's share of two points of the gross, Sondheim said, "Oh, don't bother." (He would later regret the many thousands of dollars that simple, magnanimous decision cost him.)

West Side Story was a great success but not the mythic hit it is perceived to be today. It played 732 times in its first engagement, making only a minimal profit. Prince takes the blame for curtailing the run, saying he booked a tour and closed the show while there was still a clamor for seats. After a short tour, *West Side Story* returned for another run of about six months.

The critiques were mostly raves, with Brooks Atkinson, the senior *New York Times* critic, reversing his habitual thumbs down for hard-hitting shows. Here he led his fellow aisle-sitters with hosannas. "The subject is not beautiful," he wrote. "But what *West Side Story* draws out of it is beautiful."

Other reviewers found it the logical successor to *Porgy and Bess.* John Chapman of the *Daily News* found "the bounce, the restlessness and the sweetness of our town in a show that takes up the musical idiom where it was left when George Gershwin died." Sondheim's contribution, which undoubtedly goaded Bernstein to compose his finest score, was largely overlooked.

In retrospect, *West Side Story* was certainly one of the most groundbreaking shows of the decade of the '50s. It was the first to blend music, book, lyrics, and dance in a fluid, almost cinematic way; the first to abandon the anonymity of a chorus and give each of the gang members a name and personality of his own; the first to call for a complete lighting designer. Bernstein called it a show that was done "with a kind of bravery in which all the collaborators fortified one another to follow their instincts and follow one another's instincts in order to produce something new, something that has never been envisioned before. It's not so much what it's about, it's how bravely it's done."

For Robbins, what was important about *West Side Story* was its "aspiration."

In attempting this noncompromising show he was testing the laws of the commercial musical theater of his time. Why, he wondered, "couldn't we 'long haired artists' bring our crafts and talents to a musical. . . . Why did Lenny have to write an opera, Arthur a play, me a ballet? Why couldn't we bring our talents together?"

At season's end the show was nominated for a Tony Award but did not win. Certainly the score, the subject matter, the choreography, and even the overwhelming performances may have been too hard-hitting for what was still perceived as musical-comedy.[13]

Even though *Oklahoma!* had been billed as a musical play, the critics were not ready to accept a tragico-choreographic drama masquerading as a musical. But in the intervening decades since its premiere *West Side Story* has chalked up an enviable record. In the autumn of 1999 it had twenty-one major productions in high schools and colleges across the United States as well as many performances abroad. Bernstein's angular music has lost none of its bite—it only becomes more poignant with familiarity. Sondheim's lyrics are moving or hilarious in turn, and Laurents's dialogue refuses to date.[14] The play's construction is still a marvel and its message as potent as ever.

West Side Story slugged it out with a charming—but not groundbreaking—show and lost. *The Music Man* captured all the honors for the season of 1957–58. It won the Tony as well as the Drama Critics' Circle Award. Meredith Willson, who had written most of the book and all the music and lyrics (a feat that only Noël Coward, Frank Loesser, or Sandy Wilson seemed capable of), was the most honored luminary of the year.

Once the show opened, Sondheim—now more respected by the theater community—looked forward to writing *music* along with his words for a new show. He enlisted the help of his friend Burt Shevelove, whom he had known and whose work he had admired since his college days. Burt had been toying with the idea of turning some of Plautus's ribald plays into a musical. When Sondheim read them and found them "terribly funny," he called Jerry Robbins, who, after the heaviness of *West Side Story*, was eager to direct a farce. Shevelove

[13] The show's greatest popular acclaim came after the movie version was released. By that time the songs, most of which are not easy to sing because they use unfamiliar intervals like the tritone or wide skips, had become more widely known.

[14] One of the bones of contention between Laurents and Cheryl Crawford that was partly responsible for the creative group's leaving her office en masse was the then-popular phrase "that's the way the cookie crumbles," which the producer wanted included in the dialogue. Laurents rightly turned thumbs down, explaining that including current slang would make the show outdated when the cliché went out of vogue.

eventually suggested he bring in Larry Gelbart[15] as co-librettist to fashion the book first called *A Scenario for Vaudevillians*, then *The Roman Comedy*.

They finished the first draft quickly. Sondheim wrote a few songs, Shevelove and Gelbart completed a presentable draft, and they presented it to Jerome Robbins. They knew they wanted Robbins to direct it, but after the hosannas *West Side Story* had elicited, Robbins was Broadway's most sought-after director. He had been offered many projects and had already tentatively accepted *Gypsy*, whose book Comden and Green were even now struggling to adapt as a musical for Ethel Merman. *Gypsy*, basically the story of a dancer's journey through vaudeville to burlesque, looked like a project that would allow Robbins's dances to shine.

Gypsy already had its financing and was scheduled to go into rehearsal in a matter of a mere six months. Robbins said he would direct the low comedy Roman play immediately after. He even persuaded David Merrick—the co-producer of *Gypsy*—to option the upcoming Roman farce. Then, when Comden and Green dropped out because of motion picture commitments, Robbins asked Sondheim to do music and lyrics for *Gypsy*.

Although *Gypsy* was not the kind of musical with which Sondheim had envisioned making his composing debut on Broadway, he accepted the challenge. He and Robbins did not, however, count on the power of their star. When Robbins, touting Sondheim, said he could do a splendid score for her, Merman turned thumbs down. She was just recovering from one of the few commercial failures of her career. *Happy Hunting*, which her fame alone had kept alive through 412 torturous performances, was crafted by longtime professionals except for its composer, Harold Karr, who was actually a practicing dentist. She now insisted she would not have a newcomer writing her music.

Irving Berlin, who had created *Annie Get Your Gun* and *Call Me Madam* with Ethel's clarion voice in mind, and Cole Porter, who had written five hits in a row for her but by now was in a bad physical state, both declined. Merman suggested Jule Styne,[16] with whom she had become friendly as far back as 1936, when she was rehearsing *Red, Hot, and Blue*.

---

[15] Larry Gelbart (1923–) is a Chicago-born writer who began penning comic sketches while still in his teens. In 1958 he won an Emmy for an *Art Carney Special*. After his success with Sondheim on *Forum*, he won a Peabody Award for the television series M*A*S*H. He was to become one of America's most respected writers of comedy, with movie credits that include *Oh, God* (1977) and *Tootsie* (1982). Besides winning the Tony for his collaboration with Burt Shevelove on *Forum*, he won a solo one for his libretto to *City of Angels* in 1990.

[16] Jule Styne (1905–94) came to Broadway from Hollywood, where he had written several hit songs for Sinatra. His first musical, *Glad to See You!* (1944), closed out of town, but he soon turned out a string of successful shows, including hits like *High Button Shoes* (1947) and *Gentlemen*

Styne, who in addition to being a composer of special material was also an excellent vocal coach, had filled in when Merman's regular coach took sick. Merman felt confident that Jule Styne knew voices in general and hers in particular. As for choosing the lyricist for the new show, Styne had no habitual partner. He had written *High Button Shoes* with Sammy Cahn, *Gentlemen Prefer Blondes* with Leo Robin, and *Bells Are Ringing* with Comden and Green. Surely Merman (and Styne) could have no objection to Robbins's proposal that *Gypsy*'s words be supplied by the now highly respected young lyricist of *West Side Story*. But she could and did, finally accepting Sondheim grudgingly.

Sondheim went to Oscar Hammerstein, who by this time was treating him as a colleague. He had two gripes he wanted to discuss with his mentor. First, he wanted to complain about his treatment by his collaborators. "It had been agreed that I'd write both the music and the lyrics [for *Gypsy*]. The deal with Leland, Merrick, Laurents, and Robbins was firm, I thought."

Sondheim's second misgiving was that he felt that Styne's previous shows had been in the traditional musical comedy mold, and he didn't know how Styne would adapt to another way of thinking, whether he'd be willing to keep his eyes and ears on character and story rather than on hit songs.

Hammerstein persuaded him to do *Gypsy*. He said that the chance to work with these people and particularly to write a show for a star—which he had never done before—was invaluable. Also, the show was to have a very short schedule, Sondheim told the members of the Dramatists Guild in a panel discussion. "At worst, it would be six months out of my life. So instead of doing music and lyrics, I did just lyrics—and I haven't regretted it for one second."

Prefer Blondes (1949). *Bells Are Ringing*, which premiered in 1956, was still playing to packed houses when *Gypsy* was in the planning stage.

Words and—Finally—Words and Music

GYPSY, WHICH HAD ITS NEW YORK OPENING on May 21, 1959, turned out to be one of the glories of the musical theater. The role of Rose, mother of the famous "stripteuse," Gypsy Rose Lee, tailor-made for Ethel Merman, is a true star turn. It was stunningly re-created in London (and in its New York revival) by Angela Lansbury. Perhaps Lansbury's performance was a shade too ladylike to be credible as the tough Rose Hovic, but she certainly acted the role with great bravura and sang the songs splendidly. By contrast Bette Midler, who attacked the role in a TV special, accented Rose's tawdry pigheadedness. In its 1990 Broadway incarnation, Tyne Daly gave the brash, cheap, self-centered central character arguably its best interpretation.

With a plum of a role, one that far outshines that stalwart *Hello, Dolly!* for a middle-aged actress, *Gypsy* is the best backstage musical ever. (Perhaps one should consider *42nd Street* and *A Chorus Line* in the running, but the former is about that "one big break" and the latter is concerned with dancers, "gypsies," auditions.) Forget that the central character is self-centered and repugnant; by the end of the evening Rose's utter tenacity and defiance of the disaster that confronts her as each of her daughters outgrows her demand that an audience admire her. This writer is convinced that having all those qualities, including an insight into the stage mother psyche as well as a nondelusionary story of theatrical ambition, *Gypsy* will continue to be revived and produced as long as musicals are performed.

When Gypsy Rose Lee published her memoir, David Merrick[1] was the first to

---

[1] David Merrick (1911–2000), a razor-sharp businessman, was originally a lawyer. He came to Broadway from St. Louis in 1939 to "learn the business" and began by co-producing serious plays. In 1951 he secured the rights to Marcel Pagnol's *Fanny*, which he finally brought to the musical stage four years later. Before *Gypsy*, in addition to *Fanny*, he had produced *Jamaica, Maria Golovin, La Plume de Ma Tante,* and *Destry Rides Again*. After *Gypsy* the most notable titles among the

option it. He brought Leland Hayward into the project and shortly after suggested that Ethel Merman read the book too. She liked what she read and, being between shows—with none offered to her—agreed to keep herself available if the libretto and score suited her. Signing this "first lady of the musical," although she was then nearing fifty, would have spelled cash in any producer's pocket.

At that point, unbeknownst to Merman, the project was like a house of cards, with Hayward telling Arthur Laurents that Robbins would direct the show if he, Laurents, would write it. Comden and Green, who had wrestled with the script for a year, conceived the musical as Gypsy's story and bowed out because they simply could not find a way to make the musical work. Laurents was not keen to work again with Jerry Robbins, since they had had a falling-out during the creation of West Side Story, but he was too canny a theater man to let a good project slip by him.

"I was not interested in the strip-tease queen of America, and I did not think anyone else would be," Laurents was to say. "Then one day, a lot of people dropped by my place at the beach for a drink and I heard one young woman talking about Gypsy Rose Lee's mother . . . a plump, curvaceous blonde—sort of like Shirley Booth . . . but an absolute killer."

This intrigued him, and he soon "came up with the idea of parents who lead their children's lives." But it was not enough for him to accept the assignment. "I told them that if I could figure out a way that the star could top the strip number at the end, I would do it." When he got the idea for "Rose's Turn," originally conceived as a ballet, Laurents signed on.

From this eleven o'clock number, Laurents quickly sketched in the rest of the character of this self-centered stage mother. His idea was that the musical would be super-realistic. Then Arthur Laurents, who had never met Merman, called for a conference with her, insisting they be alone. "This woman is a monster," he recalled telling her. "How far are you willing to go?"

"I want to act and will do anything you want," said Merman, who was renowned for her leather-lunged singing style but whose acting ability was considered rudimentary. Her stage persona had always been the simplistic heroine, at the most recent, the well-meaning matron.

With Robbins, Laurents, and Merman signed on, even minus a score or script, producers Merrick and Hayward easily raised all the financing without giving a

---

thirty-odd shows he produced or co-produced were Irma La Douce, Carnival, Stop the World—I Want to Get Off, Oliver!, Hello, Dolly!, Funny Girl, The Roar of the Greasepaint, I Do! I Do!, Promises, Promises, Mack and Mabel, and 42nd Street. In 1996, despite being deprived of the power of speech by a stroke, he was still producing, notably a musical version of Rodgers and Hammerstein's film, State Fair, his last show. Having made so many enemies among the show business fraternity because of hard bargaining, he was given the soubriquet of "the abominable showman."

single audition. At that time the only producing organization capable of attracting angels without their hearing the songs was Rodgers and Hammerstein.

Laurents, strongly in control of the project, then put Styne through the indignity of having to audition. Sensing the same fear that made Sondheim leery of taking on the assignment, he told the producers, "Jule is a great pop songwriter, but this is a dramatic entity." Yet when he heard some of Styne's recent work he approved wholeheartedly. "It was a wonderful collaboration," Styne recalled many years after. "I've done some twenty-five shows but never had a collaboration like this. The show practically wrote itself."

On the first day Sondheim and Styne began their work together, Jule handed Stephen thirteen songs "from his trunk." But since Jule Styne was one of the most prolific songwriters in the business, Sondheim said, "Let's try to write fresh for this show." One tune Sondheim had heard Styne play at a party and had thought would be ideal for their show, however, was missing from the sheaf. It had a lyric by Sammy Cahn and was written for a movie called *Pink Tights*, which was never made. It was originally titled "You'll Never Get Away from Me" and later retitled "Why Did You Have To Wait So Long?" Sondheim's new lyric reverted to the original Cahn title. Once *Gypsy* opened Sondheim was annoyed to discover the song had an even *earlier* publication. Styne had kept mum about its use in the film *Ruggles of Red Gap*, this time with a lyric by Leo Robin that went, "I'm in pursuit of happiness / Because the constitution says/ I've a right to be . . ."

This was not the only song that was resurrected from Styne's trunk. With some changes, a song called "In Betwixt and Between" was to become one of the pivotal songs of the musical: "Everything's Coming Up Roses."

Like Cole Porter, rather than repairing or changing a tune, Styne preferred to create a totally new melody if any of his collaborators rejected a section of a song he had written. In his biography, *Jule*, Styne stated that "in most cases I wrote the music first and then Steve wrote the lyrics, but frequently he wrote additional lyrics or suggested using a release of one song as the motive of another." Sondheim disputes this, saying, "In fact, it was the reverse. I wrote the lyrics and sketched out rhythms of melodies for him. The music was written first in the case of the vaudeville numbers and variations thereof."

From the paragraph above, we know that "You'll Never Get Away from Me" had had a former incarnation. "I even sketched out part of 'Everything's Coming Up Roses,' " Sondheim adds.

This method sent Jule into fresh forms, away from his habitual AABA or ABAC. It is noteworthy that Styne wrote "up" in his collaboration with Sondheim. Like Bernstein with *West Side Story*, but in quite a different fashion, Styne never was to turn out a score to equal his collaboration with Sondheim.

Gypsy's songs are not only tuneful and beautifully crafted, they capture the essential spirit of the vaudeville era.

Before he got too deeply into the story, Laurents conferred with Gypsy Rose Lee and her sister, actress June Havoc. Gypsy gave the writer no trouble, confiding that she had "imagined" much of her memoir, her only stipulation being that the musical's title must be *Gypsy*. Every time Laurents talked with her she had a different account of how she got into show business and how she started in burlesque. She left it to Laurents to make up his own story, even to figure out how she came by her nickname, confessing, "Honey, I've given fourteen or fifteen versions of that. Yours will be as good as mine." When she read the part, pure fiction, about Herbie, her mother's boyfriend who eventually walks out, she said, "God, I wish I had thought of that for my autobiography!"

But when Laurents discussed adapting Gypsy's book with her sister, Havoc disapproved strenuously.

"Why do you want to make a play of this?" she asked.

Laurents replied that he found the subject touching.

"I'm touching," her sister snapped. "Not her. She's cheap. She eats out of tin cans."

Havoc threatened an injunction unless Laurents changed the first act to show that when she runs away from home she is "only eleven or so." Laurents said, "This would have made the mother beyond horror, and, of course, would have made June's elopement impossible." Laurents refused to make the change, and June Havoc refused to sign the release. David Merrick came up with the legal loophole of changing the character's name, which only confused the actors and gave the plot a fictitious air, as Havoc was a well-known actress. But nothing worked until, as Sondheim recalled, "Havoc was given a percentage of the show. She ended up getting pieces from both the producers and from Gypsy. That's what it really came down to—money."

Although the gestation period for *Gypsy* was short, because of differing emphases it was very costly. And because Laurents and Robbins, already antagonists, were eager to express their own points of view, the show was overly long, lasting three and one half hours in Philadelphia. While Laurents saw the show as Rose's story, Robbins—certainly in the beginning—saw the musical as a panorama of vaudeville. To that end, the collaborators auditioned, according to Sondheim, "every vaudeville actor who was still alive." When it was decided to emphasize Rose's personal story rather than theatrical history, all the jugglers, dog acts, tumblers, and aerialists (who were not eliminated until the Philadelphia previews) were let go.

Scenes were cut; costumes, many of them never worn, were discarded and new ones ordered. Merrick's patience frazzled as he went far over his budget.

Eventually he and Robbins had a blow-up. Robbins swore he'd never do another show with Merrick—and kept his promise.

One of the fortunate breaks in this melee was Faith Dane's audition. A professional stripper, she came in and did her bumps and grinds while playing the trumpet—sometimes bent in two, back to the audience and still trumpeting through her legs. She was hired on the spot to perform this athletic solo in "You Gotta Have a Gimmick," one of the second act's two showstoppers.

Originally the show began with a skit, a backstage drama of the mother-sacrifice-for-daughter variety. This concept of the show as a satire was soon cut, and Merman came down the aisle—which had always been planned—interrupting a kiddie show in progress with her clarion call, "Sing out, Louise," which, incidentally, has become a sort of backstage idiom. The entrance is subtle and brash at once, serving to introduce the star while giving the audience a glimpse of Rose's disruptive, intrusive character.

The number she interrupts also has a dual edge. "May We Entertain You," sung by young June, becomes "Let Me Entertain You," orchestrating Gypsy's hastily put together debut in burlesque near the musical's end. With lines like "and if you're real good, I'll make you feel good—I want your spirits to climb," the lyric serves both the saccharine kiddie show and the sensual strip tease. With its rhythm changed from a clog-waltz to a raunchy strip it serves yet another purpose—reprise, one of the pillars of musical comedy.

Merman's introductory number, "Some People," was an angry song directed at her father. The song originally culminated in her telling him to "go to hell." Presented with the lyric, Merman reneged on her promise to do anything her collaborators asked of her. "Ethel told me that her public would be alienated if they heard her tell her father to go to hell," Sondheim said. "So the passage was cut."

When he began working on his lyrics for "Some People," Sondheim remembered coming to Arthur Laurents with a draft. Laurents had given him the idea for the song, but Stephen was afraid it was going to be just a list song showing a woman's anger at having to settle for less than she felt she deserved. What Sondheim had already learned from Laurents was the concept of subtext, and he was to build it into all his future work. Subtext can as well refer to a performance that contradicts the text—as when words belie their meaning. For example, an actor who bids his lover to "have a wonderful time," all the while meaning "be bored, don't go," can have a field day playing the subtext—the negative hidden behind the positive words—of the scene.

Sondheim defines the term as giving the performer something extra to play. "Rose wants a plaque that's hanging on the wall behind her father's head for which she can get eighty-eight bucks, which is what she needs. And she is using the entire song as an excuse for borrowing money from him—and when he doesn't fall for the song she goes and takes the plaque. She can play the money *and* the plaque."

Sondheim felt strongly about this crucial song since it is Rose's credo. In the interlude, with the words "I had a dream," she tells her father and the audience that she lives in her fantasies. This theme and its words will become a sort of leitmotif picking her up whenever fate knocks her down. The fantasy recurs in dialogue when Rose dreams of revamping the act—adding, of all things, a cow. She uses it again as a ploy to lead into the song that closes the first act after one of her daughters leaves her, and the phrase recurs with even more urgency in the show's climax, "Rose's Turn."

From Hammerstein, whose "Ol' Man River" suffuses *Show Boat*, Sondheim had learned the unifying value of a recurring motif. His mentor had also taught that musical comedy must be wary of long-windedness. Song and dialogue immediately have to define character. This is especially apparent in Sondheim's lyric for "Small World," Rose's introductory ballad. The lines "you're a man who likes children" followed by "I'm a woman with children" are tantamount to showing Rose as a fast worker, almost saying, "Let's get married." Jule Styne, on the other hand, who always kept his eye on the commercial possibilities of his songs, deplored the fixed gender of that lyric. "With those lines, it can't be sung by a man," he complained to Sondheim. "That cuts out half its recording possibilities." But the composer was overruled.[2]

Sondheim had his problems at the end of the first act trying to write the closing song. Arthur Laurents had given specific stage directions for the kind of number he was expecting. The song would cap Rose's speech at the railroad station after June elopes and even the boys she has picked up along the way walk out on her act. Her sights set on Louise, she roars:

> "I'm going to build a whole new act—all around you! It's going to be better than anything we ever did before! Better than anything we ever dreamed! (*Like a gallant joyous express train*) It *is* for the best! The old act was getting stale and tired! But the new one? Look at the new star, Herbie! She's going to be beautiful! She *is* beautiful! Finished? We're just beginning and there's no stopping us this time!" (*Her face alive with fight and plans and happiness, she roars into a violently joyous song about how great everything is going to be.*)

Sondheim said one of the problems was to "sail off that speech," and one of the wonderful things about Styne's melody is that it starts at the top of its register—shooting off the sparks Rose has created with her determined words.

---

[2] After *Gypsy* opened and "Small World" became one of the show's most popular numbers, Sondheim did alter the lyric, and the song became a hit for Johnny Mathis and was then recorded by several other male singers.

Finding the title, "Everything's Coming Up Roses," of which Sondheim is justly proud, took him a full week. "The point was to find a phrase," Sondheim recollected, "that sounded as if it had been in the language for years but was, in fact, invented for the show." Robbins, however, did not understand the reference and asked, "Everything's coming up Rose's *what?*" Sondheim, patently annoyed, laid his faith in the phrase on the line. "I'll tell you what, Jerry," he quipped, "if anybody else has that confusion—anybody connected with the production, in the audience, any of your relatives—I will change the title."

But it is not only the title that gives the song its impetus, it is the song's entreating, nay, its desperate tone, that almost makes one believe Rose can pull it off. We are catapulted into the intermission presuming she can turn this clump of no talent into a "star" by sheer force of will. Sondheim and Styne end the song by going gloriously over the top, creating what musicians call a quadruple evaded cadence wherein Rose pulls her sweetest fancies from her imagination—all calculated to seduce her child. (Notice who comes first in this coda's last line.)

> Honey, everything's coming up roses and daffodils,
> Everything's coming up sunshine and Santa Claus,
> Everything's gonna be bright lights and lollipops,
> Everything's coming up roses for me and for you!

As remarkable as "Everything's Coming Up Roses" is, it had to be topped for the conclusion of the second act or the whole show would be lopsided. As previously noted, Rose's replaying of her life, her reminiscences—what Hammerstein called her "public nervous breakdown"—had originally been planned as a ballet, but it was turned into a song because "Jerry [Robbins] said he would not have time to stage the ballet," Sondheim said, "and direct the show as well."

"So it devolved on us," Sondheim was to add, "Jule and me, to try to carry out Arthur's idea of climaxing the show this way, but with no help from anything except the singer herself." What they created, in a way, was a kind of musical comedy aria, using a stream of consciousness technique.

Jack Klugman, who created the part of Herbie, Rose's suitor who eventually walks out, remembered how emotionally involved the whole company was with this final number, written when the troupe was already three weeks into rehearsal.

"We were at the Amsterdam Theatre, and Steve and Jule came in late and announced that they'd just finished 'Rose's Turn.' We stopped the rehearsal and Jule sat down at the piano and played it, and Steve got up and sang it with such feeling and such awareness of what it was about that I just fell apart and bawled like a baby. It was so brilliant. I will never forget that moment. When

Steve did 'M-m-momma, M-m-momma' and couldn't get it out, Ethel and I just burst into tears."

On stage, in the New York production, the scena—one cannot call it a mere song—is helped enormously by Jo Melziner's setting, which recalls Gypsy's Minsky triumph, one scene earlier, with "GYPSY ROSE LEE" spelled out directly under the proscenium in big marquee lights. When Rose begins her tirade, the "GYPSY" and the "LEE" are extinguished and only the "ROSE" and one naked stage arc bulb are lit. They contribute hugely to the eerie picture. Then, over a persistent rhythm, Rose begins with "HERE SHE IS WORLD!!!" During the song she employs quotes from past numbers, even some reminiscent dialogue, making the scene a neurotic musical scrapbook. "Some People," "Everything's Coming Up Roses," and a good bit of "Momma's Talking Soft," a song that was cut from the score, all with nightmarish reharmonizations, are reprised.

The long soliloquy had no ending and went right on into the final scene, a rapprochement between Gypsy and her mother. "I insisted the number not reach a hand. A woman having a nervous breakdown," Sondheim said, "should not get applause from an audience. I forced Jule to have it fade out with high scratchy violin sounds with those last chords when she's screaming—not singing, but screaming—'For me, for me, for me.'"

When Oscar Hammerstein came down to Philadelphia to see the show, he found very little wrong with it but was not happy with this scene. He advised that "since the scene that follows is what the entire play is about, if you want them to listen, you must let them release themselves. That is what applause is for." At first Sondheim bristled at the thought, but he eventually realized that was exactly what was needed. Laurents and Sondheim were criticized by some critics for *not* ending the show with "Rose's Turn." Robbins especially sneered that by inserting this final scene, Laurents had changed *Gypsy* from musical into a "book show," but in this writer's opinion, the off-again-on-again relationship between this mother and daughter is exactly what would occur.

When *Gypsy* opened, most of the accolades were for its star, whose contract guaranteed her name be above the title and whose picture dominated the show's poster. John Chapman wrote, "What this town had needed is Ethel Merman. What Miss Merman had needed is a good show. We got her and she got it last evening when *Gypsy* opened at the Broadway Theatre." Brooks Atkinson's critique in the *Times* likewise talked about the joy of having Merman back on the stage. Atkinson did not even mention Sondheim. Walter Kerr too glossed over the songs, simply calling Sondheim's lyrics "dandy."

Perhaps the most offensive criticism was written by Walter P. Cook in the *Wall Street Journal.* "Merman is so strong that it seems to have prevented listeners from realizing that Jule Styne's music is not memorable, and while his tunes further the story [how tunes can further the story is beyond this writer] well

The final scene of Gypsy, when Gypsy (Sandra Church) lends Mama Rose (Ethel Merman) her sable coat and they leave the stage together. © Museum of the City of New York.

enough, they do not linger in the mind." There was no mention of Sondheim in the entire review.

But the show was off for a run of 702 performances, and David Merrick reported that its original engagement netted a profit of a million dollars. *Gypsy* should have run forever, but tourists and the garment industry theater stalwarts didn't rush to its box office. The sleazy millieu coupled with the heaviness of the story kept them away.

Sondheim has his own definition of what makes a smash hit: "Everything turns out terrific, and in the end the audience goes out thinking that's what life is all about." *My Fair Lady*, he says, "tells the old Cinderella story; *The Sound of Music* says you can eat your cake and have it too; *Hello, Dolly!* says that a loud, middle-aged lady can get the man she wants. *Gypsy* says something fairly hard to take: that every child eventually has to become responsible for his parents . . . they become your children. It's something everybody knows but no one likes to think about."

"That," Sondheim believes, "is what kept *Gypsy* out of the smash hit status." He was not rolling in money, yet with his full share of royalties this time, coupled with what he had earned from the best-selling movie sound track of *West Side Story*, Sondheim was able to buy a townhouse on East 49th Street in New York. He would ever after refer to his residence, directly next door to Katharine Hepburn's, as "the house that *Gypsy* built."

Gypsy lost to other shows at season's end when the prizes were given out. The show received seven Tony nominations but did not win a single award. Mary Martin in *The Sound of Music* won for Best Actress in a Musical. Merman, who was justifiably seething, began to miss performances and did not stay with the show beyond the run of her contract. Even though *Gypsy* was a hit, it needed a star of the first magnitude to propel it into blockbuster status, and with Ethel gone, none was available. Because of Merman's pique, no London company was planned right away;[3] in fact, after it closed on Broadway, *Gypsy* languished unplayed for more than a decade until Angela Lansbury agreed to star in it in the West End.

The Sound of Music swept all the awards and even tied with *Fiorello* (given a Pulitzer Prize as well) for Best Musical. As with *West Side Story*, at prize time Sondheim's contribution was largely ignored. (This was two years before Tonys were instituted for music and lyrics; otherwise Stephen would have been pitted against Oscar.)

Oscar's last show, *The Sound of Music* opened in New York on November 16, 1959, to good notices but not unqualified praise. While noticing its "hand-

---

[3] According to Sondheim, a London company starring Elaine Stritch *was* planned but something happened, "either Elaine got a movie or she fell ill."

someness," and "substantiality," Walter Kerr in the *New York Herald-Tribune* called it "too sweet for words but almost too sweet for music."[4] Most of the critics for the workaday papers mentioned the professionality of Mary Martin's performance and the aptness of the score, but the reviewers for the intellectual journals had a field day lambasting the show's saccharinity. Still, none of the reviews dampened the public enthusiasm. They came in droves throughout *The Sound of Music*'s 1,443 performances, allowing it to run twice as long as *Gypsy*.

Sondheim's glossing over by the critics helped him develop what has become a lifelong aversion to them. He says, "I never read them because if you believe the good ones, you have to believe the bad ones." Even though the writing of *Gypsy* had been a joyous experience, and, as Oscar Hammerstein promised, it had taken only half a year out of his life, he was not prepared for being ignored again. Now, in order to wash away the whole experience of being considered exclusively "a lyricist," he continued writing music *with* lyrics for the Roman farce. "Music is the fun part, lyrics the hard part," he would always say. But he had barely dug into the fun when he was informed by Dorothy Hammerstein that Oscar was dying.

Hammerstein had gone for his routine annual check-up in mid-September, during which time he complained of stomach pain. His doctor gave him the usual tests and X-rays to determine if he had an ulcer, and when they read the lab reports it was determined that he had cancer. The carcinoma was Grade IV, which meant it was so advanced that they had to remove three-quarters of the patient's stomach. Even with such radical excision they predicted Oscar would be dead in six months.

Throughout the spring of 1960, Oscar's doctor monitored his condition, which outwardly seemed not to have changed much, and began giving him liver and vitamin shots to bolster his waning energy. Two months later, in early July, he showed his patient the most recent X-rays, which indicated the carcinoma was now advancing rapidly. He suggested chemotherapy. Oscar said he had considered the matter carefully and decided that he would prefer not to spend his last months in the hospital but to die possibly a little earlier on his beloved farm in Doylestown, with his head "on Dorothy's pillow."

Once he had made the decision, he planned to continue to live as before until death overtook him. Nor would he allow its shadow to keep him from being driven to New York where he scheduled a series of luncheons with one after another of his dear friends. He invited Sondheim to one of them, and they talked merely of theater, exchanging pleasantries. Sondheim realized later that it was Oscar's way of saying goodbye. Richard Rodgers too recalled one of their

---

[4] The "sweet" libretto was *not* Hammerstein's but the work of Howard Lindsay and Russell Crouse. Oscar Hammerstein, ill at the time, bowed out from attempting *The Sound of Music*'s book.

last lunches at the Plaza Oak Room. Oscar, who ate very little now, was pecking listlessly at his food, when a man at a nearby table came over to ask them to sign his menu. "You're the most successful team on Broadway," he said. "Tell me, why do you both look so sad?"

Oscar even acquiesced to a last party. Here is an excerpt from his last journal entry:

> Today is July 12, 1960, my birthday, I am sixty-five. This is the accepted age of retirement. I do not want to retire, am in no mood to retire. This is considered a good time to come to a stop. Perhaps it is, but not for me ... Some day I may leave the theatre, but I couldn't walk out suddenly. I would have to linger a while and take a few last looks, I would have to blow a few fond kisses as I edged towards the stage door . . ."

On that very day, before his celebratory dinner, he inscribed copies of a handsome photograph of himself which he gave to each member of his extended family—always including Sondheim. Acknowledging his student's emancipation, he penned, "To Steve—my friend and teacher, Ockie" on the photo. (Sondheim would pay his own posthumous homage in turn to *his* friend and teacher when he dedicated the score of A *Funny Thing Happened On the Way to the Forum* "To Oscar Hammerstein II.")

On Monday, August 22, Dorothy was with Oscar when he became delirious and began reciting the names of baseball players from the past. Ten minutes later he was dead. The following evening the lights all over Times Square were dimmed for a minute of reverence for this great theatrical spirit.

Sondheim has called *Gypsy* "the last good show in the Rodgers and Hammerstein form." His new show, because of its long title usually referred to as *Forum*, was not to turn out like an R & H opus, but was to be the kind of zany comedy Rodgers had written with Lorenz Hart. Very much like their final show, *By Jupiter*, but avoiding all the topical and anachronistic references, it was pure musical comedy. Sondheim's songs, far from helping the plot along in the Hammerstein tradition, simply sit like jewels (sometimes rhinestones) on the scenario. Most of them have witty and amusing lyrics supported by rather routine, forgettable melodies. Perhaps the reason why, here again, Sondheim's contribution was little noted was simply because the comedy, the script, the mugging were the stars here, and the songs were, in a way, a chance to let audiences dry the tears of laughter from their eyes. "When we were putting *Forum* together," Sondheim told Dan Sullivan of the *Los Angeles Times* in 1971, "I realized that the songs had to *not* progress the action." By the same token, and to Sondheim's credit, the songs had to *not* draw attention to themselves either.

Forum's plot is carefully worked out, and at every turn it is always logical and amusing. It was a long time a-borning—from its conception even before *Gypsy* opened in 1958 until its premiere in May 1962, the show went through about a dozen complete rewrites. During that time, Sondheim, eager to write music, was not willing to sit around and wait for the final version of the farce. In addition to his work on *Gypsy* he outlined Giraudoux's serious comedy, *The Madwoman of Chaillot*,[5] for a musical, worked with Mary Rodgers on a version of *The Lady or the Tiger?*, wrote incidental music for a play, *Invitation to a March*, and began work on his next musical, *Anyone Can Whistle*.

It was at about this time that the film version of *West Side Story* was released. Its motion picture sound track recording, selling into the millions, was to make Sondheim, if not a household name, at least quite wealthy, allowing him for the rest of his life to pick and choose his projects. His only worry, he reported at that time, was that *Forum* might not work. "I thought it was the funniest show I'd ever read in my life and I wanted to be part of it. But I didn't have any real worries about the music; I thought the book would carry everything, which in fact it did."

Part of the perpetual hilarity of farce is the opening and closing of doors: one character entering on the heels of another's departure. To this end, Tony Walton designed the simple yet serviceable set the script calls for. With its three houses and an attendant number of doors, it is ideal.

Recounting the plot of a farce is a little like offering stale beer. The taste is recognizable, but the effervescence and bite have dissipated. So is reading the story without seeing the hilarious Marx Brothers–like happenings, hearing the rapid Neil Simonesque one-liners, or watching the ribald mugging of the actors, with which the musical is filled. If *Gypsy* burlesques burlesque and vaudeville, then *A Funny Thing* burlesques farce and low comedy.

Briefly, it is the story of a slave, Pseudolus, who is promised his freedom by his pubescent master, aptly named Hero, if he can secure for him the maiden with whom he has fallen in love. Hero has been smitten with the girl, Philia, a newcomer to the House of Lycus, the brothel next door. Both Hero and Philia are handsome but rather slow-witted. The complication is that Philia has been sold to the military captain, Miles Gloriosus, who is coming that very afternoon to collect his bride. Pseudolus convinces Lycus that Philia is dying of the plague and installs her as a maid in Hero's house. When Senex, Hero's father, who had been away, returns unannounced and attempts to seduce Philia, she is moved

---

[5] In 1969 a musical version, *Dear World*, with a much underrated score by Jerry Herman and book by Jerome Lawrence and Robert E. Lee, had a short run on Broadway.

next door to the vacant house of Erronius—absent searching for his long-lost son and daughter, stolen by pirates in infancy.[6]

More intrigue happens when Miles Gloriosus appears, and Pseudolus, under threat of being speared to death by Miles, has to convince the other family slave, Hysterium, to pose as Philia, dead of the plague. Matters come to a head with a funeral pyre for Hysterium, but as in all good farce, at the breakneck ending Erronius returns. When he spots the family crest, a gaggle of geese, on Miles's finger ring—and a matching one on Philia's—he realizes Miles and Philia are sister and brother—his children. Pseudolus is granted his freedom, and the lovers, Hero and Philia, are united as the curtain falls.

If the machinations of *Forum*'s plot are convoluted, they have nothing on the backstage intrigue that preceded the show to Broadway. By the time Sondheim came back to the project, *Gypsy* had already opened, and Leland Hayward, who originally evinced some interest in the project, had dropped out. Phil Silvers, for whom the leading role was conceived, rejected the part as "old shtick," missing the point of the farce completely.[7] The show's creators hoped Hal Prince would become its producer, but he turned them down. David Merrick was the next to option the show.

Sondheim, Shevelove, and Gelbart wanted Robbins to direct, but after Robbins's blow-ups with Merrick during *Gypsy*'s staging, he swore never to work with Merrick again and bowed out completely. Merrick, acting in an uncustomary gentlemanly manner, agreed to release his option on the script.

Sondheim returned his advance of $4000 to Merrick, and when Hal Prince picked up Merrick's option, Robbins came back to the project. Then Robbins went on an extended vacation in Paris; when he returned he said he had changed his mind and was *not* going to direct this show. Prince (who had come in as producer by now), in exasperation, engaged his former boss, George Abbott, to direct. Sondheim wrote an apologetic letter to Merrick, stating that he owed him a favor mentioning how Robbins had "once again slithered away."

The show was choreographed by Jack Cole, but its movement was not working in the previews. In Washington it played to only fifty people one matinee. The critic in the local papers cried "Close It!" It was at this point that Sondheim

---

[6] Erronius was instructed by the oracle to begin his quest by circling Rome seven times. One hilarious production found Erronius trotting through the theater lobby at intermission, mumbling, "second time around . . ."

[7] In 1965 Silvers was hilarious as Marcus Lycus (not the part for which he was originally intended) in the film version of *Forum* and in the 1972 revival of *Forum* was somewhat less successful in the part of Pseudolus.

In the 1996 revival of Forum, Pseudolus (Nathan Lane) feigns shock while witnessing Vi-brata's (Mary Ann Lamb) seductive dance. Photo: Joan Marcus. © Museum of the City of New York.

suggested they bring in Robbins to look at the show, and Prince agreed. Robbins reset the opening. Now the show seemed to work like magic.

There had been two opening numbers before "Comedy Tonight," the one in use today, was decided upon. "Comedy Tonight" is as close to a Sondheim hit song as this show ever comes. But the first one, "Love Is in the Air," which Sondheim calls "perfectly charming," is a light ballad that might have been written by any one of a dozen professional Broadway songwriters. It treats love as a disease bordering on an epidemic. It is obviously inspired by the "plague" idea that suffuses the play's text. I quote from its A2 section:

Anyone exposed	Leave your house and lose your reason,
Can catch it.	This is a contagious season,
Keep your window closed,	Love is going around.
And latch it.	

It was cut from the opening in Washington, where it was replaced with "Comedy Tonight." Sondheim and his collaborators realized that "perfectly charming" set the wrong tone for this farce. Sondheim had written another extended number, "Invocation," that told the audience what to expect and which Robbins called "perfect for the show," but, according to Sondheim, added, "but George [Abbott] won't have it. So you've got to write another version." This writer agrees that "Invocation" is a stylized plea to the gods of the theater, which suggested "high comedy" rather than "low." Although, as Abbott put it, "not hummable," it fits the play like a tattered glove.

Bless our little company and smile on us.	We offer you rites and revels,
Think not about deep concerns,	Smile on us for a while[8] ...
Think not about dark dilemmas.	

By the time Jerry Robbins came back to doctor the show, when "Love Is in the Air" had been reinserted at Abbott's request because it *was* hummable, he told Sondheim to "tell the audience what the evening is about because the show is perfectly terrific." Most theater pundits have agreed that was wise advice.

"The first song is what makes or breaks the show," Sondheim always maintained to his classes in musical theater. "You start off with the right opening, and you can ride for forty-five minutes on the telephone book. On the other hand, if you start off with the wrong one, it's an uphill fight all the way."

---

[8] "Invocation" was not to be totally lost. Its verse, called "Invocation to the Audience," was used as the opening number of a musical version of Aristophanes' *The Frogs*, which Sondheim and Shevelove wrote and which gave performances in the Yale Swimming Pool in 1974.

"Comedy Tonight" was substituted for "Love Is in the Air[9]" before the first New York preview. Sondheim insists that this change turned the show around, but an interview with Madeline Gilford brought forth another theory contrary to Sondheim's. Madeline, whose husband, Jack, played Hysterium, never missed a preview performance at Washington's National Theater and blames the Washington audience for the lack of response. "We knew it was bound to be a hit with New York theatergoers, but those up-tight Washingtonians are afraid to laugh," she insists. Sondheim counters with "what about New Haven, where the audience did not think the show was funny?"

In any case, whether disaster in Washington may be turned around to SRO on Broadway by a new opening is moot. What is evident is that "Comedy Tonight" is a rousing, funny, tuneful romp—ideal for the ensuing farce.

"Comedy Tonight" has a typically commercial form: A1, A2, Release, and A3 with extension. Perhaps the most interesting thing about it is the way it builds excitement by narrowing metrically—shorter phrases with fewer syllables—toward its end. After several choruses interspersed with dialogue and movement Sondheim sums up the evening ahead:

Stunning surprises,	Philanderers,
Cunning disguises,	Cupidity,
Hundreds of actors out of sight!	Timidity,
Pantaloons and tunics,	Mistakes,
Courtesans and eunuchs,	Fakes,
Funerals and chases,	Rhymes,
Baritones and basses,	Mimes
Panderers,	Tumblers, grumblers, fumblers, bumblers,

Then, with an old but infallible showbiz trick, the main theme returns fortissimo with a slow and deliberate beat coupled with a lyric that ties everything together:

No royal curse,
No Trojan horse,
And a happy ending, of course! . . .

Besides the opening number, there were other changes, simplifications made earlier, when George Abbott came in. According to Larry Gelbart, "The show didn't work[10] because by the time it opened we had put it through a strainer and taken out a lot of the plot. So we put it all back."

[9] This tune, too good to sacrifice, was kept in the show and used as a prelude to the second act, but it suffered the indignity of being presented wordlessly and being shorn of its final A3 section.
[10] One amusing anecdote concerns a quip by George Abbott, famous for his knack of saving plays in trouble. Standing in the back of the theater and listening to the audience *not* laughing at the mayhem on stage he said "I dunno. Maybe you had better call in George Abbott."

"Free" is the show's pivotal number. In it Pseudolus savors all the ramifications of freedom. At one point he almost declines the offer and sings: "I have a roof / Three meals a day . . . / And I don't have to pay / A thing. /I'm just a slave and ev'rything's free. / If I were free, / Then nothing would be free . . ." But he soon comes to his senses, and the song ends climactically and hilariously as the illiterate slave, savoring each delicious letter asks his master to spell the word out again. Hero sings, "F, R Double—" "No," interrupts Pseudolus, "the long way."

Two wonderful songs had to be dropped from *Forum*, but fortunately they can be heard on recordings. "Once Upon a Time," one of this author's favorites, was deleted from the score. The more obvious "Lovely" was substituted for it because it could be reprised and act as a hilarious moment in the second act when it was sung by Hysterium, now in drag.

"The Echo Song," a witty and hilarious gem, was deleted as well. Following in the pattern of "Pretty Little Picture," this is a situation song—as Sondheim says, "a song that can be accomplished in one line of dialogue." It was reinstated and became for this listener one of the high spots in the 1972 Broadway and the 1995 Utah Shakespeare Festival revivals.

There are enough extra *Forum* songs in the Sondheim trunk to give any enterprising director leeway for any production. There is even one called "A Gaggle of Geese," which has never, to my knowledge, been used in any production.

The show was carefully cast for ensemble hilarity. The girthy Zero Mostel wowed the critics as Pseudolus, a role originally written for Milton Berle. Prune-faced Jack Gilford made a hysterical Hysterium, while lanky John Carradine of the stentorian voice played Lycus, the dealer in courtesans. *Forum* went on to win Tonys for Best Musical, Best Producer, Best Book, Best Director, Best Actor, and Best Supporting Actor and ran for two years. Again Sondheim's contribution was overlooked, but it must be mentioned that *Oliver!*, a humdinger of a show won for best score. In addition to *Oliver!* the critics nominated a meandering, practically one-man show *Stop the World—I Want to Get Off*, which Anthony Newley co-wrote and starred in, and *Little Me*, another episodic musical that boasted the combined talents of Cy Coleman, Carolyn Leigh, Neil Simon, and television superstar Sid Caesar. Both of these had first-rate scores. But presumably to fill out the ballot, the Tony committee incomprehensively added *Bravo, Giovanni*, a fourth-rate musical that is clearly head, shoulders, and trunk below the *Forum* score.

Many have wondered how a show can win a Best Musical award without having the best score. It is incomprehensible to this writer, but Sondheim's own feeling about the inappropriateness of his songs to the zaniness on stage may give some clue.

"It's a very elegant, low comedy libretto and it's a drawing room score. The score is clever, and the book, though it is brilliantly clever, never shows that it's clever. It's always essentially on a clown level. Too many of the songs are on a written level. A song like 'Free,' which I'm very proud of, simply is not the right style for that show, whereas a song like 'Impossible' is. I'm afraid that about three-quarters of the score is wrong."

As a curious sidelight to *Forum*'s billing and the power of entrenchment leading to acclaim, when the show was first presented in 1962, Sondheim's name was listed last after Shevelove's and Gelbart's. For the revival in 1972, after he had added *Anyone Can Whistle, Company*, and *Follies* to his dossier, the critics hailed it and called it Sondheim's *A Funny Thing Happened on the Way to the Forum*.[11]

[11] Since everyone knows by this time that *Forum* is Sondheim's, the hit revival that had a long run in 1996 and '97 could afford to put the name of its star, Broadway's newest farceur, Nathan Lane, above the title.

Lloyd-Webber and Rice—The Sixties

CONTRASTED WITH ANDREW LLOYD-WEBBER, who, try as he might, would never attain that state of insouciance known as "shag," Tim Miles Bindon Rice *was* practically born shag. The event occurred November 13, 1944, in Amersham, Buckinghamshire—about twenty-five miles north of London. He had grown up near Hatfield and St. Albans in Hertfordshire. His father, an executive with de Havilland Aviation, necessarily moved the family around a great deal, giving Tim a wide scholastic sampling—they even spent a year in Tokyo. In his formative years Tim had gone to various religious schools, but he took his secondary education at Lancing College in Sussex, on the coast near Brighton. In his early teens there he'd sung with a rock and roll group called The Aardvarks.

His real aim was not to be a mere singer with a group but to be the star. From his earliest days Tim Rice had developed a great interest in popular music, was an avid record collector, and by his late teens had acquired an encyclopedic knowledge of its performers.

Wanting to "taste life" and assess qualities in himself besides musicianship, he talked his parents into letting him take a course at the Sorbonne in Paris. Tall, blonde, blue-eyed, gregarious, affable, and intensely handsome, he had, according to one interviewer, "sampled quite a large measure of life and many of the coed students abroad." Nor was he celibate on his return to England.

Back at home he took a menial job as gas station attendant until he was able to get one in music. He studied the whole rock repertoire avidly until he had it at his fingertips—who wrote what, when the song was released, and how high it went on the charts. Keen to make a record, he taped some songs he'd written. When he played them for a group called Night Shift, they liked "That's My Story," for which he had written words and music. They agreed to record it. The record sold poorly, "only twenty copies," Tim deplores, but adds that "the point was that it was something I could talk rather grandly about to publishers."

It was Tim Rice's mother who knew Desmond Elliott, the publisher and incipient agent. She told him about her son's background and asked him to entertain Tim's idea for a book about the history of the Top Twenty rock hits. As he was now a "recording artist," his father helped him get a job as a "management trainee" (which means gofer) with EMI, the great British recording firm that was handling many of the emerging giants of rock and roll like Elvis Presley, Cliff Richard, and The Shadows. Although his contact with these idols was nonexistent, he was near enough to get glimpses of them occasionally and access to their recordings. The proximity made him think more about his own capabilities as a singer-songwriter, and he began to seek an outlet for his capabilities.

After their interview, during which Elliott was more impressed with young Tim's creative abilities than his scheme for a rock compendium and gave him Lloyd-Webber's address, Rice wrote the following:

> 11 Gunter Grove
> London S.W.10
> April 21, 1965

Dear Andrew,
  I have been given your address by Desmond Elliott of Arlington Books, who I believe has also told you of my existence. Mr. Elliott told me that you "were looking for a 'with-it' writer" of lyrics for your songs, and as I have been writing pop songs for a short while now and particularly enjoy writing the lyrics I wondered if you consider it worth your while meeting me. I may fall far short of your requirements, but anyway it would be interesting to meet up—I hope! Would you be able to get in touch with me shortly, either at FLA 1822 in the evenings, or at WEL 2261 in the daytime (Pettit and Westlake,[1] solicitors, are the owners of the latter number).
                    Hoping to hear from you,
                              Yours,
                              Tim Rice.

Only a few days after he posted that letter, an impatient Tim popped around to Andrew's flat in Harrington Court. "I have written eight musicals," Andrew boasted almost upon opening the door to his future collaborator—and in case the latter did not believe him he quickly moved to the piano to play extracts

---

[1] Pettit and Westlake, a Baker Street law firm, had given Rice a job a year earlier. While there, totally bored with his job, his interest became even keener in popular music. After two uneventful years as an intern at the law firm it was painfully clear to Tim and his parents that his future did not lie in a courtroom, and in 1966, when he was twenty-two, he simply quit. By that time he was well on his way into his songwriting career.

from *Cinderella Up the Beanstalk*, *Socrates Swings*, and many of his toy theater opuses.

Rice was duly impressed. In his own way Andrew was overwhelmed. "I knew almost immediately that he was exactly right," Lloyd-Webber remembered. "As soon as we started to work together I saw how much better he was than all the people I was ever likely to meet at Oxford."

But it was not an ideal collaboration at the start. Their goals and experiences were different. Tim Rice's knowledge of the world outshone Andrew's narrow background. They both shared an idolatry for the heroes of rock and roll, even though Tim was more knowledgeable about their recordings. Yet their interest in their idols was more for their successes than for their music. Tim felt "Andrew had this burning ambition to be Richard Rodgers while I sort of wanted to be Elvis," and it would take them at least a half year to discover a songwriting direction they both could find congenial.

Andrew had planned a last holiday that summer of his graduation from Westminster, a tour of Italy with four friends from school. Ivon Asquith (who would later serve as an executive at the Oxford University Press), David Carpenter (who would become a university don), William Bach (who went into law), and the most shag of the group, Gray Watson. Watson, tall, handsome, dark, and witty, was Andrew's closest friend. "His Wildean flamboyance," says Lloyd-Webber biographer Michael Walsh, "was looked at askance by his classmates and privately led to speculation about the real nature of his relationship with Andrew. That relationship appears to be purely platonic," Walsh adds, explaining that "Lloyd-Webber's lifestyle has always been committedly heterosexual."

Ivon Asquith recalled the tour they had taken: "It took us to Florence, Rome, Assisi, and Ventimiglia on the way back, where we stayed with Andrew's aunt." Aunt Vi had given up her pursuit of a theatrical career and with her physician husband had retired to that Italian coast city several years before. Childless, she often came to London to be near the bohemian, theatrical side of her family— especially her favorite nephew, who was so passionate about showbiz. Her villa in Italy, flower strewn and overlooking the sea, was always open to Andrew, who came often. This was the first time he had brought his friends.

Gray and Andrew were the tour leaders and selected the itinerary because of their knowledge of art and architecture. When the group was not inspecting ruins or masterpieces, basking in the warm Mediterranean sun, or taking side camping trips, the seventeen-year-olds became embroiled in political discussions. Asquith, Bach, and Carpenter deplored Italy's role in World War II, but both Lloyd-Webber and Gray held opposite views and pointed out that Mussolini had certainly improved Italy's architecture—Andrew's forte. His right-wing political slant led him toward "Tory anarchism," despite what he later called "a strong

Socialist tendency—almost to the point where I joined the Communist party." (This last was obviously Jean's influence.)

That autumn Andrew began his first term at Magdalen College at Oxford with heavy misgiving. Putting his music aside, and propelled by the past summer's political discussions, he tried to examine his own political penchants. "At school everyone had a point of view. Mine was that I'd always believed, hugely, in the British liberal tradition with a small "l." Mentioning the lack of political training or interest among Molly, Jean, William, Julian, and himself, he said that "as a family, the only things we really felt very deeply about were the preservation and care of buildings, architecture, and music."

But this most nonliterate of young men was beginning to think now on his own and to deplore the possibility of his future—spending four years embroiled in academia. Unequivocally, the terms of his scholarship obliged him to "read history," which was becoming abhorrent to him. Being swallowed in the literate life and the study of architecture and art history paled before the possibility of collaborating with a true shag, from whom he felt he might learn to be more "with-it."

Andrew's interest in Tim Rice as an ideal collaborator had never left him. But Tim was fifty miles away working in London. Choosing second best, Andrew renewed his contact with Robin Barrow of the *Cinderella* and *Socrates* musicals. Barrow was now in his last year at Oxford, but after three years apart Andrew found his former collaborator wasn't interested in writing any more. "Like all composers, I wanted to cling on to lyricists, but I think Robin had a rather changed direction. At school [Westminster] he'd been a rock 'n' roller. Then against all odds he became a classics don."

It was not sour grapes. Andrew Lloyd-Webber would have worked with anyone, so eager was he to get started. His room in Magdalen New Buildings was a little apart from the others, rather gloomy, and, for the first time in his life, he was without a piano. It was small solace, but now he began to build up his interest in recordings. And like his father's, his choices were eclectic. William Cran, who lived beneath him, remembered hearing sentimental pop coming from Andrew's room. Middle-of-the-road singers like the Everly Brothers, Neil Sedaka, and Bobby Vee seemed to be his favorites. Show tunes and light classics like "The Warsaw Concerto" were played over and over.

He still maintained his interest in Victorian architecture and had developed a taste for the quasi-romantic paintings of the Pre-Raphaelite school. These pursuits, which were to involve him throughout his life, made him fit in less at Oxford than he had at Westminster. From his perch as one of the world's preeminent creators of musicals in 1996 he was to remark that these were "the least fashionable things you could possibly be interested in: the Pre-Raphaelites,

Puccini and Rodgers and Hammerstein. They were all *loathed* in smart circles. I loved them anyway."

Callas's *Tosca* at Covent Garden eventually rehabilitated Puccini for the cognoscenti; the Pre-Raphaelites have by now become the most interesting and choicest paintings to collect; and Rodgers and Hammerstein's works, now that their creators are gone, are considered classic musical models, constantly revived, with Rodgers being looked on as the last font of hummable melody and Hammerstein dubbed Tin Pan Alley's only true poet. So much for vogues.

The musical life at the college was multifarious with organ recitals, choral groups, madrigal societies, chamber orchestras, jazz groups, and pop and swing bands. But nobody seemed to be interested in musical theater[2]. Gradually he began to come down to London, sometimes for a day to see the family and maybe to attend the matinee of a musical. During the week, when he was definitely obliged to stay at Oxford, there were long telephone calls, with Andrew alternately angry, tearful, or contrite. Soon he began coming home for the weekend, after which he always returned to Oxford with a heavy heart.

Champing at the bit to work with Tim Rice and afraid that so erudite a lyricist might be snapped up by another composer, Lloyd-Webber decided to leave Oxford at Christmastime. He knew Jean and Molly, who had sacrificed so much so that he might have a classical education and who believed he would never succeed in music, would be appalled. So fearful of their reaction (and perhaps a bit insecure as to his own future) was he that he talked the university into allowing him to take a two-term leave of absence instead of closing the door permanently.

Once his parents were assured their son knew what he was doing, they gave their blessing. William's reasoning was clear enough. He rationalized that since "fate" had denied him the chance to become a creative artist, why should he deny that chance to his son? Jean came to her decision with more difficulty. Andrew's course in life thus far had mystified her, a natural fatalist. It was clear to her that Julian was the gifted one, and so she had pushed him hard into his calling. It was just as clear to her that Andrew's talents did not lie in music, so she hoped he would become the historian of his childhood wishes. When he developed his passion for the theater, Jean was totally at sea. Now she realized it was time to let him go and find whatever the gods had in store for him.

---

[2] Cambridge, not Oxford, was far more advanced in the field of theater—specifically musical theater. "Everybody came from Cambridge," Andrew stated. "You look at David Frost, John Cleese, Trevor Nunn, and Jonathan Miller—it was just incredible." Oxford lacked any kind of musical theater department until 1991, when Cameron Mackintosh established a chair in musical theatre. Its first visiting professor was Stephen Sondheim.

He moved back home for good now. Fate came to the rescue again when the three-bedroom flat next door became available, and Molly moved in at once. What would she do with the two extra bedrooms? They could be rented out for a few additional pounds a week. One would be perfect for John Lill and his grand piano so that Andrew could have his old bedroom to himself. The other, of course, would serve as a dandy studio-sleeping arrangement for Andrew's collaborator, Tim Rice.

To the sheer sound pouring out of this dwelling Tim Rice now added his rock gramophone records, played at top decibel. When this was added to Andrew's piano and French horn (he also liked the tuba), Julian's perpetual cello practice, John Lill's glittering piano etudes, William's playing his special piano fitted with organ pedals, or, when he was not at the keyboard, playing Tchaikovsky or Puccini records fortissimo, the hammering of Jean's students on *her* piano, and Molly's television set, on which, in self-defense, she turned up the volume as she grew deafer, Number Ten Harrington Court was a veritable musical Tower of Babel.

For Tim Rice the sheer eclectic bohemianism of life at Harrington Court was a revelation. Musicians came and went, meals were served at odd hours—or not at all. At first he was shocked, for Tim had never heard parents use scatological words in front of their offspring, but in this uninhibited household, nothing was verboten. If he stayed out all night (one interviewer remarked that he had "a practically inexhaustible supply of girls"), it was not remarked upon the next day.

But in addition to the freedom, life at the South Ken flats also incorporated frequent bickering between Julian and Andrew Lloyd Webber—now the older brother was no longer the star attraction. He could not boss his younger sibling as he had done in the days of the Toy Theater. Molly sensed the conflict and, in order to give everyone a modicum of peace, supplied a small weekly stipend so that Andrew could move into a basement flat nearby. The brothers were kept further apart when Andrew, preparatory to his work with Tim, thought he'd better catch up on the musical crafts he lacked and began to study orchestration, conducting, and piano orthography.

There has always been some controversy as to why Andrew's mastery of these crafts, essential to every musician, was so sketchy and came so late. Lloyd-Webber confesses to "a slight battle with my old man to get him to allow me to go to the Royal College of Music because . . . he said it would be a mistake to be too formally trained. He thought it was better to pick it up by practical experience." Certainly William, torn between his love of light popular music and his heavy academic musical training, must have thought that his theoretical erudition had done him in and hoped to protect his son—whose pure melodic gifts he foresaw—from becoming a modernist or, worse, an atonalist, which all the conservatories in Britain and abroad were turning out by the dozens.

Tim Rice was mightily impressed with Andrew's facility for tunes, but he was equally taken with Jean Lloyd Webber's dedication: her helping to educate and thereby elevate those children of the East End. Never having known any zealots to a cause, he became especially close to Jean. Andrew's mother's philosophy and the whole subject of social reform began to appeal greatly to him—so much so, that he and Andrew decided their first musical would be based on the life of Thomas Barnardo (1845–1905), who had pioneered in the care of underprivileged children.

Dr. Barnardo founded the East End Juvenile Mission in 1870 with the aid of the seventh Earl of Shaftsbury. This boys' home was the first of his famous Dr. Barnardo homes, which soon spread throughout Great Britain and British possessions[3]. A musical based on his difficulties in setting up these philanthropic shelters had all the earmarks of being in the mainstream of British theater. Lionel Bart's *Oliver!* and *Fings Ain't What They Used To Be* had dealt amusingly with the underprivileged, and both had been wildly successful. Tim and Andrew decided to have a go at the same genre. It was an ambitious decision, but it was doomed to fail because its material had already been recycled. In 1990 Lloyd Webber was to say that "of the tradition of sob-*Olivers*, our Dr. Barnardo show was probably at the bottom of the heap."

Desmond Elliott, now their manager, put his literary stable of writers and celebrities at their service and enlisted one of his clients, Leslie Thomas, the best-selling author of *The Virgin Soldiers* and *Orange Wednesday*, to handle the libretto. Then Elliott found them a producer, Ernest Hecht, who gave them their first advance, a pitiful £100—but to the new team it carried the seal of professionality.

Their show, to be called *The Likes of Us*, would include everything that Dickensian London had to offer. Leslie Thomas fashioned an eclectic book that included urchins, sex, love, fortunes lost and found, all to songs and accents mostly cockney, with a bit of Mayfair thrown in. Working practically round the clock, the Rice–Webber team began to flesh the story in with songs.

They began with the title song. Coupled with the gentle melody Andrew wrote,[4] Tim's self denigrating lyric for the ragamuffins, although a bit treacly, works to inspire audience sympathy for the urchins from the start.

---

[3] There are presently over one hundred homes in Britain and others in Australia and Canada. Barnardo was instrumental in securing the passage (1891) of parliamentary legislation for child welfare.

[4] This melody which actually was written earlier, during the Toy Theater days, would eventually resurface as one of the main themes for *Variations*, ALW's composition based on the 24th Caprice of Paganini.

'Ave you seen my bruvver Johnny?
Not since yesterday.
Is it going to rain tonight?
It's kind of 'ard to say.
'Oo 'as got me blinkin' rug?
I need it for me bed.
No one knows the likes of us
Are sleepin' over'ead.

I picked up a wallet
From a fancy coach today,
I got fourpence cleaning boots
Down Stepney Market way.
Ain't no one seen Johnny yet?
Perhaps they took him in.
No one knows the places where
The likes of us have been.

Pitter Patter, Pitter Patter
We can feel the rain,
Little silver water drops
Are falling down again.
We ain't gonna bother,
It's no matter if it falls,
For we know the likes of us
Are going to stay outdoors.

Time to doss us down to sleep,
They're putting out the light.
When they make it dark and quiet
Is when we say goodnight.
We don't mind the things we got,
And we ain't gonna fuss.
This is what we know is proper
For the likes of us.

"Going, Going, Gone," the auction phrase, is an irresistible concept for a song. Stephen Sondheim used it as the final words to his moving song "Good Thing Going" from *Merrily We Roll Along*, a show which, somewhat like *The Likes of Us*, is concerned with juveniles. Sondheim's rueful ballad approaches love as a waning metaphor, whereas the Webber–Rice version has no such subtext. The latter is sheer Monty Python Music Hall and makes its auction theme great fun to boot.

Here I have Lot 1 in this beautiful auction—a
    beautiful parrot in a magnificent cage.

Here I have a lovely parrot, sound in wind and
    limb,
I can guarantee that there is nothing wrong
    with him.
Pretty feathers, very clever, do I hear a call?
20, 30, 40, 50—Goodness, is that all?

This parrot is a sturdy fellow, you can plainly
    see,
His habits are impressive, he has a wide
    vocabulary.
60, 80, 90, 100—going for a song,
Going to that well-built lady, going, going, gone.
    . . .

Other songs were not so successful. Rice himself would describe them as "square and dated." But the show had a complete score, including some songs in which the concept is inherent in its title, such as "Strange and Lovely Song," "A Man on His Own," "Where Am I Going?," "Will This Last Forever?," and "You Won't Care About Her Any More."

The Likes of Us might never have gotten off Tim's typewriter or Andrew's keyboard if it had not been for Alan Doggett. Doggett was an enterprising and adventurous musician, an intensely nervous man. As choir director of Colet Court, which is the preparatory school for St. Paul's School, Doggett was top notch. In the few years since he had come to Colet Court he had revolutionalized the way the choir was taught. He trained them as professionals in the style of the Vienna Boys Choir; that is, they were prepared to sing four-part harmony as distinguished from the usual English two- or at the most three-part harmony sung by church boy choirs.

Doggett was also a discreet homosexual who developed a fruitless letch for Lloyd-Webber. He admired the boy's sensitive looks as much as his phenomenal aptitude for creating tunes. He had come to know William and Jean Lloyd Webber when he taught music history in the days when Andrew and Julian were students at Westminster, before his step up to Colet Court, and had often been to their flat. From time to time Doggett helped the young composer with his compositions, assuring that there were not five beats in a bar that was written in 4/4 and making subtle suggestions about the contour or singability of his work.

When the score was somewhat complete, Lloyd-Webber persuaded Doggett to arrange for his off-duty Colet Choir to record the songs, hoping that the demo would lead to a theater performance. Tim's having worked in the EMI recording studio provided the entree.

Now with a demo record of their show, the group was ready to go forward to the stage. Oxford was a logical choice for the musical's debut, especially as Andrew Lloyd-Webber, who had taken a leave of absence, was still a matriculated student there, but Desmond Elliott had grander ideas. He felt the show should be brought into the West End. Elliott was not canny in the ways of mounting a musical, for even in 1966 it was a question of many thousands of pounds to present one in the mainstem of London. A publisher and literary agent, he could not know that there would simply be no backers for a show by a team with no track record that consisted of a composer still in his teens and a lyricist hardly out of them.

In the long run it was a mistake not to produce the show at Oxford, for although their excursion into London's slums was déjà vu, Andrew Lloyd-Webber and Tim Rice had written a real show, and seeing their work performed, similar to the experience Sondheim had with *All That Glitters* at Williams College, might have shown them at that early and receptive stage of their careers more about what makes a true musical succeed. Actually, *Joseph*, *Superstar*, and, to some extent, even *Evita* began basically as ideas for recordings. To get them into shape for the musical stage they needed directors with minds and wills of steel to mold them into theatrical productions. As it turned out, after *The Likes of Us* languished unproduced in his trunk, Andrew did not begin properly thinking of music theater written purposely for the stage until his collaboration with a true man of the theater, Alan Ayckbourne, and their production of their first flop, *Jeeves*. Prior to that, and in spite of the tremendous success Lloyd-Webber's works achieved, they must properly be called sound shows, swelled to full-length musical size.

In the spring of 1967 when Andrew had just turned nineteen, *The Evening Standard*, one of London's highest-circulation newspapers, announced a contest to find "The London *Evening Standard* Girl of the Year," whose life in the year to come would be chronicled on its pages. According to David Ballantyne (who would later become Julian's brother-in-law), Tim and Andrew "scoured London for copies of the newspaper carrying entry coupons for the contest and filled in dozens of voting forms." The girl they voted for, and who won, was Ross Hannaman, an attractive blonde singer with a smoky, chanteuse-like voice. As part of her first reward the *Standard* saw to it that she was given a debut engagement at the Allegro, one of London's fashionable cabarets, an adjunct of the elegant Quaglinos restaurant.

Almost immediately Rice and Lloyd-Webber, sensing their proprietary interest in Hannaman's triumph, wrote to her, offering to become her managers. A meeting was arranged at the newspaper offices on Shoe Lane. In *Fanfare*, writer Jonathan Mantle reports that "Tim and Ross Hannaman were, to Andrew's dismay, instantly attracted to each other," while the journalist Angus McGill, whose idea the "Girl of the Year" had been, "took a shine to Andrew." Mantle continues, "McGill became a friend and something of a father figure, the latest in the succession of older men to complement the role of his reclusive father. Like them, he was a useful contact."

Ross Hannaman agreed to record two of the team's songs for EMI's Columbia Label. As yet the songs were unwritten, and Rice, smitten, tailored the first one, "Down Thru' Summer," to the husky sound of Ross's voice. On the "B" side they threw in "I'll Give All My Love to Southend," an upbeat pop filler. Thus, on June 23, 1967, the team had its first commercial recording.

"Down Thru' Summer" was not a hit, but its genesis as a super-romantic torch song is interesting. Its lyric, "Sadness now, but my life goes on / Night and morning gone / Lost in the air / Now I watch for the afternoon / Why does it come so soon? / Life isn't fair. . . . ," is the kind Tim would refine and polish as the years brought him more technique; its melody, once the record was a decided flop, was to be put aside and recycled. When it was brought out again and polished it would become the first section of one of the team's biggest hits, "Don't Cry for Me Argentina."

In autumn of that same year, Ross recorded another pair of the team's songs, this time for Southern Music. "1969," a hard-rock apocalyptic epitaph for flower power contained lines like "A hundred tongues began to shout / And then a panic in the hall / I heard them call / We can't get out . . ." Its melody souped and beefed up, was Beethoven's "Für Elise," a piano piece well known to every beginner. The "B" side of this record had a poignant lyric about infidelity called "Probably on Thursday":[5]

Can you see all of me?	I spend all my precious time
I am hiding nothing	Wishing you would love me
Must you stay so far away?	You are trying hard to find
Won't you whisper something?	Ways to get rid of me.
You're going to leave me.	You used to love me
Don't have to tell me, don't have to tell me,	Look at you now love, look at you now,
You'll be unfaithful	You'll be unfaithful
Probably on Thursday,	Possibly on Wednesday
Probably on Thursday.	Probably on Thursday.

If "1969" owes its patrimony to a well-known Beethoven piano piece, "Probably on Thursday" goes slightly more contemporary. Its tune is a dead ringer for the theme from Dvořák's *New World Symphony*, familiarly known as the spiritual "Goin' Home." It seems that Rice and Lloyd-Webber, so eager for success at any price, might attack any fad, even one as passé as adapting pop classics. "Moon Love," "Tonight We Love, and "The Lamp Is Low" had all become megahits in the '40s and '50s, but these numbers didn't stand a chance in the late '60s. Biographer Michael Walsh deplores (as does this writer) the lack in "1969's labelling of any indication that the song is anything other than an original work of Andrew Lloyd-Webber."

For that matter, the team's next offering, after all the unsuccessful ones, a number which would eventually become a gigantic hit, was also—this time unintentionally—cribbed from a classic. It was a lovely melody that Andrew wrote and upon which Tim foisted an inappropriate, folksy title. "Kansas Morning" he called the melody that the world was later to recognize as "I Don't Know How to Love Him." "There is one occasion in *Jesus Christ Superstar*," Andrew told a reporter for the Los Angeles *Village Times* in 1993, "where I know I must have heard something else, because 'I Don't Know How to Love Him' sounds very much like the Mendelssohn Violin Concerto. Probably because of my family background. I just absorbed that."

But Mendelssohn or not, the melody is an expansive one, and it was only Tim's misguided eagerness for success that made him suggest "Kansas Morning" (whose A section is printed below) for this melody that is redolent of religious longing. When the song went nowhere, the team decided to put it aside.

---

[5] This lyric, which uses the motive of the day of the week to signal the end of a love affair, reminds the writer of "Tell Me on a Sunday," Don Black's far more trenchant version of a split up.

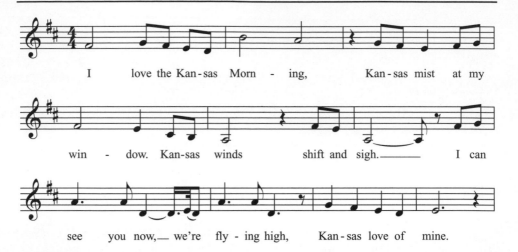

I love the Kan-sas Morn - ing, Kan-sas mist at my win - dow. Kan-sas winds shift and sigh.———— I can see you now,— we're fly - ing high, Kan-sas love of mine.

By now the collaborators had a small trunkful of songs and very little money. Fortunately there was Tim's job and Molly's weekly stipend to take care of rentals and recordings. Worse, they were at odds about the direction of their work. Tim Rice still wanted to pursue heavy pop, while Andrew Lloyd-Webber was aiming for some kind of musical theater.

Fortunately Alan Doggett, who had helped prepare *The Likes of Us*, reentered their lives with a request that they turn out a short piece, say fifteen or twenty minutes long, for an end-of-term concert at Colet Court. It was to be the last concert in the old Hammersmith building, and he wanted it to be a memorable one. Next year both Colet Court and St. Paul's were preparing to take possession of new premises.

Although Doggett did not insist, it was implied that the work should have some religious significance, as it was for the St. Paul's Underschool. Doggett had had great success the previous year with *The Daniel Mass*, a biblical cantata by Herbert Chappell, and had gone so far as to record it. In essence, the combination of the Bible and contemporary music was just coming into vogue in Britain, where "Jonah Man Jazz" would become a best-selling record. Although the musical of *Hair* had brought rock and a sense of irreverence, into the theater, Americans would not find their own biblical-rock theater work until Stephen Schwartz's *Godspell* struck gold in 1971.

After Lloyd-Webber and Rice discussed the pros (at least they would have an audience of parents dragged to the concert by their offspring; Novello, the publisher was offering a hundred guinea advance—and the possibility of recording) and cons (the old Assembly Hall where their work would be performed was small, not much more than a three-sided corridor; there could be no orchestra, just a piano), they agreed and—working practically around the clock—in the space of two months had completed the work.

Tim chose wisely, for the story of Joseph and his eleven brothers was ideal choir material. He did not go to the extended Genesis version of the Bible, in which the story is related in fourteen closely packed pages, but chose *The Wonder Book of Bible Stories*, which begins:

Joseph, a young man of seventeen, was tending the flock with his brothers . . . Now Israel loved Joseph more than any of his other sons, because he had been born to him in his old age; and he made a richly ornamental robe for him. When his brothers saw that their father loved him more than any of them, they hated him and could not speak a kind word to him.

On March 1, 1968, a rainy Friday afternoon, the parents of the Doggett choir-boys, only some sixty of them, heard the fifteen-minute mini-oratorio. Ian Hunter, Doggett's assistant, played the piano and Julian played the cello. After the concert, the parents took their sons home for the school holidays. Some remarked that this concert was less boring than the usual concerts before spring break. Some remembered the intriguing title, *Joseph and the Amazing Technicolour*[6] *Dreamcoat*; most were struck by the bright tunes, the admixture of swing and pop, the anachronistic lyrics that were amusing but never antireligious.

But no agent called, and no offer of further production was tendered.

William Lloyd Webber, fearful that Andrew might become discouraged and give up music entirely after his and Tim's second major work was so summarily dismissed, arranged for a gigantic concert performance hardly ten weeks later at London's immense Central Hall, where he was organist. He rationalized his involvement in an alien field when he subsequently told a reporter for the *Daily Mail* that he "thought his son should have a shot at what he wanted to do because if he didn't he'd be fed up all his life."

It was to be a curiously inbred family affair, and for their two shilling sixpence admission, the audience of over two thousand (mostly parents) received a healthy helping of eclectic music. John Lill opened the proceedings with piano solos by Haydn, Prokofiev, and Chopin. He was followed by Julian, who played the Saint-Saëns cello concerto accompanied by his father on the piano. Then William moved up to his organ loft to perform the majestic Bach Toccata and Fugue in D Minor.

Joseph and the Amazing Technicolor Dreamcoat in expanded form came after intermission. At this performance the whole Colet Court School Choir was joined

---

[6] Once the piece got into professional venues, MGM, the owner of Technicolor, demanded the Americanized spelling as well as the © sign whenever their trademarked word was displayed. Lloyd-Webber and Rice, pulling rank, refused to keep the copyright sign in the title and threatened to call their piece *Joseph and the Eastmancolor Dreamcoat*, at which point Technicolor relented.

by a rock group called The Mixed Bag, their forces augmented by a full orchestra and Ian Hunter, this time on harpsichord, and William Lloyd Webber on organ. At last Tim had an opportunity to vent his rock and roll fantasies, singing an Elvis Presley take-off, "The Song of the King," his solo with the rock group.

Several critics attended, and one of them called the concert "overlong and poorly planned." Meirion Bowen, writing in the *Times Literary Supplement*, found William's solos "indifferently played" and implied that he spoiled Julian's rendition of the concerto with his "tepid piano accompaniment." Nor did Bowen care for the evening's major work. Deploring its lack of dramatic structure, he said that it boiled down to a "series of pop tunes of the crusading type featured by Cliff Richard." But he went on to single Andrew Lloyd-Webber out by adding, "he certainly has the skill and talent to become a successful composer/arranger."

That might have been it—a so-so notice in a paper that catered only to a few intellectuals—had not Derek Jewell, Britain's foremost pop and jazz critic, been there too. Jewell's son Nicholas, a pupil at Colet Court, had come home one night and, according to his father, had begged, " 'Dad, you've got to come to this concert, it's really great.' And I said 'Oh, Lord, have I?' Because I hear a lot of music and I love most of it, but school concerts are not particularly my thing, especially when I knew perfectly well that my son was not musical and could scarcely sing in tune, though he was in the choir."

But Jewell and his wife did agree to come and listen to Nicholas's choir. His review appeared the following week in the *Sunday Times*. Entitled POP GOES JOSEPH, it began with the quatrain sung by Joseph's groveling brothers when they come to Egypt because of the famine in Canaan: " 'Give us food,' the brothers said. / 'Dieting is for the birds.' / Joseph gave them all they wanted / Second helpings, even thirds." In quite a lengthy critique he went on to extol *Joseph*'s "beat rhythms and Bacharachian melodies and its infectious character."

It was not all rave, for Jewell mentioned that it needed "more light and shade" and complained that beyond the beautiful melody of "Close Every Door to Me," "the snap and crackle of the rest of the work tends to be too insistent, masking the impact of the words which, unlike many in pop, are important."

Still, his next paragraph was pure gold.

"But such reservations seem pedantic when matched against *Joseph*'s infectious overall character. Throughout the twenty-minute duration it bristles with wonderfully singable tunes. It entertains. It communicates instantly, as all good pop should. And it is a considerable piece of barrier-breaking by its creators, two men in their early twenties—Tim Rice, the lyricist, and Andrew Lloyd Webber, who wrote the music."[7]

---

[7] As mentioned in Jewell's review and as listed on the program (and eventually on the printed score and recording), Rice's name, because of seniority, preceded Lloyd-Webber's.

Jubilation broke out at Harrington Court, as Lloyd-Webber and Rice distributed photocopies of Jewell's review to all and sundry. Novello immediately announced they would publish the work; Decca soon offered to record it and did so eight weeks later. With such notice being taken of their work another performance that November was easily scheduled, this time in London's commodious St. Paul's. Tim and Andrew, adding what they hoped would be some hit songs to the cantata, lengthened it to thirty-five minutes. The new songs would be retained for yet another mammoth concert, this time a Central Hall encore.

Throughout that summer of 1968, a time when *Hair* and hair were *in*, Lloyd-Webber and Rice waited for the release of their album. Success seemed near but still elusive. Decca had paid them a mere £100 each for the rights, and they were forced to make do on what Molly gave Andrew and what Tim was able to earn from his job. It was not only frustrating, it was ironic, for when they tried to write something that reflected their indignation at the state of education in England they were told it was unmountable. When they wrote something that was timely, Decca refused to release it until the temper of the times changed.

They were not the only ones in a state of limbo. The world seem to be exploding around them. April had brought Martin Luther King's assassination, with Robert Kennedy's only two months later. There were student clashes in Paris and in Mexico City, and disturbances were beginning in Northern Ireland; protests against the Vietnam War were everywhere. The world was clamoring for change.

Young people were even beginning to *look* different. Men began to wear their hair long and to grow beards; women started to wear less or no make-up and adopted a natural look. In the States most wore the universal uniform of youth, blue jeans, while in Britain the Carnaby Street, Edwardian, or poetic look was the uniform. Drugs, especially marijuana and LSD, became very popular even among high school students. Across America hippies, then "flower children," and finally "Jesus freaks," commune-dwellers, and dropouts shocked their elders.

Andrew Lloyd-Webber, always much given to wear bizarre clothing but especially so after this bit of notoriety, took to wearing Mozartian velvet frock coats with the collar always turned up in Beau Brummell fashion. Tim too cut a dashing figure with his long, flowing blond tresses and handsome figure. The team's unusual looks contrived to make them catnip to the press, and they were much photographed as London's new mod rock-poppers.

The January 1969 release of *Joseph* was hailed in all the press. The *Record Mirror*, England's top recording journal, raved: "Some excellent lyrics and melodies and really all absolutely splendid." But the album sold only three thousand copies in its first month, and those went mostly to Londoners who had been to the concert.

The pair had yet to arrive.

From 1968 to 1982, *Joseph* traveled through so many versions in its at least five incarnations,[8] during which it was so blown out of proportion, that the best one can do is to try to discuss the original, pristine work as differentiated from the exaggerated. Starting from a fifteen-minute cantata for a few voices (with no narrator) and finally ending up as an hour-long staged piece, the difference is enormous. Both versions have merit if one looks for different things, but as Lloyd-Webber himself says, *Joseph* is best served when performed by the small choir group for which it was originally intended. First the original.

It opened with an intriguing sense of verve. Rice's lyric,

Way, way back many centuries ago,   Jacob lived in the land of Canaan,
Not long after the Bible began,   A fine example of a family man.

coupled with Lloyd-Webber's almost simplistic rock, which used the Mixolydian[9] mode, started the piece off with energy.

Two numbers down the road, the composer let the lyricist shine by using a single note (over the three essential rock chords) in describing the many colors of the coat: "It was red and yellow and green and brown / And scarlet and black and ocher and peach / And ruby and olive and violet and fawn / And lilac and gold and choc'late and mauve / And cream and crimson and silver and rose / And azure and lemon and russet and grey / And purple and white and pink and orange and blue."

Sometimes the tunes are so pragmatic as to maintain a joyful stance even though the situation and words might lead another composer into darker areas. Look at Andrew's naive melody when Joseph is sold into slavery and the narrator asks:

---

[8] After the Colet Court original in March 1968, there was the slightly longer one heard twice at Central Hall and St. Paul's. A third version was offered in 1972 at the Edinburgh Festival, and yet another when the production moved to the Albery Theatre in the West End. This version included an expanded section called "Jacob's Journey," which contained a good bit of spoken dialogue and in the tale some incidents in the life of Joseph's father as a young man. However it soon became clear that the combination of through-sung and dialogue was not working, and so by the end of the run "Jacob's Journey" was phased out. The fifth and last version was presented in Brooklyn in 1976, toured the United States, and came to downtown New York's Entermedia Theater in November 1981. This version was such a success that in January 1982 it transferred uptown to the Royale Theater, where it chalked up 747 performances.

[9] See Glossary.

Poor,   poor   Jo - seph,—   what-cha gon - na do?

Things look bad for you,   hey,   what - cha gon - na do?

However, one has to agree with *Joseph*'s first critic, Derek Jewell, and admire the melody of Joseph's lament from jail, "Close Every Door," written in a minor key. That its genre, which is more Judaic than Hebraic, would make it feel more at home in *Fiddler on the Roof* matters little. Its second strain, wherein it modulates to the relative major, is truly moving. It seems like a template for the later minor–major melodies that would pour from Lloyd-Webber's keyboard and find their way into *Phantom* and *Sunset Boulevard*.

In the mid '60s "go-go," a precursor of disco, was all the rage, and the next number, "Go, go, go, Joseph," with its use of "sha, la la," the typical syllables of

The company in a scene from Joseph and the Amazing Technicolor Dreamcoat. *Photo: Craig Schwartz/Jay Thompson.* © *Museum of the City of New York.*

the flower children, if a little behind the times, still conjures up the period. Actually this particular song, with its high school cheerleading yells and bonhomie, distills the essence of the entire cantata. It's a clear affirmation that the story will have a happy end.

One cannot discuss *Joseph* without mentioning Rice's controversial rhyming. From an American's point of view, Rice's much-criticized couplet in the next number, "Pharaoh's Dreams Explained"—"All those things you saw in your pajamas / Are a long range forecast for your farmers"—should not be dismissed as bad rhyming. Rice, like many of the theater people to follow him, would never insist on perfect rhyming in his lyrics but would broadly "Britishize" words by vowelizing the last consonant[10] ("saw" rhyming with "before" [pronounced "befaw]; "yawn" with "corn"). He would also use the imperfect rhymes that, having crept in from country music (mostly the confusion of "m" and "n"), unfortunately were becoming acceptable in pop and even theater music ("time" / "mine"; "fine" / "time"; "dream" / "mean").

Sometimes he was just plain careless, as when he rhymed "man" and "hand," or "biscuit" with "district." Imperfect rhymes, although Jerry Herman, Fred Ebb, Sheldon Harnick, and Sondheim avoid them, seem to be like microphones, a by-product of imperfect speech and imprecise diction, the calling card of the late twentieth century.

Even though we consider the theater the last bastion of the perfect rhyme, many of the pop oriented have so grown up on imperfect rhymes that I'm afraid they wouldn't recognize them by sound. At the risk of driving the subject into the ground I'll quote one of the great theatrical costumers of all time, Helene Pons, who, when I asked her about the eroding standards in theater, replied simply: "They don't know that they don't know."

Another brickbat often thrown at Rice in this and later works is his use of Britishisms like "beyond the pale," or "have a go," and even Americanisms like "a piece of cake," which add to the fun.

But aside from its occasional slipshod rhyming, one cannot be too hard on a youthful work written in two months. *Joseph* is full of charming concepts, as the description of Potiphar below makes clear:

Potiphar had very few cares,	Potiphar had made a huge pile,
He was one of Egypt's millionaires,	Owned a large percentage of the Nile,
Having made a fortune buying shares	Meant that he could really live in style—
In pyramids.	And he did.

---

[10] Lorenz Hart inimitably impaled this type of rhyming in his verse to "The Lady Is a Tramp." "Alas, I missed the Beaux Arts Ball / But what is twice as sad / I was never at a party / Where they honored Noël Ca'ad."

Robert Torti as Pharaoh. Photo: Craig Schwartz/Jay Thompson. © Museum of the City of New York.

In a later number, "Stone the Crows," which comes after Pharaoh has taken Joseph's advice and averted famine by filling his storehouses, Rice makes Joseph a hero while insinuating a subtle hint of Britain's then recent wartime rationing history when he writes, "Seven years of famine followed, / Egypt did not mind a bit, / The first recorded rationing in hist'ry was a hit."

With Joseph's success in Egypt, Rice inserts his message to the children that "anyone from anywhere can make it, if they get a lucky break." He goes on to say, "This could be a happy ending, perfect place to stop the show / Joseph after all has got about as far as he can go."

Now the story should be over, Tim Rice says, but he has yet to give out the moral, so he continues by including the lines, "But I'm sure that Jacob and his other sons have crossed your mind / How had famine hit the fam'ly Joseph left behind?" And like any good dramatist brought up on the British pantomime, we are off again into the question of guilt or forgiveness, in this case bringing the brothers back to Egypt, allowing Joseph to frame Benjamin with a golden cup, and letting the brothers redeem themselves by offering to take on Benjamin's punishment. Thus, with the moral of forgiveness coming from all these prepubescent larynxes, the first version of *Joseph and the Amazing Technicolor Dreamcoat* ended.

We have seen that ambition drove Rice and Lloyd-Webber and have mentioned how that meant they had to swell the show out to half an hour for an LP record—and somewhat double that length for a staged musical with an admission charge. An overture was added; the final number, "Any Dream Will Do" (which won a Grammy Award in 1982), was then introduced so the show would appear as flashback. "One More Angel in Heaven," a clip-clop imitation western, referred to by Michael Walsh as "one of the worst songs Lloyd Webber ever wrote," was added, as well as the showstopping Elvis number, "The Song of the King."

Doo-wop, which is so effective in this Elvis-like number, was already long out of vogue. Used in the '40s and '50s, it served to develop rhythmic patterns and was used as a filler under held notes. "Bap shu was du wa bap, bap shu was du wa," intone the boys when Pharaoh pauses while reciting his disturbing dream to Joseph.

"Those Canaan Days," another addition, was intended to be parody, and in truth it works quite well even if what emerges is more Jewish than the French it tries to satirize. One line, "*Eh bien*, raise your berets to those Canaan days," always wrenches a wry smile from this listener.

The last addition, the "Benjamin Calypso," is my nominee for the most uninteresting Rice–Lloyd-Webber single. It is another copycat song in a dated form inserted simply to try to snare another hit. But there is no doubt that at every performance I've attended it always brings down the house.

In sum, *Joseph*, although it works best in its original version, has a naive charm that it seems to retain, no matter how much fat is larded between the original numbers. Like much of Andrew Lloyd-Webber's music and Tim Rice's words, it has a way of looking simple and sounding extraordinary. It is immediately accessible. Accessibility, according to Stephen Sondheim, is tantamount to unoriginality, but the pastiches and take-offs that fill out this work are intended purely to jog memory. The trick is creating a simplistic, lighthearted view of the Bible. And its frequent revivals attest that it is a stunt that seems to work right down through the generations.

Sondheim in the Eclectic Late '60s

LOOKING BACK on the early career of Stephen Sondheim, one can see that no matter how much he was dragged, kicking and screaming, into writing lyrics only, one man alone was responsible—even until the '70s—for most of Sondheim's work that reached Broadway. He was not Oscar Hammerstein, his coach and mentor, nor was he Hal Prince, his theatrical confidant, or even Burt Shevelove, whose work and friendship Sondheim so cherished.

He was Arthur Laurents, whose meaningful plays and unusual theatrical concepts were to intrigue the composer. Laurents, after all, had led (maybe "pushed" is a better word) him into *West Side Story* and had been the force that kept *Gypsy* from becoming a vaudeville and dance show. Because they respected each other's theatrical ingenuity they had worked smoothly together. And together they would tackle two more musicals in the '60s. Neither would come anywhere near the success or have the popular appeal of *West Side Story* or *Gypsy*.

The first would be a musicalization of Laurents's original idea that was announced in 1961 as *The Natives Are Restless* and later called *Side Show*. Eventually produced as *Anyone Can Whistle*, it would be a joy to write. The second was a version of Laurents's Broadway and cinema success, *The Time of the Cuckoo*. The latter was a project Laurents had brought to Oscar Hammerstein back in the late '50s suggesting a possible collaboration, one Oscar had liked but felt should be postponed a few years because its film adaptation, *Summertime*, starring Katharine Hepburn, had recently been released.

Anyone Can Whistle was Sondheim's initial opportunity to create music and lyrics for a show that would be built from the ground up, an original musical that would "say something" and would break with tradition. It intrigued the composer because the musical segments were to be different from anything he had yet tackled. According to Sondheim himself, the "songs would comment on the action instead of advancing it."

Oscar Hammerstein had taught his pupil well, and Sondheim had observed his mentor's formulas in all his early work. In the new musical of the '40s and '50s songs were inserted generally to *further* the action, sometimes to develop character. The old musical comedy pattern of song or specialty being entertainment, unessential to the plot, had disappeared once Hammerstein transformed the musical with *Oklahoma!*

West Side Story, Gypsy, and, to some extent, the early *Saturday Night* had hewed to furtherance of plot guidelines or the character-enhancement principle. But *Forum*'s songs needed to break the pattern because of the shenanigans going on stage. Sondheim had been warned by Shevelove that the songs needed to be "a respite from the sidesplitting action, as they were in Plautus's plays" and had written his score with that in mind. But two months before the show went into rehearsal, when it was too late to change the entire score, he realized he had written what he calls "salon songs." In face of the fact that *Forum* was his most popular show, Sondheim admits to being "proud of some of the songs," but adds that "everything in the score, except 'Impossible,' is really wrong for that show."

Anyone Can Whistle would take a different tack, still avoiding the Hammerstein template of continuing the action. Sondheim's new score would *comment* on the action and deepen the audience's understanding of the characters. As it turned out, *Anyone Can Whistle*'s remarkable score is a showing off of the tremendous musical and lyrical talent he possessed. Pages of the ballet (which, contrary to Broadway tradition, he wrote himself) are Ravel-like; others could easily be Bernstein. Ned Rorem says that "minor artists borrow, great ones steal," and he goes on to call all art clever theft. "Conscious that he is stealing," the composer continues, "the artist seeks to cover his traces. In so doing he expresses himself despite himself. The act of covering one's traces is the act of creation." But Sondheim's work in *Anyone Can Whistle* is not lifted from anyone. It seems to be an amalgamation of past musical influences, filtered through his own musicianship. It is a brilliant, eclectic score, and, as we shall see, one that does not comment on the action but augments it.

Anyone Can Whistle bears very little similarity to the second Laurents project, *Do I Hear a Waltz?* In both works Sondheim's and Laurents's heroines were unexpected types. But the shows separate when it comes to the question of sexual equality that had begun to emerge in the musical. The women in Sondheim's shows are far from the female prototype whose expectations are love and marriage.

The strong heroines that had dominated Sondheim's work from the beginning are not absent from *Anyone Can Whistle*. Maria shows her strength by controlling the violence around her. Rose, even if she does drive everyone away, does offer her daughters something beyond the safety of marriage. Whereas Jerry Herman's heroines, Mame and Dolly who are contemporaries of Sondheim's, still exist in the traditional world of family values, in which becoming a wife (Dolly) or a maternal figure (Mame) defines a woman and makes her whole.

The form of the lyric theater allows for much freedom, but musicals had become, as Sondheim says, "a little stodgy. *Whistle* has a lot of experimentation in it, some of it whimsical, some of it arch, and some of it, I think, very successful. It's a mixed bag, but it has a real core of vitality even though at its worst it's very, very bad. At its best it's very, very good."

Anyone Can Whistle has become a cult musical since its opening on April 4, 1964, although it had a run of only nine performances. With its closing, its entire investment of $350,000 was, of course, lost. Its backers included four stalwart theater men who had faith in the project—Irving Berlin, Frank Loesser, Richard Rodgers, and Jule Styne. The day after its closing, Goddard Lieberson, Columbia Records' musical executive, felt obliged to make a permanent record of it, despite the fact that according to his contract he had no need to. The recording has been selling steadily ever since.

The plot of the musical is simple; it is its diversions and deviations that make it complex. This complexity is generated because the characters are symbols rather than realistic, and with reality suspended the author tried to create a social satire. Unfortunately, it turned out to be utterly humorless in spite of frequent attempts to be funny. As satirist, Laurents allowed himself to go on spouting good, noble ideas at great length. Because Laurents was also the director as well as the librettist, there was no overseer with a stopwatch. "Convention be damned" was the byword throughout the show's three (yes, three, in a musical form that was generally limited to two) long acts.

Basically it is the story of Cora (played by Angela Lansbury), the mayoress— back in the time when women mayors were so called—of a corrupt and bankrupt town where a tourist "miracle" is created: water flows from a rock. To the rock comes Nurse Fay Apple (Lee Remick) with her loonies from the town's mental asylum, known as the Cookie Jar. The loonies and the sane citizens then mix. Doctor Hapgood (Harry Guardino) has a brief affair with Nurse Apple. Soon another miracle is discovered in a nearby town, and the tourists then move on there.

Lest one complain of the paucity of plot in this innovative musical, it must be added that *Anyone Can Whistle* is *really* about government intervention, price gouging, false advertising, totalitarianism, craziness, sanity, syllogistic logic, inhibition, slander, sacrilege, panic, plague, and temporal values, among other things. Retelling the story in synopsis gives no clue to the musical's importance. It came in the middle of a season that presented *Hello, Dolly!*, *Funny Girl*, and *Fiddler on the Roof*, so it's easy to see that musical and lyrical upheaval wasn't exactly what was jingling the cash registers at box offices along Broadway.

If the book was preachy and disorganized, the score and the production were not. Right from its overture, a kiddie-type song gone awry, we sense we are in for something out of the ordinary. At the rise of the curtain we *know* we were right—the set is askew. Soon Cora enters, carried on a litter by four chorus boys. She is not your archetypal musical comedy diva. Who does she symbolize? Some have said Ethel Merman, whose refusal to take *Gypsy* abroad scuttled the foreign production; others have said she is a stand-in for Sondheim's mother.

This show was Angela Lansbury's debut in the musical theater, and she was cast true to type, for in most of her films she had played a bitchy, domineering woman. Here she is an unremitting scoundrel, crackerjack clever and power mad. Even though her voice had been dubbed in the musical film *The Harvey Girls*, Arthur Laurents sensed she could really sing and talked Stephen into flying back from Copenhagen to Los Angeles to listen to her. Sondheim auditioned her as well as Lee Remick on a single afternoon. They both were impressed with what they heard, and in Lansbury's case were "responsible for starting me on a whole new aspect of my career."

Sondheim calls her opening number "a Hugh Martin–Kay Thompson pastiche" after the Hollywood team noted for the now dated musical comedy schtick, a solo woman surrounded by several males. Set to a thumping blues, this number concerns a lady who deals in attitudes instead of emotions. (Much of the song was in "rap," a combination of rhythmic declamation and singing. Sondheim said he was imitating a number written by Kay Thompson which was sung-spoken by Judy Garland in the film *The Ziegfeld Follies*.)

Me and my town,
Battered about,
Ev'ryone in it would like to get out.
Me and my town,
We just wanna be loved! ...

Come on the train,
Come on the bus,

Somebody please buy a ticket to us,
Hurry on down,
We need a little renown,
Love me,
Love my town.

The next number, "The Miracle Song," sung when the arranged "miracle" happens, was one of the pastiches that are sprinkled throughout this score—usually given to the chorus. An interesting exception is the song given to Fay when she gets into disguise in Act Two. She assumes a phony French accent and sings, "Come Play Wiz Me," another pastiche song—written purposely in that style *because* Fay has now become an imitative or pastiche character.

Throughout this show's many interpolations, one cannot but be reminded of the Rice–Lloyd-Webber *Joseph and the Amazing Technicolor Dreamcoat*. In *Joseph* they are more generic to the text, and the style chosen was elected for variety,

Lee Remick as Nurse Fay Apple (disguised as The Lady from Lourdes) and Harry Guardino as Dr. J. Bowden Hapgood sing "Come Play Wiz Me," a song in which the characters speak in French clichés that are translated as subtitles under the proscenium. © Museum of the City of New York.

but in both cases they allow their creators to indulge themselves in take-off. For Sondheim, pastiche and parody would become the curtain behind which he could write songs that were too obvious or clearly "over the top"; for Lloyd-Webber, these styles would be his passport to commercialism. It must be added that once their careers got into high gear, both artists essentially put pastiche aside. "The Miracle Song" is pure rousing gospel.

"There Won't Be Trumpets" is Lee Remick's (she was also making her musical debut) optimistic opening number. Her credo announcing that "there are heroes in this world" is sung shortly before the arrival of Hapgood, when Nurse Apple is hoping to get even with the town's crooked comptroller and police chief, "those smug little men with their smug little schemes." It is a wonderfully extractable number—actually Sondheim's first song hit—that never became a hit.

It was cut from the Broadway production. Why? Sondheim gives the following explanation:

> She [Remick] had a long and very brilliant monologue that Arthur had written directly preceding it—brilliant both in its concept and brilliant in its effect. I mean

it really sparkled, and it brought the house down. She then followed it with the song which had the same kind of force, I mean it's aiming for the same thing. So there was not only the same kind of repetitiousness, there was the same kind of anticlimax—not big, but just enough so that the hand for the song was not as much as the hand for the speech. And that's a bad way to do it. If it had been reversed, it would have been fine, but it was impossible to reverse the song and the speech because the song is what drives her away from the stage. So we decided reluctantly to cut the song in New York. So we went to her—because we knew she loved singing it, and it wasn't that her singing was bad—it was just that when you're really tightening a show, and trying to make it as sharp as possible, you have to watch out for things like that.

Both speech and song were exhilarating. The speech, according to Arthur Laurents, was "very long and was delivered by Lee Remick at tremendous speed, seemingly without pause for a breath, to the accompaniment of a running musical figure which kept switching to a higher key." Here is a brief excerpt from the diatribe, which touches on many injustices—this section a plea for equality for the races, for the handicapped that gives a small clue to the speech's theatrical power:

Why do I want my Cookies to take your waters? I'll tell you why. Because my Cookies are people, Schub, they are human beings, and they are to be treated as such and have the same rights as everyone else! You let them sit in your movies, Schub, although you make them sit in a segregated section. You let them charge in your stores, Cooley—although you make them pay on the ninth and on the tenth of the month. So you both can bloody well let them dip into that leaking drain pipe. If you don't, I'm not saying I'll go to the police because I am no fool. Nor will I go to the Mayoress because she is. But this is a free town in a free state in a free country and I am a free woman with a free mouth and if you say No to my Cookies, I will open up that mouth and talk—and I am telling you here and now that when I talk, I talk LONG AND LOUD!!! (*Music finishes with a crash*)

The action is frozen to allow for "There Won't Be Trumpets."

Unfortunately because the speech was so intense, it meant the song, whose originality and power can be glimpsed in the excerpts from the lyric below, had to be cut. It, like many other Sondheim songs refused to stay in the limbo of his proverbial trunk and has had a life in cabaret. It does more to cut away the dross-covered image of heroism than any I know.

There won't be trumpets or bolts of fire	Doesn't matter,
To say he's coming.	Just as long as he comes along...
No Roman candles, no angel's choir,	We can wait,
No sound of distant drumming.	What's another day?
He may not be the cavalier,	He has lots of hills to climb,
Tall and graceful,	And a hero doesn't come till the nick of time
Fair and strong,	. . .

The song begins on the leading tone, a note of unrest that wants to resolve somewhere. First, Sondheim moves it upward. Then in its second phrase the note resolves downward, so it seems the melodic line jibes with the iconoclasm of the concept. Even at the song's end, the phrase moves up to the supertonic— as though the heroism could not be contained on the tonic but had to overshoot its goal.

There are other gems in the score, including, of course, the title song, which many assume to be the Sondheim credo[1]—the intellectual as misfit in society; "Everybody Says Don't" ("Well, I say do! / I say walk on the grass, it was meant to feel! / I say sail! / Tilt at the windmill / And if you fail, you fail!"); "There's a Parade in Town";[2] and one of the composer's most successful and affirmative songs, "With So Little to Be Sure Of."

Musically simple and pure, beginning with the common I (or its substitute III)–VI–II–V harmonic cliché, this song is a perfect example of how to be inventive though using worn materials. The number fit snugly into the score but never achieved much notice or applause at the time, because an uncompromising Sondheim let it whimper away into the drama at its end. Its lyric, printed below, shows it to be a song in which a man and woman separate with an equanimity and a mutual respect that was unusual not merely in the world of the musical but in the real world as well.

Hapgood: With so little to be sure of
If there's anything at all,
If there's anything at all
I'm sure of here and now, and us together.

All I'll ever be I owe you,
If there's anything to be.
Being sure enough of you
Makes me sure enough of me.

Thanks for everything we did,
Everything that's past,

Everything that's over too fast.
None of it was wasted,
All of it will last.
Everything that's here and now, and us
    together.

It was marvelous to know you,
And it isn't really through.
Crazy business is this life we live in,
Don't complain about the time we're given,
With so little to be sure of in this world . . .

"The show seemed to be jinxed," Arthur Laurents reported. "Audiences were hostile, sometimes booing, from the start. During the first preview in Philadel-

---

[1] When asked by an interviewer if he had chosen to conclude his performance in a 1973 concert of his works with his own performance of "Anyone Can Whistle" because it was autobiographical, Sondheim replied, "No, it's because it was easy to play." Speaking candidly, Sondheim says he performed the song because Lee Remick, who was supposed to sing it, was indisposed.

[2] This song was added before rehearsals, Sondheim explains, to give Lansbury "a number separate from the pastiches that she was involved in." As it happens, it joined the group of "parade" songs that coincidentally appeared on Broadway that season: the ruminative "Before the Parade Passes By" from *Hello, Dolly!* and the determined "Don't Rain on My Parade" from *Funny Girl*.

phia, a fire broke out in the ladies room and the whole theater was smoky. I had to go onstage and make an announcement and quiet the audience. Then one night later in one of the numbers where the cast all ran forward, someone overshot the stage and fell into the pit. An announcement had to be made that what happened was an instrument was dented, which was what I thought. However, the musician with the dented instrument had a heart attack and went to the hospital and died. And just before we came into New York, Henry Lascoe, who played opposite Angela Lansbury, had a heart attack and died. We were just killing them off."

Things reached near panic as the company approached the Broadway opening. Everyone involved in the creation of the show had a different reason as to why it wasn't working. Sondheim believed it "was about so many things that . . . they weren't able to establish in the first few minutes exactly what it *was* about." Lansbury blamed the director and composer for vacillating on how the role should be played. Laurents blamed the producer, Kermit Bloomgarden, for not raising enough capital. "We spent too much time auditioning for money rather than working on the show," he said. And Bloomgarden blamed Laurents for not directing it properly or rewriting. Things flew out of control during the series of previews, with Laurents demanding more time of his producer to work on the show, and Bloomgarden insisting it open on schedule.

One senses that more time to polish the script would not have helped much. So open it did, and on time. Most of the reviews were coruscating. Even Sondheim's former collaborator on the *Topper* series, George Oppenheimer, had to admit it was "less way out than way off." But one critique is worth reading. Whitney Bolton in the London *Morning Telegraph* wrote, "If *Anyone Can Whistle* is a success, the American Musical Theater will have advanced itself and prepared the way for further freedom from now old and worn techniques and points of view. If it is not a success we sink back into the old formula method and must wait for the breakthrough. The new musical is not a perfect commentary by several chalks, but it is a bright first step toward a more enlightening and cerebral musical theater, musical theater in which that kind of show can say something about its times and the mores of those times."

Bolton went on to talk about Sondheim's work: "The lyrics are of a mental piece with Mr. Laurents's philosophies. The music has size and structure. It has not a whistleable song in it, neither has Copland. But Mr. Sondheim is a good, resourceful, sound musician and his score has musicianship redolent in it." Comparing a score to one written by America's most prestigious serious composer, no matter how flattering it is, is like sounding the death knell at the box office. So it was that *Anyone Can Whistle*, barely eking out its nine performances, expired at the end of the week.

*   *   *

In 1960, the last year of Oscar Hammerstein's life, he spent most of his time on the Doylestown farm but occasionally came to New York to meet with his many show business friends. Chief among them, of course, was Richard Rodgers, who in his biography recalled that Oscar thought "I should try to find a younger man to work with; it would prove stimulating for me and he was sure that my experience would be of great help to someone just beginning. We discussed many things that day, two somber, middle-aged men sitting in a crowded restaurant talking of the imminent death of one and the need for the other to keep going."

The category of "younger man, collaborator" to whom Hammerstein was referring certainly would have included Sondheim. And at the time, Sondheim seemed to be the only "young" composer around capable of writing lyrics in the R & H tradition. Rodgers, then fifty-seven, was eight years younger than Hammerstein and possessed a bonhomie that gave him the appearance of a much more youthful individual.

But after his partner's untimely death, Rodgers became involved in an emotional relationship with Diahann Carroll and decided to write a show for her. Armed with the knowledge that he had "assisted" on lyrics with his former partner, Larry Hart, and trying somewhat to dissipate the shock of Oscar's death, he chose to work alone. In 1962 he created *No Strings*, whose score, music, *and* lyrics were far above the average of what was then being offered on Broadway.[3]

The show was innovative on several counts, notably that there was no fixed pit orchestra. The musicians worked offstage as a group or occasionally wandered about onstage alone or in small combinations, insinuating themselves into the story. The stage was set and reset by the dancers or sometimes the actors using an unconventional assortment of vari-colored lights, frames on hinges, and platforms that served to let the action flow to various locales—Paris, Deauville, Honfleur, and the Riviera.

For the first time in a Rodgers show, there was no overture. From the moment when the curtain rose on a darkened stage with Diahann Carroll singing "The Sweetest Sounds" to a flute obbligato, followed immediately by Richard Kiley's reprise of the song while a clarinetist near him is playing the accompaniment, one knew this show would break conventions. Even though they sing together (which presages their romance), they are unaware of each other's existence.

Earlier in that same season (and this was three years before the Civil Rights Act was passed), another musical tried to create a romance between black and white protagonists and failed miserably. *Kwamina*, with a score by Richard Adler, featured Sally Ann Howes and Terry Couter as the lovers. Adler gives some

---

[3] In 1963 Rodgers created both music and lyrics for the additional songs in the film version of *The Sound of Music*, released in 1965.

reasons why he believes the show failed to succeed although it had a superior score and exciting dancing choreographed by Agnes de Mille.

> Hate mail roared in even before we opened and spat forth from the mailbox long after we closed. It was particularly devastating for even though Richard Rodgers' show dealt with miscegenation, it was a story about a *white* man in love with a *black* woman. That made all the difference in the world, for before the Civil Rights movement, there was a Janus-headed Southern heritage that informed American tradition. It had, in 19th century America, been perfectly acceptable for white plantation bosses to have their way with black female slaves. But let a black man touch a white woman and a lynch mob would have him before sunrise. We'd dared to place the black man–white woman equation on the musical stage, and so while Dick Rodgers' story remained unresolved, as ours did, the public accepted its relationship, while angrily rejecting ours.

In *No Strings*, the instrumentalists too, though in full view, are meant to be only musical abstractions. Most resourceful, besides the relationship that crossed the color line with its unorthodox casting of back and white protagonists without ever mentioning it, was the literal use of no strings in the Ralph Burns (dictated by Rodgers) orchestration. In the long run, perhaps some of the warmth violins can give was missing, but using brass, woodwinds, and percussion exclusively did create a fresh, noncompromising sound.

With *No Strings* so inventive, it was something of a letdown for the avant-gardists for Rodgers to opt for so passé a work as *The Time of the Cuckoo* as his initial collaboration with the young groundbreaker who had written the score for *Anyone Can Whistle*. But Rodgers was keen to work again with a partner, as he had all his life. He came into the project not only as composer but producer, as he had the know-how and would easily be able to raise the money. Being the producer would mean he could rule the musical's direction, a power thing he reveled in. The vogue then was to adapt successful plays and movies into musicals, and *Cuckoo*, which had a healthy run on Broadway starring Shirley Booth and a bit more on the screen when it was renamed *Summertime* and rewritten as a vehicle for Katharine Hepburn, looked as if it should go on to become a hit musical.

For his part, in accepting this story of a near frigid, somewhat unpleasant spinster who has a brief fling with an Italian during her maiden trip to Venice, Sondheim was squaring his debts to Oscar while discharging his obligation to Laurents, who had first brought him into the theater with *West Side Story*. Laurents was a powerful enticer. "Dick Rodgers had asked me to write songs with him," Sondheim reported, "and although I didn't want to write just lyrics ever again, I told Dick I'd be honored to write with him if a project came up that excited me. . . . Somehow Arthur and Mary Rodgers, after a great deal of pressure, convinced me to write lyrics for Dick's music to *Do I Hear a Waltz?*" The project represented quite a sacrifice for Sondheim, who had already written complete scores for *Forum* and *Anyone Can Whistle*, a reversion to earlier times of having his capacity limited to writing lyrics.

Rodgers had come to a stall in his brief embryonic partnership with Alan Jay Lerner (they spent several frustrating months working on a story about extrasensory perception which, with music by Burton Lane, would become *On a Clear Day You Can See Forever*) and was "eager to get going again." Lerner, a notoriously slow and fussy—albeit magnificent—lyricist had remained true to his reputation—his persona of notorious procrastinator. Rodgers, always a prolific and demanding partner, should have suspected that their collaboration was doomed in advance.

The new relationship between Rodgers and the lyricist who was half his age seemed ideal at first because each man respected the other as well as the other's enormous talent and flexibility. Rodgers, accustomed to composing the melody after which Hart would write the lyric, had shifted gears when he collaborated with Hammerstein. From the beginning of their partnership he had set Oscar's poetic lyrics. By now he was free enough to work either way. "Sometimes a quatrain would start me thinking of a melody; sometimes it would be a completed lyric," Rodgers was to say. "Occasionally I thought of a theme first and Steve would then write the words. I was working again and I was happy again."

The collaborators had elected to steer clear of all the clichés one might easily fall into with a story about an American tourist in Venice. Rodgers decided the score must avoid anything like a tarantella, saltarello, or other native dances.[4] Unfortunately, when they saw their play on stage, it was clear to them that they had written a sad little comedy with songs about American morality versus Italian sexuality—with very little musical excitement.

Leona Samish, the heroine, was a taciturn and rather vindictive character— quite out of keeping with the uninhibited, liberated woman of the mid '60s. Sondheim has called her "a lady who, metaphorically, can't sing."

The choice of a young actress in the role must be laid at Arthur Laurents's door. "An attractive lady has been libeled," he was to tell a newspaper reporter. "For over ten years she has been called a virgin and worse. My theory is that the actresses who played her were too old for the part. The story of an aging woman who could not give herself physically is something small and rather dirty," he continued. Laurents concluded that what he wrote was the story of a woman young enough to have a chance at the future.

---

[4] However, the best song in the show, "Take the Moment," has the rocking rhythm of a Venetian boat song.

Yet when Leona sings out her loneliness in "Here We Are Again" in the first act, meaning that for her, "we" is "I and me," we don't believe her. Bright, pretty, dynamic as she is, any Venetian would be attracted to her. The role is a plum for a mature actress, and Anne Bancroft or Mary Martin, the original choices for the role, just might have elicited enough sympathy to have pulled it off. Shirley Booth and Katharine Hepburn had done it in a previous decade, but Elizabeth Allen, young and beautiful but without the star appeal of a Hepburn or Booth, was never believable as the lovelorn spinster.

Not only was the main character unbelievable, the show was static. Rodgers, Sondheim, Laurents, and the director, John Dexter, had made one fatal mistake. They had decided at the outset that there should be no dancing in their Venetian odyssey. No choreographer was hired, only an associate in charge of movement. At last when the show was in previews a desperate search for choreographer was begun. Herbert Ross was brought in to assist in the enormous job of putting some dances into a danceless show, but he found he could make little headway.

Coming after the brilliance of *Forum* and *Anyone Can Whistle*, Sondheim's contributions seemed bland, especially in the romantic ballads that had the typical Rodgers lilt. But he was able to summon up his wits on the lighter subjects: tourism in general in "This Week Americans"; "Bargaining"; "No Understand"; and the following excerpt from "What Do We Do? We Fly!" Here are a few lines excoriating airline food from that one:

The shiny stuff is tomatoes, Anything that is white is sweet,
The salad lies in a group. Anything that is brown is meat,
The curly stuff is potatoes Anything that is grey—don't eat!
The stuff that moves is soup.

As for the ballads, they are typical Rodgers, this time perhaps a bit more chromatic, but always respecting the long line. All the release sections seem finally to bog down with slow-moving notes. Sondheim's lyrics, not terribly imaginative in the ballads, seem to fall flat at their endings too, especially in "Take the Moment," the best ballad in the score, and the title song. "Do I Hear a Waltz" has a strange, almost uncomfortable prosody: "Do *I* hear a waltz? / Very odd, but I *hear* a waltz . . ."

The shifting of accent and the uncertainty in the lyric, coupled with Rodgers's rather four-square use of ¾, are not very convincing. One also cannot comprehend why this Venetian idyll should have a title song so suggestive of Vienna. Throughout the score one misses the unequivocal Nellie Forbush of *South Pacific* and her shouting about being "in love with a wonderful guy." Unlike Nellie, Leona never quite hears that confident waltz that will sweep her past her doubt to a final embrace with Renato.

By February 1, 1965, when *Do I Hear a Waltz?* was previewing in New Haven, the show was a mess because it had no real raison d'être. Something drastic had to be done. Rodgers wanted to soften Elizabeth Allen's edges, to make her more sympathetic to audiences, by altering the crucial scene in the second act where Leona gets drunk and tells a young wife that her husband has had a dalliance with the owner of their *pensione*, but Laurents, who joined with Sondheim in their adamancy about retaining the realism of the play, objected.

"The more we worked on the show, the more estranged I became from both writers. Any suggestions I made were promptly rejected, as if by prearrangement," Rodgers was to complain. There is no doubt that by preview time the factions had polarized—Rodgers insisting that the roles be played sentimentally, Laurents and Sondheim wanting a tough, dry interpretation. Allen, their star, was shredded between the two. Unfortunately, Sergio Franchi, as the Italian lover, was sterile, as he had nothing to work with. When Rodgers, never known for his equanimity, would come into the theater, the cast would whisper, "Here comes Godzilla." Rodgers himself hated the whole in-crowd cabalistic atmosphere and was scathing about many of Sondheim's offerings.

One day while the show was previewing in Boston, Sondheim came in with a new lyric. In front of the entire company, Rodgers said, "This is shit!" Mary Rodgers says that the combination of her father and Sondheim was "ghastly, for they were incompatible from every point of view." Rodgers, who was never noted for his forbearance or modesty, is reported to have been so sure of his tuneful fecundity that he once announced, "I can pee a melody."

But he showed remarkable restraint in his autobiography when he wrote of that time: "I can't say that all this tension was to blame for the production being less than the acclaimed triumph we had hoped for, but it certainly didn't help. *Do I Hear a Waltz?* was not a satisfying experience." Yet shortly before the show opened on Broadway, he let his full venom out when he told a reporter for the *New York Times*, "The first time I saw Stephen Sondheim was when I was working on *Oklahoma!* . . . I watched him grow from an attractive little boy into a monster."

The show received a few favorable, but mostly tepid to poor, reviews, with one critic calling it *Dearth in Venice*. Sondheim himself has always considered it his least favorite work,[5] calling it a "why? show" and explaining the term by saying that "it had no real energy—no excitement whatsoever. . . . It need not have been done."

---

[5] Ironically enough, Sondheim *did* receive his first personal Tony award nomination on this occasion. The season was full of good musicals like *Golden Boy, Bajour, Baker Street, Half a Sixpence, Flora, the Red Menace,* and *The Roar of the Greasepaint.* Of course, *Fiddler on the Roof* ran away with all the awards in the musical category.

Perhaps Martin Gottfried summed up the critical feeling in *Women's Wear Daily*: "*Do I Hear a Waltz?* is a tasteful, good-looking and perfectly mundane unmusical musical that lobbed itself gracefully into the 46th Street Theatre last night without fluttering a feather of a spectator, it is so completely four-square." But John McLain went one step further by noting in the *New York Journal-American* everything that was lacking in the musical by simply listing only "two spectacular things about the show . . . the scenery by Beni Montresor and the portrait of a slipshod Venetian maid by a young Greek lady name Fleury D'Antonakis." When a critic is forced to single out the decor—as most of them did—and a bit player's performance for praise, any musical is in deep trouble.

Because of the magical Rodgers name, the musical did manage a run of 220 performances and did not lose more than half of its $450,000 investment. In Rodgers's post-Hammerstein oeuvre, *Do I Hear a Waltz?* came somewhere between the successful *No Strings* and the subsequent *Two By Two*.[6] As it turned out, the show ran far longer than Rodgers's last two musicals, *Rex* and *I Remember Mama*, combined.

After the debacle of *Anyone Can Whistle*, *Do I Hear a Waltz?* was a double blow to Sondheim. One has to assume that had the first project with Laurents had more success, the second might never have taken place. As it was, the two flops in a row were to delay Sondheim's getting a new musical on Broadway until the next decade.

"Jim Goldman and I had been working on what eventually became *Follies*, namely a show called *The Girls Upstairs*, for a year," Sondheim was to say in a radio interview. In the course of the program he was being queried by Paul Lazarus about the origin of his telemusical *Evening Primrose*.

> And Jim's then wife, Marie, was about to have their second child and he needed a larger apartment. He had read in the paper or had heard about this program on ABC called Stage 67 where they were soliciting original plays and musicals, and I think I had mentioned to Jim earlier that the guy who was in charge of it at ABC was an old friend of the family, a fellow named Hubbell Robinson. So I had the nerve to call Hubbell and say would you give Jim Goldman and me a chance to write an hour-long musical. Would you commission one? For Jim's rent money? And that's what we did.

The telemusical, a macabre story that bears a slight similarity to *Sweeney Todd*, was aired on November 16, 1966. It scraped the bottom of the ratings for the

---

[6] "Two By Two," one of the more interesting songs in *Do I Hear a Waltz?*, was cut before the New York opening. Its melody and lyric bear no resemblance to the title song of the show by Rodgers and Martin Charnin that opened in 1970.

big networks, coming in well below NBC's Danny Kaye variety hour and CBS's *I Spy.*

Sondheim wrote four songs and much instrumental music for the show, whose story concerns escapees from the pressures of the outside world who live out their lives in a department store. There they exist, posing as mannequins by day and stepping out into a world of freedom and complete luxury at night. When the guard on his rounds approaches, they "dummy up."

Into this bizarre haven comes Charles, played by Anthony Perkins, a young (and from the quality of the poems he recites, dreadful) poet. He is no sooner in the store when he is spotted by one of its denizens, a fellow intellectual, and introduced to Mrs. Monday, doyen ruler of this small crowd of night people. In Mrs. Monday's luxurious quarters, Charles is smitten with her maid, Ella, who, quite unlike all the other fugitives from society, has come to the store as a lost and unclaimed child. As the relationship grows more loving, Ella explains to Perkins that alliances are verboten in the store and that should one occur, Mrs. Monday will call the "dark men," who are taxidermists from a nearby mortuary who drain the blood of any miscreants and turn them into dummies.

But Charles will not be dissuaded and becomes intrigued with teaching Ella, who was brought into the store when she was six, to read and write. Ella soon convinces Charles they must leave together, and during Mrs. Monday's birthday party they decide to break out. Unbeknownst to them, Mrs. Monday has already called the dark men, and as the closing credits roll by we see mannequins of Charles and Ella, dressed as bride and groom, in the show window as a couple resembling them hold hands while looking on from the outside.

It was a bold idea and one that any producer in today's commercial television would have softened with a happy ending. Most of the critics remarked that the scenario was too crammed and convoluted, but Sondheim's debut television score, which served to introduce him to the nation, was heartily applauded. Joseph Sullivan in the *Boston Herald* wrote, "It carried with it the same class he has brought to the stage."

Of the songs, three of the four are top-notch. The opening number, "I'm Here," trips along brightly and ends with a crowing octave skip, not unlike the coming *Follies* theme song, "I'm Still Here," while the closing song, "Take Me to the World," eminently whistleable, ends the show on an optimistic and very romantic note. But "I Remember," a sad threnody for Ella, is by far the best of the lot. It has been recorded by Bernadette Peters, Cleo Laine, Geraldine Turner, and Evelyn Lear, among others.

Sondheim's song owes its genesis to Goldman's script. He admits this is the closest he has ever come "to taking everything the book writer had done." Looking at both works gives one a glimpse into the reasons why Sondheim is so insistent on close collaboration with his book writer.

I remember snow. It's
white as bedsheets and as
cold as frozen food. It
comes down from the
sky. I remember sky. It's
blue as ink and very far
away, as far away as
mommy. I remember her
a little. She was big, as
tall as trees. Oh, trees
with leaves as green as
spearmint. Leaves rustle
when the wind blows. I
can hear them. Nothing
in the store sounds like
leaves in the wind. I re-
member rain, it comes
down from the sky like
shower-water and makes
the grass grow tall and
soft, like carpet. But grass
is lovelier than carpet,
and a shower isn't rain
and thirteen years aren't
like one minute of the
sky. Oh, I'd do anything
for snow, I'd even die,
I'm so unhappy here.

I remember sky
It was blue as ink.
Or at least I think
I remember sky.
I remember snow,
Soft as feathers,
Sharp as thumbtacks,
Coming down like lint.
And it made you squint
When the wind would blow.
And ice like vinyl
On the streets,
Cold as silver,
White as sheets,
Rain like strings,
And changing things, like leaves.
I remember leaves,
Green as spearmint,
Crisp as paper.
I remember trees,
Bare as coatracks,
Spread like broken umbrellas ...

And parks and bridges,
Ponds and zoos,
Ruddy faces,
Muddy shoes,
Light and noise,
And bees and boys
And days.

I remember days,
Or at least I try,
But as years go by
They're a sort of haze.
And the bluest ink
Isn't really sky.
And at times I think
I would gladly die.
For a day of sky.[7]

Evening Primrose was scheduled to be shot in Macy's on a Sunday night, after business hours. Shortly before the prearranged date, the store said it could not

[7] In discussing his work on this key number in the show with this author, Sondheim gives a clue to his lyrical procedure of solving the end shortly after he has conceived the beginning of a song. "The major thing is that Jim started out with this lovely phrase, 'I remember snow,' and I kept trying to work with it and all I knew was at the end I wanted to use the word 'die' and it took me hours before the light went on and I thought, 'Oh no, if it's called, 'I Remember Sky,' then I can repeat it at the end and it would rhyme with 'die.' The light flashed and I was able to go ahead with it."

allow the TV crew to work there when it was dismantling its gigantic Far Eastern exhibits. But the *New York Times* report was that Macy's had decided that a show such as *Evening Primrose* might not be flattering to its security system. "How could it be explained," the report continued, "to the canines [Dobermans] Macy's uses for nighttime security that the television crew was friendly?" With Macy's defection, it was decided to film most of the show in the studio. One day's shooting however was done in Stern's, a nearby department store.

In recent years *Evening Primrose* has become as much a cult subject as *Anyone Can Whistle*. It was a fortunate digression and diversion during the years Sondheim was toiling with Jim Goldman on *The Girls Upstairs*, a murder mystery with a Follies background. The latter would never have a satisfactory book, but its score would represent to most, even more than *Anyone Can Whistle*, the chef d'oeuvre of Sondheim's early period.

The Team Comes of Age

DURING THE YEARS from 1965 to 1970 the British musical seemed to be trying to come out of its rut and keep pace with the American one. English actors and dancers could play and sing as well any of the Americans, but to do that they needed the roles. Throughout the U.K. the creative end of the musical was in short supply: directors, set designers, and especially choreographers were desperately needed. The few hardy souls acting as producers tried delving into stories from their long history or literary past with mixed results. *Robert and Elizabeth*, based on the romance of the Brownings, ran for two years, and *Canterbury Tales* chalked up over two thousand performances. In the light of such homegrown successes others were tried, seemingly surefire projects—*The Four Musketeers*, *Lock Up Your Daughters*, *Anne of Green Gables*, and [*A Tale of*] *Two Cities*—but each one failed.

As Sheridan Morley, discussing the last year of the decade, says, "Six productions losing half a million pounds in less than six months even at 1960s values did not exactly add up to a climate in which the British musical might yet again be reborn, and the decade ended with some despair."

The only thing that paid its way were the shows that transferred from Broadway, for the American product was thriving handily. Apart from the works of Stephen Sondheim, who stumbled during those years and had yet to find his unique style as a composer/lyricist, the Broadway musical was at its apogee. It was a period comparable to the last hurrah.

The stalwarts like Rodgers and Hammerstein, Frank Loesser, Cole Porter, Irving Berlin, and Harold Arlen may have been gone or nonproductive, but there were plenty of new voices being heard. If Jerry Bock and Sheldon Harnick had already peaked with their reigning hit of the decade, *Fiddler on the Roof*, their counterparts, John Kander and Fred Ebb, were waiting to take over with *Cabaret*, *The Happy Time*, and *Zorba*—all presented in the last half of the '60s decade. Alan Jay Lerner working with Burton Lane, whose *On a Clear Day* was premiered in 1965, would produce little more of lasting value, but Jerry Herman could set Broadway singing with *Mame* and the sensitively scored *Dear World*. Other composers of the caliber of Charles Strouse, Cy Coleman, Mitch Leigh, and Harvey Schmidt were turning out memorable works. Besides those shows listed above, *Man of La Mancha*; *Sweet Charity*; *Superman*; *I Do, I Do*; *Hallelujah, Baby!*; *You're a Good Man, Charlie Brown*; *Your Own Thing*; *Jacques Brel Is Alive and Well*; *Hair*; *Dames at Sea*; *Curley McDimple*; and *1776* all opened during that period.

Politically it was an unhappy time for the United States, an era that climaxed in youthful rebelliousness and disorderliness at the Democratic Convention in 1968, with the police acting more like gestapo than officers of the law. But in spite of it, the musical theater seemed to remain aloof from bureaucratic or governmental ramifications. The musicals in the paragraph above (except perhaps for *Cabaret*) show how Americans were not losing their appetite for escape.

Even more than demonstrating political insouciance, the creators of musicals buried their heads in the sands of the past. For except for an occasional inclusion of a rock song, more on the order of pastiche, musicals took no notice of the split, nay, the chasm that was developing between what was sung on stage and popular music as broadcast on radio. Nor was it conscious of the burgeoning record industry, which would grow to enormous size as the importance of music broadcast over the airwaves diminished.

When the Beatles arrived in the States in 1964, a different kind of music exploded across the land. It was, of course, not the kind of music that illuminates characters in a continuing story or even comments on the action. It was worlds away from the standard show tune in harmony, lyric, and form. In 1968, the year of *Joseph*'s debut, the best-selling album was their *Sergeant Pepper's Lonely Hearts Club Band*. The two works seemingly had very little in common, except that they were both British in origin, able to fit on an LP record, and had a vaguely cyclic feeling. Neither was a musical in the traditional sense (although *Sergeant Pepper* too would eventually be staged), but they were both breakthrough works.

Tim Rice understood the import of *Joseph* and knew that although he and Andrew Lloyd-Webber were "writing records," not musicals, they were on the track to creating material that would eventually be mountable as a new form, "the pop opera."

A year after *Joseph*'s first performance, once the hosannas had died down, after the Decca recording had been made but not released, both Tim and Andrew missed the publicity and acclaim. Worse, they were becoming desperate for funds. Molly helped out a bit with the rent, and Tim still had his job to enable him to eke by.

At last Andrew came up with an idea to use Tim's encyclopedic knowledge of pop and rock trivia, and together they drafted a letter to Sefton Meyers. Meyers was a wealthy friend of one of the singers who had sung on the *Joseph* recording, and, according to Andrew, reputed to be "youngish, very wealthy and with a strong interest in the theater." What they proposed was a pop music museum—one that would include Elvis's guitar, the tail section of Buddy Holly's plane, a door from the Cavern Club in Liverpool where the Beatles had played, and other pop artifacts. Andrew proposed himself as the museum's curator and enclosed two attestations to his suitability for the job: Derek Jewell's review of *Joseph* clipped from *The Times* and an advance copy of the unreleased Decca recording.

Meyers, although only forty-two, was a sick man, but the letter intrigued him so much that he listened to the recording. He agreed with the erstwhile *Times* reviewer about the "immediacy" of *Joseph* and thought the pair just might have possibilities. Then he persuaded his partner in a company called New Talent Ventures, Inc., to do just that—venture to hear the other works of these young men.

David Land, Sefton Meyers's partner, agreed, and Lloyd-Webber and Rice were summoned. They brought along recordings of *The Likes of Us* and *1969* as well as several demos from *Joseph* to their interview. After the museum idea was discussed and hastily dismissed, Land and Meyers offered to become their managers.

Compared to the New Talent Ventures offer of £2000 each for their first year, £2500 for their second, and £3000 in the third, with an option to extend the contract for ten years, their present arrangement with Desmond Elliott, which garnered them £100 per song, was pitiful. What Land and Meyers wanted in exchange for their handsome stipend was 25 percent of anything Rice and Lloyd-Webber wrote while under their aegis, whereas Elliott had been satisfied with only 10 per cent.

The offer was tempting, but not the least troubling would be their need to dump Elliott. It was a hard decision to make, but the young are often able to rationalize, and with sang froid they reminded each other of Elliott's insignificant advances as well as his botched job of presenting *The Likes of Us* on the West End. Worse than that, Elliott had not handled the contracts dealing with theatrical rights to *Joseph* to Andrew's liking, generating harsh words between them. A 25 percent commission charge was not so bad considering what they stood to make from this highly professional firm. The clincher was, of course, the down payment. One could live rather respectably on the yearly advance New Talent offered them, and neither had ever had such a lump sum in his account. Not wanting to appear too eager, they said they would give their answer within three days—although they had already made up their minds.

Once they called and signed the necessary papers, they were gleeful. At last they were employed in the profession each of them had always dreamt of adopting. Now it was a question of finding their next project.

Tim Rice liked the idea of writing about people who had short lives but whose existence changed history. He mentioned John F. Kennedy, Hitler, Robin Hood, Jesus Christ, and Richard the Lionhearted.

In the summer of 1969, the trade magazine *Record Retailer* announced, "Tim Rice and Andrew Lloyd Webber are planning a follow up to their *Joseph* album." Based on Richard the Lionhearted, Richard I, *Coeur de Lyon* fit into Tim's description of shag. He was king of England from 1189 to 1199. He fought the Third Crusade against the Moslem empire, was captured and ransomed by the Austrians, and died young while fighting the French. Even more appropriate to the subject, he loved music, especially the songs of his troubadour, Blondel.

The choice of Richard offered another dividend. With Britain going through a period of bad industrial relations exacerbated by high inflation and loss of their extensive colonies, the protagonist of their record might just stand as the symbol able to impress his countrymen that Britain was in need of a genuine hero— hence their work's title, *Come Back Richard, Your Country Needs You.*

Once the collaborators fixed on the idea, they began, Andrew creating the melodies as always and Tim supplying the words after. They worked out a forty-minute show and put it on at the City of London school where Alan Doggett was now teaching. "We thought we'd got it," Tim was to say later, "but it was an enormous flop. We had to begin thinking again." The title song, "Come Back, Richard," was recorded as a single on the RCA-Victor label and was released in 1969, but it went nowhere. Now the other numbers they had written for *Richard*[1] went back in the trunk.

The whole endeavor was a mistake. They knew it at once, realizing they had no experience in the musical field, *The Likes of Us* having never been produced. Back to their list they went, and this time, for some assurance from their past success with *Joseph*, they chose a biblical story.

Tim Rice set the tone. The story would be about the last six days in Jesus' life. But Jesus would not be the central character. In Rice's search for freshness, he delved far more deeply into the psychological implications of the Passion than he had in *Joseph* and came up with an unexpected protagonist, Judas. Rice, an

---

[1] Tim Rice was still intrigued with the idea of Richard the Lionhearted and in 1983, a decade after he and Webber split up, he resurrected the story, this time concentrating on Richard's courtier. *Blondel*, with music by composer Stephen Oliver, although not a long-running success, was a fine, witty musical, full of anachronisms and gentle barbs.

agnostic, had always felt the story as related in the Bible was too pat and simplistic.

This time he had no intention of gearing his libretto to children, and so he could let his most mature ideas hang out—and with an adult subject, so could Andrew. He felt the story was far more significant and powerful than that of *Joseph*. Best of all, they could both go as deeply into hard rock as they wanted to.

Betrayal as a theme intrigued Tim Rice. In the story of Jesus here was another aspect of perfidy, for just as Joseph's brothers had sold him into slavery, so had Judas betrayed Christ. Yet, in his scenario, the thirty pieces of silver was an afterthought. Judas would become far more complex than was possible with any of the eleven brothers of Joseph. Like James Dean in *Rebel Without a Cause*, he would become the prototype of the nonrepentant antihero.

As the story developed in Rice's mind, Christ's followers became a metaphor for communal living, and Christ became their guru. Judas's main complaint was that Jesus, so eager for adulation, had developed too many followers, too big a cult for the Roman authorities to ignore. Rice's Judas is obviously in love with Christ in an unconsummatedly homosexual way—hence the betrayal with a kiss. In becoming a "superstar," Jesus is ignoring Judas's advice to "cool it" and is responsible for bringing down the wrath of those in power not only on himself but on all the apostles.

Some of these iconoclastic themes were not totally innovative. Nikos Kazant-zakis's 1955 novel, *The Last Temptation of Christ*, had already shown Jesus as a pawn of his disciples, and the popular 1964 film *The Gospel According to Saint Matthew* treated Jesus quite humanly. But Rice's scenario which would play fast and loose with time, coupled with a visceral rock score that Lloyd-Webber was eager to write, would make the Passion more immediate and accessible. Although still a dream, it would be their first theatrical production under the terms of their contract with Meyers and Land.

But before beginning their first "popera" or rock musical, they decided to encapsulate Judas's philosophy on a single record to test the waters, and during the summer of 1969 they wrote the title song. After turndowns from Decca and RCA, Land finally interested Brian Brolly[2] of MCA-UK in sponsoring the recording by offering an option on a complete recording of an album, should one ever be made.

It was magnificently recorded at a cost that far exceeded its £10,000 budget, but Brolly backed them all the way, and the recording, which received splendid reviews for its technical, musical, and lyrical virtuosity, caused a

---

[2] Brolly, who was at the time head of the British MCA, later left that company to become chief executive of Lloyd-Webber's producing company.

sensation. Putting Rice's typical anachronistic words in Judas's mouth set against Andrew Lloyd-Webber's hard-driving multi-chord rocker that metamorphoses to a luminous quasi-hymn at the end, they came up with what certainly was their best song thus far. According to Tim Rice, his intention was to write lyrics to give "a fairer hearing to people like Pontius Pilate and Judas Iscariot, who get cursed every day . . . and never seem to have a fair hearing at all."

The single, recorded by Murray Head, who had played in the London production of *Hair*, was originally called "Jesus Christ," but at the last minute Tim borrowed a concept from Andy Warhol and changed it to the more provocative—and appropriate—"Superstar." Scanning the lyrics, one can see Tim's use of anachronism, humanity, and theatricality.

Everytime I look at you I don't understand
Why you let the things you did get so out of
  hand.
You'd have managed better if you'd had it
  planned.
Why'd you choose such a backward time and
  such a strange land?
If you'd come today[3] you would have reached a
  whole nation.

Israel in 4 B.C. had no mass communication.
Don't get me wrong,
I only want to know.
Jesus Christ, Jesus Christ—
Who are you? What have you sacrificed?
Jesus Christ—Superstar—
Do you think you're what they say you are . . .

Of course there was a public outcry and banning on the BBC, not disastrous in Britain, where Cliff Richard had recorded "Jesus" and gotten away with it. At most it was "how could those nice boys barely out of their teens, who had produced the gentle biblical story of Joseph, write such heresy?" But abroad the record caused more controversy. The church became involved with some clerics applauding Lloyd-Webber's efforts to "bring Christ home to the people, make Him more real and take Him down from the stained glass windows," while others called it blasphemous.

Brian Brolly relished the controversy and decided MCA could use it to its advantage. That autumn he commissioned a double-length recording and riding on the publicity pro and con filled the papers with talk of the search for singing actors to play Mary Magdalen, Christ, and the Apostles. Meanwhile the single was slowly rising on charts all over the world.

But there was still no score, only Rice's vague lyrical ideas and thematic snatches that Lloyd-Webber had notated. In December, Andrew and Tim went off to closet themselves to put the pieces into concrete form. They found a little

---

[3] In stressing the folly of Jesus' coming at an inappropriate time in history, Rice, perhaps more prosaically, is actually giving us the same message—on far grander scale—that Stephen Sondheim contributed to "Send in the Clowns."

hotel in the village of Stoke Edith in Herefordshire, locked themselves in a room with a piano, and began to put together their somewhat eclectic score.

Dipping deeply into their trunk, they resurrected "Kansas Morning," which became Mary Magdalen's showpiece, "I Don't Know How to Love Him," and turned a kitschy ragtime number called "Those Saladin Days," penned for *Come Back, Richard*, into one of the show's more successful numbers, "King Herod's Song." Michael Walsh accused Andrew of more "borrowings," saying "the Grieg Piano Concerto provided an instrumental theme symbolizing Judas's betrayal, a lick from Carl Orff's *Carmina Burana* made a fleeting appearance in the Gethsemane scene, and the ominous trudge of Prokofiev's 'Battle on the Ice' from *Alexander Nevsky* materialized as well."

Yet one has to take Lloyd-Webber's eclecticism as part of his total personality. All of his output is a combination of rock, show music, pop, and semiclassics. Fortunately show music and semiclassics do not figure heavily in this work and so, in this listener's opinion, *Superstar* emerges as one of Andrew's finest achievements.

One has to say the same of Tim Rice's work, for although they were only to do one more major work together[4], this shows the lyricist/librettist at the top of his form. Christ is depicted as manipulative, cynical, unsure, and given to easy anger. This is apparent beyond the occasions when his anger is righteous, as when chasing the moneylenders from his temple, but also in the unexpected—when he backs away from the crowd who begs him to heal them. "There's too many of you, don't push me, don't crowd me," he complains in true celebrity superstar fashion.

The double-length recording begins with "Heaven on Their Minds," sung, no, shouted at the top of Judas's range against a strong ostinato. In the lyric, "Jesus, you've started to believe / The things they say of you / You really do believe / This talk of God is true / And all the good will soon get swept away / You've begun to matter more than the things you say," Judas sets out the basic premise of the opera.

Character development comes in swiftly as the Apostles are shown to be self-centered and sycophantic, demanding Christ tell them the "news of the rialto" in "What's the Buzz?" Later they will be portrayed as even more bitingly ambitious, when, after they drink at the Last Supper, Rice gives them the ironic lines, "When we retire we can write the gospels / So they'll all talk about us when we've died."

---

[4] After *Evita*, Rice and Webber were to create *Cricket* as a masque for the Queen. On his own, besides *Blondel*, Rice was to write *Chess* with the Swedish group ABBA as well as the lyrics for Disney's animated features (later, Broadway musicals) *Beauty and the Beast* and *The Lion King* and for Broadway's *Aida*.

But we are soon introduced to Mary Magdalen, who sings, "Everything's Alright," a soothing cantelina, intoned while she anoints Jesus. Handling the awkward 5/4 rhythm masterfully and giving us a lovely tune at the same time, Andrew has here turned out one of his finest melodies. The homosexual theme is flaunted again when Mary is interrupted by a jealous Judas, whose complaint is that Magdalen's ministrations would be better served if she cared for the poor.

"Hosanna" is a lyrical shout that resembles the themes sung by the flower children of San Francisco in the mid '60s. Its melodic line, hard to sing because it is so chordal, is infectious. The lyric, written in the same school as Gertrude Stein or Colette at her best, transports the sacred words into nonsense syllables singable by Everyman.

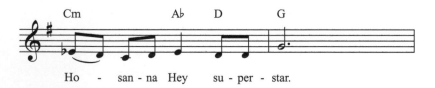

Pilate is introduced in his "Dream," a vision of the coming tragedy of Jesus' crucifixion. Lloyd-Webber's most soulful melody, in the morose key of B-flat minor, weeps under Rice's lyric, wherein Pilate envisions his coming vilification. Throughout the musical, Judas and Pilate are given the most moving melodies—a canny trick one finds in Puccini's *Tosca*, wherein the villain, Scarpia, sings the opera's most erotic theme.

By the time we get to Jesus's big solo, "Gethsemane," the humanity of Christ is brought home clearly. This soliloquy begins with the lines, "I have changed, I'm not as sure / As when we started / Then I was inspired, / Now I'm sad and tired," and ends with a somewhat unsure Christ as He asks of no one in particular, "Bleed me, beat me, Kill me, Take me now—before I change my mind."

This is followed almost immediately with "The Arrest," the crowd becoming a definite stand-in for the contemporary paparazzi.

Perhaps the only number in the score that seems out of place is "King Herod's Song," as mentioned before, a ragtime solo brought in from *Come Back, Richard* and obviously included for light relief before the heaviness of the trial and the sadistic thirty-nine lashes. Then the score ends with "Superstar," the original hard-rock single, by this time already fairly familiar to audiences.

The album was released in the beginning of October 1970 in Britain and available in the United States by the end of that month.[5] Because it was contained so much music and was so provocative, it was given far more serious attention than the single.

Now Andrew Lloyd-Webber and Tim Rice made their second crossing to New York[6]. They were in the city for only a few days when the reports began filtering to them that although the album was down on the charts in Britain, it was a smash hit in the States. Most churchmen in both countries generally applauded it and viewed it as a tool for teaching church values. The petulance of Christ and Judas's real reasons for betrayal were apparently either chalked up to human failings or lost on them.

Rave reviews were received from all the recordings journals. Even *Time*, which compared the work to Bach's Saint John and Saint Matthew passions, said it built "to considerable impact and evocativeness, in part because it manages to wear its underlying seriousness lightly. What Rice and Lloyd Webber have created is a modern day passion play that may enrage the devout but ought to intrigue and perhaps inspire the agnostic young." Interviewed by New York journalists after a party to launch the album at Saint Peter's Church, Lloyd-Webber expounded on his eclectic musical influences: "Bill Haley and Stravinsky," he pointed out, citing the latter's Symphony in Three Movements as an object lesson for a rock band. Rice, on the other hand, was far less pedantic. "It

---

[5] Alan Doggett, who had done such a fine job conducting the boys choir at Colet Court for *Joseph*, struggled through the hard-rock sections of the *Superstar* recording. He would be replaced for the film version by André Previn. Doggett's career went into a tailspin when he was let go at Colet Court because he had sexually molested one of the choirboys. He then conducted The London Boy Singers, bringing them to international fame. He even composed a fine cantata, not unlike *Joseph*, for them. Again accused of molestation—this time presumably falsely—he was forbidden to have any contact with his chorus. Depressed because he would never be able to hear his beloved choir sing his original work, he traveled to his birthplace in Buckinghamshire, lay down on the railroad track, and was killed. Later, at a moving memorial observance in Albert Hall, his choir performed his cantata.

[6] They had come to New York several months earlier ostensibly to attend a staged performance of *Joseph*, but additionally because the "Superstar" single recording had been launched.

happens that we don't see Christ as God, but simply as the right man in the right place at the right time," he told a reporter.

Ellis Nassour, publicity man for MCA, was assigned to take Lloyd-Webber and Rice about the city. Neither artist had any money. David Land's stipend had been spent long ago. Nassour had been instructed to pare the expenses to the bone and even domiciled Rice at his Greenwich Village apartment. Eventually he was moved into the suite at the moderately priced Drake Hotel, where Andrew was being put up.

The pair were in New York only a few days, Nassour remembered, when he got a call from Robert Stigwood. "He said he'd heard their record of *Superstar*, knew that MCA was putting it out in the States, and sensed that he might have a lot to offer the young, obviously talented, but equally inexperienced pair." When Andrew and Tim agreed to talk with him, Stigwood sent a limousine to the Drake Hotel. Young then, and impressionable, Lloyd-Webber later recalled, "Managements were calling us from all over, but Stigwood was the only one sensible enough to send a car."

Robert Stigwood, a major force in British show business, then manager of the Bee Gees and Cream and known as the Dino de Laurentis of recordings, immediately became interested in the possibilities of staging the recording. His company had gone public and owned *Hair*, *Oh, Calcutta*, and *The Dirtiest Show in Town*.

But how would he wrench the rights from Meyers and Land? Easily. He bought their company. The Stigwood Group simply issued some 400,000 shares of new stock and gave them to New Ventures Theatrical Management plus some £50,000. It was a steal for Stigwood, one of which financial journalist David Palmer said, "Midas himself would be proud." But at the time, before Stigwood stock soared and made everybody very rich indeed, the future of *Superstar* was chimerical.

Crafty as this machination sounds, it was especially fortuitous for Meyers. He had just been diagnosed with terminal cancer and having stock at an easily determinable value would be a boon to his estate and heirs. Land too could not have had any objections to the buy-out, for he knew he had not the experience or know-how to stage a rock opera.

Stigwood signed his new clients to a five-year contract, keeping the same 25 percent percentage as New Ventures had taken but forming a new company with Tim Rice and Andrew Lloyd-Webber as principals (Land too was retained on salary and commission), which he christened Superstar Ventures Inc. As his first act of management he succeeded in persuading MCA to double the 2.5 percent composer/lyricist royalty on *Jesus Christ Superstar*. It was not as altruistic as it sounds, for Stigwood also came in for his 25 percent of the increased royalties.

With contracts signed and a rosy future ahead, the team headed back home. It would seem that Lloyd-Webber had all he could ever want. A certain amount of fame was assured, and at least a moderate income would be guaranteed from this one album. It was entirely possible that he might be able to move out of the basement pied-à-terre.

He had always envied Tim Rice's shag, but no more so than now. Tim talked constantly about his current "dolly bird." Indeed, this was driving a wedge between them. Tim wanted to work when "he felt like it, or only while the mood was upon him" and to spend time with his girlfriends when he was so inclined. Since Tim had moved out of Harrington Court their relationship had lost much of the friendship aspect and was fast becoming one of a business collaboration.

Although Andrew had made some close male friends in the mansion block where he had his apartment, he missed having a "dolly bird" like Tim's. What he craved was someone close, a companion, a dear friend—in short, a lover. He felt even worse when he was introduced to the young lady with whom his eighteen-year-old kid brother was going steady and wondered, "Why not me?"

It was obvious to all that he was an uncomfortable mixer, tense, with darting eyes and unaccustomed to chit-chat. Michael Walsh describes him as "awkward around people of both sexes; he also lisped slightly. Even by the standards of the times, Lloyd-Webber cut an eccentric figure in his cinch-waists, shocking pink velvet jackets, flowered shirts, tight pants, and shoulder-length hair."

One evening in January 1970, he found himself at loose ends, and a friend offered to take him along to a party in Oxford. There he met Sarah Jane Tudor Hugill. Although Sarah's world was light years away from Andrew's, she was a good listener, wowed by his enthusiasm, and sincerely interested in his ambition. They hit it off splendidly. Only sixteen years old and still in school, because she was so commonsensical she gave the appearance of being considerably older.

Ten days after their meeting Lloyd-Webber asked her to dinner. He looked very young, and even though he was twenty-two and well in charge of the evening, Sarah reported that she "sat through the whole meal wondering if he expected me to pay my half when the bill came."

In due time he approached her parents. Her father, Anthony Hugill, a director of the white sugar firm Tate and Lyle, was especially disappointed to learn that his daughter was planning marriage rather than attending university. But there was no doubt to anyone that the pair were deeply in love, although intimates recall that both were too inhibited to display many outward signs in public.

That Christmas Andrew invited Sarah to Ventimiglia to meet his favorite aunt, Vi. "Her mother kept ringing up," Vi reported, "and asking me to keep an eye on them. Of course, nothing improper would take place under my roof."

Sarah Hugill's pride in her fiancé was obvious, for by this time, the recording of Andrew's single, "Superstar," could be heard everywhere they went. And even when the pair returned to London and Sarah was forced to resume her studies, her heart was elsewhere. Andrew, whose flat was in the neighborhood, not far from Harrington Court, dutifully would call for Sarah after classes at the Queens Gate school. At last they fixed the date of the wedding for summer.

In the months before his wedding, the phenomenal sales of the record, while seeming to put Lloyd-Webber and Rice on easy street by netting them each $50,000 in music royalties in 1971, were only the tip of the iceberg. Stigwood had his eye on the "grand rights," theatrical performances, from which everyone would be making millions.

He started by mounting a touring production of the show beginning across America. It was an inexpensive show; the few necessary loincloths and the minimal scenery were transported by truck, and the young cast, no stars among them, were content to travel by bus and were not paid large salaries. Stigwood estimated that this company alone would gross over twelve million dollars. It proved more successful than that, so much so that he immediately mounted another company to criss-cross the first one.

Even though they received conventional royalties and no extra percentage of the profits of the show, Rice and Lloyd-Webber, would become wealthy within a year. Tim was ecstatic. "We'll make a packet," he crowed to a reporter for the *New York Times*. Andrew, who was never to wear his purse on his sleeve, was more circumspect. "Over a period of ten years we may bring in two or three million." Then he went on to denigrate his the team's attainment by saying it was nothing to what the Beatles or Stones made on a single record.

But he could not hide his success from the world for very long, for even though it was common knowledge that Sarah was in charge of organizing *him*, no one could stop his overwhelming ambition or his ability to wring the best out of every contract. He really believed there were millions to be made from the stage performances of *Superstar*.

When they had finished putting together the material for the *Jesus Christ— Superstar* album and were flush with early success, in his frequent interviews Lloyd-Webber had often told reporters, "We want to stay together and be a recognized team just like Rodgers and Hart." He was right in his choice of Rodgers working with Hart for even though he much admired the later works of Rodgers with Hammerstein, he had read accounts stating that Rodgers set his music to Hammerstein's lyrics. This working arrangement would be impossible to him. He envisioned himself a Rodgers, the organized fecund toiler, and Tim to be Hart, the mercurial, imaginative lyricist who managed somehow to fit his words *into* Rodgers's most convoluted melodies. Like Rodgers, Andrew would be a business-minded stay-at-home, and like Hart, Tim represented the dissolute, profligate literary genius.

In their later life, Andrew Lloyd-Webber and Tim Rice were to defy being categorized, but for the time being, Andrew's announcement of his intention to pattern his life after one of musical theater's most famous pairs was prophetic indeed.

Prince & Company

T HERE IS NO DOUBT that Harold Prince has been responsible, almost single-handedly, for shaping the post-Hammerstein musical into the daring new form he visualized. Gradually under his guidance the story-song-story-song construction metamorphosed into today's free theatrical form. Since 1963, when he added directing to his considerable talent of producing, Prince has been recognized as one of the leading forces—perhaps the most propulsive engineer—of the world's musical theater.

Hal Prince is doubly important with respect to the principal protagonists of this book for his work with both Sondheim and Lloyd-Webber. He has staged six Sondheim musicals in the United States and abroad (*Company*, *Follies*, *A Little Night Music*, *Pacific Overtures*, *Sweeney Todd*, *Merrily We Roll Along*) and left his mark on others, notably as producer of *West Side Story* and *A Funny Thing Happened on the Way to the Forum*. He even produced the Broadway version of a revue called *Side by Side by Sondheim*, which was based on the composer/lyricist's songs. Sondheim's friend since undergraduate years, Prince enlisted his lyrical help revamping and rewriting his acclaimed circuslike production of the Bernstein-Hellman-Wilbur-and-God knows-who-else *Candide*.

As an eclectic, involved wherever his showmanship could be put to good use, Prince's vision took him beyond the exclusivity of working with Sondheim, and his staging of the Rice–Lloyd-Webber *Evita* (1979) practically eclipsed the input of the creators of its book, lyrics, and music. Eight years later, Prince scored again with his phenomenal direction of one of Lloyd-Webber's lushest and certainly most successful works, *The Phantom of the Opera*, and involved himself in 1996 with the composer's *Whistle Down the Wind*, a musical that even he was

Harold Prince and Stephen Sondheim. © Museum of the City of New York.

unable to get into shape for Broadway.[1] Prince's incalculable effect on British directors like Trevor Nunn, Nicolas Hytner, and others is evident in their mammoth stagings from *Les Misérables* to *Miss Saigon* to *Sunset Boulevard*. Without Prince's template, those blockbuster, through-sung extravaganzas might never have surfaced.

One would assume that steering the works of these two giants of the musical would occupy any musical director/producer fully, but there is much more in Prince's dossier, including four scores by Jerry Bock and Sheldon Harnick (*Fiorello!*, *Tenderloin*, *She Loves Me*, and *Fiddler on the Roof*); four by the team of John Kander and Fred Ebb (*Flora, the Red Menace*, *Cabaret*, *Zorba*, and *Kiss of the*

---

[1] *Whistle Down the Wind* was finally presented in the West End in 1998. According to one reviewer it was miscast, but that did not seem to stop the Lloyd-Webber fans from attending. As of the present writing, there are no plans to bring it to New York.

Spider Woman); and two scores that he produced at the outset of his career by Richard Adler and Jerry Ross (*The Pajama Game* and *Damn Yankees*).

Somewhere in between, Prince managed to produce *A Call on Kuprin, They Might Be Giants*, and *Take Her, She's Mine*. Other shows that came under his aegis as director were the Sherlock Holmes mystery musical, *Baker Street*, and the Strouse and Adams work with the unwieldy name of *It's a Bird . . . It's a Plane . . . It's SUPERMAN*. He also has had his share of flops: in addition to the two last-mentioned musicals, the uncomic comedy *Some of My Best Friends*, the aforementioned *A Call on Kuprin* and *They Might Be Giants*, and Arthur Kopit's *End of the World*; the drama *Play Memory*; the musicals *Roza* and *Grind* (the latter a failed attempt at what Prince succeeded in doing so brilliantly in *Cabaret* and *Follies*—using showbiz as a metaphor for the dislocations of reality). He even tried a topical musical revue on baseball called *Diamonds*. *A Doll's Life*, the daring musical that tells us what happens to Nora Helmer after she closes that door on *A Doll House*, was another failure, and yet another—but a highly respected one—was *Parade*, the debacle about a lynching that had a short run at the Vivian Beaumont Theater, Lincoln Center, in 1998–99. In the smash hit column one cannot overlook *On the Twentieth Century* (1978) and a 1993 revival—no, a rethinking and rewriting—of *Show Boat*. Here at last the second act, which dissatisfied Hammerstein so intensely that he himself tinkered with it throughout his life, is finally brought into line with the first one.

From his apprenticeship with George Abbott, with whom he did seven shows, Prince observed how a musical is produced and put together. He learned about movement from working on two musicals with Jerome Robbins. But his impeccable taste, daring, and vision has to have been inborn, and this was apparent to the theatrical community from the first show he produced *and* directed, *She Loves Me*.

It was a startling departure, and many of the principles that were seen for the first time on stage in that show metamorphosed into the Stephen Sondheim works he directed.[2] Without *She Loves Me*'s small, nonpadded cast of seven principals, *A Little Night Music*, with its equal number of major roles, would have been impossible. Prince also realized when he put on *She Loves Me* that stars were as unimportant as "hit" songs.[3] "What counts," he stated, "is how good the show is."

---

[2] Sondheim told this writer that his first professional show, *Saturday Night*, which "Hal knew about, although it was not produced," gave Prince the idea for the small cast of *She Loves Me*.

[3] Julie Andrews was eager to do the part of Amalia Balash and asked that the production be delayed for six months until she fulfilled a prior commitment. Prince stuck to his resolve that a star was not essential in this kind of ensemble show and hired Barbara Cook, then a musical comedy stalwart. Daniel Massey, in his first musical role, was chiefly known as the son of cinema

She Loves Me was hailed as a gem of a musical, akin to Jerome Kern's intimate and tasteful Princess shows. Its failure to make money is reputedly due in large part to a miscalculation in the choice of theater, which was too small to support it financially. But the superb score and the imperishable romanticism of the story were not to be defeated. In 1993 the show was revived on Broadway and in London's West End and went on to have an extended run and garner the critical awards (but only a little more of the financial success that had been denied it in 1963).[4]

Knowing that the concept and libretto are the point of departure without which the score cannot be instituted, Prince initiated the process of asking his librettist to write the book *before* the songs were inserted. Joe Masteroff gave Bock and Harnick an outline with no moments for songs marked. It was the composer/lyricist team who decided where the songs should be. That principle was continued in 1966's *Cabaret*. "I wrote the scenes," says Masteroff, "and Fred [Ebb] and John [Kander] plucked the songs out of them." So it is with Stephen Sondheim who, although he deplores Brecht's dramaturgy, agrees with the German playwright when he says that the ideal way for him to write a musical would be to see the script staged and then to come back six months later with the score.

Prince was aware of Sondheim's involvement for the past several years in *The Girls Upstairs*, a murder mystery with a book by James Goldman. He had read the first draft, simply as a friend would, back in 1965 when he had gone out to East Hampton to work out some snags in the script of *Cabaret*. Although they had remained on close terms (Hal and Steve had last worked together on *Forum*), Prince did not involve himself in Sondheim's two flops, *Anyone Can Whistle* and *Do I Hear a Waltz?*, but took a keen interest in *The Girls Upstairs*.

In spite of that, when the play came up for production, Hal Prince was not asked to either direct or produce it. Sondheim had said, "Hal won't produce anything he can't direct, and I don't think he can direct this." So Sondheim and Goldman approached David Merrick, who *did* option it. Merrick believed so firmly in Prince as a strong director that he had asked him to stage two of his biggest hits, *Hello, Dolly!* and *Promises, Promises*, but he was not about to go against the wishes of the composer/lyricist and librettist James Goldman, who

---

star Raymond, who perennially portrayed Abe Lincoln. As for the songs, only the title song achieved some mild popularity; the rest of the score are "book" songs of pure gold.

[4] When this writer asked Sheldon Harnick recently to explain *She Loves Me*'s lack of financial success he answered simply, "It's caviar," and then went on to explain that this kind of musical attracts an elite theatergoer and its rave reviews pull in many more. But after that wears off, the people from "the hinterlands come in, and they are not terribly impressed by a small sensitive musical whose tickets cost the same as a big scenic extravaganza and they don't rave to their friends. The important 'word of mouth' is missing," the lyricist added, "and the empty seats start showing up."

were adamant about Prince's unsuitability for the project. Perhaps Sondheim's comment was sour grapes, because after reading the first draft Prince said, "I found the script to be awful."

After compounded delays during which time the team created their TV musical *Evening Primrose* in 1966, Sondheim, sans Goldman but with Leonard Bernstein, John Guare, and Jerome Robbins, began to work on a play by Brecht called *The Exception and the Rule* (later retitled *A Pray by Blecht*), but not liking Brecht to begin with, and ending up by abhorring this project in particular, Sondheim dropped out, and the project remained in limbo.

Later that year, David Merrick decided not to renew his option on *The Girls Upstairs*, although the score was half completed. Prince read it again after Stuart Ostrow, the producer of the Brechtian opus, had picked it up. Again, Prince was seduced by the songs, and wrote a three-thousand-word critique outlining just what he thought was wrong with Goldman's script. After sending the letter to them and receiving no reply from Sondheim and company, and feeling Steve had merely tossed his long critique into the wastebasket, Hal dismissed *The Girls Upstairs* from his mind.

But not quite.

He was always fascinated by Sondheim's musical and lyrical daring, nowhere more evident than in the few songs, several of which were pastiche[5] that Sondheim had written for *The Girls Upstairs*. So it was a shock to him and all the show business fraternity when the papers announced the show was scheduled for the 1970–71 season, with Joseph Hardy—better known in the field of straight plays—scheduled to direct.

In the meantime, George Furth,[6] a friend of Sondheim's, had asked Steve to give his opinion of a series of seven short plays he had written for a one-woman show to star Kim Stanley, which was scheduled to be presented on Broadway in 1968. The plays, which were collected under the title *Company*, were about some of the marriages he, Furth, had known on the West Coast. Most of the

---

[5] One should differentiate among the terms *pastiche*, which the dictionary defines as a piece openly imitating the previous works of other artists, often with satirical intent; *parody*, which implies comic effect or ridicule; and *travesty*, which brings in the exaggerated or grotesque. In his score of *Follies*, Sondheim's imitative works are pure pastiche, reminiscent of other styles. They never stoop to parody or travesty.

[6] George Furth (1932–) came to New York after graduating from Northwestern University and earned a master's degree from Columbia University. In 1961 he entered the theater as an actor in *A Cook for Mr. General*. Offered a film contract, he appeared in a score of films including *The Best Man*, *The Boston Strangler*, *Myra Breckinridge*, and *Butch Cassidy and the Sundance Kid*. *Company* was Furth's initial attempt at playwriting, and it was followed in 1972 by *Twigs*, which employed some of the sketches not used in *Company* and which ran for 312 performances. Furth also did the libretto for Sondheim's *Merrily We Roll Along* in 1981 and coauthored their play without music, *Getting Away with Murder*, which had a brief run on Broadway in 1996.

plays dealt with three people, usually the couple and an outsider, but not the same outsider. But by January 1969, by which time the producer had been unable to raise the necessary backing, Furth called Sondheim in despair and asked for his suggestions. "I know who's the smartest in this realm," Sondheim answered, "and that's Hal Prince, who's one of my best friends, and he'll give you the best advice in the world. And to my astonishment Hal said, 'why not make a musical out of it?' It never occurred to me."

Prince remembered telling Sondheim that he thought it wasn't viable to have Kim Stanley, one of the country's best actresses, "running around having seven makeup jobs and seven wigs and being seven different people." But he found the writing superior and thought it would be "a terrific idea for a musical."

"But they are so unmusical, so unsingable—George writes nonsinging people," Sondheim insisted.

"That's what's interesting about it," Hal responded.

"You've got me hooked," Sondheim capitulated.

"So George came East," Sondheim continued, "at Hal's behest and we met over a period of weeks and hammered this thing out and it seems obvious now that the things that the plays had in common were the couple and the outsider, and we thought, what if the outsider is the same outsider?" Of those original seven skits only the karate sequence and part of the marijuana piece remained. (Four of the discarded playlets were used in Furth's off-Broadway success, *Twigs*.)

For the past several years Prince had been hoping to do a musical about contemporary marriage. He wanted to explore attitudes toward wedlock, the influence living in cities had on the desire to get married, and what he called "collateral problems of especial interest to those of us in our forties" (which Prince then was).[7]

When Sondheim introduced Furth to Prince and they began to work on this *modern* musical, it was decided this show would be plotless. From the beginning they rejected the kind of Rodgers and Hammerstein format in which the characters express their feelings in song, as Furth's characters are indeed, as Sondheim noted, the kinds of people who do not sing. Sondheim and Prince also felt that to have others, the cast or an ensemble, try to amplify the characters was not feasible either, because Furth's people were presented in vignettes. The focus would be on the five married couples who, in the public exposure of their marriages both intrigue and repel the protagonist, Robert,[8] a thirty-five-year-old bachelor.

---

[7] In 1976 Prince told a reporter for the *New York Sunday News* that *Company* "was me making my decision to marry Judy."

[8] The name Robert was not casually chosen. Sondheim sought a name that sang boldly and could be as varied as possible. Bob, Robby, Bobbie, Bubi, Baby, Rob, Rob-o are all diminutives by which his friends refer to him.

Although Sondheim had recently given up work on *A Pray by Blecht* mostly because, as noted before, he could not stand Brecht, he opted for the Brechtian approach in this work. That meant comment and counterpoint. It would be a difficult assignment, treating each song as an episode, especially as he had been schooled by Hammerstein to integrate his songs into the musical fabric of the show. It was his first show in which the dialogue doesn't necessarily build to a music cue.

As Sondheim began to work on the songs, it looked as if he would be in the enviable position of having two musicals opening in the same season. The debut of *The Girls Upstairs* was scheduled for autumn 1970, and Prince had planned to bring in *Company* late in the spring of 1971.

Prince was to remember (although Sondheim's memory disputes this):

> The summer came and I was in Germany, making the film *Something for Everyone*, and we were on long distance phone at night and he [Sondheim] was anguishing because suddenly . . . Joe Hardy wasn't happy with the script and they wanted to postpone *The Girls Upstairs*, and would I postpone my show a season? And I said I would not. And I served notice. "I'm working, I'm ready, my set is designed, my costumes are designed. You haven't written any god-damned music, but my show's ready." And he said, "I can't write any music, so your show is *not* ready. I feel like a father with a kid and I've been over this kid for five years and I cannot write *Company* until I've done *The Girls Upstairs*."

Prince then agreed to read *The Girls Upstairs* again and to try to reconstruct the notes he had sent the authors three years earlier. The crux of what he now felt was that the people were small, mean, and petty. He appreciated Sondheim's remarkable score, and he knew with proper direction the project could be steered onto a valid dramatic course. Prince went out on a limb and promised Sondheim that if he would go ahead and write the score for *Company*, he would guarantee a production of *The Girls Upstairs* for the following season.

Knowing and admiring Goldman's play *The Lion in Winter*, Prince had confidence in the playwright's ability to "write people *big*, and if they're small, *really* small." Prince had thought of Ben and Phyllis as though they were "the Kennedy fellow and the Kennedy wife. If he could write that king and queen in *Lion in Winter*," he asserted, "Goldman could write these characters for me. This show is not *The Girls Upstairs*, this show is *Follies*."

Once he had Prince's guarantee, Sondheim eagerly went ahead with his score for *Company*. Building on only one and one-half of George Furth's plays, the scene was moved from the West Coast to Manhattan. "In discussing why," Sondheim said, "the three of us discovered a pertinent metaphor; one that was not just laid on, not arbitrary, but something inherent in the material."

Comparing that "obdurate island" with "the institution of marriage" soon became the hidden rebus, the epoxy that connected these fragments. Both contain portions of torment and delight. Life within each is a war of nerves, and a marriage that exists in Manhattan—not the Bronx, Brooklyn, or Queens—must function at fever pitch. Individuals live together on their own terms, in their own cocoons—called apartments.

Manhattan's dehumanizing effect was paramount to the understanding of the metaphor. Nowhere was it more strongly suggested than in the focal concept of the whole show as created by Boris Aronson's towering set, a skeletonized structure of plexiglass and steel that dramatized the individuality, the claustrophobic cellular modularity of a chic apartment house.

The musical opens with a surprise party for Robert's thirty-fifth birthday—a scene that recurs at the end of the first act, again at the opening of the second, and at the play's end. Whether these are four different parties or aspects of the same one is purposely left ambiguous. "Pinteresque in feeling," explained Prince, "the first [party] was giddy, somewhat hysterical; the second, an abbreviated version of the first; the third hostile and staccato; and the final one at the end of the show, warm, loving, mature. Since Robert never arrives for the final celebration, the enigma is compounded. Does he not attend because he was never really there to begin with or has he gone and found himself a love object, leaving his friends forever?" Prince and Sondheim believe it is one and the same party, because "*Company* is about a fellow who stays exactly the same."

Both Prince's and Sondheim's views of Bobby's immutability would have to be challenged if we are to believe his final song, "Being Alive," which states that although marriage may be difficult, being alone is not being alive. This song was arrived at after Prince and Sondheim decided to delete the romantic "Multitude of Amys" because the plot was changed and the song no longer worked. This cascading song was originally intended for Robert to sing on his way to Amy's house to propose. "We removed that sequence," Sondheim said, "and we had him propose to her at the end of the first act instead, on the day of their supposed wedding." Then, before "Being Alive" was chosen, Sondheim had written the cynical "Happily Ever After" and "Marry Me a Little," a threnody for sitting on the fence.

But it is true that except for the contrived ending, Bobby does not change. This tremendous departure—lack of growth and little plot development—makes *Company* an exemplary concept musical. Of course, the concept in large terms would be seen to be marriage. But beyond its construction, taken in even more essential terms, *Company*'s concept deals heavily with ambivalence. And because of this, its hero (although we see him in seductive scenes with several young women) has often been labeled homosexual or bisexual. The five wives, who find him a nonthreatening stimulant to their marriages, give us the first clue to

Dean Jones, center, surrounded by the entire cast of Company. *Going through his own marital troubles, he would play the part of Bobby for only a few weeks, being replaced by Larry Kert.* © *Museum of the City of New York.*

his emotional uncertainty. From the curtain's rise, Robert, at the first birthday party, wishes for nothing beyond the status quo. Robert's uninvolved reaction to his friends in the opening number sets the tone of the show. But his friends *are* involved, and they talk about the pattern of their threesome existence. "Bobby come over for dinner! / Just be the three of us, / Only the three of us." It is an old psychological cliché: the presence of young, handsome, available, and flirtatious Robert makes their mostly mundane or hostile marriages sexually exciting and thereby tolerable. Later, in the "Side by Side—by Side" number we have a blunt outpouring—in vaudeville terms to obfuscate the ménage à trois theme—of a common homosexual fantasy.

Recounting the first notes he ever made about *Company*, Sondheim told a seminar at the Dramatists Guild, "We sat around and talked about how to turn these one act-plays into a musical. We talked about the central character and Hal Prince said, 'It would be nice to have a number called "Company." ' Then Hal said, 'And also I would like it to introduce the various styles of the show, the way we are going to cut back and forth; also I would like it to introduce the main character and include all the other characters; also I would like it to use the set.' So I replied in my usual grudging way, 'Well, I'm not sure if I can, well, let me see if I can do it, and maybe I can write the score. I don't know.'"

But he did it. The opening catches the nervous telephone throbbing beat of Manhattan. Like most of what Sondheim writes, this number has tremendous rhythmical energy.[9] It begins with a vamp, a figuration he uses as a continuo while he writes the song over it, and the number serves to introduce all the characters. By the time it is over, Sondheim has accomplished all that Prince had suggested. And more. Once Sondheim had delineated all the principals, Prince had them move back into their individual apartments on different levels of the set. Robert could now sing in staccato phrases about what "company" is (love is company, three is company, friends are company, etc.). And the show was off and running.

Of *Company*'s five couples, Sarah and Harry, who will later display their hostility in a karate bout, are the first to be introduced. Next, Peter and Susan, who have an amusing vignette about getting a divorce, come on. (In the second act they will represent the epitome of Manhattan sangfroid when they show the audience the blissful state they have arrived at by living together *after* their divorce.) Then Jenny and David, whose big moment will be the marijuana smoking scene, are developed slightly. Paul and Amy, who are about to be married, if Amy can get her courage up, have an intense scene that will end Act One, and Joanne and Larry have their big plot moment toward the end of the musical, when Joanne propositions Robert. These five couples, plus three girlfriends of Robert's and a female quartet back-up group called "The Vocal Minority," make up the entire cast of eighteen—remarkably small for a major Broadway musical. What is also unconventional is the preponderance of women. And even more unusual is the fact that all the men, including Robert, are ciphers,[10] so dissatisfied with their wedded state that they sing "Marriage may be where it's been, but it's not where it's at!" They goad Robert into maintaining his perpetual bachelorhood by quizzing if he likes being greeted after work with a kiss, or a home-cooked meal, and then springing the punch line, "Then waddaya wanna get married for?" At the musical's end their about-face urging Bobby

[9] It took four days for the cast to begin to make sense of this difficult ensemble number, which John Cunningham, the original Peter, describes as "similar to climbing Everest." Cunningham recalled recently that "at one point Stephen took Hal outside, and to give you an idea of how lovely this man is, he said to Hal, 'Is this too difficult for them? If so, I'll rewrite it.' Hal repeated this to us, and collectively we went, 'No! We'll get this thing.'"

[10] "Of course," replies Prince, "he is a cipher, an empty vessel—but who says you can't do plays about empty vessels? The world is filled with walking empty vessels." Prince's comment notwithstanding, the emptiness in Robert may have been the reason why, in spite of enthusiastic reviews, the show played to a half-empty house. Although it closed its Broadway engagement with a small profit, *Company* never had a sold-out week and ran for only twenty months.

to marry rings hollow. This cuts into the believability of the men. None of the husbands has a personality anywhere approaching the definitive ones of the women.

Enigmatic as the characters may be, there is nothing indefinite about the score. *Company* is full of wonderful, trenchant songs, with hardly a misstep in tone and sensitivity in the entire musical. "The Little Things You Do Together" is a list song, one that starts almost innocuously with "Hobbies you pursue together, / Savings you accrue together, / Looks you misconstrue together" and talks about what makes marriage a joy. But it soon becomes an honest catalogue of human faults: "Concerts you enjoy together, / Neighbors you annoy together, / Children you destroy together / That keep marriage intact." Soon we are into the bitchy invective that Sondheim would use to even better advantage in *Follies*, "Leave You" with lines like "It's 'I do' and 'You don't' and 'Nobody said that' / And 'Who brought the subject up first?' "[11]

The karate scene that sets off "The Little Things" proclaims the wife the clear victor, and it melts into "Sorry-Grateful," which, although the song looks ambivalent on the face of it, has perhaps the most honest and perspicacious lyric in the score: "You're always sorry, / You're always grateful, / You hold her thinking, 'I'm not alone.' / You're still alone." The song expresses Sondheim's personal viewpoint, for he has said, "Ambivalence is a basic quality that everybody has but that not everybody likes to admit, because they're ashamed of one-half of the ambivalence. They're feeling a little annoyed, but they feel guilty that they're feeling annoyed because they love you so much." Perhaps more important, the song tells us that marriage is no cure for personal loneliness.

But Robert is not convinced. Later in the score he will amalgamate all the loveliest characteristics of the five married women in the show into a seductive waltz:

Someone is waiting,
Cool as Sarah,
Easy and loving as Susan—
Jenny.
Someone is waiting,
Warm as Susan,
Frantic and touching as Amy—
Joanne...

Would I know her even if I met her?
Have I missed her? Did I let her go?
A Susan sort of Sarah,
A Jennyish Joanne,
Wait for me, I'm ready now,
I'll find you if I can...

[11] Sondheim's first sketches for the lyrics to this song—The little ways you josh together, / Wash together, / Nosh together, / That make perfect relationships. / Making little slips together, / Trips together, / Whips together, / That make marriage a joy—were discarded. They are obviously too specific for general audiences.

Robert is affected by all the qualities of these five wives so drawn to him, but the only one of the group to gain the audience's sympathy is Amy. Her fragility and insecurity, indeed, her terror at making the commitment to marriage in spite of her obvious love for Paul, is similar to Robert's own ambivalence. It draws Robert and Amy together and will end the first act in a blaze of confusion.

In explaining the genesis of the song "Getting Married Today," Sondheim restated the axiom that *content dictates form.* And in order to make the scene work, he chose to contrast Amy's hysteria and singing at breakneck speed with a serene, but almost intrusive, wedding choir.

Climaxing the scene is Amy's obvious lie to Paul, telling him she does not love him enough to marry him. After an emotionally shaken Paul walks out, Robert offers to marry Amy. Now we get the best line in the play when Amy reconsiders. "Isn't this some world?" she begins. "I'm afraid to get married, and you're afraid not to. Thank you, Robert. I'm really . . . it's just that you have to want to marry *some*body, not just some*body*."

It begins to rain, and Amy, snatching up Paul's raincoat, rushes out after him, saying, "He'll get pneumonia. I've got to catch him," whereupon Bobby throws her wedding bouquet to her. "I'm the next bride," Amy declares, as the scene ends.[12]

The second act has three of Sondheim's finest numbers, each in totally different style. After the "Side by Side—by Side" number that opens the act, we see Bobby at his seductive best, in a vignette. The duet, called "Barcelona," has a strong erotic beat, somewhat suggestive of the city itself, and resembles the kind of cabaret-skit number that used to be so popular in the 1950s. It can stand well apart from its context, yet it works marvelously in the musical to illuminate Bobby's character.

In the scene he is trying to seduce April (Susan Browning), an airline stewardess with whom he has spent the night, to delay leaving and remain for a morning encore. He cajoles her to "stay a minute," and when she refuses, saying she must be aboard Flight Eighteen to Barcelona, he persists. At the end of the song he finally gets her to capitulate: "Oh, well, I guess okay." An astounded

---

[12] While the show was still in its early stages, this scene was written differently. Amy didn't marry Paul at the end of the act. Bobby came to her in the second act and sang "Marry Me a Little" with the lyric slightly altered, more referent to Amy than the published version. But the song was too "knowing." Sondheim and Prince feared that the audience might not get the lie Robert is telling himself, so Sondheim went back and wrote a song about Bobby thinking he's in love. "Multitudes of Amys / Crowd the streets below. / Avenues of Amys, officefuls of Amys / Everywhere I go." The song ended with "I know what it means, Oh, wow!/ I'm ready, I'm ready / I'll say it / Marry me / Now." This fine song was scrapped. Actually no Sondheim songs are scrapped, for they usually have a life outside the theater, but this one was deleted because, as Sondheim puts it, "the plot changed."

Company's seduction scene. Dean Jones as Bobby with airline stewardess April (Susan Browning), who insists she must fly to "Barcelona" in the morning. Although Bobby tries to get her to spend the day in bed with him, he is flabbergasted when she assents. © *Museum of the City of New York.*

Robert asks, "What?" "I'll stay," she surrenders. "But ..." he rhymes and, trapped, he mutters, "Oh, God!" before the stewardess disappears beneath the covers and the stage blacks out.

"The Ladies Who Lunch" is one of the bitterest songs ever written, one which Sondheim, master of understatement, says he "likes a lot." He has packed it full of inner rhymes which give it a tightness that makes us feel much of the singer's vitriol: "Here's to the ladies who lunch, / Aren't they too *much*? / Keeping house but *clutch*ing a copy of *Life* / Just to keep in touch."

"The clutch is hidden," Sondheim explained to a class in songwriting, "and it occurs in each of the sections." (I have italicized the subtle inner rhyme, but an examination of the lyric will show that this pyrotechnic happens in each verse.) "There's always that little inner rhyme, but there's not a musical pause there. There's no way of pointing it out. It's just there to help make the line tenser." In Elaine Stritch's[13] ferocious and definitive performance in the original cast, it became more of a diatribe than a song. But, like the rest of the score, it coruscated several segments of female society, uniquely Manhattanesque, utterly useless and outdated. "The dinosaurs surviving the crunch" is what Sondheim calls them.

But why *are* some of them dashing to the gym and others rushing to classes in optical art or attending the Philharmonic? Why are those who play wife busy with their extension classes and others (like Joanne herself) disapproving and half drunk? The answer is simple. "Everybody dies." It is not a subject often mentioned in musical theater, but the song's angry propulsion seems to cover and make us quite ignore the lugubrious message. As Shaw theorized, "The audience can take in only one theme at a time."

After the song, Joanne, married to Larry, wealthy and brash, overtly propositions Robert. He refuses her come-on. Finally she offers to "take care of him." Robert, whatever else he is, is not the stuff of a kept man, so he replies, "But who will I take care of?" This line, as mentioned, leads to Bobby's decision to marry and is expressed in one of Sondheim's supreme achievements—whether or not it is corkscrewed in to fit the play.

Much of what any musicologist writes may be conjecture, but throughout my analysis in the succeeding paragraphs it seems to me that Sondheim, with his word puzzle–solving mind, might have been stymied here in this, his fourth attempt at a finale.[14] He and Prince, more so, were aiming for the kind of song that his mentor, Oscar Hammerstein, might call "ennobling."

"Being Alive's" rhyming scheme may well have been necessitated by the hard-to-rhyme word "love" (which rhymes with glove, above, shove, dove, and a few more trite words, none of which would be appropriate to this song). In the play, Robert has come to realize that what he lacks and what he seeks to change from his bachelor existence is someone to love. "Love" needs to be an important word here.

The only way to make it climactic is to use it in the final A section; the best way to make a word stand out is to use it at the end of a line. If he had the title, "Being Alive," the song's unusual rhyme scheme comprising a rhymeless first line may have been dictated by the A3, which begins, "Somebody crowd me with love." Thus with "alive" rhymed with "survive," the song sums up the two major goals of the protagonist—survival and loving. Craftsman that

---

[13] Stritch was the only one of the performers for whom the role was written in advance.
[14] Other finales Sondheim had tried were "Multitudes of Amys," "Happily Ever After," and "Marry Me a Little," which was restored to end the first act in the 1995 Roundabout Theatre production.

Sondheim is, in each of the preceding A sections, the first line is likewise left unrhymed. An analysis of the first and last A should make the scheme clear:

A1		A3	
Somebody hold me too close,	A	Somebody crowd me with love,	A
Somebody hurt me too deep,	B	Somebody force me to care,	B
Somebody sit in my chair	C	Somebody make me come through,	C
And ruin my sleep	B	I'll always be there	B
And make me aware	C	As frightened as you	C
Of being alive.	D	To help us survive	D
		Being alive,	D
		Being alive,	D
		Being alive.	D

With the score written, final casting began. Prince had hired Michael Bennett,[15] one of the theater's most brilliant choreographers, to stage the musical numbers for this group of singing actors—basically nondancers, for although there is a lot of moving around the plexiglass and steel set in *Company*, there is not a lot of dancing. The main number involving the whole cast is "Side by Side—by Side" early in the second act.

After several tries in which he got nowhere in teaching them a choreographic routine, Bennett's inspiration, which he bounced off Sondheim, was to suggest the cast imagine themselves as members of a Parent Teacher Association, about to do a show. Then he attached a theatrical identity to the number by giving the group straw hats and canes. The unique concept worked like magic. As Walter Kerr noted in his *New York Times* review, Bennett often used "traditional devices . . . in provocative new ways, letting the hats slash the air and canes slap the floor to stress the harshness of what is being stomped out." The one professional dancer, Donna McKechnie, had the only dance solo.

Anthony Perkins was slated to play Robert but, preferring to try his hand at directing, bowed out. Dean Jones was chosen for the role. Sondheim's agent, Flora Roberts, felt Jones was an inspired choice. "He broke your heart . . . he looked so dopey and innocent." Jones made an acceptable Robert but was not happy with the role as far back as the Boston previews. Going through his own divorce, Jones said, "The show was anti-marriage and at the time I was anti-marriage." Prince offered him an out, saying that if he stuck with the show through opening night, he would release him from the contract shortly after-

[15] Michael Bennett was born Michael DiFiglia in 1943 in Buffalo, New York. He was an extraordinary dancer and a choreographer with great vision, having proved himself with his work on *Henry, Sweet Henry, A Joyful Noise, Coco,* and *Promises, Promises* before having been hired by Harold Prince to choreograph *Company*. They worked together as codirectors on *Follies*, after which Bennett moved out on his own and became the acclaimed choreographer-director of *A Chorus Line, Ballroom,* and *Dreamgirls* before being struck down in his forty-fourth year by AIDS.

wards. Jones gave a fine performance at the Broadway premiere and left the cast two weeks later. The news release said that he had contracted hepatitis. Jones is heard to good advantage on the recording that was done shortly after the opening. Fortunately Larry Kert, who had starred as Tony in *West Side Story*, stepped in and made an outstanding Robert throughout the musical's extended run. He even had the honor of being the first replacement star nominated for a Tony award. Thomas Z. Shepard, who produced both the American and British recorded versions of *Company*, overdubbed Kert's voice so one could hear Kert's moving performance, but because of contractual arrangements, the recording was allowed to be sold only abroad.

To facilitate rehearsal, Hal Prince did something no other producer had done. He had a replica of Boris Aronson's complicated and expensive set built so the actors could get the feeling of moving and dancing on its many levels and stairs.

Stephen Sondheim at a recording and taping session with Company *cast members Susan Browning, Donna McKechnie, and Pamela Meyers, practicing one of the show's most amusing numbers, "You Could Drive a Person Crazy." © Museum of the City of New York.*

Company had its out-of-town tryouts in Boston, where it opened to mixed notices. The critic for the *Boston Evening Globe* called the show "Brilliant, just brilliant!" and then added, "*Company* is destined to become a classic in the American musical theater," but *Variety* had a totally different view: "Who cares what happens to Bobby-Booby is only one of the problems affecting Harold Prince's unconventional musical. The songs are for the most part undistinguished. It is evident that the author George Furth hates femmes and makes them all out to be conniving, cunning, cantankerous and cute. As it stands now it's for ladies' matinees, homos and misogynists."

The show opened in New York on April 26, 1970, to much more favorable reviews with the notable exception of Clive Barnes, then the all-powerful representative of the *New York Times*, who wrote:

> The conception has two difficulties. In the first place these people are just the kind of people you expend hours each day trying to escape from. They are, virtually without exception . . . trivial, shallow, worthless and horrid. . . . Creatively, Mr. Sondheim's lyrics are way above the rest of the show; they have a lyric suppleness, sparse, elegant wit, and range from the virtuosity of a patter song to a kind of sweetly laconic cynicism in a modern love song. The music is academically very interesting. Mr. Sondheim must be one of the most sophisticated composers ever to write Broadway musicals, yet the result is slick, clever and eclectic rather than exciting.

Walter Kerr, too, praised the craftsmanship but ultimately disliked the show, saying:

> I left *Company* feeling rather cool and queasy, whatever splendors my head may have been reminding me of, and there is a plain reason for that. At root, I didn't take to Mr. Jones' married friends any more than he did . . . On the whole I had difficulty . . . empathizing.

But the landmark musical survived and went on to win the Tony for Best Musical. More important, Sondheim won his first set of Tonys for music and lyrics and was no longer considered just a lyricist.

As a milestone in this book devoted to the *new* musical, *Company*, the first collaboration of Sondheim as composer-lyricist and Prince as producer-director, seems to have covered all bases and certainly stands in the forefront of the handful of musicals that provide an alternative to the Rodgers and Hammerstein method of writing a workable musical[16]. Certainly the future would produce

---

[16] By the time of its 1995 revival, *Company* was being revered as one of the "handful of greatest musicals ever written."

blockbuster hits like *Annie* and *La Cage aux Folles* that would hark back to that earlier tradition, but *Company* seemed to turn the tide that was eventually to lead to the large-scale acceptance of bold concept shows like *A Chorus Line*, *Cats*, and *Starlight Express*.

As for its British incarnation, with Larry Kert and Elaine Stritch in leading roles, *Company* managed only a six-month run. Yet even though it closed at a substantial loss, the investors said they were glad they had been involved in it. "We've lost our money happily," some told Craig Zadan, who reported their feelings in his book, *Sondheim & Co*. That tradition has continued and spread even to Broadway. Sondheim has no trouble raising the capital for his shows. Contrary to showbiz economics, investors do not expect to make a killing at the box office but are content to savor the prestige of being part of an elitist Sondheim oeuvre.

Company started the worldwide love affair intellectuals in the English-speaking world have developed with the works of Sondheim. Considering that British native son Andrew Lloyd-Webber would use the concept theme to perhaps more universal acceptance in many of his works, *Company* is even more of an anomaly as a stepping-stone into the world of the contemporary musical.

And because of its somewhat surrealistic construction and the multivaried meaning of its text, the show inspires creative directors to seek new interpretations of the Sondheim-Furth opus. In 1995 several *Company* productions caused newsworthy controversies. A lesbian and gay group, The Alice B. Theater of Seattle, Washington, changed the sex of several of the major characters, even going so far as to alter into a gay encounter the morning-after scene in which Bobby and the flight attendant duet on "Barcelona." The *Seattle Weekly* critic felt that Bobby is gay and that the truth could not be told in 1970. Music Theater International, which granted the rights to the show, threatened to sue but dropped the case as the production had already closed.

Sondheim was furious and wrote: "Like those directors who wanted to stage *Who's Afraid of Virginia Woolf* with a cast of four men so . . . [the directors] distort what George and I wrote in order to point attention to themselves. . . . Their changes make the show ring completely false. . . . If George and I had meant to write a gay central character we would have." (The Albee play Sondheim was referring to has often been criticized for portraying two criss-cross homosexual relationships as bitchy heterosexual ones.)

Later in the year a major London staging at the Donmar Warehouse tried to put the question of Robert's homosexuality to rest and only added fuel to the fusillade. Sam Mendes, the director, reverting to the text of one of Furth's original playlets, has Bobby admit to Peter that he has had a homosexual experience, then qualify the confession by asking, "Who hasn't?" Then he rejects Peter's proposal for two friends to "show how much they love each other." The change of text and introduction of Peter as homosexual raises the question: Is Bobby a gay man who is trying to go straight, or do men simply not appeal to him?

Had the sold-out Roundabout revival that opened in New York in the fall of 1995 simply been transferred to the Booth Theater as planned, even these critical rumblings might have been forgotten, but when plans for the production fell apart amid recriminations, questions of *Company*'s content and intent began to surface.

In the *New York Observer*, January 22, 1996, Jeffrey Hogrefe recounted all the mud-slinging that surrounded the nontransference of the revival, wondering whether "it was a casting dispute or a flaky producer. The real issue was whether the character of Bobby is gay. Producer Hart wanted to bring the question into the open and imply that Bobby could be grappling with his sexuality as was done in the then current London production."

The article continues, alleging that Hart suggested changing the scene in which Bobby and his friend Peter talk, allowing Peter to make a pass at Bobby— as it was done in the London production. Sondheim calls that reportage "completely untrue." But the sticky wicket of whether Bobby was gay or not never had to be faced—the final transfer was not effected because, according to Sondheim, "Hart couldn't raise the money."

With *Company*, having garnered thirteen Tony nominations and having won seven of them, now seeming into a long and profitable run, Hal Prince moved to fulfill his promise to Sondheim, turning his attention to *The Girls Upstairs*. The libretto had originally come into being when James Goldman read an article about the reunion of the Ziegfeld Girls Club and thought the setting would be interesting for a murder mystery—not a whodunnit but a who'll do it. Admitting to borrowing a device from Chekov, he had invented four characters, each of whom had a motive for murder, and he told Craig Zadan that he "had incorporated something I was always very taken with, [a scene] where people are driven by anguish to the point where someone fires a gun . . . Our show dealt with desperate feelings, but nothing bad ever happened." On the more symbolic side, Goldman and Sondheim were intrigued with the concept of unfinished business, and the murder attempt, supposed to be a "crime of passion," would be the climax of the play.

Follies, as *The Girls Upstairs* was soon renamed by Prince shortly after he came into the project, would have nothing to do with the mayhem but everything to do with the magnetism of the Ziegfeld era. He would concentrate on the memories and reminiscences of its showgirls, giving audiences in 1971 a sort of Proustian view of its ghosts as they linger in the memory of theater people who were involved in and who, for better or worse, lived on beyond the *Follies* heyday in the '20s and '30s.

Prince patterned the musical he was directing after Fellini's masterpiece, 8–1/2. Goldman's main character, Benjamin Stone—his stage name wisely chosen—approaching menopause and on the cusp of a nervous breakdown, became an adamant monolith. Prince, then forty-three, was obviously comparing himself with Stone, the leading man in the show, as played by John McMartin, when he told a reporter for the *New York Sunday News* that McMartin's character, "realizing his youthful dreams and ideals were lost forever—that was me getting scared about getting older."

Prince's new title would be a quadruple play on words. It could suggest the *Ziegfeld Follies*, the English word "folly" (the word translates easily into the theme of the musical—the folly of living in yesterday), the French word *folie*, which can mean anything from a bagatelle to infatuation, and, minus its "i," *folle*, an underground French word for blatant homosexual or drag queen. As it turned out, he overlooked Webster's last definition, which so aptly describes this leviathan, overproduced musical which lost almost its entire investment: "a costly undertaking having a ruinous outcome."

A photograph of Gloria Swanson taken by Eliot Elisofon had impressed Prince heavily. She was standing supreme and glamorous in the rubble that had once been the famed Roxy Theatre—and some of that indomitability must have inspired the show's logo. David Edward Byrd designed a Greek statue modeled on the one in Fellini's *Juliet of the Spirits*. Byrd's statue wore the title, *Follies*, as a tiara crowning her rather psychedelic blue tresses, but as indication that we are entering Sondheim–Prince land and that this will not be a Follies à la Ziegfeld, there is a crack developing from the "e" in "Follies" and spreading as it runs down the goddess's face, from her left temple to her determined chin. The face, with clear eyes and a square-cut decisive jaw, suggests an exquisite gargoyle protecting a crumbling, once beautiful theater. As well, the fissure represents the lines that come with age and, metaphorically, the cracks that develop in our relationships. (It is curious that Gloria Swanson's mystique, that of a woman who had outlived her movie roles, should also be the metaphor for Andrew Lloyd-Webber's 1995 musical *Sunset Boulevard.*)

A masterful set was designed by Boris Aronson, fresh from his triumph with *Company*. The proscenium, missing great chunks of crumbling plaster, the theater already ravaged by the wrecker's ball and open in some parts to a glowering sky, greets the audience at curtain's rise. Here the denizens of the Weismann Follies, who had cavorted on this stage in the period between the wars, 1918 to 1940, will gather for a macabre party. It will be their last reunion before the once elegant theater suffers the final indignity of being turned into a parking

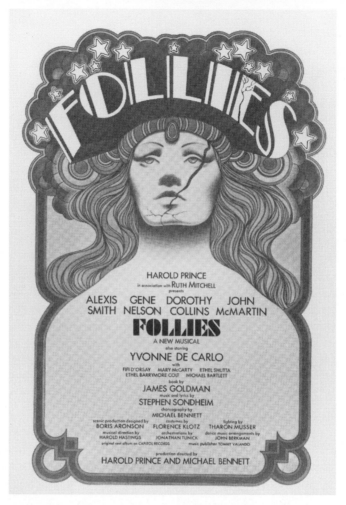

The original "cracked face" Follies *poster, a brilliant concept by David Edward Byrd, was inspired by a photo of silent film star Gloria Swanson standing in the sunlit rubble of the Roxy Theatre. © Museum of the City of New York.*

lot. "A final chance to glamorize the old days," their old impresario confides, "stumble through a song or two, and lie about ourselves a little."

The chief liars among this group of ex-showgirls (and assorted husbands), the youngest of whom is in her early fifties, are the four major characters, two unhappily married couples who inhabited Goldman's libretto from the beginning: the aforementioned Benjamin Stone, a former politician, now the head of a charitable foundation, and his cool and elegant wife, Phyllis (Alexis Smith). Phyllis and Sally (Dorothy Collins) were roommates thirty years ago when the women were frivolous Weismann (read Ziegfeld) Girls and dated college students—the proverbial "stagedoor johnnies." Both of them were in love with Ben, although Sally was dating Ben's college pal Buddy Plummer (Gene Nelson), who has since become a sales representative for a company making oil rigs. Ben, ambitious, unscrupulous, and thoroughly unlikable in spite of his ineffable charm, had seduced Sally and then lost respect for her. He married Phyllis, who with her detached practicality and keen mind eventually turned into the perfect corporate wife.

Buddy, Ben, and Phyllis have little respect for the fidelity of their marriages and in the course of this very evening are seen to make passes at others. The only one true to her ideals is Sally, who has come in from Phoenix against her husband's wishes to make one last—and eventually unsuccessful—stab at winning Ben away from Phyllis. It is a foolish hope, but then Sally, the most likable of the group, is really a romantic naif.

Every member of this quartet is deluded, we are told quite late in the evening in the extended "Loveland" section, during which tall lovely showgirls descend the legendary staircase. Soon each of the major protagonists has the chance to show us his or her own folly. Sally is in love with romance, Buddy is self-loathing, Phyllis has a confused identity, and Ben, who has a mini–nervous breakdown in midnumber, wonders if "the road he didn't take" is the cause of all his woes.

Prince's belief that Goldman was capable of writing any kind of character, because he had succeeded so admirably in *The Lion in Winter*, was ill founded. For once this infallible director was misguided. No matter how many times Prince sent Goldman back to his drawing board, these four protagonists kept emerging from the libretto as merely uninteresting people—as Clive Barnes had said about the characters in *Company*, the kind of people one spends hours seeking to avoid.

Prince hoped to clarify the story of how these four became the unhappy souls they are today by including another quartet, their younger selves. That way he was able to show some of the action on stage, action that otherwise would have had to have been merely talked about.

They are "so much ectoplasm," Prince says. "They wander as silent memories across the paths of their present selves." He even latched onto Michael Bennett's idea of materializing the ghosts of old showgirls in the old Winter Garden Theater by having six-foot two-inch beauties, dressed in black, white, and grey gauze and made up with a glamorous pallor, slip in and out of the stage production and even move into the audience. Both ideas made for a fresh and fluid staging[17]

---

[17] One can see the influences of Prince's daring concept in serious plays as varied as Larry Kramer's *The Destiny of Me* and Edward Albee's *Three Tall Women*.

and added to the resonance of the production, but they only served to point out the trivialities of the book.

The show is a reunion of ill-assorted Follies girls, most of them coming on to do individual songs, and that, in itself, would necessarily make for a fragmented musical. Even Prince's original metaphor, a concept musical about aging, might have been workable with a better book. Or lacking that, perhaps *Follies* would have been more successful as a revue with just a wisp of a story. Codirector Michael Bennett wanted to bring in Neil Simon to rewrite the book, but Prince and Sondheim overruled him.

One of the many "ghosts" bearing fantastic headdresses reminiscent of those worn in the Ziegfeld Follies. They paraded through the theater throughout the performance. © Museum of the City of New York.

In a musical play it is difficult for an audience to empathize with more than one (Mame, Dolly, Bobby, Lili, Pal Joey, etc.) or two (Anna and the King, Curley and Laurey, Eliza and Higgins, etc.) major characters. But here we are asked to explore the psyches of these four truly troubled people, none of whom really intersect. Unlike *Company*'s Robert, who has, however hokily, embraced the concept of saving his life by loving *some*body when, at evening's end he puts himself firmly on the right track, these four quit the stage without catharsis. Oh, yes, they *seem* to see the light before the play's chaotic denouement but the resolution is a sham. When they go home with their disgruntled mates to plod through the rest of their lives, we are left with one thought only. Do we care?

Not for them, but only for Sondheim's haunting and haunted twenty-four-

A costume design for Follies. *Illustration: F. Klotz. © Museum of the City of New York.*

song score.[18] Ghosts abound. Remnants of the past mostly sung by the aging chorines keep surfacing along with contemporary book songs. There are even songs like "Losing My Mind" or "Live, Laugh, Love" that walk a middle ground; they are extractable—that is, not particular to this show—yet they help us to know more about the character who is singing them. Still, even though these pastiches are beautifully integrated into the score, and the book songs elucidate the story far better than Goldman's dialogue, even they serve to heighten the schizophrenia and our final confusion at the end of this interminable (and unfortunately intermissionless) evening.

Perhaps it is ignoble to complain, as each of these excesses is infused with its own originality. "Beautiful Girls," the number that introduces the company, has a parallel in Irving Berlin's showgirl-down-the-staircase standard "A Pretty Girl is Like a Melody," but Sondheim adds his signature to "Beautiful Girls" by taking his show tune to unexpected places, something Berlin would never do. From the outset Sondheim gives us most literate and elaborate rhymes. I quote from the second chorus:

Careful, here's the home of
Beautiful girls,
Where your reason is undone.
Beauty can't be hindered
From taking its toll.
You may lose control.
Faced with these Loreleis,
What man can moralize?
Caution, on your guard with
Beautiful girls.

Flawless charmers every one.
This is how Samson was shorn:
Each in her style a
Delilah reborn.
Each a gem,
A beautiful diadem
Of beautiful—
Welcome them,
These beautiful girls!

Sondheim intended his score to include stylistic imitations of the great songwriters of the times. "The Story of Lucy and Jesse" and "Ah, Paris" could easily have been penned by Cole Porter. "You're Gonna Love Tomorrow" and "Love Will See Us Through," two songs that have Kern-like melodies, work in delightful counterpoint, so popular at the time. Sondheim says he modeled one of the most popular songs in the show, "Broadway Baby," on those of DeSylva, Brown, and Henderson and felt that "One More Kiss" was written in the tradition of Friml and Romberg, but to this writer the sweeping appoggiaturas of his lovely waltz have a greater affinity to those of Noël Coward. Close as these tributes are, they all have much of Sondheim's unique way about them. As he himself notes, "there's always something of me added . . . my own comment on style."

Although Sondheim's songs were not major hits outside their theatrical ven-

---

[18] Two songs, "Can That Boy Foxtrot!" and "Uptown, Downtown," were cut before the New York opening.

ues, in recent years three of the pastiches from *Follies* have become better known through cabaret performances—"Broadway Baby," "Losing My Mind," and perhaps the best of the lot, "I'm Still Here." The last has become the anthem of the "senior" showbiz divas since Yvonne De Carlo sang it originally. Subsequently Millicent Martin, Dolores Gray, Nancy Walker, Julie Wilson, and Carol Burnett, among others, have had a crack at it. Eartha Kitt's version even bordered on parody, changing lines to give the song more references to her own career.

The number, which chronicles the vicissitudes of a theatrical life, is set to a rueful Ellingtonian blues and moves through the decades from the '20s through the '60s, hitting every "good time and bum time" squarely on the head. The last verses recapitulate the singer's career:

. . . First you're another	Then you career
Sloe-eyed vamp,	From career to career.
Then someone's mother,	I'm almost through my memoirs,
Then you're camp.	And I'm here . . .

In contrast to the pastiches, the book songs go deeply into the souls of the major characters. But we don't get into the seriousness at once. "Waiting for the Girls Upstairs," a song redolent of backstage, introduces the quartet and their younger counterparts.

Just a glance at the jumpiness of its line gives the reader an idea of the youthful brio inherent in the melody. Add a look at the harmonic intricacy (as

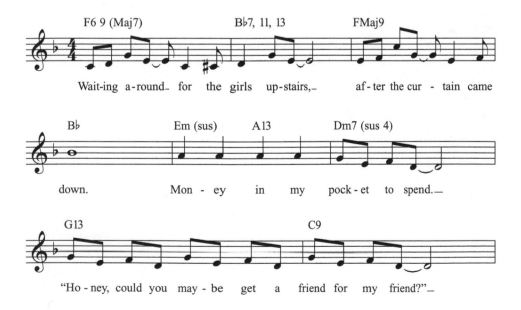

listed in the chords above the melody), and the reader will get some idea of the harmonic complexity[19] of a typical Sondheim creation.

The principals of *Follies* are so dishonest with themselves that Sondheim was forced to tell the audience not to believe them through the music he gave them to sing. A song's melody, especially in the musical theater, has always been able to confirm or deny what the character on stage is telling us. The lyric to "Free Again," for example, proclaims how delightful it is to be liberated from a long love affair, but its hysterical, minor melody denies the joy the singer takes in her freedom with every measure. Jerry Herman's "Time Heals Everything" has such a rueful melody that we know all along that time heals nothing.

In *Follies*, "The Road You Didn't Take" has a musical texture that really elucidates Ben's character. It is built on a typical Sondheim nervous vamp, a kind of ostinato. As the composer himself noted, "It is a man saying, 'oh, I never look back on the past, it just wouldn't be worth it.' And he's doing it to con himself as well as the lady he's with [Sally, whom he has not seen in years]. In point of fact, he's ripped to shreds by the past." One hears stabbing dissonances in the music that tell us how shattered he is inside and warn us to disbelieve his words.

Similarly, Sally's "In Buddy's Eyes," one of the most moving songs ever written, is another song of self-delusion. This time it is the actress who must put it across. "For those of you who want a lesson in subtext," Sondheim told a group of students, "watch what Dorothy Collins does with 'In Buddy's Eyes.' . . . She says everything is just wonderful and she's having a terrific time and is so happily married. Nothing in the lyric, not a single word, tells you that maybe it isn't true. Nothing in the music tells you (although there's something in the orchestration), but the actress has to tell you. And if you watch Dorothy deliver that song—she feels she was jilted by Ben twenty or thirty years ago.—Watch the anger with which she does it. The whole song has a peculiar quality to it. It isn't quite what it seems to be.

"Jonathan Tunick understands subtext as well because every phrase that refers to Buddy, her husband, is dry, all woodwinds; whenever it refers to herself it's all strings. Not one person in a thousand would get this, but . . . it's there and it helps inform the song."

Follies bears out Sondheim and Prince's conception that the old style musical was dying. The show bids a fond farewell to the feather boa, the Busby Berkeley production number, the showstopping belted number, and the inextinguishable torch song.

---

[19] Sondheim has often mentioned his distaste for the "lead sheet" form in quotations of his work, because it doesn't express one of the key elements of the harmonic fabric, the arrangement. This arrangement, however, was purposely chosen in this case to give the lay reader some idea of the harmonic complexity hidden in a seemingly simple melodic line.

Most of the critics noted this daring message and gave it generally favorable reviews—usually for the score. The musical also received negative ones across the board for its libretto. Audiences perceived it as a love-it-or-loathe-it show, with some of the public coming to see it again and again and others complaining bitterly of how depressingly bad it was. The *New Yorker*'s Brendon Gill wrote:

> I admire Mr. Sondheim for not hesitating to explore again the wastelands of alone-ness and self-repugnance that he opened up for us in *Company*, and I hope it is clear to him that what has proved unworkable in *Follies* is the subject matter and not his great themes.

Time magazine reported, "Goldman's book lacks the dry brilliance called for by Prince's direction," while *Newsweek* called it "wonderfully entertaining, ex-traordinarily intelligent and having both a stunning direct appeal and a rare complexity of feeling and structure." *Newsday*'s George Oppenheimer, Sond-heim's collaborator back in the *Topper* era, wrote that it was far better than any musical of that season. "It is, in truth, more of a revue than a musical play, but it is a cornucopia out of which pour scores of rewards in the form of superior entertainment by superior entertainers," he added.

In the beginning all the raves translated into cash at the box office, and the show, with all its lofty aspirations and lavish sets and costumes, looked like a shoe-in at award time. It did win the New York Drama Critics' Circle award for Best Musical, but the Tony Committee must have noticed the hollowness of the libretto, for they judged *Two Gentlemen of Verona*, a tepid takeoff on the Shakespeare play, Best Musical. Sondheim's score, however, captured the Tony,[20] and *Follies* won prizes in lighting, costumes, and sets categories. Prince and Bennett were singled out for direction and choreography, and Alexis Smith won the award for Best Actress in a Musical.

But in the end, *Follies* lost $685,000 of its $800,000 investment. It needed to play to 70 percent capacity just to break even, as its running costs were $80,000 a week. But most weeks it played to half-empty houses, and even though it gave 522 performances, it rarely had a week in which it finished in the black. By the time it closed on July 1, 1972, *Follies*' dismal box office record had succeeded in eroding the confidence of Harold Prince's most loyal investors. He needed a surefire hit for his next production.

George Oppenheimer's critique, that *Follies* would have made a better revue, is a valid one, one whose worth was demonstrated in September 1985, fourteen years after the Broadway premiere. A monumental, all-star production, con-

---

[20] Actually, the 1972 Tony Awards were somewhat of a clean sweep for Sondheim musicals. Larry Blyden and Phil Silvers each won an award for their roles in the splendid revival of *A Funny Thing Happened on the Way to the Forum*.

Lee Remick in discussion with Sondheim after the 1985 concert performance of Follies *at Lincoln Center. Remick played Phyllis Stone—the role originated by Alexis Smith. AP/Wide World Photos.*

ceived and presented by record producer Thomas Shepard, omitted most of the book portion of the show and concentrated on what most have called "ideal" presentations of the songs.

Shepard's extravaganza, which ended up feeling more like a revue than a concert, came about because, at that time, the *Follies* score was only available on the Capitol original cast recording. Prince admits it had been folly to sign the contract Capitol presented, because under its terms they were not obliged to record all twenty-two songs of this score. Prince wanted them to release a two-record LP at that time, but they felt that would not be commercially viable. So Capitol cut some songs, omitted others, and generally patched the score together. Shepard's recording was intended to rectify this, and it certainly has.

When has a musical's score been presented so aptly? When has the magnificent New York Philharmonic (under Paul Gemignani's knowing baton) been enlisted as a "pit-band?" When have past, present, and even future stars of the caliber of André Gregory, Barbara Cook, George Hearn, Jim Walton, Howard McGillan, Mandy Patinkin, Lee Remick, Liz Callaway, Betty Comden, Adolph Green, Liliane Montevecchi, Elaine Stritch, Phyllis Newman, Carol Burnett, Licia Albanese, and Erie Mills all joined together to perform a masterwork? Not before or since.

After that, *Follies* refused to lie fallow. In 1987 a revival was presented at the Shaftesbury Theatre in London with a revised book and some new numbers. It starred Diana Rigg, Julia McKenzie, Daniel Massey, and Dolores Gray. Goldman had made some changes in the book which, according to Julia McKenzie, fell flat.

"Although I never saw it, from listening to the recording and seeing the Lincoln Center concert version, I liked the other [Broadway] version very much more than the one in London," she told this writer recently. "I think they made an enormous mistake to take out "The Road You Didn't Take," which I think is the motif for all the characters. James Goldman redid the script, and it lost its poetry for me then. The earlier script had a poetry which matched Steve's contribution very well. The new script became a bit more pedestrian. But you can't dispute the score, and that score is just supreme whatever you do."

In 1998 *Follies* was given a splendid revival at the Paper Mill Playhouse in New Jersey, one that almost made it to Broadway, and in April 2001, too late for discussion but not for mention in this book, New York's Roundabout Theatre Company mounted another production. Directed by Matthew Warchus, the Roundabout production starred Blythe Danner, Gregory Harrison, Judith Ivey, and Treat Williams and featured Polly Bergen.

By this time, because of its splendid score and despite its inadequate book and petty, bickering characters, *Follies* has attained the status of a beloved classic, growing in popularity and critical esteem with every incarnation. It now has joined the pantheon of distinguished musicals that includes (in this writer's opinion), *Show Boat, Porgy and Bess, Carousel, Gypsy,* and *A Chorus Line.*

Superstars on Broadway and Jeeves

WHEN HAL PRINCE clambered on stage of the Booth Theater in 1972 to accept the Best Director of a Musical Tony for *Follies*, it may have crossed his mind that but for a slip-up in communication, he might just as well have been standing there accepting the award for directing *Jesus Christ Superstar*. For after having heard the rock opera's English recording, Prince had sent a telegram to Andrew Lloyd-Webber expressing his interest in producing and directing the work. The wire lay unopened at his parents' house in Harrington Court for several weeks. At the time Lloyd-Webber was in the States meeting with Robert Stigwood, and by the time he learned of the offer, it was too late to act upon it, for Stigwood had already hired a director.

Lloyd-Webber knew of Prince's work and had great admiration for him, but that cable came at a time when the composer had more on his plate than he could handle. *Superstar*, which had been touring in small productions, was being readied for Broadway, and Andrew as well as Sarah were exceedingly involved in wedding plans.

They were married on Saturday, July 24, 1971, in the Church of the Holy Cross at Aston Keynes, Gloucestershire. The rustic church in the village where Sarah's parents lived is just a half hour's drive from the hotel where Andrew and Tim had closeted themselves to hone and polish *Jesus Christ Superstar* a mere year and a half before.

Sarah, who celebrated her eighteenth birthday only a month prior to her marriage, had just finished what would be the equivalent of her high school education; in fact, her final exams were still lying on her teacher's desk waiting to be marked.

The service was simple and colorful, but the congregation made an odd contrast. According to one of the guests, Sarah's reserved family, members of the middle class, sat on one side of the aisle, speaking to each other in hushed tones.

On the other, the bohemian Lloyd-Webber clan, agents, rock musicians, and theater people Andrew had recently come to know were gossiping and chattering loudly. Both sides, however, listened in absolute silence as Andrew's parents, Jean and William, shushed the invitees. Then a singer initiated the brief ceremony with a romantic setting of The Lord's Prayer that Andrew had composed as a gift for his young bride.

After the ceremony, and before the reception, the bride and groom posed for wedding pictures like any newlyweds. One sees them as an odd pair: Sarah with her long brown hair, toothsome smile, and slightly protruding upper jaw—a look that gave rise to Andrew's nickname for her—"the vole"[1]—and Andrew, small, thin, with darting black eyes, raffishly dressed and unable to stand still. Once the last canapé had been devoured and the last glass of champagne quaffed, the young couple flew off to a honeymoon in Vienna.

Shortly after the wedding Andrew Lloyd-Webber bought their first home: Summerlease Farm, a six-acre property in Dorset, about eighty miles from London. The location was always to be a problem for Sarah and especially Andrew, whose work and heart were in London. To locate that far out of the hub was a mistake, and the couple would spend most of their time in a flat in town.

It was a fortuitous time for them and a healthy start for a marriage that would produce two children and last a full twelve years, during which Lloyd-Webber would become the world's best known composer.

But the road to that fame had already been cobblestoned.

Although the Superstar recording had had only so-so success in Britain, it was selling briskly in the United States. Now, in order to quell all the pirated theatrical performances, unauthorized productions of Jesus Christ Superstar that were springing up by any group who could afford to buy a recording, Stigwood decided to stage the show on Broadway. He booked the Mark Hellinger Theatre—one of New York's largest and most beautiful, where My Fair Lady had run for five years—and announced the opening for late September. The stage production was budgeted at $750,000, huge for the times but $100,000 less than Follies, which had opened only six months earlier. To add to the hoopla, Stigwood trumpeted that a motion picture version of Superstar would begin filming in Israel the following year. He predicted it would outgross Gone With the Wind.

The album was becoming more successful in Britain, while in the United States, the recording reached Number One on the Billboard charts and (by the time the show opened) had sold over three million copies. This, coupled with

[1] According to the American College Dictionary a vole is "any of the various rodents of the genus Microtus and related genera resembling rats or mice but having a shorter tail and limbs with a heavier body."

much advertising plus controversy from religious groups,[2] some of whom thought the idea was heresy, others who thought it was bringing religion into the twentieth century, kept the box office at the Hellinger jingling. By the time it opened, *Jesus Christ Superstar* had chalked up the biggest advance in history—a million dollars.

Veteran director Frank Corsaro, familiar with both musicals and opera, was hired on June 1. But less than two months later, after he saw Corsaro's dark scenic designs and heard of his rather serious plans for the rock opera, Stigwood was not so sure he had made the right choice. Unfortunately—but fortunately for Stigwood—Corsaro was in an automobile accident that landed him in the hospital for several weeks, during which time Stigwood was able to buy him out of his contract.

As replacement he chose the flamboyant, pony-tailed Tom O'Horgan, fresh from his success with *Hair*, who permuted the original concept. Suddenly the character of Jesus was overwhelmed by O'Horgan's over-the-top production. The director not only put the emphasis on the colorful and sometimes grotesque scenery of Robin Wagner and outlandish costumes, but introduced bizarre stage effects and jejune symbolism.

Herod emerged as a campy drag queen in platform shoes. Christ made his entrance emerging from a silver chalice and exited nailed to a golden triangle. (O'Horgan changed his mind at the last minute about the crucifixion—his original plan was to have "a vinyl-clad, hip Christ" crucified on the handlebars of a Harley-Davidson motorcycle.) The director resorted to vulgar imagery, such as having priests suspended from a framework of dinosaur bones or Judas dressed in silver jockey shorts, on a trapeze filled with beautiful girls and peacock feathers.

In a time when most Broadway shows were hardly miked, this one, in an effort to re-create the feeling of the recording, broke the decibel level. By having the cast stroll around the stage passing microphones from one member to another, any sense of theatrical reality was abandoned. Committed to these outlandish concepts, O'Horgan must have been following Samuel Goldwyn's prescription for a successful production: "one that starts with an earthquake and works up to a climax."

Lloyd-Webber and Rice were dumbfounded when they attended the rehearsals of O'Horgan's extravaganza. Andrew had an entirely different view of the piece, and, according to Gerald McKnight, he "was very unhappy and nursed gloom over the outcome which he confided to Sarah."

She had come over from England with him and was suffering as much as her

---

[2] Billy Graham, America's unofficial chaplain, straddled the fence when he told a reporter: "The music, in my opinion, is excellent, but the lyrics, while at times reverent, at other times border on the sacrilegious."

husband through the tension and depression of these weeks. Of course, with Lloyd-Webber, it was mostly frustration over his inability to control the medium. Only twenty-three, but already canny to the collaborative ways of the musical, he knew that producer Stigwood and director O'Horgan were in the drivers' seats. As the score had been prewritten and prerecorded, rehearsals left the composer irate but impotent. One has to understand that the chief driving force in Andrew Lloyd-Webber at the time was not the desire to compose or see his works on stage, it was the urge for control. But beyond that, abhorring what he saw there, he could not understand how those of the public who came to see the previews actually liked the mayhem that was happening nightly on stage.

Years later he was to wonder "what Corsaro would have made of it. It *might* have been a complete disaster." He must have mused too on what Hal Prince, whom he greatly admired and with whom he was to collaborate on his most successful works, would have done with this score. For even though the music was well sung, especially by newcomer Ben Vereen[3] in the key role of Judas, the production was so busy that it did the score in.

During the interminable break-in period (the official debut had to be postponed because the sound level O'Horgan demanded took weeks to adjust), the staid Mark Hellinger Theatre smelled strongly of marijuana. O'Horgan's unorthodox way of rehearsing included arranging Vereen and Jeff Feinholt, who portrayed Jesus, in cruciform shape on the floor. Then he insisted the blindfolded cast touch them "in order to think about what the Crucifixion was." According to one member of the company he covered Feinholt's prone body with honey and encouraged the other actors to lick it off.

Jesus Christ Superstar finally opened on October 17, 1971, and was able to chalk up a long run, if not a record, of 720 performances in New York. When it was produced in London with a different director and more traditional staging it ran for eight years. Of the Broadway reviewers, two endorsed the show, four wrote mixed reviews, and five condemned it in scathing terms.

Although one critic said "the evening proceeds from orgasm to orgasm," most admired the score but were appalled by the direction. Clive Barnes, writing in the *New York Times* seesawed and called Lloyd-Webber's music "neither inventive nor original," but a paragraph later termed it "the best score for an English musical in years." Barnes went on to aim his most venomous darts directly at O'Horgan:

> Ever since his beginning at La Mamma, Mr. O'Horgan has tried to startle us. Once he startled us with small things, now he startles us with big things. This time, the

---

[3] Vereen won a *Theater World* award for outstanding new acting talent and was nominated for a Tony for Best Supporting Actor in a Musical.

things got too big. The stage is full of platforms, carriages descend from the heavens, and even the stars over Gethsemane are captured in a blue plastic box. The total effect is brilliant but cheap . . .

Barnes was not alone in skewering O'Horgan. Critic John Simon, master of vitriol, lambasted him—and Lloyd-Webber and Rice as well.

What we get at the Mark Hellinger is closer to rock bottom than rock opera: a mediocre score with less than mediocre lyrics, in an overinflated megalomaniacal production which, for all its going off like a dozen Roman candles in twelve simultaneously diverging directions, cannot hold a candle to a modest, innocently imaginative, and truly felt little musical like *Godspell*.[4] I shall not even try in such limited space to describe what O'Horgan hath wrought in terms of sliding panels and all-engulfing fabrics, pieces of scenery and actors lowered and hoisted through the air . . . creepy objects like inverted metallic elephant trunks with tongues hanging out at the wider end or enormous silver dentures carried about as if they were cymbals, merchants selling what appear to be mummified babies and soldiers in armor cunningly designed to facilitate instant sodomy. Clearly, a man who could invert an elephant's trunk would stop at no imaginable inversion.

Douglas Watt, critic for the *New York Daily News*, alone gave the production unqualified praise. "A shattering theatrical experience," he wrote, "unlike any other I can recall. It seems likely to be around for a long time to come."

On opening night after the performance, Stigwood arranged a party at the Tavern-on-the-Green for a thousand guests that rivaled the excesses on stage. "Transvestites nibbled at hams decorated to look like Indonesian masks," Jonathan Mantle reported, "and topless models danced to live rock music into the small hours." The guests, many of whom were members of the British press, flown over to dilute what were certain to be scating American reviews, were oblivious to the mob that had begun picketing the theater, brandishing placards on which the "Superstar" following Jesus Christ's name had been crossed out and replaced with "Lamb of God," or "Our Hope."

The next morning church groups too began airing their resentments. Catholics and Protestants, particularly Baptists, were more than voluble and offended by the musical's implication that Mary Magdalen's love for Jesus went beyond the platonic. Blacks were incensed at Vereen's being cast as Judas, and their spokesman in *Jet Magazine* panned the show, saying that Vereen's acting might be the only thing of relevance to black audiences that *Superstar* had.

But the loudest objections came from the Jews. Rabbi Marc Tannenbaum,

---

[4] *Godspell*, with a book by John-Michael Trebelak and revival-like songs by Stephen Schwartz, had opened five months before. Although given a small, off-Broadway production, this splendid musical based on the Gospel According to St. Matthew was to run downtown and eventually on Broadway for more than five years.

representing the American Jewish Committee, wrote that the show "unambig-
uously lays the primary responsibility for Jesus' suffering and crucifixion to the
Jewish priesthood . . . it is if nothing else, insufficiently thoughtful, potentially
mischievous, and possibly a backward step on the road to Christian–Jewish
relations."

The box office had already built up a healthy advance and shortly after *Superstar*'s opening performance was sold out for six months in advance. Eventually, as the show settled in for a long run, the demonstrators grew tired and the
black and religious groups, powerless to stop the show, left off their picketing.

Looking back from the vantage point of three decades after its premiere, one
sees that the essence of Andrew Lloyd-Webber lies in his score for *Superstar*.
Certainly it heralded his success as it rode the rock-opera trend and introduced
his bag of tricks—catchy pop songs, melodies with broad dramatic arcs, open-
throated arias, and, later, special effects. Encouraged by the success of *Superstar*,
what he has continued to deliver is entertainment designed to overwhelm. A
critic for the *Los Angeles Times* said that "his musicals guarantee not just jaw-
dropping staging, but crescendo after crescendo as the heart-swelling backdrop
to an easily followed story line. And he hammers hooks home, making it impossible for theatergoers to walk out on the street without at least one melody
stuck in their heads. In other words Lloyd Webber treats his customers as if
their enjoyment meant more to him than anything." On the other hand, it is
this writer's opinion that Stephen Sondheim doesn't care about the enjoyment
of his audience, only what he perceives as truth.

At the 1972 Tony Awards ceremony, for the first time an Andrew Lloyd-
Webber musical was pitted against one of Stephen Sondheim. Earlier that year,
the twenty-three-year-old Andrew won the Drama Desk Award as most promising composer of the season. The Tony committee wiggled out of the competition by announcing that as *Superstar* had been a recording translated into a
staged performance, it was ineligible to be considered in the Best Musical category. But everywhere else—in the categories of costumes, lighting, and scenic
design—the committee chose *Follies* over *Superstar*. O'Horgan was furious. "Have
you seen *Follies*?" he asked an interviewer. "It's the saddest, most boring show
you ever saw in your life," he quipped.

Certainly it was O'Horgan's folly that broadsided such an intrinsically exciting
musical as *Superstar*, denied it its rightful kudos, and kept it from going beyond
nomination to minor awards. The Tony committee, notoriously chauvinistic,
didn't quite know what to do, but as if meting out theatrical justice, not one of
the critics nominated O'Horgan in the Best Director category.

Once the show was off to a running start, Lloyd-Webber returned to England,
eager for him and Rice to get started on the rewrites for the upcoming movie,
but even more important, for them to begin a new project.

Stigwood had suggested they do a musicalization of *Peter Pan*, and although they both approached the idea tepidly, as nothing else was in the offing they agreed to try. But over his collaborator's objection, before beginning the project, Rice wanted an extended holiday in Japan and couldn't be talked out of it.

It was the beginning of a crack in their relationship that would develop into a full-blown fissure by the end of the decade. Just a hint of their disagreement had begun earlier. While they were still in New York, Lloyd-Webber, uptight and straitlaced, had been vociferous about O'Horgan's obvious homoerotic vulgarizing of *Superstar* and had expected Rice to join him in denouncing the director. Tim, with his habitual laid-back attitude, could not get wildly excited by the fact that O'Horgan and crew sometimes wore full drag, an attitude that Andrew took as betrayal. Even Stigwood felt Lloyd-Webber, like all composers, should be seen and not heard. Besides, he was demanding to look at the books and wondered publicly, according to one biographer, whether he and Tim were getting paid on *Superstar*'s gross or net. Tim Rice thought that vulgar and unnecessary.

After Rice's Japanese odyssey, the team went to Israel, ostensibly to give their input to Norman Jewison's production of the *Superstar* film. They soon realized that they were personae non grata here as well, for this director too had unequivocal ideas about production. Jewison envisioned a group of tourists getting off a bus and doing the musical as a sort of morality play. The film version of *Superstar* was not a critical success. It was released in 1973 after the musical was an accepted hit on stage, but whatever the rock opera's merits in the theater, something was missing on screen. One critic called the picture "one of the true fiascos of modern cinema." Few have disagreed with him.

Both returned to London, and as the money from the Broadway production and others worldwide and the recordings kept rolling in,[5] both bought townhouses. Tim Rice chose the fashionable Bayswater section and filled his home with a Tibetan terrier and a growing collection of paintings of Christ, while Andrew Lloyd-Webber, whose grandmother, Molly, had died the year earlier, chose to be nearer his parents and his roots. He bought a six-story Victorian mansion on Brompton Square, less than a mile from his parents' flat in Harrington Court.

Lloyd-Webber began to collect pre-Raphaelite paintings (and has gone on to

---

[5] According to an item in *The New York Times*, up until 1990, *Jesus Christ Superstar* earned $16.8 million at the box office in London alone. The album grossed $100 million worldwide, and the film earned about $30 million. On stage the show was produced in more than twenty countries, and revivals and tours continue to this day. Using his new-gained assets and wanting to buy back the rights to his own works, in an astute move Lloyd-Webber paid £1.6 million in 1989 for the copyright to *Joseph and the Amazing Technicolor Dreamcoat*, which belonged to Filmax Limited— a company that had acquired the work in 1968 from Novello.

amass one of the world's great collections of the art of this era.) As to why he became so embroiled in the paintings of this serene English school of the mid-nineteenth century, one interviewer opined that "there is something about their perfectly sanitized world that appeals to him."

Andrew and Sarah did not stay long in Brompton Square. For one thing the house was easy prey for burglars, and after it was once broken into, the young couple lost heart. They refused to install additional iron gates and barred windows that would make it robbery proof. Lloyd-Webber sold the place after a year (clearing a £100,000 profit) and in 1972 bought a country home, nay, a stately home located on twenty acres near the village of Kingsclere and the town of Newbury in Hampshire. He also sold Summerlease Farm, which they had bought shortly after their marriage, this time at a £40,000 loss.

Sydmonton Court, a huge old house that had sections that dated back to the sixteenth century, was a true country estate. With its Victorian arches and large rooms it would make a perfect setting for their burgeoning art collection and Lloyd-Webber's new collection of pinball machines. Its purchase price, £220,000, was secured by the sale of the Brompton Square property and the house and land itself. Tim Rice, too, bought a country estate. His was called Romeyns Court and stood outside the village of Great Milton, Oxfordshire. The old house was surrounded by nine acres of verdant fields—plenty of room to build a cricket pitch to indulge his favorite sport.

Now with the expenses of refurbishing and running a big estate, the Lloyd-Webbers were "land poor." With obligations mushrooming, Andrew felt he and Tim had better get down to work—and fast.[6]

No sooner had the they tackled *Peter Pan* than they realized its fantasy was far too juvenile for them. Rice reiterated his desire to continue with projects similar to ones with which they had been successful in the past: protagonists who led short, exciting lives that changed the course of the world. They had already explored Dr. Barnardo, Richard the Lionhearted, and Jesus with varying degrees of success. Joan of Arc, Mata Hari, and another woman whose story had recently been turned into a radio play were on Rice's short list. He had tuned in late one night and caught only the last half of the drama, but had been mesmerized. He knew Eva Duarte, dead at thirty-three, wife of Argentina's president Juan Péron and the woman over whom the entire nation was still mourning, would make a fascinating subject for a musical.

He told Lloyd-Webber excitedly about the rise to power of this superbitch, saying that with her cruelties, her hypocrisy, and the use she had made of men,

---

[6] It should be mentioned that at that time taxes on significant incomes in Britain were monstrously high. For those earning beyond £100,00 the government took some 85 percent of one's net income, in some cases this went as high as 97 percent.

Sydmonton Court. Photo: Irene Clark.

her story would make an exhilarating musical play—actually the reverse of the coin of *Superstar*. Andrew listened and was intrigued with the idea, for which he could create Argentinean tangos, *paso doubles*, and the like with touches of De Falla and Ravel, his heroes, thrown in.

But he ultimately was forced to reject the idea, saying he didn't want to do "another piece about an unknown who rises to fame at thirty-three and then dies . . . we've just *done that* with *Superstar*." The project he was in favor of was at the same time both more and less ambitious. He wanted Rice and Lloyd-Webber to be a well-rounded team—a sort of Rodgers and Hart—and felt it was time they joined the establishment and created a proper musical comedy. He eagerly anticipated them going forward with a story that had originally been Rice's idea, one with which they had been toying haphazardly for some time.

Both cricket enthusiasts, they had had some of their best camaraderie amid laughter when they sketched out the story of P. G. Wodehouse's unflappable butler, Jeeves. Andrew and Tim saw great humor in the author's evocations of a Britain that never was, a carefree land of shallow aristocrats and devoted help. Besides, as the new royalty, the master of Sydmonton Court, the notion of writing about the upper crust of British society had a strong appeal to Lloyd-Webber.

Still, the more Rice investigated Eva Duarte, the more avid he began to feel about postponing the *Jeeves* project in favor of one he called *Evita*. Eager to find out all he could about this glamorous blonde whose flamboyant use of her body had never been seen as vile enough to quench the mesmeric ardor of her subjects, in 1973 he whisked his then secretary, Jane Mackintosh, away to Buenos

Aires on a research trip that proved so impassioned he married her. When their first daughter was born the next year he named her Eva (after the Argentinean bombshell) Jane.

Frustratingly committed to the *Jeeves* project, Rice argued with his collaborator back and forth about the tone of the upcoming musical project. Eventually, after he had written a few songs that weren't hugely inspired, he announced that he could not seem to get a handle on Wodehouse's characters.

From Rice's point of view, his confusion made a lot of sense. The very organization of the Bertie Wooster stories demanded an alternation of dialogue and song, and Tim had very little interest in lighthearted traditional musical comedy. Besides, with the many characters that comprise the Bertie Wooster stories, Rice had trouble keeping the narrative from becoming fragmented. Knowing he would not be able to use the sung-through style that worked so well in *Joseph* and *Superstar*, he was insecure about the project.

But he was willing to journey to Long Island in tandem with Lloyd-Webber to see Wodehouse and gain his permission and perhaps some insight into the musicalization of his work. Andrew was thrilled to meet the grand old master of the Jeeves stories and chose to ignore Wodehouse's caution that "it's been tried before and it's failed." Perhaps Wodehouse's negativism affected Rice, for shortly after their return from America, Rice threw in the towel, declaring that he was not a librettist and would serve only as the lyricist.

Leaning over backward, Andrew Lloyd-Webber brought Alan Ayckbourn,[7] who shared his interest in money and pinball machines, into the enterprise, hoping Tim would still agree to serve as lyricist to the project, but Ayckbourn's haughtiness rubbed Rice the wrong way. When the playwright exclaimed, "Who the hell is Jeeves? I mean he's just a figure who says lines!" Rice soon made it clear that he was no more disposed to working with Britain's top comedy writer than he was with Andrew on this project. On Tim's refusal, Ayckbourn felt he might have a go at the lyrics, and Andrew, who had learned much about vocal placement and prosody in general from Tim, agreed to let him try.

The new collaborators had an early rapport, for they were both obsessive workers. Perhaps Lloyd-Webber was more obsessive than Ayckbourn, for the mere thought of having his musical staged at Her Majesty's Theatre filled him with almost uncontrollable excitement. The recorded musical was a totally different thing—second rate. It was nothing at all like drinking umpteen cups of black coffee while working feverishly to get it right for the previews in Brigh-

---

[7] Often characterized as Britain's Neil Simon, Ayckbourn, a highly skilled chronicler of the foibles of middle-class British society, had written *Absurd Person Singular* in 1973 and a trilogy, *The Norman Conquests*, the following year. He had never written a musical; actually, it was rumored that he detested them.

ton—Britain's equivalent of New Haven. Now he was composing the way his idol, Richard Rodgers, had and with a proper lyric-librettist to boot.

When Stigwood and the director, Eric Thompson, first saw Ayckbourn's script they realized that with the addition of Lloyd-Webber's songs, the show would run over four hours. The cause, according to Andrew's music director Anthony Bowles, was that "Alan hadn't the remotest idea of how to write a musical. . . . He produced the most *involved* plot. Very ingenious . . . a very good Wodehouse pastiche. But it was so enormously long!"

It was also totally escapist, and by the '70s musicals had to have some resonance with contemporary life. Ayckbourn and Lloyd-Webber erred on the grounds of pure malconstruction as well. The first four numbers went to Bertie, and the audience sat for half an hour watching the proceedings before a female, a dancer, or an ensemble appeared.

The initial read-through took, according to Bowles, five and one-half hours. Later this was cut to a preview that lasted four and one-quarter hours. But because of the convoluted plot it was impossible to cut the show any further. When you snipped away scenes, the audience could no longer follow the story. The cast members too seemed to lose their motivation and were as confused as those sitting out front.

As the show approached its London opening things became even more ominous. Wodehouse died, and Ayckbourn, who had little talent for lyrics, struggled valiantly with his rhymes while trying to juggle the cuts that the director was demanding. Lloyd-Webber, who had written a sort of Palm Court kind of score, was having trouble getting the jazz band orchestration he needed. In desperation he asked Anthony Bowles to do the orchestrations for him (subject to his approval). He offered to pay the conductor extra for the job, but he wanted no mention in the program that these were Bowles's orchestrations. When Bowles refused to work anonymously, he was asked to do (and be given credit for) the vocal arrangements. Lloyd-Webber farmed out the orchestrations eventually among Keith Amos, Don Walker, and David Cullen, taking some of the credit for himself.

One wonders why Lloyd-Webber did not want his lack of technique in instrumentation known. It was a given that top Broadway composers like Jerry Herman, Jule Styne, and Stephen Sondheim, pressed to create new songs in the last weeks before an opening, did not do their own orchestrations. They left that to the men like Sid Ramin, Jonathan Tunick, Luther Henderson, Bill Brohn, and others who had rapport with their scores and had developed the craft of instrumentation to a considerable art. In fact, Robert Russell Bennett's orchestrations for Andrew's idol, Richard Rodgers, were highly acclaimed—and Rodgers always acknowledged that the reason his music sounded so "alive" in the theater was due to Bennett's arrangements.

With *Jeeves* scheduled to open at Her Majesty's Theatre as soon as it finished its break-in period at Bristol's Hippodrome, rehearsals were held in a virtual theater of war. According to Michael Walsh, director Thompson, Lloyd-Webber, and Ayckbourn fought about everything from cuts to the proper sequence of musical numbers. "They fought about the chorus of the Drones Club, the all male singing sextette that accompanied Bertie," Walsh writes, "and they fought about the role of the leading female character, Aunt Dahlia—who eventually was written out of the show altogether. During a meeting with Thompson and Walker at Harvey's Restaurant in Bristol the atmosphere grew especially heated and Thompson called Lloyd Webber a vulgar expletive. Shattered, Andrew returned to his hotel, sat down on the stairs and wept."

Everyone begged the producers to replace Thompson, who seemed to have no idea of how to handle the large forces musical comedy demands. But with true British loyalty he was kept on until, only a few days before the London opening, when everyone could clearly see the project, like a dreadnought, heading for disaster, he was let go, and Alan Ayckbourn took over the reins.

An author never likes to cut his own dialogue, and so after a few more leviathan performances, for better, but mostly for worse, the show opened. Its premiere soon allowed British aislesitters to trot out their most vicious metaphors. "It is longer than *Parsifal* and not half as funny," one said. "The effect is like a dream of all Wooster novels combined into the ultimate ghastly weekend," wrote Irving Wardle in *The Times*. Jack Tinker of the *Daily Mail* did him one better. "*Jeeves* is the all-British musical launched with the unsinkable formula of a *Titanic*. It sinks like a stone, fatally holed by an iceberg of immeasurable boredom."

The failure of *Jeeves* was to haunt Lloyd-Webber for years. At a Dramatists Guild seminar as late as 1991, the composer was to admit "*Jeeves* was a catastrophe. Nothing in it worked. It was all over the place. Hal Prince came to see it and wrote me this note: 'You can't listen to music if you can't look at it.' He was right. Its concept included . . . imaginary scenes in all sorts of physical locations, and it just couldn't work. I learned from Hal that a musical has to look right, that's the most important thing of the evening."

Of course the statement is simplistic. A show needs more than just "to look right." Beyond talent in its collaborators, it needs fire and purpose—more so, collaborators who are artists on the same wavelength.

Had *Jeeves* opened on Broadway, after receiving comparable critiques it would certainly have closed by the end of the week, but in a country with a far kinder tolerance for theatrical mediocrity, the musical hung on. It had opened on April 22, only a day after another comedy of manners, *A Little Night Music*, had premiered in the West End and garnered a sheaf of splendid reviews. Sondheim's musical had been directed by Hal Prince, who had since become a friend, and as *Jeeves* kept playing to half-empty houses for those four weeks until it finally expired on May 24, 1975,[8] the awareness that Prince's vision had shepherded this successful musical to the Broadway and eventually British stage must have rankled Lloyd-Webber.

Now Andrew Lloyd-Webber was determined to take fire from Prince's wise words and Tim's enthusiasm for *Evita*. They would go away, leave England, and in some peaceful place, as they had turned out *Superstar*, they would write their next show. Who knows? They might even get the great Hal Prince to direct it.

[8] By the spring of 1996, Lloyd-Webber had rewritten *Jeeves*, adding several new songs. Ayckbourn had revised the libretto, and the show, now called *By Jeeves*, had turned itself around and received rave reviews in its incarnation at Scarborough. The production opened in July and had a rather successful run in London's West End. It was also produced at Connecticut's Goodspeed Opera House in 1998.

A Masque and an Oriental Odyssey

ANDREW LLOYD-WEBBER had known it from the beginning, nor was he alone among astute theater people: Hal Prince had an uncanny eye for what was classy and what would play on the musical stage. He alone should shepherd Andrew's next production to the stage, for among all the high-powered directors, Prince was the only one to have these talents in tandem. Jerome Robbins, Bob Fosse, Michael Kidd, Gower Champion, and Michael Bennett each had a string of hits to his name, but they were basically dance directors who could bring to musicals the movement that was now in vogue. Prince had the rare talent to know what made the dramatic sections of a musical hold together—especially now, in the '70s, when the book was paramount. Prince also possessed the daring to try new things. Musicals were going through flux and change after the "golden '60s." By now the traditional song and dance show had become totally passé. And as if all those abilities weren't enough, he was gifted with a great sense of confidence—apparent since the time he had been in his early twenties.

Sondheim told Linda Winer, a reporter for USA Today, how Prince projected their future years ago. "I remember walking down the street and his saying, 'It's going to be terrific. We're going to be able to do anything we want to do.' And I'm thinking 'Oh, God, he's crazy. . . . We're going to be starving or dead in the gutter in two years.' You see, he was always the positive one. I was the pessimist—and he turned out to be right."

Secure in his glowing optimism, Prince can be notoriously persuasive. In their previous collaborations Prince "had a notion, a vision," says Sondheim of Company, "and I followed him to his vision." Similarly with Follies, he adds, "It went through two processes. First I went to James Goldman and said 'I want to write a musical with you.' . . . When we bought it to Hal, Hal had a vision of it that was entirely different from ours, and we entered his vision again."

Their next collaboration, *A Little Night Music*,[1] had its genesis back in 1957 when Sondheim and Prince talked about doing a gracious court masque. As Prince perceived it in his autobiography, *Contradictions*, it was to be "a chamber opera, probably about sex, a gavotte in which couples interchange suffering mightily in elegant country homes wearing elegant clothes."

Around the time of *West Side Story*, the pair asked for the rights to Jean Anouilh's play *Ring 'Round the Moon*, their first choice, but were turned down. Ten years later they asked again, and that play was still unavailable to them. Now Sondheim suggested they have a look at Bergman's 1956 film, *Smiles of a Summer Night*, a kind of Gallic sex comedy set in turn-of-the-century Sweden. It contained many of the elements he and Prince were looking for: a weekend at a summerhouse, a play within a play, young and old lovers, below-stairs servants who take their sex lightly as contrasted with the *weltschmerz* of the upper classes. They decided to "lyricize the various aspects of love."[2] The film also had a mystery and a darkness that appealed strongly to Sondheim.

Prince was looking for a great success. He *needed* a great success. *Follies* had lost a large amount of money, and his runaway megahit *Fiddler on the Roof* had just closed. He had nothing playing, not even anything in the works at the moment. This was no time to think of a musical based in metaphor, concept, or even Kierkegaardian symbolism. He wished to play down *Smiles of a Summer Night*'s ambivalence and gloominess, traits he felt had kept *Company* and *Follies* out of the smash hit column, and to play up the romantic, happy-ending idealism—while still keeping the show a "class act." To that end he brought in Hugh Wheeler,[3] a well-rounded intellectual playwright.

Sondheim's first—rather daring—idea was to treat the story as "theme and variations which would coincide with a musical theme and variations." Hugh

---

[1] The title, a translation of Mozart's *Eine Kleine Nachtmusik*, is somewhat inappropriate to the farcelike operetta-masque that was nameless until late in its creation. Ingmar Bergman gave Sondheim and Prince the rights to use anything they liked from his film, from which it was adapted, *except* the title, *Smiles of a Summer Night*. *A Little Night Music* was the (more appropriate but) discarded name of the television musical eventually known as *Evening Primrose*.

[2] The phrase is Prince's, but it was coincidentally the title and theme of Andrew Lloyd-Webber's 1989 musical, which was adapted from the 1955 novella by David Garnett.

[3] Hugh Wheeler was born and educated in London. He became a naturalized American citizen in the 1930s and wrote mysteries under the name of Patrick Quentin and Q. Patrick. Four of his novels were made into motion pictures. In 1961 he wrote his first play, *Big Fish, Little Fish* for Broadway followed by *Look, We've Come Through* (1965) and *We Have Always Lived in the Castle*, an adaptation of Shirley Jackson's story (1966). His writings also included screenplays for *Something for Everyone*, *Cabaret*, and *Travels with My Aunt*. After *A Little Night Music* he was to produce the libretto for Sondheim's *Sweeney Todd*. Wheeler also assisted Prince and Sondheim in the 1973 restaging of *Candide* and contributed additional material to the 1984 off-Broadway revival of *Pacific Overtures*.

Wheeler even wrote one act in that fashion, but "it didn't pan out well," Sondheim says, "and so we decided to write a straightforward version" adapting Bergman's screenplay into a story that largely concerns Désirée Armfeldt, a mature actress in turn-of-the-century Sweden.

Before we see her, we are introduced to her former lover, forty-nine-year-old lawyer Fredrik Egerman, whose attempt to renew (in Wheeler's phrase) "his unrenewable youth" has led him into a frustrated marriage with a sexually reticent eighteen-year-old. Now Fredrik, the father of Désirée Armfeldt's daughter (in Bergman's film, of her son), has decided to take his impressionable young wife, Anne, to attend Désirée's performance at a local theater. He has not seen Désirée in years, but she notices them in their box and plays her lines directly to Fredrik. Anne suspects her husband and Désirée's former liaison and leaves their loge in tears.

Fredrik decides to visit Désirée in her rooms. When he confesses that his wife is still a virgin, the actress's sympathetic consolations soon lead to their lovemaking. Afterwards, they are surprised by an unscheduled visit from Count Carl-Magnus, a pompous dragoon, whose mistress Désirée has become.

Désirée and Fredrik manage to wiggle out of their *flagrante* situation but only halfway convince the jealous, argumentative, and self-centered Carl-Magnus that their liaison was a business appointment. After a long look at her life, which she deems to be one extended theatrical tour, Désirée plans a daring attempt to win Fredrik back. She has her rich mother, a retired courtesan, invite the Egermans, Henrik (Fredrik's son by a previous marriage), and the lady's maid to a weekend in the country. Henrik, a divinity student, is in love with Anne, who is near his age, and he is torn with angst and guilt. When the jealous Carl-Magnus learns of this weekend rendezvous, he persuades his masochistic wife, Countess Charlotte, to join him in a trip to the country, and, although uninvited, they show up and are accommodated at Mme. Armfeldt's home as well.

So ends the first act, with all the pieces for farce and intrigue in place.

In the second, the trysts multiply until the couples gradually get properly sorted out. Carl-Magnus challenges Fredrik to a duel that ends in a minor skirmish, after which, his honor redeemed, he can end his affair with Désirée and return to his wife. At the last, when he learns that Anne has run off with Henrik, Fredrik realizes the folly of his searching after youth and wisely settles on Désirée, a woman nearer his own age. Everything ends logically. Even the servants are paired off.

Prince had planned the show as an operetta, a form that might be considered *derrière-garde* but which, considering its basis in Bergman and the fact that it would have music and lyrics by Sondheim, could not possibly be considered passé. "I am willing to tell any story that interests me," said Sondheim. "I don't think in terms of breaking new ground, and I doubt if Hal does either. . . . What

Désirée (Glynis Johns) comes to visit her wealthy, ex-courtesan mother. © Museum of the City of New York.

we tried to do was infuse some rejuvenating life into the operetta form, because that is what the material seems to call for. Hal kept saying, 'Let's not resist it just because it's called operetta. Nobody has done it in twenty-five years but maybe it isn't old hat.' Well, I think it's always a mistake to think about what you are doing. Just tell it."

Both collaborators came into the project gingerly. "The first reading had either no music or one number," Prince told a Dramatists Guild seminar, "and so in fact it was a play. It sounded sensational and Steve and I thought there was absolutely no need for music in the piece." Sondheim remembers *Night Music*'s genesis differently. "I had three and a half songs at the first reading; possibly four and a half. Two of them are no longer in the piece. Although one of them is called 'Now' it was a different 'Now,' and there was an opening called 'Numbers.' "

But of course Prince is going out on a limb; there was a need for music, and, as is typical in operetta, the music fills in and helps to satisfy the emotional peak the dialogue has worked up to. By the second reading Sondheim had written a few more songs, but they were dark because he was really writing to Ingmar Bergman rather than Hugh Wheeler, and Prince wanted the score to have what Sondheim calls "darkness peeping through a whipped cream surface. We could see it going right off the track. If we hadn't had that reading we wouldn't have seen it. I threw out practically all the songs I had written and started over again. If you don't take care of that in the beginning you end up in the third week of rehearsal having your first run-through and seeing that the book is here and score is there, and it's too late to rewrite the entire score."

So that the musical would have an uninterrupted flow, Prince made a conscious effort to utilize the movie technique that had worked so well in *Company* and *Follies*. "The last scene in *Night Music*, which takes place *everywhere* on the estate, appears to be happening only on the lawn," he told Craig Zadan. "What no one else realizes is that the young wife and her stepson are running along a hall and down an alley and off to the country. Désirée is having her scene with her lover in her bedroom. The countess and Fredrik are having a conversation on the lawn, and so on . . . I told Hugh Wheeler not to worry about it, to write it as though it were a movie . . . I don't think the audience quarreled with it."

Sondheim too was interested in the flow of the piece, but as its composer his aim was to create unity and to that end had decided from the outset that all the score's time signatures would be in multiples of three. He was searching for an interrelatedness, a smooth-flowing quality, and a uniqueness. "Obviously when you have dialogue in a show," he has stated, "it can't be through-composed. But it occurred to me that you can make a score more cohesive than just a group of disparate thirteen or fifteen songs—that they can have interrelationships and act like movie music does, in that it will arouse in the audience resonances acting like reprises by just the use of themes again—something that keeps a score together so that this score can only be written for this show. Just as the individual songs must be written for just these characters—Oscar's principles—the score belongs to this show. Another score belongs to another show . . . It's not so much that the songs are interrelated but that the tone is. By keeping everything in multiples of three there's a sense that they're all part of one show."

That does not mean *Night Music* is all waltzy or "Viennesy," as it has been so often (and erroneously) pegged. *A Little Night Music* has its share—as do all Broadway operettas—of waltzes. Here they most closely resemble Ravel's sensual *Valses Nobles et Sentimentales*, but sometimes they remind one of Sibelius's nostalgic *Valse Triste*. Both these masterpieces use *hemiola*[4] liberally.

Without getting too technical, it should be explained that 3/4, whose best

[4] See Glossary, p. 421.

known outgrowth is the waltz, had its precursor in the minuet. This developed into the *ländler* in Austria and the mazurka and the polonaise in Poland. All these variations or colors brought with them their varied nationalistic moods: the polonaise became heroic; the mazurka, dancelike. In addition, as the symphonic form grew more impetuous, the third movement, an obligatory minuet, began to be transmogrified into a scherzo, sometimes stormy, as in Beethoven, at other times playful, as in Mendelssohn. These various rhythms and moods make up the major part of Sondheim's ingenious score.

Another curious effect of triple time is that in rapid movement, what is referred to by conductors as "in one," the three beats that comprise a measure become one. Because of the natural rise and fall inherent in all music, this single strong beat is always followed by a weak beat. Thus a rapid 3/4 becomes *strong* two three, *weak* two three, *strong* two three, *weak* two three, and as speed develops, the pulse is no longer perceived as triple time but as *strong, weak, strong, weak*. Thus duple.

And then a slow 3/4 can translate into 3/2, as in Henrik's lugubrious solo, "Later," or Mme. Armfeldt's dawdling "Liaisons." In these cases Sondheim's melodies are so shifty we forget about the underlying pulse. It is easy to imagine 3/4 translating into 9/8 ("It Would Have Been Wonderful") or even 12/8 ("Send in the Clowns"), but a bit more difficult to imagine it as 6/8—which musical textbooks usually term a duple meter. But 6/8 is flexible and can be thought of in its usual *one* two three *four* five six (as Sondheim uses it in "Every Day a Little Death"[5]) or combined with *one* two *three* four *five* six (as Leonard Bernstein does in *West Side Story*'s "America."

One can see then that Sondheim's conscious choice of this thread of unity that tied his score together would not imprison or enchain it but rather open it to great variety while consolidating its force. Perhaps it is this very homogeneity that makes the score of *A Little Night Music* hold together so well and has given it the cachet of being called Sondheim's finest by most reviewers.

Those critics who call him elitist have often carped that his songs are not simple to sing—in a word, "hummable"—and his reaction to that complaint has always been immediate and vociferous. "Nobody notices that any songs of mine are immensely hummable," he told one interviewer. "The only reason 'Send in the Clowns' became such a hit is that two years after the show—two years— Glynis Johns was singing it at the top of her lungs—two years they were playing

[5] Although Sondheim's meter here is duple, he explains that each section of the song is composed of three phrases. But this is a common set-up in all songwriting: two declarative phrases and a consequent one. No, while the message of "Every Day a Little Death" clearly belongs to this score dramatically, musically it steps out of it.

it in the *boîtes* around—it took Judy Collins to listen to it and make a record—which became Number One in England. Then Frank Sinatra heard there was this Number One song, so *he* made a record of it here. Between the two of them, I've a hit. They could have picked up "Losing My Mind" or "With So Little To Be Sure Of," or "Anyone Can Whistle." . . . I write lots of simple and passionate stuff—when it's called for."

There is no denying the rueful passion in "Send in the Clowns," which is certainly Sondheim's best known song with probably his least understood lyric. Extracted from the play, the lyric and even the form make little sense.[6]

"Send in the Clowns" uses popular (and show) music's most common template—A1, A2, contrasting release, A3—used dozens of times by composers from Kern ("Can't Help Lovin' Dat Man"), through Rodgers ("The Lady Is a Tramp"), through Gershwin ("The Man I Love"), through Herman ("The Best of Times"), Lloyd-Webber ("I Don't Know How To Love Him"), and even Sondheim himself ("Being Alive," "Losing My Mind"). In the musical there is an A4 which comes after some bridging dialogue, and it serves rather as a reprise of the A3.

The song is beautifully put together. The motives of the A section and the release are different melodically, but Sondheim uses a clever device to move the listener smoothly from the A sections to the release. His singer finishes the A1 section one bar before the orchestra, and ends it on an incomplete dominant suspension. That urges us into the next section, and here the composer ends that section on a comfortable tonic (see motive A). But although, as I have said, the release is contrasting, its motive (see motive B) is practically the same as the comfortable ending of the A2—yet this "patch," sending us off into minor chords, begins the wonderful free-flowing, arching release.

Motive A

Motive B

[6] Barbra Streisand wanted to record "Send in the Clowns" for her Broadway album (released in 1985). In a telephone conversation she said to Sondheim, "I never understood the song. What would you think about writing a second bridge [release] that would kind of tell us more about this relationship?" Sondheim wrote a second release that was placed after the A3, and apart from the show, in that version the song stands more squarely and clearly on its own.

Fredrik's speech, which leads into the song, talks about why he came to the weekend in the country:

> When my eyes are open and I look at you, I see a woman that I have loved for a long time, who entranced me all over again when I came to her rooms. . . . But when my eyes are not open—which is most of the time—all I see is a girl in a pink dress teasing a canary, running through a sunlit garden to hug me at the gate, as if I'd come from Timbuctu instead of the Municipal Courthouse three blocks away.

Sondheim thought that speech would lead into a song from Fredrik and had even started one. Hal Prince felt the response should come from Désirée. "While I was writing it, I figured it would be the man's song because the impulse for the scene, the impulse for the singing was the man's as far as I was concerned. But Hal directed the scene in such a way that the impulse became the woman's."

Désirée's sung response to Fredrik's speech of rejection is both clever and heartbreaking, all the more so because of the sand-papered voice of Glynis Johns, the original Désirée, which was not large, but wonderfully expressive. With its short, breathy phrases, the song was not difficult for her to sing, and placed where it is, it becomes in fact the emotional highpoint of the musical. Here Sondheim forgets to be tricky or to indulge in pastiche, often his barrier when the emotional waters run deep.

The reference to sending in the clowns is an in joke, a phrase that was coined by circus folk (and adopted by theatrical ones) as a cure for the dire circumstances when things were getting too theatrical or too maudlin—mostly, when the audience was getting fidgety. In showbiz, this is the long overdue cue that a change of pace is needed. In the play, we have just witnessed Countess Charlotte playing the theatrical charade of throwing herself at Fredrik, as well as an "over-the-top" performance by his son, Henrik, climaxing when he smashes a champagne glass. The moment is heavy and propitious.

Now, after Fredrik's confession, Désirée can look at herself and sing about being anchored to the ground while describing her love's fascination with Anne as his being still aloft. Later she adds to her evaluation that they are in mid-farce when she compares them to lovers, one of whom is frantic, the other, frozen.

Sondheim learned from Hammerstein that the bridge must take a different, often the opposite, track, and here he narrows his canvas to describe only the feelings of the actress: No longer hysterical, at the peak of her career, in this section Désirée faces the ultimate theatrical nightmare—playing to an empty house.

As Fredrik rises and prepares to leave her, she begins to apologize, but she quickly sizes up the situation for the farce it is and instead of asking again for clown relief, she realizes that she and Fredrik are the real buffoons.

The song is essentially over, but after Fredrik walks out, Désirée does not go to pieces but sings to herself a reprise of the A section as she queries why she lost her timing this late in her career. Then, looking candidly at the situation, she ends on a quixotic note, a hope that things will be better next season or next year.[7]

"Send in the Clowns" was written a few days before the company went off to Boston for the first previews, and Sondheim played it for Prince on the eve of the preview for the actors—what is called the "gypsy run-through." After Prince approved the song, Sondheim played it for Glynis Johns, who was enchanted by it and asked if she could sing it for the assembled actors, who would certainly have no trouble understanding the song's lyrical allusions.

There are three other gems in *Night Music*'s remarkable score that must not be overlooked. The first is indicative of the composer's philosophy and the second of his development. By this time in his career Sondheim, in his mid-forties, had cast off most of Oscar Hammerstein's optimism, a philosophy that could create "Oh, What A Beautiful Mornin'," and exchanged it for one that would be able to beget "Every Day a Little Death" even in his sunniest, most sanguine operetta.

The song is first sung by Charlotte, Carl-Magnus's wife, who has gone to Anne to inform her of Fredrik's dalliance with Désirée. Eventually she convinces the young bride of how love can be a stinging, demeaning business, and Anne joins her in a canonic counterpoint. In the course of the number we glimpse an ideology that first appeared in *Company*—the erosion of feelings over time.

This continuing outlook, unfortunately only too often true, that increasing familiarity will only lead to a destructive situation will be further explored in forthcoming shows, notably *Sweeney Todd, Sunday in the Park with George*, and *Merrily We Roll Along*. In the last, one of Sondheim's best and most extractable songs contains the nihilistic line, "and while it's going along, you take for granted some love may wear away."

The other number, "A Weekend in the Country," the one that shows a Sondheim in a remarkable creative step forward, occurs at the end of Act One. In his autobiography, Prince describes its genesis:

---

[7] Sondheim inserted three dots after the word "year." Although they cannot be heard, they certainly help the singer project Désirée's perpetual optimism, a sanguine "more to come" attitude.

The final scene in Act I was a sequence for the entire company, to be musicalized, a miniopera. I got tired of waiting and one day with some ad lib from Hugh, I began to move the actors around: "You go here and you hand this person an invitation and you say, "Look what happened. We've been invited to a weekend at the Armfeldts' in the country." And you say "Well, I don't want to go," and you say "Oh, please," and you say, "Well, I'll reconsider," and so on.

I took the company through these little scenes, perhaps six of them. Each time I came to the end of one, I would say, "Now you sing" or "You two sing" or "All four of you sing." And catching the spirit, with vocalizing and appropriate gestures, they make a mock opera of it. Simultaneously I choreographed the birch trees to go with the scene changes and dialogue.

I invited Steve to see what we'd done and he went home that night and wrote a fifteen-minute sequence so specifically that Pat Birch was able to choreograph the company without altering the blocking.

Sondheim finds Prince's account of the creation of this sextet a bit simplistic and denies that he wrote this fifteen-minute, through-sung finale to specification. ("I look back at my notes," he maintains, "and in my first routining of the show, long before we went into rehearsal, I have something at the end of the first act called "Invitation Song.")

But in writing this extended finale to the act he moved the musical theater a step further into its alignment with opera—*opéra buffo*, to be sure, but nevertheless suitable for that grander venue. Still this finale keeps its other foot in the land of operetta, where a concerted number is obligatory prior to the intermission.

This writer disagrees with those theatergoers who have often called *Night Music*'s first act curtain a twin to Hammerstein's extended "Bench Scene," which carries the action forward in *Carousel*. In my mind this bright finale, which begins small and gradually adds voices to build up to a considerable climax replete with auto horns and movement, bears a closer resemblance to the way the curtain descends on the first act of *Show Boat*. By this time all the pieces are set into place. Magnolia and Gaylord are united. Everything seems logically tied up. Only the dread of the second act—in *Show Boat*, Gay's gambling; in *Night Music*, Fredrik's indecision—will follow. But we know true love will out, for this is operettaland. Désirée and Fredrik are just as sure to be united at the lowering of the second act curtain as Magnolia and Gaylord were.

Perhaps he was saving his tour de force for last, but the "eleven o'clock number" is often credited as one of the most brilliant of his entire oeuvre. It comes in just after Anne and Henrik have found out they love each other and as the plot is beginning to resolve itself. In her song, "The Miller's Son," Petra, the servant girl, outlines her philosophy of living sexually in the present, fantasizing about marrying a wealthy business man or even the Prince of Wales. As she outlines her invention, she tells us that once a week she and her mate will go dancing. When she comes to her ultimate illusion, a wedding with royalty, Sondheim magically transforms the line from "we'll go dancing" to "we'll *have* dancing." If she must return eventually to her own class and marry the miller's son—as she tells us at the song's conclusion—life and lust will not have passed her by. In that she seems far wiser than her effete masters crudely playing at the "game of love."

On the whole, in this, Sondheim's most luminous score, he seems to have come into his element. Permitted for the first time to deal with characters from the upper reaches of society, he revels in the opportunity to use these individuals' extensive vocabulary, which he couples with his own fanciful sense of rhyme. And for the star, Désirée, and most of the others, the images here are "pure theater" as distinguished from the show business facsimiles he was dealing with in *Follies*.

Always within character, none of his sometimes far-fetched but rarely forced rhymes seems inappropriate. He even shows off a bit, finding rhymes for a rhymeless word like "moustache" in "You Must Meet My Wife." When Fredrik, besotted with his virgin bride, recounts to Désirée how his bride caters to and dotes on him, Sondheim writes it into the comic number, pairing "moustache" with "just ash." He pulls off a tour de force by rhyming "cigar butt" with "Bizarre, but."

One should not leave any discussion of *A Little Night Music* without mentioning the considerable contribution of Jonathan Tunick's orchestration to this unique score. Although when Sondheim plays through his piano-vocal score for his orchestrator he often indicates what instruments he is hearing, he leaves the major choices up to his orchestrator. He will not tell him, "I need four cellos here," or, "this should be taken by the bassoon." According to Sondheim, sometimes he'll say, "I hear this. Is that a good idea? And [the orchestrator will] say 'yes' or 'no.' It doesn't happen often, but it does happen. I remember particularly the score of *Stavisky*, in which I heard the airplane cues done entirely on strings, and Jonathan said, 'Yes, it's a good idea' and it sounded terrible. And I said, 'Why did you listen to me?' And he said, 'There weren't enough strings in the orchestra. Had there been, it would have sounded good.'" Before Tunick tackled *Night Music*'s orchestration Sondheim told him, "This score should sound like perfume."

And it does.

A Little Night Music opened on February 25, 1973, with a cast that in addition to Glynis Johns included Len Cariou as Fredrik, Laurence Guitard as Carl-Magnus, and Hermione Gingold as Mme. Armfeldt. Sondheim's score and Boris

Aronson's stage of tall white birch trees that moved in and around the stage received almost unanimously glowing reviews, with the few naysayers faulting the libretto.

"The triumph of Bergman's film," wrote Jack Kroll in *Newsweek*, "was that it set up among all these characters crystalline conjugations of libido and love as complex and alive as a DNA molecule. . . . But the show has a period flavor that swaddles rather than releases its energy." John Simon, writing in *New York*, was far more brutal, calling Mr. Wheeler "the archetypal hack." Comparing Wheeler's characters to Bergman's he goes on:

> All of Bergman's complex characters are simplified down to monochromes and flattened out into drugstore cutouts. The Count, a Byronic Don Juan, becomes a blustering boob whose stupidity elicits gales of unearned onstage laughter; the Countess, a touching, because wounded, schemer, who sometimes involuntarily reveals the pain beneath her glitter, becomes a typical uneasy, neglected wife; lawyer Egerman, a delightfully sophisticated and ever so slightly fatuous bon vivant, becomes a rather plodding Midwestern would-be philanderer; his exquisite child-wife Anne becomes a somewhat overgrown vapid drum majorette, and so forth.

But Simon joined most of the others in saying, "Sondheim has composed, to his customary polished, easefully and richly rhyming lyrics, some of his best tunes so far. . . . [He has] laced their carefree forthrightness with daring little twists in the melodic line; unexpected wry modulations, deliberately wrong notes, a fine gray overcast on the sunniness."

Douglas Watt of the *Daily News* best put his finger on the little that ails the show when he wrote, "Exquisiteness is so much the concern of *A Little Night Music* . . . that there is little room for the breath of life. . . . It reveals the work of superior theatrical craftsmanship. But stunning as it is to gaze upon, and as clever as its score is with the use of trio and ensemble singing, it remains too literary and precious a work to stir the emotions." His co-critic on the same paper, Bob Sylvester, was harder: "The music for this epic is by this year's hallowed Stephen Sondheim, who can do nothing wrong for the cult. I found Mr. Sondheim's music interminable and ditto for the entire show."

But the *Times* critic, Clive Barnes, called it "heady, civilized, sophisticated and enchanting" for a start and then pulled out even more superlatives. "It is Dom Perignon. It is supper at Lasserre. It is a mixture of Cole Porter, Gustav Mahler, Anthony Tudor and just a little Ingmar Bergman," he added. His colleague Walter Kerr, writing the Sunday column in the same paper, obliterated any further carping when he called the score "a gift," found the ladies delightful, and raved about Prince's staging.

A Little Night Music won both the Drama Critics' and Tony Awards as the year's best musical. Sondheim won another Tony for music and lyrics; Hugh Wheeler won for best book; Florence Klotz won for best costumes. Glynis John and Patricia Elliott (Countess Charlotte) won Best Actress in a Musical and Best Supporting Actress in a Musical, and the box office boomed. Having a smallish cast, the musical was able to pay off its investment within six months, and for the rest of its six hundred performances on Broadway was into profit.

In the decades since its opening, *Night Music* has never been off the boards for any length of time. The Broadway production spawned a touring company, and then Hal Prince successfully produced it in London with Jean Simmons in the role of Désirée, Joss Ackland as Fredrik, and David Kernan as Carl-Magnus. Thomas Shepard, who has recorded most of Sondheim's major work, repeated his original craftsmanship and produced a superb British album.

In 1976 Hal Prince directed a movie version of the musical, moving the locale to Vienna. The film emerged looking less like a Prince–Sondheim creation than an anachronistic paraphrase of *The Student Prince*, and it was touch-and-go finding U.S. release. Sondheim himself called the film "ghastly." Elizabeth Taylor, blowsy and Rubenesque, impersonated Désirée, and Diana Rigg was trapped in the role of the Countess. Three of the best songs, "The Glamorous Life," "Liaisons," and "The Miller's Son," were dropped, and the show's theme, a *valse triste*, "The Sun Won't Set," whose lyric mentions how Swedish summer days tend to last until midnight, would obviously not work with that Austrian backdrop. In a rare condescension to popular taste, Sondheim changed its lyric to "Love Takes Time."

Movie musicals had, by this time, moved on to more popular rock forms like *Saturday Night Fever*, so *A Little Night Music* seemed quaint and precious. Hal Prince's stodgy and stagy direction made it seem static as well.

But *A Little Night Music*, the musical, keeps marching along as a perennial and has had many revivals, most notably the lovely one at the New York City Opera starring Sally Ann Howes, of whose performance Sondheim said, "You *are* Désirée" (this writer concurs), and one at Britain's National Theatre in 1995.[8] The show, one of Sondheim's most felicitous and frequently performed, along with *Company* and *Forum*[9] has become a classic and been produced all over the world, so that by now audiences who would formerly wait for *Send in the Clowns* might come out whistling *A Weekend in the Country* or *The Miller's Son*.

[8] The "all-star" British production at the National Theatre in 1995 starred Dame Judi Dench as Désirée, Sian Phillips as Madame Armfeldt, and Patricia Hodge as Countess Charlotte. "My Husband the Pig," cut from the Broadway version, was reinstated to give Hodge a solo, and Laurence Guitard, who created the role of Count Carl-Magnus in New York, was moved up to the leading role of Fredrik. So successful was it that the National, a repertory company, scheduled the production for an unprecedented eight performances per week in the summer of 1996.

[9] According to Sondheim, *Into the Woods* is his most popular show.

A *Little Night Music* was not truly innovative, but because it was so cleverly staged and so carefully crafted, it seemed to be miles ahead of its Broadway competitors of 1973 and the recent past. Musicalizations of warhorses like *Cyrano*; popular successes from an earlier decade like *Raisin in the Sun* and *Two for the Seesaw*; revivals of *Irene*, *Where's Charley?*, *Gypsy*, or *Good News*; songbooks based on the works of Noël Coward, Sammy Cahn, Kurt Weill, or Ogden Nash seemed to be the best that Broadway could muster. In this welter of mediocrity and déjà vu, *Night Music*'s gold lit up Broadway.

But the street wasn't totally dead. Here and there one could spot attempts to break through, ideas waiting to be born, like the brilliant staging Hal Prince would show was possible in his 1974 revival of the Lillian Hellman–Leonard Bernstein *Candide*. He had commissioned a new book from Hugh Wheeler, new lyrics from Stephen Sondheim, cut down the orchestra, and let the action explode in various parts of the Broadway Theater. It was more a happening than a musical, but it contrived to resurrect Bernstein's remarkable score of 1956 and let it speak to a new audience.

Prince's production also let theater owners know that their prosceniums, and their very walls, were not sacrosanct or safe from his idea of total theater. His daring and belief in his work paved the way for audacious "happenings" of the '80s and '90s that were to go far beyond revolving stages or the runway into the audience he would be using in *Pacific Overtures*. Although it looked like what Sondheim calls "a free-for-all," it was—as all of this director's work—carefully planned. Other directors took up his torch, usually with less imagination and success, and so the Prince esthetic where "anything goes" would have to lie fallow for a while.

In 1975, the all-black version of *The Wizard of Oz*, called *The Wiz*, whose music contained elements of soul and rock, endeared it to audiences young and old, intellectual or naive, thus assuring it a long run—without costing a lot of money.

Shenandoah and *Chicago* are two of the very different musicals of 1975, neither great, but they must be mentioned for the way that each moved the form a notch further on its path toward the present. *Shenandoah* is the story of the Anderson family, who tried to stay clear of the Civil War. It is only when their youngest son is kidnapped by Union soldiers that the father gets fighting mad. Even though the show was indifferently produced and contained tepid songs, its pacifistic point of view, in keeping with the U.S. recent involvement with the unpopular Vietnam War, put it into the category of "a musical with a cause."

Kander and Ebb's *Chicago* was another story altogether. It boasted a rip-roaring score, highly amplified, and an unwholesome tale that purposely took no moral stand. In that attitude it was akin to *A Little Night Music*'s refusal to preach, perhaps even a harbinger of the Webber–Rice *Evita*. *Chicago* was based on a true story of two murderesses who are acquitted of their crimes and who form a successful nightclub act. Evoking the "roaring 20s" with transvestism, masochism, and blatant sexuality in the forefront, the show was so strongly reminiscent of *Cabaret* that it only needed a Hal Prince point of view to put it into its predecessor's league. But Prince, who had produced and directed *Cabaret* less than a decade before, had moved far beyond that kind of Bauhaus expressionism and, like Sondheim, never looked back.

No help from anyone was necessary when *A Chorus Line* debuted a month after *Chicago*. Originally mounted by the New York Shakespeare Festival in April 1975, it conquered Broadway, although it had only mild success in the West End. Its incredibly successful long run Broadway record of 6,137 performances in fifteen years was only broken in January 1996 by *Cats*.

It was a phenomenal success, one that is looked back upon today with love and nostalgia, and one muses on what made *A Chorus Line* so endurable. Certainly its triumph was due in part to composer Marvin Hamlisch's unique and moving score (Hamlisch has never risen above mediocrity in his later works, *They're Playing Our Song* or *Smile*), plus totally honest and, except for Sondheim's, the most literately moving lyrics ever heard on Broadway, by Edward Kleban. Then there was Michael Bennett's awesome choreography. But mostly it was the unusual "first person" point of view. The choreographer, a detached voice, seeming to emanate from somewhere in the audience itself, is selecting his chorus of eight from seventeen applicants. These hopefuls not only have to sing and dance for us, but each has to recite his or her history. In song or soliloquy we learn about their backgrounds—bickering parents, homosexuality, or frustration—as well as their resolve, beliefs, and hope. Every audience member, therefore, feels like he or she is taking part in the selecting process. This is the backstage musical that Rodgers and Hammerstein were looking for when they wrote *Me and Juliet*, for here is the ring of truth.

A Chorus Line opened on Broadway only a few months before Sondheim and Prince's next musical, the controversial *Pacific Overtures*. Prince was riding high, flush with success, and felt he could make almost anything work. In late 1974 he had been able to return their original investment to his *Night Music* angels plus a 10 percent profit. (Those who had been canny enough to invest in his two other great successes, *Cabaret* and *Fiddler on the Roof*, had received even bigger checks. *Cabaret* made a profit of $2,075,000 on an investment of half a million dollars, while *Fiddler* had made over nine million dollars on an investment of $375,000.)

Pacific Overtures came about when John Weidman[10] submitted an intriguing

---

[10] John Weidman was then a law student and a budding dramatist. Prince had produced Jerome Weidman's (his father's) libretto for *Fiorello* in 1959, which won the Pulitzer Prize.

script to the producer-director, and Prince, liking the play and its message, asked him to adapt it first into Kabuki style and then as a libretto of a musical. Eventually Hugh Wheeler came into the project, mostly working on dialogue. The libretto was aimed, according to Prince, to be done as if it were "written by a Japanese in that style, with the Americans the traditional Kabuki villains." At first Sondheim told Prince he thought *Pacific Overtures* should be a play with incidental music, but he was overruled. Prince became obsessed with this Kabuki odyssey, and he dragged his usual collaborators, "kicking and screaming," according to orchestrator Jonathan Tunick, into the project.

"We—Steve, Boris Aronson, me, everyone—didn't want to do a Japanese musical," Tunick continues. "We don't know anything about Japanese culture. Who are we to do this?" Although the cast was almost entirely Asian, Sondheim, along with Prince, had spent only two weeks in Japan trying to absorb the musical and theatrical innuendoes. But Prince's challenge was so powerful that it really brought out the best in all the collaborators, and if they didn't produce what this writer calls a work of art, they created an innovative musical. Because they had worked together for such a long time, Sondheim dedicated this score to Prince.

As it turned out, the musical used only the armature of *Kabuki* in its insistence on a mostly male cast, many of whom play the women's roles, a trio of musicians seated on one side of the stage accenting the action (yet with the balance of the orchestra in the pit), and a reciter narrating the story. But there are touches of *noh* in the use of masks, and the ramp known as a *hanamichi*, which is used by performers to enter from the auditorium, as well as *bunraku*, the Eastern puppet theater. Unfortunately these pure styles have been watered down with mixtures of vaudeville, agitprop, and the conventions of a Broadway musical.

The main story concerns Commodore Matthew Perry's 1853 uninvited visit to Japan to open up the country for trade with the West. Foreigners had been forbidden to come ashore on the islands for over two hundred years, but Perry anchored four threatening gunboats in the Tokyo harbor and proceeded to make—in his own words—"pacific overtures."

His diary recounts how he informed the shogun of President Millard Fillmore's resolve that if the Japanese did not accept these overtures he was prepared— again, Perry's own words—"to introduce them to Western Civilization by whatever means are necessary."

These "four black dragons" in the harbor gave Japan the dreadful shock that catapulted their feudal kingdom into the mid-nineteenth century. In working on the project, Sondheim says, "Hal was interested in dealing with ideas, but he and Weidman were more interested in dealing with character and the clash of two cultures."

Weidman's original play had a kind of scrapbook structure, and in the end

Sondheim in a pensive pose with the score of Pacific Overtures *(1976).* AP/Wide World
Photos.

Prince gave in and threaded the stories through these vignettes of history, certainly inserted for human interest, of the "Americanized" fisherman Manjiro,
who is caught fishing on the property of the shogun and relegated to the job of
sending the Americans away. While he is off in his boat, his grief-stricken wife,
fearing he will never return, commits hara-kiri. We are also given the tale of
the lowly samurai Kayama Monzaemon, who rises in stature together with Man-

jiro from dealing with the Americans. The fisherman becomes more traditionalist, while the samurai gets Westernized, soft and corrupted, and they end in fatal conflict like the heroes of a Kabuki drama.

There are others, hardly more than sketched in, like the story of the sailor who has been to Boston and knows the real barbarians are not the foreigners but the feudal lords who fear change will mean their loss of power.

The story is told as if by a radical Japanese theater group, with Asian actors in whiteface playing Western roles, and achieves what success it will eventually have in its early portions. Boris Aronson's delicate scenery evokes a floating world while Sondheim tells us that they are floating in the middle of the sea where realities remain remote. "Gods are crumbling somewhere, / Machines are rumbling somewhere, / Not here."

Then the mass of Perry's black ship with forward portholes gleaming like bloodshot eyes and its smokestack belching flames threatens them by anchoring in the harbor. *New York Post* art critic Emily Grenauer called the scene "an eye-filling adaptation of a famous wood-block print.[11]"

The Japanese are no match for Perry and, his technology, and eventually, although they resent the intruders, they are obliged to accept them. They invite the Americans to land on a strip of beach carpeted from the sea to the "treaty house," which they construct for the occasion—and will deconstruct once the intruders depart. Thus they can save face by saying that the barbarians, not having actually set foot on Japanese soil, could not have desecrated it, and pushing this logic a bit into abstract philosophy, that they were never really there.

In this work—especially in the first act, remote in time—Sondheim frequently uses the pentatonic scale, which is usually thought to have no basic tonality. But he senses and differentiates between the Japanese and Chinese pentatonics, saying, "The Chinese one has a minor modal feeling, and kept reminding me of de Falla, a composer I admire a lot. . . . Finding that, I was able to relate to it, because it had a Western feeling at the same time as having an Eastern one." One of Sondheim's favorites of all his theater music is the song "Someone in a Tree," which comes in a scene in which the reciter deplores the fact that there is no official Japanese account of what took place on that historic day. An old man who was on the beach when Perry landed remembers that meeting with the Emperor's emissaries behind tissue paper–thin walls in the treaty house and offers to give an eyewitness report. The old man says he saw it all by

---

[11] Aronson's settings and Florence Klotz's costumes full of demons and deities were the only Tony awards this show garnered. Klotz's contribution must, of course, be considered in the light of Hal Prince's decision that even the Americans like Perry would be wearing stylized dress—a sailor suit with kimono sleeves and floor-length white hair for his traditional "Lion's Dance."

Haruki Fujimoro as Commodore Perry performs the traditional Lion Dance in Pacific Overtures. *Photo: Van Williams. © Museum of the City of New York.*

climbing a tree and looking into the hut's open eaves. "I saw everything. I was younger then." Kabuki stylization comes to the rescue, and a younger performer takes his place and scales the tree for him. Then another eavesdropper tells how he slipped below the boards of the treaty house to listen. He too gets only snips and patches. Unfortunately nothing comes of the scene, although, like most on-the-spot reportage, it is interesting—almost maddeningly so—because of its complexity and length. But the terms of the truce remain unknown. The faults of the scene are basically the failings of the entire show: pattern without substance. Walter Kerr put his finger on what is wrong with *Pacific Overtures* when he wrote in the *New York Times* that "we are really only attending to the *manner* of doing things on a stage; matter is ill-defined or nonexistent."

The final scene of the play jumps to the present, which was then 1976, with the company shedding their obis and donning modern dress and sunglasses. They carry Sony transistor radios, flash cameras, and Seiko watches. These trinkets, of course, add up to their loss of identity. By the time we get deeply into the evils of Westernized Japan, Sondheim, Prince, and Weidman are up on their soapboxes.

The concept is simplistic, suggesting that the American opening of Japan led to the establishment of military power, organized defense, and eventually to World War II. However, the Weidman–Wheeler book never tackles those important tenets head on but plays around them. World War II is omitted; it is as if it never happened. The premise seems to be anti-American satire, seemingly saying that if we hadn't been such imperialists, Tokyo wouldn't be polluted today.

Writing in the *New Yorker*, Brendan Gill found the final scenes, culminating in an arch musical number called "Next," an about-face that didn't seem to fit in with the rest of the evening,

> a bitter indictment of contemporary Japanese life. And the burden of the indictment is that the Japanese have consented to become as dangerous to the world as we westerners, whom they first learned to imitate and then surpass, giving themselves up to the manufacture of cars, watches and silly plastic gadgets and to the pollution of the air, earth and water. A shocking show stopper, for which no foundation has been laid, and in which for only the second time all evening, Miss Birch [the choreographer] gets a chance to display her talents and, for the first time all evening, girls are welcomely present.

Pacific Overtures opened on January 11, 1976, to vociferously contrasting reviews. *Newsweek* gushed: "No other team in the American theater could have achieved this show's integration of elements, its harmony of form, color, sound and movement." Its competitor *Time* had its thumbs way down: "Prince and Sondheim's moonwalk musical . . . proves to be as arid and airless as the moon." *New York* critic Alan Rich wrote that the musical "stuns our senses and expands our theatrical horizons to a point just this side of infinity." Douglas Watts at the *Daily News* disliked it intensely and damned it by calling it "a pretty bore," while his confrere Richard Watts of the *New York Post* went further calling the show "an irritating bore."

Perhaps the most succinct critique was given by Edwin Wilson, writing in the *Wall Street Journal*:

The premise of *Pacific Overtures* is that a Japanese theatrical producer, a Nipponese Harold Prince, as it were, is presenting a Broadway musical in Kabuki fashion, but this is where Kipling's dictum comes to mind. Are we seeing a Japanese work through Mr. Prince's eyes, or are we seeing an American musical through the eyes of his imaginary Japanese counterpart? It cannot be both, though Mr. Prince seems to want it that way. Brecht understood this. When he incorporated oriental settings and techniques in his work, he still wrote from his own perspective."

With mostly negative critiques, *Pacific Overtures* was forced to close when its advance booking ran out and it had exhausted the considerable cult audience that Sondheim–Prince musicals had built up in New York by that time. In sum, for all its stylistic audacity, *Pacific Overtures* proved too alien for most audiences. Closing after having given fewer than two hundred performances and losing its entire investment, it comes near the bottom of the list of Sondheim musicals.

After three strikes (*Company, Follies,* and *Pacific Overtures*) and only one hit (*A Little Night Music*), Prince's situation was as dire as it had been after *Follies*. To make matters worse, he had invested some of his own money in *Overtures* because of the poor reception in its Boston previews. Hal Prince was to write: "The show lost me my shirt, but was something we were very proud of." *Pacific Overtures* has gone on to have many productions since its initial Broadway run. It was given a splendid off-Broadway revival in 1985 that brought out its tissue-paper origami qualities in an intimate venue. By contrast it had a production that was successful with critics and public by the English National Opera in London's cavernous Colosseum. In this vast auditorium, however, the words were incomprehensible and all delicacy of feeling was lost.

After *Pacific Overtures*, lest his stable of investors fall away or those remaining think *Night Music* was a fluke, Prince needed a genuine, mainstream hit. He found one in *On the Twentieth Century*, a show whose only message was to have a good time. With words by Betty Comden and Adolph Green and music by Cy Coleman, it was an adaptation of a 1932 farce set entirely aboard a coast-to-coast streamliner. The dazzling art déco train was designed in sections that enabled it to carry out Prince's wish for it to move electronically as part of the choreography, and the train became the star of the show.

Now it was time for Prince to move on. There were interesting things being created across the sea. Yes, Prince would return to work with Sondheim on two more shows, but now the Andrew Lloyd-Webber–Tim Rice team, back together again, had sent him some of the remarkable recordings they had made for their new opus—the saga of Argentine heroine-monster Eva Peron. He would not let it slip through his fingers as he had *Jesus Christ Superstar*. "Evita," he told Carol Ilson, "is the beneficiary of *Pacific Overtures*. Neither is lineally constructed."

Prince admitted he was "boring" in the latter. "With *Evita*, I knew how to stop and move at the right place and get the rhythm right."

And with his next show, he would not only get the "rhythm right," for here he would be operating at his most theatrical, but he would also make heaps of money.

A Rainbow Goddess

ARLY IN THE MORNING after the debacle of *Jeeves*, Andrew Lloyd-
Webber received a telephone call from his mother. She was the first to
offer words of solace. "It wasn't *that* bad," Jean's perky voice chirped across
the wire. But Andrew knew it was. He suddenly understood that the way *Jeeves*
had been cobbled together with dialogue, jokes, and songs had spelled its doom.
With the fall of *Jeeves*, the success of his next project became that much more
important.

The chastened composer returned to Tim Rice, the collaborator he knew.
"We have got to get down to writing again," he told a reporter, adding somewhat
facetiously, "even if what we write never sees the light of day . . . We had a very
intense period of working together—and then it all happened [two enormous
hit shows] and we allowed people to come between us. It's ridiculous. Tim and
I are very close, actually."

Carrying out his resolve, he asked Rice to prepare an outline of the history
of Eva Peron, the project he had been so excited about for so long. His partner
gave him the following "obituary":

Buenos Aires, July 26, 1952: "OUR SPIRITUAL LEADER IS GONE!" Those words broadcast at 9:42 tonight told the Argentineans that Eva Peron, their little Evita, was
dead. The next morning the headlines screamed the details of how the President's
wife succumbed to ovarian cancer at age 33.

While the "descamisados," the "shirtless" poor of Argentina prepare for a month
of mourning, a few members of the middle class and the opposition prepare to
breathe a sigh of relief. Eva Peron was a charismatic woman, certainly more popular
than her husband, Juan Peron. She was also on occasion ruthless.

Born Maria Eva Ibagueren at Los Toldos, she was the illegitimate daughter of a
cook. When Colonel Peron met her she was a budding fifteen-year-old singer and
actress. He made her his mistress, not an unusual thing for the Secretary of Labor

to do. Especially since this Secretary of Labor had a notorious penchant for pubescent girls.

In October 1945, when Peron was arrested on a treason charge, Eva took to the airwaves, beseeching the masses to rally and free him. Panicky higher-ups in what was already a corrupt government let him go, and in gratitude for her pleas to the people, two months later Peron married her. When he was installed in the Presidential Palace, a year later, Evita was by his side.

Eva championed women, labor, and the poor. She got women the vote and legalized divorce. But *she* was the number one woman in her canon and amassed a tremendous collection of jewels and furs. Some of her unscrupulous acts were simply petty, yet she was quick to anger and when anyone challenged her or the Peron regime reprisal came swiftly. She shut down opposing newspapers, and filled the jail in Buenos Aires with those who offered the slightest offense. She professed admiration for Adolf Hitler and Benito Mussolini and levied a charity tax that found its way into her private Swiss bank account.

As the years went by, "disappearances" and cases of torture multiplied. From her vantage point as Minister of Health *and* Minister of Labor she had a finger in every Argentinean pie. In the summer of 1951 she proposed to fortify her position by running for Vice President, but when the army objected she renounced her intentions. She did not try to overturn their decision, for she alone knew that she was already riddled with the cancer that would kill her.

As Andrew Lloyd-Webber read more about this Argentinean spitfire he found himself warming to the idea.[1] Soon he and Tim Rice decided that they would follow the same pattern that had served them so well in *Joseph* and *Superstar*. Get the concept and write a rough draft of the story, leading to ideas that would give the musical its high points. Then he would compose the music and Rice would set his melodies with lyrics. Last of all would come the recitatives, providing a through-sung, seamless work. They would then go about casting the main singers, and finally, as before, make a full recording of their opera. In contrast to *Joseph* and *Superstar* this work would be written so it *could* be transferred to the stage. This time Lloyd-Webber even planned to do all the orchestrations.

In retrospect, from the vantage point of more than two decades, the method and planning sound elementary and give no idea of the fire that Lloyd-Webber caught from Rice. The failure of *Jeeves* had convinced the composer that a musical must be "all of one piece." He sensed more than he had ever felt with *Joseph* or *Superstar* that the songs needed to be far more than interludes—they

---

[1] Rice was not the first to think Evita's story would make a good libretto for an opera. According to Joan Peyser's biography, in the early '70s, while his wife Felicia was still living, Leonard Bernstein showed some of his colleagues a libretto for a show based on Evita Peron that he was thinking of treating. He said he saw things in common between his own wife and the dictator's consort who had been so effective in her political efforts on his behalf. But conducting and other compositional duties took precedence, and Bernstein never took the project any further. By the time Felicia Bernstein died (of cancer as had Evita) in 1978, the Rice-Webber *Evita* was ready to open.

must carry the story forward. Lloyd-Webber's zeal coupled with Tim Rice's obvious passion, inspired the team to produce their finest theater work thus far. *Evita* as the recording quickly revealed, was no ad hoc affair like *Superstar*, which evolved as it went along. When it was released it had more than the feeling of a double rock album. It was an oratorio, one the collaborators pretentiously called an opera, conceived directly for disc.

When Lloyd-Webber spoke to a seminar at the Dramatists Guild he recalled the political forces in his country that had impelled him to take on the story of a dictator of a country in another hemisphere. Both he and Rice found great relevance in the shaky Argentinean economy to that of their own country and felt the form of a serious musical—the form it had been proven they knew how to write—was needed to make a statement to the world. He recalled in an interview given to the *London Evening Standard*.

> Nineteen seventy-four and five was a very bumpy time in England, particularly because we had an elected government basically overthrown by the trade unions. There was serious talk of private armies, and people were really thinking that the country was going to nothing. In fact there was a point at which one of the major banks was about to default. We kept seeing parallels in the story of an attractive extremist and pointing out how very dangerous an attractive extremist could be. We made quite a lot in the show of the shutting down of *La Prensa*, a liberal newspaper like the London or New York *Times*. We were writing a cautionary tale of our time. A lot of artists thought very deeply about the questions we were raising in the piece.

But *Evita* had to be more than a piece of political propaganda or a retelling of the rise of cruel dictators. In order to achieve that it would need a naysayer, a sardonic commentator—the same Everyman (Judas) that had served Tim so well in *Superstar*. Tim needed an observer, a narrator, at times simply a device to place Eva in a situation where she is confronted with direct personal criticism. This time he chose a character he called simply "Che."[2]

Eva Peron and Che Guevara may never have met, but their pairing on stage was no accident. It was a Stoppard-like inspiration. Guevara was Argentine born in 1928 and would therefore have been seventeen when the Perons came to power. Even as a very young man he was strongly opposed to the Peronist regime during Eva's lifetime, and it is not unreasonable to suppose that his later activity in Cuba and elsewhere was in part a reaction against the government he had known in his youth.

With the major characters Eva, Peron, and Che in place, Rice was able to

---

[2] Rice gave him no surname, but when Hal Prince came into the project he insisted his singing-actors model themselves as closely as possible on Ernesto "Che" Guevara.

tackle the scenario, which hewed closely to Evita's life. It began dramatically in a cinema in Buenos Aires (in both the London and New York productions, a clip from one of Eva Peron's own movies was used). The movie grinds to a halt, and protestors to the interruption of the show are awestricken when a voice announces the death of Evita.

A requiem, more like a lamentation, is then interspersed with Che's caustic comments, made doubly effective by the diametrically reversed musical styles. The chorus in four-part ecclesiastical obeisance is juxtaposed with Che, who sings a driving, decibel-breaking hard rock.

...Instead of government we had a stage	Sing you fools? But you got it wrong
Instead of ideas a prima donna's rage	Enjoy your prayers because you haven't got
Instead of help we were given a crowd	long
She didn't say much but she said it loud...	Your queen is dead, your king is through
	She's not coming back to you.

A flashback then reverts to 1934, where the third-rate tango singer Augustin Magaldi is holding forth. A teenage Eva, who has somewhat brightened up his act, wants him to take her with him to the capital city. She sings her own rock number, whose chorus repeats, "I want to be a part of B.A.—Buenos Aires— Big Apple." Ruthless from the start, she gets her family to blackmail Magaldi and take her along.

Once there, she goes through a series of lovers, and eventually the young actress, now a radio personality, meets Peron. Again with astonishing candor, singing "I'd Be Surprisingly Good for You," she takes over the reins of the relationship and casts out his present mistress. The deposed sweetheart is given one of the best songs in the show, however ("Another Suitcase in Another Hall"), and Evita moves in for good.

Together with Peron, in spite of objections from "The Aristocrats," who sing "We have allowed ourselves to slip / We have completely lost our grip / We have declined to an all time low / Tarts have become the set to know," and "The Army," who counter with "The evidence suggests / She has other interests / If it's her who's using him / He's exceptionally dim / Bitch! Dangerous Jade!," they rise to the top. To the theme of Evita's running the show, "I'd Be Surprisingly Good for You," she retaliates:

It doesn't matter what those morons say	Keeping out of everybody's way
Our nation's leaders are a feeble crew	We'll—you'll be handed power on a plate
There's only twenty of them anyway	When the ones who matter have their say.
What is twenty next to millions who	And with chaos installed
Are looking to you?	You can reluctantly agree to be called.
All you have to do is sit and wait	

Peron, who by this time has stolen enough, wants to leave and retire with their riches in Paraguay, but Evita is made of sterner stuff, and she urges him to stay on and run for president. Lloyd-Webber and Rice created a grandiose martial hymn, "A New Argentina," that would sweep anyone into office. During its singing the chanting of Evita's name gradually eclipses that of Peron. Now, from the balcony of the Presidential Palace, the Casa Rosado, they make their first public appearance after their triumphant victory. Peron appears first and gives the people the same tired political clichés, but soon Evita appears and sings her stunner, "Don't Cry for Me Argentina,"[3] which closes the first half of the recording.[4]

Rice tried to create interest, but in the second half, the pettiness and eventual decline of the dictators had to be a letdown. After a short ride on the crest ("High Flying, Adored" and "Rainbow High"), during which Evita tries unsuccessfully to woo all of Europe, she returns home a little less successful than when she set out. To compensate she establishes the charitable organizations but soon begins to skim money from them—"The Money Keeps Rolling In (and Out)." Che keeps interrupting more now as the people, especially the children, increasingly become duped by Evita. He sneers at those who adore her and openly questions her about her motivations. She realizes that she is ill but keeps the news to herself.

Along with the anti-Eva feeling growing in the military comes Peron's realization that he is losing his grip on the government. Evita, however, refuses to give in and resolves to become vice president. Rice wrote a classical sonnet[5] that Lloyd-Webber set to music to enforce her resolve, but opposition from the army is too great and more importantly her body can no longer be relied upon. Knowing she is dying, she makes a final broadcast to the nation—saving face, for it is a position she knows she could never have won.

Now comes a montage: fragments of her life flow through her consciousness, including the army officers, Che, Magaldi, Peron. Finally, reprising the melodic line of "Don't Cry for Me Argentina" with perhaps Rice's finest lyric (again, cut down when it was staged), she sings about her youth and her options:

---

[3] Although British books and newspapers often add a grammatically correct comma between "Me" and "Argentina," Rice never used it. As a lyricist, he plays fast and loose with the usual laws of punctuation.

[4] In the staging, Hal Prince wisely decided to have the act break after "A New Argentina" and to use the scene with the Perons on the balcony of the Casa Rosado that climaxes in "Don't Cry for Me Argentina" to open Act Two.

[5] Again, Prince's sense of theater saved the day when he cut down the fourteen-line political harangue, retaining only the sonnet's final sextet.

The choice was mine and mine completely
I could have any prize that I desired
I could burn with the splendor of the brightest
    fire
Or else—or else I could choose time.
Remember I was very young then
And a year was forever and a day

So what use could fifty, sixty, seventy be?
I saw the light and I was on my way.
And how I loved! How I shone!
But soon the lights were gone!
Oh my daughter! Oh my son!
Understand what I have done!

Long before the script was completed, Lloyd-Webber and Rice tackled that all-important main song. After *Jeeves*, Hal Prince had suggested that Andrew "bank" the score and move on. Searching in his "bank," Lloyd-Webber found several moving melodies that had been used unsuccessfully before. Topping them all was the single "Down Thru' Summer," which they had written at the start of their collaboration for Ross Hannaman, the *Evening Standard*'s "Girl of the Year." While he was in Bristol, waiting for the first performance of the tour of *Jeeves*, Andrew remembered "playing around, developing the melody and getting a lot of it right."

Later, when the first recordings of *Evita* were planned, they hired Julie Covington, a singer with a big voice, who earlier in the year had appeared on the TV show, *Rock Follies*. Rice wrote a new lyric for the soaring main strain of the melody:

It's only your lover returning.
The truth is I never left you,
All through my wild days,

My mad existence
I kept my promise
Don't keep your distance.

The song, passing as "It's Only Your Lover Returning," was not to have its now world-famous title of "Don't Cry for Me Argentina" until the entire double album had been recorded. It was only when they listened to the playback that they noticed the opening line of that chorus—"It's only your lover returning"—while making good sense and seeming to sing well wasn't truly memorable. The melody stuck, but the lyric lacked what songwriters call the hook. And they were depending on that song to climb up the charts and pull the balance of the album with it.

The song had been recorded at an early session, and Tim Rice recalled that they were almost on the last session while he was pressing Lloyd-Webber to agree on one of several titles. "Oh, look," Rice said, "stick it in as 'Don't Cry for Me Argentina' [which had been used in the funeral scene, when the opera began]. It sounds nice and we'll alter it later for the stage show." Julie Covington was called back into the studio. "She sang the line over," Andrew added, "and we dubbed it onto the track."

The ballad, more like an operatic *scena* rather than an aria, became one of the biggest hits in all songdom. In the two years between the release of the album and the stage show, more than ninety versions, from brass bands to Greek accordion ensembles, surfaced. Yet it almost defies pigeonholing except in the serious realm of opera. "Don't Cry for Me Argentina" divides into a recitative, a refrain, and coda. Its recitative is built on many of the same harmonies as Bach's first prelude from *The Well-Tempered Clavier*—the one that Charles Gounod used to counterpoint his famous melody of the "Ave Maria." But this recitative, unlike Gounod's impassioned melodic line, stays within a limited, almost parlando range and is further anchored by a long pedal point. When the main soaring, expansive melody, a song that is easily sung and remembered, hits us after this quiescence, it is more than a relief. It is a gorgeous melody to wallow in.

This short strain, which Lloyd-Webber marks as "Slow Tango Feel," is one of his finest. Written in his favorite lyrical key, D-flat, it is as rangy as the recitative is static and begins with a splendid motive whose appoggiatura (see Glossary) gives it an added kick (Example A). This is succeeded by two short sequences (Example B) and a pair of balancing phrases (Example C) to close up the section.

Example A

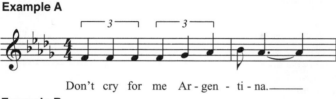

Don't cry for me Ar - gen - ti - na._____

Example B

All through my wild days, my mad ex - ist-ence,

Example C

I kept my pro-mise. Don't keep your dis-tance.

Then the recitative and the cantabile return. After several repeats, the *scena* ends with a quiet and tentative coda, a dead ringer for the couplet Mimi sings in *La Bohème* when she apologizes for importuning on her neighbor. Here Evita asks the hushed crowd:

Have I said too much? There is nothing more I can think of to say to you.

But all you have to do is look at me to know that every word is true.

But a song is a combination of music and lyrics, and popular appeal often lies, as we have seen with "Send in the Clowns," in the mystique of a literary phrase. Certainly "Don't Cry for Me Argentina" is intriguing, but Rice's lyric offers us much more. Just as Sondheim's song, replete with stage images, makes us empathize with the irony of lovers who miss the trapeze when it is thrown at them, so Rice's lyric, as the verses below attest, allows the woman who wants the whole country to love her to speak from the heart. In truth the songwriters *have* to give us more, because they are working only with sound, whereas Sondheim, whose very being is instilled with theater, has those images to play with. Evita's words seem to hide nothing; she is enlisting the crowd as confidantes while recounting her rise from poverty. And in doing so, the moment becomes the capstone of the show.

Yes, one can carp about the forced artiness of a Briticism like "a woman dressed up to the nines, at sixes and sevens with you," or "staying down at heel." And Evita's final lines in this recitative—"the answer was here all the time"— smack more of Dorothy in *The Wizard of Oz* than they do of the late 1970s. Yet if the entire project was criticized for extolling a monster, a fraud, is it not that this lyric is so honest that coupled with its music and a superb performance by Elaine Paige, Susannah Fellowes, or Patti LuPone, or those Evitas who came after, it could even melt the most anti-Fascistic heart?

It won't be easy, you'll think it strange
When I try to explain how I feel,
That I still need your love after all that I've
    done.
You won't believe me,
All you will see is a girl you once knew,
Although she's dressed up to the nines,
At sixes and sevens with you.

I had to let it happen, I had to change
Couldn't stay all my life down at heel
Looking out of the window, staying out of the
    sun
So I chose freedom
Running around trying everything new—
But nothing impressed me at all.
I never expected it to.

(Don't Cry for Me Argentina, etc.)

And as for fortune, and as for fame
I never invited them in,
Though it seemed to the world they were all I
    desired.
They are illusions,
They are not the solutions they promised to
    be.
The answer was here all the time.
I love you and hope you love me.

(Repeat chorus)

"Don't Cry for Me Argentina," like all the other songs in the score, provided Lloyd-Webber with the opportunity to write for his heroine's public and private personality. "Eva Peron's public utterances range from the rabble-rousing extremist to the slightly cynical use of sentimentality," Andrew explained. "Thus it is possible to set up a straightforwardly romantic tune in a dramatic context." Creating music for Evita's "two sides" gave Andrew the opportunity to exercise a wider palette than ever before in his score. "From then on, I looked for the 'highs' and 'lows' in the story that would work dramatically and musically."

Nor was he intimidated as to the difficulty of his melodic line. Throughout the music one finds bars of varying meters, abrupt key changes, pitches that demand chest tones in the upper tessitura. According to Susannah Fellowes, who sang the role as an alternate with Elaine Paige in London, "It was really an exhausting but rewarding part. The score is complicated. The time signatures are constantly changing. And *Evita* included a lot of extraordinary things where you'll sort of pick a note out of thin air. He'll finish a phrase and you have to start vocally in a completely different arena." Comparing the difficulty of singing a major Sondheim score to one of Lloyd-Webber's, Fellowes, who has sung both, felt that their musical partitions were equally complicated. "Andrew's just doesn't sound it," she concluded.

But, if Lloyd-Webber let go in writing a complicated score, he did not consider the difficulties insurmountable because he felt "there are now more rock singers who can handle complex music, so the melodic line can be far more adventurous."

Rice too could be more expressive of his personality and less concerned with rhyme and evenness of his scanning than he had ever been before. He knew Lloyd-Webber was capable of stretching a musical phrase to accommodate any number of syllables he needed to express his thought. Although they still followed their usual format, with Andrew writing the music first, there were times now when Andrew would set Tim's words.

With this new-found freedom Tim Rice could write as the existentialist he was at heart. One of the tenets he espoused was that lovers use each other. At one point he has his principals sing what he believes in:

There is no one, no one at all
Never has been and never will be a lover
Male or female
Who hasn't an eye on
In fact they rely on
Tricks they can try on

Their partner
They're hoping their lover will help them or
    keep them
Support them, promote them
Don't blame them, you're all the same.

Casting Paul Jones as Peron and Colm Wilkinson (who would later cause a sensation as Jean Valjean in *Les Misérables*) as Che, Andrew and conductor Anthony Bowles coached their singers through the latter half of 1975 and all of 1976. Now, with the full London Philharmonic Orchestra as their backing, Rice and Lloyd-Webber were ready to go into the studio to make the recording.

Having performed the songs earlier at the second Sydmonton Festival[6]—a try-out—they knew it would work, at least in the recording studio.

With the balance of the album ready for release, Lloyd-Webber talked Rice into flying to Majorca in the summer of 1976 to play the album for Harold Prince. They had already auditioned the tape for Lord Harewood, the queen's cousin who had offered to stage it at the English National Opera in the London Coliseum, but they knew that a stuffy classical venue was not for them. Staging of their work needed a proper showcase and showman. Prince, who had already directed Puccini for Chicago's Lyric Opera and Kurt Weill's *Silver Lake* for the New York City Opera, had succeeded in musicals as well as on the lyric stage.

After listening and liking what he heard, Prince agreed to become involved. "After all," he quipped, "any opera that begins with a funeral can't be all bad." He would not, however, be free of prior commitments for two years. Now Lloyd-Webber and Rice were not so sure. In the meantime Prince wrote a three-thousand-word memo to the team outlining his suggestions. Chief among them was his suggestion to reveal different aspects of Evita's character by having her played by three different actresses (a concept that stemmed from his earlier flashback staging of *Follies*). He also thought there should be some changes in their recording, whose release was imminent. Now it was the authors' turn to reject Prince. They wrote a rather curt note saying they were postponing all thought of theatrical production until the album was launched.

In October 1976, after six months' solid work, the first recording, "Don't Cry for Me Argentina" backed with "Rainbow High," was released. The record caught on immediately, soaring to the top of the charts. The song on its "A" side catapulted Lloyd-Webber and Rice into the household name category. It was the hit they had been seeking for more than a decade. The next month the album appeared, and it too was an instantaneous hit, quickly going gold.

To cap that, when a second single, "Another Suitcase in Another Hall" backed with the harrowing "Requiem for Evita," was released a month later, it too soon began spiraling up the charts as well. Even the critics jumped on the bandwagon. Derek Jewell, the Rice–Lloyd-Webber champion since the first performance of *Joseph*, raved.

What made the work so unique was a quality that all the critics missed. Most creators of musicals, whether they be on record or stage, were so aware of the back catalogue they couldn't crawl out from under it. They knew what made a

---

[6] The year before Andrew had originated a musical concert of various numbers climaxing with his brother Julian's playing a cello concerto at his country home. At the second festival in 1976, *Evita* was not performed live, but the Sydmonton guests and colleagues were entertained with an audiovisual show. Slides depicting Eva Peron's life were shown while the sound track consisted of what they had completed of their forthcoming album. The reaction was eminently favorable.

hit or a flop. They knew too much. Lloyd-Webber and Rice were so ignorant of construction, balance, and form that they could more or less get away with anything. They wrote pop music and lyrics, and in doing so they managed to do what Broadway's established composers and lyricists were now failing to do, which was to keep faith with the pop quality that the American musical always had had fifty or sixty years ago.

Seven months later, when the collaborators began to think again of staging their work, they quarrelled bitterly over coming back to Prince. Rice had refused to even consider "this mush," and both had ignored all of Prince's suggestions and had gone ahead with the recording as they envisioned it. Eventually Lloyd-Webber prevailed, and he and Tim appeared at Prince's Broadway office to offer him the score. Prince, recognizing the enormous theatrical possibilities of their work, agreed to stage it. He would be ready to put the score into rehearsal in early 1978. Meanwhile, he said that the record selling so phenomenally could only add to the public's excited anticipation of a full theatrical performance.

When he began to direct it the following May, he changed very little, the only deletion being Che's rock number, "The Lady's Got Potential." His one addition was a song for the officers called "The Art of the Possible." Prince requested the latter to show Peron's rise and staged it memorably. The five members of the G.O.U., a right-wing grouping of officers within the military group that seized power in Argentina in 1943, including Peron, are seen moving slowly back and forth in rocking chairs. During the song, every time the music stops, the officers rise and one chair is removed. By the end of the scene there is just one chair left, occupied by Peron.

Susannah Fellowes recalls the rehearsal period: "It seemed like we rehearsed five weeks and I think about three and a half of them were on the opening. And then we rehearsed a huge Latin mass at the end for her death So we spent days and days learning this authentic, lengthy Latin mass which was then cut. We thought we were in trouble, we were all muttering under our breath saying, 'Oh this is going to be a disaster.' "

During that time, while the set was being built, set designers Timothy O'Brien and Tazeena Firth approached Prince, saying they felt something was missing. A few days later Prince spent several days in Mexico City. Wandering through Chapultapec Park, he saw murals by Diego Rivera and David Siqueros, and he knew immediately the answer to his designers' problem. He had great murals depicting Argentinean peasants prepared to flank the proscenium.

Fellowes has a vivid recollection of the difficulty with the costuming this change in set elicited. It was solved with typical Prince resourcefulness:

"You were supposed to be on benches at the very beginning, watching a film when someone stands up and announces that she has just died. We had all these monochrome costumes, which Hal didn't like at all, and he threw them out. So they went to Oxfam [a charity outlet store] and all kinds of secondhand shops and got racks of used clothing and put them in the back of the stalls bar, and we were instructed to go and collect something to wear. It was like a shopping spree, and we chose whatever we thought we might want to wear as our character. Then we did a dress parade, and the designer said, 'Oh that looks nice but that needs a hat, that needs gloves, that needs a different pair of trousers,' and we costumed the show that way.

"We also had all the very snippy aristocracy who were constantly down on Eva Peron. Their costumes had been designed as from the Edwardian period—very exaggerated clothes where the hats were five feet across and there were beads to the floor and all the men had huge padded bellies with rows of medals on their chests and big top hats that were two feet high and everything was like a cartoon. The point was that we'd been choreographed to move very tightly together to move as one unit, and we couldn't get anywhere near each other because of the costumes. Hal took one look at us and said NO! NO! NO! and immediately the whole group had to be recostumed. They thought black and white—that looks classy, that looks easy—and they cut new costumes and made us costumes within three days."

One of the female chorus members recalled that prerehearsal period:

"I was struck with the kind of things that were 'combined.' All thirty of us sat down one afternoon at a screening of a documentary about Eva Peron, and in it they had local, well-known Latin tunes, and scenes of the crowds. In the background, I heard one of the songs from the show. Yet no one said anything. And it was a direct lift. I don't know whether Andrew would attribute it to another source but that certainly was it. Sometimes I think it's accidental. Many of us who know Andrew's shows go through the show and pick out all the tunes that we think he lifted from others, and it could be something that we lay onto him just because we're feeling slightly malicious at the moment. I don't think he does it that intentionally. It just happens. His language is music and he absorbs things and as anybody does, you absorb stimulus and it comes out as having been computed through your own being, it becomes yours. It's like any actor. You absorb a situation and then you exhale it into a part."

In his own defense on this allegation, Andrew Lloyd-Webber told a reporter, "I listen to my shows a lot because I have to, and I know they're not derivative. They're not. One has to admit there are only so many notes on the piano."

With Elaine Paige as Evita, David Essex as Che, and Joss Ackland as Peron, *Evita* opened in London on June 21, 1978. The critics were about evenly divided on the merit of the work, but they were unanimous in praising Prince's contribution. Prince himself allowed that he had learned from his recent production of *Pacific Overtures*. "They're both documentary revues; incidents; highlights," he told a reporter for the *Hollywood Drama-Logue*. "Neither is linearly constructed. I found out where I was boring in *Pacific Overtures*; with *Evita* I knew how to stop and move on at the right place and get the rhythm right. Things last too long in *Pacific Overtures*."

Derek Jewell trotted out all his superlatives in the *Sunday Times*: "*Evita* is a quite marvelous modern opera, exceeding in stature even *Jesus Christ Superstar*. Lloyd-Webber's score, so full of glorious melodies apart from the well-known "Don't Cry for Me, [*sic* comma] Argentina" is an unparalleled fusion of 20th-century musical experience. . . . It is the interweaving of pop, rock, jazz, Broadway, Latin and other elements which makes the brew so astonishingly potent . . . , Lloyd Webber is perhaps the most remarkable musical child of his generation. In Tim Rice he has a partner of perfection. Rice writes trenchant, witty, modern lyrics superbly married to Lloyd Webber's ambitious score."

But Bernard Levin, Britain's most intellectual reviewer, writing in the *Times*, called *Evita* "one of the most disagreeable evenings I have ever spent in my life, in or out of the theatre," objecting strongly to this "odious artifact . . . that calls itself an opera . . . merely because the clichés between the songs are sung rather than spoken."[7] Levin saved his most vitriolic words to complain about the glamorizing of a heartless dictator. "Next, we'll have a musical about Hitler," he concluded.

What Levin was referring to was perhaps the most daring concept in staging: Prince's conception of the first act finale. The stirring strains of "A New Argentina" are sung at a political rally celebrating Eva and Peron's accession to power, replete with flowing banners and flaming torches and all culminating in a foot-stomping climax. The audience also sees the political opposition beaten with clubs by jack-booted storm troopers. At the end of the act some members of the audience rose to their feet to applaud the theatricality of the scene, while others remained seated, clearly shaken by the suggestive depiction of Hitler's Nuremberg rallies presided over by a posturing Peron and a beaming Evita.

Rice countered Levin's accusations of glamorizing Evita. "If your subject happens to be one of the most glamorous women who ever lived, you will inevitably be accused of glamorizing her," he said, while Hal Prince brought out his similar point of view as to their protagonist. Prince wrote that "she is a villain, corrupted by all that power. But there's also a sympathetic part that draws me to her. . . .

---

[7] Prince has gone on record in the *San Francisco Sunday Chronicle and Examiner* as to his feelings about opera: "Opera is, and always has been, musical theater of its time, presented in a form using limited dialogue. Puccini and Verdi—who are the musical heroes of Andrew Lloyd-Webber, incidentally—were pop composers of their era. . . . There are certain elitist lines of rigidity drawn around opera. The word tends to carry with it a type of awed reverence that has been a barrier to acceptance of the contemporary opera works. But those operas by Verdi and Puccini were the show biz musicals of their time."

Evita, illegitimate and a woman, a 10th class citizen in Argentina. And she made it sexually. It's grim and grimy stuff. . . . The rage of ambition at work."

Yet the pros and cons of Argentinean politics mattered not a jot because during the nine preview performances, the press came—not the critics—and heralded the show as groundbreaking news. "DON'T CRY FOR EVA—ARGENTINA'S A HIT," one headline screamed. There were lines at the box office from the first day, and they got longer daily. For over two years there was a return ticket line of 150 to 200 people hoping a bus with ticketholders would break down and allow them a chance to get in.

Prince had inserted a clause in his contract with Lloyd-Webber, Rice, and Stigwood that barred them from any performances in the United States without his express permission. He was not sure there ever *would* be a Broadway mounting because he knew that what was acceptable to the British might not go down well with Americans.

> I did not think it was for American audiences and . . . I did not want it seen in America without my permission. So they very unwisely (from their point of view) gave me a contract which would have made it possible for me to embargo the production. What happened was that . . . I was delighted that it should be seen everywhere. It is also, obviously, the show that has given me the financial independence that everyone thought I always had!

When he decided to present the show on the other side of the Atlantic, he made deep cuts in both the opening and the ending of the musical. But the major change was that he decided to be "more political in the U.S. and that Che should be the force that drove the story along." Mainly Prince "toughened" the show, calling it a change of "emphasis" that made it more abrasive.

"We were dotting all the 'i's' and crossing all the 't's'," Lloyd-Webber added. It was a matter of underlining Che's remarks to show his anger and revulsion at how Evita was becoming a saint in the eyes of the Argentine masses. All the changes that were made in the American version were gradually incorporated in the finished score and used in the British production as well.

In order to break it in (so the British wouldn't feel he was robbing their thunder or stars), Prince chose to have the American production cut its teeth in Los Angeles and San Francisco, bringing it to Broadway only after several months on the West Coast, where it built up anticipation and excitement enough to guarantee an unheard of $2.4 million advance by opening night.

For the mercurial star he chose a recent graduate of the Juilliard School of Music, an alumna of their drama department. Patti LuPone,[8] whose belt voice

---

[8] Miss LuPone is the great-grandniece of opera singer Adelina Patti, from whom she takes her name. Although she is a belter, she believes that any vocal role should respect the original keys

can be compared only to Ethel Merman's, amazingly seemed to be able tirelessly to take the score's several high 'E's in full chest. She succeeded in bringing the overacting dictator to stunning life by playing her "over-the-top." As Che, Prince cast the sensitive cantorial tenor Mandy Patinkin, who, although he won a Tony award for this impersonation, would later be elevated to stardom when he was given the role of his career as Georges Seurat in Sondheim's *Sunday in the Park with George*.

A different *Evita*, then, opened on Broadway September 25, 1979, fifteen months after its London debut. The reviews, better than they had been in Britain, were still not outstanding.

Brendan Gill in the *New Yorker* could not understand "what prompted these creators of *Jesus Christ Superstar* to devote their extraordinary talents to the present trifle," which he called "an oratorio striving ambitiously but in vain to become an opera . . . The difficulty is that being an oratorio, *Evita* is content to narrate a sequence of events instead of dramatizing them. In only two scenes do characters effectively face each other and contend together."

Walter Kerr, drama critic for the *New York Times*, called it "a bold step backward into the medieval morality play." He termed the evening "emotionally icy, psychologically monochromatic, a cut-and-dried sermon with capital letters to burn." His review was diametrically opposed to Clive Barnes's opinion. The latter thought Prince had given his audience "a virtually faultless piece of Broadway fantasy," adding, "I have rarely if ever seen a more excitingly staged Broadway musical."

Evita settled down for a four-year run at New York's Broadway theater. It won seven Tony Awards for the 1979–80 season: Best Musical; Best Actress (LuPone); Best Featured Player (Patinkin); Best Direction (Prince); Best Score (Lloyd-Webber and Rice); Best Book of a Musical (Rice); and Best Lighting (David Hersey). It also won six Drama Desk Awards, including another one for Prince as director, and the New York Drama Critics' Circle Award for best musical. The show eventually spawned three touring companies and was seen in eighteen productions worldwide.

For Andrew Lloyd-Webber and Tim Rice, who were accredited successes in their native land, the American reception and lavish awards meant they had really arrived. Beyond that, for its director, *Evita*'s overwhelming success was patent proof that Prince could also stage shows that were not cold and cynical as his work with Sondheim had been called. "I sure as hell would like to do anything Steve ever writes," he told one interviewer who thought the extremely successful partnership with Lloyd-Webber might signal a break with Sondheim.

---

of the score. Accordingly, in talking about the movie version of *Evita*, which starred Madonna, LuPone deplores that Madonna used much lower keys.

"But I can't just wait for Steve because then I'll work too rarely. I need to work—all the time."

Although the public at large, which pays very little mind to a show's director, may not have known about it, during the time Prince had been readying the British version of *Evita*, that is, since 1977, he had been working closely with Sondheim on *his* new opera, *Sweeney Todd*.

A Revue and a True Opera

STEPHEN SONDHEIM WENT TO LONDON in 1973 to oversee the West End revival of *Gypsy*, his grand success that had never been presented in Britain. Because Ethel Merman had been denied the role of Rose in the cinematic version, she had washed her hands of the show, thereby drying up any touring or foreign performances. Now *Gypsy*'s star role, a tour de force stage mother, had been selected by Angela Lansbury for her next musical, so the trip afforded Sondheim the opportunity to anglicize some of his showbiz lyrics, as well as the delight of renewing old acquaintance with Lansbury. After all, he had given her her first starring musical role—the mercurial mayoress in *Anyone Can Whistle*. Subsequently Lansbury, who had a powerful musical voice plus great acting ability, went on to win a Tony for her performance in the title role of Jerry Herman's musical *Mame*. A real trouper, she was now about to resurrect *Gypsy* and bring it to glowing life on both sides of the Atlantic. And although he did not know it then, Sondheim was soon to create for Lansbury one of the best roles of her musical career.

While he was in London, Sondheim attended a performance of Christopher Bond's new adaptation of *Sweeney Todd* (*The Demon Barber of Fleet Street*). Sondheim had an abiding interest in Grand Guignol and melodramatic horror. "My two favorite horror experiences in my childhood," he was to say, "were reading *Night Must Fall* and eventually acting it in college, and seeing *Hangover Square*, my favorite horror movie."

Nor was Sondheim a novice to writing of the macabre. As far back as 1966 he had collaborated with James Goldman on the grotesque—but beautiful—television musical *Evening Primrose*, in which those ostracized from a select society are drained of their blood and turned into department store mannequins. And after *Sweeney* he would certainly involve himself with what conductor Mark Dorrell calls "the darker side of human nature dealing with *Into the Woods* and *Assassins*."

Christopher Bond came to *Sweeney Todd* as a young actor/novelist working in a repertory company at the Victoria Theater, Stoke-on-Trent. In a previous season his company had had great success with a melodrama called *A Ticket-of-Leave Man* and, without seeing the script, had advertised *Sweeney Todd* as their forthcoming shocker. Two weeks before rehearsals were to begin, members of the company read the crude, repetitive, and simplistic script that had been one of the staples of the "blood tub" theaters in mid-nineteenth-century England. Written by George Dibden-Pitt, it had originally been published in the "penny dreadful" sheets that sold for a copper and were roughly equivalent to today's tabloids.

Bond had been assigned one of the few sympathetic roles, that of Tobias Ragg, in the creaky melodrama his company was about to put on, and a single reading showed him that the play had no character development and hardly any plot— just a series of slaughterings. The two chief characters were Sweeney, a psychopath who killed and robbed, and Mrs. Lovett, a harridan who baked the bodies into meat pies. Bond realized that the show in its original form would be impossible to be taken seriously by today's audiences. When the director of the company left it to Bond to do any doctoring the show may have needed, he volunteered to rework the material into his first play.

"It didn't need doctoring, it needed a heart transplant, and preferably new lungs and balls as well," Bond was to say. "I crossed Dumas's *The Count of Monte Cristo* with Tourneur's *The Revenger's Tragedy* for a plot; added elements of pastiche Shakespeare in a sort of blankish verse for Sweeney, the Judge, and the lovers to talk; borrowed the name of the author of *The Prisoner of Zenda* for my sailor boy; remembered some market patter I'd learnt as a child; and adapted the wit and wisdom of Brenda, who ran the greengrocer's shop opposite my house, for Mrs. Lovett's rumination upon life, death, and the state of her sex life."

The play was a great success and produced by several theater companies in England, one of which performed it at the theater where Sondheim saw it. He thought it was wonderful, as "it had a combination of charm and creepiness, and it was still a melodrama, but also a legend. It was elegantly written, part in blank verse—which I didn't even recognize until I read the script. It had a weight to it, but I couldn't figure out how the language was so rich and thick without being fruity. . . . It struck me as a piece that sings." And then, intrigued with the mystery, he bought all the original versions of the play, read them through, and thought they were terrible. Bond's play, he now realized, was far richer than the earlier versions, and he felt it would make an opera because although it remains true to the melodramatic tradition, *Sweeney Todd* was "larger than life as a story and larger than life in technique."

Bond, with endearing modesty, plays down the work's excellence, saying that "whilst I have great affection for the play, until Steve performed his alchemical miracle on it, it remained a neat pastiche that worked well if performed with sufficient panache, but base metal nevertheless. But the transformation to pure gold was about to begin."

The metamorphosis began when Sondheim, seeking an option to musicalize Bond's work, discovered that producers Richard Barr and Charles Woodward were also bidding to present *Sweeney Todd* in America, but as a straight play. When Sondheim, who had just committed himself to Harold Prince to do *Pacific Overtures*, suggested they all join forces to make a musical of Bond's play, they agreed to wait until he had finished his other commitment. "I didn't get around to *Sweeney Todd* until the summer of 1977," Sondheim was to say, remarking on the five years Barr and Woodward stood patiently by.

Much earlier Sondheim approached Hal Prince to join the enterprise. It was a role reversal, for this was the first time Sondheim had initiated a project, but Prince was not persuaded that this gory melodrama was for him. "I thought it was a little on the campy side," he told Carol Ilson for her biography, *Prince*, "about serving meat pies at intermission and hissing the villain." But as he delved deeper he realized that Sweeney and Mrs. Lovett were driven by revenge. "Today your ensemble must populate the piece with a shared experience," he added. "Our way to shared revenge became the incursion of the industrial age on the human spirit. For that Eugene Lee designed a factory to house our musical, and our cast—*all* our cast—became victims of the class system."

After fulfilling his commitment to *Pacific Overtures* and its subsequent demise, Sondheim busied himself with rewrites and new material for *A Little Night Music*, which was due to begin filming in September 1976. Around that time, *The New York Times* announced that he would do the libretto *and* music and lyrics for *Sweeney Todd*, a mammoth task that only Frank Loesser, Nöel Coward and Meredith Willson had managed successfully. "I started it," he told Craig Zadan in *Sondheim & Co.*, "because it was really all going to be sung. . . . I did the first twenty minutes and realized I was only on page five of Bond's script. So at that rate the show would possibly have been nine hours long. And I realized I didn't know how to cut it, so Hal suggested I call Hugh [Wheeler] because he had written mysteries and he was British and he would understand the tradition of the play." The actual writing began the following summer.

Meanwhile, during the middle 1970s, the Sondheim name and the great body of the work he had accomplished until then was disseminated to a larger public—by, of all things, a British quartet: singer-actor David Kernan, enlisting producer-author-chat show host Ned Sherrin and well-known singer Millicent Martin as well as the energetic singing actress Julia McKenzie. These four converged and put together *Side by Side by Sondheim*, an evening of songs excerpted

from Sondheim musicals that made him, if not a household name, at least a
familiar one on theater marquees.

It was David Kernan's idea, conceived when he was in the West End run of
A *Little Night Music* playing the key role of Count Carl-Magnus. "Cleo Laine
has a small country theater in the stables of her country house," he told this
writer recently, "and she phoned me and asked if I could persuade Jean Simmons
[then starring with him in *Night Music*] to come down and do a benefit. I said
I would try. Much to my amazement, Jean agreed and asked, 'What do you want
me to do?' I said, 'Oh, I thought we'd sing four or five Sondheim songs.' 'Which
ones?' she asked. 'You could do a couple of songs from *Follies* and I could do
one or two from there, and then you could do a couple of songs from our show.'
So we worked out sort of a little quarter of an hour program and trooped down
to Cleo Laine's. They loved it. That endorsed my feeling that every song Sondheim wrote is a one-act play with a beginning, a middle, and end. You can
extract all those songs and string them together with themes and you have a
wonderful evening. I then wrote to Stephen to ask if we could try this. He wrote
back, 'By all means have a go, but I can't think of anything more boring except
possibly the Book of Kells.' So we tried it."

Then he approached Ned Sherrin, who had once produced the BBC show
That Was the Week That Was. "Ned was in the doldrums then," Kernan continued. "His film company had gone down the tubes, and he was not a happy man.
'This will sort of cheer you up,' I said. And he asked, 'Who are we going to
have in it?' and I said, 'Well obviously Milly [Martin], she's perfect for it.' 'Who
else?' I replied, 'I've seen this terribly good girl who has been *the* understudy in
the West End for God knows how long and is always "Miss Takeover." I've just
seen her in *Promises, Promises* and she's terribly good. Her name is Julia Mc-
Kenzie.' He said, 'Never heard of her.' 'Trust me,' I said. And so I asked Julia
to do it."

Small revues built around the songs of one man with a little patter or history
of his life had been quite successful at that time in London. These intimate
revues often originated at the 200-seat Mermaid Theatre, and as they built up
a following usually moved on to larger West End houses. In 1972 there had
been a Nöel Coward evening called *Cowardy Custard*, and two years later a Cole
Porter revue. Both had been successful; the difference here was that unlike Coward or Porter who were seventy or dead at the time of their retrospective tributes,
Sondheim was only forty-five.

"We rehearsed for a couple of weeks," Kernan continued, "and then we tripped
off to Cleo's theater, Wavendon in Hertfordshire, and did one performance. It
was overly long, but one could see a huge potential there. We did a bit of
trimming and we did two other nights, one in a town called Bury St. Edmunds
and then one at the Greenwood Theatre."

"We still didn't have a producer," added Ned Sherrin. "Several came and didn't think it was worthwhile, except one small backer of Cameron Mackintosh's, who somehow had missed seeing it. The backer came for the first time and he was bouleversé about it. We all went out and had supper afterwards, and he said, 'I will ring Cameron in New York tonight—I don't care what time it is there, I will wake him up. He must do it!'

"Now this sweet man never put more than a hundred pounds into a piece, but he did phone Cameron. Cameron became excited and got in touch with Helen Montagu, who was working for the H. M. Tennent Organization. She hadn't seen it either. Neither of them had any product, so in it went to them. Then they couldn't find a theater for it. Julia bumped into a director who said Bernard Miles, the director of the Mermaid, was desperate for something. The theater was running, but they were running down, and he had no play to go in a few weeks. So I took a tape recording, an appalling recording. Bernard got bored with it after about two minutes and said, 'You're all so bloody wonderful! It's too bloody good, and we can't let this bloody opportunity go.' So in we went under the management of Tennent's and Cameron Mackintosh for a budget of fifteen thousand pounds—or it may have been twelve—and Stephen came over and did a very good master class. They sang the show to him one day and he gave them notes the second day."

"We opened on May 4, 1976, after an intensive *two weeks' rehearsal*," Kernan corrects, "with the maestro himself. He actually, in my opinion, directed the show, much to Ned's total annoyance. Sondheim was the director. Ned had been the referee up till that point saying, 'Well, move over here, or move over there.' Suddenly we had in-depth direction. And so tactful and clever. He never undermined you. He knows exactly how to spin you into the right mode for the song, and it was a wonderful two-and-a-half weeks. And when the show opened there was a standing ovation every night."

Much of the success of the revue, which played for two years in the West End, was due to the inclusion of a few of the better known songs of other composers, for which Sondheim had written lyrics. "Richard and Mary Rodgers, Jule Styne and Leonard Bernstein," Kernan says, "break it a little bit, because some of Steve's music is pretty demanding on the ear, however wonderful it is."

Ned Sherrin feels that Sondheim would have been happier had the revue stuck only to songs for which he had written both music and lyrics. "But," he adds, "*we* put the show together, and the earlier numbers were more or less there. It was very funny when Lenny [Bernstein] came to see it. Steve said, 'Tell me everything he says. I'm sure he's going to say, "pity the later stuff isn't as good as the earlier stuff." ' In fact, Lenny couldn't have been more diplomatic."

Millicent Martin noted that before *Side by Side*, most of the English had not heard of Sondheim as many of his shows had not been presented in England.

Sondheim (left) with Millicent Martin and David Kernan, two of the stars of Side by Side *by Sondheim. Julia McKenzie and Ned Sherrin were also in this revue. All were nominated for Tonys. AP/Wide World Photos.*

She took this as an advantage, one that helped the singers create a fresh evening. "Since we had not seen all of his shows, there was no temptation to copy anyone else. We sang from the printed page and created our own interpretations."

The production at the Mermaid soon became a sell-out. Later, after the show had been moved to the West End, so popular was it with public and critics alike that it almost won out over *A Chorus Line* as the best musical in town.

Hal Prince, who had not produced the show in London, decided to bring the revue to Broadway with the original cast as his first British import. He capitalized the show at $250,000, which, by the way, illustrates the tremendous disparity in the '70s of producing a show in the U.S. or U.K. "It was a natural for me," Prince said, "it was material we had worked on together, so it seemed I should have something to do with it."

Actors' Equity protested the scheduled appearance of all four English performers, claiming that Dick Cavett could do Sherrin's role and Americans could handle the singing assignments as well as the foreigners. Only Prince's persuasiveness, his pointing out that the show had been conceived and arranged by the performers themselves, who were unique to the material, obtained a waiver of the rules. But it was not total victory over Equity, for Prince promised that once the show got a foothold on Broadway, the foreigners would be phased out.

Among the twenty-nine songs culled from various Sondheim works, perhaps the most unusual were two sung by Kernan that are usually performed by women, the *West Side Story* duet "A Boy Like That" and "Could I Leave You?" from *Follies*. The latter is a bitchy diatribe that could easily have been directed at an older man and come from the mouth of a younger kept man. "I did that song much against Ned's will and against Stephen's will," Kernan says. "On reflection, I think some of the lines are inaccurate. Lines like 'ten elderly men from the U.N.,' only a woman, a bored wife would have put up with those elderly men from the U.N. I don't think a young guy would have put up with that [referring to the young man's confessional]. 'Boy in the grass, bet your ass,' oh sure, that works a treat."

During the rehearsal period in New York only minor musical modifications were made. "Hal wanted some changes, but I said to the great man, 'You bought a show. When shows come from Broadway to London, we don't demand changes. Why should you?' I was absolutely trembling in my boots—because he is so adamant. He said, 'Well, it's not going to work.' 'Let's give a few previews to see if it works or not,' I said. So we played two or three previews and they loved "A Boy Like That." So we made no changes whatsoever."

Side by Side by Sondheim[1] opened at the intimate Music Box Theatre on April 18, 1977. There was no orchestra, only two pianos and percussion, and the performers were taken to heart by sophisticated New Yorkers. Sherrin, an articulate Oxonian, seated on a stool on the far side of the stage, interspersed the songs with topical jokes that seemed to be plucked from the news of the day. "I'd established a sort of formula of my sitting on the side of the stage and making comments, trying to relate the songs not just to their content, but to what was going on in the world. I read the newspapers daily and added something different every night."

Halfway through the run, which turned out to be a substantial 384 Broadway performances, Sherrin recalled the night when the Americans took over. "One of the Broadway producers said to Hal, 'You see? You didn't need the English after all,' mentioning the four replacements: Hermione Gingold as the narrator

---

[1] Originally prosaically called *The Sondheim Songbook*, the show's title was suggested by Burt Shevelove after the performance in Bury St. Edmunds. According to Ned Sherrin, "We were then thinking of calling it *Side by Side*, and he suggested *Side by Side by Sondheim*. That's how he got Sondheim's name into it."

and singers Georgia Brown, Nancy Dussault, and Larry Kert. And I said, 'I think Hermione Gingold and Georgia Brown might be said to be English anyway.' " Sherrin noted with his customary sangfroid that his role as narrator "had been played in various parts of the world by Hermione Gingold, Cyril Ritchard, Peggy Lee, Arlene Francis, and Dorothy Lamour, and those two puppets [Burr Tilstrom's Kukla and Ollie] who came in from Chicago, and all those people who talk like Sheridan Morley." Actually, he was even played by Sheridan Morley.

According to Prince, the show "paid off, but did not make any money for anybody to speak of." Yet when Tony time came, all four of the original cast were nominated. *Side by Side by Sondheim* was beaten out by *Annie*, which deservedly won most of the musical awards in a lackluster season. But its very accessibility with the introduction of by now familiar and tuneful material took away some of the intellectual bugaboo that attending a Sondheim show had formerly signified.

In the ensuing decades *Side by Side by Sondheim* has been produced at small theaters everywhere and has become a staple of college campuses with hardly any updating. Its success has spawned two other Sondheim revues that use more current material as well as songs that have been dropped from other productions: *Marry Me a Little*, a two-character revue that opened in 1980, and *Putting It Together*,[2] which had a run in 1993 and a revival in 1999 and offered a quintet of singers.

As Sondheim visualized *Sweeney Todd*, his design concept was to have the actors practically commingling with the audience. "Smoke, some street lamps, fog rising from the floor," is all the composer felt was needed for his thriller, "and somebody would pop up beside you and scare you half to death."

Hal Prince knew that intimate kind of theater would never hold enough people to be economically feasible on Broadway. He figured he could get the same effect in the Broadway Theater, whose large seating capacity had been reduced to nine hundred to present the short-lived rock musical *Dude*. Prince found the theater, with seats, bleachers, and various playing areas, ideal for his circuslike version of the revised Bernstein-Wheeeler-Sondheim *Candide*, which exploded all over the house. What he called "environmental theater" would also be a fine venue for a "scary" musical like *Sweeney*. He hoped the theater owners

---

[2] This revue originated in Oxford and was directed by Julia McKenzie, who by this time had become somewhat of a Sondheim specialist. (Since her first Sondheim show, *Company*, she had starred in *Follies* and played the Witch in *Into the Woods*. She was also instrumental in bringing about the 1994 revival of *Sweeney Todd*, in which she was a splendid Mrs. Lovett.) Cameron Mackintosh brought *Putting It Together* over to New York for a limited engagement at the Manhattan Theater Club, where the ensemble included Julie Andrews. The 1999 revised version of the show, which starred Carol Burnett, had a limited run.

would keep it as he had left it, but because of all the delays in getting the production together, the Shubert Organization, which managed the theater, was forced to revert it to its original capacity. What was available to the production was New York's largest auditorium, the 1700-seat Uris Theater (now the Gershwin).

This meant *Sweeney*'s concept would become bigger rather than smaller. Prince knew he was going against Sondheim's wishes when he offered him "an epic style. You'll lose some of the scary part but you'll gain size," he said. When Eugene Lee found he could acquire an unused Rhode Island iron foundry and reconstruct it to resemble the play's mid-Victorian factory setting, Sondheim remembers Prince's "calling excitedly" with the news. "Hal was not looking for a foundry, it's just that Eugene thought it would make the stylish setting that Prince was looking for." The drawback was that the scenic paraphernalia was so huge that the show would be unable to give out of town tryouts and would have to open "cold" to a demanding preview audience.

For his part Sondheim went along, saying, "Hal is the one I want to do it, so let's see how it works his way." Sondheim felt that Prince "has a sense of arc, a sense of design, a sense of what theater is about." And he felt that someday it would be done small.[3]

This writer, who has seen several productions of Sondheim's masterwork, feels that Prince was prescient in opting for the large theater. Perhaps it was the director's relentless search for social meaning that made him think so metaphorically that he connected this simple tragedy of revenge with the enormous panorama of the whole Industrial Revolution. The massiveness worked on stage, however, and the gargantuan venue certainly may have influenced the grand passions that Sondheim (not to underestimate the brilliant contribution of orchestrator Jonathan Tunick) was able to bring to this score.

With the size of the production decided on and Hugh Wheeler's adapting Bond's play, Sondheim could start work on the score. "Even Bond's version was that absolutely unreal, old melodrama where you boo the villain," Wheeler was to say. "We wanted to make it as nearly as we could into a tragedy. I wrote it as a play, but I encouraged Steve to cannibalize it and make it nearly all music."

That is an appropriate word for Wheeler to use, for cannibalism is at the heart of this opera. In center stage was a large rotating box that served as Sweeney's tonsorial parlor, which was atop Mrs. Lovett's pie shop. When, in the course of the play, Sweeney slits the throats of his unwary customers, he pulls the handle

---

[3] The eminently successful 1994 production at London's intimate Cottesloe Theatre used a reduced cast and reduced orchestra. According to Julia McKenzie, Sondheim thought it was *Sweeney Todd*'s best production. The twenty-seven-piece orchestral arrangement was scaled down to nine: synthesizer, violin, cello, double bass, trumpet, horn, clarinet, bassoon, and percussion.

A striking view of the gigantic set of Sweeney Todd, *a real factory transported in its entirety from Rhode Island. Angela Lansbury dominates Act Two as she sells her famous "meat pies." Sweeney (Len Cariou) and his barber chair are just behind her. Photo: Van Williams. © Museum of the City of New York.*

on his chair and they slide ever so neatly down into Mrs. Lovett's shop, waiting to be baked into pies. This central area, a module and a few stairs, unjustly criticized by the press as "using a gigantic stage and yet confining the action to a close area," is purposely seedy and crowded. It is eminently down-at-the-heels Victorian, and Prince was justly proud of his concept. "While the superstructure of the set was huge," he stated, "the show itself was very small and intimate."

Ragtag members of the ensemble moved the setting around to represent Mrs. Lovett's modest parlor or shoved it aside when the full stage was needed. This almost dizzily shifting about helped to create a seamless production without the use of drops or scrims, with music and lighting changes propelling the audience from one part of London to another. This is what Prince calls "the motor, how the scenes will look and how the people are going to move around in telling the story." This is the essence of the play, without which he could not begin to direct it.

From concept to opening night took a relatively short time for such a complex work, "under two years," according to Sondheim, and although Prince at first was not eager to join in the collaboration and worried that he might be the wrong person to stage it, "as he started to work on it," Sondheim recalled, "he fell in love with it too."

Prince has always said that exchanging ideas is one of the most important things collaborators can do while creating a musical. Now each of the collaborators had a different idea: Prince's was that it was a romance, a play of passion, while Sondheim still felt that it was a musical thriller. Wheeler was the leveling force; having wide experience in playwriting and mystery novels, he opted for the "well-made play" and, according to Sondheim, structured the love story between the two young lovers. He put their scenes in different places than where Bond had placed them and introduced their love scenes earlier. In the finished product, each man's contribution is liberally represented. Amazingly, instead of making the piece discursive, these various pulls actually give *Sweeney* balance and much needed variety.

The evening begins as the audience enters the theater, somewhat trepidatiously, as though they are entering a funeral parlor, for an organist is improvising a discursively ghoulish theme[4] while two gravediggers are excavating the front of the stage. A drop curtain showing a diagram of the British Beehive, a symbol of industry and harmony, is before us. From bottom to top it represents the laborers, tradesmen, and other working classes. Above them are the commercial and educated and then figures representing the law, equity, religious freedom, trial by jury, and, at the very peak, the royal family, with Queen Victoria depicted as queen bee. The supervisor of the gravediggers enters and starts some wheels turning, the music buzzing and humming complacently. *Voila*, the grim Industrial Age springs to life.

A screeching whistle, part factory signal, part agonizing scream, shatters the mood at the same time as the Beehive is torn down to reveal a smoke-stained London backdrop. This earsplitting shriek begins the Prologue, a rumbling ensemble number called "The Ballad of Sweeney Todd," not unlike, at least in tone, the "Moritat" that begins another unsavory tale, the Weill-Brecht *Threepenny Opera*. "Attend the tale of Sweeney Todd," we are told in true Victorian rhetoric, a warning, especially from the double meaning of the word attend, that there is a moral here for our consideration.

---

[4] The music only sounds as if it is improvised, and it is carefully arranged. Beginning with minor triads, it has a baroque effect. In execution it is rather like a journey through the five species of basic counterpoint, becoming more and more florid as it goes along.

The individuals soon become an ensemble. "Swing your razor high, Sweeney," they sing to the tune of the *Dies Irae*, the Day of Wrath (Example A) section that has been part of the Catholic funeral mass since the early sixteenth century. The very pitches themselves can be terrifying to anyone familiar with the service. This theme (Example B) will appear in various guises throughout the opera, just as the blood-chilling opening factory whistle will be heard throughout the evening—every time Sweeney glides his razor over the throat of a victim.

Example A

Di - es   i - rae,   di - es   il - la

Example B

Swing your   ra - zor   wide,   Swee - ney!

Now, members of the ensemble tell us of the evening's protagonist and his quest for revenge.

Back of his smile, under his word,   Sweeney pondered and Sweeney planned,
Sweeney heard music that nobody heard.   Like a perfect machine 'e planned . . .

At last the Prologue rises to a climax, culminating in a vocal scream—the sopranos on a brutally high C-sharp—that rivals the factory whistle. The entire ensemble seems to be evoking an undead, ghostly Sweeney and Mrs. Lovett. They arise and join in the ballad, and after Sweeney sings a couplet with wry humor—"What happened then—well, that's the play, / And he wouldn't want us to give it away" —they all slink away.

This Prologue, and its matching final Epilogue, is entirely Sondheim's work. There is nothing in Bond's play quite so evocative of the era. And, of course, suggesting that this is a fable, even one with a moral, makes all the bloodletting to come merely theater—bloody, but unreal.

The story that follows is as tightly constructed as a wound spring. It begins as Benjamin Barker, who has taken the assumed name of Sweeney Todd, is returning to London after fifteen years in an Australian prison. Convicted on a trumped-up charge because the corrupt Judge Turpin desired Todd's wife, he is eager to find the family he left behind. Todd's wife, raped by the judge, had swallowed poison, we are told, and their daughter, Johanna, Todd learns, has become the ward of the insidious judge.

Todd was rescued while escaping at sea by a young sailor, Anthony Hope, as optimistic as his name implies, kind even to a half-crazed beggar woman who inhabits the dock area. Like most of the major characters in the opera, he has his own leitmotif, a jaunty sea chanty. Hope and Todd are approached by the bedraggled creature, straight out of a Hogarth etching; she pleads pathetically for alms but once given a coin lifts her skirts, offering, "Wouldn't you like to push me crumpet? / It looks to me, dear, / Like you've got plenty there to push."

Sondheim gives us a clue to her identity in the music of her salacious offer. It is the same music that will be slowed down and serve as the minuet when we see a dumbshow of the judge's party during which the wife is raped. We may or may not know that this demented creature is Sweeney's wife, and her approach to him, when her foggy brain recognizes him and she asks, "Hey, don't I know you?" is pathetic at the same time as being key to the plot. It is also good mystery playwriting, for the clue to her identity has been dropped for us to connect at the evening's end.

After the fashion of melodramatic coincidence, Anthony passes by the judge's house as soon as he leaves Todd and falls instantly in love with the daughter. It is Anthony who gets to sing the score's most moving song, "Johanna," whose simple but exquisite theme (Example C) should lay to rest, once and for all, the charge that Sondheim is unable to write flowing melody.

Example C

I feel you, Jo - han - na, I feel you.

Todd, in returning to his former shop on Fleet Street, renews acquaintance with Mrs. Lovett, who admits in song that times are hard and customers scarce. The song has a driving rhythm, broken periodically by Mrs. Lovett's pounding her dough or swatting an insect as she prepares "The Worst Pies in London." Here Sondheim gives his character definite stage business, all fitted in time with the music. In discussing her character's opening number, Julia McKenzie, who played the role in its 1995 London revival said, "It was dog eat dog (no pun intended) in those days. We didn't have the ethics we have now." So Mrs. Lovett intimates to Todd that her rival Mrs. Mooney has succeeded by what she calls "Enterprise, / Popping pussies into pies." We get the idea that Mrs. Lovett would do the same, but she adds, "and I'm telling you them pussy cats is quick."

Todd asks her why she doesn't rent the room above her shop, since times are so hard and she answers with the second verse of the same aria Todd sang to Anthony earlier in the act, when he hinted about his past. Again the repetition, the uncompleted musical sequence is far more like opera than musical play. Musicals, even operettas, always seek to develop a number through repetitive choruses reaching the apex to applause rather than to fragment a theme.

There was a barber and his wife,	A proper artist with a knife,
And he was beautiful,	But they transported him for life . . .

sings Mrs. Lovett, before she tells him the story of Benjamin Barker and "why no one will go near that room upstairs." At the climax of her tale, when the wife is raped, Todd can endure no more and emits an agonized scream.

"So it is you," she confronts him, and soon, after offering him a place to live, she brings forth his razors, which she has kept all these years. When they are returned to him, he sings the opera's most passionate music: its theme, a moving inversion of the *Dies Irae* theme—a love song to his razors.

"Till now your shine / Was merely silver, / Friends, / You shall drip rubies . . ." As he vows vengeance, he declares, "My right[5] arm is complete again."

Aiming to build back his former reputation as a first-class barber so he may get the judge, who has told his ever-present beadle that he plans to marry Johanna, into his chair, Todd challenges a street mountebank, Pirelli, to a shaving contest. With the beadle as moderator, he wins handily.[6] But the loser, a former apprentice of Todd's, recognizes his mentor's silver implements and appears with his young assistant, Toby, at the shop, threatening blackmail. While Mrs. Lovett entertains Toby, Todd kills Pirelli and puts the body in a heavy trunk, keeping, of course, his purse. Just then the judge, recommended by the beadle, comes in for a shave. Todd is about to slit his throat when Anthony

---

[5] Sondheim told this writer that they had to lose the word *right* on the recording because Len Cariou, who starred as the original Sweeney, is left-handed. "When George Hearn took over," Sondheim adds, "I thought at last I can have the proper line—but George Hearn turned out to be left-handed too."

[6] Barbers in Victorian times were also dentists, and in writing this number Sondheim had a field day with a succeeding contest, a tooth-pulling bout. The number was cut in previews, but its lyric lead-in is too good to omit:

Perhaps, signorini, signori,	That a-though to begin
You like-a I tell-a	She's a screaming-a murder,
Da famous-a story	She's later-a swoon-a wid
Of Queen Isabella,	Bliss an' was heard-a
Da queen of-a Polan'	To shout:
Whose toot' was a swollen,	"Pull all of 'em out!"
I pull it so nice from her mout'	

Hope bursts into the shop, and the judge, recognizing the sailor as his ward's unwanted suitor and swearing to lock her up where no young man can get at her, wipes the lather off his face and leaves angrily. The realization that his quarry slipped through his fingers sends Todd over the edge, and his "Epiphany" becomes the turning point of the musical.

It took Sondheim a full month to write this key number on which all further action and believability in the play depends. Now instead of vowing vengeance on one guilty man, he pledges to murder humanity, shouting, "They all deserve to die!"

Discussing this, the first of Sweeney's multiple murders, Julia McKenzie finds "Mrs. Lovett a very human being with strong sexuality. Once he commits the first murder, I found, he became, in her eyes, more sexually attractive. And where she'd had a fondness for him before, in my interpretation I take on more seriously with him after he commits the first murder—I suppose the sadism and sexuality cross over there. It's something to play, and that's the way I'm playing her."

Mrs. Lovett, always practical, takes the purse from the body upstairs, and she passes on to Todd the grim idea of grinding Pirelli into her meat pies. The act ends with a lively waltz "A Little Priest," as Todd and Mrs. Lovett fantasize on the joy of eating the many flavors of humanity. "Priest," for example, she says, "is too good." Grocer is green and piccolo player is "piping hot."

By Act Two, Mrs. Lovett's business is such a roaring success that she has created an outdoor eating garden. We are treated to a truly operatic segment: Toby hawking and serving the pies, full chorus extolling their excellence, Mrs. Lovett being baker, waitress, major-domo, and cashier simultaneously, while Todd, his tonsorial parlor now a success, paces anxiously, waiting for his chair with the tricky lever to arrive. At last it does, and he drags a reluctant Mrs. Lovett away from her enterprise to have a look. "It's gorgeous," is the best she can muster before returning to her customers. Now Sweeny sings a passionate song to the chair, based on the theme of the one he sang to the razors, saying he has "another friend." This chair completes *his* mission. He tells Mrs. Lovett that when he pounds three times on the floor, she is to collect the body. This whole ten-minute number, which thrusts the plot forward, has an interwoven mosaic of themes. With overlapping vocal lines over a full chorus generally screaming "God, that's good!" as they swill pies and ale, it is as complicated and many-faceted as Verdi's second scene of *Aida* and certainly as intense.

Soon Todd's many customers supply plentiful raw ingredients, but Todd is still deeply interested in getting the judge back in his shop. He instructs Anthony on ways to rescue Johanna and immediately writes to the judge that she will be brought to his shop before the pair elope.

Mrs. Lovett and Toby change the mood in a tender scene in which the young man tells his protectress, "Nothing's gonna harm you, not while I'm around."

Sweeney Todd (Len Cariou), lost in his own angry world, tells Mrs. Lovett (Angela Lansbury) why "they all deserve to die" as he sings his "Epiphany," the high point of Act One. Photo: Van Williams. © Museum of the City of New York.

Again, as in opera, phrases are interrupted here and there so the plot may move forward, and themes move in and out, creating a total musical fabric.

When Mrs. Lovett takes out the slain Pirelli's purse, the boy now senses the truth, and Mrs. Lovett has no alternative but to lock him in the piehouse for disposal later. After the beadle comes to the shop to investigate, because neighbors are complaining of the stench from the pie shop, he too is dispatched in Todd's chair. The beadle's entrance sets the plot in whirlwind motion to its end. Carnage, escapes, mistaken identity—all the paraphernalia of melodrama come into play as the story rushes headlong to its conclusion.

It begins when Toby, grinding the meat, finds a fingernail and knows the rest of the truth. Mrs. Lovett urges Todd to do away with him, but Todd has other business, because he knows the judge will be there soon. Now Anthony rescues Johanna from the asylum, dresses her as a man so they may slip aboard ship, and brings her to Sweeney's to wait while he gets a carriage. She hides in the big trunk that once held Pirelli. Then the beggar woman too comes and sits in Todd's chair just as he sees the judge coming up the street. It is his moment, and in a frenzy he dispatches her and slides her body down the chute just as the judge comes up. This time the magistrate does not elude him, and as the factory whistle screams, he slits the judge's throat. Sweeney now sings his fervid theme and puts his razor away, seemingly for the last time, saying, "Rest now my friend, rest now forever."

But the mayhem is not nearly over, for picking up his razor to dispatch Toby, he notices the disguised Johanna and attempts to kill the stranger. But she eludes him narrowly and runs to the street as he hurries down the stairs into the area of the huge bake-oven. Looking for Toby while dragging the bodies over, with an agonizing cry he suddenly recognizes the beggar woman as his beloved wife, Lucy. Her first words to him, "Don't I know you?," resound in the agonized murderer's head. Confronting Mrs. Lovett, she admits that she didn't tell him his Lucy lived because she herself loved him. The waltz music that ended Act One begins again, and Sweeney, with a demonic look on his ashen face, twirls Mrs. Lovett around ever and ever more wildly until he throws her into the gaping bake-oven.

The bloodletting is all but over when a crazed Toby, somewhat representative of Shakespeare's fools, picks up the nearby razor and cuts Todd's throat. The whistle screams for the last time as Todd falls across the body of his wife. The music of Sweeney's ballad whirrs again, and the ensemble sums up the play with a short Epilogue, a kind of multipurpose curtain call, scare tactic, and moral. The frightening part was Sondheim's idea, grudgingly staged by Prince and sung by the entire company while they hint that dozens of Sweeneys are sitting in the auditorium:

Sweeney wishes the world away,	(*Pointing around the theater*)
Sweeney's weeping for yesterday,	
Is Sweeney!	There! There! There! There!
There he is, it's Sweeney!	There! There! There!
Sweeney! Sweeney!	

This time the music does not peter away, but all the characters on stage build to a shattering climax—with just the hint of a moral. "To seek revenge may lead to hell," shouts an unrepentant Sweeney, while Mrs. Lovett exonerates him slightly by adding, "But everyone does it, and seldom as well." Now an unrueful, still angry Todd—like Mozart's Don Giovanni—slams the door on salvation as he exits into the underworld. The music gives a final fillip somewhat reminiscent of the *Sorcerer's Apprentice*, and the stage blacks out.

Ever since *Forum*, Prince held readings of his projects as they went along. *Sweeney* was to be no exception, and so in May 1978, when Wheeler had completed a draft of the first act and Sondheim had seven songs, they held their first one. It was, according to Prince, "A very serious, heavy, relentless, misanthropic business with no humor—none anywhere." Included in the songs Sondheim had completed at this time was Mrs. Lovett's seductive charmer that would appear in the second act, "By the Sea." Even though another of these songs was Mrs. Lovett's truly funny "The Worst Pies in London," Prince felt the work was too dreary. His first idea was to have more of the young lovers, thereby relegating the older couple to the background.

But by the second reading Prince saw his folly, eliminated some early scenes for the lovers alone, and, when it finally came time for *Sweeney Todd* to go into rehearsal, only one song (plus the harum-scarum finale, which because of its complications would need working out on stage) was yet to be written. By preview time, audiences were responding enthusiastically, but the show was running long. Pirelli's tooth-pulling section and the judge's song were eliminated.

The judge's song, which is sung as he is spying on Johanna through a keyhole while flagellating himself, was a daring foray into prevalent Victorian hypocrisy, for the judge's voyeurism coupled with his religious exhortations for deliverance from his filthy thoughts lead him to spontaneous orgasm. Just as the pounding of Mrs. Lovett's dough was built into her song early in the play, so these self-inflicted beatings are built into the music.[7] The judge's song was cut because Prince didn't like it or know how to stage it. "It was so explicit," he admitted, adding, "and I thought it was pretty gruesome." Some cast members intimate the real reason for the cut was that the number was too controversial and off-putting from the main thrust of the story.

Sweeney Todd opened on March 1, 1979, to mostly enthusiastic reviews for the musical and raves for its stars, Len Cariou and Angela Lansbury. But *Variety* noted that "It seems improbable that the general theater public will want to attend *Sweeney Todd* or that party and matinee audiences will be diverted by or even attracted to it. There have been reports of numerous intermission walkouts during the previews."

Martin Gottfried, writing in the *Saturday Review*, went even further, wondering "why anyone would want to see it. . . . Stage works must give us something, entertain us in some way; frighten or enlighten or move or simply divert and

---

[7] The judge's song was included in the recording and restored in the New York City Opera staging. Its lyrics were printed in the addendum to the libretto, with the excuse given for its omission being "reasons of time," although a note said that "the authors feel it helps particularize the character of Judge Turpin."

amuse. They must control us, set our lives by the curtain's rise and fall. They must have something theatrical to accomplish. This musical . . . seems in the end but a brilliant exercise."

But Douglas Watt called it "a staggering theater spectacle and more fun than a graveyard on the night of the annual skeleton's ball." Jack Viertel, writing in the *Herald-Examiner*, said, "In writing Sweeney's song, Sondheim has laid out before him the very elements that he seems most to thrive on: overt madness and passion betrayed by human frailty."

Richard Eder, critic for the *New York Times*, had mixed feelings and felt the show dictated a "confusion of purpose." He said that "when the cast lines up and says there are Sweeneys all around, the point is unproven." "That was Steve," Prince acknowledged. "I didn't feel it." Neither man understood that Sondheim did not mean the evil he pointed out was contained within the theater walls. It was out there on the side streets near Broadway and in London's East End.

From our vantage point more than two decades later, Sondheim's metaphoric prognosis has proven true. There are more serial killers, more Sweeneys, everywhere. Thomas Shepard feels "you're dealing with some pretty unpleasant people . . . bloodthirsty. Sweeney Todd is certainly a sociopathic killer. The judge and the beadle are crooked." Julia McKenzie too believes Sondheim was prescient "in pointing out the 'Sweeneys' among us, here and in *Into the Woods*. I think we are living in a dehumanized society and so I think Steve is very realistic. He's telling the truth. People are wrong when they say he has a jaundiced view."

As for Sondheim's penchant for mystery and horror, Shepard believes it is "a reflection of . . . a dark secret side to Sondheim which may or may not be hinted at in his work, but for sure he's a very complicated and probably a very disturbed person. How much of it really comes through in his work, I don't know."

In spite of the varying opinions, from horrific to brilliant, *Sweeney Todd* settled in for a run, awaiting the Tony Awards to be handed out two months later. It won eight of the nine awards for which it was nominated: Best Musical, Best Score, Best Libretto, Best Direction, Best Set, Best Costumes, Best Actress in a Musical (Angela Lansbury), and Best Actor in a Musical (Len Cariou).

This bonanza was immediately reflected at the box office, and most of the reviews thereafter were positive. The cavernous Uris Theatre was packed on weekends, which helped to defray the cost of the midweek's empty seats. The critics had never been lukewarm; now some of them changed their spots and got behind the show. Audiences who had stayed away were now coming to see what all the fuss was about. Thomas Shepard produced a two-record version of almost the entire score, which also helped to popularize the work.[8] Prince was ecstatic and in an interview with Dick Cavett said that *Sweeney* swept away the feelings that Prince and Sondheim were "bad for each other." It looked like it might be a money maker.

Lansbury and Cariou played the show for a year and were replaced by Dorothy Loudon and George Hearn, who received equally extravagant reviews, but business plodded along after the two original stars left, and it closed on June 19, 1980, after having given 558 performances.

The London edition presented by the Robert Stigwood Organization did not fare very well, managing to eke out only a four-month run at the Drury Lane. Sheridan Morley deplored its shameful treatment at the hands of British critics, which "caused it to be ignored by most theatregoers. But," he promised, "it would eventually emerge as one of the most important and influential musicals of the century." And he was indeed prescient, for *Sweeney Todd* has been presented by theatrical troupes all over the world and taken its rightful place in the repertory of many of the world's opera houses, including Helsinki, Cologne, Munster, Opera North, Chicago Lyric Opera, and the Metropolitan Opera in New York.

Sweeney Todd lost a great deal of money for the Stigwood Organization, but they were making it up on productions of Andrew Lloyd-Webber, whose *Evita* in the year that followed would win almost as many Tony awards as *Sweeney* had.

As for its Broadway staging, Prince had not been involved as producer and was paid his salary as director. Nevertheless, in spite of its sixteen-month run on Broadway, the show only repaid 59 percent of its investment. As Prince says: "It may have won every award in the book, but it didn't pay back." That meant it would be much harder for Prince to raise money for the next Sondheim venture *if* he cared to produce it.

Soon enough, shortly after *Sweeney* closed on Broadway, Prince's wife, Judy, who had been nagging her husband to do a musical about young people, got her wish. Prince thought of a show he had enjoyed when he himself was a teenager: *Merrily We Roll Along.* He was *eager* to produce it. He called Sondheim, and, as Prince recalled, "It was the first time he ever said yes on the phone."

Now, for the last time, the team was off and running again.

---

[8] "On stage when Sweeney pulls the lever on the chair," Shepard said recently, "the sound of the body falling is vertical—from top to bottom. You can't do that in stereo, so I had to make all the body falls horizontal. There it goes from speaker to speaker."

Song and Cat Dancing

B Y THE END OF 1978, with *Evita*'s London opening behind him and ticket lines around the block proclaiming its megahit status, Andrew Lloyd-Webber had become one of the musical theater's exceptional commodities: a critic-proof composer. Not only had his new musical succeeded in cleansing his name after the debacle of *Jeeves*, but *Evita*'s original cast album, from which the stage musical had been adapted, was still high on the charts. The success of its Broadway opening anytime it deigned to go abroad was assured.

Sheridan Morley, one of Britain's finest critics, had proclaimed that "what mattered about *Evita* was . . . that for the first time in eighteen years since *Oliver!* London could actually boast a musical which could be exported across the Atlantic with a feeling of pride instead of the usual deep embarrassment."

In 1981 Paramount Pictures would buy the film rights, beginning a star search whose outcome supplied theatrical gossip columnists for more than a decade. The winner was not to be chosen until 1995, when Madonna was finally cast as the blonde spitfire and the film began shooting at last.

From the vantage point of the end of the '70s Lloyd-Webber could look back at a time in June 1971 when the Broadway Drama Desk had voted him most promising composer of the year. Certainly now, with three hits out of four times at bat, he had satisfied their faith. Promising and ambitious, too, were his plans for Sydmonton, where since 1976 he had held his annual festival. It was a beautiful spot for the performance of music, and Andrew, now an estate holder and paterfamilias—his first child, daughter Imogen, had been born that year— wanted everyone to see how successful he had become. His belief that audiences should be exposed to all kinds of music, from popular to serious to rock, spawned these summer weekends of music making. He might envision a new kind of festival where the performances at his stately home would one day rival those at England's most chic. Soon Lloyd-Webber would become ambitious enough to want to acquire the lands surrounding the manor house, as far as the eye could see. Eventually he did.

The first festival featured a cello recital, works by various composers played by brother Julian. But the motives behind the yearly festival were not totally altruistic. *Evita*, which was premiered there the following year, had profited by its country performance. As did Sondheim in his "tryouts" instigated by Prince, Lloyd-Webber learned from hearing his works in embryo, although he could be more easily swayed from polishing a work due to an enthusiastic audience reaction than could Sondheim.

Since the initial days of the festival, Andrew and Julian, distant throughout their teens, had become closer. The two had been collaborators as boys in the toy theater days, but as they grew older, their musical and even their social paths diverged. Julian had little interest in popular music and had been giving concerts since he was in his early twenties. He had already recorded works as diverse as a collection of Bach solos and an album of modern British cello music and was considered one of the finest cellists of his generation.

The brothers had last worked together in 1974 when Andrew had been asked to compose incidental music for Ronald Neame's film *The Odessa File*. The background score featured Julian and a rock band, and although neither the picture nor his score had been successful, Andrew liked the iconoclastic combination of instruments and squirreled away the sound in his mind.

For three years after that, Julian had been after his older sibling to write a piece for cello and orchestra he could premiere, "Because," he wrote, "I felt he would approach the cello in a new and creative way. For a while he stalled on the idea . . . because he was busy with other projects." But in the end, the *Variations*, which would be Andrew's next work, was created because he lost a bet to Julian.

Both brothers attended football matches, rooting lustily for their favorite team, the Leyton Orient. In the 1976–77 season the O's, notorious losers, were at their nadir—in last place. They had to get at least a draw in their final home match to remain in the league. Andrew, pessimist that he was, believed they would lose, while Julian "*knew* the lads would pull through." If they did not win, Andrew was to write the piece without delay. It seems that Julian had nothing to lose from the wager.

On May 17, Orient somehow managed a 1–1 draw with Hull, and Andrew, true to his word, began the piece: *Variations*, a series of twenty-three variations on Paganini's Twenty-Fourth Caprice for Solo Violin. The well-known theme, which was first arranged for the piano as a finger-breaking solo by Franz Liszt, also attracted Brahms so mightily that he wrote two complete books of variations for the instrument. Later, Rachmaninoff penned one of his most enduring compositions for piano and orchestra. Nor had this melody's popularity been con-

Julian Lloyd Webber. Photo: Roger Elliott.

fined to the serious music area. There was a *Variations* that made the charts much earlier. In the mid-1950s, Winifred Atwill's "Variation on A minor Caprice" by Paganini reached number nine in the popular music charts. It took *chutzpa* or naïveté to risk the implicit comparisons that such an undertaking would imply, but Andrew had a generous supply of both.

Lloyd-Webber was much taken with *Electric Savage*, a solo recording, which consisted mostly of improvisation on synthesizers along with heavy rock drumming performed by a group called Colosseum II. He thought they could provide a perfect background for the cello solos. For his new composition, which he termed a dialogue for cello and rock band, besides the synthesizers, he decided to add yet another melodic soloist—a wind—and he knew he would need a fine instrumentalist, one who could read flute and alto flute parts as well as being able to double on tenor and alto saxophone. He found just such a versatile musician in Barbara Thompson, who happened to be band drummer John Hiseman's wife.

For source material, besides the Paganini theme, he included two songs that came out of his trunk. Both had been excised from earlier musicals. One was taken from *The Likes of Us*, the Barnardo musical, his first work with Tim Rice, and the other had almost made it into *Jeeves*. The second, in A major, seems more appropriate to the *Variations*, although it must be admitted that neither has the genetic feeling of having sprung from the original theme, which is the way variations are generally written. It may be hard for the lay listener to appreciate the relationship, but even Rachmaninoff's famous eighteenth variation in his well-known quasi-concerto, which has a popular melodic line that seems to have little connection with the original melody, is simply an inversion of Paganini's theme in major.

Variations was first performed at the Sydmonton festival in August 1977, and then after two weeks of concentrated eight-hour sessions at Babson's Morgan Studios in Willesden, the same studios where Mick Jagger, Rod Stewart, and the Beatles had recorded, the score was put on tape. The recording was not released until January 3 of the next year, and by the following morning it had rocketed to eighth place on the charts. In a few weeks it soared to the number two spot and stayed there.

Variations was the first of Andrew Lloyd-Webber's compositions to be released under the banner of the Really Useful Group, Ltd.,[1] a corporate entity he formed to protect any of his income that was not directly related to his contract with Stigwood. He was still seething under the terms of the ruinous contract negotiated in 1969 by Myers and Land. Under its terms, he and Tim Rice split a 10 percent royalty on their works—*but they paid one quarter of it back to Stigwood as his management fee*. It had been an inequitable deal from the outset, arranged before the Rice–Lloyd-Webber success, and Andrew, canny in business affairs, had little respect for, and much less trust of, Stigwood.

As for Stigwood, he was glad Lloyd-Webber would be getting out of his hair. He would continue to manage *Joseph*, *Superstar*, and *Evita*, but it would be a relief to him not to have to work with Lloyd-Webber any more. Although he had made a great deal of money from the Rice-Webber works, by the time his contract with them was about to expire, the Robert Stigwood Organization had moved on to producing blockbuster films such as *Saturday Night Fever* and *Grease*.

Stigwood had little patience with Andrew Lloyd-Webber, who was almost paranoid about being cheated, always checking and rechecking the books. But Lloyd-Webber, unlike Tim Rice, had paid careful attention to the financial ar-

---

[1] The name was derived from Wilbert Awdry's book about trains, a childhood favorite of Lloyd-Webber's and a concept he was itching to develop into a musical. It would eventually blossom as 1984's *Starlight Express*.

Andrew Lloyd-Webber shakes hands with Tim Rice on the occasion of the launch of the Really Useful Group, Ltd. (RUG) on the London Stock Market in 1986. First shares opened at £3.20 ($4.58). AP/Wide World Photos.

rangements of shows he was involved with and, like most theater denizens, knew that producers generally lived off the profits of a show. Unless one got royalties from the gross, there was rarely anything left for the net. He also knew that producers were able to charge planes, parties, even yachts—Stigwood had bought himself one—to the production and manipulate the books so a hit show could actually appear to be running at a loss.

In the '70s the Inland Revenue tax laws were stringent on royalties—as much as 90 percent of annual income could go to the government. As one was paid royalties as a salary, they could never be considered a capital gain and spread over a period of years, which would have decreased the tax bite. A producer, however, could call his income a capital gain by stretching his profits over a period of several years, and Lloyd-Webber knew that if he could set himself up as his own producer and managing agent, he could immediately lower his effective tax rate from the high 90s to a manageable 30 percent.

Thus when he signed the recording contract for *Variations*, for the first time his name was listed as composer *and* producer. Soon he was to set up a company to publish his own music. Knowing how successful he had been on his first foray with *Variations*, he wanted to have more works in his catalogue.

He called Rice, who came up with the idea of a television show cycle about an English girl and the problems in her love life. Rice's idea, a return to the small, which Lloyd-Webber latched onto with pleasure, would provide a congenial antidote to the giganticism of *Evita*. Andrew began some melodies and Tim sketched out a few lyrics for the piece, keeping in mind the voice of Elaine Paige, who was then starring in *Evita*.

It was known to all theaterfolk that Tim Rice, married and the father of two children, was carrying on a blatant affair with Paige. Lloyd-Webber was especially offended, and he knew if the song cycle came to fruition, it would have to star Paige, making him almost a third party to the relationship. Besides Rice's flagrant liaison, his laid-back quality—working when he pleased, vacationing at will—had always vexed Andrew. He felt there was no way out but to search for a new lyricist for this project. It did not look like the team had come to the end of the road, just a small parting of the ways until Tim's love life got sorted out—but indeed, except for *Cricket*, a short piece written in 1986 for Queen Elizabeth's sixtieth birthday, there would be no more major collaborations between Lloyd-Webber and Rice. At thirty years of age, already a world-renowned composer, Andrew Lloyd-Webber was still the impetuous child of the toy theater days, unable to sit still, unable to enjoy his fame. Eager not to let a day go by during which he was not adding to his catalogue, he knew he had to work with a dedicated professional. The experience of working with Alan Ayckbourn, whose first musical *Jeeves* had been, was still sticking in his throat.

He chose perhaps the best unattached lyricist in Britain, Don Black. Black, who had wide experience in stage musicals, had made a name for himself in movie music, writing about a hundred lyrics for cinema, mostly main title songs. He had consistently worked with the best, people like Elmer Bernstein, Quincy Jones, Michel Legrand, Neal Hefti, and Charles Aznavour. His lyrics for "Diamonds Are Forever" and "Thunderball" were spot-on, and "To Sir, With Love" had gone to number one on all the charts. He had even won an Academy Award for "Born Free."

After some years in Hollywood, Black's ambition led him away from Tinsel Town into writing for the stage. There too, as had happened to Lloyd-Webber, fortune smiled on him the first time out. "When John Barry came into my life," Black said recently, "and thought *Billy Liar* would make a great musical, I loved the idea of it because it was all in the North of England and I could use language like Sondheim did in *West Side Story* with his Puerto Ricans."

Black understands theater lyrics; his work has a warmth and theatricality that Rice seems to lack. He is not as rebellious or as adventuresome as Rice, but that implies, to his credit, that he is never pretentious as Rice can often be. His mind doesn't run to literary showing off like "a woman at sixes and sevens— dressed to the nines." His work has evolved through popular songs to stage songs of character. Theater was the natural area into which his work would develop because he is aware, as he says, "of what you can say on stage that you cannot say in pop songs. It's not just looking for a title and a hook, it's character development—you can be funny, you can be heartbreaking, you can be solemn, you can be stupid in a theater. Whereas with a pop song it's a matter of how's it go? Where's the hook?" In Lloyd-Webber's case, Black might have added, it was really: how high is it going to go on the charts?

"After *Billy* I started on a journey of musicals—some of them failed musicals. I once compared doing musicals to doing your own root canal work. You can spend a couple of years writing it and nothing happens and in the end you lose the tooth. But I remembered Alan Lerner once telling me not to worry about failure. He said that good things often happen from something that's failed. *Bar Mitzvah Boy*, a musical I did, was a great opportunity. Martin Charnin, who wrote the book and had directed *Annie*, staged it, and the legendary Jule Styne wrote the music. But it didn't work. It was a great adventure and I found it easy to write with joy about a Jewish boy—my roots. We screwed it up. We made too much of it. I was really quite heartbroken. As often happens with musicals you can get a great idea, and before you know where you are, people are dancing on pianos—it's a big production. And you say 'hang on. What happened to our little dream?'

"However, just as I was feeling really shattered by that blow, two or three things happened. One, I got a cable from Michael Bennett saying 'best lyrics I've heard on the stage for years. Love, Michael,' which was wonderful when the reviews that came in were terrible. The other one was from Hal Prince; I've still got it. He said, 'Bravo, bravo. Your work is superb.' The other thing, which is probably the main thing, was that I got a phone call from Andrew Lloyd-Webber. He said, 'Let's have lunch.' And I did have lunch with him, and he said he loved *Bar Mitzvah Boy* and he loved my work. And Alan Lerner's words, that things happen from failure, came back to me."

At that lunch, Lloyd-Webber told Black that he wanted to do a one-woman show about an English girl. When Black asked who the girl was, he said he didn't know. "Could it be about an English girl in America?" Black offered. "There are so many of them." Lloyd-Webber was taken with the suggestion and came back to Black's apartment in Knightsbridge. "He played me some tunes— one turned out to be a song I called 'Tell Me on a Sunday,' and another which I called 'Take That Look Off Your Face.' And we started. The third tune he played me was what I called 'Capped Teeth and Caesar Salad.' Andrew was bowled over by the title, and by then we knew we had something."

Built on Black's libretto, the work wrote itself very quickly, aiming for a premiere that September at the 1979 Sydmonton festival. As Black has proven in all his subsequent collaborations with Lloyd-Webber, the work of the newly formed team is written to be *seen* as well as heard. This would be the first time (discounting *By Jeeves*) Andrew would be writing something that was not committed to vinyl first. And the very first time he wrote with a particular voice in mind.

Marti Webb, who had been playing the *Evita* matinees to take some of the strain off Elaine Paige, was the one they chose. "What I like about Marti is her wonderful ordinariness," Black said. "I wanted the story to be about an average girl who is overawed by New York, Hollywood, the glamour and the buildings. She couldn't be a sharp girl."

Black had years of managerial experience, having looked after the career of singer Matt Monroe in earlier days, and when both men decided that Marti Webb's rather strident and "ordinary" voice was the one they wanted, Lloyd-Webber asked Black to manage her.

According to Black, "Andrew was nervous about her, and he was monitoring her career. . . . He was very worried that we would write this major work for somebody and then she'd be handled by an idiot." Of course, with Black steering her career, the Really Useful Group could easily negotiate favorable terms with their budding star.

Tell Me on a Sunday is the story of Emma, a talented hat designer (what used to be called a modiste), "an ordinary British girl from Muswell Hill," who comes to America. As it is a monodrama, it needs several imaginary characters for the protagonist to sing her thoughts to. Chief among them, besides the various men in her life, are her English chum, Viv, who has come to New York a year earlier, and her Mum back home.

When Emma first arrives in New York to live with her boyfriend, a musician, her opening number, "Take That Look Off Your Face," is sung to Viv, and it will work as a bookend to the end of the musical. In it, she tells us she is frightened of turning into the hard-bitten city career girl, or worse, the user of men that she hears so many English girls in America have become. On the night she arrives, shortly after she rubs the stardust of the city's imagined grandeur from her eyes, she discovers her beau has many other girls. Promising to pay him back the fare that he lent her—once she gets her green card—she walks out. She moves in with Viv and shortly afterwards meets Sheldon Bloom, a Hollywood producer who relocates her out in Tinsel Town. Sheldon, about whose plastic lifestyle we learn little except his obvious ambition, soon becomes too busy to see her, and Emma heads back to New York.

But Emma, through Black's eyes, is a sharp observer, and in one of the show's more successful songs, "Capped Teeth and Caesar Salad," she has much to say about the mores of Hollywood. I quote the first verse:

Capped teeth and Caesar salad, good old Beverly Hills.
With ev'ry deal that's done, an award is won.
You can rent a car, or rent a star.

Suntans and Sunday brunches, sprinklers sprinkle away.
It's like a fairy tale, long as you don't inhale.
I'll call back and have a nice day ...

Back in Greenwich Village she meets Joe, a salesman, now the real love of her life. But after a while, once they have planned a more permanent relationship, Emma finds out that Joe is not always out of town on the days he says he is. After they split up, she takes Viv's advice, which is that new men make her feel she belongs in New York. Then she meets Paul, who is married, settled, with four kids. The new relationship, plus the acquisition of a green card and her burgeoning career, help her forget Joe's terrible fear of commitment. In her song "Nothing Like You've Ever Known," she comes to accept the noon to two relationship that allows her to get ahead with her career.

On the day Nieman-Marcus buys her whole collection, she is ecstatic until Paul appears at her flat that night and announces that he has told his wife of their love and wants to marry her. She is horrified at the home wreck she has caused for two reasons: first, that she does not love Paul, whom she sends away, but, more important, because she realizes she has used him and despises the user that she has turned into. Promising (a bit hollowly—a contrivance that tries to create an "up" ending) that she will return to the idealistic person she once was, she now sings "Take That Look Off Your Face" to her mirror. In the song she vows to become the Emma, pure and trusting, who landed at JFK a year earlier.

The doormat quality of Emma is hard to believe in the era of the liberated female. Worse is the static quality of a one-person narrative, especially as she only tells us about the other characters. But with telephone conversations, her letters to her Mum, and confrontations with Viv, Black has almost created the illusion that there is some dialogue going on on stage.

Most of Emma's correspondence with her Mum is nostalgic and sentimental, yet it is told with humor and often insightful: "Sheldon's so dynamic he is sweeping me away./ He is funny, he is handsome ... strangely handsome,/ Well, there's no words to describe him./ You can't imagine Sheldon Bloom unless you know L.A." Later, after the affair has ended, Emma writes: "I never hear from Sheldon, but I read what he is up to, / He's working on a musical, 'bout Rommel as a boy / Mum, I've never seen a drink here that isn't full of ice-cubes / And I've never met a waiter here who doesn't say 'Enjoy!' "

There is no denying this is a three-handkerchief saga, but the haunting concept of the title song set to one of Lloyd-Webber's most memorable melodies treads the delicate ground between pride and despair.

Don't write me a letter when you want to
   leave.
Don't call me at 3 A.M. from a friend's
   apartment.

I'd like to choose how I hear the news.
Take me to a park that's covered with trees
Tell me on a Sunday, please.

Tell Me on a Sunday, as the work eventually was called, was heartily approved by the Sydmonton audience, who heard it balanced with a one-man show by Edward Duke called *Jeeves Takes Charge*. That November the cycle, arranged for orchestra and still with Marti Webb, was transferred to vinyl. The recording went on to great success, and because the story is such an intimate one, it seemed ideal for the small screen. A television performance was hastily arranged. Like all of Lloyd-Webber's earlier works for the stage, this one had an audience already familiar with its songs, thus *Tell Me on a Sunday* was so well received on the BBC that a repeat was telecast the following February.

During those months in late 1979, with *Evita* now a huge hit on Broadway (where it would remain for four years), Lloyd-Webber was not content to let *Sunday* remain a TV one- or two-shot, and he began thinking about what kind of piece he could pair his cantata with. He had toyed for some time with the idea of doing a one-act opera about the friendship between Puccini and Leoncavallo, which turned to bitter rivalry when both of them decided to write an opera based on Murger's *Scènes de La Vie de Bohème*. Lloyd-Webber even began an aria based on Puccini's heroine's "Mi chiamano Mimi," creating a different melody.

But he knew that Italian opera was too far away from the odyssey of an English girl abroad and would never make for a balanced evening. Then he tackled and rejected Dickens's gloomy tale, *The Signal Man*. At last he left his solo cycle alone and only occasionally fretted about the other short work that might balance *Sunday*. Its theme would one day occur to him, he knew.

Better to begin a new project entirely. But since 1978, ever since *Evita* opened, he and Tim Rice could not come to any agreement on what their next project might be. Tim was never open-minded or flexible. Now he was talking about doing a play about two chess players, one Russian, the other American, competing for the love of the same woman. But gamesmanship and an adversarial story did not appeal to Lloyd-Webber. If there were to be rivalries, they had better be musical ones like the Puccini-Leoncavallo feud.

Then he chose a middle course and suggested something really dramatic to Tim Rice: *Sunset Boulevard*, the *grand guignol* movie, he felt would make a blockbuster musical. But Rice nixed the idea, saying he didn't see how one could improve on Billy Wilder's film. Still Lloyd-Webber persevered and, wanting to intrigue his collaborator, played him one of the best melodies he had ever written. This moving strain, originally intended for the Puccini opus, was to accompany the silent film star after having killed her lover, as she descended the grand staircase to relive what she thought were her past glories.

The theme, which anyone who has had enough training in sight-singing will recognize as "Memory," Grizabella's haunting song that was to become the centerpiece of *Cats* and achieve world-wide celebrity, was indeed borrowed from the Puccini opus. After he had written it, Andrew Lloyd-Webber had called on his father and, as the melodic line smacked so of the verismo composer's style, asked, "Does this theme sound like anything, to you?"

"Yes," William shot back, "it sounds like a million pounds to me."

Lloyd-Webber put it away and was not about to take it out until a year later. Meanwhile, eager to work at something, anything, almost as a lark, he had been setting T. S. Eliot's verses from *Old Possum's Book of Practical Cats* simply because he loved the poems. Back in 1972 during all the crossing and recrossing of the Atlantic that the staging of *Jesus Christ Superstar* entailed, Lloyd-Webber had come upon the book in an airport bookstore, and, since then, a copy of it was never far from his briefcase or the desk of his piano.

Setting these verses about Jellicle cats to music was like reliving his past. His family had never been without a multitude of felines throughout his early days in Harrington Court. He was not sure if a song cycle based on the Eliot verses could be given a story and hammered to fit with *Sunday*. But no matter, it was a joy to work on the settings, and the poems brought out some of his most felicitous music. In this endeavor he was not unlike Oscar Hammerstein, who reveled while working on *Carmen Jones* because "his collaborator was always at hand."

But it was more than that with Andrew Lloyd-Webber; it was a challenge. "I wanted to set existing verse to music," he was to say. "When I have written with lyricists in the past we have agreed together on the dramatic structure, but for the most part, the lyrics have been written to the music. So I was intrigued to see whether I could write a complete piece the other way 'round."

By the summer of 1980, Lloyd-Webber presented his song-cycle at Sydmonton. Fleshing out the program, he presented the *Missa Brevis* by Alan Stuckey.

Having planned an elegant and serious evening, he invited T. S. Eliot's widow, Valerie, then a woman of fifty-two (she had been forty years younger than her husband). She was delighted with the young composer's treatment of her husband's work and even offered to supply him with some letters about the poems and to hunt down an unpublished eight-line fragment about Grizabella, the Glamour Cat, which Eliot had omitted from the collection because he felt it was too somber for the young.

Cameron Mackintosh was at Sydmonton that summer too. He approved of the amusing song cycle and thought the songs would make a brilliant *coup de théatre*, but he had no idea how they should be put together. When he learned that Valerie had papers and some unpublished verses he felt there might just be a show lurking in Lloyd-Webber and Eliot's felines.

Cameron Mackintosh's place in the British musical of the last third of the twentieth century runs a close parallel to Harold Prince's on Broadway. Both men were drawn to things theatrical, especially musical theater, from their earliest days, and each in his youth became a walking encyclopedia of stage lore. Both eventually came to dominate the musical theater not only in their native countries but throughout the world. Besides working with the era's two major players, Andrew Lloyd-Webber and Stephen Sondheim, each man's vision spilled over into the area of discovering other great musical works, shaping them to his own image and shepherding them to the stage. "When I started off," Mackintosh says, "I was given a book about Cochran, the great British producer, who was giving advice to aspiring young producers. He said 'never put a show on for audiences, always put it on for yourself.'" It is advice Mackintosh has followed slavishly, so much so that his shows always have an intense Mackintosh stamp.

Hal Prince once revealed why he felt the English would never produce a good musical. "They are too polite," he explained, adding that the one in charge must be ruthless, able to give a flat out "no" to a dance routine, a costume or set, a new song, or even a whole scene that represents weeks of diligent and thoughtful labor of one of his collaborators.

But Prince did not know Mackintosh. He has, according to Lloyd-Webber, "strong creative views on practically everything." Andrew deplored the interruptions of his producer. "Sometimes we'd be doing a song and Cameron would say, 'I don't like that.' And I'd say, 'Cameron, just wait a minute! Let's get through to the end and then we'll work it out.'"

His opinionated and stubborn traits go back to his earliest days. Like Prince and Lloyd-Webber, Mackintosh had a toy theater where he and his brother would give puppet shows. "The shows have to start on time," he told his parents. "If you're late you can't come in." So his Maltese mother and Scottish father responded, "But, if we don't come in, you'll have no audience."

"Never mind," the boy retorted, "to every show you want to be on time."

In 1954, when he was eight, he attended his first show, Julian Slade's *Salad Days*, and admits he was "captivated by this enchanting tale where a piano could make all of London dance." The young Mackintosh insisted on an interview with Slade. The composer spent serious time with the boy, and, not unlike Hammerstein who immediately gave of himself when young Sondheim showed theatrical aptitude, he gave Cameron a tour of the backstage and showed him how the production was run.

"I'd like to do this when I grow up," Cameron declared.

He left school at sixteen for a course at the Central School of Speech and Drama but eventually deserted that for actual experience: a job backstage at Theater Royal, Drury Lane. To earn extra money, in the mornings he also cleaned the theater. Before long he had cadged office space from a theatrical agent, had cards printed, and enlisted his mother as secretary.

"When someone calls what am I to say?" she asked.

"Never say you are my mother. Simply say Cameron Mackintosh Productions."

Looking far younger than his twenty years, he effected a grand manner, took a tiny room in Mayfair so he might have a chic address, traveled everywhere by taxi. Before the year was out he began touring low-budget mysteries, mostly by Agatha Christie, around the country.

Ambitious, precocious, and thinking he knew everything, he decided to bring Cole Porter's *Anything Goes* as his first big production into the West End. Every calamity that could happen to a production befell that one: "Backers withdrew, the leading lady left, scenery fell down. If I knew anything about the theater I'd have pulled the plug. In my ignorance I assumed this was what it was always like. We closed in two weeks." The lesson he learned has served him well: that it doesn't really matter how good the songs are, but if the book isn't really strong and the songs don't grow out of it, you don't have a good musical."

After *Anything Goes* and a stage version of *The Dales*, a popular radio serial, which was an even worse failure, Mackintosh found himself deeply in debt and went back to stage managing until he returned to solvency. As soon as his checkbook was in the black he got the urge to produce again, but he had learned never to invest his own money. This time he produced Julian Slade's *Trelawny*, adapted from Pinero's *Trelawny of the Wells*, and a production he nursed from scratch, *The Card*. Both were critical successes but failures with the public. Yet along the way there were some hits: *The Rocky Horror Show*, *Godspell*, and, as mentioned earlier, *Side by Side by Sondheim* which he produced for £6,000 and which eventually netted more than £100,000.

It was at about this time that Mackintosh and Lloyd-Webber had their first contentious meeting. It was at the Society of West End Theatre Awards in 1978, which Mackintosh was producing. *Evita* had been named best musical that year, and a group of songs from his show had been prepared by Lloyd-Webber. They were to be performed before he gave his speech accepting the award. Mackintosh had asked only for "Don't Cry for Me Argentina," but Lloyd-Webber stuck to his guns and insisted on the medley. Mackintosh had not planned on the use of multiple microphones in the *Evita* segment, and halfway through the several songs the sound system went awry and a horrible caterwauling ensued.

In his acceptance speech Lloyd-Webber thanked all those involved with the show. "*Evita*," he concluded, "was a great show because it had a great director. That is exactly what this show needed tonight. Thank you very much."

Cameron Mackintosh was furious and, fortified by claret, threatened to go to Lloyd-Webber's house and punch him in the nose, but he passed out in the back of the taxi.

A few days later Mackintosh received a letter of apology from Lloyd-Webber, saying he had not intended to upset Mr. Mackintosh with his remarks. It was obvious that Andrew realized he and Mackintosh were two tremendous forces— the most important talents in their country's musical theater. Like an electro-magnet, they could either repel or attract each other. Andrew also remembered the cardinal rule of showbiz: never, NEVER, close a door on ANYONE. You can't know in which future production you will be working together.

With the arrival of the letter Mackintosh realized he had been dealing with a man who was routinely prepared to work himself up into a manic frenzy to achieve his ends but could come down to earth when he had overstepped. He accepted the apology and told Lloyd-Webber that he would be busy for the next months with his productions for the Arts Council, but they would get together when he finished his tour.

Leicester Haymarket was putting on *My Fair Lady* so Mackintosh had cleverly gone to the Arts Council and suggested a coproduction. The council was very pleased because it was the start of a way to bring subsidized theaters and com-mercial productions together. Mackintosh oversaw a lavish production and tour of the classic using mostly unknowns but featuring Anna Neagle as Mrs. Higgins. The next year he had little trouble persuading the Arts Council, whose coffers were now replenished, to launch a tour of *Oklahoma!* This really propelled him into a career as a major producer.

For almost two years composer and producer kept clear of each other until one day in 1980, Andrew Lloyd-Webber called and invited Cameron Mackin-tosh to lunch at the Savile, his club. Across that table each could recognize his need for the other, and, accepting their common volatility and headstrongness, they knew they could contain their tempers in their mutual quest for success. They chuckled when they realized that each man had an inordinate fondness for wine and good food, but they were utterly serious when they looked at the qualities that made each of them run—incredible ambition and passion for musical theater.

Mackintosh felt that Lloyd-Webber was the hope of the emerging British musical and allowed that the American product, apart from Sondheim, was on the way down. Nobody on Broadway even admitted that the Beatles, Elvis Presley, or the Rolling Stones existed.

At the turn of the century, he claimed, the American musical was built on European talent. Most of the forefathers of what would become the American musical—Sigmund Romberg, Oscar Straus, Rudolph Friml, Emmerich Kalman, even Gilbert and Sullivan—had their roots in Europe. He declared the success of *Joseph*, *Superstar*, and *Evita* in America had happened because Lloyd-Webber and Rice's work was pop oriented, and Europe, notably Britain, would once again lead the pack.

And he was right. In hindsight, from Mackintosh's vantage point in 1980, one can see that Irving Berlin's popular songs and Rodgers and Hart's sassy pop music had injected the imported Broadway musical with invigorating new life. The form (always with the exception of the work of Stephen Sondheim and Harold Prince) had become routine, clinging to a carbon copy of past successes, still emulating the golden musicals of the '60s. It had now lost the voice that formerly spoke to large numbers of the population. Even Sondheim and Prince's intellectual musicals were aimed at an elite group, and although Sondheim's music has an exciting rhythmic restlessness, it is a far cry from pop.

When one looks at Mackintosh's later productions of Claude-Michel Schönberg and Alain Boublil's *Les Misérables* and *Miss Saigon*, it is obvious that they grow out of international rock, where the composer and lyricist began. ABBA and Tim Rice, who went on to write *Chess*, had their roots in pop music too. Pop music, plus clever marketing of the blockbuster hit before the show opens,[2] is behind the resurgence of the British musical.

After that lunch, Lloyd-Webber invited Mackintosh back to his flat in Eaton Place and played him his settings of the *Cats* score. He admitted that he had pitched them at several people, but nobody thought there was a musical there.

Mackintosh did.

And he suggested that Trevor Nunn, the director of the Royal Shakespeare

---

[2] The custom of trying to create several song hits before a show opened has been declining in the United States since the early '60s, as the libretto became more important and songs were integrated into the story. Hit songs and reprises only served to stop the action. The late Jule Styne remembered how it used to be: "At the time of *Gypsy* or *Bells Are Ringing* I could walk into a record company and say, 'Here it is: So-and-so will record this number and so-and-so will do that one.' And you had eight hit singles before the show opened."

Company, was a creative enough director to mold *Cats* into shape for the stage. Although Nunn had never directed a full musical, the year before he had staged a delightful fifteen-minute tribute to Hollywood musicals as the finale of George S. Kaufman's *Once in a Lifetime*. Lloyd-Webber, badly burned by his experience with Ayckbourn in their *Jeeves* collaboration, asked Jamie Muir, a close friend, about Nunn. "Clever Trevor," came the reply, was not a man to let politeness stand in the way of performance. In fact, it was known in theater circles that "his bite was worse than his bark." Cameron Mackintosh and Andrew Lloyd-Webber both knew Nunn had his finger on Eliot's poems combined with the pulse of contemporary British theater in a way that Hal Prince could never understand.[3]

At first Nunn tried to make a story out of the poems, stringing them together like *Alice Through the Looking Glass*, but he realized this would never work because they weren't written as narrative. Then he fine-combed Eliot's correspondence and letters of the period of *Old Possum's Book of Practical Cats*. Among copious notes that Valerie Eliot had so graciously provided, he found a letter denying Walt Disney the rights to turn his felines into a cartoon. He also found a monodrama written by composer Alan Rawsthorne that had been read over a performance of his music. At last he came upon a reference to "the Heaveside Layer." The poet described this as a kind of paradise to which a worthy animal, having lived through nine unhappy lives on earth, might be transported. This tribal aspect became the show's concept: a loner who wanted to rejoin the community.

Combining this idea with the fragment of the poem:

She haunted many a low resort	And the postman sighed as he scratched his
Near the grimy road of Tottenham Court.	head
She flitted about the no-man's land	You'd really have thought she'd ought to be
From "The Rising Sun" to the "Friend at	dead.
Hand."	And who would ever suppose that that
	Was Grizabella, the Glamour Cat?

might just provide enough of a plot. If one was to have a memorable song, something, say, of the quality of "Don't Cry for Me Argentina," and a luminous star to sing Grizabella, might that almost be enough to hold the show together?

Knowing that the opening must set the tone of the show, Nunn called lyricist Richard Stilgoe, and they cobbled together a premise inspired by sections from Eliot's poems and lines of unpublished verse called "Pollicle Dogs and Jellicle

---

[3] Indeed, when Andrew Lloyd-Webber first showed Hal Prince the "book" of *Cats* Prince asked if it was some kind of elaborate British political metaphor that, as an American, he might not understand. "No," he was told, "it's simply about cats."

Cats." The idea was to humanize the animals and to establish the theory that cats behave a lot like humans.

As for the scope of this groundbreaking effort, it was decided to make it as spectacular as possible. Yet Nunn seemed at cross purposes with this light-hearted, mostly danced show when he hired his associate at the Royal Shake-speare Company, designer John Napier, who had created the sets for *Nicholas Nickleby* but had never done a musical. He took other chances as well, enlisting Gillian Lynne, an English choreographer. This would seem to be suicide, as dancing would be the raison d'être of the show and Lynne was to be co-director. Everybody knew that the English were no match for the Broadway dance direc-tors. Lynne had choreographed many British musicals and had even done some on Broadway, but none of her work had the pizzazz needed for a totally dancing show. Then Nunn took another gamble and hired Judi Dench, their name star, to play Grizabella. Dench was a fine actress but an unknown commodity as a singer.

Even Lloyd-Webber looked like he was set to scuttle the show when he raved on the phone to Cameron Mackintosh about finding the perfect venue for their musical. Lloyd-Webber had been the subject of a surprise edition of *This Is Your Life* televised from the New London Theatre. "Come right over," he babbled, after crew and audience had gone home. "I'm standing in the perfect theater for *Cats*. It's got a revolving stage."

"You have to be kidding," Mackintosh told him. "That theater is the white elephant of all times. It hasn't had a success in ten years."

But he did go over with Nunn and Napier the next day, and even though the New London in Drury Lane was in a drab office block, with a cramped airport departure lounge of a foyer, the theater itself was spacious. No matter that it was hired mostly for conferences, lectures, and television, its first front rows revolved and it had excellent sight-lines throughout. All three envisioned it as perfect for an audience-in-the-round watching what they planned to be a revolutionary dancing show. Besides, it was available at a low rent. They decided at once to make a set that would be unique to this building: a gigantic rubbish heap, all the pieces greatly enlarged so the cats would look normal size. Central to the set was a gigantic tire that would ascend to the heavens near the end of the show, transporting Old Deuteronomy and the Glamour Cat.

With negotiations for the theater finalized by December, Cameron Mackin-tosh was free to call on his usual group of angels to finance the necessary half a million pounds that the production would cost. But nobody wanted to invest.

"I can give you the objections," Mackintosh was to tell an interviewer some years later: "Andrew Lloyd Webber without Robert Stigwood and without Tim Rice; working with a dead poet; with a whole lot of songs about cats, with Trevor Nunn, who's never done a musical in his life . . . working in the theater

Members of the cast of Cats, *the longest-running show in Broadway history. Photo: Carol Rosegg. © Museum of the City of New York.*

with the worst track record in London; asking us to believe that English people can do a dance show when England had never been able to put together any kind of dance entertainment before."

At last, desperate, he placed ads in financial newspapers inviting the general public to invest in shares of not less than £750. In the end 220 angels came forth.

George Barnett, one of them, said, "I saw an article about a producer looking for backers for a new musical. I wrote to him and said I'd like to invest £5,000 in the show. I went to his office carrying a bag of small change and a few big checks from some of the money my mother had left me. The producer said, 'Do you realize you could lose all this money? The nature of show business is that shows do close and some close quite rapidly.' And I said, 'Well, I do realize that but I've got a hunch. I like Andrew's music . . . and it could be a good show.' "[4]

Casting then began in earnest, and the principals were quickly chosen. Besides Judi Dench, the exciting cast included Paul Nicholas, a well-known rock singer,

[4] As of the writing of this book, Mr. Barnett said he has had a return of double his investment every year, which would make an approximate return of £300,000 on his £5,000—and still counting.

and Wayne Sleep, principal dancer with the Royal Ballet. Then an open call for dancers was announced, and hundreds of dancers appeared at the first auditions. Bonnie Langford, Finola Hughes, and Sharon Lee Hill, all experienced dancers, were chosen on the first audition. Sarah Brightman, a twenty-year-old singer-dancer with a most unusual voice, auditioned as well.

Brightman, then married to Andrew Graham-Stewart, was the lead singer of a rock-dance group called Hot Gossip, a collection of black boys and white girls. Slinky, slender, and sexy, her hair cut in spiky punk style and dyed blue, she had recently left the rock group to seek a career in the theater. At her audition she sang a few lines and was dismissed. Imagine her surprise when, a few days later, she received a call from Lloyd-Webber's assistant, Bridget Hayward, to come to his Eaton Place flat for a further audition.

None of Andrew's friends suspected there was anything wrong with his marriage. Nor was the composer known for any "playing around" in a profession notorious for adultery. His apartment in town was not the usual "casting couch." Sarah, in spite of difficult pregnancies complicated by her diabetes, had been a veritable Penelope during their nine years of marriage. She had borne him two children who were the light of his life—Imogen, now five, and young Nicholas, almost three. To all it looked like an ideal family. Besides, everyone knew that the "steam" that made Andrew run was theatrical ambition, not sex.

"But Sarah Brightman was different," wrote Michael Walsh in his biography of Lloyd-Webber. "Sarah Hugill was a pretty, domesticated homemaker; Brightman was a forbidden fruit, ripe and luscious. There was about her more than a whiff of forbidden sexuality. Her racy image in Hot Gossip—and before that, with the television dance company Pan's People—all fishnet stockinged legs and heaving bosom, was only part of the attraction. Even more important, she was, like Andrew, entirely a creature of the theater."

Lloyd-Webber auditioned her several times, always at Eaton Place so he might get a close-up look at her, and, satisfied, he gave her the minor role of Jemima.[5] At rehearsals she was, according to Jonathan Mantle, "different from the other members of the company . . . She floated in and out of the theatre in different dresses; she carried credit cards. She did not appear calculating; she just seemed to blow along with the wind."

In its early rehearsals *Cats* looked like a disastrous flop because numbers remained to be written. Lloyd-Webber called it "the blind leading the daft." Cameron Mackintosh compared it to "a most expensive workshop production. "What we were doing should have been done in the back yard, but we were doing it in the theater using all the forces of the theater." It was a vast and expensive project.

[5] In the Broadway production the character was renamed Sillabub.

The large cast was two weeks into the routine when Nunn felt the lack of the big song, the one that after a reprise would be whistled by the audience as they exited the theater. Lloyd-Webber pulled out the fragment he had written for the Puccini opus, which he now planned to put into his projection for *Sunset Boulevard* some years down the road. Nunn asked him to make it even more emotional, and the composer obliged. When it was finally completed, and he played the wordless melody for the assembled cast, Nunn asked them to remember the date and hour because "you have just heard a smash hit by Lloyd-Webber."

Lloyd-Webber knew this melody intended for the Glamour Cat's ascent into the great beyond urgently needed a strong, moving lyric, and he asked Tim Rice to consider it. Rice turned the project down until Judi Dench tore her Achilles tendon and had to leave the cast. When Mackintosh chose Elaine Paige as her replacement, Rice was once again interested.

Meanwhile, with Rice's refusal, Nunn had begun his own lyric, and soon a race ensued to be the author of the hit song. There was so much hard feeling, even threatened lawsuits, that at one point Lloyd-Webber and Mackintosh wanted to close the show. Nunn eventually came up with the lines (somewhat inspired by Eliot's poem "Rhapsody on a Windy Night"), which, if not better than Rice's, were more appropriate to the character. They have made him a millionaire.[6] Paige, loyal to Rice, fought against using Nunn's lyric until, against her will, she was forced to begin rehearsing the lyric written not by her lover, but by her director. Then she recorded the song, and her rendition is actually the key to the enormous success of the show. The teapot tempest over the lyric is quite immaterial. With Lloyd-Webber's gorgeous melody, Nunn could have substituted the New York City telephone directory for his lyric.

Suddenly "Memory" started shooting up the charts, and by the time of the opening the box office had a healthy advance.

Cats's score is a curious amalgam of styles. Its melodic roots hark back to *Joseph*, although the songs are far inferior to those of that early work. What propels the show is its enormously energetic dancing. From the beginning, when cats' eyes peep out from the darkness at every conceivable angle and about a quarter of the New London Theatre's audience revolves along with the playing area, *Cats* is more an experience than a show.

The critiques were not good, with most of the critics calling the source material minor doodles of a major poet. Even Sondheim, notably close-mouthed about Lloyd-Webber's work, told an audience at the Chicago Humanities Festival in 1995 that he was "for spectacle and spectacular things, but when there's no substance, it gets boring. . . . I remember going to *Cats* and wondering why

---

[6] By most conservative estimates, "Memory" has pulled more than five million dollars in royalties.

they just didn't stack five million dollars on the stage." But as Mark Steyn said in the *Observer*, "Nobody liked it but the public."

The show was a sell-out from its beginning. Andrew, who had become wealthy from his earlier musicals, now became rich,[7] and Cameron was to say that besides giving him overnight acclaim as a producer, "*Cats* gave me enough money so that I only had then to do shows I wanted to."

[7] By April 15, 1999 (the latest figures available), having given 6,141 performances, *Cats* had grossed £115,363,000 (almost $230 million) in its original New London Theatre engagement. It still holds forth at this theater and is still booking seats months in advance.

The Broadway company, which opened at the Winter Garden Theatre on October 7, 1982, closed after an eighteen-year run on September 10, 2000—the longest-running show in Broadway history, a title it had held since mid-1997.

Since its opening, *Cats* has been presented in twenty-six countries and over three hundred cities, including Buenos Aires, Seoul, Helsinki, and Singapore. At present writing there is still a company touring Australia and booked well into 2001. It is estimated that the combined performances of the show have earned more than $3 billion.

The song "Memory" has been recorded by more than 150 artists, including Barbra Streisand, Johnny Mathis, Liberace, and Barry Manilow, whose version was a Top 40 hit in the United States.

Not So Merrily

ANDREW LLOYD-WEBBER'S enormously successful *Cats* opened in London at the New London Theatre on May 11, 1981. It seemed to be defying convention and breaking new ground (as well as new box office records) in the definition of what a musical show could be. Some called it "a happening," recalling the arena-like events that were popular in the '60s. Others considered it a dance extravaganza similar to the Bob Fosse and Jerome Robbins entertainments of the '70s. Whatever genre it was listed under, its slogan, "now and forever," looked like truth. As of this writing *Cats* is, like its only competitor in the long-run musical department, *The Fantasticks*, a fact of life, continuing in London after closing a record-breaking eighteen-year run on Broadway in 2000.

Only six months after the London debut of *Cats*, Stephen Sondheim's *Merrily We Roll Along* arrived. It too holds a pair of records. It was the first time a musical had been told backwards, that is, from the present to the past. Its other record is that of the shortest run of any of the Sondheim-Prince collaborations— sixteen performances. When the final curtain fell on this youthful, melodic, and very Broadway musical, it also sounded the death knell of the creative partnership. Critic Martin Gottfried in his book *Sondheim* implies that Sondheim equates his separation from Prince almost melodramatically to that of a married couple divorcing after their child has died.

Yet the show has a glorious score, with several songs among Sondheim's best. Its Broadway failure could be blamed on several things: the libretto's superficial dialogue; the unattractiveness of its set, and the practically nonexistent costumes; the amateurish performances given by its inexperienced cast; but most of all, the built-in awkwardness of telling a story in reverse. This-is-where-we-are, and I'll-show-you-how-we-got-there takes away all sense of suspense. It is not nearly as interesting as watching lives unfold.

Merrily We Roll Along was a Prince-Sondheim reaction to the acrid bitterness of *Sweeney Todd*. Its theme was first suggested to Hal by his wife, Judy, a close friend of Sondheim's, who asked her husband why he didn't do a show that reflected the vision of their two teenagers, Charley and Daisy Prince, who were then eighteen and sixteen years old.

One morning while Prince was shaving he remembered the play *Merrily We Roll Along*, a moralistic comedy with which George S. Kaufman and Moss Hart had had a mild success in the 1934–35 season. He would have been too young to have seen the original production, but he remembered his erstwhile partner Robert E. Griffith had appeared in the original show, and that the play had ended with Polonius's advice to his son, "This above all, to thine own self be true," which was one of the messages he wanted the musical to deliver. He knew at once the framework of this play could be bent to serve his purpose—to cast young people in its major roles—and give him a platform to say what he wanted about the often disillusioning events of the last twenty-five years. He phoned Sondheim who, according to Prince, "agreed right away. He has rarely ever agreed to do anything so quickly," Prince added.

The original told of a misguided playwright who loses sight of his earliest objectives. Richard Niles, the protagonist, is determined to write only fine plays at the outset. Gradually he loses his ideals and becomes a hack who turns out successful and fashionable Park Avenue comedies. Along the way he loses the friendship of Jonathan Crale, a dedicated painter, less ambitious than Richard, who remains true to his muse, and Julia Glen, a sharp-tongued writer who works only to keep herself in whiskey. Julia's dissolute portrait was a direct slap at Kaufman and Hart's nemesis, Dorothy Parker. When asked why she did not sue the playwrights, Parker replied, "I've been too busy fucking and vice versa."

The original comedy featured over-the-top melodrama and scandal to hammer home its message: sell-out. Chic it was, like so many plays of the time, full of barbs to titillate the intellectual theatergoer who doted on vitriol, but *Merrily We Roll Along* was full of redundancies and trivialities even in 1934. It seemed pointless to a critic of the times like Herman Mankiewicz, who wrote: "Here's this playwright who writes a play and it's a big success. Then he writes another play and it's a big hit too. All his plays are big successes. All the actresses in them are in love with him, and he has a yacht and a beautiful home in the country. He has a beautiful wife and two beautiful children and he makes a million dollars. Now the problem the play propounds is this: How did the poor son-of-a-bitch ever get in this jam?"

Hal Prince hired George Furth to do the libretto and collaborated with him and Sondheim, stretching the narrative to include other dimensions—the fragility of friendship, and how with ensuing success, all the crises in our lives seem to be played out in public.

To give the musical a relevancy to our generation, Prince advanced the story's time frame to the then present. The libretto moved back from 1980 to 1955, a period during which Americans had become fragmented, egocentric, and avidly in search of instant fame.

The story centers on three friends. Franklin Shepard, a talented young composer, and his collaborator and lyricist, Charley Kringas, start off by composing their high school graduation song ("The Hills of Tomorrow") and go on to write three Broadway musicals. Keeping step with the two men is Mary Flynn, a talented novelist-turned-film reviewer in love with Franklin, who turns alcoholic when she can't cope with success.

The show begins at the 1980 Lake Forest High School commencement where Franklin Shepard is the guest speaker at his alma mater. To the surprise and scorn of the graduates, he talks of the necessity to compromise in life, seeming to justify his own sell-out. From there the story moves back in time covering the intertwined lives of the three. In the middle of Act One we are confronted with Charley's breaking away from Franklin in plain view of a television audience. Then we are given the reasons for the break-up. At an opening night party (again the scene is being played out in public) Mary gets drunk, becomes disgustingly outspoken, and is ejected. Along the way back, Frank marries his producer's bitchy ex-wife and sheds his own naive, sentimental young marriage.

Near the end of the musical we find the three atop their building in New York, private at last, where they are watching Sputnik and talking about the ideals they have for changing the world. The song is "Our Time," which ends with "It's our heads on the block, / Give us room and start the clock. / Our time coming through! / Me and you, pal, / Me and you!" Not since *Gypsy*'s first act closing which, it will be remembered, is "Everything's coming up roses for *me* and for you," had Sondheim been faced with a more self-delusionary or self-centered protagonist.

At the *finale ultimo* we are back in the graduation exercises, and now Franklin seems to advocate idealism as a contrast to the earlier part of his speech. The playwright's aim to make Franklin sympathetic adds to the falseness of the plot and is only one of the many slips that made the story confusing and unbelievable to its Broadway audience.

Although the show had been announced as early as 1980 and the score was almost complete by the fall of that year, *Merrily* ran into delays and didn't cast its principals until the spring of the following year.

If the book is preposterous and sketchy, the score is not. It attests to Sondheim's mastery of his material that the songs, and the way they are presented, help create whatever motivations are needed to make audiences understand the inner emotional regression and evolving opportunism of Franklin. The lyrics help give reasons for his friends' disillusionment with him. Sondheim used the gimmick of telling the story backwards to splendid advantage, presenting songs in reprise at first and gradually letting them take their more elemental form. The technique is not unlike one Vincent d'Indy used in his long symphonic poem *Ishtar*, where, according to biblical legend, the warders stripped Ishtar as she passed through each of seven gates. The multitextured melodic line becomes more elemental and transparent with the passage through each of the seven long variations, the theme shining forth unadorned in glorious nakedness at its final variation.

Merrily elicited much of Sondheim's puzzle-constructing cleverness. "Usually you start with the song in the first act and then you might have fragments or a full reprise in the second act," Sondheim explained. "I thought, well, suppose we start with the fragments."

And he did just that. The melody of "Our Time" appears in the release of "Rich and Happy." The accompanying rhythmic figure in "Like It Was" becomes the melodic motive of "Old Friends," and "Good Thing Going," the "hit" song of Shepard-Kringas's first show, was really the third incarnation of a song that started life as their high school collaboration, "The Hills of Tomorrow." Along the way it was adapted as a motto for the team's first success, "Opening Doors."

Sondheim's consolidation of themes that parallels the reverse order scheme of the play puts one in mind of the unification he achieved by writing all the songs in *A Little Night Music* in triple time signatures. Many members of the audience were unaware of either feat, but on frequent rehearing and reexamination, those unifying techniques become clear.

Sondheim, who by now had turned fifty, found this score a challenge because in addition to keeping the material genetic, he was trying "to get back to what it was like to write songs when I was twenty-five years old." He wanted to suggest the period of the late '50s and early '60s and write with a kind of innocence without making a comment. No one is better than Sondheim at writing pastiche, but except for one cabaret turn, "Bobby and Jackie and Jack," he chose to extend the range of popular musical theater by placing his own signature on a basically familiar form. Thus he elected not to copy the pop forms of each of the earlier eras—avoiding the bebop, folk, and rock styles which were the mainstays of that generation—but to maintain his own acerbic and rhythmic musical profile. *Merrily We Roll Along*, then, is more in the vein of *Company*, coupled with some of the nostalgia but none of the tribute to period that is found in *Follies*. Sondheim admits he found the score "extremely hard to write," and told a reporter that he was "very proud of it because it does sound intimate."

Two other running themes, time and continuing friendship, helped to bring unity to the score of *Merrily*: "Old Friends" (relationships that last); "Like It Was" (nostalgia for the past connections that never were); "Good Thing Going"

(how alliances erode in time). Even songs whose titles give away their connection with the passage of time, like "Not a Day Goes By," "The Hills of Tomorrow," and "Our Time," are the mainstays of the score.

The casting of talented but inexperienced adolescents was part of Prince's search
for raw energy and excitement in the production. "Think with speed. Audacity
is what I want," he told these juveniles at their first rehearsal. They took him
at his word and whizzed through their roles animatedly but with little subtlety.
His avoidance of seasoned actors and dancers was perhaps his biggest mistake,
for every one of these youngsters was at sea in the opening scenes of the play,
which required them to play themselves a quarter of a century older. Hardly any
could dance, so production numbers had to be rudimentary. Prince's daughter,
Daisy, who had appeared in her own high school musicals, was cast in a minor
role, a clear-cut cue for critical barbs when the reviewers complained that the
production looked like it had been put together by the kids at Dalton, her high
school.

     With a large cast and not much of an advance in the box office Prince thought
twice about billeting the company and readying the show out of town. Because
it had worked in his staging of Sweeney Todd, and he had actually built up
audiences in its Broadway previews, he decided that Merrily would not try its
wings in New Haven or Boston but would give a series of previews at the Alvin
Theater. It was another gigantic mistake, for after six weeks of rehearsal, the
breaking in of a new leading man in the pivotal role of Franklin Shepard while
the show was in previews, and the firing of his choreographer, the show was a
sheer disaster.

     The new lead, Jim Walton, had a baby face and was utterly unbelievable as
a man of forty-three. He was passable at the end of the play, when he is supposed
to be a teenager. Besides those changes, before the first preview the costumes
had been totally changed. The characters wore formal clothes in the beginning,
lavish or surrealistic outfits for the scenes in the '60s. They had been designed
to represent the lifestyles of the twenty-six characters in the cast. But shortly
before the first preview, when the teenagers tried them on, they looked ridicu-
lously overdressed. They were scrapped in favor of sweatshirts that read, "Charley," "Ex-wife," "Ex-ex-wife," "Producer," or "Secretary," which clarified who the
person represented. With the addition of a stole or a hat, they were suddenly
"costumed."

     The set too was drastically changed. Prince junked a surrealistic, tinker-toy
construction and wanted a bare stage à la Our Town. When this seemed too
barren, he used a series of bleachers that were appropriate for the high school
gym and disassembled and reassembled were supposed to make various combinations. Besides being ugly, they never worked right and were largely discarded.

For the front curtain, Eugene Lee designed a blow-up collage of a *Life* cover, a drop depicting the events of the last quarter century, but even this was scrapped after a few performances.

"This show had more changes than I am used to," Prince admitted to a reporter from the *New York Times*. "One of the biggest problems was that we were charmed by the 'rawness' of the twenty-six youthful actors . . . I was charmed by the beginnings of their artistry, the roughness of their craft, their inexperience. I was charmed as hell by that, but we realized that other people were not as charmed, and they wanted more polish. They were also very confused by twenty-six characters, and so much information . . . so we decided to settle on six major characters for clarity. We did this after we realized that the audience was getting confused in the previews, and when an audience gets confused it gets hostile."

Prince's report was an understatement. At thirty-five dollars a ticket, people were storming out of the theater, often demanding their money back. *Merrily's* troubles became such a hot item that Liz Smith, a widely syndicated columnist, wrote a piece called "Not So Merrily They Roll Out of the Theater," which recounted Prince and Sondheim's troubles and almost encouraged the docile to oblige and head for the nearest exit. A great percentage of the audience did not return after the intermission. "At the top of Act Two," Jim Walton, who played Frank, reported, "we were sitting in these bleachers onstage, and we could count the empty seats in the mezzanine." Things got even worse during the second act. Daisy Prince came home one evening and reported to her father, "The first eight rows were empty by the time we took our bows."

To change the look of the show and to give Furth a chance to shorten the overlong libretto, Prince postponed the opening for three additional weeks. Toward the end of this postponement the hostility stopped coming from the audience, but at curtain-call time the reaction was a mixture of tepid applause and a few boos.

"It didn't become what it was until the last five previews," Sondheim said optimistically. "We changed a lot. It turned out to be very good." But, of course, it was not good enough, and with stiff Broadway competition from Lauren Bacall in *Woman of the Year*, Lena Horne in a one-woman show, and Mickey Rooney and Ann Miller touting a return to good times and burlesque in *Sugar Babies*, all competing for the musical theatergoers' dollars, *Merrily We Roll Along* with a cast of unknown kids didn't stand a chance.

There was so much wrong with the show that even a Sondheim-Prince enthusiast like Frank Rich had to call it "a shambles." Sondheim's score alone escaped total shredding by the critics. Coming in for the most vociferous complaints was the basic premise of the backward idea. "It's like watching a series of Walt Disney nature films in reverse," said Jeremy Girard. "Drama depends," he continued, "on the accumulation of motives to achieve its ultimate payoff: imagine, for example, *Oedipus Rex* beginning with the king gouging out his eyes. Instead of depicting growth that leads to maturity or to downfall, *Merrily's* book falls from a cynical present to its heros' innocent past: from denouement to climax to setting out. There's nothing for an audience to achieve in this setup and nothing for an actor to build in the way of character. It is instead, a continuous emotional dressing-down."

Brendan Gill, writing in the *New Yorker*, found George Furth "breathed little life into a book bristling with clichés of attitude and language, and for once Mr. Sondheim was unable to turn into memorable song those feelings of alienation and abortive affection he has so often given melodious utterance to."

It was left to John Simon, writing in *New York* of the most recent production—there have been five rewrites since the original 1981 production—to put his finger upon the show's unfixable flaw: "The retrograde structure is strategically self-defeating. We might care enough about decent people as we watched them gradually turning into rotters, but people we loathe on sight are unlikely to move us with the buried sweetness of their early days."

Simon, who Sondheim says "has never given me a good review," insists that "[Sondheim] lacks the natural gift of melody as it spontaneously and idiomatically wells up from the likes of Cy Coleman, Jerry Herman and Charles Strouse . . . Except for three genuine songs—"Old Friends," "Our Time" and especially "Not a Day Goes By"—an aura of laboriousness attaches to this score, a sense of stubborn doodling, more kinetic than incantatory."

Simon misses the crux of Sondheim's intentions as a composer. It is simply that he is too involved fitting the theatrical situation to bother to write a "hit song." According to reports, he doesn't really want to. He doesn't think in terms of "hook" (repetition of a basic idea), range (keeping within the compass of the less than average voice), or easily sung intervals (skips of an octave or a seventh, interesting but hard to sing, are frequent in his melodies). But in this show it was almost a necessity to have one genuine hit, especially in what is supposed to be the hit song of Franklin and Charley's musical. "Good Thing Going," a song which even Sinatra's splendid recording could not propel to the top of the charts, is appropriate, moving, and beautiful. (The melody does contain awkward skips like an augmented fourth, intervals of a ninth and octave; its range is an octave and a fourth with half of its release staying in the upper tessitura.) Its lyric is a marvel of inner rhyme without forcing, and its closing lines are as close as Sondheim ever gets to cliché without tumbling over the brink into parody.

. . . And if I wanted too much,	You never wanted enough
Was that such a mistake at the time?	All right, tough, I don't make that a crime.

And while it's going along,
You take for granted some love will wear away.
We took for granted a lot, and still I say
It could have kept on growing

Instead of just kept on.
We had a good thing going...
Going...gone.

Many of Sondheim's creations might be termed breathtaking, brilliant, exciting, moving, or even hilarious. But he does not write hits. His one melodic hit, "Send in the Clowns," seems almost accidental. That elusive quality that Rodgers brought to "If I Loved You" or that permeated Kern's "Smoke Gets in Your Eyes" seems to elude him. Theater composers of late are not notorious for having their songs climb up the charts, but Jerry Herman has had best sellers in "Hello, Dolly," "Mame," and "The Best of Times," and, of course, Andrew Lloyd-Webber has been able to lead the pack.

Although the show is not at all self-referent, as neither Prince nor Sondheim could be accused of "selling out," there is one song in Merrily that does refer to what some have called Sondheim's obtuse kind of melody. It is sung by the crass producer trying to get young Charley and Franklin to write more commercially:

There's not a tune you can hum.
There's not a tune you go bum-bum-bum-di-
    dum.
You need a tune you can bum-bum-bum-di-
    dum—

Give me a melody!
Say, can't you throw 'em a crumb?
What's wrong with lettin' 'em tap their toes a
    bit?
I'll let you know when Stravinsky has a hit...

That said, the producer turns the young team down and exits humming "Some Enchanted Evening."[1] The quotation from Rodgers and Hammerstein was not wasted on the reviewers, who immediately began comparing Merrily in Sondheim's oeuvre to Allegro or Me and Juliet, two of his late mentor's biggest fiascos.[2]

Certainly parallels abound, and although Allegro is about ideals being subverted and Me and Juliet bears resemblances in its backstage atmosphere, the only real parallels the musicals have are their mutual lack of success.

Merrily We Roll Along was shuttered after a two-week run. Shortly before it closed, Thomas Shepard,[3] along with Tommy Valando, Sondheim's publisher,

[1] Sondheim finds the joke not in the producer's humming R & H's evergreen hit as he exits, but that he hums it incorrectly.
[2] With the passage of years and increased "plugging" by cabaret and recording artists, several of Merrily's songs, notably, "Old Friends," "Not a Day Goes By," "Our Time," and "Good Thing Going," have become well known, certainly to aficionados of show tunes.
[3] The choice of Franklin Shepard's name in the musical is mere coincidence, according to record producer Thomas Z. Shepard. Since their initial collaboration on the album of Company, Mr. Shepard produced all of Sondheim's original cast recordings (with the exception of Follies and the U.S. version of A Little Night Music) through Sunday in the Park with George.

convinced the powers that be, notably Bob Summer, the president of the record division of RCA at the time, of the excellence of the score, and that even though the show failed, an original cast recording should be made. With such a curtailed run, RCA was under no obligation to honor its commitment, but Shepard, feeling "that the score was like a reversion to the old Sondheim with those terrific songs, like a return to the melodic outpouring of *Follies*," spoke up. When he added that RCA would always have Sondheim's catalogue and that this show should sell well to the composer's burgeoning audience, Summer agreed.

The morning after the show's closing the cast gathered at the recording studio to sing the *Merrily* score one final time. This recording, full of presence, managed to keep the score alive as it moved more and more into small productions on college campuses. Shepard too was disappointed with the physical appearance of the show and its libretto. He "didn't want the album to sound the way the show looked. I wanted to make sure it sounded elegant and polished . . . The material is very precise. . . . I thought it should sound sort of like *Company* . . . it should have that kind of sparkle."

Shepard was not the only one who was disappointed with the production. We know how this show put the axe to the Sondheim and Prince partnership. George Furth, too, was dissatisfied and resented the way his book was savaged in the press. He sent a tape of the show to James Lapine, whose staging of *March of the Falsettos* for Playwrights Horizon, an off-Broadway organization dedicated to supporting the work of promising playwrights, had impressed him mightily. He had seen its Los Angeles incarnation and hoped Lapine would agree to direct a new production of *Merrily*. He thought that given time, he could improve his work on the libretto. Lapine thought it would be a good idea, but since he had recently met Sondheim, he felt, *if* they were to work together, it was preferable to attempt new material. *Merrily* was then put on the back burner. Lapine didn't get around to a new production until 1985.

It is understandable that after a fifteen-year partnership in the Broadway arena with Prince, the two of them constantly buffeting a public that, like the producer in *Merrily*, demanded hit songs that were not up the Sondheim alley, the more relaxed off-Broadway workshop idea that was Lapine's milieu would have great appeal. As a Broadway producer, Prince was constantly in a position to face up to his investors,[4] but Lapine had worked mostly downtown away from the harsh

---

[4] As mentioned earlier, Prince's career took a Broadway tailspin after *Merrily We Roll Along* with the failures—commercial but not necessarily artistic—of *A Doll's Life* (1982), two straight plays, *Play Memory* (1983) and *End of the World* (1984), and the musical *Grind* (1985). But he had several successes in the field of directing opera: *Willie Stark* for the Houston Grand opera (1981); *Madama Butterfly* for the Chicago Lyric Opera and *Candide* (1982); and *Sweeney Todd* (1984) for

Sondheim points out score changes to Thomas Z. Shepard, producer of the cast album of Merrily We Roll Along, *before the recording session, November 30, 1981. Photo courtesy Thomas Z. Shepard.*

spotlight of criticism, where audiences were different. Intellectualism was a plus in Greenwich Village or in the small theaters that had recently mushroomed on far West 42nd Street. Viewers would sit enthralled, cogitating précis they

the New York City Opera (1982), as well as *Turandot* (1983) for the Vienna State Opera. He was to bounce back splendidly when he directed *The Phantom of the Opera* in 1986. Two more splendid productions were to follow, *Kiss of the Spider Woman* in 1992 and a glorious revival of *Show Boat* in 1994.

didn't understand or atonal musicals. If a show was a smash, talk might erupt about bringing it to Broadway, and sometimes that actually panned out. If it was a turkey, it died unmourned under the heading of growing pains for an author who had something to say but who did not yet possess the technique to make his voice clear. Angels were prepared to gamble where costs were lower, and a fiasco did little harm to the reputation of its creators.

James Lapine, almost two decades younger than Sondheim, had first become involved with theater in the mid-1970s while working as a graphic designer at the Yale School of Drama. It was there he had his first directing experiences, staging Gertrude Stein's *Photograph*, which basically was a dramatic poem whose centerpiece was a collection of photographs. When he came to New York he wrote and directed for off-Broadway, what the British call "fringe theater."

Table Settings was an unconventional satire focused on family frictions, and *Twelve Dreams* was a Jungean fantasy, an intellectual exercise, about a young girl tortured by prophetic dreams concerning her own premature death. Sondheim attended the latter, and it started him wondering "if that man could write a musical." He was too shy to ring him up and ask so he let it go.

Sondheim was recovering from several months of depression, "feeling a hatred on Broadway that was directed at Hal and me," and the despondency of having to close a show like *Merrily* that was getting better with each performance. But he was aware that the Broadway he knew with its expectations of hits and hit songs he could not write was no longer for him. It was time to turn in another direction.

New Collaborator, New Venue

I N FEBRUARY 1982 Sondheim received a call from producer Lewis Allen, inquiring whether he would like to collaborate with James Lapine on an adaptation of Nathanael West's novella, *A Cool Million*, and he jumped at the chance for a meeting. But after rereading the book, he realized that he had pretty much covered the same ground in his and Prince's adaptation of Bernstein's *Candide*, and Sondheim told Lapine as much at their first meeting. Still, they met once a week to search for a project.

The idea that was to develop into *Sunday in the Park with George* was born when Sondheim and Lapine were spending an evening together discussing ideas. Sondheim remembered that Lapine "had brought some photographs and drawings and was juxtaposing them against each other and we got talking about visual arts." That led Sondheim to show Lapine an old issue of the French magazine *Bizarre*, which was devoted to various aspects of the *Mona Lisa*.

"A little later in the evening, James mentioned *Sunday Afternoon on the Island of the Grande Jatte*, which hangs in the Art Institute of Chicago and which Lapine had used in his play *Photograph*, and we began speculating about the people in the picture." Both Sondheim and Lapine wondered why some were looking beyond the canvas and some were facing front, speculating that perhaps some surreptitious affairs were going on and that was the reason some were staring off in the distance.

According to Sondheim, "Jim then said, 'Of course, the main character's missing,' and I asked 'Who?' And he said, 'The artist.' "

Sondheim felt that once they got the idea that the artist had manipulated this disparate group into appearing here on a sunny afternoon, they decided that, as Sondheim put it, "This was a character worth looking into and a story worth telling." The interrelationships of the characters in the painting would make up the plot. It would, of course, be total fantasy. Both men were interested in form and decided their new musical would be a theme and variations.

Sondheim and Lapine thought at first it would be a tour de force to try the form theatrically, using Seurat's painting and showing how it was made in the first act. Then, the second act could be a series of variations or comments on the painting. But Lapine's playwright's instincts took over, and he insisted that form alone would never sustain audience interest enough and some form of narrative was necessary to make the second act viable.

Searching for narrative made the writers dig into the life and career of Seurat. He was intensely private, so little is known about him, certainly not enough for a biographical musical in the sense of *Gypsy* or *Fiorello*, but what little there is is dramatic and therefore intriguing. For the second half of the play the writers abandon Seurat and project the cause of "art" and the "artist" into contemporary times.

Georges Seurat was born into a middle-class Parisian home on the colorful Boulevard Magenta in 1859. His eccentric father lived away from the family, but he'd return every Tuesday evening for a family meal of lamb. Having lost an arm in battle, he'd distribute the meat with his hook.

Georges left this odd family as a teenager when he discovered painting and with it the decadent pleasures of Parisian lowlife. One of the greatest of the French neo-Impressionists, he devised the technique of painting in tiny dots of pure color. His method, called divisionism or pointillism by critics, and chromoluminarianism (from color and light) by Seurat himself, obsessed him. Each of his mostly sizable canvases consisted of thousands of dabs from his brush. These dabs are mixed by the eye when observed from the considerable viewing distance the size of the work requires. Although Seurat's technique was a systematic refinement of the broken color of the Impressionists, which makes his paintings seem to shimmer and glow, he was ridiculed by the public and shunned by his successful contemporaries like Monet, Renoir, and Sisley, who found his work rigorously scientific. After all, the Impressionists mixed their colors on their palettes, often creating breathtaking emotional effects, while Seurat expected the viewer's eye to do the mixing. Microscopic examination of his work has shown that he often applied primary and secondary colors in several layers with the full technical understanding of getting the subtle hue he desired. Because his technique was so bizarre and misunderstood and his output so meager, he never sold a painting in his lifetime.

But color is not all there is to Seurat. His composition displays a tremendous rigidity of form, an almost mathematical working out of line, shadow, and shape. Today he is recognized as one of the most intellectual artists of his time, one who had great influence in restoring harmonious and deliberate design and a thorough understanding of color combination to painting at a time when sketching from nature had become the mode. In *Sunday Afternoon on La Grande Jatte*, for instance, one sees the strong lines of the trees, but this is contrasted with the horizontal shadow that pervades the painting; the somewhat statuesque verticality of the figures looking out at the water is softened with the rounded forms of parasols, bustles, and animals.

The sliver of land in the middle of the Seine chosen for this large (81 by 120 inches) masterwork was habitually the holiday refuge of the Parisian working class, but Seurat included a few fashionably dressed members of society, which gives the painting a universality. Even though Seurat's colors are muted, the painting has the feeling of a mural teeming with vibrancy.

"He led a double life," Sondheim told a reporter for the *New York Post* in 1983, when he first began to work on the score. "On the one hand, every Sunday he'd go to his mother's home for dinner, but when he died in 1891, it was discovered he'd kept a mistress and had a baby by her."

Sondheim and Lapine deduced (or fantasized) that Seurat used his mother, his mistress-model, and the baby in this painting that caught their fancy. They chose the obvious name of "Dot" for the mistress, Madeline Knoblock, an Alsatian whom Seurat met in 1888 while painting *The Sideshow*, which now hangs in the Metropolitan Museum. She moved in with him immediately and had his baby a year later. Soon after, Seurat developed a constant sore throat and suddenly choked to death on March 29, 1891. The child must have caught his father's virus, for he died two weeks later of the same mysterious disease (some suspect meningitis, others claim pneumonia).

The authors rewrote history by making the baby a girl, naming her Marie, rather than basing the character on the actual boy, Pierre, who was Seurat's only issue. Their plot has her being brought to America and living to the age of ninety-eight. Marie becomes the dea ex machina of the second act when she inspires her grandson George to pursue his own artistic vision, the undiscovered aesthetic of Georges Seurat, whom she knows is his great-grandfather. The concept is a tour de force for the two principal players. George (Mandy Patinkin in the New York production) gets to play the bearded painter in the first act and a contemporary light-sculptor in the second, while Dot (Bernadette Peters) dons heavy make-up and a whimsical voice as Marie. (Both principals received Tony nominations.) In writing a play about an uncompromising life in art, Lapine opened his collaborator to criticism that George *is* Sondheim. The basic question of the libretto is how does the artist relate to the world and to other people. Together they addressed the problem of the nature of art and the conflicting demands of art and life. In answering these questions Sondheim was to create his most personal work.

Both Sondheim and Seurat approach their work intellectually. The former's mastery of word puzzles, some of which spills over into his lyrics, is tantamount to the painter's obsession with his pointillism. Both bring an assiduous concentration to their work, and Sondheim's preoccupation with the correctness of even the minutiae of his compositions is on a par with the painter's.

"In almost every Sondheim show, at least one character stands apart and comments," said a *Time* profile of him in 1987. This is perhaps because he has been so taciturn about his personal life, becoming such an enigma that reporters impute the characters he creates to be self-portraits. Some critics have compared Bobby in *Company* to the composer; likewise *Merrily*'s Franklin Shepard (although they know better than to hint that Sondheim sold out). These self-portraits have been suggested throughout the gamut of his whole career, from the intellectual who is unable to whistle (read relax) in *Anyone Can Whistle* to the soldier Giorgio in *Passion*. Of all his characters, Seurat most closely resembles, at least outwardly, what we know of the composer. His unromantic opinion that music is a series of small decisions and a lot of painstaking work, a principle he learned from Robert Barrow at Williams College, has served him throughout his life. Noting the perhaps millions of decisions Seurat was faced with throughout his brief lifetime and comparing them with his own, Sondheim said, "That is what art is. You spend four days working out the flower on the hat, then you spend ten days working on the hat. Then you have twenty other hats to do. Then all the hats are part of a pattern. Then you start working on the face." Substitute for hats the songs in a musical score.

As an aural art, music resembles Seurat's clinicalization of the visual. "Music is the organization of a certain number of variables," he told an interviewer for the *New York Times*. "Seurat experimented with the color wheel the way one experiments with a scale. He used complementary color exactly the way one uses dominant and tonic harmony. . . . The more I found out about Seurat, the more I realized, 'My God, this is all about music!' What makes up the diatonic scale has a clear mathematical basis." An octave is not just an interval to Sondheim, but a series of twelve variable colors, what is known as a chromatic (from color) scale. And in some harmonic systems these twelve semitones may be subdivided into 24 or even 48.

Even Sondheim's methodology resembles Seurat's: "I always start with motifs. . . . Small musical ideas are expanded into large structural forms. . . . I've always taken that to be the principle of art. If you look at a Bach fugue you see this gigantic cathedral built of these tiny little motifs. I've always composed that way, and I think that's why I'm attracted to the kind of musical . . . that offers opportunities to take characters and assign motifs to them which can grow with them."

In creating the theme, Sondheim and Lapine put us inside Seurat's head. At the outset we are presented with a white stage, white floor, and a proscenium arch that has been squared off and extended above the orchestra pit to create a picture frame. Seurat enters and states his principles of art: design, composition, balance, light, and harmony. Each of these is punctuated by an arpeggio, the last accompanied by the theme of "Sunday," built on one of the most harmonious intervals, the ascending sixth. Along with the other elements, the stage has, by this time, gradually been transformed into the green island in the middle of the Seine early on a bright summer morning. Seurat now places Dot into model position.

By the time the first act is a just few minutes old, we have surrendered our belief in realism and are in the kingdom of the artist's imagination. Trees have been flown in, moved, or done away with at the painter's whim. Boats float on and cut-out characters appear, sometimes arriving from slots below the stage. Soon the painter's cantankerous mother and her nurse come on.

Dot, Seurat's model, is a complainer too; although she is illiterate, she frequently stops to give us insight into George and her love for him:

The petticoat's wet,
Which adds to the weight,
The sun is blinding,
All right, concentrate . . .
George's stroke is tender,
George's touch is pure.
Your eyes, George.

I love your eyes, George
I love your beard, George,
I love your size, George.
But most, George,
But most of all,
I love your painting.

Other characters move in, including an academic painter who does not approve of George's work; then, much to the other artist's disapproval, a tableau vivant of *Une Baignade Asnières* (*Young Boys Bathing at Asnières*) is paraded before us. It seems as if our guides want to give the audience a lesson in history now and again, when the scene changes to George's studio and we see Dot powdering herself at her vanity as another of his paintings, *La Poudreuse*. But we pick up the plot. He has promised to take her to the Follies but loses himself in his feverish commitment to the *Grande Jatte*. As he does, we get more of the pointilistic, almost minimalistic music. Seurat admires Dot as his model "for the way she catches light," and he understands her needs for relaxation and frivolity, but he cannot break away from his obsessive urge to "finish the hat."

Soon we are back on the island, where George is painting Dot while she is learning to read from a child's primer. She lets us hear her lesson and makes amusing notes in the margin of her text. Lapine has created all sorts of intrigue and diversions for the many personages in the painting. Two young girls and their flirtation with two soldiers (one of whom is a cutout dragged along by his live companion); a pair of dogs, a boatman's mutt and a lady's lapdog, whose lives Seurat will imagine, emitting barks, yelps, growls, and sniffs while he sketches them;[1] an obese American couple who will eventually take Louis, the baker, and Dot back to Charleston with them; a provocative and willful child who will later expose her father's dalliance with a cook. Near the end of the act, the group's excitement, anger, and argumentativeness will spill over even to Seurat's mother and her nurse. All the characters begin losing control, and at the moment the melee is at its most intense, Seurat freezes the action by calling for "Order."

Now, while singing a chorale-like "Sunday," the characters move to the places and poses the artist has assigned them. The act's choral ending is chillingly beautiful, not only for the tone clustered dissonances that will eventually disappear leaving a major triad, cold and pure, but for the exquisite tableau vivant mat Sondheim and Lapine arrange to close the act:

(The music becomes calm, stately, triumphant, GEORGE turns front. The promenade begins. Throughout the song, GEORGE is moving about, setting trees, cut-outs, and figures—making a perfect picture)

ALL
Sunday,
By the blue
Purple yellow red water
On the green
Purple yellow red grass,
Let us pass
Through our perfect park,
Pausing on a Sunday

By the cool
Blue triangular water
On the soft
Green elliptical grass
As we pass
Through arrangements of shadows
Towards the verticals of trees
Forever . . .

Admittedly, that glorious first act curtain where Sondheim and Lapine take a back seat while Seurat shows off his masterpiece would be hard to surpass in the finale ultimo. Nor do the writers try—they simply reprise the number before the ending.

But they open the second act with the same tableau; a kind of denouement of the first. "It's hot up here," Dot complains, while the other characters join her griping about being transfixed for all time. "To find you're fading is very degrading," another moans. Then they begin a mutual discussion of the painter, a sort of history lesson. Dot tells us she was in Charleston when she heard he

---

[1] Sondheim's score, which has been called Ravelian, is perhaps inspired by the impressionist composer here. The writer feels the song involving the two dogs is comparable to Ravel's duet for two cats in *L'enfant et les Sortilèges*. Sondheim rebuts this hypothesis: "That song is a duet, and it is the imitation of cat sounds. Except for the fact that they both involve two animals, I don't think they have anything at all to do with each other. First of all, the song for the dogs is really a song for the man, and it is sung by the artist."

had died. She and all the other characters exit, and we are introduced to a new beardless George, our contemporary.

He is an inventor-sculptor showing off his latest invention, his *Chromolume #7*, to an invited audience at a museum. As the characters disappear we realize how unimportant they are to the playwright—a device into whose lives we have had a brief glimpse. It is as though they knew these cameos only existed to be manipulated into a painting.

We have been moved forward from 1884 to the then present, 1984, but we hear the same ostinato figure that accompanied Seurat's daubing, only this time played on a synthesizer. A few moments later Dot is wheeled on, having been transformed into her own daughter, rechristened Marie, and now a ninety-eight-year-old woman. It is a tour de force for the actress, and we understand at once why Lapine had to change the sex of Seurat's issue—to build up a substantial part for his leading diva.[2]

Young George (in a very unlikely move) has brought her along to spout more of the history lesson that attempts to tie the past to the present and give the whole evening a unity. Marie, a bit dotty, claims she is Seurat's child. George denies this, but his grandmother produces the little red grammar book Dot had been so assiduously studying in Act One. Now it is time for us to see George's "art," and after some sputtering and a blow-out he eventually shows off his invention. It refracts colors from the *Grande Jatte*, sending laser beams around the auditorium to the accompaniment of a twelve-tone row and atonal chords, an enormously exciting theatrical-visual effect.

When one of the onlookers demands to know how his enormous color-casting machine ties in with the painting, the libretto somewhat glibly spouts Sondheim's original premise: "It is theme and variation." Soon the rest of the assemblage begin talking in art clichés while George is buffeted with the same misunderstanding of his work that afflicted his great-grandfather. But we soon realize that young George is a product of his (and our) times, and where the pointillist insisted no one intrude into his art, this George's enormous mechanical construction (like "a musical" and like Sondheim himself) depends on the cooperation of a great many people. George capitulates easily and in what seems almost a replay of Franklin Shepard's sell-out in *Merrily We Roll Along*, he sings "Putting It Together."

> What's a little cocktail conversation,　　　Leading to a prominent commission
> If it's going to get you your foundation　　And an exhibition in addition?

---

[2] Sondheim disagrees with this theory and says "the whole idea of its being a daughter is to relate the mother-son relationship in the first act to the grandmother-grandson relationship in the second act."

Critics and public join in the discussion of the merits of George's new work. The majority opinion is that George could keep on doing "Chromolume after Chromolume—but there are new discoveries to be made." The discussion turns into a melee similar to that in the first act, and George frames the group, freezing the action into a tableau, just as his great-grandfather did in Act One.

After all the excitement Marie, who has quietly drifted off to sleep, awakes to find most of the assemblage gone in to dinner. She brings the plot around to one of Sondheim's most profound and gentlest songs, "Children and Art," in which she confirms that these are the two greatest things one can leave behind. Marie could be a twin to Mme. Armfeldt in *A Little Night Music* in her ruminations of the past—except that Marie's motives are benevolent where Mme. Armfeldt's were grasping. Marie wants George to connect with his family. Like all splendid ideas, the one she sings about has always been self-evident—only nobody wrote about it before. First the art:

...You should have seen it,	But, Mama, the things that he does—
It was a sight!	They twinkle and shimmer and buzz—
Mama, I mean it—	You would have liked them...
All color and light—!	It...
I don't understand what it was,	Him...

Then the children:

This is our family	After I go, this is
This is the lot.	All that you've got...

With a final, "Goodbye, Mama," Marie falls asleep and is wheeled offstage. It is the last we see of her, but her alter ego, or rather her spirit in the form of Dot, will reappear to young George when, confused and in search of direction for his art, he visits the Island of the Grand Jatte. He is there on commission to set up the latest Chromalume, which by now has only served to stagnate his art, and he notices how much the island has changed, surrounded as it is with ugly high-rise buildings. As if corroborating Marie's thesis of the permanence of children and art, he has brought along all he has left of family, her red grammar book.

As he leafs through it he sings a soliloquy whose subtext is that both his family and his muse—even his assistant—have deserted him. Dot appears and, mistaking him for Seurat, compels him to look at the beauty inside himself. She deplores the paralyzation of his work since she has left him and encourages him to seek new possibilities:

Move on.	If you can know where you're going,
Stop worrying where you're going—	You've gone.
Move on.	Just keep moving on.

Then, as Dot begins to give back some of the principles he has taught her, her spirit seems to be championing both Georges:

Stop worrying if your vision	Look at what you've done,
Is new.	Then at what you want,
Let others make that decision—	Not at where you are,
They usually do—	What you'll be . . .
You keep moving on.	

At last George gets the message, and as the characters in the first act promenade on stage to the elegant hymn that is "Sunday" we have almost visual proof that George is on the track of the artistic principles laid down in the first act. As George reads the postulates—"Design," "Tension," "Composition," "Balance," "Light"—the ugliness of the surroundings begins to disappear. And then, their work done, the characters in the painting retreat gently into the shadowy past leaving George alone while a pristine canvas descends. "White," he reads from Marie's book. "A blank page or canvas. His favorite. So many possibilities . . ."

Never has Sondheim had so much of importance to say in a score, and never has his message as delivered in his lyrics been more succinct. He does not try to dazzle us with rhyming technique, but he astounds us just the same. He creates axioms that stick in the imagination, as when Seurat tells Dot: "You will not accept who I am / I am what I do," or when he instructs his mother on what represents beauty to an artist: "Pretty isn't beautiful, Mother, / Pretty is what changes. / What the eye arranges / Is what is beautiful."

Unfortunately, much of the musical aspect of Sunday in the Park with George was stifled by Sondheim's minimalist and repetitive accompanying figures. In trying to match the painter's dots to close-knit motives, the music remains obsessively nervous, interesting for a few minutes because of its rhythmic jumpiness, but eventually strait-jacketed. It tries almost pathetically for moments of songfulness and lightness, as when Dot, powdering herself, sings about the Follies, or when she oohs about Louis the baker's gooey cakes.

And yet there are moments of overpowering beauty, as when characters arrange themselves according to Seurat's plan for "Sunday," and the minimalist lyrics become almost inaudibly unimportant as the chorus, orchestra, and ennobling music take over. This happens again with the love relationship's apotheosis, "Move On."

"Move On" is truly the song that expresses the heart of passion between both Georges and Dot/Marie. Sondheim says that the song is not "completed until the end of the show, and it is an amalgamation of all the themes involving their relationship, including every harmony and every accompaniment." Early in the score, in the song "Sunday in the Park with George," Dot begins a lyrical theme that is picked up later in "Color and Light," and it develops and starts to reach a climax when each says "I could look at her (him) forever." Just at that point, the pregnant moment is broken off for dialogue. Then, in "We Do Not Belong Together," the melodic line is further developed. The theme is thwarted once more, when Dot, leaving for America, sings, "I have to move on."

At the end of the second act, where Sondheim believes "their love is finally consummated," it all comes together and becomes a completed song in "Move On." Not only should Sondheim's methodology go a long way toward stifling those critics who saw no continuity in the second act of *Sunday*, but if they listen to the material they will realize the composer has incorporated all his motivic and harmonic material to lead us through a relationship that takes place over a hundred years. "It is," he admits, "one way of threading the theme through time."

In contrast to the way the musical would have been handled had it been produced and directed by Prince, the show played a four-week engagement, a sort of summer workshop, at New York's minuscule Playwrights Horizon, followed by a series of previews at one of Broadway's smaller houses, the Booth. In previews, Sondheim and Lapine were still working on it, and audiences were disappointed especially in the second act. "Children and Art" and George's soliloquy, which Sondheim titled "Lesson #8," undoubtedly two of the most moving moments in the musical, were not completed until two days before the scheduled opening, necessitating a postponement of the premiere from April 23 until May 2.

The new songs helped, but the show was a hard sell from the outset, and most of the critics turned thumbs down. "The overlong first act seems even longer because there are no human beings. There's no drama, no conflict, no story," carped Joel Siegal on WABC-TV, while John Simon in *New York* called it "a musical without a single song in it." The respected critic Benedict Nightingale found the musical "delightful—for at least a quarter of an hour," but eventually sided with the public, who found the work hard to take. "As a crusading artist," he concluded, "Sondheim has my admiration, but as a group of people who seemed often to feel he was crusading against them, the audience had my sympathy."

Of all the major critics, Frank Rich of the *New York Times* went out on a limb to champion the show. One must remember that Rich's first critical assignment for the paper was as a second-string art critic whose reviews generally praised the avant-garde rather than the establishment. Certainly the art critic in him must have been mightily impressed by the pictorial magnificence of the ending of Act One.

"Even when it fails—as it does on occasion—*Sunday* is setting the stage for even more sustained theatrical innovations to come," he wrote of the premiere. Then, in an extended piece some three weeks later, he spelled out the musical's strengths when he called it ". . . this season's strongest reminder that guts and imagination can still transform our theater. . . . It is a work about an intellectual process—the creation of art . . . It's a show that asks us to believe that time can leap ahead and backward 100 years without explanation; that an entertainment can tell a story about states of mind instead of plot events; and that the meaning of songs and characters and images can converge in our heads when we're home."

Rich's critique was instrumental in helping *Sunday* chalk up a run of 604 performances. It won the Drama Critics' Circle Award and was considered to be a shoo-in for the Tony. But it was bested for that major accolade by *La Cage aux Folles*, whose victory was considered by some to be a vote *against* the "new musical of ideas."

Jerry Herman, the show's composer-lyricist, took a swipe at Sondheim in his acceptance speech when he crowed: "There's been a rumor that the simple, hummable show-tune is dead on Broadway. Well, it's alive and well at the Palace."

Business sagged when *Sunday* lost its Tony nominations in all categories except the visual, but a year later, when the show was awarded the Pulitzer Prize, it seemingly had the last laugh. Yet in spite of a considerable run, playing at the Booth, which has only 783 seats, it could only make back about 75 percent of its $2.3 million cost.

For once the Broadway moguls, who generally can only see the bottom line, were not concerned. "Nobody would produce a musical in the Booth to make money. We did it because it was the only way *Sunday in the Park with George* could be creatively fulfilled," said Bernard Jacobs of the Shubert Organization. "I don't regret a thing," he concluded. " 'Great' and 'popular' are two different words."

Sondheim had relished his journey into the fantastic, the ability to stretch the parameters of the musical that collaboration with the poetic Lapine allowed him. He found that writing for off-Broadway rather than the main stem's tired-business-man or revival-prone large houses so revitalizing he was eager to do it again.

Almost immediately after *Sunday* opened he and Lapine began thinking about their next collaboration. He had long wanted to create a quest tale, along the lines of *The Wizard of Oz*, and after deciding that they didn't want to either invent a fairy tale or expand an existing one, they combined several tales, even adding one of their own.

Wisely they rejected their first idea, a literal retelling, because fairy tales, as Sondheim says, "are very simple and short-form stories and as you try to expand any given fairy tale to an hour or two, you run into padding and filler, as Rodgers and Hammerstein proved. You simply can't, and that's what led us to smashing all the fairy tales together."

Lapine wrote what they called "interior monologues," and in tandem the collaborators decided they should be about the essence of experience and not about the retelling of adventures of being swallowed by a wolf or traipsing through a wood or climbing a beanstalk. "We retold a number of stories," Sondheim says, "and then interspersed them with each other. You'll find that in the first act, the stories are actually told in quite a traditional plotting, and because they intersect, they have all kinds of fresh and odd complications."

Lapine did not subscribe to Bruno Bettelheim's philosophy, which the psychologist expounds in *The Uses of Enchantment*. Bettelheim states that characters and actions in fairy tales are two dimensional, and largely symbolic. "The fairy tale simplifies all situations," he argues. "The figures are *not* ambivalent, not good and bad at the same time as we all are in reality." Rather, Lapine inclined to the theories of Carl Jung, whose main objection to the stories was that he felt they offer too pat a happy ending. Sondheim's theories went even further, feeling that these childhood *contes* advocated social irresponsibility and selfishness. Both Sondheim's and Lapine's feelings of the deep psychological morass that lies beneath these seemingly harmless stories would be brought out in their musical.

Into the Woods had its first reading at Playwrights Horizon, the Manhattan theater that launched *Sunday*. From then on it went to the old Globe Theater in San Diego's Balboa Park. Some of the second act that had been used in that production was discarded, and Lapine and Sondheim began writing a new one for another New York workshop production. They hadn't decided what should be its focus—whether it should be on community responsibility or on the parent-child theme. In the end they used both of these important themes. With the second act now in place, the musical finally opened on November 5, 1987.

Into the Woods bears a great similarity, if not in content, in construction, to *Sunday*. Both were perceived by some critics to have strong, arresting first acts that lay out the predominant ideas and preachy, weak second ones. Their second halfs even open similarly, with what seemingly was an idea beginning to cloy. Each ran down somewhere before its 11 o'clock number, and no amount of tinkering could seem to improve the later part of each show, although Sondheim—so often inspired by a crucial deadline—added fine songs to each.

The musical begins with the obligatory "Once upon a time," but we are soon aware of the concept, which is "I wish." We are introduced to the borrowed characters and an original tale that Lapine thought up about a Baker and his Wife—they wish for a child. The familiar characters are Cinderella, wishing to go to the King's Three Day Festival; Jack of the beanstalk fame, wishing he could keep his cow; his mother, wishing for money; and then Red Ridinghood, who will wish for sweets.

Almost at once Sondheim introduces the song "Into the Woods" which will become the musical's theme. The song uses a straight four-beats-to-the-bar rhythm to support a childlike theme whose rhythm, 12/8, resembles "Here We Go Round the Mulberry Bush."

Eventually we will be introduced to Cinderella's family, Rapunzel, and two Prince Charmings. Soon we are involved in Lapine's quasi-fairy tale: A childless Baker and his Wife are enchanted by a Witch who lives next door. Because the Baker's father stole some magic beans from the crone, she has rendered the family sterile. But she asks the Baker:

You wish to have   Bring me these
The curse reversed?   Before the chime
I'll need a certain   Of midnight
Potion first.   In three days time,
                                          And you shall have,
Go to the wood and bring me back   I guarantee,
One: the cow as white as milk,   A child as perfect
Two: the cape as red as blood,   As child can be.
Three: the hair as yellow as corn,
Four: the slipper as pure as gold.

"So what they have to do," as Sondheim puts it, "is to go in and screw up everybody else's fairy tale." The interplay between the stories was something Sondheim, with his puzzle-loving mind, as well as Lapine reveled in. All the members of this fairy tale tribe have more dimension than the usual characterless interpretation of these imaginary people. Sometimes, when the storyline boxed them into a corner, Sondheim and Lapine sawed their way out with fairy tale's stock-in-trade, a healthy dash of coincidence.

Early on we learn that the Baker is the brother of Rapunzel (she of the long hair, as yellow as corn), and by donning the coat his father wore, the Baker finds the six magic beans his father stole from the Witch. It is these he will trade for Jack's cow (only five—the last will be used to thicken the plot of the second act). We are soon off on this insistently doggerel-like theme with the Baker and his Wife trying to get the items we have already been shown: Jack's cow, Red Ridinghood's cloak, Rapunzel's hair, and Cinderella's slipper.

Cinderella was the character Sondheim and Lapine discussed the most, and along with the Baker, his Wife, and the Witch, is the most fully developed personage in the musical. When we first meet her we realize she is a modern heroine, very different from Sondheim's teacher Oscar Hammerstein's protagonist in the musical he and Richard Rodgers wrote for television. Both Cinderellas are clever in different ways: R & H's lets her innate goodness bring about her fate, but S & L's is not content to just sit back and let things happen to her. She commands her own magic by enlisting the birds to help her get to the Prince's festival. After her stepmother reneges on her promise to allow her to accompany them to the ball, she is the first of the fairy tale characters to ask questions: "What's the good of being good?" she muses. Nor does she sit by the fire waiting for a fairy godmother. She *goes* to the spirit of her mother lodged in a tree in the woods. The birds bring her the ball gown and slippers, and she's off and running through the woods with the other characters. Later in the act, when she meets up with the others, she is given perhaps the most amusing song in the show, "On the Steps of the Palace."

Sondheim often writes about ambivalence ("Sorry-Grateful" from *Company*, "Now" and "Soon" from *Night Music*) but has never done so more amusingly than in this song. Cinderella tells us just how smart the Prince is, for after her hasty retreat on the first night of the festival, he took no chances when she reappeared. He spread pitch on the stairs.

"I was caught unawares.	Better stop and take stock
	While you're standing there stuck
And I thought: well, he cares—	On the steps of the palace."
This is more than just malice.	

Earlier in an encounter with the Baker's Wife we learn that Cinderella was not very comfortable in her first encounter with the Prince, and she might just opt for a life of mistreatment that she knows to a relationship she doesn't. So she comes to a most human decision. (Sondheim rhymes dizzily, shattering Cole Porter's long-standing record set in "I Get a Kick Out of You"—*fly*ing so *high* with some *guy* in the *sky* is my *i*dea of nothing to do.)

Then from out of the blue,	And then see what he'll do.
And without any guide,	Now it's he and not you
You know what your decision is,	Who is stuck with a shoe,
Which is not to decide.	In a stew,
	In the goo,
You'll just leave him a clue:	And you've learned something, too,
For example, a shoe,	Something you never knew,
	On the steps of the palace.

Different from the other characters who get what they seek, Cinderella eventually lets the Prince marry her, but instead of forgiving her wicked stepsisters as some versions of the fairy tale have it, the birds, her allies, blind them. This is only part of the unnecessary cruelty that indeed is written into many fairy tales but is highlighted throughout the show—vengeances, blame, and perfidy we are unprepared for. But here, early in the proceedings, one of the stepsisters cuts off a toe to fit into the slipper and the other slices off her heel.[3] Red Ridinghood too does not come out of the woods unscathed. Sexually excited and matured by her meeting with the wolf (whose genitalia were highlighted in the Broadway performances), after her sojourn in his bowels we like her a lot less. But her unpleasantness works in with the plot. She is now haughty and so upwardly mobile, sporting a wolf stole her grandmother stitched from the animal's hide, that by now she has outgrown the simplicity of her red cape and willingly lets the Baker have it.

Jack, a simpleton at the musical's outset, has exchanged the Baker's beans for the cow. Once he climbs the beanstalk, he too matures, becomes by turn sensitive and greedy, that is, human, and steals the hen that lays golden eggs. Pursued by the giant, he turns and kills him—the evening's first murder—and scurries down the beanstalk. In short, all the characters have had to lie and cheat a bit to get what they want. Sondheim even lets the Baker's Wife pun that "if the end is right it justifies the beans." But she and her husband have both grown from their experiences. Their love has deepened, and they look on each other with newfound respect. It is obvious that the writers are trying to make this an *adult* fairy tale, glossing over none of the "scary parts."

The Witch too has been humanized and becomes maternal—but controlling. Entreating Rapunzel, who is clearly unprepared to make her way in the world, not to leave her, she cuts her hair and tries to isolate her, but her Prince rescues her. Now everything seems to come aright, the Baker supplying the four requisites to end the Witch's curse. At the last moment Lapine adds to the suspense by having Rapunzel's hair being ruled out of the scavenger hunt. A minor character substitutes some corn silk.

Suddenly the Witch turns into a beautiful woman, the cow is reunited with Jack, the Baker's Wife has conceived a child, Cinderella's and Rapunzel's Princes have found their mates, and to the sing-songy melody of the beginning, the company chants euphorically that once you take the journey into the unknown to conquer your fears and will now live "happily ever after," the act ends. The ensemble does not notice that a beanstalk—the one extra bean that the Baker's Wife threw away in a fit of pique—is growing rapidly on one side of the stage. But we know we are in a Sondheim musical where things do not get tied up in a ribbon that easily.

Act Two begins, as hinted above, with the same group now overjoyed at having their wishes granted. Humanly, and to the same tune, they wish for a bit more: Cinderella would like to *sponsor* a festival, Jack misses his kingdom up

---

[3] These mutilations are present in some of the German Grimm versions of Cinderella, but not in the French version.

in the sky, and the Baker wishes more room in his tiny cottage now that the baby's here. "Why," the Baker asks, "does he always cry when I hold him?"

But their exhilaration soon evaporates. With a crash, the Giant's Wife has come down the beanstalk to avenge her husband's murder. With a footstep she has caved in the Baker's house, killed Red Ridinghood's mother, and ruined the Witch's garden. Now the group takes on more human qualities, somewhat banding together but often splintering away for their individual survival. They are forced to go again

Into the woods,	You're through, and then,
It's always when	Into the woods you go again
You think at last	To take another journey.

When the Giant's Wife asks for the lad who killed her husband, the group offers up a scapegoat in the form of Cinderella's lackey. But the ogress is not satisfied. Jack's mother, protecting her child, becomes a symbol of isolationism and then confrontation. The group, trying to silence her, is responsible for her death. Rapunzel too is killed by the Giant's wife, as her mother, the Witch, begins one of the show's most haunting melodies, proclaiming that "children won't listen."

In trying to elude the Giant's Wife, the Baker's Wife, a practical character, is not above having a brief dalliance with Cinderella's Prince in the woods. She has developed into a true twentieth-century woman. Her philosophy: "There's the answer, if you're clever: / Have a child for warmth, / And a Baker for bread, / And a Prince for whatever—"

The Princes, both philanderers, now sing a reprise of the light barcarole "Agony," the show's most comic number—and the only one that sounds like a full-fledged show tune. These characters, similar to Miles Gloriosus in *Forum* or Carl-Magnus in *Night Music*, are the kind of macho popinjay Sondheim loves to make fun of. And he does it better than anyone. In the first act they were given to comparing the frustration of one being ten steps below his inamorata, Rapunzel, while the other was ten steps behind his Cinderella. Now in the reprise they sing about the frustration of getting to their recent discoveries, Sleeping Beauty and Snow White.

Cinderella's Prince:

High in a tower—	Agony!
Like yours was, but higher—	No frustration more keen,
A beauty asleep.	When the one thing you want
All round the tower	Is a thing that you've not even seen.
A thicket of briar	
A hundred feet deep.	

Rapunzel's Prince:

I've found a casket
Entirely of glass—
   (As *Cinderella's Prince starts to protest*)
No, it's unbreakable.
Inside—don't ask it—
A maiden, alas
Just as unwakeable— ...

Agony
Such as princes must weep!
Always in thrall most
To anything almost,
Or something asleep . . .

When Cinderella learns of her husband's infidelity, his rejoinder—"I was brought up to be charming, not sincere"—brings down the house. But we have more serious business to attend to, for the group, having finished with their in-fighting, is suddenly silenced when the Witch announces that it's "The Last Midnight," and if they refuse to give Jack to the Giantess it will be all over for them. The Baker answers with his own philosophy, "No More," in which he tells the group that you can't run from the truth, you simply must face it. "Run-ning away only leaves you more undefined," is the way Sondheim puts it. But the song, overlong and preachy, rings hollow. We need to rush to the conclusion.

Soon the group decides to enlist Cinderella's birds to peck out the ogress's eyes, spread pitch on the ground so she can't move, and, while Jack climbs a tree, they batter her to death. Now comes another moral, this one on how all our actions affect each other (the tune sounds a little bit like a popular song of a decade before, "The Candy Man"):

Mother cannot guide you.
Now you're on your own.
Only me beside you.

Still you're not alone.
No one is alone, truly.
No one is alone.[4]

Is the show over? Well, it should be, but the Witch has not given us *her* final warning: Sondheim has the Witch tell us her philosophy, reversing what she said after Rapunzel's death to tell us to be careful of what we say because "chil-dren *will* listen." This advice is perhaps the deepest message of the show, but it comes too late in the evening for us to care. At last, with a reprise of the title song, and a final "I wish," the musical is ended.

Into the Woods is so full of plot, machinations, and movement, all set to an extremely clever script with lyrics that are a tour de force, that it is perhaps ungrateful to ask for distinguished music. But Sondheim's short motifs, devel-oped and varied as they are, while according perfectly with Seurat's pointillism,

---

[4] Sondheim explains the lyric this way: "[It] is about how all our actions affect each other. It's not about walking through a storm and having somebody by your side. 'Say the slightest word,' that's what the song is about—it's not about 'you'll never walk alone.' "

add up to a somewhat tiresome, almost tuneless evening here. John Simon, who generally dislikes Sondheim's work, was particularly vitriolic, reviewing the composer's entire output and saying that "Sondheim's early, show-bizzy, relatively unself-conscious phase yielded some captivating tunes, but the rivulet quickly ran dry. . . . By *Sunday in the Park*, it was all tuning up, getting revved up; but no melody really took off. *Into the Woods* is even more desperate: endless introductions to songs, and by the time we cry, 'Enough of this foreplay!' the thing is over—that intro was the song."

Although most critics praised the production and the performances, they gave mixed reviews to the work itself. The *New Yorker* review stated that "what it adds up to is little more than a hodge-podge of clichés," while the *Daily News* critic found that "an inviting but unrewarding idea has been lavishly expounded upon to create an unworkable musical."

Jack Kroll in *Newsweek* hedged, writing that Sondheim's show "seems to be an uncertain expression of what may be an artistic and emotional pivotal point. At 57 he may be trying to shape a new vision away from his role as Broadway's leading laureate of alienation and anxiety. If so, he's not out of the woods yet." *Newsweek*'s opposite, *Time*, raved that it was "strikingly original yet completely accessible," adding, "the best show yet from the most creative minds in the musical theater today." Clive Barnes, generally not a Sondheim fan, wrote, "I find it exciting in its acceptance of simplicity and its quest for an acceptable musical usage to bridge the gap between Broadway and its future." And Frank Rich, by now habitually in Sondheim's corner, found the musical leaning delightfully on Sondheim's trademarks, scavenger hunts and puzzles, and added that "it may be just the tempting unthreatening show to lead new audiences to an artist who usually lures theatergoers far deeper and more dangerously into the woods."

Rich's review was prophetic. The show won Tonys for Best Score and Best Book and won the Best Actress in a Musical Tony for Joanna Gleason, who played The Baker's Wife. It faced stiff competition from Lloyd-Webber's *Phantom of the Opera*, which walked off with the majority of the other awards.

But the fairy tale opus did lure a youngish audience into the theater. They were amused by the juvenile criss-crossings of the first act and perhaps bored by the overlong and preachy second one, even though they seemed to react well to the violence in the act. The show made some money, the first Sondheim show since *Night Music* to do so. It played the Martin Beck Theater for 764 performances and then had a rather successful tour.

Into the Woods asks many questions and gives us few answers. It is full of undertones of violence and overtones of sex. Once again Sondheim's women have taken over the most important perceptions. They are like Rose in *Gypsy*,

Désirée in *Night Music*, and all the women in *Company*, the strong ones. They are not defined by the relationships in their lives but solely by their hard fought and often moving journeys toward self-knowledge.

The musical does not present the fairy tale in its usual setting as a study in black and white. Lapine's Witch usually tells the truth. Even honest people like the Baker's Wife can lie. And good people die. But eventually the characters' deeds and misdeeds bring them closer together and empower them to act against the "giants" in our society.

However close they become to other members of their community, the individuals of *Into the Woods*, as well as those of *Sunday in the Park with George*, make us look deeply into the parent-child relationship. Sondheim was fifty-seven when *Woods* opened, an age at which most of us are mellow enough to imagine how our parents might react in a similar situation. The reconcilement of the generations seems, according to Stephen Banfield, to have taken place somewhat later and "was still far from complete as far as his mother was concerned when she died in 1992."

Just as Voltaire's *Candide* discovers this is not the "best of all possible worlds," so the characters in *Into the Woods* learn there is no "happily ever after." All of this helps to leave us with a positive message—often untrue—that however bleak things may seem, we'll muddle through because help is nearby—"no one is alone."

Into the Woods's final morals are clear, but Sondheim's next musical, like this one, contains many themes. It will explore the seeds of violence and become one of this writer's and Sondheim's favorite works—and the least popular with the establishment and the American critics. In fact, *Assassins* will not even make it to Broadway.

A Tale for Children

A S   S O O N   A S   *Sunday in the Park with George* closed, a company called Broadway Showtime (in conjunction with producer Emanuel Azenberg and the Shuberts) decided to make a videotape of this Pulitzer Prize–winning work and aimed to come as close as possible to the freshness of its early showing by enlisting the original stars. Patinkin was available, but Peters was starring in Lloyd-Webber's *Song and Dance*. In an unprecedented move, the producers bought all the seats for two performances, and the Royale Theatre remained dark in mid-October 1985, only a month into its run, while the cast recorded *Sunday* at the Booth. The shuttling of Peters back and forth was a rare instance of entrepreneurship between Sondheim and Lloyd-Webber.

It was ironic that Bernadette Peters, having been nominated but passed over for a Tony for her work in Stephen Sondheim's *Sunday in the Park with George*, would win one for Andrew Lloyd-Webber's *Song and Dance*. But with the ministrations of Richard Maltby Jr., who supervised and reconceived the dramatic cantata that was *Tell Me on a Sunday* and who brought in Peter Martins of the New York City ballet to choreograph the Paganini variations that make up most of the second act, Peters managed to melt Broadway audiences' hearts, making them lap up the somewhat soupy tale of Emma, the Cockney modiste's odyssey in America. The restyled *Song and Dance* turned a mediocre London evening into a New York success—a mild one in the Lloyd-Webber canon, but one that was able to play out the season and then some.

There is no doubt that Peters' wistful charm suited Emma's mercurial character far better than Marti Webb's straightforward characterization, even though the part was written for Webb. But it is also true that Maltby worked his own special magic by tying the show together, Americanizing many of Don Black's lyrics, and bringing Emma back on stage for a forced but happy conclusion with

Joe, the Nebraskan from the first part whom we recognize from his baseball jacket and red boots. He is to be, we assume, after Emma has sown a fieldful of wild oats, the one continuing love of her life.

In the British original, the "dance" part of *Song and Dance* is merely that; in the Broadway version, Joe encounters everyone from a youth gang in a subway station to Wall Street brokers in gray flannel suits. En route he meets a tap dancer who, for no reason at all, teaches him that art. At last he meets up with Emma again, and they and the other dancers sing "An Unexpected Song," one of the show's strongest ballads.

Ms. Peters, who, incidentally, shares a birth year with Lord Lloyd-Webber, has been singing and dancing professionally since childhood. She first achieved notice in the 1968 spoof *Dames at Sea* and the 1971 revival of *On the Town*, going on to win acclaim as Mabel Normand in Jerry Herman's *Mack and Mabel*. After bringing her special magic to the role of Dot in *Sunday* for almost a year, Peters was, by this time, a bona fide star, and there is no doubt that *Song and Dance* gave her several tuneful melodies to interpret and a chance to have the stage all to herself to sing, dance, and emote in the reconceived musical.

The show, opening on September 18, 1985, three and a half years after its London debut, sharply divided the two major critics. Clive Barnes, writing in the *Post*, called it "the best thing that Lloyd Webber has written for the theater," while his competitor at the *New York Times*, Frank Rich, turned thumbs down: "Empty material remains empty, no matter how talented those who perform it. Emma is a completely synthetic, not to mention insulting, creation whom no performer could redeem."

Peters did sustain the show and is one of the reasons for its American success. She would shuttle back to the Sondheim camp two years later to assume a major role in *Into the Woods*.

At around that time Lloyd-Webber was into his own children's fantasy, a show that would eventually be called *Starlight Express*. He had premiered some of the songs for the new work at the Sydmonton festival of 1982, and they were quite well received, but it was to be a work that he would malign at a Dramatists Guild forum by saying, "I will make no defense for [it]. It was written for my children. I really don't like the show anyway."

His children, Imogen, six, and Nicholas, four, caught some of their father's fire when he talked of the great railway journeys and trains. He had been obsessed with trains from his childhood, and their favorite bedtime adventure was to hear Daddy read the classic story known in the States as *The Little Engine That Could* and in Britain as *Thomas, the Tank Engine*. Several times he tried and put away sketches that musicalize the saga of the little train that repeated, "I think I can," while it climbed the mountain. As it surmounted the peak it changed its doggerel to "I thought I could." Although it sounds like there is not enough in the moralistic tale for a musical, one must admit that this simple *Rocky*-like story is infallible. *Cats* was built on far less.

The urge to write the piece was revived again when he had taken his youngsters for a ride on the Valley Railroad in central Connecticut, a restoration of what the old engines, passenger compartments, and cabooses were like. He was keen to compose music about American railway trains, he told a reporter, "because they make lovely noises and have marvelous names, and because even more than Britain, the railway is about America."

His idea was to combine the railroad motif with the Cinderella story, making the hero a steam engine. Cinderella's ugly brothers were to be a diesel and an electric train, while the traditional fairy godmother would be a magical train known as the Midnight Special. She would lend the steam engine special equipment to keep up with his brothers on condition it was all back by midnight when the Special was scheduled to leave. En route to get back in time the steam engine dropped a piston, and, as Lloyd-Webber recounted it, "the Prince went around America to find the engine which the piston fitted."

He planned to have the actors driven around the stage in little trains from which they would emerge to act out the plot which was obviously suitable only for a children's show or a Christmas pantomime. He did not press forward with the project until a year later because of a series of other involvements, but before he left the project suspended, he chose John Napier and David Hersey to repeat the wizardry they had shown in setting and lighting *Cats*. In a stunning move toward modernism he selected choreographer Arlene Phillips, the leader of the rock group *Hot Gossip*, and with young Richard Stilgoe, who had managed to redo some of Eliot's verses as lyricist, he left the entire production on "hold" in the capable hands of Trevor Nunn.

First on the urgent 1982 agenda was the Broadway premiere of *Cats*, which had been sold out since it opened in London in 1981. Lloyd-Webber hoped the New York version would "make the English one look like a touring tryout." With an advance of six million dollars, he and designer John Napier had gone out on a limb and spent $2.5 million tearing apart Broadway's venerable Winter Garden Theater to create a garbage dump that included junked cars, tires, scattered fish skeletons, cream cartons, and enormous trash cans. They had even extended the set to take in the theater's mezzanine, which necessitated cutting a hole in the theater's ceiling and removing the roof to create the "Heaveside Layer." (Lloyd-Webber and Mackintosh's contract obliged them to restore the theater to its original condition whenever the show moved out—a renovation that was estimated at $1.5 million then, but which has escalated to five million of today's dollars.)

The work done on the set was only part of the metamorphosis that the American incarnation of *Cats* would entail. Lloyd-Webber had moved Sarah and the children into a suite at the Mayflower on Central Park West and was busy reworking and polishing the score. He reset three of the songs and added a completely new song for Mungojerrie and Rumpelteazer. "I've rewritten a good third of the show in the last two weeks," he told the *New York Times*. "One of the things that has astonished Trevor Nunn and me, working here, is the range and depth of the performers . . . If you're suddenly given a whole lot of extra forces to use, it is imperative that you use them—otherwise you're not doing what you ought to be doing as a composer. You can't see some of the performers we've seen here and not want to write for them."

The changes he made that were incorporated into the Broadway version have become a part of subsequent versions of the show. If one sees a touring *Cats*, one sees a clone of the American version. Perhaps the show was sung and danced on Broadway with an élan that the British version lacks, but like the Gucci, Godiva, or Body Shop stores, the production aims for an identical feeling from company to company. One can well understand why. Except for the main two or three performers, cast changes were easily accomplished by switching a performer from Berlin to San Francisco. Like a traveling executive of a large corporation, the assistant choreographer or director looks in periodically on various companies to see that the performances remain consistent and vitally up to snuff, be it in Boston or Budapest.

Cats was the first of first of the megamusicals that would be sold in a way not vastly different from merchandising a new car or launching a new resort. With 331 theater parties booked even before its opening night, and enormous hullabaloo before its opening, it was guaranteed to run for years. Its yellow cat's eyes logo that shows two dancers, and its slogan, "now and forever," became part of popular culture.

Writing in the *Post*, Clive Barnes called it "the most long-awaited show in history," and then went on to say that "for audiences hungry for musicals and novelty, *Cats* is made to order. It has an intriguing amalgam of feline behavior, the snob appeal of Eliot's poetry . . . lyrically undemanding music that sounds vaguely classical and sheer genius in its staging."

Time's T. E. Kalem called it a musical "that sweeps you off your feet but not into its arms. It is a triumph of motion over emotion, of EQ (energy quotient) over IQ. . . . In *Cats*, the spectacle is the substance."

Objections to the contrary, it was obvious even before its opening that *Cats* was in for a long run. Part of the joy Andrew Lloyd-Webber took in *Cats* hitting America's jackpot was because his parents were present at the spectacular star-studded premiere and the gala celebration at the Waldorf-Astoria that lasted until dawn. One could hardly walk down Broadway without wallowing in the strains of Barbra Streisand's recording of "Memory." Lloyd-Webber could show his parents Jean and especially William that he was able to set and orchestrate the words of one of Britain's major poets. Maybe his work didn't elicit bravos from the traditionalists, but it sure made the box office jingle. And wasn't this what Puccini, Verdi, and even Mozart did?

But the son's elation was short lived, for shortly after returning from New York, in early October, William entered the hospital for a routine prostate operation. After the surgery, he seemed to have made a full recovery, although he was subject to frequent blood clots. As the doctors were able to dissolve them, he was given some blood-thinning medication and scheduled to be discharged. Preparing to go home, he went off for a bath in which he collapsed.

Jean was told to come at once and bring her sons. Julian drove her over and Andrew came in from Sydmonton, but by the time they arrived, Bill had died. They were told that both his kidneys and heart had failed. The father had died just three weeks after his son's gala opening.

William Lloyd Webber, always the *compositeur manqué*, had been a difficult man to know. He had not been close to either of his sons, but he had supported both of them in their attempts to reach their goals. His own eclecticism, which had kept him from achieving fame, had been their salvation. He could talk Bach suites for the cello alone with Julian, but he did not object if Andrew wanted to cut his teeth on Elvis Presley or the Rolling Stones. For a conservatory director, traditionally enmired in academia, Bill was not pedantic or stodgy. He had encouraged his sons—and one of Britain's foremost pianists, John Lill, who had been almost a foster son to him—to follow their own stars.

But if he was not narrow-minded about things musical, he was straitlaced when it came to family. He had hoped his sons would follow his example: one relationship, children, and music were all that was important in life. As Sondheim's Marie declares, "Children and Art." Perhaps it was his father's death that allowed the church organist's son to break the mold and seek to follow his own libido, for the following year was to bring the composer into a whole new emotional relationship.

Andrew Lloyd-Webber's marriage to Sarah had been lackluster and routine for some time. Sarah had a serious case of diabetes and was more comfortable at home with the children rather than jetting around the globe accompanying her husband. Andrew was no angel (nor were his associates among his show business circle; Trevor Nunn, then married to actress Janet Suzman, and designer John Napier had both formed attachments to dancers from *Cats*). A press release in the early '80s had hinted Lloyd-Webber had taken a girl identified only as "the golden golliwog" off to Paris, and then on his return had written her a song. For Christmas '81 he had given her a golden golliwog brooch with diamond eyes.

Sarah, who was generally close-mouthed about her husband's exploits, retaliated by telling the press about how neurotic Andrew could be and how he would lose control of his temper when things did not go his way. "If you marry young, you either grow together or grow far apart," she added, allowing readers to make up their own minds as to which direction the marriage had taken. It was not long before the tabloids were able to point out her route.

Lloyd-Webber went to see a production of Charles Strouse's *Nightingale*, a children's opera that starred Sarah Brightman. This was the second show in which the esteemed composer of *Bye, Bye, Birdie, Applause,* and *Annie* had featured Brightman, and as she had received glowing personal reviews for this one, Andrew wondered what all the fuss was about. As he sat there listening to the show, he was taken with her voice. He remembered that when he auditioned her at his flat for a small role in *Cats* she had used her chest, or belt voice, but here in this musical she had been given an opportunity to display her enormous range. And it was truly phenomenal, going from G below middle C all the way up to a coloratura high D. Almost three octaves! Why even Streisand, for whom he had played when she first wanted to record "Memory," couldn't run that gamut.

After the performance he went backstage to congratulate her, and when he remarked on the change in her style she explained that she had been working with the noted coach of the Scottish Opera, Ian Andrew. He was struck with her beauty; with the pinkness of her complexion and the blackness of her eyes, she seemed to have stepped out of one of the pre-Raphaelite paintings he had been avidly collecting. He stood there not a little flustered and stammered that if he had known she had such an enormous range he would have given her something special to sing in *Cats*. Then he asked her over to the Eaton Place flat so he could hear her at close range. By the time he had played through some Rachmaninoff songs, which she sang in the original Russian, it was all over for him; he found himself in the grip of a passion he had never known before.

Over the years, as his acclaim had heightened, he had become more sure of himself—especially around beautiful women. Gone were the twitches and the eye-rolling, for by now he was aware that success is a powerful aphrodisiac. Now his worldliness, charm, and position seemed to work like magic on Sarah Brightman.

They went out to dinner and talked about musicals—how she wanted to star in them and how he wanted to make them. She told him about her early career, how she had got a job dancing on the BBC's *Top of the Pops* when she was only sixteen, how she moved the next year to *Hot Gossip* and made her first record that got into the top ten. She had no need to remind Andrew that she was allowed to audition for *Cats* because of that recording. Two years later, wearing a jeweled body stocking, she performed a single called "Adventures of a Love Crusader." The tabloids reported that around that time she had moved in with a forty-six-year-old property developer named Max Franklyn, and when asked why she thought he commuted from his home in Minorca to see her in London, she answered that she supposed he "loved her freshness and youth."

She told Andrew Lloyd-Webber of her brief marriage to Andrew Graham-Stewart, from whom she had been separated for some years, and he in turn recounted how his wife (who would eventually be dubbed Sarah 1) had been his first romantic experience—which was over by now. After they met again, he asked her to come away with him for a weekend in Italy, and it was there that she accepted him when he asked simply, "What are we going to do about getting married?"

The hasty decision was typical of Lloyd-Webber. As in his first marriage, or

Andrew Lloyd-Webber at the time he announced publicly that he was divorcing Sarah Hugill.
AP/Wide World Photos.

Sarah Brightman at age twenty, when she was lead singer with the group Hot Gossip. AP/ Wide World Photos.

his choice of aides, once he had cast the right person in the part he moved straight ahead. He foresaw no problem in the dissolving of Brightman's marriage because there was little community property; as for his own, he was confident that Sarah would consent to part, for he knew she loved him enough to want to put his happiness in the forefront. He was rich enough to have no compunction about giving her whatever she asked for. He must have recalled how

Sarah had helped him through the struggling years. When nobody wanted to invest in *Cats* she had called their friends and had kept a list of those who put up money and those who had refused.

The yellow press had a field day, and in an attempt to throw sand in their eyes, he announced that he was writing music for Brightman. He told the papers that he was interested in writing for someone who had a range of more than a dozen notes. Additionally, what he liked about his new protégée was that "unlike most operatic sopranos, she took care not to distort vowel sounds." In truth, although Brightman's voice does lack color, her diction is impeccable and she was soon cast to take over from Bonnie Langford in the updated American version of *Pirates of Penzance*. Lloyd-Webber gave her what little help she needed with the role, and they were together most of the time.

To save face, it was Sarah who set the date of the separation, which by coincidence was the same one on which her husband's Really Useful Theatre Company's first wholly independent production in the West End, *Daisy Pulls It Off*, was to open. On Monday, April 18, 1983, Sarah, Imogen, and Nicholas came in from Sydmonton and set up housekeeping at 11 West Eaton Place.

With the children at home with their nanny, a stoic Sarah attended the opening performance of this jejune comedy seated next to her mother-in-law. After the curtain came down, knowing that Sarah Brightman would be attending the gala opening night party in Pimlico, Sarah chose to go out with Jean for a light supper. She asked Andrew to put them in a taxi, he obliged, and they said their goodbyes in the street. The cab had hardly taken off when Sarah broke down and could not control herself enough to risk being photographed in public. Jean told the taxi to drive them back to her flat in Chelsea, stopping on the way in Brompton Road to pick up some snacks at an all-night food market in case a disconsolate Sarah could be persuaded to eat a bite.

The papers were brutal, saying that Lloyd-Webber had attended the play with his wife and went to the cast party on the arm of his mistress. The next morning, in order to crawl out from under, he issued the following statement:

> In the past two weeks there appears to have been speculation about my marriage to Sarah Lloyd Webber. I want to record that my affection for Sarah is still very great, but unhappily we will be seeking a divorce in the near future.
>
> I also want to confirm my great friendship for Sarah Brightman. Sarah Brightman and I have known each other professionally for several years but it is only recently that our relationship has developed.
>
> Both of us are entirely aware that our personal circumstances do not allow us to take our friendship further for the moment. However it is our present intention to marry when we are honourably able to.

The controversy over Britain's premiere composer's ditching the Penelope who had stood by him throughout the lean years for a sex kitten might have died down had Lloyd-Webber not been blatant and been photographed locked in a passionate embrace when he took Brightman to New York. The celebration was given because with the advent of *Cats* and the continuing success of *Evita* and *Joseph*, Lloyd-Webber now had tied Richard Rodgers's record of having three shows running simultaneously on Broadway.

Now he was really riding high, the most successful composer of his generation. Desperately in love with Brightman—her voice, her beauty, her gentle laugh— he moved her into a flat at 51 Eaton and bought another house at 20 Greek Street in Soho to use as offices. The pair shuttled back and forth between London and New York, and by September, when Sarah 1 had moved out of Sydmonton, Sarah 2 moved in.

The terms of the divorce were kept secret even though the tabloids ballooned the settlement price by headlining that it would cost Lloyd-Webber seven millon pounds. The correct figure was a modest seven hundred fifty thousand pounds in cash, plus the house on Eaton Place, as well as three hundred fifty thousand pounds in trust for Imogen and Nicholas.

For a man of his wealth, one might consider he got off cheaply, since at almost the same time, he was to spend nearly twice that for the Palace Theatre.

Caught up in the urge to have his own theater, Lloyd-Webber had first offered a million pounds for the Aldwich, but in 1982 his bid had been topped by the Nederlanders, American theater owners. Disappointed, he then bid half a million pounds for the Old Vic, but this time was outbid by the Canadian Ed Mirvish. Determined not to lose out, when the theater built originally by Richard D'Oyly Carte with some of the fortune he had made from his entrepreneurship of Gilbert and Sullivan and known initially as the Royal English Opera House came up for sale in August 1983, Lloyd-Webber bid high enough to assure it would be his. He snapped up the property as soon as it came on the market, paying £1.3 million for this grand old gem at the top of London's "Broadway"—Shaftesbury Avenue. The Palace, a terra-cotta Victorian wonder, commands Cambridge Circus, and because it is set far back into its plot, it gives even a more majestic impression than the Royal Opera House or the far larger Coliseum.

The Palace had long held a special attraction for Lloyd-Webber, for his *Jesus Christ Superstar* had given 3,358 performances there, and his then current production, *Song and Dance*, was actually playing there when he made the deal.[1]

---

[1] In 1985 the blockbuster musical *Les Misérables* transferred to the Palace after its first performances at The Barbican and by 1993 had broken *Superstar*'s longevity record, racking up at the same time a tidy profit for the theater's new owner.

Andrew Lloyd-Webber's dream comes true. On August 23, 1983, he became the owner of the Palace Theatre, designed for D'Oyly Carte and built as London's grandest opera house in 1891. His own Song and Dance *was followed by the long-running* Les Misérables. *AP/ Wide World Photos.*

With *Cats* running so successfully, Andrew Lloyd-Webber was now able to turn back to *Starlight Express*. Richard Stilgoe was deep into the lyrics for his Cinderella story when Trevor Nunn announced that he found that concept to have "a depressing and cosy Englishness." If trains run on wheels, why not make the actors run on wheels? The answer was to put the cast on roller skates.

He communicated this revolutionary idea to John Napier, who eagerly came up with a plan to gut the Apollo Victoria Theatre after other sites—warehouses and defunct department stores—had been rejected. Taking a page from the havoc he had wreaked on Broadway's Winter Garden Theater when he staged *Cats*, Napier connected the stage to the mezzanine with a track on which the human trains would hurl themselves around and through the audience at speeds of some forty miles per hour. Transparent crash barriers would rise from the floor to separate the racers from the viewers, and a massive suspension bridge would move into place at just the right second so the racers could hurtle over it.[2] This roller derby would need an additional track for racing around the orchestra floor, known in Britain as the stalls. To banish collision with the actor-racers, ushers would ensure that audiences were seated or barred entry during the races. And so that everyone, even those sitting in the cheap seats, could see the "races," two huge television monitors were set up on either side of the stage. To turn the theater into this skating arena, almost half the seats would have to be ripped out, but the team believed in the project and went blithely forward.

The story is a simple one. Rusty, a lovable steam engine, inspired by his lovable, folksy father, takes on his more modern rivals and wins the final race over Greaseball, the cheating diesel, and the electric train called Electra (what else?). Rusty's Poppa tells him of the days when trains were trains and inspires Rusty to see and to be the Starlight Express. As the engines and rolling stock come under the controller's orders, the only one that cops out is the British advanced passenger train. The cast, assembled without major stars, had no need for great singers but needed energetic dancers adept at break-dancing, body-popping, and, of course, fancy roller-skating. When this writer asked an associate who had seen the show in previews what it was like, he replied, "They whoosh around the auditorium three times in the first act, and luckily only two times in the second."

Actually, the racing is the best part, for the score is perhaps intentionally naive, but played at eardrum-piercing volume. No one is credited with the book, and the kindest word one can say about the lyrics is that they are simply banal.

The overamplified songs are performed on synthesizers, certainly computerized. One must admit that *Starlight Express* shows off Lloyd-Webber's ability to

[2] This idea was introduced by Hal Prince in the massive iron bridges Eugene Lee contrived for *Sweeney Todd*.

clone songs from the '50s to the '80s. Beginning with rock and '50s group sound, traveling through R&B, rap, funk, rockabilly, country, and ending up with soul and gospel, there is something here for everyone. But it all adds up to the weakest score Lloyd-Webber had written. Certainly he was attempting to connect the pop music sound with the theater, but this is an eclectic score in which, for example, a typical blues is almost a rudimentary lesson in how to write one.

> The first line of the blues, you don't waste a
>   second's time,
> The first line of the blues, you don't waste a
>   second's time
>
> By the time you get to the third line, you got
>   time to think of a rhyme.

Starting with "Rolling Stock," a hard-driving rock song with perhaps the most memorable tune of the evening, followed by "Pumping Iron," an Elvis Presley takeoff (not nearly so amusing as the one in *Joseph*), and continuing with lyrics that are replete with sexual images, the show ends up being more offensive than it is boring. But then isn't the very Freudian image of trains coupling and un-coupling, hurtling into tunnels an erotic one?

Unfortunately its creators didn't know which audience, adult or juvenile, they were aiming the show at, but most of the ticketholders have been preteens. What possessed the creators to invent a character like Electra and give him/her perhaps the most annoying song of the evening: "AC/DC, It's O.K. by me, / I can change my frequency"? Maybe they felt the innuendoes would go over the heads of their youngsters, but without prudery one can say that enough remains for this writer to consider it sleazy.

The engines are all male, except for the androgenous Electra, and the invariably female coaches that are coupled behind them are mere sex symbols, outlandishly costumed. The dining car tells us, "Buffy at your service, / Ever open wide," while Belle, the sleeping car, is the cliché whore with a heart of gold who leeringly invites all comers to "climb aboard."

Distasteful as distinguished from pitiful, the lyrics hit rock bottom in the imagination department with one that is reprised countless times: "Freight is great, / We carry freight, / 'Cause we are great, and / Freight is great."

Critics were divided, most of them at a loss to describe the set, the cost, and the decibel level. Jack Tinker of the *Daily Mail* called it "not much of an innovative musical, with synthesized echoes of many an old score to be picked up along these tracks. But it is one hell of a roller coaster spectacle." The *Guardian*'s Michael Billington complained that "not since Lionel Bart's *Blitz* has London seen a musical where the technology so totally dwarfed the minuscule content."

But the *Sunday Telegraph* called it "a triumph," although it qualified the success as mostly technical, and the *Mail on Sunday*, one of the few that hailed the score, said it was "a vibrant show . . . with stunning spectacle and Lloyd Webber's driving, inventive, evocative score." London's theatergoers are not swayed by critiques to the same extent as those in New York. The British are more prone to making up their own minds, coming to see a show because it features a favorite star or has been written by a creative team they admire. Every bit of theater they attend need not be advertised as "the event of a lifetime."

Additionally, the economics of Broadway make it imperative that the theater be 90 percent sold at each performance, whereas on the West End (more true at the time of *Starlight Express* than today) a show can limp along with half-full houses until it finds its audience. Additionally, in a city with so many daily and Sunday newspapers, one can always find some positive quotes to plaster on billboards or to affix to the buses. *Starlight*'s few positive reviews, plus a large overcall, plus the loyal public Lloyd-Webber had built up by this time were enough to energize its human trains to keep them running for almost a decade. And since the closing, there have been frequent revivals.

Andrew Lloyd-Webber had celebrated his thirty-sixth birthday just a few days before most of the critics tore this work to pieces. Two days earlier, on March 20, his final divorce decree came through. That very afternoon he had married Sarah Brightman at the magistrate's office in a little village near Sydmonton. It had been a quiet ceremony, barred to photographers. Brightman's mother and David and Lisa Crewe-Read, old friends of Andrew's, were the only guests. It was reported that after the brief ceremony the newlyweds hurried back to London just in time to dress in evening clothes and to get to the theater.

Mr. and Mrs. Andrew Lloyd-Webber arrived in time for a preopening gala that had been announced months before. That performance, a benefit, was to be attended by Queen Elizabeth and Prince Philip, and Andrew pulled off the feat of presenting Sarah to the Royals not as his mistress, but as his bride.

In March 1987, three years after its London premiere, *Starlight Express* was brought to New York's Gershwin Theater under the sponsorship of Martin Starger and Lord Grade, with the major portion of the money coming from MCA and a New Zealand investment company. Lloyd-Webber revamped the score and added a big ballad called "Only He." The Nederlanders, who owned the theater, would not let their auditorium be torn apart like the Apollo-Victoria had been, so what had been the show's chief excitement, the races in which the trains raced through and around the audience, had to be done as a proscenium show with the public mere spectators. One wonders how much the production might have cost had they been allowed to tear up the theater—as it was, it set a startling record for the time. "I find it quite amusing," Lloyd-Webber said, "that my little train musical, which was written for my son Nicholas, has ended up costing someone eight million dollars." That "someone" was the key word, for Lloyd-Webber had not invested a penny in the American production.

Perhaps because he suspected that with the technology limited to the stage, thereby robbing his extravaganza of half its punch, the Broadway critics were going to clobber his score, he inserted a long disclaimer in the program. Trying to shift the blame and save his reputation, it somewhat cravenly blamed Trevor Nunn for changing the concept from "a concert sung by all the schools of the City of London," à la *Joseph*. He also admitted that the pop score and the roller skates were all Nunn's idea. "Frankly, some of us had doubts. I hope Trevor," Lloyd-Webber continued, "and my other collaborators will forgive me for saying that despite the commercial success the show has had in London, something of the joy and sense of pure fun that was the original intention seemed to get lost, and *Starlight Express* was not quite what we intended."

Here was Lloyd-Webber waiting to be crucified by admitting his failure. It was more than the critics needed—especially *New York Times* guru Frank Rich, who was passionately in the Sondheim camp.

> Andrew Lloyd Webber modestly explains that he conceived . . . *Starlight Express* as an entertainment "event" for children who love trains. Over two numbing hours later, you may find yourself wondering exactly whose children he has in mind. A confusing jamboree of piercing noise, routine roller-skating, misogyny and Orwellian special effects, *Starlight Express* is the perfect gift for the kid who has everything except parents.
>
> Instead of aspiring to his usual Puccini variations, Mr. Lloyd Webber had gone "funky," English style, by writing pastiche versions of American pop music—with an emphasis on blues, gospel and rap. . . . Soul music couldn't get much more soulless than this.

In the light of Rich's harsh critique, one can hardly blame Andrew Lloyd-Webber when some years later he bought a gelded race horse and named him Frank Rich. Yet Rich was not wholly responsible for *Starlight Express*'s lack of success in New York. The production tried to play into Americana by a cute trick—naming the stops on the itinerary after major U.S. cities—and thus anchored to reality, the show lost its out-of-this-world quality. Moreover, American youths, accustomed to the exciting rides in Disneyland, found *watching* the races on stage less than exciting.

After running close to two years, exhausting its $4 million advance, selling tickets at a discount, and still playing to less than full houses, the show closed. It repaid only about 80 percent of its investors' outlay. Its closure did little damage to Andrew Lloyd-Webber's reputation and, because he had not invested in the production and was merely collecting his composer royalties, no harm to his pocketbook.

By the time *Starlight Express* closed, Lloyd-Webber had stretched his wings by writing two showpieces for his beloved Sarah. The first, which he called *Requiem*, served the dual purpose of honoring William's memory and partnering his prima donna with opera's superstar, Placido Domingo. The second would carry his fame all around the world. Based on the famous Gaston Leroux novel, it was to be his finest work thus far—*The Phantom of the Opera*.

Two Pieces for Sarah

S ARAH BRIGHTMAN LLOYD WEBBER had no intention of retiring from the theater, even though her new husband had enough money to keep her in a style to which one could easily become accustomed. Andrew, passionate about his bride and electrified by the enormous operatic range of her voice, could think of nothing else but the music he would write for her. Wouldn't she be wonderful in the opus based on the Puccini-Leoncavallo feud he had long wished to compose? But, no, the two men were the stars of this, the women merely incidental.

He might have put her name in lights on the marquee of his new show, but he had rejected the thought of putting her into *Starlight Express*, even though she was a good skater, because the piece lacked a starring role. Instead, he featured her in a TV version of the first part of *Song and Dance*, the solo cantata *Tell Me on a Sunday*. The show was seen on the BBC and, later, on U.S. television. Still, that impersonation, which had been written for the belt voice of Marti Webb, used only half of Sarah's remarkable range. And the leading lady of the piece was supposed to be close to thirty. Sarah was twenty-three and looked far younger. It was a showcase, but not an ideal one.

Lloyd-Webber had been working recently on music for David Garnett's no-vella *Aspects of Love*, but here, too, the tone was confidential, and the songs that would seem appropriate for this tale that somewhat resembled *La Ronde* in its dissection of liaisons would be small, whispering, and intimate. The whole piece would have the feel of a chamber opera. No, this Pygmalion needed to write a bravura piece that would allow his Galatea's voice to soar and reverberate throughout the auditorium. Because of her youth, Sarah Brightman had the power and the stamina and, because she had been working with a fine operatic coach, now had acquired the extended range.

Just a few months after they were married Sarah had been offered the starring role in Ken Hill's version of Gaston Leroux's *Phantom of the Opera*, which was then being staged at a small theater, Stratford East. Lloyd-Webber and Mackintosh went to see the production, not particularly thinking of it as a vehicle for Sarah but more as a show they might produce.[1] Hill, who was a playwright, had adapted the story, making it a scary comedy—what Andrew called "wildly jokey"—that used real operatic arias of the period. Both Mackintosh and Lloyd-Webber rejected the idea as being too light, too camp for presentation under their aegis, while Andrew thought that the idea of Sarah's singing operatic arias in her London debut—especially ones written by Gounod or Meyerbeer—was inappropriate. If there were operatic arias to be sung, he himself would compose them. But the idea, now a mere glimmer, behind *Phantom*, which had obsessed him since he read the book, refused to leave him.

It is hard to know when Lloyd-Webber turned his thoughts to the *Requiem*, an extended piece of liturgical music that would feature his wife and serve as homage to his late father at the same time. He was much moved by the horrors of the killings in Northern Ireland and the senseless 1982 bombing outside Harrod's, but what stirred him to action was an item buried in an obscure corner of the *New York Times*. The story concerned a Cambodian boy who was faced with the choice of killing his mutilated sister or being killed himself. That gave him the idea of scoring the *Requiem* for a boy, a girl, and a man—that is, boy soprano, soprano, and tenor. Because of this dramatic idea, the mezzo-soprano, baritone, or bass soloists common in most requiems purposely would be omitted.

"The soprano should be young," he told a journalist, "and have a special connection with the solo boy, and let's say there is an imprecise theatrical structure concerning the boy and the tenor. The girl is the bridge between them." The tenor would represent the world at large, and, according to Lloyd-Webber, the whole piece would be a diatribe against "the manipulation of children in wartime."

It was a glowing concept. The project would allow him to thumb his nose at those critics who had applauded his seriousness after *Superstar* and *Evita*, proclaiming him Britain's premiere composer, and who had then deserted and lambasted him for *Starlight Express*. He would show them that he could be far more than the parodist of American popular music they had labeled him after *Starlight Express*.

After a short draft of the *Requiem* was tried out at the Sydmonton festival in the summer of 1984 to positive reaction, Lloyd-Webber forged ahead with an eye to a New York debut of the forty-seven-minute work in February 1985.

---

[1] The Really Useful Company, which had produced *Daisy Pulls It Off* in 1983, offered a succès d'estime the following year with Melvyn Bragg and Howard Goodall's fine musical, *The Hired Man*. In the years ahead they would present two hit shows: *Shirley Valentine* and *Lend Me a Tenor*.

Almost nothing was allowed to interfere with the writing, and by October he had completed the score; by the end of the year the orchestration, which he and David Cullen did together, was ready.

The first performance took place February 24, 1985, at Saint Thomas Episcopal Church at Fifty-third Street and Fifth Avenue in New York. The British premiere took place two months later on April 21 in Westminster Abbey. In both cases the principals and the conductor, Lorin Maazel, were the same: Sarah Brightman, of course, had the major role, and the boy soprano, Paul Miles-Kingston, sang the child's part with purity and feeling. Placido Domingo, a longtime friend of Andrew's, had been after the composer for some time to write a piece for him, and Lloyd-Webber obliged by tailoring the stentorian tenor part to his voice.

In a book devoted to the development and changes in musical theater, Andrew Lloyd-Webber's large liturgical work would seemingly have little place. But because the composer himself occupies an enormous niche, the techniques he developed in writing *Requiem* were to serve him well when he tackled *Phantom of the Opera*. Here the extensive part and choral writing move strictly along classic lines. Some of what he learned is apparent in the ensemble writing in *Aspects of Love* and *Sunset Boulevard*. Lloyd-Webber admits that his writing might not always be academically correct, adding that his father "insisted that I should not be overtrained musically."

Academic training is precisely what is lacking here, for in spite of Lloyd-Webber's having created interesting, sometimes ravishing themes, the larger forms, such as the "Dies Irae" and "Offertorium," lack development. Some development is necessary for every extended piece, whether it be augmentation (stretching the pitches out) or diminution (cramping them together), retrograde motion (playing the tones backward) or crab inversion (upside down *and* backward). It is boring to listen to the same statements repeated in the same way or simply gussied up with different orchestration. Where is the lovely craft of music, the tossing about of motives or even bits of motives? Where are subtle modulations that move us gradually from key to key?

In this work what you hear first is all you get. Perhaps for compensation Lloyd-Webber works up to some tremendously dissonant, theatrical climaxes and then stops abruptly, but the effect is merely astonishing, not musical. Worse than that, in his zeal to use every note in Brightman's and Domingo's extended ranges, the composer sets the keys for his soloists achingly high. He pushes Brightman to a high C sharp that comes out as a jarring scream, and although he is kinder to Domingo, his vocal writing does not progress gracefully or gradually into the upper tessitura, and so the tenor's voice sounds bumped and strained.

Most of the slow music resembles medieval plainsong gone amok, while the driving fast choral passages remind one of nothing so much as Carl Orff's *Carmina Burana*. There are, however, two genuine totally honest moments: the toe-tapping "Hosanna" and the lovely hit tune "Pie Jesu." The latter has been called the *Requiem*'s "Memory," partly for its similarity to a Puccini aria. Yet, in spite of a slight resemblance to moments in *Gianni Schicchi*'s "O Mio Babbino Caro," Lloyd-Webber's melody truly works. Here is a case in which development is unnecessary, and the cantalina, introduced by the soprano, reprised by her and the boy singing in thirds, and encored with the chorus, which finally melts away in the two high voices, is gorgeous, liturgical, and appropriate.

Since the *Requiem* had its premiere in New York, the American critics were the first to take a swipe at the composer who at the time of *Superstar* had been roasted for his operatic pretensions. Now they complained that this "pop" tune-smith had inordinate chutzpah to consider himself able to write in a form so successfully managed by Mozart, Brahms, Verdi, and Fauré.

"It promised much," wrote Bernard Holland, doyen music critic of the *New York Times*, "but fell back too often on massive claps of thunder and other coups de théâtre, most of which startled rather than moved. Thus Mr. Lloyd Webber was least effective when he tried the hardest. The intended force of the 'Dies Irae' merely grated, while the massive outburst that interrupted the boy soprano at the final lines served to vulgarize his sweet singing, not to set it off."

Martin Bernheimer of the *Los Angeles Times* went even farther. "It aspires to the pure fragrance of churchly incense, but it ends up reeking of cheap perfume." Bernheimer went on to excoriate Lloyd-Webber for his "eclecticism," while Peter Davis in *New York* magazine deplored the presence of Domingo and Maazel in this "pretentious and crushingly trivial hunk of junk."

Yet in spite of all the complaints, "Pie Jesu" *was* a hit, quickly entering both the pop and classical music charts. In fact, the entire album stayed in the Classical Top 20 in Britain for some four years. In America, the *Requiem* won the Grammy award as the best classical album of 1985. Soon, in a marketing phenomenon, stores were flooded with videocassettes, singles, sheet music, excerpts, and full scores. Since its debut, performances of the entire work have been frequent, perhaps because of the popularity of its hit song. Lloyd-Webber was not above exploiting its market appeal and soft pedaling its religiosity. He booked a week of performances into his own Palace Theatre, the first half of which would be his *Variations*, followed by what he called simply *Requiem* (as though it were a theater piece), starring Sarah and Paul Miles-Kingston.

In sum, even though its marketing is suspect, one cannot say that *Requiem* itself is dishonest, for the passion and struggle are evident on every page. As Lloyd-Webber himself said, "I don't know what place it will find in the music of today, but to me it is the most personal of all my compositions." In a way it is his conservatory graduation thesis, a serious composition that would have

The Archbishop of Canterbury, Dr. Robert Runcie, presents gold albums to composer Andrew Lloyd-Webber, his wife, soprano Sarah Brightman, and Paul Miles-Kingston, boy soprano soloist, for Requiem, *which at that date (March 29, 1985) had sold more than 100,000 copies and was Number Five on the album charts. AP/Wide World Photos.*

made his father William proud. "It was a great exercise, and one that I got only about sixty percent right," the composer was to admit. "I'd like to go back over it one day." And he probably will.

From *Requiem's* genesis through its rehearsal and performances, every vocal effect, every melodic trick he had learned to handle in its composition had been stashed away and would be taken out and used to tremendous effect in *The Phantom of the Opera.*

Andrew Lloyd-Webber had made his preliminary sketches for *Aspects of Love*, the freewheeling David Garnett novella about a family ruled by sex, before he had left for New York to ready the *Requiem*. Trevor Nunn was slated eventually to direct the work, and because clever Trevor had crafted if not a fine, at least a best-selling lyric for "Memory," Lloyd-Webber thought he might do the same for the score of *Aspects*. His mind's eye saw the musical as a chamber opera, a thoughtful piece sung by characters who were emotionally inhibited, albeit libidinously erotic, and he knew the music he had given Nunn was too lush, too openly romantic.

But the idea of musicalizing *The Phantom of the Opera*, a Grand Guignol classic, did not come to him until he had a conversation with Hal Prince at a meeting of Tony Award nominees. After Prince's several flops he was smarting under an accusation that his shows were fairly cold. "I asked Hal what he was up to, and he said, 'I'm looking for a romantic musical.' And I said, 'So am I. Do you think you'd really like to do a musical about straightforward romance?' 'Yes,' he answered, 'I'd like to do a musical where somebody actually comes out and says "I love you" and that's that.' "

Lloyd-Webber knew that the melodies in Nunn's hands would be right for whatever was to be Prince's "romantic musical," and he was reminded of Leroux's tale of the ill-starred composer, a deformed genius who roamed the subcellars of the Paris Opéra, fell in love with a beautiful young singer, and eventually lost her to a handsome, empty-headed aristocrat.

"I wanted to use real opera and all of that," he was to recall. "My entire exposure to the story had been through Lon Chaney movies and a blurred one about somebody who threw acid over somebody's face." That last cinema version had starred Claude Rains and was more like a version of *Little Shop of Horrors*, for it bore no relation to the original novel. "But now," he added, "I wanted to romanticize it."

It was not only for himself, for he knew at once that this operatic venture was just the vehicle to bring Sarah Brightman the éclat she deserved. Yet he could not in all conscience ask Nunn to shift gears and rewrite the lyrics he had begun for *Aspects* to suit the startlingly different project. Allowing that he had signed no contract with Nunn, and risking the loss of their friendship, he decided to ask him to put the *Aspects* project on hold, just as he had done with *Starlight Express*. Because loyalty to the director of *Cats* meant less to him than what he imagined the magician who had staged *Evita* could do with high romance, he took the melodies back from Nunn and began to rethink them for *Phantom*, with an idea that Prince would direct it. This time, however, Prince would not produce. Cameron Mackintosh was raising 40 percent of the money, and Lloyd-Webber's Really Useful Theatre Company was responsible for the balance.

In their preliminary discussions Prince cautioned Lloyd-Webber not to fall into the trap of unmitigated horror that had, he believed, curtailed the run of Sondheim's *Sweeney Todd*. He wanted the Phantom to be "desirable." He also warned that there must not be any hint of camp or bogeyman in the work. He advised Andrew to give the lovers a glorious duet with an expansive melody, pointing out that Sweeney and Mrs. Lovett were given the main numbers while the lovers sang a frenetic duo. All their amorous solos were relegated to subplot. As he had taken back that sheaf of melodies from Trevor Nunn and already had written some more, he now had to find a lyricist. He knew that Tim Rice was busy with the Swedish group ABBA creating *Chess* and felt Don Black was not right for this project. Taking a chance, he went straight to the top. That meant Alan Jay Lerner, who, having married his eighth wife, Liz Robertson, was then living full time in London. As one of the world's premiere composers of musicals, Lloyd-Webber felt he could command the world's foremost living lyricist, the creator of *My Fair Lady*, *Brigadoon*, *Camelot*, and *Gigi*, the man who lived "romance" and could write it with one hand tied behind his back. Lloyd-Webber wrote for an appointment.

Lerner, then sixty-six, was involved in an adaptation of *My Man Godfrey*, but once he understood the utterly idealistic approach Lloyd-Webber was aiming for in *Phantom*, eagerly agreed to put *Godfrey* aside. Lerner had already written the lyric for the big second act choral number, "Masquerade," when he began having dizzy spells. Then his memory began to fail him, and he assumed it was writer's block. His daughter, Liza Bibb, told this writer she felt he was suffering from a brain tumor that was never diagnosed. Reluctantly, although committed to do the show, he wrote to Lloyd-Webber telling him he couldn't work with him any longer.

Lloyd-Webber was more saddened than annoyed, but with his usual persistence he wasted no time before engaging Richard Stilgoe, who had provided the words to *Starlight Express*. Stilgoe began afresh, disregarding any work Lerner had done on the project. He worked fast and had completed enough of the lyrics and book of *Phantom* to present much of the first act at the Sydmonton Festival of 1985.

The result was a sensation even to the first-act ending, the famous dropping of the chandelier that, after a free fall, was caught on wires and hovered half a foot above the heads of a frightened audience.[2] But Lloyd-Webber, finding the score more rock than opera, was not satisfied with anything about the work as it stood then, except some of the melodies and the set and costume designs of Maria Bjornson.

Hal Prince did not attend the Sydmonton performance, preferring to keep an

---

[2] The final decision to have the chandelier discovered in pieces at the musical's opening, then reassembled and hoisted by wire up to the center of the theater, is a mistake that robs the ending of the act, when the huge luster falls, of any tension. It is obvious that the fixture will be guided back on stage by the same wires.

open mind on the direction the production should go. He too was dissatisfied with the lyrics, the book, and the style, and not knowing where to turn, decided to get his direction from the novel. This called for a visit to Paris and a tour of the magnificent opera house designed by Charles Garnier and built in the late 1860s. He walked its stage, the auditorium, the loges, galleries, corridors, rehearsal rooms, and backstage areas. He was amazed to discover that the massive playing, rehearsal, and audience areas comprised only one fifth of the Opéra's seventeen stories from its sub-sub-subbasement to its copper rooftops, which are on a level with the top of the Eiffel Tower. Then he investigated the nearly four-acre plot, examined the basement, which once housed a stable of horses, and visited the lake five stories below the stage, whose water was used to operate the hydraulic stage machinery. With Leroux's book in hand, Prince found the novelist's settings remarkably authentic.

But Prince did not have his necessary "metaphor," without which he has never been able to conceive a show, until he happened by chance on a BBC documentary called *The Skin Horses*. The film consisted of a series of interviews with handicapped people interspersed with scenes from the 1930s movie *Freaks* and the famous scene from *The Elephant Man* in which the actress kisses the deformed creature.

"Some of those interviewed spoke willingly, eagerly of their sexuality," Prince was to say. "It was an element which had been missing in the design of the *Phantom* and which, indeed, informed the subsequent rewritten drafts of the libretto."

The novel was then simplified. Characters important to the written page, like the omnipresent Persian, a kind of passe-partout who reports to the reader on the goings-on in the bowels of the opera, could be eliminated because of the visual nature of theater. This took away much of the cloak-and-dagger aspect of the book. The hero's brother Philippe, Comte de Chagny, a witless villain, was expendable for the same reasons. The "Prince-ipals"—Christine, Raoul, and the Phantom—need only be surrounded by managers, costume mistresses, dancers, and a rival prima donna, helping to accentuate the opera house milieu.

Back in New York, Prince advised Lloyd-Webber and Stilgoe to stick closely to the novel but to infuse it with desire, humanity, carnality. With Bjornson's dark designs and Leroux's book viewed through contemporary eyes, he felt that if Lloyd-Webber could come up with some really smashingly romantic music, they would have a hit of enormous proportions. Stilgoe worked on the book, but his lyrics were prosaic indeed, and Lloyd-Webber and Prince went in search of a vital, hopefully ardent lyricist.

It was Cameron Mackintosh who suggested young Charles Hart, who had been runner-up for the Vivian Ellis competition that encouraged young composers and lyricists. Andrew gave him a melody to lyricize, and the young man came up with three "solutions": "Look at Us," "Knowing Him," and the one that finally was used, "Think of Me."

Judging Hart's lyrics for his initial contribution, one wonders what possessed them to hire the fledgling, for although this is supposed to be an operatic aria in the style of Meyerbeer,[3] his poem is of monumental triviality. I quote the first verse:

Think of me,   When you find
Think of me fondly   That once again you long
When we've said goodbye.   To take your heart back and be free,
                                          If you ever find a moment,
Remember me,   Spare a thought for me . . .
Once in a while,
Please promise me you'll try.

Hart's lyrics do not improve as the show goes on, but the music and the story seem to carry the day.

The Phantom of the Opera opens with the provocative sound of a gavel striking an auctioneer's block while the musty curtains and turn-of-the-century costumes establish place and time. "Sold," the auctioneer shouts, "a papier-mâché musical box in the shape of a barrel organ. Attached, the figure of a monkey in Persian robes playing the cymbals." The words have an exotic sound and seem to move us back in time. The language that follows is rich, fruity, like Sweeney Todd's industrial-age circumlocutions.

When the monkey is purchased by the now aged Vicomte de Chagny, whom we will meet shortly as the young hero, he sings sotto voce and philosophically, wondering if the music box will play after we are dead. The mystery and the foreignness of the venue are apparent at once. Who is this man, we ask? Why are they all here? Then the auctioneer opens the bidding on the chandelier, saying that it figured in the famous disaster. He mentions that if it were lit it might help to frighten away the ghosts of so many years ago, and as the huge crystal mass is illuminated, the organ and orchestra launch fortissimo into the overture. The curtains fall away, seeming to move us back to the nineteenth century, transforming whatever theater we are sitting in into the Paris Opéra.

Four ominous chords, descending chromatically and then rising similarly, hint that we are in for melodramatic pastiche—and we really are. It is a mock Mey-

---

[3] Giacomo Meyerbeer (1791–1864) is remembered for his overblown but spectacular French grand operas. Short on inspiration but long-winded and showy, his Robert le Diable (1831), Les Huguenots (1836), Le Prophète (1849) and L'Africaine (1865) were staples of French opera houses in the nineteenth century. He fell out of fashion well before the twentieth.

erbeer opera in rehearsal, and a splendid way to get the musical going. During the rehearsal's stops and starts we are introduced to the opera's stars, the new owners of the theater, Firmin and André, and the old costume mistress, Madame Giry, who functions as a go-between the Phantom and management. When a piece of falling scenery frightens off Carlotta, the girthy diva, the girls of the chorus begin to scream, "He's here! The Phantom!" Mme. Giry steps forward to explain that the falling scenery was a sign of the Phantom's puissance to the new landlords and that they are to continue to keep his Box No. 5 available for his personal use and to remit through Mme. Giry the habitual 20,000 francs "protection" money every month.

Christine Daaé gets to complete Carlotta's aria, "Think of Me," and soon is singing it in a concert. When asked by her friend Meg, Mme. Giry's daughter, how her voice has so improved, she tells her she has been having lessons from an "angel of music," one she equates with her dead father, who was a violinist. Raoul, the Vicomte de Chagny (the handsome young man who we know will end up getting the girl), knew Christine as a young girl. He has been in attendance at the concert and, coming back to congratulate her, waits outside her dressing room. But she does not come out.

In the first of what will be several coups de théâtre the Phantom appears to her, formally dressed and caped, elegant and with his half-mask.[4] We see him standing in her dressing room mirror, and they sing their first duet, "Angel of Music," after which the Phantom takes his willing protégée through the mirror down into his subterranean domain. In a dazzling effect, they travel by boat across a shimmering candlelit lake.[5]

Prevented by fire laws in both London and New York from using real flame, lighting designer Andrew Bridge devised a series of tiny lamps whose bulbs flicker inside a tube, giving off the impression of moving flame. To create the shimmer of light on water, he used motorized wheels and rotating disks.

The song that accompanies this excursion is one of the musical's four hits to have made the charts: "The Music of the Night." Originally written for *Aspects of Love* and titled "It's a Miracle," it has been judged by some to stem from an old tune called "School Days." Others remark on its similarity to Lerner and Loewe's "Come to Me, Bend to Me" from *Brigadoon*. The similarities bring up

[4] The now-famous Phantom half-mask was Maria Bjornson's inspiration after she had looked through books depicting the masks often created for veterans who had been maimed in the First World War. To hide the scars of battle these masks were commonly painted to match the color of the wearer's skin.

[5] Prince's original concept was to have the lake full of rats with flashing red eyes. According to David Firth, one of the principals, when the director saw the effect, he yelled to his assistant, " 'Cut those rats!' So they came right out. I don't know how much they cost, but he knew they were wrong."

The Phantom (in this photo, Mark Jacoby) carries his inamorata, Christine (here, Karen Culliver) to his subterranean lair beneath the Paris Opéra. The roles were originated by Michael Crawford and Sarah Brightman. Photo: Joan Marcus. © Museum of the City of New York.

the frequent critique that Lloyd-Webber's music "sounds like . . ." But it must be mentioned in his defense, or that of any composer, that a melodic motif is merely a point of departure, and it is what the composer does with it afterward that shows his mettle. In this, as so many songs from other composers that occasionally borrow a phrase, the main body of the song is what really counts. For the record and for comparison the opening phrases for "Music of the Night" and "School Days" are printed below:

Soft - ly,   deft - ly,   mu - sic shall car - ess   you.

School - days, school - days,   dear old gold - en rule   days.

Hart's lyrics (here he had an assist from Richard Stilgoe) for this song are the sexiest and the best of the evening. The Phantom is a mighty seducer, and his song invites not only Christine but every audience member into a fantasy:

Close your eyes, surrender to your darkest
  dreams!
Purge your thoughts of the life you knew
  before!
Close your eyes, let your spirit start to soar
And you'll live as you never lived before! . . .

Floating, falling, sweet intoxication!
Touch me, trust me, savour each sensation!
Let the dream begin,
Let your darker side give in,
To the power of the music that I write—
The power of the music of the night.

In the next scene we get to understand the Phantom's dedication to his music. He is hard at work on his opera when Christine steals up behind him and tears off his mask. Because he is cleverly directed here, with his back to the audience, we do not get to see his face, but the horror we see on Christine's is far more chilling.

When Christine is returned to the world above, so she can star in an opera the Phantom has chosen for her debut, the management risks incurring his wrath by preferring to have Carlotta sing the role. Lloyd-Webber wrote "Prima Donna," a charming waltz, one worthy of Noël Coward, with which the managers reassure her of her eminence in her field. As it is reprised, it becomes an ingenious ensemble number, but at its end, over the series of descending chromatic triads which we have by now come to associate with the Phantom, he warns: "So—it is to be war between us! If these demands are not met, a disaster beyond your imagination will occur." We know we are nearing the moment of the falling chandelier.

But not yet.

The opera goes on, but Carlotta hardly begins to sing when the Phantom, ventriloquist that he is, makes her sound like a croaking frog. The managers call out the ballet until Christine can be substituted for the hoarse diva, who has now left the stage amid catcalls. In the confusion and a backstage murder, Christine and Raoul flee to what seems to them the only safe place, the rooftop of the opera house. We are at last out in the open, away from the claustrophobic stage areas, free of the stifling velvet curtains, and are given the best song of the musical—"This Is All I Ask of You." This is certainly Lloyd-Webber's finest achievement—the glorious, romantic melody Prince requested. David Firth, who sang in the first Sydmonton production, remembered that when he heard this love duet, "I thought it was absolutely beautiful . . . I thought here was a central theme. And I thought well, if this work takes off it will be because of this."

It is a melody that spins itself out in almost through-composed fashion. Hart and Stilgoe take credit for the inconsequential lyric full of misplaced accents and cliché, but it is a melody that stomps over the mundane words.

With an elegant eight-bar verse lead-in, the refrain of this melody, which gains much of its tension by beginning on the supertonic, is somewhat of a departure for Lloyd-Webber: it is reminiscent of nothing else. As such, it was a harbinger of much original work to come. Listening to it, one can sense that the rock period of *Joseph* and *Superstar* and even the later *Evita* and the *Variations* were merely a phase. Perhaps it is a sweeping statement but this writer believes that the true disciple of Richard Rodgers was afraid to be laughed at, and so he assumed a "with-it" mod guise. With this duet he seems to have unmasked himself. At the very least, it is a direction from which he has not since veered.

There on the rooftop, Raoul and Christine have their first passionate embrace, and as they sing yet another reprise of their duet, they are joined by the Phantom, who turns their duet into an operatic trio when he mentions his feelings of being betrayed.

We are quickly transported back to the opera stage, where Christine has replaced Carlotta and is taking her bows to thunderous applause. The Phantom, jealous, angered because of what he has witnessed on the rooftop, sends the chandelier crashing to the stage.[6] Prince's wizardry has it set off a flare that temporarily blinds the audience and sends them reeling into the intermission.

The second act, which begins six months later, features the musical's major dance offering. Set on the grand staircase of the Opéra, splendidly costumed, it is megamusical at its most opulent. This "Masquerade" scene was inspired by Poe's "Masque of the Red Death," and the revelry is broken off when the Phantom appears at the top of the stairway clad in—what else?—red. He announces that he has written a new opera and demands the managers produce it.

In a succeeding scene, when they and the singers examine the difficult, avant-

---

[6] Leroux's book describes the scene: "The immense mass of the chandelier was slipping down, coming toward them, at the call of that fiendish voice. Released from its hook, it plunged from the ceiling and came smashing into the middle of the stalls, amid a thousand shouts of terror. A wild rush for the doors followed.

"The papers of the day state that there were numbers wounded and one killed. The chandelier had crashed down upon the head of a wretched woman who had come to the Opéra for the first time in her life."

The novel's account had its basis in fact. According to a newspaper report of 1896, what fell and killed the woman, a concierge, who had indeed attended the opera backstage for the first time in her life, was the chandeliers's counterweight, weighing about four hundred pounds.

garde score, *Don Juan Triumphant*,[7] they decide to use the production of the phantom's opera to set a trap for the man himself. During the rehearsal of a particularly troublesome passage, the cast is having difficulty singing the score when the stage piano mysteriously points out the correct notes. Christine thinks it is a message from her father and rushes off to his gravesite. She sings a tender melody called, "Wishing You Were Somehow Here Again."

The Phantom appears and tries to lure her back with a reprise of "Angel of Music," but Raoul, too, has followed Christine and pulls his love over to his side. Deserted now, the Phantom realizes Christine loves Raoul and shouts, "Let there be war on you both!"

The scene shifts back to the opera house for a segment of *Don Juan Triumphant*. This is inspired by Mozart's opera, in which a cloaked and masked Don Juan and his servant Leporello switch places. The Phantom does away with the leading tenor, dons his costume, and without the audience's being aware of the exchange sings another of the musical's most interesting numbers. Here the lyric is passable, the title, "The Point of No Return," is perfect.

She alone knowing who her singing partner is, Christine unmasks the Phantom—this time in full view of the audience. It is the moment we have all been waiting for. His face is not horrible, merely twisted. He shrinks and becomes a somewhat pitiable child, but during the confusion when the tenor's body is found, the Phantom escapes, abducting Christine as hostage to his lair.

Raoul follows immediately, but he is no match for the masked man, whose magic quickly overpowers him. The stalwart hero is clamped into an iron maiden-like torture device while we, the audience, are presented with another quasi-operatic situation—this one reminiscent of Puccini's *Tosca*. The Phantom proposes Christine marry him in exchange for Raoul's freedom. Here the plot really gets contrived, but as with a Hitchcock movie, we are so caught up that we are not aware of inconsistencies. Christine realizes how her captor longs for love. "God gave me the courage to show you you are not alone," she sings nobly, and proceeds to kiss him full and lingeringly on the lips.

This, the first gesture of love that has ever been shown him, is enough for him to set the lovers free. Then, in typical operetta fashion or perhaps like a scene out of *Frankenstein*, the townspeople, brandishing flambeaux, have found their way to this subterranean lair, while the Phantom, fearless, wrapped in his cape, sits majestically on his throne. The orchestra thunders out "The Music of the Night," at which point Meg, Christine's friend, pulls aside the cloak. Nothing is in the chair but a wisp of smoke—and the mask.

---

[7] We all know that Mozart's villainous Don ends up in Hell. It is Leroux's switch that makes us expect, maybe even hope, that the Phantom will get away and "triumph" with his nefarious deeds.

Even though four of the songs in the musical made the charts, one must allow that Lloyd-Webber's aim in this work was not merely for commercial success. A few singles came out, but no cast recording was released before the premiere, which took place October 9, 1986, at Her Majesty's Theatre.

The Phantom of the Opera had everything going for it, including a peculiar tenet of the times, the appeal of the ugly. A "beauty and the beast" mentality was sweeping the world. (Indeed the actual musicalization of *Beauty and the Beast* was to be produced by Disney and become a full-fledged stage success in a few years.) The handsome hero is the less exciting of the two rivals for the fair lady. Ask a woman seeing the production whether she would rather go to bed with Raoul or the Phantom, and the latter usually wins. The production team knew this, and they cast that title role against type.

Michael Crawford, before then known primarily as a light comedian, had the right voice, presence, and athleticism for the demanding role. "Everybody came thinking they were going to get somebody swinging on a chandelier," Lloyd-Webber was to recall, "and saying 'Boo' every now and again." Although Crawford created the part, the role is open to many interpretations—as the great variety of every ethnicity who have worn the Phantom's mask have proven.

Coming after *Starlight Express*, the quality of this musical is all the more startling, and one would have expected the reviews to be rave. Not so. Most thought Lloyd-Webber overreached himself in the opera sections. Several took aim at the composer himself, the most vitriolic being David Shannon, who headed his critique in *Today* as "Andrew's trite night at the opera."

> Andrew Lloyd Webber's new musical is, he says, "about a man who is hideously ugly who falls hopelessly in love with this girl and is only able to express himself through his music." Only those of a very cruel frame of mind would suggest the musical was at all autobiographical.

Frank Rich came abroad to report on the show in the *New York Times*. He praised only his countryman Harold Prince, noting that it is "invigorating to see what a crack Broadway director at full throttle can do." He dismissed Hart and Stilgoe, saving his harshest words for his bête noire, Lloyd-Webber. He called the operatic sections "insufferably smug" and wondered if a show "that is sold out until 1988 [that was in 1986] need sell itself out quite so much."

But there were some good notices as well. Michael Coveney cheered the production, performances, and music, noting in the *Financial Times* that "the final moments as Christine rips off the mask and the lovers' triangle is resolved in a descent to the lair and an emotional farewell are almost unbearably moving." And there were consistent raves coming especially from the tabloids.

None of it mattered. The show was to play to 100 percent capacity in London for the next fifteen years. It would break all records and go on to become a theatrical phenomenon. Queues would line up at dawn, in rain, shine, snow, or heat wave, outside Her Majesty's Theatre waiting for returns for that evening's performance.

Everything was set for a Broadway opening when American Actors' Equity refused to allow Sarah to repeat her role, saying she was not essential to the production. Andrew was furious. Supported by Prince, he threatened to cancel the plans to bring *Phantom* to New York. And he was not bluffing. At last Andrew realized his overwhelming theatrical power when he brought Equity to its knees. They agreed to allow Sarah to star in the show for six months, and to save a bit of face, made him promise to cast an "unknown" American in his next British show. Andrew obliged by casting Ann Crumb in *Aspects of Love*.

Now the ads for mail orders began to appear, and the show was scheduled to open at Broadway's Majestic Theater on January 26, 1988 (where it remains today). The first day tickets went on sale, the box office nearly broke down with a record of almost a million dollars. By the time of the show's opening, it had taken in sixteen million dollars.

As expected, the majority of the reviews were negative, with most of the critics complaining about the derivative nature of the score. John Simon said, "It's not so much that Lloyd Webber lacks an ear for melody as that he has too much of a one for other people's." Brightman too came in for her share of Webber-bashing from him when he called her casting "a triumph of uxoriousness."

But none of the reviews could dent the show's enormous popularity. The casting and hoopla alone guaranteed an exciting performance. Michael Crawford, an enormous favorite with the British and known to Americans for his role in the film version of *Hello, Dolly*, made a charismatic Phantom. Sarah Brightman's crystalline voice and Pre-Raphaelite looks were a perfect foil for him, and although her tone was at times harsh and edgy, that could be an advantage in a heavily amplified theater where young audiences are accustomed to considering such sounds contemporary.

Phantom has sold over ten million double album sets across the world. Lloyd-Webber believes "that's not the theatergoing public that bought them because there just aren't that number of people who could possibly have seen the show."

At present writing a company in addition to the ones holding forth on Broadway and in London was touring the United States and selling out in San Francisco, Seattle, and Tulsa. There was as well a company in Germany. The show has played in ninety-six cities from Singapore to Basel to St. Paul and been seen in eighteen countries worldwide. It is booked solid through 2001. It has already taken in over two billion dollars. Cameron Mackintosh has estimated that *Phantom* will make far more money than *Cats*.

Andrew Lloyd-Webber is sanguine about the show's success, sensing the common appeal of his maimed creature: "There's no one who doesn't feel they wish they had been born different, that their fingers were longer, or something." But he is able to sum up the show's success by adding, "At the end of the day, it's overwhelmingly high romance."

He expects to develop the romance more deeply when a film is finally made of his musical. "In the film I want to go even further with the exploration of Christine and the Phantom through music. I have the feeling that there's still a lot that we didn't touch on. Love that exists through music is a very different love from the physical love that she feels for the boy . . . there is a real love between her and the Phantom."

The various aspects of love would be examined in his next musical. And the succeeding one would be a melodrama with a monster antiheroine not unlike the Phantom in her quest for love. Andrew Lloyd-Webber had finally found his metier.

Acts Villainous

B Y THE LATE 1980s both Stephen Sondheim and Andrew Lloyd-Webber had their aficionados. As his body of work grew, Sondheim's group, because it was composed largely of people who took an intellectual approach to musical theater, might be considered the aficionados of the "musical of thought." Even though the man in the street had known of *West Side Story* since the early '70s, if you asked who wrote it, he was sure to respond: "Bernstein."

Sondheim's work, even his contribution to *West Side Story*, remained unknown to the public at large and except for his hit song, "Send in the Clowns," was largely unknown to middle America. (Query many of those who owned the hit record and they would tell you Judy Collins wrote it.) Those who had seen the Broadway review *Side by Side by Sondheim* found that his songs, when taken out of their show's context, were not so off-putting. By 1985 with the release of Barbra Streisand's multimillion-selling recording, *The Broadway Album*, a sheaf of Sondheim's songs—still not his name—were becoming known beyond the metropolises where his shows could be seen. It was not until 1992, when the film *Dick Tracy* was released and the best and most popular song in this popular entertainment, "Sooner or Later," won the Academy Award, that an intellectual who mentioned the name of Sondheim might not receive a puzzled shrug in Omaha. By the time Streisand's *Second Broadway Album* was released and featured more of his songs, many of them totally unfamiliar outside the theater, in arrangements geared to the pop market, Sondheim was becoming known. By now his work has gone far beyond cult status and begun to spawn newsletters and magazines published (and a group of composers and lyricists searching new directions for the musical). Both Britain and the United States have periodicals devoted to his work. One of them, *The Sondheim Review*, now in its seventh year of publication, has as its slogan: "Dedicated to the Work of the Musical Theater's Foremost Composer and Lyricist."

Just where does that leave Andrew Lloyd-Webber?

Of course, Lloyd-Webber is not a composer *and lyricist* but many have felt that *he* is the "Musical Theater's Foremost whatever." His fame and works spread over the entire world (where Sondheim's oeuvre is hardly known outside the English-speaking sphere) practically from the first performances of his three groundbreaking works with Tim Rice, *Joseph*, *Superstar*, and *Evita*. Once the partnership was disbanded, Rice went his own way, turning out such fine shows as *Blondel*, *Chess*, and lately *Aida*, while Lloyd-Webber's musicals, especially *Cats*, *Starlight Express*, and *Phantom*, carried him to even greater triumph than the former collaboration had. Now he made sure that his name and his alone floated *above* the musical's title. Collaborators, lyricists, and directors might be listed on the inside of the programs, but Andrew Lloyd-Webber's celebrity is what sold the tickets. A master of marketing ever more canny, he was to continue to release one or two hit songs, songs with easily spottable melodic motifs, from the forthcoming show, which invariably were given a great deal of airplay. These were timed to come out six to eight months before the tickets went on sale. Then pop music fans rushed to the box office on the wings of a "Don't Cry for Me Argentina," "Memory," or "Love Changes Everything." In keeping with this tradition, the single of "No Matter What" from *Whistle Down the Wind* went to No. 1 on British charts in 1998—and stayed there.

Sondheim's shows feature no "hit" songs. He is against the showstopper because, as a journalist said, "It's difficult to get the show started again." He is against reprises per se, because he feels that later in the show the characters are in a far different place than when the song was originally introduced. His lyrics avoid the expected rhyme, which makes them feel "uncomfortable" to those anticipating a singsongy construction. As for melody, he creates his own unique kind that takes a bit of getting used to. Many of his songs are hard to sing but beautiful to listen to.

Although both Sondheim and Lloyd-Webber refuse to be goaded by the press into criticizing each other's work, they have the musical theater's two most distinct voices. Aside from Claude-Michel Schönberg and Alain Boublil, whose *Les Misérables* and *Miss Saigon* are supermusicals that fit into the mold that Lloyd-Webber originated, there is nobody in the Broadway arena whose work when announced can create a box-office line around the block. (If you ask the average theatergoer who wrote *Les Misérables* he or she will usually answer Andrew Lloyd-Webber.)

The snobs and the so-called intelligentsia look down on Lloyd-Webber not only because his shows are so popular and because he is so rich, but because his work is so easily accessible. Sondheim's audiences rarely enthuse about a Lloyd-Webber musical. But Joe Public, enthralled by either Sondheim or Lloyd-

Webber, returns to see their shows again and again. Because his work and lyrics do not give up their secrets easily, Sondheim's fans return to better understand what they have witnessed; Lloyd-Webber's fans want to wallow again in his genuine romantic effusions.

The two and their work were inextricably linked at awards time in 1988. Whether by design or mere coincidence, producers have been careful recently to keep their shows from coming up for judgment in the same year. Even the most bloodthirsty critics do not want a repetition of the musical awards section of the Tony ceremony of 1988.

Joanna Gleason was chosen Best Actress in a musical for *Into the Woods*. Michael Crawford won the parallel award for his work in *Phantom of the Opera*. Then the Tony committee cited Sondheim's music and lyrics and Lapine's book as the best of the season but incomprehensibly chose *Phantom* as the Best Musical. *Into the Woods* was the Drama Desk's choice for Best Musical, but they gave the Best Music award to Lloyd-Webber while giving the Best Lyrics award to Sondheim.

It was clear that the Tony committee was practicing its own kind of favoritism by nominating a trivial musical, *Romance, Romance*, while ignoring Tim Rice's provocative *Chess* and looking askance at Lloyd-Webber by not even nominating Sarah Brightman for the award of Best Actress in a Musical. It was as if they were negating Andrew's hard-won right to have his wife star in the musical he had written for her.

Lloyd-Webber had the last word, however. As he held his Tony high, thumbing his nose at the Broadway establishment over whom he had clearly been victorious, he trumpeted, "This one's for Sarah." The phrase was not lost on the critics and theater owners sitting there. He reminded them that if the United States had "class" as represented by the musicals of Sondheim, the big blockbuster musicals that kept Broadway solvent were all coming from England.[1] The man was invincible. He could put on whatever show he liked and it was almost certain to have a run.

In his way, Sondheim had reached the same plateau. Perhaps he was not a sure moneymaker like Lloyd-Webber, but he had attained an enviable stage of notoriety, with books and articles about him and his work in all the intellectual media, such as *Atlantic*, the *New Yorker*, and especially the *Sunday New York Times Magazine*. By now it was almost a philanthropic thing to lose money in a Sondheim show. Investors and funded theaters clamored to be part of the next

[1] Equity was to lose another fight when Cameron Mackintosh almost pulled back his *Miss Saigon* because they didn't want Jonathan Pryce, its British star, to repeat his role on Broadway.

Cameron Mackintosh and Andrew Lloyd-Webber have a playful tug of war over the Tony
Phantom of the Opera won as Best Musical of 1988. AP/Wide World Photos.

work. Even if it didn't succeed in its first showings, they knew that as with his
dogged persistence with *Merrily We Roll Along*, he would work to repair what
was wrong. Eventually he would turn that failure into a classic that could well
march into the twenty-first century. The score, the libretto, and the recordings
would never go out of print. Cabaret singers ultimately would get around to the
individual songs. Angels would *eventually* get their money back, and if by some
outside chance they didn't, it would be an honor to lose in the cause of genius.

Such was the climate surrounding Sondheim's next show. It was to be about
the killing of the President of the United States, and the idea came to him back
in 1973, when he merely saw the title of the play *Assassins*, which had been
written by Charles Gilbert. "Oh, my gosh, what an idea!" he was to recall. "I
don't even know why I thought it was a wonderful idea."

When John Weidman, the librettist of *Pacific Overtures*, whom Sondheim
enjoys working with, came to him with a political idea, one that took place
during the First World War, he didn't care for it but told him, "I once came
across an idea. When I said it was called *Assassins*, his eyes lit up. And I said

to him, 'You're having the same reaction I did—the word alone—I don't know what it is, but wouldn't it make a great musical?' "

The subject, of course, is a taboo, and before Weidman and Sondheim could think about drafting a libretto, much less writing its songs, they needed a point of view. Here is what Weidman wrote about the show, after it had opened:

> Thirteen people have tried to kill the President of the United States. Four have succeeded. These murderers and would-be murderers are generally dismissed as maniacs and misfits who have little in common with each other, and nothing in common with the rest of us.
>
> *Assassins* suggests otherwise. *Assassins* suggests that while these individuals are, to say the least, peculiar—taken as a group they are peculiarly *American*. And that behind the variety of motives which they articulated for their murderous outbursts, they share a common purpose: a desperate desire to reconcile intolerable feelings of impotence with an inflamed and malignant sense of entitlement.
>
> Why do these dreadful events happen *here*, with such horrifying frequency, and in such an appallingly similar fashion? *Assassins* suggests it is because we live in a country whose most cherished national myths, at least as currently propagated, encourage us to believe that in America our dreams not only *can* come true, but *should* come true, and that if they don't, someone or something is to blame.

It was a groundbreaking idea, but one that might have been expected to come from the team that had already pointed out the shameful bullying tactics of the United States in the matter of opening Japan to trade. And although *Pacific Overtures* was not a hit, it had left its mark on musical theater. In this show Sondheim and his collaborator would be forcing those who bought tickets to their shows to reexamine their conception of history.

Almost all of the musicals Sondheim has been involved with have asked audiences to reconsider their fixed ideas: The nostalgic past in *Follies* ended up looking tawdry; the question of just who is sane was propounded in *Anyone Can Whistle*. Art was looked at from the point of view of following an obsessive vision in *Sunday in the Park*, and the sell-out that usually accompanies success was examined in *Merrily We Roll Along. Into the Woods* concerned the responsibility of the individual to society, and continuing relationships versus playing the field was the focus of *Company. Assassins* would be the most demanding for audiences, and because of its insistence that we gaze for almost two hours at this underbelly of the beast, the most provocative.

In the Hammerstein or, even earlier, the George M. Cohan tradition of the musical, we await the ennoblement, often patriotic, at the end. We are accustomed to looking at, say, Benjamin Franklin or Thomas Jefferson as they were portrayed in the musical *1776*. With pride. We were puffed up by their signing of the Declaration of Independence on stage, but it was never mentioned that Jefferson was a slave owner. *Bloomer Girl, The Golden Apple*, and *Shenandoah*, all

classic musicals, if not always hits, resuscitated the Civil War as a benign time
of fighting for freedom. When they went on tour, Bill "Bojangles" Robinson,
Paul Robson, and Lena Horne, each a star, were not treated the same as the
white members of their companies. Robinson was gratified by his recognition
from white organizations and announced, in monumental self-delusion, that he
was "tremendously proud of his triumph over race prejudice."

"But he remained cast in the stereotypical roles of the Jim Crow Negro,"
Anne Edwards writes in *Shirley Temple: American Princess*. "When appearing in
theaters across the country, he had to enter through rear doors, could not eat
in the same restaurants as other members of the cast, or use the same toilets."
Even in the liberal world of show business there were many ethnic wrongs that
needed to change.

"*Assassins* is *Sweeney Todd*," Sondheim said. "It's about righting a wrong, and
how, if you do it the wrong way, you're in a lot of trouble." Sondheim's simplistic
comparison does not go far enough. In equating his two "monster" musicals, one
must realize that audiences can empathize with *Sweeney*. As a piece of stagecraft
his story is far different in *Assassins*. Sweeney's motive is revenge for a genuine,
not a perceived, wrong. The judge who raped the barber's wife and wanted to
seduce his daughter is an out-and-out villain. Sweeney is an avenging angel at
first. And even his first murder of a blackmailer is somewhat justified. It may be
Mrs. Lovett's influence, her lurid cannibalism disguised as "thrift," that gets the
grisly humor going. It eventually sends him over the edge into psychopathy and
turns the couple into an industrial revolutionary family of Borgias.

Louise Gold, who played Lynette "Squeaky" Fromme in the London production of *Assassins*, seems to have gotten a different message. She talked to this
writer recently and had some cogent thoughts about acting one of these misfits:

> It's a black show, but there is a lot of heart in it, because it's not saying in any way
> that assassination is a good thing. As an actor it is asking me to identify with the
> character I'm playing. It's saying these people are not necessarily monsters. Some-
> thing in the American dream or in what is held up to be the American dream, the
> cliché that anybody can *be* a president, is perverted and twisted into anybody can
> *kill* a president, or become famous by association. This belief in America has been
> held up, perhaps in a way to keep people down, or to help them get through life.
> The statement is simply not true. To aspire to the presidency you have to have a
> lot of money and power. . . . The characters in *Assassins* fell for the dream or the
> platitude and were disillusioned and spun out of control when this didn't work out.
> Not everybody kills somebody because their dream doesn't work out, but it's very
> easy for people who've never had these thoughts to say "those who have are mon-
> sters—we could never do that," and not try to understand. Not that we love them
> and they're great people—we just must try to understand where it came from. There
> is a pattern. Before acting the roles we all studied their backgrounds—their child-
> hood, upbringing; there did seem to be some pattern.

As far back as 1984 John Rockwell, music critic for the *New York Times*, wrote: "As a man of today, Sondheim refuses to accept the pat, sweet directness that once defined our national character, at least as that character was projected in musicals and in musical films."

The intermissionless show, whose sixteen scenes most resemble what used to be called a topical revue, opens to calliope music in a fairground shooting gallery. The Proprietor lights up his slogan—HIT THE "PREZ" AND WIN A PRIZE.[2] As the cast saunter on, he tries to drum up business by singing, "Hey, pal—feelin' blue? / Don't know what to do? / Hey, pal—I mean you—/ C'mere and kill a President." His song's big sweeping intervals make the verse seductive, but in the chorus he changes it to a more elemental Jerry Herman–type show tune—irresistible and eerier because the melody is so wholesome. Even the lyric sounds virtuous, so apple pie that we do not even notice the words "right," "different," "extremes," "aim," or "shot."

> Everybody's
> Got the right
> To be different,
> Even though
> At times they go
> To extremes.
> Aim for what you

> Want a lot—
> Everybody
> Gets a shot.
> Everybody's
> Got a right
> To their dreams.

As the song goes along we are introduced to the assassins. First comes Leon Czolgosz, who assassinated President William McKinley in 1901. Later in the evening we find out his history when Weidman humanizes him by writing a speech in which he explains his job in a bottle factory for which he is paid six cents an hour—five, if one of the bottles breaks. He tells how he stands at the oven's door, holding his breath so his insides won't cook. "A bell rings and I reach into the oven. I wear gloves. Inside the gloves my hands are rubbed with grease and wrapped in rags. But still each time my hands begin to burn." He then shows the other would-be assassins his scarred hands and neck, and when some of the more privileged among them suggest he should change jobs, he declares flatly, "There is no other job!"

Young John Hinkley, who would attempt to shoot President Ronald Reagan, enters next. In a later scene he will write a letter to film actress Jodie Foster telling her he will do one brave historic act that is certain to win her love. After that he will sing a moony pop ballad à la Barry Manilow which, inciden-

---

[2] In the Los Angeles production of 1994, a relatively innocent-looking huckster, dressed for Fourth of July, pushes a cart of the kind that dispenses hot dogs and ice cream on stage. We learn quickly that the cart contains guns.

tally, proves that had that been his goal, Stephen Sondheim could easily have cashed in on the pop song market.

Then comes inky-bearded Charles Guiteau, dressed all in black, wearing a broad-brimmed jet felt hat. An archangel of doom, Guiteau, who assassinated President James Garfield in 1881, had written a book called *The Truth*. He rants about his omnipotence, telling the others that he had been an attorney and an evangelist. Next week, he says, he is going to be the ambassador to France. When President Garfield comes on the scene, Guiteau makes his ambassadorial request.

"Mad as a hatter," Garfield says to his aide as he turns aside.

Guiteau shoots him in the back.

For his march, rather a Bill Robinson–like step dance, to the gallows, Sondheim has given him a remarkable cakewalk interrupted by a Joan of Arc–like refrain on "I am going to the Lordy." In words that are strangely reminiscent of *Follies*'s "You're Gonna Love Tomorrow," the evangelist sings:

Wait till you see tomorrow,	Or you can be President—
Tomorrow you get your reward!	Look on the bright side . . .
You can be sad	

Giuseppe Zangara, a tiny, angry man who speaks with an accent, is next. He was executed in 1933 for his attempt to assassinate Franklin Delano Roosevelt in Miami. When he comes on stage his stomach pains are so obvious, the Proprietor addresses him in stage Italian.

What's-a wrong, boy?	(*Holds out gun*)
Boss-a treat you crummy?	Here, give some
Trouble with you tummy?	Hail-a to da Chief—
This-a bring you some relief.	

Zangara's segment will be a tour de force, for it will be mounted opposite a group of bystanders singing to Sousa marches about how they deflected the bullet aimed at FDR. Their lyrics are taken from the actual testimony of eyewitnesses to the crime. Their one-upping each other and mugging for publicity is counterpointed with the words of the gunman on the other side of the stage. The contrast makes it easy to see that both the group and the assassin are pleading for public notice. Zangara is strapped in the electric chair. He tells us about how he first thought he would kill Hoover, but the weather in Washington was too cold for his peptic condition. That's why he went down to Miami.

No laugh!	Roosevelt, Hoover—
No funny!	No make no difference
Men with the money,	You think I care who I kill?
They control everything.	I no care who I kill,
	Long as it's king!

With Zangara defiantly asking the prison officials to pull the switch, the chorus cheers out the letters "F"–"D"–"R" with a long dimming of lights and an electrical hum between each letter. Perhaps for the first time on the musical stage we have been witness to an execution. In the small theaters where the show is usually mounted, you can almost smell the burning flesh.

Lynette "Squeaky" Fromme and Sara Jane Moore, each of whom attempted to kill President Gerald Ford in the same month, November 1975, soon enter. They show us their ineptness at handling guns, and the Proprietor has to turn their gun barrels away lest he himself get shot. Later in the vaudeville they will practice shooting by firing bullets at a bucket of Kentucky Fried Chicken.

The group is all assembled when, as the music quiets down, a dapper young man in a black frock coat enters. He is John Wilkes Booth. He will be their organizer; the Proprietor calls him their pioneer. He turns, looks up to an imaginary theater box, and we have the first assassination: Abraham Lincoln.

The next scene introduces the Balladeer, who now and again will try to keep the narrative going. His style is folksy and guitar-plunking, and it seems as if we are going to have some moralizing. He sings of how Booth, a twenty-seven-year-old actor, fleeing after the assassination, shot himself while the marshals set fire to the barn in which he was hiding. He jokingly asks if Booth did the act out of pique for his bad reviews. Booth denies it all, and with brilliant rhetoric and vehemence he accuses Lincoln of deliberately provoking the Civil War. His ardor is so impassioned that he almost sways us to his cause. He begs the balladeer let his side be heard and to tell us

How the country is not what it was,
Where there's blood on the clover,
How the nation can never again
Be the hope that it was.

How the bruises may never be healed,
How the wounds are forever,

How we gave up the field
But we still wouldn't yield,
How the Union can never recover
From that vulgar,
High and mighty
Niggerlover,
Never—!

By the time he gets to the end we are aware of Booth's rabid racial bigotry and are somewhat resentful of the impassioned music with which Sondheim manipulated our feelings. In a coda, the Balladeer tells us he does not buy Booth's reasoning. He tries to mollify us with one of Sondheim's most cogent and theatrical quatrains:

But traitors just get jeers and boos,
Not visits to their graves,

While Lincoln, who got mixed reviews,
Because of you, John, now gets only raves.

Succeeding scenes alternate between attempted assassinations, executions, and rantings—incoherent and tiresome tirades. Boredom sets in, especially when we are subjected to a long monologue (fortunately divided into two scenes) by Samuel Byck, who appears in his habitual outfit, a filthy Santa Claus suit. He complains that Leonard Bernstein never "picked up a phone and said, 'Hey, Sammy, how's it going?'" which incomprehensibly set him off on his attempt to assassinate Richard Nixon.

Along the way there is a rather touching scene when Czolgosz meets anarchist Emma Goldman, who tries to inculcate some sense of self-respect in him. At scene's end she offers him a pamphlet about social justice and gives him a kiss. Her lines will be reiterated when he later wraps his gun in his handkerchief and waits his turn to get to the head of the line. As he shakes hands with President McKinley he shoots him in the stomach.

But the last three scenes are the ones we have been waiting for.

This final sequence begins with the Balladeer telling the assembled assassins that their acts didn't make a bit of difference, "It didn't mean a nickel, it just shed a little blood." But they soon overrule him and maintain that they march to "Another National Anthem." The song is an astonishing piece of work that announces a reversal of their nihilism. They say that if you can't do what you want to do, then you must try again to do what you can.

Their song dissolves into a beautifully written scene of a surreal meeting during which John Wilkes Booth, who by now seems to have become the father of all assassins, enters a room where Lee Harvey Oswald, his only peer, is busily writing. They are on the sixth floor of the Texas Book Depository. Booth picks up and reads to us Oswald's suicide note. Gradually and insidiously, taking his cue from what his fellow assassins have just sung, he imperceptibly gains Oswald's confidence, and, promising everlasting fame on a par with that of Julius Caesar's killer, he almost persuades Oswald to shoot John F. Kennedy. When Oswald falters, the other assassins appear and appeal to him to join their family, to make valid what they have done. "Without you we're a bunch of freaks. With you we're a force of history," they maintain. They talk about the power within his grasp, for the havoc, grief, and despair that he can create by merely moving his little finger is unimaginable. In that single trigger motion is there not power indeed?

Booth points out that Oswald's defecting to the Soviet Union and distributing Cuban literature were only examples of his ineffectuality. He argues that killing the president will send a message that will make them "pay attention." Riding on Oswald's alienation, his lone wolf attitude, he offers membership in a community. The others join and say that his act will validate theirs and remove them from being thought of as individual aberrations. "Bring us together. Connect us. Empower us," they yell. At last, when they say "you are our future" and they tell him of how they respect and admire him, Oswald can resist no more and fires the bullet that was to change the world.

Where can one go after that? The New York production reprised the assassins' singing their theme song about how everyone has the right to be happy and to dreams; again the American dream gone awry.

With the tension of the Texas Book Depository scene, the short reprise of a light show tune seemed too abrupt before the audience was sent out into the night, and so for the London production a year later, Sondheim added a buffer. "Something Just Broke" is sung by the common folk recalling the moment they heard President Kennedy had been shot. The song is based on the idea that everyone remembers where he or she was the moment they first heard about the assassination. It is moving, but still somewhat of a cliché.

The intense scene is best left with the drums and *trauermusik* that Sondheim added after the shot. Perhaps it would be have been better to have ended the show there. By building up to this inevitable scene Weidman and Sondheim created a moving climax to a chilling and provocative evening in the theater, while at the same time boxing themselves into a troublesome corner. One must heartily agree with Martin Gottfried, who wrote that the writers "underestimated the continuing trauma of Kennedy's murder."

Assassins (like *Sunday in the Park* and *Into the Woods*) opened at the 137-seat Playwrights Horizon Theater on January 27, 1991, in the middle of the Persian Gulf War. *Sweeney* had been dark, but it had enough humor and two genuine stars in Cariou and Lansbury to appeal to general audiences. Now with such a provocative title, this work promised to be a return to the deepest shadows. By the end of the first day of box-office sale, its two-month run was entirely sold out.

It must be mentioned that had the show *not* been by Sondheim, it might have had trouble getting even an off-Broadway production. Playwrights Horizon is a partially funded operation that (when it has a work by a writer of Sondheim's caliber) is assured a substantial run—and a percentage of the take *should* the musical go on to Broadway.

In spite of the musical's being tuneful, rhymeful, accessible, and by the man who was by this time considered the genius of the American musical, *Assassins* was roundly trounced by the critics. John Lahr, never in Sondheim's corner, writing in the *New Yorker*, said the subject offered Sondheim "the extraordinary panorama of American psychopathy and infamy, but from it he drew merely a dark cartoon." Others felt it was incomplete, pointing out that there were only eight musical numbers, while still others called the subject matter an affront. *Time*'s William A. Henry III dismissed it as "glimpses of looniness" and wondered how such a show could be put on—more than that, he wondered "why?"

Mostly, because of the realism of the sketches, the critics did not seem to understand whether the playwrights were on a soapbox or, as respected critic Robert Brustein put it, whether "it was history as seen through the eyes of show business."

All the critics were scathing, but it was left to John Simon, not known for his restraint, to note that "one could write a searching, perhaps, even moving, show concentrating on one such person, but it would have to be compassionate, analytical, philosophical." Simon ended up calling *Assassins* "an uneasy amalgam of bleeding-heart liberalism and high camp."

André Bishop, the Playwrights Horizon producer, said that "at the time we didn't know if [the Gulf War] would help the show by delivering nightly audiences who were stirred up and willing to be stirred up further, or hurt because they were feeling patriotic . . . and might not want to see something that presented a darkly comic version of the killing of a number of American presidents."

Bishop feels that the reason it never transferred to Broadway had nothing to do with the Gulf War. He is right. *Assassins* is not Broadway material. It has no place in the "establishment." It is, however, material for off-Broadway, college groups, theatrical societies, and small and large town splinter groups to stage, and throughout the English-speaking world they have latched onto it. By 1994 it was having more productions than *Company*.

Perhaps it is the use of pastiche, and simple pastiche, that makes the score appear lighthearted and offensive to older audiences. More than that, the still-open wound of the Kennedy assassination sends waves of pain through the raw nerves of any American who lived through 1963. But at every performance this writer has attended, younger audiences become very involved with *Assassins*, admiring the build-up at the end. Having grown up in a climate of violence, they are not put off by it. They relish the various historical figures and accept the melodic score within its historical context.

One might compare Sondheim's pastiches to (the original version of) Andrew Lloyd-Webber's *Joseph and the Amazing Technicolor Dreamcoat*, even though all of *Joseph*'s characters inhabit the same time frame. Both composers used melodic material suggestive of many historical periods in order to make their points.

The show is easy to stage. It can be scored for a three-piece orchestra, as was done at Playwrights Horizons, or expanded to full orchestra as it was on the recorded version. For the London production, which reopened the Donmar Warehouse in 1992, Mark Dorrell used an eight-piece group.[3]

In spite of its reception by the media, *Assassins* is the only show Sondheim says he cannot see himself improving on. The book, he contends, is the best libretto he's worked with—"versatile, witty, powerful. And in general the whole show is just as close as I've gotten to perfect."

---

[3] That production put *Assassins* squarely in the forefront as one of Sondheim's finest musicals. Reliable accounts state that *Assassins* reopened the Donmar Theatre and helped make Donmar's reputation as one of the most adventuresome and best theaters in London. It received splendid reviews, winning the London Critics' Circle award for the best new musical.

The "La Ronde" Family

I F SONDHEIM'S TIMING of *Assassins*, coming as it did in the middle of the Persian Gulf War, was unfortunate, it could not have been foreseen. Saddam Hussein, Iraq's premier, had determined to reclaim his right to annex his neighbor Kuwait. The nations who responded to this act of aggression moved quickly, and the invader was forced to retreat. *Assassins*, which had been scheduled months before, was caught in the middle of the hostilities.

Lloyd-Webber's paean to free love and sleeping around, *Aspects of Love*, was also caught in the middle of a war—the war on AIDS—but although the show was begun years before the disease took a strong hold, following through to its presentation in the West End and later on Broadway was a monumental miscalculation—for a variety of reasons.

As far back as 1980, when Andrew Lloyd-Webber and Tim Rice were still a team, still looking for the stimulating idea to follow *Evita*, the two had traveled to Eugénie-les-Bains in search of the same kind of inspiration that had engendered *Jesus Christ Superstar*. Rice talked again of creating an original musical focusing on two international chess players, one American and one Russian, competing to win not only the game but the love of a beautiful woman. Rice wanted the work to star his inamorata, Elaine Paige—which it eventually did—but Lloyd-Webber would have none of it.

The two oenophile millionaires brought vast quantities of vintage wines to the spa, hoping to find their muse in their cups. Rice brought along a novella by the Bloomsbury author David Garnett as well. The book, *Aspects of Love*, had been sent to him by film producer Jason Pollock, who hoped the team might contribute a couple of songs to the scenario he was planning. A Rice–Lloyd-Webber agreement might turn a passé romantic script into a bankable proposition. They decided not to write any songs for the movie, but they were intrigued by the novella.

Rice told Lloyd-Webber that he thought the story was thin, but he sensed there was something in the saga that spanned love affairs across three generations that would be suitable to their through-sung type of musical. Still, they went no farther with it. Then, when Lloyd-Webber was overseeing an Australian production of *Evita*, he gave a copy of Garnett's book to Hal Prince.

"I've read through it," Prince told him after an hour. "You can't turn this into a musical." (Those were, incidentally, the same words Rodgers and Hammerstein used when Alan Jay Lerner asked why they had abandoned their musical treatment of Shaw's *Pygmalion*.)

Lloyd-Webber ignored Prince's advice, and the following summer when he and Rice met again, he firmly closed the door on *Chess* and stayed with the romantic effusions of *Aspects*. At last Tim Rice bowed out, but not before the team wrote an ardent ballad to be placed in *Aspects* which was eventually recorded by Placido Domingo. Then in 1983, to Trevor Nunn's lyrics, Lloyd-Webber presented the first *Aspects* cabaret at Sydmonton. The work was intended for Sarah Brightman's debut, but it will be recalled that when the prospect of *The Phantom of the Opera* was conceived and he realized he could avail himself of Sarah's three-octave range, Andrew snatched those lush melodies away from Nunn and recycled them for *Phantom*, leaving *Aspects* in limbo.

Trevor Nunn was incensed. One would have thought Britain's most prestigious director, the former head of the Royal Shakespeare Company, would have nothing further to do with the composer. After all, in spite of Nunn's tour de force staging of *Cats*, Lloyd-Webber had publicly disowned his work on *Starlight Express*, humiliated him by divorcing Nunn's *Aspects* lyrics from their melodies, and fallen out with him over the planning of *Phantom*—assuring him he would be the show's director and then going back on his word, eventually replacing him with Hal Prince. Moreover, Lloyd-Webber had publicly announced at a big party in his Trump Tower aerie that he wanted Nicolas Hytner, the rising young star of the British Opera, for *Aspects*. Both Hytner and Nunn had been put "on hold" by Cameron Mackintosh to direct his forthcoming *Miss Saigon*, but it was not long before it was announced that Hytner got the job. That left Nunn *without* a job.

But there were plenty of other offers on Nunn's horizon, so when Lloyd-Webber offered him *Aspects*, his first reaction, out of pique, was to turn it down. Yet on reflection he realized he had already devoted a lot of time to this project. He had sheafs of notes on the novella from the first time he had worked on it, and he really believed it would make a marvelous romantic musical. From his home in the south of France came word that he would put aside the book on subsidized theater he was compiling and return to the project. As to lyricists for the project, Don Black, whose remarkable sense of humor, maturity, and strong technique had kept *Song and Dance* from becoming a soupy melodrama, was chosen to work with young Charles Hart, *Phantom*'s wordsmith. The latter's lines were often romantic effusions that could easily go "over the top," however appropriate they were to the melodrama. Black, the veteran of many shows, ended up doing most of the lines, keeping Hart in check, and if the lyrics don't always sound newly minted, at least they do not have the frenetic aura of opera about them.

Much of the score was to be material that was already in Lloyd-Webber's trunk, some of it far down at the bottom like the *Chanson d'Enfance*, which went back to his toy theater days. At least five of the other tunes were taken from *Cricket*, a short *piece d'occasion* for which Lloyd-Webber and Rice united briefly in 1986 to honor Queen Elizabeth's sixtieth birthday.[1]

One of his songs written back in 1984 that had been the theme of a TV show called *Executive Stress* was also borrowed back and fitted out with new lyrics by Black and Hart. Rice was infuriated, for with *Aspects* an entity, it meant that *Cricket*, which had been extremely well received, was a dead item. But it must be added that years later when journalists asked Rice if he intended to expand *Cricket* into a full evening's musical he had the forbearance to say simply "I believe some of the tunes have been reused in *Aspects of Love* . . . You know what composers are like.[2]"

The master plan for *Aspects* went into action when the four got together at Lloyd-Webber's villa in Cap Ferrat in the summer of 1987. They wrote out a "quasi-libretto," actually a synopsis of the story that left room in the margin for Lloyd-Webber to write hints of what music he would use. Most of it had been decided on by that time. He entered his songs under titles such as "Damn-the-Boy Theme," "Love Duet," "Renunciation Theme," "Ghost Motif," and so on. Then he and his lyricists set about developing them according to the lines of the synopsis. By the end of the year they had completed the first act. Act Two was finished less than six months later, in spite of the interruption during the

---

[1] Edward Windsor, the Queen's youngest son, who had joined the Really Useful Company as staff assistant that year, commissioned a short musical as an honor to his mother. *Cricket*, that peculiarly English game, was Rice's special passion and had been an important diversion for Andrew as well. Directed by Trevor Nunn, the performance of the "musicalette" that took place on June 18 at Windsor Castle was spiritedly amusing indeed. The cast included Ian Charleson, John Savident, and Sarah Payne. The band was the rock band who had first played *Variations*. *Cricket* was shown again that summer at Sydmonton and was reprised in the autumn as a benefit for Tim's favorite charity, the Lord's Taverners.

[2] Composers have frequently recycled and often improved material that was unappreciated in its original incarnation. One thinks immediately of Richard Rodgers, who adapted the theme of *Victory at Sea* into "No Other Love," the hit song from *Me and Juliet*. Librettist-lyricist Alan Jay Lerner took the duet "I Remember It Well," a dud in his and Kurt Weill's musical *Love Life*, and turned it into a charmer for the Lerner-Loewe film *Gigi*. Later in life, Lerner suppressed revivals of *Love Life* because, he said, he had pilfered so much from its score.

heady time when all except Nunn flew to New York to look in on the readying of *Phantom*. Thus one might consider *Aspects* a musical designed by committee and built to specifications.

The story tells of seventeen-year-old Alex (a stand-in for Garnett himself), an Englishman traveling through France, waiting to be called up for the army. In a provincial town he falls madly in love with a young French actress, Rose Vibert. She is a few years his senior, a good performer whose play is so sparsely attended that the company must disband. They will start up again in Lyon two weeks later. Alex, knowing she has no money, impulsively asks her to come with him to Pau, where he says he has a villa. The villa, with a magnificent view of the Pyrenees, belongs to his Uncle George, a successful painter of forgeries (a poet in the novella), and once the uncle enters the scene, Rose throws over the nephew.

Two years later Alex, now on military leave, decides to visit his uncle. In George's Paris flat he finds Rose. She takes him to bed but asks him to leave the next morning. Incensed at her duplicity he tries to shoot her, but the bullet grazes her arm when it is deflected by the almost melodramatic arrival of George, who grabs his nephew's pistol and spoils his aim. Uncle George, whose libertine philosophy that one can love two people at once is the main thrust of the story, has not married Rose. To point up his philosophy, he has also been having an affair with an Italian sculptor, Giulietta. Rose is introduced to her, and now the three form a happy combination. Near the end of the act George marries Rose with Giulietta in attendance as "best (wo)man." Giulietta claims her wedding attendant rights and gives Rose a passionate kiss. George is delighted. At the curtain's fall we see Alex in his army uniform wretchedly reading a letter that tells us George will soon be a father.

Act Two begins twelve years later. Rose has become a successful actress on the stage and in cinema and, easily adopting George's philosophy, has taken a lover, Hugo. When Alex, now handsomely in his prime, comes backstage to see her, she is so delighted that she asks her lover to go on a weekend holiday and takes Alex back with her to Pau to see his Uncle George and to meet their daughter, Jennie, now twelve—who could well be Alex's daughter. We assume Rose's old yen for Alex has not cooled.

At the villa we discover that George has lost all his money; Rose is now the breadwinner. Jennie and her father have a tender relationship, but as soon as Rose walks in with Alex, Jennie is attracted to him. Alex is urged to stay on and he does so for three years, during which time Jennie falls deeply in love with him. Jennie tries to seduce Alex, but he realizes at last that besides this being an incestuous situation (even if she is his niece and not his daughter), Jenny is only fifteen. He decides to be noble and to leave. The stage is split now and we see Alex saying goodby to Jennie in her room. George suspects the worst of his daughter and his nephew. Overcome by emotion he has a heart attack in the stairwell and dies outside the bedroom door.

At the wake, Giulietta returns and has a roll in the hay (literally) with Alex, which is observed by a now much disillusioned Jennie. But she still loves Alex, and citing Juliet's passion for Romeo at thirteen as her example, she begs him to take her away—or at least to wait for her until she reaches the age of consent. (Incest is never considered.) Meanwhile the newly widowed Rose, who has always feared solitude, sings "Anything but Lonely," after which she begs Alex to stay on with her. In an ending that Hollywood would say, "can go any one of three ways," he decides to leave with Giulietta.

For some reason, Lloyd-Webber revered the largely self-aggrandizing book by David Garnett[3] and insisted his director and the lyricists stick closely to it. "Garnett himself was really the old man in the book and also the boy, so you have a sort of double autobiography about a man obsessed by cats, and wine, and girls," he told critic Sheridan Morley. "I'd rather we didn't explore that analogy in too much more detail," he added, perhaps wearing his heart on his sleeve and hoping the public would grasp the somewhat naughty reference to the girls. His mania for cats and his fondness for the grape were by this time well known.

Garnett's 1955 novel depicted the then-fashionable idea which the author espoused of having multiple relationships. Certainly the wealthy profligate landowner, Sir George (in the book), and his mistress are representative of the Bloomsbury Set. In the musical, George's insincerity, as well as his great wit, is hinted at. Somewhat like Lord Henry in *The Portrait of Dorian Gray*, George has no trouble perverting the character of Rose. Alex, too, the tortured protagonist, quickly learns that multiple relationships are better than a single love. Giulietta, the strong, and Hugo, the weak, are born hedonists. At the end,

---

[3] David Garnett (1892–1981) was an editor, novelist, and a member of the Bloomsbury Group, whose painters, poets, and artists were considered the sina qua non of British aesthetic circles in the first half of the twentieth century. Lytton Strachey, father of the modern biography, was the leader of the set. He espoused the cause of free love or multiple relationships with either men or women. Garnett was actually a minor member of the coterie whose work is now largely forgotten. Apart from two relatively sensitive novels, *Lady into Fox* (1932) and *Aspects of Love* (1955), he is probably more important for his associates, about whom British intellectuals continue to write esoteric books, than for his own achievements. Born into a literary family, he married Angelica Bell, the supposed daughter of Clive and Vanessa Bell—she, Virginia Woolf's sister. (Angelica was young enough to have been Garnett's daughter.) It was only at maturity that Angelica discovered her real father—homosexual painter Duncan Grant, who was Garnett's lover. Garnett, a notorious libertine, announced his intentions to marry Angelica after seeing her in her cradle. It is certain that the randy, incestuous, bisexual characters in *Aspects of Love* spring from this background.

George summons up some moral fiber only when faced with the possibility of the seduction of his daughter. She is the only one who stands for true principles, and we almost suspect that once the curtain is down she too will become as licentious as the rest.

Aspects contains a great deal of infidelity, and each affair, Garnett insists, is a different aspect of love. The curious thing about these multiple relationships is that there is so little objection by the "injured" party. When Andrew was asked in 1993 at a Dramatists Guild meeting in New York why he chose such obviously controversial characters to people his musical, he defended Garnett's philosophy:

> I know that from my observation, you'd be away for a year and come back and find that people got married . . . or the other way round—and nobody minded. All very much of the '60s, although Garnett was writing in the '50s. The final line is "Hand me the wine and the dice, and perish the thought of tomorrow," not immediately the most commercial subject to put on in this town of all places. It's something I've wanted [to say], that's been in my system, and I wanted to get it out of my system. I want to write what I want to write and I'm lucky enough that I *can* write what I want to write.

Those comments were, of course, made after the fact, and one senses that the composer, now almost forty, was feeling his own sexual prowess. Certainly its subject, as he might have imagined, would be a deterrent, for even though at first the musical was received with some enthusiasm, it soon wore out its welcome with the British public and chalked up the shortest British run of any of Lloyd-Webber's major works—three years—a runaway hit for anyone else but only a ripple in the Lloyd-Webber canon. And less on Broadway.

The score is perhaps Lloyd-Webber's most romantic, yet it does not contain any of the surpassing melodies he produced for *Phantom* or the memorable music he was to write for *Sunset Boulevard*. He seems to be holding himself in check, perhaps because the first sketches were made when he thought it would be a Rice–Lloyd-Webber creation, and he was looking for a return to "shag." Even in the rangiest songs, the emotion is constrained. He comes closest to letting it out in the ardent ballad "Seeing Is Believing," which is almost done in by stereotyped lyrics that contain lines like "I dreamt that it would *be* her" rhyming with "And in my arms I *see* her." But the melodic line deserves some analysis, for in examination it shows some of Lloyd-Webber's strengths and weaknesses.

See - ing   is   be - liev - ing,   and   in   my arms   I   see   her.   She's

here,   real - ly   here,   real - ly   mine   now.   She seems at home here …

One will notice at the outset the six-note motive: G, F#, E, D, A, E. Four notes descend gracefully from the tonic, then scoop up to the super tonic (A) and the submedian (E). The title, as mentioned before, is a cliché, but it and the repeated motive give us a sense of the familiar, a comfortable lullaby. Nor does the harmony disturb the idyllic feel, pedal-pointed as it is on the tonic (G). But by the fifth bar we start to get the ardent Lloyd-Webber. The melody becomes impassioned, rising on the words "here" and "mine" to the melody's climax.

This is intensified by the harmony: the E-minor chord (VI) and the B-minor (III) are typical of the composer's fervor as well as that of Puccini, Mascagni, and Giordano. This sequence is one of the reasons why Lloyd-Webber's compositions have so often been accused of sounding like these verismo composers, whose melodies lean heavily on III and VI chords.

But there is more. After the melodic and harmonic climax of bars six and seven, a new phrase is introduced in bar eight. It will become part of the release, and this release, built mostly on minor chords, will be a sort of *parlando* bridge, with very little melodic interest, purposefully going no where until at *its* end we will be catapulted through a strong A^7 (dominant of the dominant) into a passionate D^9 to return to the theme.[4]

Unfortunately *Aspects*'s big song, one that stayed on the charts for weeks, "Love Changes Everything," never creates that intensity. Part of the reason is that it is built on three chords. According to journalist Mark Steyn, Lloyd-Webber, who admired the rock band Creedence Clearwater Revival, "always wanted to write a three-chord song." One wonders why a composer with his palette, as evidenced in *Phantom*, would want to write "down." Isn't even the most unsophisticated theatergoer entitled to some challenge? Eventually, even though the accessible melodic line is belted out in pop style by the show's stentorian Michael Ball, who played Alex, and is given innumerable reprises, with such a limited harmonic means it ultimately becomes tiresome.

Another song, one that the critics fell for, owes much to Jerome Kern's "They Didn't Believe Me," only it's not quite as good. Its lyric pushes redundancy beyond incomprehensibility: "I want to be the first man you remember, I want to be the last man you'll forget."

---

[4] This same kind of sequence closing the release of "As If We Never Said Goodbye" had the intensity to bring the house down at every performance of *Sunset Boulevard.*

The lack of melodic inspiration in *Aspects of Love* might be understandable except for the fact that Lloyd-Webber and his artistic collaborators took the work so seriously. And because he was working without Hal Prince, even without Cameron Mackintosh, he seemed impelled, according to one cast member, not to cut anything. "The most marked differences from 1978's *Evita* to 1988's *Aspects* was that in the early days Andrew was very amenable to cutting. If Hal said 'This section's too long, get some music out of here,' Andrew would be up with the scissors. When we got to *Aspects*, he would fight tooth and nail. It's interesting that as he gained more assurance and more popularity, he stuck to his guns more."

Lloyd-Webber called *Aspects of Love* his chamber opera and referred to it, with no little self-aggrandizement, as "Mozartean." Sensing it had an intimate story, he tried to narrow its scope. He scored it for a dozen instruments. But he was eventually done in by the libretto. Being short on wit and style, it replaced interest with set changes, of which there were an amazing thirty-nine. That means that with the show's 150-minute playing time there was a set change every three and a half minutes. With nothing to say, changing the visual became the only alternative.

When that didn't work, music from other numbers was reprised as a sort of recitative. Forced to stick with these mundane characters, who probably were more interesting in bed than out of it, Black and Hart could come up with nothing but platitudes. Lightness, charm, and wit were in short supply. If by some chance the story had appealed to Stephen Sondheim, his collaborators might perhaps have injected some distinction into the libretto. But he would never have been interested because he had already written *A Little Night Music*, whose characters share many of these dissolute traits but possess a keener sense of discernment. Their sex comedy is a bagatelle, a flirtation.

Aspects of Love's program carries no credit line for libretto, so one must assume the recitatives between songs were cobbled together by Nunn, Black, and Hart. We know they all agreed that this was to be a through-sung musical, a genre Lloyd-Webber had founded, although this particular work was to be somewhat operatic. But styles may differ from work to work, and here he creates musical points of reference by using compositions over and over again not as reprises, but in the manner of what the musicologists of early music call *contrafactum*. This term refers to a piece of vocal music whose text has been replaced by an entirely new one, often totally unrelated to the original. In the Renaissance, when stylistic distinctions between sacred and secular music began to crumble, it was common to convert one sort of piece into another simply by according it a new set of words.

For example, to the tune of "Love Changes Everything," near the end of the musical Jenny sings:

No one said that Romeo (4 bars musical interlude)
Was a monster— What, what are you frightened of?
Why are you? When you know . . .
I'm as old as Juliet . . . You know you love me . . .

One wonders why these *contrafactums* are being used as the replacements for "recitative." Why don't we have the plunked Mozartean chord followed by the voice that fills in some of the story? Then when the singer sings "Love Changes Everything," we can accept it as an aria. Of course, the answer is that we are in the *commercial* musical theater, and the composer wants us to take that *tune* home with us.

Okay, so it's not opera. Why would anyone want to call it by such a high-falutin name? Wouldn't that put off the ticket buyers? No. Not coupled with the name of Andrew Lloyd-Webber.

But what is musical-opera anyway? One of the things that led to a rapprochement of more serious works on Broadway and the West End was a breakdown of terms. The press is totally confused with *Carmen Jones*, which contains the same music and very much a translation of the original Bizet-Halevy score. What could account for calling it (as it was so named) a musical play when it debuted? It had the same spoken dialogue as the opéra comique version.

In spite of being called musical plays or musical comedies or operettas, these forms are somewhat interchangeable. Although I think of *Evita* as a musical, because it is through-sung and deals with a serious subject who dies in the end, some critics have called it opera. Ridiculous. Those are not the criteria for opera.

The difference lies in the expectations of the audience. Put *Pacific Overtures* in an opera house, as it was done in the English National Opera, and the audience will think of it as opera. Even though it is sung in English you will find them doggedly trying to follow the libretto. (And as so many opera singers are guilty of a lack of clear-cut diction, who can blame them?) Stage it on Broadway and, *voilà*, it is a musical. The cast will be chosen for their acting-singing-dancing ability, not, as in the opera house, primarily for their voices. Keys will be altered to suit the singers, a great taboo in opera. Diction will be stressed, even at the sacrifice of vocal purity. That is why I prefer to hear Kurt Weill's *Street Scene* and Gershwin's *Porgy and Bess*, both of which started out on Broadway, in the theater rather than in opera houses.

Whether Lloyd-Webber writes in through-sung fashion or Sondheim writes a fifteen-minute concerted number followed by dialogue is immaterial. One can think of Sondheim's extended "Weekend in the Country" as opera, for it contains all the elements of grand opera. Through-sung, it exposes character and moves the plot forward at the same time. That's what opera is supposed to do. *Sweeney Todd* is truly opera, when done in an opera house. In Britain's

National Theatre's tiny Cottesloe theater the audience comes to watch a blood-and-guts thriller and gets just that.

But to make matters even more confusing, one must be wise enough to separate out the true operas, *The Telephone*, *The Medium*, *The Rape of Lucretia*, and others—works that had their debuts on Broadway because of economic factors but which rightly belong in opera houses.

What, then, is operetta? The same confusion exists. *A Little Night Music* is by and large operetta (although it lacks one of its criteria, the huge chorus of *The Student Prince* or *The King and I*). But *Night Music*'s first act ending with its through-sung, multi-voiced seventeen minute section throws it, for that quarter hour, into the realm of pure opera.

What Lloyd-Webber seems to misunderstand in his through-sung musicals is not what opera is, but what recitative is. It is not sections of a song. He must not saturate us with these melodies coming over and over. "Have an armagnac," "There's a woman's shoe here"—these deserve recitative, not snatches of his best tunes. This trivia is less apparent and less bothersome in *Phantom* and in *Sunset* because their plots involve us, and the fat can be cut out. But in *Aspects* the story is cobbled together with these *contrafactums*.

Aspects of Love opened in London on April 10, 1989, less than a year after *The Phantom of the Opera* had blitzed New York. It amassed a huge advance there, partly because "Love Changes Everything" had permeated the airwaves the way "Don't Cry for Me Argentina" had done. There was also a flurry at the box office when it was announced that James Bond interpreter Roger Moore was slated to play George. Unfortunately it was discovered that the actor couldn't sing. However, Kevin Colson went in and came out with splendid personal reviews. The critics were divided about the show as a whole, although Lloyd-Webber felt that he had received some of his best reviews of his career, the best the *Sunday Telegraph* could muster being "surprisingly bearable." But after the show played a year, new actresses were brought in to take the key part of Rose. Even Sarah Brightman, who, it was rumored, had asked Andrew for a divorce, was brought in to keep the show running.

In *Punch* Rhoda Koenig totally wrote off the London production, saying, "The more one looks at the story, the more the limpid Frenchy charm devolves into Bloomsbury bullshit." Another critic noted that the creators took this tale "so seriously and so humourlessly that there is little fun, not much bite and no excitement."

Aspects of Love was plagued with further bad luck, as Susanna Fellowes, who first played Rose opposite Michael Ball's Alex in the Sydmonton production, recounted to this writer. She was scheduled to star in the West End version, but "because of a previous deal that Andrew had made with Actors' Equity, when the union would not allow Sarah to do Christine in *Phantom* in New

Sarah Brightman and Andrew Lloyd-Webber at the gala charity premiere of Aspects of
Love, *April 10, 1989—a command performance before Queen Elizabeth. AP/Wide World
Photos.*

York, he had told them that he would swap his wife's role for an American
actress to come and play the lead in his next show in London. They held
Andrew to this agreement so I could not then open in the show."

So they brought over an American called Ann Crumb, who opened in the show
and played the lead for about four or five months, at which point they contacted
me and asked if I would now take over the role. And I said, "yes, I'd love to." And
within two weeks they rang me up frantically and told me that she had had a

terrible accident. There were two travelators which brought all the scenery onto the stage, and where the flat went round to form the kind of loop, if there was anything on the end between the gap, things would get trapped. And she unfortunately had been doing a scene with an understudy who didn't realize that this was a very dangerous moment; the actor who normally played it knew about it and knew he had to steer her away from the edge of this travelator. So she was playing the scene and not looking down and walked straight into the edge of the travelator—and it ate her foot. Screams could be heard in Leicester Square. And they had to stop the show. It was a matinee. They rang me straightaway and asked could I possibly start at once. . . . I started rehearsal on Monday and went in two weeks later. They put Ann's understudy on for two weeks, that understudy who had to go on for her that very night, and *she* was still walking with a limp. She had been the previous victim of that same travelator. I'm sure you will hear in your investigation that it wasn't the first time an accident of such gravity had happened. Then they changed it, took out all the mechanism and put guards on the end so that it wouldn't happen again.

The Broadway production opened at the Broadhurst Theater a year later on April 8, 1990, with twelve-million-dollar advance booking. Ann Crumb, her leg healed by this time, appeared as Rose and the rest of the principals were brought over from London.

The musical was roundly trounced, one critic noting, "We hear 'Love Changes Everything'—a repetitive insistent tune—endlessly. At first I tried to clock its recurrences: After the initial hearing at 8:08 it reappeared at 8:25, then at 8:37. But 8:20 we had heard the second take-home tune, 'Seeing Is Believing,' which was reprised by 8:30. I wish the 'C' Train came this often."

In spite of its reviews, with much attendant publicity, Lloyd-Webber was able to keep the show running until the advance was depleted. Besides, it was a heady time for him. He was in love with Madeline Guerdon, nicknamed "Guerdy," and would marry her next February. She was a horsewoman and came from what even the English call "old money," the pedigree being more important than the quantity. Sarah, naming Madeline in the action, had been bought off quite amicably at what the tabloids declared was six million and more reputable journals reported as two million pounds.

But Andrew Lloyd-Webber had not abandoned Sarah Brightman any more than he had Sarah Hugill. Her voice and her sound in his music still captivated him. In fact, he thought so highly of her that after the divorce, he featured her in the Broadway company of *Aspects*.

Aspects was nominated for six Tony awards but did not win a single one, perhaps because there had been a flurry of excitement that year in Broadway's musical theater. *City of Angels*, a whimsical detective story pastiche, whose gimmick was a split stage, would capture the public—and, incidentally, all the awards. *Grand Hotel*, an old-fashioned "musical play," and *Meet Me in St. Louis*, an "expansion" of the movie musical, would be worthy rivals. And so when *Aspects* had used up its advance, it simply expired.

It mattered little financially to Lloyd-Webber but bothered him deeply emotionally. He was still trying to crack the critics in "the Big Apple." That year, with *Cats, Starlight Express,* and *Phantom* acknowledged fixtures of the city's theatrical scene, *Aspects* running in the West End, and revivals of *Joseph* and *Superstar* coming in from the hinterlands, he set a world record, one that it seems could hardly be broken. Six shows running simultaneously in London and three in New York. It looked like he had *almost* everything he ever wanted.

Cracking the Nutshell

I N M A Y 1 9 9 2 Stephen Sondheim was one of the dozen nominees selected by President George Bush to receive perhaps the nation's most prestigious honor: The National Medal of Arts, given since 1985 in a ceremony at the White House under the sponsorship of the National Endowment for the Arts—familiarly known as the NEA.

Sondheim refused the award. His letter stated that it "would be an act of utmost hypocrisy" to accept it. The composer wrote President Bush and the assistant to the endowment's chairman, Susan Houston, that he was "flattered and honored" by his selection, but he immediately zeroed in on the reason for his rejecting the medal.

> When I served on the Endowment in the 1970s [as a member of the music and theater panels helping to choose grants recipients], I was glad and proud to be serving a governmental organization devoted to American arts and artists. Although severely underfunded, it seemed noble in intent and clear of purpose.
>
> In the last few years, however, it has become a victim of its own and others' political infighting, and is rapidly being transformed into a conduit and symbol of censorship and repression rather than encouragement and support.

What he was referring to specifically was the NEA's unwillingness to grant monies that had been recommended by their peer panels to exhibits at MIT's List Visual Arts Center and Virginia Commonwealth University's Anderson Gallery. These included graphic depictions of sexual organs and bodily functions. Sondheim's refusing the medal was a stand against the ultraconservatism of the lawmakers and even the public at large, a plea that any organization that called itself an endowment "for the arts" not be subverted by the policies of the far right.

Sondheim was not the first prominent musician to turn down the medal. Three years earlier, Leonard Bernstein made headlines for the same act. At the

In the East Room of the White House Sondheim (second from left) receives the Kennedy Center Medal of Honor in 1993 from President and Mrs. Clinton. His cohonorees are, from left to right, Marion Williams (singer), Sir Georg Solti (conductor), Arthur Mitchell (founder of the Dance Theatre of Harlem), and Johnny Carson (entertainer). AP/Wide World Photos.

time Bernstein was protesting cancellation of an NEA grant to a Manhattan gallery for a show on AIDS. At least Bernstein's uproar did some good, for it convinced the then chairman, John Frohmeyer, to change his mind and restore the appropriation. But Sondheim's objection, falling on a Congress with little respect for artistic license, caused hardly a ripple.[1]

It did have its artistic ramifications in his work. His next musical, *Passion*, with a libretto by James Lapine and based on both the unfinished novel by Iginio Tarchetti and on Ettore Scola's 1981 film *Passione d'amore*, was a great breakthrough for him. Sondheim, the master of ambivalence, who had been contending since *Anyone Can Whistle* about how little there was "to be sure of" and who had the central character in *Company* avoid stifling commitment in

[1] Sondheim was not reluctant to accept the Medal of Honor given by the Kennedy Center for distinguished contribution to American culture through the arts in 1994. The award, presented by President Clinton, is the artistic counterpart of a British knighthood.

his search for love, was about to take a step in the other direction. *Passion* is about "how the force of somebody's feeling for you can crack you open," he told a reporter, adding, "and how it is the life force in a deadened world."

Sondheim relates that this is only the second musical that has gotten on stage that he started himself. The first came about when he saw Christopher Bond's version of *Sweeney Todd*. (One cannot count the instance when he suggested the title of *Assassins* to John Weidman, for Sondheim had no idea where the spark would take them.) But on viewing the Scola movie in New York, he "wanted to sing it, and thought some day I want to do that." At the time he had just begun writing *Sunday in the Park with George*, and after that they went right to *Into the Woods*. So it wasn't until after these projects were out of the way that Sondheim started thinking again of *Passione d'amore*.

The film tells the story of Giorgio, a callow but sensitive officer, who leaves his married mistress, Clara (her name means "light"), in Milan to join his garrison in a dreary mountain town. There, the colonel's cousin, Fosca (whose name signifies "dark"), a sickly, hideous creature, conceives an unbridled passion for him and will not leave him alone until he loves her. When at last he returns her love, she dies. At the end of the film, Scola has a dissolute Giorgio tell his story to a dapper dwarf. After the narrative the dwarf erupts into gales of laughter, saying the story is preposterous.

"On Fosca's first entrance in the film, I started to cry," Sondheim admitted, "because I couldn't believe the story I was about to be told; not about how *she* falls in love with *him*, but about how *he* falls in love with *her*. It's a bizarre situation, because he's this very handsome young man who has been having an affair with a very beautiful woman and there's no reason on earth that he should be the least bit attracted to this strange, selfish, willful, unattractive woman, but it is in fact the story of her passion that breaks him. The story just kept inexorably getting there. And when it happened, I burst into tears."

"There was some personal connection clearly," Sondheim told Michiko Kakutani. "I think it's about a desire to open up, a desire to be like Giorgio." In 1973 he told Charles Michener of *Newsweek*, "One of the reasons I've been in analysis for years is there are things I miss like having a permanent relationship and I don't know how to work for it." Fifteen years later he disclosed to a *Time* magazine reporter that he had never been in love, but he now says his life "has changed a lot" recently, "and it's one of the coincidences that happened while I was writing *Passion* and vice versa." But the affair that ran parallel to the composition of *Passion* came to an end, and in November 2000 Sondheim told Sunday *London Times* interviewer David Benedict that he was no longer wearing the ring that had been given to him by his ex-lover, Peter, adding, that "It's a familiar feeling. I was single most of my life."

According to his collaborator, whose first adaptation this was, seeing the film is what drew Sondheim to the material. But Lapine's own involvement came from the novel. "I've only seen the film once," he said after the musical was completed. Rather than the beauty versus ugliness metaphor, Lapine prefers the allegory of illness, which became the moving thrust of his libretto. Illness of gigantic proportion pervades Tarchetti's Gothic novel, which was written in the late 1860s. So bizarre and somewhat unbelievable is it that it has been compared to *Vampira*. It would have to be so, as the novelist, ill throughout his life, died of tuberculosis when he was twenty-nine, and the work was completed by a colleague.

One doesn't know if Tarchetti, who was associated with the *scapigliatura*, a group of bohemian painters, composers, and writers whose art was intended to shock, meant this work seriously. One wonders if his romantic soap opera was just tweaking its nose at the cultural values of nineteenth-century bourgeoisie.

Certainly Scola's film noir is understandable, and we would not be romanticizing to exchange the Giorgio in the film for the author. He has delicate features and he looks innocent. (Unfortunately, the part in the musical was played by the brawny and self-assured Jere Shea, who John Lahr called "a package of military testosterone.")

In the film, Fosca almost looks like a vampire. She is emaciated, with coal-black eyes and enormous teeth, and one really feels she is sucking the life out of her victim. But we soon realize this is her one chance to reclaim her humanity, and we feel for her. It makes the movie very powerful but still almost impossible to believe, and even when one understands the symbolism in the movie and the novel, it is hard to see how one would ever find the subject attractive as a musical.

Passion has no overture. It begins with an ominous drum roll, after which, as the lights come up, we see Clara astride Giorgio in full coitus. (Placing Clara in the superior position becomes Lapine's subtle hint as to Giorgio's passivity and malleability.) It was a daring and compelling decision, coupled as it is with truly fervent music. The pair interrupt each other in their intense ardor, recalling their earliest meetings and singing out their happiness. We also learn that their affair is clandestine and that Giorgio is being transferred. This only intensifies their lovemaking. Hungrily they begin again as the lights dim.

The next scene happens over a period of days, and in it we get to sense military life at the northern outpost to which Giorgio has been transferred. We meet Giorgio's commanding officer, Colonel Tambourri. (As with the names Clara and Fosca, it does not take much imagination to connect his name with a military snare.) He tells us of his cousin Fosca's passion for books. Then we hear a penetrating scream from her quarters above, followed by eerie Chopinesque trilling, a demented piano nocturne. The surreal style the musical will take, as well as the script's epistolary manner, is introduced in this scene, for Clara appears from time to time in the background reading from Giorgio's letters. The three characters will intersect, frequently joined by the military men, throughout the rest of the musical.

Counterpointed to the military horseplay, we learn of Fosca's illness and get a glimpse of a tortured and humorless Giorgio, who cannot wait to be back again with his beloved Clara. Then, one morning alone at breakfast, Fosca comes down to join him and to thank him for the books he has lent her. She apologizes for her tardiness at returning them, illness having prevented her, she explains, and when Giorgio responds that perhaps she is now feeling more normal, she demurs: "Normal? I hardly think so. Sickness is normal to me, as health is to you." This launches her into her recitative-like aria, which begins:

I do not read to think.	I know the truth,
I do not read to learn.	The truth is hardly what I need.
I do not read to search for truth,	I read to dream . . .

One will note that throughout this exceptional musical, intricate rhymes, almost a Sondheim signature, are missing. Previously he has equated elaborate rhyming, especially internal rhyme, with erudition. Fosca is well schooled, yet tells us that her dreams are without expectation. It all adds up to a relaxed lyricist who can let his poetry come out at will, without pyrotechnics.

After her confession Fosca tries to interest Giorgio in seeing what there is of this town, especially the ruined castle, and when he mentions that he has not seen a flower since he arrived, she brings him a few. Then, with a piercing scream, she faints at his feet.

In the next scene they visit the castle. Clara, reading a love letter materializes, and Giorgio unwisely tells Fosca about his ardor "that floods every living moment." She lashes out at him for speaking to her of love. She has watched him from her window and thought he'd understand. "They hear drums, you hear music, as I do." She is somewhat mollified when, to appease her anger, he says she can rely on his friendship.

Reporting his exasperation to Clara, she warns him to keep his distance. But after remonstrances from Fosca when he returns from maneuvers, he begins to feel sorry for this poor creature. He senses he is trapped yet he is unable to pull away. Frustrated, he takes a five-day leave to be with Clara. Before he goes Fosca extracts a promise from him that he will write her daily. Seated on one side of the stage Fosca reads Giorgio's words. His letter becomes a mordant note in a reprise of his and Clara's original song of happiness. She joins their happiness duet, making it a soaring trio. Once and for all Giorgio tells her that there can be nothing between them because of his love for Clara. With touches of Fosca's

Giorgio (Jere Shea) is unresponsive to Fosca's (Donna Murphy) plea for love, in a scene from Passion. *Photo: Joan Marcus. © Museum of the City of New York.*

Chopinesque piano trilling peeking through the orchestration, we feel just a bit that he is deluding himself.

On his return Fosca is cold and reproachful, and Giorgio feels himself well out of this wretched situation, but three weeks later the company doctor persuades him to visit her, saying her obsession will kill her if he does not. When Giorgio says he does not want to get involved, the doctor answers that he is already involved, and then as a final shot tells him that Fosca's life or death lies in his hands.

Giorgio visits her chamber late in the night, and indulges her by lying on the bed next to her while she sleeps. Knowing he must leave before dawn, Fosca asks him to write a letter before he goes, and this musical piece (the songs are not listed as such in the program) becomes the cornerstone of the musical. It is a love letter, one from him to her. It ends:

> ... I don't know how I let you
> So far inside my mind,
> But there you are and there you will stay,
> How could I ever wish you away?
> I see now I was blind.
>
> And should you die tomorrow,
> Another thing I see:
> Your love will live in me
>
> I remain always ... Your Giorgio.

In the next scene the Colonel tells Giorgio of Fosca's history. An unattractive woman, faced with forever being a daughter or a wife, she was duped into marriage by a bogus count who after some time squandered her dowry. (Here Lapine's plot differs from that of Scola's film, in which the count absconded the very afternoon of the wedding, leaving his bride a virgin.) One day while marketing she meets a woman who claims to be the scoundrel's wife. Faced with truth the count unremorsefully admits his past and his misdeeds, but he says that it was a fair bargain. To a scherzando waltz, he sings:

You gave me your money, I gave you my looks,
And my charm,

And my arm.
I would say that more than balances the books.

The Colonel takes some responsibility for Fosca's situation because he introduced his cousin to the man, and he explains to Giorgio that is why he took his now ill and penniless cousin to live with him. Through the number we also get to understand why Fosca covets beauty and why she is attracted so desperately to the sensitivity and handsomeness of Giorgio.

Later, Giorgio seeks out a quiet place to read a letter from Clara. Fosca follows him there and he furiously asks her

Will you never learn
When too far is too far?
Have you no concern

For what I feel,
What I want?

After his angry outburst, Fosca collapses. As Giorgio is about to leave the stage, it begins to rain. He returns, covers her with his coat and carries her back to camp. When he awakes two days later, he has a raging fever and is given a forty-day sick leave. (We will notice how the healthy man is beginning to take on the mantle of illness.) But just as he starts to board the train Fosca appears, wanting to accompany him to Milan. She sings of her love, telling him it is beyond her control, then she says she would die for him. "Would Clara do that?" "I'm taking you back to the base," he answers.

Back at the base he writes to Clara that he is forgoing his long leave and taking only four days. The doctor, feeling remorseful that he has involved Giorgio so deeply by suggesting he be kind to his patient because of her illness, threatens to arrange for a transfer for his own good. During the few days leave in Milan, Giorgio tries to test for himself how deeply Clara's love runs. He asks her to go away with him, but of course she cannot leave her husband and child.

At the officers' Christmas party we learn Giorgio is indeed being transferred. A hysterical Fosca throws herself at him and leaves the room in tears. The Colonel follows to tend to his distraught cousin while we hear Clara's final letter—their affair is over. The Colonel reenters in a fury. He has discovered the love letter Giorgio had written at Fosca's request. Giorgio does not explain, but the Colonel, believing the letter dishonors his cousin, challenges Giorgio to a duel the next morning.

Giorgio asks the doctor to arrange for him to see Fosca that night. "You understand this woman could never be your lover. Her physical condition—" But he goes to her anyway to tell her he had nothing to do with the transfer and that his relationship with Clara is finished. He realizes that no one had ever truly loved him before. Adding:

Love without reason, love without mercy,	Love unconcerned
Love without pride or shame.	With being returned—

Giorgio tells her he realizes that *he* loves her. She leads him to the bed, and when he tells her "we can't," she overrules his caution, saying, "To die loved is to have lived."

There are two more scenes, the brief duel that ends with Giorgio's scream of pain which sounds exactly like Fosca's initial outcry, and the final one, in a hospital.

A nurse brings a letter from the doctor informing Giorgio that Fosca died three days after the night he visited her. She knew nothing of the duel, the Colonel's injuries, or Giorgio's collapse. Now with the full company in a glowing reprise of the letter Fosca wrote, the work ends as a dazed and debilitated Giorgio joins Fosca (and the chorus) in the happiness music Clara sang at the outset. It trails away, leaving only Giorgio and Fosca with the repeated line, "your love will live in me." A hushed F#-minor chord, somewhat reminiscent of the sick-room last act of *La Traviata*, fades away.

Passion is a beautifully heartfelt work with lush romantic themes—almost too repetitive and unrelieved. Because of its brevity (it is less than two hours long), it was erroneously reported to have been intended as part of a double bill, but according to Sondheim, "It wasn't conceived as part of a double bill, but as a one-act piece. Then James had this idea for another show, *Muscle*, and then we thought of putting the two together." But that idea was wisely vetoed, and *Passion*, far too intense to be paired with another musical, stands glowingly on its own.

The whole project seems done in by compression. We miss the expansion, the filling in, that a full evening's two acts would have allowed. We want to see an early Giorgio and Clara, and we certainly need time to adjust to Giorgio's about-face, which is hardly convincing. Given more time, it would not seem that only after Clara's refusal to run away with him, he suddenly sees Fosca in a new light. Giorgio, who is not portrayed as being particularly cerebral, makes us feel as though losing his vision of what love is is worse than losing the object of it.

The settings and smallness are apparent throughout. It is, after all, a piece for three singers. The addition of the military is perfunctory, limited to drumrolls and a few soldierly clichés. Fosca's attendants, too, feel like a false diversion, so sketchy are they. They appear in only one scene, seemingly brought on because they were needed to sing the frequently reprised choral parts and were hanging about backstage.

The "happiness" theme that begins and ends the work is surpassingly beautiful but overused. That is not to deny that the "loving you" confession and what is known as the "letter song" are two of the most remarkable arias in the Sondheim canon.

Sondheim says he was aiming to write a score "closer in style to *Sweeney Todd* or *Sunday in the Park* as opposed to *Night Music*." That would bring it closer to operatic tragedy, which it resembles indeed. *Passion* summons up innuendoes of many of the tragedies of the mid-nineteenth century, but in its connection with the inexorable it seems particularly like Prosper Merimée's *Carmen* as well as the film *The Story of Adele H.* But times have so changed since those characters walked the stage that it is hard for audiences to relate to someone like Giorgio, on whom the plot revolves.

In the nineteenth century Don José was a typical romantic hero, but in our time we seem to write him off as a spineless weakling. He follows a path like Giorgio's that leads to his own destruction. The film about Victor Hugo's daughter is more realistic. Adele Hugo followed a soldier to an island, but in this case, he would have nothing to do with her. Her tale of obsession and degradation is a familiar one in our society.

During the first week of previews, while the authors were readying the show, there were occasional outbreaks from the audience during some of the scenes. Some reacted violently to what they considered the preposterousness of the turnaround in Giorgio's character, and laughter broke out where it was not intended. Others who were enjoying the show almost got into fistfights with those who vociferously objected to the gloominess of some scenes. *Newsweek* announced that it "would be the most argued-about work of Sondheim's career," and the prognostication was correct. But by opening night, audiences began listening intently, even though they may have argued when the house lights came back up. Still, even today no two Sondheimists agree on the place of *Passion* in his oeuvre.

The *New York Times*'s Vincent Canby, while calling the show "a major work," suspected Sondheim was not through tinkering with it and wrote that he hesitated "to write about *Passion* as if it were fixed and finished. No Sondheim show ever goes quietly into the night."

Most of the other reviewers were amazed at Sondheim's "direct take on love reciprocated and attained." Many of the critics objected to the end, calling it commercially compromised. John Lahr criticized the conclusion, which says "Your love will live in me," attributing it to "box office reasons" and saying that Giorgio and Fosca never prove the validity of that line. "In fact," he continues, "everything we've been shown in the musical belies the purity of the finale's romantic ardor." Even those critics who accepted their ardor like *Time*'s William Henry III said that "the message that love is unworthy unless it recklessly risks everything may fit the *Anna Karenina*-style sensibilities of 1863, when the show is set, but now it feels adolescent and irresponsible."

In the end, the good reviews won out. Clive Barnes raved that "the show was "just plain wonderful—emotional and, yes, passionate. . . . It will enrich you and it will touch your heart. This is the most thrilling piece of theater on Broadway." *Newsday*'s Linda Winer seconded the compliment, writing, "We live in an age when a beautiful score is nothing to take for granted, and this show has one of Stephen Sondheim's most ravishing."

Controversy aside, in a dolorous season that offered only a pretentious extravaganza based on *The Red Shoes* that closed quickly, yet another tired *Cyrano*, a stage version of Disney's *Beauty and the Beast*, not nearly as imaginative as the animated movie, and an inane sequel to *The Best Little Whorehouse* that had very little to offer beyond its provocative title, there was no way the Tony committee could overlook the distinction that *Passion* brought to Broadway. The show won the Tony for the Best Musical.[3] Sondheim and Lapine each received awards for Best Score and Best Book. In the role of Fosca, Donna Murphy was a shoo-in for the award and was acclaimed as a new star.

But even after winning four Tonys and being given those grudgingly great reviews plus personal accolades for Donna Murphy, *Passion*, which opened April 23[4] at the intimate Lyceum Theater, played only 340 Broadway performances,

---

[3] According to *Variety*, the heavy betting was on the Disney show—commercial enough for children of all ages and a definite moneymaker.

[4] On March 26, 1996, almost two years after its New York premiere, *Passion* opened in London, starring an intense Maria Friedman as Fosca and "a fatally bland" Michael Ball as Giorgio. Jeremy Sams directed a much more leisurely, less austere production than Broadway's. Sams's production even included an intermission in what Sondheim was certain had to be an "intermissionless show." But after watching several previews he came to feel that one was called for. The critiques were mixed, which caused the show to limp along playing to half-empty houses. Quotes ranged from "a piece from the heart" to "pretty but vapid." Alastair Macaulay's comment in the *Financial Times* was perhaps the most succinct: "Sondheim's cynicism is virtually nowhere in sight—and I almost

falling far below the number chalked up by *Forum, Company, Follies, Night Music, Sweeney Todd, Sunday in the Park with George,* and *Into the Woods.*

In sum, what can one say of Sondheim for having chosen to identify with a subject who seems to have mistaken self-immolating masochism for love? Perhaps the *Passion* he intended was unbearable suffering for that is the meaning of the Latin *passio,* translated from the Greek *pathos.* Giorgio's passion may be equated with Christ's Passion—quite different from the sensual meaning of the word. In any case, capitulation to "the spirit, the idea of love" is as far as Giorgio goes. Although the show confuses them, obsession and love are not the same thing. But to equate them as Giorgio does is frightening and more than a little suspect. Fosca was obsessed, as Sondheim and Lapine's musical makes clear. But obsession is a remote and steely terrain, far from the earthiness of passion and miles away from love. This heartfelt musical is probably best appreciated for its romantic effusions, its blatant sensuality, and its depths of human degradation. It should be enjoyed without too much analysis. In that, it is just like love.

---

miss it. All that is left is a loudly bleeding heart, and some insights into human nature and love that would not disgrace a fortune cookie."

The Film Noir Becomes Plus Noir

S*UNSET BOULEVARD*, the exemplary film *noir* of 1950 that was to be Andrew Lloyd-Webber's next project, has an absorbing plot that cries out to be musicalized. Not only did Sondheim once consider it as a subject for a musical, but a photo of its star, Gloria Swanson, was coincidentally responsible for the metaphor of crumbling age that pervaded *Follies*. As Lloyd-Webber's descent into a world of murder and madness, the work connects the two men in a way their personalities never could have.

The transformation to musical was first attempted by Swanson, one of the silent screen's luminaries, a few years after the picture was released. In the film, Swanson plays Norma Desmond, a deluded, passé star, unable to make the transition to talking pictures.

Swanson had a fine singing voice and was planning to pull another Gertrude Lawrence coup as when the British actress was the first person to option *The King and I*. Lawrence scooped up the rights to the novel, then brought the project to Rodgers and Hammerstein, saying if they wrote it she would play the leading role. It was an offer they could not refuse.

Like Lawrence, Swanson had always been creatively involved in any film in which she appeared. *Sunset Boulevard* was no exception. When Swanson was offered the role (after Mae West, Pola Negri, and Mary Pickford had turned it down), she and Billy Wilder agreed early on that the script drew Norma Desmond too harshly and totally without sympathy. Wilder then softened Norma's character by having her visit Paramount Studios and Cecil B. De Mille. That sequence became one of the high spots of the movie—and is indeed the centerpiece of Andrew Lloyd-Webber's musical version. In it an ecstatic Norma has been telephoned to come to the Paramount lot, where she visits her old director. Believing he wants her to return to the screen, she has a devastating awakening toward the end of the film when she learns that the phone call came from another Paramount director who wanted to use her classic car, an Isotta-Fraschini, in a Bing Crosby film.

In the middle '50s, a musical titled simply *Boulevard*, heavily underwritten by Swanson and with a score by Dickson Hughes and Richard Stapley, was ready to go into production. Earlier in the decade Swanson had extracted oral permission from Paramount Pictures, which had produced the original film,[1] that it was all right for her to proceed with her plans for *Boulevard*'s musical development.

A typical product of Hollywood, Swanson understood the illusory mystique of embroidering your own real or imagined success, as the parenthetical phrase in a letter she wrote to D. A. Doran, an executive at Paramount, shows: "I shall really be marking time (with my dress business and a possible picture in Europe) until my dream can come true. *Sunset Boulevard* as a musical." When Swanson finished her supervision, she said she "hoped her role would be played by a high voltage opera star who is also a great actress."

Sunset's plot had been changed to make Norma different from the bossy harridan and eventual murderess she becomes in the movie. In Swanson's now sympathetic version, she pawns her last piece of jewelry to throw the New Year's party. At the end, instead of shooting Joe, she gives her blessing to his and Betty's union. It must be stated, without coming to Swanson's defense in what now strikes us as ludicrous changes, that a musical ending with the leading man's murder and the heroine's insanity was unheard of in the 1950s.

By grit alone, Swanson had enlisted a British producer by 1957, and the musical was well under way. But later that year, with the cast chosen and rehearsals about to begin, Swanson's years of work on the project collapsed when Russell Holman, a new executive at Paramount, wrote her a devastating letter. Claiming that they were planning to reissue the film, which had by now been acclaimed as one of the three finest films ever made about Hollywood,[2] he informed her that her oral contract was invalid and refused to grant performance rights to a stage production.[3]

---

[1] *Sunset Boulevard* was directed by Billy Wilder and written by him, Charles Brackett, and D. M. Marshman Jr. According to Wilder, the idea of the silent star's comeback stemmed from Brackett and the character of a younger man who becomes her lover was suggested by Marshman, a young reporter who sometimes joined Wilder and Brackett for a game of afternoon bridge. In 1989 the film was granted "landmark" status by the National Film Registry of the Library of Congress.

[2] The others were *A Star Is Born*, a harsh indictment of the studio system manner of building and destroying stars, and the musical *Singin' in the Rain*, the reverse of *Sunset Boulevard*'s mirror: about how careers were *born* with the advent of sound.

[3] Having listened to the score of *Boulevard*, which is preserved in the Gloria Swanson archives in the University of Texas, one has to feel that Paramount felt the work was not stageworthy in that version; and after theatrical mounting, stage rights would be dead for all time.

The film was indeed reissued and played to a whole new audience. But by 1970, after interest in the reruns had died out, *Sunset Boulevard* was once again available for optioning. Most librettists stayed clear of such a depressing story, but not Andrew Lloyd-Webber.

He had been seduced by the story shortly after he first saw the film in the early '70s, when he was only in his early twenties. Believing that music could enhance the tragic elements of the plot, he was determined to secure it. "I sort of made inquiries about the rights and they weren't really interested. Paramount in those days didn't really know who I was. *Jesus Christ Superstar* had only just come out."

Harold Prince, too, was interested. He thought this film about the dark underbelly of Hollywood would be ideal for his friend and collaborator Stephen Sondheim. Prince's concept for an adaptation would have turned Norma into a forgotten Doris Day–type heroine all the sadder for having the pug-nosed beauty and the coy wholesomeness she projected replaced by her antithesis: today's lusty Hollywood heroine. Nor had Prince forgotten that widely circulated art photo taken in 1960 of Swanson with her arms outstretched standing in the rubble of the Roxy Theater. The haunting picture was a comment on the destruction of the lavish movie palace. Swanson's film *The Love of Sunya* had opened the movie showplace in 1920, and it was actually this photo that brought about Hal Prince's concept of what *Follies* should be about. "Rubble exposed in the daylight," was the way he put it. Even *Follies'* cracked-face logo by David Edward Byrd, although modeled after Marlene Dietrich, came about because of that Swanson photo.

But Sondheim, involved in turning *The Girls Upstairs* into *Follies*, was not interested, and after a while Prince too became committed to other projects and dropped his option. Lloyd-Webber, however, proved inexorable in his pursuit of the property, and eventually Paramount learned "who he was." As Don Black puts it, "Once he latches onto something, he's like a bulldog and doesn't let go." Even in Hollywood, people couldn't ignore his track record. The studio eventually let him transform and perhaps revive interest in Wilder's celebrated cinematic effort.

"I wouldn't be doing it if I didn't think a score could bring something that gives it its own life and its own validity," he told a reporter for the *Financial Times*. His conception of the piece was that it was about the false values of Hollywood. He acknowledged that there were pitfalls in the plot, and that many would not care to see a musical about a rich woman who keeps a young man. Still, he felt that the story was even more theatrical than it is filmic and found it "desperately sad."

By 1979, after his first successful alliance with Don Black, *Tell Me on a Sunday*, wherein he realized the lyricist was the one to romanticize his music, he confided that he wanted to do *Sunset Boulevard*, which, by this time, he had under option. "We had a screening of it and he wrote a couple of tunes," Black said. "The first was Norma's theme, sung in the finale as she comes down the staircase. I called it "One Star," something about how there's only one star in the world and it's me." That, as we have seen, became "Memory" when it went into *Cats*, but only the first section had been written at that time. Then they wrote another song, this time for Max, Norma's confidante-butler and ex-husband "Madam Takes a Lot of Looking After," the essence of which is retained in the show as "The Greatest Star of All."

Then Lloyd-Webber contacted Hugh Wheeler to fashion a libretto, and he created a story sticking to Hal Prince's idea, moving the time frame closer to our own. Lloyd-Webber quickly saw that this updating wasn't going to work.

In 1991, after *Aspects of Love* was out of the way, Lloyd-Webber thought that serious playwright Christopher Hampton might be the man to adapt it, leaving the action back where it originally was, in the '50s. Hampton, who had written many plays, recently had had tremendous success with *Les Liaisons Dangereuses* which won him an Oscar for Best Screenplay when he adapted it as *Dangerous Liaisons*. His dialogue in the mordantly stylized play had a poetic ring about it that appealed to Lloyd-Webber. But he had never written a musical before and was naturally leery.

Then Lloyd-Webber hired Amy Powers, a New York entertainment attorney and lyricist, to work with Hampton. But Powers's lyrics did not satisfy either of them. Lloyd-Webber later said, "She was not untalented, but young and a little over-awed by the whole thing. This is a real play and it needed a playwright-lyricist." Amy Powers soon left the project.

As he had announced a *Sunset Boulevard* for Sydmonton in September of 1992, and all his plans were coming to naught, Lloyd-Webber was getting nervous. Some months before the invitees came, he asked Don Black if he "would consider working with Amy Powers to get the lyrics right for Sydmonton. I said yes . . . I played with some bits and pieces, and we did it there together. 'One Small Glance,' which eventually became 'With One Look,' was in that production." The Sydmonton version was not very good and did not go very deeply into the material.

"Christopher Hampton is a very brilliant man," Black acknowledged, "and I loved him from the first moment because he said to me, 'It's a masterpiece, let's not fuck around with it. Let's keep it and rewrite as little as possible.' "

The team decided to depart from Lloyd-Webber's usual through-sung style and to use spoken dialogue usually underscored. "As a dramatist," Hampton said, "I had to get used to the pacing and learn that when a song is used to make a plot point it will usually take longer to get across than a spoken line." The libretto credit was originally to be Hampton's with lyrics by Don Black, but

Hampton and Black had worked so closely that at their request the line now reads "book and lyrics by Christopher Hampton and Don Black."

And they worked fast.

From the time of *Sunset Boulevard*'s Sydmonton premiere until its opening at London's Adelphi Theatre[4] on July 12, the Lloyd-Webber publicity machine never rested. *Variety* announced that "Ballyhoo has been tremendous even by Andrew Lloyd Webber standards." The show had some help from Barbra Streisand's recording of "With One Look," which was on all the charts, plus a four-part radio documentary about the composer that was aired on the BBC. There was another difference, too. Curiosity. Mystery. In contrast to most of Lloyd-Webber's previous shows, little of the score had worn out its welcome. Except for the aforementioned "With One Look" and "As If We Never Said Goodbye" on Streisand's *Back to Broadway II* album, none of the songs had been heard before. Still, when the production opened to a five million pounds advance, it was only tepidly received by the critics. It looked as if it would soon use up its advance.

The Norma Desmond in the Sydmonton production was Patti LuPone, who had won a Tony for her interpretation of *Evita* in the New York production. At forty-three, she was a bit young to portray Norma, who was supposed to be in her late fifties. With a round face and large nose, LuPone never looked like the kind of heroine Rudolph Valentino would want to spirit away into the desert, but she had a great deal of emotional intensity and a Mermanesque voice.

Lloyd-Webber had promised to let LuPone star in the New York production, but he wanted to open the show first in Los Angeles, away from his nemeses, the Broadway critics. The West Coast debut idea had worked with *Evita*, and he did not see how it could fail with *Sunset*. The plan was for it to play the West Coast for several months, where, with a Hollywood audience, it was sure to garner rave reviews, and then take Broadway by storm.

He was right about the rave reviews, but had not counted on Trevor Nunn's taking a fresh look at the whole project when he started to direct the Los Angeles version and deciding the show needed a complete overhaul. He felt every vestige of the original Doris Day update needed to be expunged. Part of the change was due to Glenn Close's multifaceted Norma, but much was his own reconception. Where there had been brightness and sun, Nunn exchanged it for gloom. The first act was a bit sluggish, with much unnecessary dialogue. It took too long to get into the story, the best of which takes place in Norma's gloomy palazzo. The big Hollywood moments, Schwab's drugstore and the Par-

---

[4] The Really Useful Group bought 50 percent of the Adelphi freehold from Broadway theater owner James Nederlander for three million dollars. It already owned the New London where *Cats* is on permanent display, and the Palace, rented out to *Les Misérables*.

amount lot, would now be mere diversions. Extraneous musical bits now seemed redundant, overlong numbers needed cropping. Plot points that didn't come over in song had to be put into dialogue. The whole production became much tighter. When it opened at the Shubert Theater in Los Angeles on December 9, 1993, Lloyd-Webber's music, John Napier's Art Déco set, and especially Close's bravura performance received accolades.

Before the lights come up on an underwater view of a Hollywood swimming pool with a dead body floating in it we hear a ruminating theme, typical of Hollywood spellbound music, a theme that one reviewer said "Franz Waxman would have died for" (although the score of the original movie was indeed written by Franz Waxman). Built on the tritone (an augmented fourth), it will be used again and identified with Max, Norma's austere butler. Its harmony centers largely on the augmented chord, a cloying, unhealthy sound that sets the whole tone of the musical.

When the action on stage starts to a bright, flippant melody, we are on the

Andrew Lloyd-Webber and his third wife, Madeline, in Los Angeles for the U.S. premiere of Sunset Boulevard, *December 9, 1993. AP/Wide World Photos.*

Paramount lot. A group of young hopefuls are milling around singing snatches of melody whose lyrics' main thrust is self-promotion. In between, we get the hollow Hollywood promises exemplified by the song's title, "Let's Have Lunch." It is reminiscent of Sondheim's New York brush-off from *Company*, "Look, I'll call you in the morning or my service will explain."[5] Joe Gillis, a second-rate scriptwriter and ex-journalist, well known to the others, especially to his pal Artie, an assistant director, is "at the bottom of the barrel." (Actually the lyricists rhyme the line awkwardly with "fallen foul of Darryl," indicating the CEO of Fox. No scripter would call Darryl Zanuck by his first name.) Plotwise, we watch Gillis try to pitch his story to a small-time producer whose secretary, Betty, not knowing the writer is present, tells him it's not very good.

Back on the lot, Betty tries to make it up to Gillis, who she believes has real talent and with whom she would like to develop a screenplay. She agrees to divert the goons who have come to repossess his car in exchange for a promise that he will meet her at Schwab's next week for a story session.

During an amazing theatrical effect, one that features a filmed car chase through the Holmby Hills to avoid the finance men, one of Joe's tires suffers a sudden blow-out, and he pulls into the deserted driveway of 11086 Sunset Boulevard.[6] It is the home of Norma Desmond, who mistakes him for the undertaker come to bury her pet chimpanzee, which has just died. He tells her of her mistake and she furiously orders him out. But as he is leaving he looks at her and says, "Say, aren't you Norma Desmond? You used to be in pictures. You used to be big." "I am big," she snaps. "It's the pictures that got small."

These lines, like most of the trenchant ripostes in the libretto, come directly from the screenplay. At this moment, in both the scenario and the musical Norma heatedly tries to prove the superiority of silents over talkies before demanding Gillis leave, but in the musical she is given one of Lloyd-Webber's best songs, one whose pathos is so reminiscent of the early flickers that it might have come from a Charlie Chaplin one-reeler. Technically, the poignance comes from the use of upper and lower appoggiaturas (marked u. a. and l. a. on Example A), an emotional effect that the composer had just begun exploring in *The Phantom of the Opera*. Added to this, Lloyd-Webber uses modality brilliantly in the fifth bar.

---

[5] Throughout this musical, as contrasted to earlier Lloyd-Webber works, most of the recitatives are not rhymed. But because the music is composed in four- or eight-bar segments, primary and consequent phrases that cry for rhyme, this rhythmic speech leaves the ear unsatisfied. The whole effect becomes one of overplugging the tunes while telling the story. The show is far more successful in its "song" songs or in its sections of spoken dialogue with underscoring.

[6] The actual house that was filmed was not on Sunset Boulevard but rather at 3810 Wilshire Boulevard. The mansion, owned by J. Paul Getty, had been rented for filming by Paramount. They had redressed it to create the Gothic mood and installed the pool critical to the story. The house was destroyed in 1957 to make way for the Getty corporate headquarters.

Example A

With one look I can break your heart. With one look I play ev - 'ry part. I can make your sad heart sing. With one look you'll know all you need to know.

At its end, the song's pathos turns to resolve, and Norma vows to triumph in her "return" (she detests the word "comeback") to the screen. "With one look I'll be me!" she exclaims while holding a high D. Joe stands astounded at her determination, and Norma hires him to edit the massive screenplay of *Salome* that she has spent the last ten years writing as a vehicle for her return. Attracted by his candor, his looks, and even his astrological sign, she insists he move in with her and take the room over the garage while he does the work. It is a godsend for Joe, who is months behind in his rent. Max takes him there and by way of explanation for the strangeness of the surroundings, sings his expository ballad built on that ruminative theme we heard at the outset. It is a theme that does not take well to the voice, but one that is sung nevertheless. Unfortunately it is given misaccents like *cor*sage or the almost laughable line when the lyric talks about the "Maharajah who hanged him*self* [as distinguished from others] with one of her discarded stockings." Despite some awkward prosody, the song's message somehow is gotten across.

Max has confided to Joe that it is he who writes the fan mail that Norma receives by the sackful. Then, as the action switches back to Norma's gilded movie-palace living room, we see Joe and Norma immersed in readying the script. We realize that Norma is falling in love with Joe. He is now a virtual prisoner in the house, forced to look at reruns of her old films for the evening's entertainment. Norma organizes a New Year's Eve party, makes Joe cancel his plans for seeing in the New Year with friends his age, and buys him a lavish new wardrobe including white tie and tails for the occasion.

When the party gets going, the orchestra playing, Norma teaching Joe to tango on the tile floor that Valentino had her put in, Joe asks timorously when

Glenn Close as Norma Desmond. Photo: Joan Marcus. © Museum of the City of New York.

the other guests are due to arrive. "There are no other guests," Norma whispers. Feeling trapped, a furious Joe storms out to welcome the New Year with his cronies. In a splendid theatrical effect that rivals the helicopter rescue in *Miss Saigon* or the underwater lake in *Phantom*, the set rises to reveal the raucous party of young writers and starlets.

Joe is in his element at the party, and he decides to give up the gigolo life he has fallen into, leave the unwholesome house on Sunset Boulevard, and move in with his friend Artie. Artie's girlfriend is Betty, but we have seen from the outset that she is much attracted to Joe—as a man as well as collaborator.

Joe phones Norma to tell her of his decision to have Max pack his things, but the butler answers excitedly saying he cannot talk now because he must tend to Madame. Distraught, she found the razor in Joe's room and has slit her wrists. Joe rushes back to her and tells her that he never meant to hurt her; that she's the only one who's been good to him. Sobbing, her makeup smeared, and with her gauze-wrapped hands, she is truly a pitiful sight, and Joe goes to comfort her with a kiss. Like a cobra she wraps her bandaged arms around him, and in a true coup de théâtre she draws him down on the sofa as the music swells and the lights dim out on Act One.

Act Two opens in the brilliant sunshine. Joe sings the title song, a minor key ballad filling us in on his background and the artificiality of the movie industry. The song, which is in a purposely uncomfortable 5/8, has some of the most cogent lyrics in the show:

... Dreams are not enough to win a war, Out here they're always keeping score, Beneath the tan, the battle rages.	Sunset Boulevard, Headline boulevard Getting there is only the beginning.
	Sunset Boulevard,
Smile a rented smile, fill someone's glass, Kiss someone's wife, kiss someone's ass, We do whatever pays the wages.	Jackpot boulevard, Once you've won you have to go on winning. ...

Norma comes in beaming. She has had a call from the studio and assumes they want to talk to her about her script. They get out the Isotta-Fraschini,[7] and in a scene identical to the one in the film, Norma comes onto the lot. Her big number, "As If We Never Said Goodbye," the climax to the show, is a completely original tour de force. Its melodic motif (see Example B) reminds one of a trapped bird, its heart aflutter.

Example B

[7] In the original London performances no car was used, but for the Los Angeles revision an expensive classic one was purchased. Of course, another was featured in the reopened London show. The magnificent auto, which is tugged on and off stage, always elicited loud applause.

But the creature becomes more assertive as she gets to the release:

I don't want to be alone,	This world's waited long enough,
That's all in the past.	I've come home at last...

Norma's excitement as she builds the song makes it impossible for De Mille to interrupt her and tell her that he will not be shooting her script. She leaves the studio glowing with the thought of her return to the screen without even knowing that it's only her car they want. While Norma is in with De Mille, Joe renews acquaintance with Betty, who has found an old scenario of his that they can work on together. Betty's wholesomeness coupled with Joe's romantic interest in her is played against Norma's self-centered illusions and her desire to smother Joe. The story, urged on by the music, seems to be heading for a showdown.

In most Lloyd-Webber works there are the two obligatory lighter moments, usually to a formulaic reprise to the same melody. The scene in Act One in which Norma has the tailors come to the house to outfit Joe with a new wardrobe had the lyric: "So why not have it all? The lady's paying." Its counterpart in Act Two, in which Norma is being pounded into shape for her comeback, ends with "of course there's bound to be a little suffering." The frivolous diversion works the first time around, but besides being crowded and jejune, the second lyric sounds almost secondhand.

But not so the big love duet, "Too Much in Love to Care," that pours out after Joe and Betty have finished their movie script. In a more contemporary way it works as well as the romantic duet in *Phantom*. It is followed almost immediately by Max's disclosure, sung to the movie theme that was introduced as "New Ways to Dream," that he discovered Norma at sixteen, directed her in her early pictures, married her, and pleaded with her to let him remain as her servant after she divorced him.

But Norma, having discovered that Joe and Betty are in love, phones Betty and tells her that Joe is her gigolo. He overhears the phone conversation and asks Betty to come to the house to see for herself. Of course he is about to do the noble thing, send her back to her wholesome Artie. As soon as a tearful Betty runs from Norma's house, Joe himself decides to leave Hollywood to return to his reporter's job in Ohio. He does shatter Norma's illusions before he goes, telling her that De Mille wanted only her car and that Max had been writing her fan letters all along. Demented as much from the reality that Joe's words have forced her to face as well as the aging face that stares back from her looking glass, and screaming "nobody leaves a star!," she shoots him.

The final scene is patterned closely after the screenplay. Norma will not leave her dressing room, and Max will not allow the police to arrest her and drag her down the stairs. In an ironic switch, Max has arranged for the reporters' cameras to be filming and the lights ablaze as a deranged Norma, impersonating Salome, slithers towards them. She stops halfway down to make the speech taken almost directly from the screenplay that makes it clear Norma has found her own peculiar kind of happy ending:

> I can't go on with this scene. I'm too happy. May I say a few words, Mr. De Mille? I can't tell you how wonderful it is to be back at the studio making a picture. I promise I'll never desert you again. This is my life. It always will be. There's nothing else. Just us and the cameras, and all you wonderful people out there in the dark. And now, Mr. De Mille, I'm ready for my close-up.

Billy Wilder recalled that he rehearsed the final scene using music from Richard Strauss's opera *Salome* as background to Norma's descent. Andrew Lloyd-Webber's selection was his magnificent theme, "With One Look." When Norma reaches the last step, the stage is plunged into darkness.

Andrew Lloyd-Webber's music has often been accused of being unspecific to its subject and to its era. "It doesn't matter if the time is now or B.C., if the place is Argentina or Galilee, if the characters are trains or kitties. If you've seen one Andrew Lloyd Webber musical you've seen them all," wrote *Esquire* critic Martin Worman in 1990.

Some of that kind of criticism is warranted, for the composer has never been reticent about revealing how he recycles melodies from one project for use in another. But the score of *Sunset Boulevard*, for the most part, has the ring of Hollywood of the '60s about it. "There's a restlessness and sourness to it," says Don Black, "and an intensity that has never come from him before. It's much darker and yet full of melody and full of tears." Trevor Nunn agrees: "It has tremendous authority and an extraordinary sense of period. Pastiche, but never in a deriding or mocking fashion."

The reviewers for the *New York Times* agreed with Nunn, saying that "when it is good it is outlandishly good. . . . The score is full of rich and swelling melodies." Necessarily carping about the lyrics, the review went on to say that the "mediocre patches are never permitted to last too long before a surge of melody or a stunning stage effect lifts the musical out of the commonplace and sets it back on its fateful course through the palm-fringed Hollywood night."

Although *Sunset Boulevard* was overlooked in favor of the routine *City of Angels* when it came time for the British awards familiarly known as the "Larrys" (after Sir Laurence Olivier), it swept the 1995 Tony Awards with a total of seven. Glenn Close easily won the Best Actress in a Musical category, while George Hearn, who played Max, won for Featured Actor. John Napier's sets and Andrew Bridge's lighting were foregone conclusions. Don Black and Chris-

Andrew Lloyd-Webber and his wife, Madeline, arrive for the 49th Annual Antoinette Perry (Tony) Awards, June 4, 1995. AP/Wide World Photos.

topher Hampton won for Book and shared additional awards with Lloyd-Webber for Score. With *Sunset*'s winning the final highest accolade, Best Musical, Andrew now had a new statuette to put beside the ones he had won for *Evita*, *Cats*, and *Phantom*. (His only rival was Stephen Sondheim, who, over the years, had taken home Tonys for *Forum*, *Company*, *Follies*, *Night Music*, *Sweeney*, *Into the Woods*, and *Passion*.)

Sunset, with its combination of Grand Guignol and overreacting, is an easy score to deride, and some of the critics did their best, overlooking the fact that through its dramatic story told in large part with dialogue over underscoring, it was bringing Lloyd-Webber into the musical theater, away from his through-composed operatic pretension.

It is certainly Andrew Lloyd-Webber's best, most homogenous score so far, and if it was not to be as popular as *Cats* or *Phantom* in the longevity of its initial run, it nevertheless has in its central role a smashing tour de force that divas for decades to come are going to kill for.

The Road Ahead

S WE TURN OUR BACKS on the twentieth century, we are
tempted to take a sidelong look at perhaps the greatest hundred years
of mankind's advancement in recorded time. Not only has the world
made enormous strides in humanitarian causes, but the advances in science,
medicine, and the exploration of space are staggering. That is not to say we
have become kinder or evince more concern for human suffering or need. Violence and war still seem to be our preferred methods of settling disagreements.

But by harnessing energy, conquering many diseases, mastering transportation,
computerizing information, and creating an industrialized society, we have provided more leisure time for the individual as well as more money and more years
to fill with golden hours. We should be living in a utopian dream world for
human development and the arts. Unfortunately, the use of that time has grown
to be no more valid than it was in the days before this technological explosion.

Movies, which began as kinescopes with the century and quickly became
windows onto a new world, rose to epic proportions and became cinematic
marvels. But in recent years they have, with few exceptions, turned to violence,
technological exercises, and/or commercialism. Only occasionally are films of
lasting artistic value produced. Recordings, which started even earlier with the
wind-up Victrola, quickly passed through scratchy shellac to long-playing vinyl
and tape, and finally arrived at the ideal form: the compact disk, which has
excellent sound, not quite as "rich" as that of the earlier long-playing record,
but still remarkable. CDs are played by a laser beam and mass produced in a
format that can fit more than an hour's worth of music in one's pocket. Their
format has changed the way musical shows are recorded and even the way they
are conceived. The pre-CD musical was directed with an eye to the recording,
so that the high point—musically and dramatically—would come at the end of
the first act. Then the intrigued listener would rush to turn the LP or cassette

over. This often led to a foreshortened and frequently weaker second act. Now, without this break in the recording, composers and librettists aim for a seamless work, climaxing in what is known as the "eleven o'clock number" near the end. Witness Andrew Lloyd-Webber's *Tell Me on a Sunday* or Stephen Sondheim's *Passion*. But interest cannot always be manufactured at will, and although their recordings are turned out by the millions, now most shows, even those of modest success are geared to the least common denominator, hardly remembered even by their aficionados a few months after their release.

Television, which did not surface commercially until the middle of the century, has saturated the land by now, and even the kindest critic refers to the myriad hours of soaps, sitcoms, and talk shows by Eliot's prescient title, *The Waste Land*.

But even though publishing faces a threat from frivolous computer surfing, there are still books, worthwhile books. There are still plays—although fewer than there used to be—whose dramatic force can send powerful messages far beyond the auditorium. And there are still musicals whose combination of character development, story, and song can reach to the very center of our souls.

One worries about the future of books in the new century as the population as a whole, and especially the young, give up reading in favor of having a story visualized, often animated, and invariably predigested for them via the television screen or Disney.

By contrast, the world of musical theater—with Broadway, West End, off-Broadway, fringe, and regional efforts constantly expanding—is, if not in the healthiest creative shape, burgeoning to elephantine proportions and eclipsing serious stage drama. It is a tragedy, but in recent decades the popularity of the musical has caused the straight dramatic play to take a nosedive.

First to go were the drawing-room and the romantic comedies, which adapted easily to TV. Then the hard-hitting crime or preachy political dramas that were the stock in trade of the stage in the '30s, '40s, and '50s found a far more congenial medium in the cinema—either *noir* or *verité*: their realism is better suited to the big screen. That left the stage only the drama of ideas, revelation, or surrealistic fantasy often beyond the scope of what would interest the general public. Recent examples are *Angels in America, Three Tall Women, Arcadia*, and *Six Degrees of Separation*.

The roster of serious playwrights that only a generation ago had included Maxwell Anderson, Robert Anderson, S. N. Behrman, Philip Barry, John van Druten, Lillian Hellman, William Inge, George S. Kaufman, Anita Loos, Arthur Miller, Eugene O'Neill, Sam and Bella Spewack, Samuel Taylor, Thornton Wilder, and Tennessee Williams, among many others, has dwindled to Tony Kushner, David Mamet, Terrence McNally, John Guare, Edward Albee, Tom Stoppard, and a handful more. In 1961 of the twenty longest-running Broadway hits only six were musicals; while in the fall of 2000 only six nonmusicals were to be found there—and none of these (*Betrayal*, *Copenhagen*, *Dirty Blonde*, *Proof*, *The Dinner Party*, and *The Tale of the Allergist's Wife*) could hope for a run or profits comparable to those of any of the twenty blockbuster musicals whose ringing box office cash registers were pleasing Broadway managers. Whether for better or worse, musicals have developed more staying power than nonmusicals, and, as we know, a show only stays open if there are audiences to fill the seats every night.

As I hope the earlier chapters in this book have made clear, it is not the musical of the "golden age" of the '50s and '60s that is causing this boom; the largest part of the ever-increasing revenue comes from a new form—a hybrid built on the technical achievements of the last generation and geared to an audience that seeks "entertainment" above all. If the musical of the last fifty years has often transformed itself into a behemoth that seems too large to fit on the stage, that is also the fault of a society impatient with the middle ground, one that has seen everything and wants everything it witnesses to be the grandest and the biggest. If, on the other hand, what I call "clique" musicals— *Passion*, *In Trousers*, *Chronicle of a Death Foretold*, *Parade*—are too small or parochial to be self-sustaining, that is the fault of rising costs in the nonsubsidized yet full-sized theater.

The cry is that today's musical seems to lack the simpler, "hummable" songs that Irving Berlin, Richard Rodgers, or Jerry Herman turned out in profusion, songs that the average theatergoers sing on their way out of the theater.

For the most part that is true, although today's composer looks to another muse and seeks to fit the song into the drama. With rare exceptions, we don't get flowing melodies that transverse several keys like the Kern–Hammerstein "All the Things You Are," or song/dances that bombard us with fresh rhythms as Bernstein–Sondheim's "America" did. But occasionally the subjects of this book can shake us up so much that we forget about listening for hit tunes, as when Rice and Lloyd-Webber produce a musical on a political maverick like Evita Peron, or Sondheim makes us take a good look at the spoiled fruits of the American Dream as in *Pacific Overtures* or *Assassins*.

Andrew Lloyd-Webber gives us many distinguished melodies; would that he would see fit to allow them to enter our psyches by themselves instead of assaulting us with them. As for Stephen Sondheim, the former master of understatement, his use of aborted nervous motifs in *Sunday in the Park with George* and *Into the Woods* seems to have given way to the expansive and repetitive melodic line. It is as if he has caught an idea from his British colleague and seems, at least in *Passion*, to be running with it.

Beyond the works of Sondheim and Lloyd-Webber, the sameness and immensity now found in our musical theater is our own fault, for we go to a musical for the most part to have a good time, to indulge our urge for the predigested, the exotic, or the opulent, and are unwilling to let our musical ears expand far beyond the comfortable and familiar. The musical of today has changed greatly from its predecessor of a generation ago, but we and it still need to change more before it can recapture the vital place it held in our cultural lives of half a century earlier and not be considered merely the diversionary splurge.

Influenced mainly by Lloyd-Webber, Schönberg-Boublil, Charles Strouse, Martin Charnin, or Richard Maltby, the current new[1] musical's subject matter, with the exception of Sondheim's works and the more daring works of Kander and Ebb, is mostly accessible or homey. There are no provocative musicals now like *The Cradle Will Rock* or *The Golden Apple*, and only an occasional one dealing with today's generation, like *Hair* or *Rent*. As costs have risen producers have had to play safe. During the 1990s the musical theater on Broadway and the West End consisted mostly of adaptations from movies, geared to a family audience (*Big, Grease, Beauty and the Beast, State Fair, Victor/Victoria*); dance shows, again family oriented (*Cats, Starlight Express, Bring in 'da Noise*); revivals, again still suitable for everyone (*Forum, Show Boat, The King and I*); some shows with familiar music (*Swinging on a Star, Smokey Joe's Cafe, Jolson*); and a few entrenched blockbusters that may originally have been for more mature audiences but whose style has so broadened after years of performances that they have lost whatever bite they once had (*Les Misérables, Miss Saigon, The Phantom of the Opera*).

Yet there is more than a glimmer of hope on the horizon, a hope that stems in a certain way from the traditional "royalty" of the American musical. Two names, vital in earlier chapters in this book, are involved: the Princes and the Rodgerses.

Harold Prince, who has always been vitally interested in promotiong new works for the theater, and his children, Daisy and Charles, are trying to rescue the new American musical in an era when people who care bemoan the state of the theater but do little to help it survive. Harold Prince seems to have passed on his fixation with new musicals to Daisy, who is in a way a self-styled composer-scout. When she hears intriguing work in cabarets, coffeehouses, or concerts, she introduces herself to the artist and arranges for him or her to join a group that meets at her home in Manhattan where they perform songs for one another. Charles Prince is a conductor who frequently conducts concerts of new theater music. Daisy and Charles call their group Musical Theater Works and offer young and qualified composers, lyricists, and librettists the opportunity to

---

[1] At the present writing, Broadway boasts a bumper crop of revivals, including *Annie Get Your Gun, Cabaret, Chicago, Kiss Me, Kate,* and *The Music Man*. There are also what I call the "pseudo-revivals," shows that celebrate an earlier era, like *Fosse, Swing,* and *Saturday Night Fever*.

have their work produced at Musical Theater Works' eighty-three-seat theater on Lafayette Street opposite the Joseph Papp Public Theater in the East Village of New York City.

One of the group's composers is Jason Robert Brown, whose *Parade*, a quasi-opera about a Jewish factory owner lynched in Atlanta, had a libretto by Pulitzer Prize–winner Alfred Uhry. Mr. Brown conducted the work while it was on the road. The show won many awards, including the Tony for Best Musical in 1998, but still had a brief frun.

Perhaps the best known of the composers in the group is John Michael LaChiusa, a prolific and polished composer, who, like the others, is not yet popular with the general public because the themes of his works are often serious and forbidding. In the 1999–2000 season he produced two astonishing works, *Marie Christine* and *The Wild Party*.

The Wild Party was also the foundation and story of a second musical written by another member of the group, Andrew Lippa. Unfortunately, as both musicals appeared within months of each other, they seemed to cancel each other out in the public's mind, and each had a curtailed run.

Adam Guetell has Broadway lineage. He is the grandson of Richard Rodgers, and his musicological genes must have been transmitted directly to him through his mother, Mary Rodgers, the composer's daughter, herself no stranger to Broadway musicals—having written the music for *Once Upon a Mattress*, *Hot Spot*, and other shows. As the composer of *Floyd Collins*, Mr. Guetell has won much praise.

Besides Mr. Guetell, Mr. LaChiusa, Mr. Brown, and Mr. Lippa, the group also includes John Bucchino, Ricky Ian Gordon, Jeanine Tesori, Kirsten Childs, Zina Goldrich, March Heisler, Grant Sturtale, and Glenn Slater.

Talking of this worthwhile project and his longtime friend Hal Prince, Stephen Sondheim told *New York Times* reporter Robin Pogrebin that Mr. Prince was "one of the very few champions of new work in the commercial theater. New writers are interested in expanding the possibilities and most musical theater producers are interested in shrinking them."

But we must not close the door on Sondheim and Lloyd-Webber, both of whom are still capable of turning out trenchant musicals and successful enough for the public acceptance of their works to be of secondary concern. Some critics believe Sondheim is in decline, that his shows under the aegis of Harold Prince were superior to the ones with libretti by Lapine and Weidman.

"It was Hal who brought Steve into theatrical complexity, and he pushed that button well before Steve himself did," says Thomas Z. Shepard. "It was Hal who created the world in which Steve would blossom as a complex lyricist-composer. Hal had the visions of just how dark one could make a piece if one so chose, Hal, who was willing to be so complicated, so Gothic, so multidimensional.

Whether the Prince–Sondheim collaborations were successes or failures, they had an adult theatricality plus the supposition that they were being performed for an intelligent audience who were willing, even eager, to be challenged. These Prince–Sondheim works are, in my opinion, far richer—not necessarily better—but certainly more complex than anything Sondheim created prior to his collaboration with Prince. Hal has a profound respect for what 'works.' Hal has an intrinsic understanding and respect for the role of the theatrical director. And it was most certainly Hal who laid out this great big yellow brick road for Steve to run on. This road led in many directions, but it seems to me that all the destinations were carefully put in place by Hal Prince."

Many believe that after Prince, nobody is able to naysay a Sondheim idea. "Everybody's afraid of Sondheim now," reported a former colleague who preferred not to be named. "Nobody will quite admit it, now that he's a national treasure. He's a god. He gets awards from everywhere. He's filthy rich. Madonna records him as well as opera stars. He runs the gamut, so who's going to fuck around with him now?"

Many. The critics for one,[2] even though Sondheim says he never reads them and their opinions are printed after the fact. His show in progress is a collaboration with John Weidman.

"I've been working sporadically and now will get back to it intensely on something I've wanted to do since I was twenty-two years old," Sondheim told interviewer Sheridan Morley excitedly. "I read a biography of a man named Wilson Mizner, an American who, with his brother Addison Mizner, lived from the 1880s to the 1930s. They both died within three months of each other in the 1930s and had a minor cultural impact on the United States.

"The best known aspect of their influence was the Florida Boom of the '20s. Addison was an architect, one the very few Frank Lloyd Wright admired, and Florida today with all that Spanish style is very much a result of his influence . . . Wilson was an even more fascinating character than Addison. He was a con man and the most successful playwright on Broadway at one point, and he managed the welterweight champion of the world. He was a great womanizer and he prospected for gold, and I can go on and on. He was more than a jack of all trades—it was more than trades—lives. And on top of it he was probably—next to Dorothy Parker—the greatest wit of the twentieth century, aphoristic wit," he added.

---

[2] Sondheim was "shocked at the savagery of the reviews" for his *Getting Away with Murder*, a play he wrote with George Furth that was forced to close in 1996 after two weeks. "We had a great deal of fun writing it. The audiences liked it, and it was wonderfully directed by Jack O'Brien and very well acted. One of [the critics] who sort of liked it said I should write under a pseudonym. If I write under my own name they have this expectation."

Sondheim had discussed the biography, *The Legendary Mizners* by Alva Johnston, with Hammerstein back in the early 1950s. It was while his mentor was putting the finishing touches on *Me and Juliet* in 1953 that the book first appeared. His interest in the project seems to have remained intense for the next three years until David Merrick, for purposes of comparison, sent Sondheim a script by Sam Behrman of Irving Berlin's unproduced musical, *Sentimental Guy*, which was based on the same book. Sondheim, then in his early twenties, was bitterly disappointed that the musicalization of these tandem lives had been preempted, for he had aspirations as a librettist as well as a composer-lyricist in his youth and had already produced a detailed scheme of scenes and numbers, using Wilson Mizner's experience as a balladeer. He even wrote half a song for the boys' mother called "Afternoon in Benicia"—the Mizners' home town in California.

More than four decades later, when the project finally got going again, it was interrupted once more when John Weidman hurried to ready his libretto of *Big*. But once that show was launched Sondheim came back to the project.

Certainly drollery will not be lacking because the book it is based on is full of Wilson's pranks and bon mots. But the story also has a dark humor, an inexorability, that is—strange to say—not unlike the relentlessness of *Passion*. The main difference in theme here is that this is one of fraternal connection and responsibility, rather than romantic love. Addison, the poetic architectural genius who crests with the Florida land boom of 1925, will be destroyed when Wilson's overreaching topples their empire. Yes, as Sondheim says, it will be funny, but one can expect tragedy always to be waiting in the wings. It is hard to see how *Wise Guys* can but turn out to be more than two steps away from the bitter jests that abound in *Sweeney Todd* or *A Little Night Music*, which Hal Prince termed "whipped cream with knives underneath." Even Sondheim presaged its seriousness when he referred to it as "my *Citizen Kane*."[3]

With every new theatrical work of his eagerly anticipated by an international audience, lately Sondheim seems to be inching his way toward Hollywood. But Sondheim denies that he would desert the stage for La-La Land, even though he was brought up on movies. "I've always loved movies and I've had a couple of movie experiences," he said, probably referring to the disasters of *Forum* and

---

[3] Preparatory to what looked like a Broadway opening in mid-2000, *Wise Guys* was given a New York Theater Workshop production on October 29, 1999. The orchestrations were by Jonathan Tunick, and Paul Gemigniani conducted. Victor Garber and Nathan Lane portrayed Wilson and Addison Mizner respectively. The rumor was that Sam Mendes, the esteemed director of Britain's Donmar Warehouse, who had mounted fine productions of such Sondheim musicals as *Assassins Company*, and *Passion*, had returned abroad with the musical to continue working on the project. One still feels that it is merely a question of time until the work will be presented to the public.

A Little Night Music. "You know, in the theater you're your own boss. Nobody can tamper with it unless you give permission. Of course you compromise and work in collaboration with the director and your actors and even sometimes the producer. But in Hollywood, you sell your material and it is, after all, the director's medium, and the director and producer and sometimes the stars do anything they want with your material. You take your money and you go home, so you don't have control of your own work unless you happen to be the director as well—which I do not want to be, and can't be. For a writer, movies are not as rewarding as the theater, even though it's more difficult to get things on in the theater, and you spend two years and it may close in a night. At least when you do a movie, it's there for ever and ever. But from the point of writing satisfaction there's no comparison."

One can understand his point—for, actually, he is using the film medium to expand his horizons. "When Warren [Beatty] did this movie of *Dick Tracy*, he wanted me to do the background, but I didn't want to spend the time because I'm a slow writer," Sondheim said. "But I said I would do some songs, so I did five songs, and I thought it would be a new experience for me to work with a true pop artist like Madonna, who found the stuff very difficult. The songs are not that difficult to sing, but she is used to a different kind of singing and a different way of approaching songs, so it was educational for her as well as for me." The project turned out very well, winning him the Academy Award for his song "Sooner or Later" and producing a recording that went high up into the charts.

Sondheim followed that with several songs for the popular success *The Birdcage.* Besides the Mizner brothers musical, the future holds a movie of *Into the Woods*, for which Sondheim is contracted to write no fewer than four new songs. It was scheduled to go into production in winter 1996 with the Muppets as the fairy-tale creatures and an all-star cast that is rumored to include Danny DeVito as the Giant, with Robin Williams, Cher, Goldie Hawn, and Steve Martin as the voices of the other characters. At present it is still on hold. Farther down the line, a film adaptation of *Sweeney Todd* was mentioned, to be directed by Tim (*Batman*) Burton. But these projects are still, at this writing, in the talking stages.

Sondheim's work broke some records in 1996. The year was a banner one for him, in spite of its spring flop of *Getting Away with Murder*. The season was sweetened by the acclaim accorded the revival of *Forum*. Earlier, he shattered his own West End record by having three shows playing simultaneously in revised versions, thereby tying Andrew Lloyd-Webber's record. *Company* and *A Little Night Music* had taken London by storm and were firmly entrenched before *Passion* opened. Additionally, the film of the Broadway production of *Passion* was presented on PBS in the autumn.

Enormous satisfaction comes to Sondheim from his work with young people. Long passionate about teaching, he initiated the Dramatists Guild's Young Playwrights Festival in 1982 and in 1990 accepted the signal honor (and the considerable responsibility) of being the first Cameron Mackintosh Professor of Theatre at Oxford. "They had been trying for fifty years to get some sort of drama department going," said Sheridan Morley, recalling his venerable university before this breakthrough seminar. "I remember campaigning in my days as a student there for a Drama Department, and they said, 'Oh, no, we don't do that kind of thing here at all.' They thought the students would waste their time doing plays."

Sondheim had never taught formally before he began with a preselected group of thirteen composers, lyricists, and librettists. "Some were partnered already and some were solo writers," he was to recall. "One of the things I'd done was try to select as ecumenical a group as possible. We had everything from cabaret writers to rock writers to classically trained writers to musical comedy. All disciplines."

In running the class Sondheim sensed he had to encourage free discourse. "And so, within twenty-four hours I got them to trust me and each other enough so that they could criticize each other freely, because I didn't want to be the one who says . . . 'I think you should do this or that.' I believe in the Socratic method of asking questions rather than making statements . . . making suggestions so that they wouldn't feel competitive. One of the problems with musical theater is competition. I didn't want them tightening up."

The class turned out to be a triumph that did not evaporate in a single term. It grew to become the core group of a collective called The Mercury Workshop, which now numbers over thirty writers who support each other's work. Headed by Edward Hardy, who was a member of the original group and who has gone on to write the libretto of the new Schönberg-Boublil musical *Martin Guare*, the group has workshops and scheduled meetings. "They support each other's work. But it grew out of this class," Sondheim crows, "which is the thing I'm proudest of."

Sondheim's interest in fostering musical theater bore tremendous fruit in 1996. He was instrumental in helping Jonathan Larson, the author/composer/lyricist of *Rent*, get a Richard Rodgers Studio Production Award when he was writing his rock musical based on Puccini's *La Bohème*. As Larson rewrote and rewrote, Sondheim was ready with suggestions and encouragement, and when Larson called with a problem, Sondheim said he "gave him my usual five cents worth of advice."

Rent opened downtown to splendid notices, then transferred to Broadway, and international productions were soon mounted. Now, four years into its run, it continues to garner raves and audiences worldwide. As theater-watchers know, the circumstances of its creation were even more lamentable than the story of its frail heroine. Larson, only thirty-five, tragically died of an aortic aneurysm after the final dress rehearsal, his death snuffing out what seemed to be the most promising hope for the future of musical theater in America. Sondheim's influence on this extraordinary composer is only now coming to be known. But it is another example of how Sondheim, in the role of teacher and adviser, is having a profound impact on the musical theater apart from his own work.

Andrew Lloyd-Webber has a similar bearing on musicals in his own country. He too is passionate about helping fledglings in his field. He is the main sponsor of Britain's National Youth Musical Theatre Trust, a beneficent organization that has influenced musical composition in the United Kingdom by offering scholarships. Beyond that, he somewhat resembles a "renaissance man," being involved in a variety of projects, architectural, artistic, theatrical, gastronomic— he writes a pseudonymous food column and has recently invented a parlor horserace game. Knighted in 1992 and admitted to the Peerage in 1998, Lord Lloyd-Webber seems to juggle all his interests with seemingly perfect aplomb.

As the founder of the Open Churches Trust, he created a simple but revolutionary nonprofit organization financed with £1.5 million of his money. There are certain similarities between Victorian churches and Andrew Lloyd-Webber musicals. They are romantic. They are emotionally direct. They are visual extravaganzas. The Trust has opened nearly fifty historic religious buildings to the public during nonservice hours. Britain, with more than ten thousand medieval churches, has struggled for decades to combat the toll that arson, theft, vandalism, and high insurance premiums have taken on these landmarks. Financial hardship and security concerns have resulted in the locking of about half of the country's six thousand most architecturally significant religious buildings.

In early 1994, when Lloyd-Webber found himself with some spare time in central England, near Manchester, he wished to indulge his passion for visiting historic Victorian architecture, but soon he was reduced to frustration and anger when the doors to historic churches, what he calls "the country's greatest unsung asset," were locked.

Determined to have these churches stay open even when no services are being held, Andrew's Trust, which is administered by Lloyd-Webber father-in-law, Brigadier Adam Guerdon, gives them money to hire caretakers and also helps them to buy hidden television cameras and other security devices. The theory, which seems to be holding so far, is that a busy-looking occupied building is less vulnerable than a locked vacant one.

"Architecture and art were my first loves," the composer explains, and he is noted for having outbid several foreign art collectors in order to keep world-famous paintings and statuary in his homeland. He owns one of the world's great collections of Victorian and Pre-Raphaelite art and frequently lends his work out to museums so the public may share in the enjoyment. He says that eventually the collection will have to go into a foundation, as he believes it is unfair to strap any of his five children with the job of "looking after the lot. I'm not a great believer in inherited wealth. I didn't have any inherited money at all apart from the £3,000 my grandmother left me."

From those days of his toy theater at Harrington Court, it was obvious that he would involve himself in the production as well as the creative end of musicals. After all, his idol, composer Richard Rodgers was also a first class producer.

Whistle Down the Wind[4] and *The Beautiful Game*, Lloyd-Webber's latest shows, were both giving successful performances in London in 2000. The former is the story of a group of farm children who protect a man they find in their barn. The man *may* be an escaped criminal, but the children assume he is Jesus because of his manner and the wounds—bullet holes or stigmata?—on his feet. At the end of the musical they stand in the way of the grown-ups and allow him to escape capture or interrogation by a hostile adult world.

This musical returns the composer to his and Tim Rice's naive world of *Joseph* and *Jesus Christ Superstar* and, even before that, their *The Likes of Us*. It has a preponderance of songs for young adolescents, an area in which Lloyd-Webber can compose beautifully and guilelessly. The show contains a stirring choral anthem called "The Vaults of Heaven," a song for the leading character, "A Kiss Is a Terrible Thing To Waste," and a lovely ballad that is the title song.

Of course, with a large cast of townspeople and children it requires a big stage and a large theater before it can open. "It's intriguing to think that a new show of mine cannot find a home on Broadway because so many old shows [many of which are his own] are still running," he told a reporter in the summer of 1996. "When I started up, people were tearing down big theatres. Now there aren't enough."

The Beautiful Game, which opened in Autumn 2000, has been enthusiastically received. Its book and lyrics are by Ben Elton, a well-known British writer of comedy. Elton, whose work was known to the composer, had been invited to dinner by Lord and Lady Lloyd-Webber. After the meal, Andrew confided that he was interested in having Ben write some comic lines for a new staging of *Starlight Express*, but Elton refused the offer with: "If it ain't broke, don't fix it." At a subsequent meeting they came up with a story set in Belfast between 1969 and 1972 concerning the fortunes of a group of young men and young women centered on a local youth football (soccer) team. These young people have the

---

[4] This show closed January 6, 2001, and is not expected to come to the United States. It had a London run of two and a half years and did not recoup its investment.

misfortune to come of age at the beginning of a time of terrible trouble in Northern Ireland, and the drama follows their efforts to live their lives against a backdrop of ever-increasing sectarian division and violence. Some of the characters are drawn into the conflict; others stand aside wanting only to be allowed to get on with their lives in peace.

Both of the teenagers involved in the story of Father O'Donnell's football team, Del and John, have enough talent to make it big. Their girlfriends, Mary and Christine, are dreaming about what to do with their lives and concerned about the way their world is changing. Yearning for a time they can live in peace, they all learn that to escape from bigotry and intolerance will take all the courage they can muster.

The show has received excellent reviews and seems to be settling down for a long run at the Cambridge Theatre. But almost more important to the history of the theater is Andrew Lloyd-Webber's announcement in early 2000 that he— the Really Useful Group (RUG)—was buying the Stoll-Moss theater chain: ten theaters including Her Majesty's, home for the last decade to *The Phantom of the Opera*; Theater Royal, Drury Lane, one of London's largest; and The Palladium. Control of some of the group like the Queens and the Gielgud on Shaftsbury Avenue will pass to Cameron Mackintosh in 2006 as part of a preexisting arrangement, but for the time being they are Lloyd-Webber's property. If one adds to these many venues the New London, where *Cats* holds forth seemingly "now and forever," and the Palace, home of *Les Misérables*, Lloyd-Webber is one of the largest theatre owners in the world.

Like Sondheim, Lloyd-Webber has lately been gravitating toward Hollywood, where the cinematic version of *Evita*, starring Madonna, was released in 1996. It signaled a return to the collaboration between Tim Rice and the composer, who turned out "You Must Love Me" so that the film would contain new material and thereby be eligible for an Academy Award. As for the works in progress, The Really Useful Film Company is co-producing a multimillion-dollar movie version of *Cats*, and Warner Brothers and the group are ready to go ahead with a cinema version of *Phantom*. Films of *Joseph* and *Starlight Express* are in the discussion stage at several studios.

Lloyd-Webber's cinematic works will probably be received with the same critical disdain that has greeted most of his works for the stage. Critics overlook the fact that he has an uncanny brilliance about what will strike the public's fancy, and a great sense of bringing it to them at *the right time*. He also has an impresario's ability to draw the public to his musicals. He knew, for example, that a show like *Cats*, with its esoteric T. S. Eliot poetry, would never attract a following unless it was dance and spectacle and had a song that everybody knew and was waiting for—qualities that would drag them in.

In the past a show like *Cats* was called "a Happening," and Lloyd-Webber sensed it was time to revive that form. No matter what the term and the opinion of the intelligentsia, many of whom would never attend a Lloyd-Webber opus, he is the musician who has probably given more joy to more people in the theater than any other living composer.

The English-singing musical theater, as we have noted, is a far cry from the popular music of today. There is a huge disparity between rock and show music. Broadway and the West End are not happy with the outré, preferring nostalgia. Even though *Grease* and revues like *Smokey Joe's Cafe* and *Five Guys Named Moe* continue to succeed with 1950s-style rock, and theatergoers supported the Motown-style songs of *Dreamgirls* and the light funk of *The Wiz* in previous decades, they did not start any trend. Rock blossomed (one cannot say flourished) in the would-be anthems of *Jesus Christ Superstar*, *Godspell*, and *Joseph*, which were specifically aimed at proselytizing a young audience and had the box office assurance of church groups.

Tommy, a full-fledged rock opera, is also a special case. It was a huge hit when it first appeared as an album decades ago, it had already been made into a film, and it had exciting special effects. Back in the late '60s, *Hair*, which had a startling unsavoriness with its draft dodgers and drug-using iconoclasts, seemed like the breakthrough that would let the two camps join hands—its story featured children on the periphery of society—but again, no one took up the gauntlet. *Rent*, although it is very loosely based on Puccini's *La Bohème*, doesn't really bank on a quarter century of familiarity, and its tale of struggling artists, drug-users, and those who are HIV positive doesn't revolve around special effects but does empathize with those who are outside the mainstream today. The musical style is familiar, and the lyrics and libretto are surely of today. It is *Rent*'s great success and acceptance as a masterwork in both the United States and England that might encourage more young artists to write for the stage.

As for the two great artists who are the subjects of this book, one must conclude that if ticket sales or run of the show is the measure, Lloyd-Webber stands as a colossus among modern musical theater composers. None is as successful as he is. But if critical praise is the yardstick, then Sondheim, his only rival, is king of the hill.

It is curious that Sondheim, who began in the Hammerstein heart-on-the-sleeve tradition, abandoned it in his maturity for what he perceived as the honesty of ambivalence. Lloyd-Webber, ironically, once he got beyond the kind of libretto Tim Rice was creating, which demanded a rock score, opted for the Hammerstein and Rodgers kind of outsized romanticism. Both forms are still valid, and both Stephen Sondheim and Andrew Lloyd-Webber only improve in their ability to handle them with each succeeding show.

Chronology

Year	Sondheim	Lloyd-Webber	US Musicals	UK Musicals	World
1930	Stephen Sondheim born March 22, New York City. Parents: Janet Fox ("Foxy"), designer, and Herbert Sondheim, successful 7th Avenue dress manufacturer.		The Gershwins' *Strike Up the Band, Girl Crazy* with Merman in debut.	A dreary season. Only Coward's *Private Lives,* Rodgers & Hart's *Evergreen.*	Depression. Gandhi and civil disobedience. Photoflash is invented.
1931			The Gershwins' *Of Thee I Sing* wins Pulitzer Prize. *The Band Wagon, The Ziegfeld Follies, The Cat and the Fiddle.*	Jack Buchanan and Elsie Randolph rival the Astaires in *Stand Up and Sing.* Gracie Fields in *Walk This Way.*	Worldwide depression continues. Britain suspends gold payments.
1932			*Music In the Air* (Kern-Hammerstein). *Walk a Little Faster,* Vernon Duke. *Gay Divorce,* Porter. *Through the Years,* with music by Vincent Youmans. *Face the Music,* with score by Berlin.	Evelyn Laye in *Helen.* Coward's *Words and Music.*	Roosevelt is elected US President. Lindbergh kidnapping. Death of Ziegfeld. Debut of Shirley Temple.
1933			*As Thousands Cheer,* with a Berlin score.	*Nymph Errant and Gay Divorce*—Porter sweeps the West End.	Hitler becomes Chancellor of Germany.
1934	Begins picking out tunes at the piano.		Spectacle rules the day: *Revenge with Music* (Schwartz and Dietz); *The Great Waltz.* Porter's *Anything Goes* is a smash hit. *New Faces* introduces Henry Fonda and Imogene Coca.	Vivian Ellis, *Jill Darling* and *Mr. Whittington.* Coward's *Conversation Piece.*	Hitler become Fuhrer. Debut of the *Thin Man* series in films.

1935		The Gershwins' Porgy and Bess.	Ivor Novello's Glamorous Night. Tonight at 8:30 with Coward and Lawrence.	Saar restored to Germany. Swing Era begins. Jazz of Negro or Jewish origin banned from German airwaves. Garbo in Anna Karenina.
1936	First piano lessons. Attends his first musical: The White Horse Inn.	On Your Toes (direction by George Abbott). Kurt Weill's Johnny Johnson.	Careless Rapture: Novello. This'll Make You Whistle with Jack Buchanan. Anything Goes with Jeanne Aubert.	German Troops enter the Rhine; the Rome-Berlin Axis. Abdication of Edward VIII. Frank Lloyd Wright architecture is in demand. BBC begins TV service.
1937	Discontinues piano lessons.	George Gershwin dies in July. Pins and Needles, labor organization revue. I'd Rather Be Right, a topical revue. Hooray for What by Arlen and Harburg.	Crest of the Wave, by Ivor Novello. Me and My Girl by Noel Gay. On Your Toes, by Rodgers & Hart, is the hit of London.	German aggression worsens. British continue policy of appeasement. Spanish Civil War. Paris World's Fair. Lost Horizon (film).
1938		Rodgers & Hart's I Married an Angel. Hellzapoppin, Knickerbocker Holiday.	Coward's Operette is only fairly successful.	Germany annexes Austria. The New York World's Fair. The Lambeth Walk latest dance craze. Disney's Snow White and the Seven Dwarfs.
1939		Too Many Girls, Rodgers & Hart.	The Dancing Years by Ivor Novello has great success and will run for 5 years. Pop song "Roll Out the Barrel" is an enormous hit.	Germany invades Poland. Gone with the Wind (film).
1940	Parents divorce. Father marries Alicia Babé. Mother has custody of Stephen. He is sent to N.Y. Military Academy.	Louisiana Purchase, Panama Hattie, Pal Joey.	Mostly revivals. Chu-Chin-Chow. New Faces of 1940 features "A Nightingale Sang in Berkley Square."	Churchill is prime minister. Fall of France. Films: Fantasia and Chaplin's The Great Dictator.

Year	Sondheim	Lloyd-Webber	US Musicals	UK Musicals	World
1941	Studies organ at the military academy. Leaves the academy after one year.		Broadway mounts escape or army shows. *Lady in the Dark* is the only solid hit. Cole Porter's *Let's Face It*.	Revivals continue.	Lend-lease. December: US enters the war after Pearl Harbor. Both US and UK declare war on Japan. Film: *Citizen Kane*.
1942	Enters George School, Newtown, Pennsylvania.		Rodgers & Hart's last new show, *By Jupiter*. Irving Berlin's *This Is the Army*.	*Waltz Without End*, Ivor Novello.	The atomic age begins. Germans reach Stalingrad. Magnetic tape recording. Film: *Mrs. Miniver*.
1943	Becomes friendly with James Hammerstein.		*One Touch of Venus*. R & H's *Oklahoma!* revolutionizes the musical. Hammerstein also hits with *Carmen Jones*.	*The Lisbon Story*. A touring company of Irving Berlin's *This Is the Army*.	Germans surrender North Africa; Mussolini falls. Films: *Stage Door Canteen*; *For Whom the Bell Tolls*. Sinatra is the idol of teenagers.
1944	Another year of piano study.	Timothy Miles Bindon Rice born November 13.	Porter's *Mexican Hayride*. *Bloomer Girl*, with a rich Arlen score. *On the Town*, the first Broadway work of Comden & Green, with music by Leonard Bernstein.	Very little of lasting value.	Normandy landing. FDR's fourth term. Olivier's *Henry V*.
1945	Writes musical of campus life called *By George!* (3 performances). Presents it to O. Hammerstein, who criticizes it and requests that SS write 4 musicals to learn the technique.		No musicals of lasting value except R & H's *Carousel*. First collaboration of Lerner & Loewe (*The Day Before Spring*)	Operettas: *Three Waltzes*, *Gay Rosalinda*. Also *Under Your Hat* and Coward's *Sigh No More*.	Germany surrenders; FDR dies; US drops atomic bomb; Japan surrenders. Bebop becomes a worldwide craze.

1946	Enters William College, Williamstown, Mass., as a liberal arts major. Studies with Robert Barrow.		*Call Me Mister*, a mustering-out revue. *Annie Get Your Gun*, Irving Berlin's most acclaimed score. *Night and Day*, film of Cole Porter's life.	*Big Ben* by Vivian Ellis. *Pacific 1860* by Coward, with Mary Martin.	First meeting of the UN. Xerography developed. British Arts council is inaugurated. BBC's Third Programme begins transmitting.
1947	January: Acting role as part of Chorus in *Antigone*. March: Role in *Trade Names*, a play by Peggy Lamson, as well as in Wilder's *Skin of Our Teeth*. May: Plays Garth in Maxwell Anderson's *Winterset*; publishes three short stories in *The Purple Cow*, literary magazine. In his academic field, he composes a piano sonata and a piano suite. Summer: Works as a "gofer" on the R & H production of *Allegro*.		US theater finding its voice with *Allegro*, *Brigadoon*, *Finian's Rainbow*, *High Button Shoes*, and *Street Scene*.	American musicals take London: *Oklahoma!* and *Annie Get Your Gun* are big hits.	Truman Doctrine; Marshall Plan; independence for India. *A Streetcar Named Desire*. Beginning of the Edinburgh Festival.
1948	Writes more stories for *Purple Cow*. May 7: Writes book and lyrics and collaborates with Josiah Horton on music for *Phinney's Rainbow*, a revue, which is presented at the school. Three songs from show are published by BMI. May 28: Featured in *Night Must Fall*. December: Acts in *Waiting for Lefty*.	Andrew Lloyd-Webber born March 22, London. Parents: William S. Lloyd Webber, Professor of Music, Royal College, and Jean Hermione Johnstone, also a musician and teacher of piano.	Porter's *Kiss Me, Kate*. Musicals aiming for charm: *Lend an Ear* and *Where's Charley?*	The American invasion continues with *Brigadoon* and *Lute Song*. One British product: *Cage Me a Peacock*.	End of the British mandate in Palestine. In art, it is the era of Jackson Pollock and Henry Moore. Film: Olivier's *Hamlet*.

Year	Sondheim	Lloyd-Webber	US Musicals	UK Musicals	World
1949	March: *All That Glitters* (musical version of *Beggar on Horseback*), the first of OH's four assigned shows, 4 performances, 5 of its songs published by BMI. Another year of piano study. Adapts Maxwell Anderson's play *High Tor* (2nd of OH's assigned shows). Show never produced. Adapts *Mary Poppins* stories as musical. Never completes 3rd of OH's assigned shows.		The big shows take over: *Miss Liberty*, *South Pacific*, *Regina*, *Gentlemen Prefer Blondes*.	Ivor Novello's *King's Rhapsody*; also *Tough at the Top*. Coward's *Ace of Clubs*.	NATO established. China becomes Communist. Arthur Miller's *Death of a Salesman*.
1950	February: Plays Cassius in production of *Julius Caesar*. May: Contributes "No Sad Songs for Me" to college revue: *Where To From Here?* June: Graduates magna cum laude from Williams. Wins Hutchinson Prize. Summer: Apprentice at the Westport County Playhouse. Moves in with his father in NYC; studies with avant-gardist Milton Babbitt.		Berlin's hit, *Call Me Madam*. Frank Loesser's *Guys and Dolls*.	American hit: *Carousel*. British musical: *Take it from Here*. Revue: *Dear Miss Phoebe and Blue For a Boy*	The Korean War. UN building completed. Menotti's opera *The Consul* runs on Broadway.
1951	Works on 4th OH assignment, *Climb High*, an original story about a young actor in NY.	First violin lessons. April 14: Brother, Julian Lloyd Webber, born.	*The King and I*, *Paint Your Wagon*, *A Tree Grows in Brooklyn*, *Top Banana* (burlesque).	Porter's *Kiss Me, Kate*; Novello's *Gay's the Word*; Vivian Ellis's *And So to Bed*.	Electric power from atomic energy. Cinerama developed. Britain begins rating system for films. *The Archers*, sitcom. Johnny Ray is the sensation.

1952	Summer: Collaborates with Mary Rodgers on musical for TV, *The Lady or the Tiger?* (never produced). Autumn: George Oppenheimer engages him to assist in writing the *Topper* TV series. Together in LA they write 29 shows.	Enrolled at Weatherby School. Studies piano with his mother; prefers to make up his own music rather than perfect accepted repertoire.	*Call Me Madam, Zip Goes a Million,* and British hit *Bet Your Life* (adapted from *Brewster's Millions*).	McCarthyism. Contraceptive pill is developed. *The Mousetrap* opens. Chaplin's *Limelight* released.
1953	Writes score for *Saturday Night.*		A disappointing season, the only sure-fire successes being *Kismet, Wonderful Town,* and Porter's *Can-Can.*	From the US: *Guys and Dolls, Paint Your Wagon, The King and I,* and holdovers *Porgy and Bess* and *Carousel.* Two superb British shows: *The Boy Friend* and *Salad Days.*	Elizabeth II's coronation. Death of Stalin. Korean armistice. Rosenbergs executed.
1954			Small shows like *The Threepenny Opera, The Boyfriend,* and *The Golden Apple* vie with extravaganzas like *Pajama Game* and *House of Flowers.*	*Can-Can* and *Wedding in Paris.*	Salk polio vaccine developed. The H-bomb. High court bans segregation. End of Korean War. McCarthy censured.
1955	Spring: Lemuel Ayres, producer of *Saturday Night,* dies. The musical is abandoned. October: SS chosen as co-lyricist for Bernstein-Laurents-Robbins *West Side Story,* eventually winds up as full lyricist.		Wholesome, homespun shows like *Plain and Fancy* vie with sexy ones like *Damn Yankees* and *Silk Stockings.*	*The Pajama Game, The Water Gypsies.*	Age of rock is born. The Khrushchev era. Churchill steps down. US launches satellite. Peron overthrown.
1956	Writes incidental music for play *The Girls of Summer.* Starts on *A Funny Thing.*	Enters Westminster Underschool.	*My Fair Lady,* a landmark musical. The almost through-sung musical arrives: *The Most Happy Fella* and *Candide.* Also a snappy revue from London, *Cranks.*	*Fanny* and *Grab Me a Gondola.*	Elvis Presley tops all the charts. Eisenhower wins second term. The Hungarian revolt. Maria Callas takes Milan and New York by storm.

Year	Sondheim	Lloyd-Webber	US Musicals	UK Musicals	World
1957	September 26: *West Side Story* premieres on Broadway.		*The Music Man* (wins the Tony). Also Lerner & Loewe's film *Gigi* and TV special by Rodgers & Hammerstein: *Cinderella*.	*Damn Yankees* and *Bells Are Ringing*.	Shake-up in the Kremlin. Sputnik. Eisenhower Doctrine. Little Rock. Ford introduces the Edsel. Civil rights legislation passes in US.
1958	Begins writing lyrics for *Gypsy* (music by Jule Styne).	Writes *Ancient Monuments in the Home Counties*, a monograph illustrated with postcards.	*The Body Beautiful* (the debut of Bock & Harnick). Other shows are *Goldilocks, Flower Drum Song*, and *La Plume de ma Tante*.	British inventions: *Valmouth, Irma la Douce*, and *Expresso Bongo*. *West Side Story* and *My Fair Lady* from US.	Folk music vogue begins with Kingston Trio's "Tom Dooley." DeGaulle is Premier of France. Alaska is US 49th state. Best-sellers: *Lolita, Doctor Zhivago*.
1959	May 21: *Gypsy* opens on Broadway.	Rewrites *Ancient Monuments*, prices and sells some copies. Opus 1: "The Toy Theatre Suite" (six short pieces published in the magazine *Music Teacher*).	A banner year that includes *Sound of Music, Redhead, Fiorello, Destry Rides Again, Once Upon a Mattress*.	*The World of Paul Slickey*.	Hawaii becomes the 50th state. Castro takes Havana. Soviet Lunik III strikes the moon.
1960	Plans to musicalize *The Madwoman of Chaillot* starring the Lunts. Project dropped.		Another banner year: *Bye Bye Birdie, The Fantasticks, The Unsinkable Molly Brown, Wildcat*.	Lionel Bart's *Oliver!*; also *Lilly White Boys*.	Princess Margaret marries A. Armstrong-Jones. J. F. Kennedy is elected President of US. "The Twist" dance sweeps US. Isaac Stern leads campaign to rescue Carnegie Hall from destruction.
1961	Begins work on *Anyone Can Whistle*. Writes incidental music for play, *Invitation to a March*. Film version of *West Side Story* released.	Writes music for school show, *Cinderella Up the Beanstalk (and most everywhere else!)*, with lyrics by Robin St. Clare Barrow.	*Carnival*, Jerry Herman's first hit. *Milk and Honey*; also *How To Succeed in Business Without Really Trying*.	*Stop The World—I Want To Get Off* (Anthony Newley).	Soviet cosmonaut Gagarin orbits earth. Berlin Wall erected. Martial law declared in Alabama. Elvis records still top best-sellers. Nureyev defects to the West. Fashion copies Mrs. Kennedy.

1962	May 8: *Forum* opens on Broadway, wins award as best musical. Writes score for mini-musical, *Passionella*.	With same collaborator writes music for *Utter Chaos or No Jeans for Venus*. Wins scholarship for Queen's Scholars entitling him to become boarding student and leaves home. Signs contract with Noel Gay Organization for songs.	*No Strings* (Rodgers writes both words and music).	*Vanity Fair, Blitz* (Lionel Bart); Coward's *Sail Away*.	John Glenn orbits Earth. US stock market plunges in largest drop since 1929. Marilyn Monroe dies of overdose. Cuban missile crisis.
1963	Film of *Gypsy* released. *Forum* opens in London.	Writes and records his first song, "Make Believe Love" (never released).	Few good shows, but *Oliver!*, a London import, and *She Loves Me* (Bock & Harnick's gem) are outstanding.	*Half a Sixpence; Mr. Pickwick; Oh, What a Lovely War*	John Kennedy is assassinated. Johnson becomes president. Top recordings by Beatles, Peter, Paul and Mary; also "Little Stevie Wonder." Pop Art: Andy Warhol.
1964	April 4: *Anyone Can Whistle*. Closes on April 11, but cast is reassembled for a recording.	June 10: Writes and produces *Play the Fool*, his last Westminster show. Performs two satirical songs at "Midnight Cabaret," "Where There's a Will" (a parody of Shakespeare) and "Ever So Romantic," a jibe at Barbara Cartland. December: his paper on Victorian architecture wins him a scholarship to Oxford.	*Hello, Dolly, Funny Girl*, and *Fiddler on the Roof* are smash hits, but the Coward-Martin-Gray *High Spirits* is an interesting failure.	*Lock Up Your Daughters; Maggie May. Robert and Elizabeth*, based on *The Barretts of Wimpole Street*, is a great success and runs 2 years.	Harold Wilson is elected British prime minister. Beatles in US debut. Civil Rights Act passes. Johnson elected president. US planes bomb North Vietnam.
1965	March 18: *Do I Hear A Waltz?* (music Rodgers), Broadway premiere. Fall: Completes first draft of *The Girls Upstairs* (later *Follies*).	April 25: First meeting of Rice and ALW. December: Decides to take leave of absence from Oxford and work full time with Rice. Moves back home, Rice rents room in their flat.	*Half a Sixpence* (from London); *Man of La Mancha; On a Clear Day* (Lerner-Lane).	*Charlie Girl* is a big hit (2202 performances). *Divorce Me, Darling, The Passion Flower Hotel, Twang*.	First combat troops land in Vietnam. Medicare bill passes. Horowitz returns to concert stage. Presley, Beatles, Rolling Stones top recording charts.

Year	Sondheim	Lloyd-Webber	US Musicals	UK Musicals	World
1966	November 16: *Evening Primrose*, TV play with music. Lyric to "The Boy From . . ." (music Mary Rodgers).	First show, *The Likes of Us*, announced in press for autumn but never produced.	Not many musicals, but every one produced this year becomes a classic: *Sweet Charity, Mame, Cabaret, I Do, I Do.*	American imports.	Floods damage Florence. Mao's Cultural Revolution. Johnson's "Great Society." Film: *A Man for All Seasons.* Novel: *Valley of the Dolls.* Jimi Hendrix helps popularize the electric guitar.
1967		April: With Rice, two songs recorded for EMI. November: Two more, "1969" (melody taken from Beethoven) and "Probably on Thursday" (melody taken from Dvořák). 1967–68 school year: Enrolls in Royal College of Music to study orchestration.	*Hallelujah, Baby* (Styne, Comden & Green) and other mediocrities.	*The Four Musketeers; Annie.*	Stalin's daughter defects to West. Nasser closes Aquaba Gulf to Israeli ships. First heart transplant. Flower children generation. Fashion model Twiggy arrives in New York.
1968	August: Writes lyrics to music by L. Bernstein for *A Pray by Blecht.* After 3 months drops the project.	March 1: *Joseph and the Amazing Technicolor Dreamcoat* premieres at Colet Court. May 12: Expanded, revised, reorchestrated version premieres at Westminster School. November 9: Performed at St. Paul's Cathedral.	Spoofs: *Your Own Thing* and *Dames at Sea* vie with second-rate shows like *Zorba* and *Promises, Promises.* But *Hair* and *Jacques Brel* are outstanding.	Mostly American shows except for *Canterbury Tales* (2082 performances).	Martin Luther King and Robert F. Kennedy are assassinated in US. November: Nixon elected US president. Hit records by Johnny Cash, 5th Dimension, Herb Alpert, Simon & Garfunkle, and Glen Campbell.
1969		January: Recording of *Joseph* released. November 21: Recording of *Superstar* (single) released in UK. December 1: Record released in US.	*1776,* a hit, and *Dear World,* an interesting failure, among unsuccessful versions of old novels, old movies, old plays: *Georgy, Gantry, La Strada, Billy* (Budd), *Canterbury Tales.*	*Anne of Green Gables, A Tale of Two Cities, Ann Veronica,* and *Belle Starr*—lavish flops.	Astronauts walk on the moon. De Gaulle resigns. Film: *Midnight Cowboy* wins all the awards. Hit albums: *Hair, Abbey Road* (Beatles), *Blood Sweat and Tears.*

1970	April 26: *Company*, Broadway premiere. Music to "Hollywood and Vine" (lyric George Furth).	January: Meets Sarah Jane Tudor Hugill. October: Complete album (double) *Jesus Christ Superstar* released in UK and US. December: Travels to Italy with Sarah Jane.	*Purlie; Applause; Company; Oh, Calcutta.* Rodgers & Charnin's *Two by Two* stars Danny Kaye.	*The Great Waltz; Catch My Soul; Oh, Calcutta.*	Kent State student riots. Airline hijacking. Nasser dies, Sadat takes over. Betty Friedan leads US feminist march. Burt Bacharach and soft rock pop. Religious trend enters pop recordings.
1971	April 4: *Follies*, Broadway premiere.	July 12: First touring company of *Superstar* launched July 24: Marries Sarah Jane Hugill. October 12: *Jesus Christ Superstar* premieres on Broadway.	*Godspell; His Monkey Wife* (Sandy Wilson); *Ambassador; Popkiss.* From the US: *Gypsy* opens in UK at last.	*Jesus Christ Superstar* (Rice-Webber) and Schwartz's *Godspell* are successful examples of the religious musical now in vogue.	Communist China admitted to UN. Britain will enter Common Market. Voting age in US changed to 18. Bernstein's *Mass* premieres. James Levine debuts at Metropolitan Opera. Top of the charts in US: George Harrison, Janis Joplin, Carole King, Santana.
1972	*Forum* is revived and is now a great success.	August 9: *Superstar* opens at Palace Theatre in London and runs 8 years. October: *Joseph* is given a stage presentation in London.	*Tom Brown's School Days; Gone with the Wind* (music by Harold Rome).	*Grease* and *Sugar.* Very slim pickings.	Last US ground troops leave Vietnam. Break-in at Democratic headquarters. Nixon wins landslide victory. Films: *The Godfather, Cabaret, Last Tango in Paris, Deep Throat.* Top single: Roberta Flack's "The First Time Ever I Saw Your Face."
1973	February 25: *A Little Night Music*, Broadway premiere. *The Last of Sheila* (film), written by SS and Anthony Perkins. *Gypsy*, starring Angela Lansbury gets its London premiere.	Webber family moves from Harrington Court to Sussex Mansions. February: *Joseph* opens in the West End.	*Cowardy Custard* (Noël Coward revue). *The Rocky Horror Show; The Card* (Tony Hatch).	*Seesaw; Raisin.*	Watergate hearings begin. Syria and Egypt attack Israel. US Vice President Agnew resigns. Military retakes power in Greece. Leonard Bernstein delivers the Norton Lectures at Harvard. Album: *Goodbye, Yellow Brick Road* (Elton John). Elvis divorces Priscilla.

Year	Sondheim	Lloyd-Webber	US Musicals	UK Musicals	World
1974	March 8: Writes additional lyrics for a new production of Bernstein's *Candide*. May 20: *The Frogs*, Yale swimming pool. Incidental music for play *The Enclave*. Musical score for *Stavisky*. *Gypsy* (revival) opens in New York.		*Over Here* (return of the Andrews Sisters); *Candide* (rewritten and restaged); *The Magic Show*. *Mack and Mabel*, one of Jerry Herman's best, is a failure.	Mostly US imports except *Billy Liar* (Barry-Black); *Good Companions*.	Nixon resigns. Haile Selassie is deposed in Ethiopia. Solzhenitsyn is deported from USSR. 55-mile-per-hour speed limit enacted in US. *All in the Family* top TV show. "Streaking" becomes a fad. Disaster and supernatural films popular.
1975	April 21: *A Little Night Music* premieres in London.	April 22: *Jeeves* (book and lyrics by Alan Ayckbourn) premieres in London. Summer: With Rice in Biarritz, begins writing *Evita*.	*The Wiz* (soul-tinged score); *Shenandoah* (folklike); *Chicago* (Kander-Ebb); *A Chorus Line* (Bennett-Hamlisch-Kleban); *Treemonisha* (Scott Joplin).	*The Black Mikado*.	Saigon falls to North Vietnam. US and Soviet spacecrafts link up. Best-selling novels: *Ragtime*, *Looking for Mr. Goodbar*. New dances include "The Hustle," "The Bump," and "The Robot."
1976	January 11: *Pacific Overtures*, Broadway premiere. Song ("I Never Do Anything Twice") for film, *The Seven Percent Solution*.	October: First private showing of *Evita*. Recording released, which immediately tops charts. December 30: *Joseph* opens at the Brooklyn Academy, N.Y. Daughter, Imogen, born.	*Rex* (Rodgers-Harnick); *Bubbling Brown Sugar*.	*Side by Side by Sondheim*; *Mardi Gras* (Melvyn Bragg); *Teeth and Smiles*; *Leave Him to Heaven*; *Liza of Lambeth*.	Chinese president Chou En-Lai dies; also Mao Tse-Tung. Satellite lands on Mars. Concorde begins regular trans-Atlantic service. Jimmy Carter wins US presidency. US and Iran sign $10 billion arms sale. Film: *Rocky*.
1977	April 18: *Side by Side by Sondheim*, Broadway premiere. Begins writing *Sweeney Todd*.	First performances of *Variations* at Sydmonton.	*Annie* is a hit of gigantic proportions. *The Act*, a Kander & Ebb piece written for Liza Minnelli.	*Privates on Parade*; *The Point*; *Maggie*; *Elvis*; *The Magic Man*.	Carter grants amnesty to Vietnam draft evaders. US & Panama sign treaties. Alex Haley's *Roots* draws largest TV audience (130 million) in history. Film: *Annie Hall*. Top Record: *Rumours* (Fleetwood Mac). Tolkien's *Silmarillion* sells over 1 million copies in 3 months.

1978	January 3: *Variations* (on *Paganini Theme*) released. June 21: With Hal Prince directing, *Evita* opens (London). November: Son, Nicholas, born.	*I Love My Wife* and *On the 20th Century*, both hits with music by Cy Coleman. *Dancin'*; *Ain't Misbehavin'* a great success.	*Bar Mitzvah Boy* (John Barry and Don Black).	March on Washington for ERA. 900 cult members commit suicide in Guyana. Atlantic City legalizes gambling. Top Album: *Saturday Night Fever*.
1979	March 1: *Sweeney Todd*, Broadway premiere.	May 8: *Evita* opens in Los Angeles. September 25: *Evita* on Broadway. September: Sydmonton premiere of *Tell Me on a Sunday*.	*Carmelina*.	US and China establish diplomatic relations. Margaret Thatcher is elected British prime minister. Mountbatten assassinated. Russia invades Afghanistan. Height of disco craze. Film: *Kramer vs. Kramer*. Top album: *Bad Girls* (Donna Summer).
1980	October 29: *Marry Me a Little*, off-Broadway premiere.	*Sugar Babies*; *Woman of the Year*.	*Tom Foolery* (Tom Lehrer); *Colette* (John Dankworth).	US breaks off diplomatic ties with Iran. Ronald Reagan elected US president. John Lennon shot dead in NYC.
1981	November 16: *Merrily We Roll Along*, Broadway premiere.	May 11: *Cats* (London).	US shows predominate, except British, *The Mitford Girls*.	US-Iran agreement frees hostages. Reagan, Pope John Paul are wounded by gunmen. First woman appointed to US Supreme Court.
1982	February: *Joseph* opens at the Royale Theatre on Broadway. April: *Song and Dance* premieres (London). October 7: *Cats* (Broadway). October 29: Father, William, dies.	*Dreamgirls*; *Nine*; *A Doll's Life*.		British overcome Argentina in Falklands war. Princess Grace dies in auto crash. Beginning of the age of the mega-musical.

Year	Sondheim	Lloyd-Webber	US Musicals	UK Musicals	World
1983		July 2: Separates from Sarah Tudor Hugill Webber.	*Baby*; *La Cage aux Folles*; *My One and Only* (Gershwins' *Funny Face* outfitted with a new libretto).	*Blood Brothers*, a solid hit; *Jean* (Seburg), music by Marvin Hamlisch; *Blondel* (lyrics by Tim Rice).	New Roman Catholic code. US invades Grenada.
1984	May 2: *Sunday in the Park with George*, Broadway premiere.	March 22: Marries Sarah Brightman. March 27: *Starlight Express* (London). Summer: First draft of *Requiem*. October: First sketches of *Phantom*.	*The Rink* (Kander & Ebb); *The Tap Dance Kid*.	*The Hired Man*.	Soviets withdraw from summer Olympic games. Reagan and Bush re-elected. Indira Gandhi assassinated. Toxic gas leaks from Union Carbide plant in Bhopal, India, killing 2,000 and injuring 150,000.
1985		February 24: *Requiem* premieres in NY at St. Thomas Episcopal Church. April 21: *Requiem* at Westminster Abbey. September 18: *Song and Dance* (Broadway).	A fallow year on Broadway. *Grind* brings some freshness, but *Big River*, although showing little merit, wins the Tony.	*Mutiny on the Bounty* (spectacular flop). *Les Misérables* and *Time* are hits.	Gorbachev elected to take helm of USSR. Italian government toppled by political crisis.
1986		June 18: *Cricket* (lyrics by Tim Rice). October 9: *Phantom* (London).	*Me and My Girl* (another British import).	*Chess* (Tim Rice and ABBA); *Charlie Girl* (revival).	Spain and Portugal join Common Market. Britain and France plan Channel Tunnel. Space shuttle *Challenger* explodes after launch, killing all aboard. In Philippines, Marcos out, Aquino in.
1987	November 5: *Into the Woods*, Broadway premiere.	March 15: *Starlight Express* (Broadway).	*Les Misérables*.	*Groucho*.	AZT approved for treating AIDS. Waldheim, Austrian president, banned from entering US. Iraqi missiles attack US frigate in Persian Gulf. Prime Minister Thatcher elected for third term. Severe earthquake strikes LA.

1988		January 26: *Phantom* (Broadway).			US Congress overrides Reagan veto of Civil Rights bill. Bush and Quayle are elected by a landslide. Pan Am plane explodes from terrorist bomb, 247 die.
1989		April 17: *Aspects of Love* (London).	*Black and Blue*; *Grand Hotel.*	*Miss Saigon*; *Metropolis* (a huge flop).	Emperor Hirohito of Japan dies. Ayatollah Khomeini declares author Salman Rushdie's book offensive and sentences him to death. Berlin Wall topples.
1990	March: *Sunday in the Park with George* (London). September: *Into the Woods* (London).	April 8: *Aspects of Love* (Broadway). Divorces Sarah Brightman.	*City of Angels*; *Falsettos.*	*King* (with Simon Estes).	South Africa frees Nelson Mandela. End of the Cold War. Iraqi troops invade Kuwait. East and West Germany reunited. Thatcher resigns as PM of Britain; John Major succeeds her.
1991	January 27: *Assassins*, off-Broadway premiere.	February: Marries 27-year-old Madeline Guerdon. Sets a world record with six shows running simultaneously in London.	*Will Rogers Follies*; *Crazy for You*; *Guys and Dolls* (revival).	*Five Guys Named Moe.*	South African schools integrated. US and allies defeat Iraq. Unrest in Yugoslavia. Britain scraps unpopular poll tax. Gorbachev resigns; end of Communist party; breakup of Soviet Union.
1992	*Dick Tracy* (film) released. Refuses the National Endowment for the Arts Medal, saying that the NEA is "a symbol of censorship." His mother, Janet ("Foxy"), dies.	May 3: Son, Alistair Adam, born.	*Jelly's Last Jam*; *Kiss of the Spider Woman.*	*Grand Hotel*; *The Blue Angel*; *Spread a Little Happiness* (revival).	November: Bill Clinton elected US president. Fiber optic phones. Fax is common.

Year	Sondheim	Lloyd-Webber	US Musicals	UK Musicals	World
1993	March: *Putting It Together* (revue based on SS songs).	July 12: *Sunset Boulevard* (London). August 23: Son, William, born. December 2: *Sunset Boulevard* opens (Los Angeles). December 7: His mother, Jean Lloyd Webber, dies.	*Annie Warbucks; Kiss of the Spider Woman.*	*City of Angels; Crazy for You; Carousel* (revival).	Rise of the Internet. The Waco, Texas, siege. NAFTA agreement. Clinton signs Brady Bill. Toni Morrison wins Nobel Prize for Literature.
1994	April 23: *Passion*, Broadway premiere.	July 26: *Sunset Boulevard* closes in Los Angeles. November 17: *Sunset Boulevard* opens on Broadway.	*Hello, Again; Beauty and the Beast; Carousel* (revival).	*She Loves Me* (revival).	Major earthquake in Los Angeles. The O. J. Simpson case. Republican landslide in US mid-term elections.
1995	*Company* (revival). Film version of *Sweeney Todd*, directed by Tim Burton, announced. Film version of *Into the Woods* announced.	Shooting begins of film of *Evita*. Plans to produce *A Star Is Born* for the stage (an adaptation of the Judy Garland film with a Harold Arlen score).	*Show Boat* (revival); *How to Succeed in Business Without Really Trying* (revival); *Smokey Joe's Café; Victor/Victoria.*	*Mack and Mabel* (revival); *Company* (revival); *A Little Night Music* (revival).	Oklahoma City bombing at Federal Building. The war in Bosnia. Premier of Israel assassinated.
1996	March 17: *Getting Away with Murder*, a comedy-thriller by SS and George Furth (closes March 30). April: *A Funny Thing Happened on the Way to the Forum* (revival). *Passion* (London).	July 2: *By Jeeves* (an almost totally rewritten version of ALW's 1975 musical) opens in London. Working with Hal Prince on musical adaptation of *Whistle Down the Wind.*	*Big; The King and I* (revival); *State Fair* (R & H film adapted for stage); *Rent; Bring in 'da Noise, Bring in 'da Funk; Chicago* (revival).	*Martin Guerre* (Schönberg-Boulbil).	Bill Clinton reelected US president. Prince Charles and Princess Diana agree to divorce. Clinton appoints Madeline Albright as first woman Secretary of State.
1997	Working on *Wise Guys*, a new musical about the Mizner brothers.	February 10: Cancels scheduled Broadway opening of *Whistle Down the Wind*. *Cats* breaks *A Chorus Line* record, becoming longest-running show in Broadway history.	*Ragtime; Jekyll and Hyde; The Lion King; Titanic.*	U.S. imports: *Beauty and the Beast; Chicago* (revival).	Hebron agreement; Israel gives up land. Fighting in Balkans. Stock market reaches new highs. Princess Diana killed in auto crash.

1998	*Follies* revival at Paper Mill Playhouse; *Into the Woods* revival (London).	*Whistle Down the Wind* opens in London. Revival of *Starlight Express* (London).	*The Scarlet Pimpernel*; *Fosse*; *Parade*.	US imports: *Rent*; *Saturday Night Fever*.	General world prosperity. White House sex scandal.
1999	*Putting It Together*, revue of SS songs (revival).		*Saturday Night Fever*; *Footloose*; *Contact*; *Marie Christine*.	*Candide* (revival); *A Saint She Ain't*; *Mamma Mia!*, a collection of ABBA songs.	Russia drives Chechnians out of homeland. Preparations for the Millennium.
2000	*Merrily We Roll Along* (revival in London).	*The Beautiful Game* opens in London.	*The Wild Party*; *Aida*.	*The Witches of Eastwick*; *Singin' in the Rain*.	Contested presidential election; George W. Bush wins the office.

Glossary of Musical, Lyric, and Theatrical Terms

AABA A common song form in which the first theme (usually eight bars in length) is repeated and followed by a contrasting theme. This second statement is followed by a return of the first theme. All the As must be essentially the same; however, their endings may vary.

A1, A2, bridge, A3 A preferred way of referring to the AABA.

Aeolian mode Perhaps the earliest of the Greek modes. The sound can be approximated on our tempered keyboard by playing the white notes from A to A. The Aeolian mode is also know as the pure minor scale, which was in common usage until the middle of the fifteenth century.

Alberti bass Alberti, a contemporary of Mozart, is remembered mostly for the manner in which he broke chords to make them sustain on the harpsichords of his time.

alla breve 4/4 time played rather quickly, so that there are only two counts to the bar. Popular musicians call this "cut time."

anticipation A rhythmic variant in which the melody or chords intended to be sounded on the first beat of the bar are played an eighth or sixteenth note earlier. Anticipation is often used to give a "jazz" feeling.

appoggiatura From the Italian meaning "to lean." A decorative pitch not belonging to the indicated chord, usually approaching its resolution from above. Appoggiaturas create mild dissonance and can add great intensity to a melodic line.

arpeggio From the Italian word for harp, *arpa*. An arpeggio is a chord whose members are sounded individually.

augmented chord A chord whose fifth has been raised a half tone. Augmenteds have a strong pull, and their overuse can become cloying.

beguine A sensual, languid dance said to be of Tahitian origin. Its accent is on the second eighth note (quaver) in the bar.

belting Referring to a woman's using the chest voice rather than letting air pass over the diaphragm to create what is known as a soprano or "head sound."

blue note This flattened 3rd, 5th, 6th, or 7th of the scale when used in conjunction with a major harmony creates a distinctly biting (some consider it melancholy) sound typical of the blues.

bridge The B section of an AABA song. The bridge is usually contrasting in character. It is also known as the release, or channel.

burthen A somewhat pretentious term for chorus or refrain.

cadence A series of chords leading to a conclusion. The typical interminable, and sometime laughable, V-I cadence can be found at the end of most Rossini overtures.

chromaticism The use of tones falling outside the prevailing key signature.

circle of chords The natural progression of dominant sevenths to tonics. The series of chords is usually written in circular fashion (see next page):

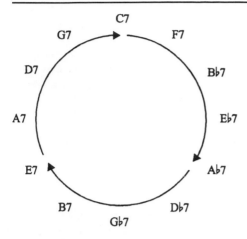

coda An extension. In popular music it is called a tag.

commercial bridge The eight bars of most ordinary releases or bridges are frequently composed of the following chord sequence: I dominant 7, IV, II dominant 7, V. In the key of C this would translate to C7, F, D7, G7. Each chord lasts for two bars.

contrary motion (see motion, contrary)

counterpoint Literally, note against note. The technique of using two or more distinct melodic lines in such a way that they establish a harmonic relationship while retaining their linear individuality.

crotchet The British term for quarter note.

cut time (see alla breve)

cycle of chords (see circle of chords)

diminished cliché My own term for a series of four chords comprising the tonic (I), a diminished seventh (usually built on the tonic or the lowered supertonic (I dim or #I dim), the minor supertonic (II), and the dominant (V). These four chords are as common in popular music as the I, VI, II, V series.

Dorian mode A Greek scale popular in medieval music. It encompasses the white notes on the keyboard from D to D.

dummy lyrics/tune Impermanent lyrics or melody line that will be changed eventually. Dummy lyrics are usually used in composing a song and are inserted so as not to impede the artistic flow.

footballs musicians' slang for a series of whole notes often found in orchestral harmony parts, so named because of their resemblance to the pigskin.

fox-trot A dance that spawned many songs, popular from 1914 to 1925. The dance, which uses a box-step, is always in 4/4 time, often with a hesitation on the third beat of the bar. This dance developed during a period of animal-named popular dances, such as the turkey-trot, monkey-slide, and bunny-hug, and is still a favorite of the older generation.

Gold Record A standard set by the Recording Industry Association of America. To reach this standard, a recording must sell a half million units *and* achieve $1 million in wholesale revenues.

gypsy A show business term for chorus dancer.

hemiola The deceptive change of meter by false accenting. For example, *one* two *three* / one *two* three. Or, as in Bernstein's "America" from *West Side Story: one* two three *four* five six / *one* two *three* four *five* six.

hold book To assist at rehearsal once the actors have memorized their lines. Holding book implies prompting and checking to see that the author's exact lines are spoken.

Ionian mode The Greek mode in most common usage. The Ionian mode is equivalent to our diatonic major scale. On the keyboard it comprises the white notes from C to C.

lead sheet Shorthand to a piano-vocal arrangement. Lead sheets list the essentials: melody, chords (often with non-root bass notes), and lyrics. They give only an approximation of the composer's intentions.

leading tone The seventh note of the scale, so called because it leads smoothly back to the tonic.

legit A shortening of the term *legitimate*, implying proper or operatic singing using resonating head tones rather than chest or "belt" singing.

list song A song whose lyrics comprises a list of items. Examples: *West Side Story*'s

"Gee, Officer Krupke"; Cole Porter's "Let's Do It."

Locrian mode The seventh Greek mode. Locrian mode is rarely used because its tonic triad is a diminished chord. One can approximate it on a keyboard by playing the white notes from B to B.

Lydian mode Ancient Greek mode, approximate on the tempered keyboard by playing the white notes from F to F. Because of the Lydian mode's odd-sounding fourth note, it is generally reserved for humorous music. Paul Dukas's *The Sorcerer's Apprentice* uses this mode for its famous theme.

measure 1) a musical unit divided by a barline. 2) A synonym for *bar*.

melisma The use of more than one pitch on a single literary syllable. Melismatic passages are most often associated with the baroque but are also frequently found in Middle Eastern, Hebraic, and "soul" music (see example of Cole Porter's "Solomon" below).

Mixolydian mode A classic Greek mode that can be approximated on the keyboard by playing the white notes from G to G. This mode is the basis of much Latin music (mambo, samba, and so on).

modality Indicating the use of a scale other than the common major (Ionian mode) or minor (Aeolian mode). *See* Dorian, Locrian, Lydian, Mixolydian, and Phrygian modes.

modulation Changing from one key to another. Modulation is not done to accommodate a singer (*see* transposition), but to create interest or to progress smoothly from one section of a song to another.

motion The movement of melody in relation to the bass. There are three kinds: parallel means the bass and soprano move in the same direction; contrary, as the word would indicate, is movement in opposite directions; and oblique means that one voice

stays on the same pitch while the other moves.

motive (or *motif*) The basic germ of a musical idea. A series of notes set in a rhythm that will be used again and again in various ways throughout the composition.

oblique motion (*see* motion: parallel, contrary, oblique)

one-six-two-five A harmonic pattern usually expressed as I, VI, II, V, indicating a series of chords (tonic, submediant, supertonic, and dominant) upon which countless melodies have been constructed. As the underpinning of songs from "Heart and Soul" to many country and rock songs of the '60s and beyond, this cliché is the granddaddy of them all.

parallel motion (*see* motion, parallel)

pentatonic scale A scale of five notes derived by dividing the octave into five equal parts. It is somewhat approximate on Western keyboards by playing the black keys. Pentatonic scales usually suggest Oriental music to Occidental ears.

Phrygian mode One of the early Greek modes. It can be approximated on a modern keyboard by playing the white notes from E to E.

piano-vocal score The song, before it is orchestrated, as generally performed in the theater, especially in rehearsal. The accompaniment will not always include the melody. Some composers insert instrumental suggestions in piano-vocal scores.

Platinum Record A standard set by the Recording Industry Association of America. To reach this standard, a recording must sell a million units *and* achieve $2 million in wholesale revenues. UK and foreign album sales are not included in these computations.

prosody The wedding of words to music.

So   o- lo-mon   had a   thou-sand wives—

Good prosody coupled with an artist's clear diction will make a lyric understandable.

punch line song A song whose lyric contains a surprise at its conclusion, preferably in its very last syllable. Example: Arthur Siegel's "Guess Who I Saw Today."

quarter note The basic pulse of most popular songs. The British term is "crotchet."

quaver The British term for eighth note.

ragtime A rhythmic style popular between 1890 and 1914, famous for syncopation and anticipation.

range The vocal palette. In popular songs before the '60s this was limited to a tenth (an octave and a third). Show tunes were permitted a somewhat wider latitude, but it was not until works by Bernstein, Bacharach, Sondheim, and Lloyd-Webber, who employed well-trained singers, that a singer's full range was utilized.

refrain The main body of the song, often interchangeable with "chorus."

reprise The custom of repeating a song, often in several parts of a show, in order to make it indelible.

segue Italian for "follow." A musical direction meaning "to proceed to the next section without a pause or break."

semitone A half tone, the next nearest pitch. In the Western musical system, the octave is divided into twelve semitones.

skip A musical interval that is more than a whole step.

sonata allegro form This form has been the backbone of symphonic music since the time of Haydn until the present day. It is the form used for most first movements of sonatas, string quartets, symphonies, and concertos. In brief, it consists of 1) *Exposition*: main theme (masculine theme), second theme (lyric or feminine theme); 2) *Development*; 3) *Recapitulation*, which is a repeat of the Exposition with different key relationships; and 4) *Coda* or ending.

spotting In the creation of a musical, finding the actual spots where songs will be inserted.

story song A song whose narrative is its most important feature. Example: "Frankie and Johnny."

subdominant The fourth degree of the diatonic scale. The subdominant is one of the three principal triads.

supertonic The second note of the diatonic scale.

suspension A non-chord member that formerly had to resolve to a chord member. Contemporary popular music uses suspension more liberally than most harmony books permit and does not oblige them to resolve. The most frequently used suspensions are the fourth and the ninth.

syncopation Misplacing accents that are normally felt on the first and third beats of the bar.

tag An extension to a song, sometimes called a coda.

tessitura The general range of a composition. Songs that remain largely around the top of their range are said to have a high tessitura, those that keep punching out the middle or bottom notes are said to have a low tessitura.

transposition Changing the key of a song or composition. Music is generally transposed to place it within the best possible vocal range of the singer.

tremolo A piano technique popular during the Victorian period. The right hand trembles, breaking the intervals of an octave or a sixth. This technique later became the mainstay of tear-jerking scenes in the old Nickelodeon movies.

triad A basic chord of three notes; two superimposed thirds.

trio The middle section of a song, originally performed in three sections. In contemporary language, this is called an interlude.

tritone The interval of the diminished fifth (or augmented fourth). The tritone was known as the sound of the devil's violin (achieved by retuning) and is assiduously avoided in all exercises in harmony or composition. Example: The first two melodic pitches of Bernstein's "Maria."

underscoring music under dialogue. Underscoring, an effect that the musicals borrowed from the cinema, is often used to heighten an emotional scene.

upbeat A lead-in or pick-up. The beat before the barline or down beat. Upbeat is so named for the position of the conductor's arm.

vamp A repeated chord pattern, usually ad-libbed until the entrance of the solo performer.

verse Before 1960, the mood-setting, expendable introductory section preceding an ABAC or AABA refrain. After 1960, a short refrain, usually one of several.

walker The musicians' union mandates the minimum number of musicians required to play in the pit for a musical. These mini-mums range in number from as many as twenty-six for a large house like the Majestic to as few as three. The term *walker* refers to a musician who walks in, picks up his or her check, but never plays. A clause enacted in 1994 allows the producer to argue the need for a smaller orchestra for "artistic reasons." *Smokey Joe's Café*, which opened in 1995 with a seven-piece band, was the first show to play a theater with a larger (in this case, sixteen) required minimum.

whole tone A full step; two half steps.

whole-tone scale A scale made up of full steps. Only two whole-tone scales are possible in our musical system, one beginning on B and the other beginning on C. All others are repetitions of these.

Bibliography

Agate, James. *Egos. Vols. 1–9.* London: Hamish Hamilton, Gollancz, Harrap, 1932–48.

Aldrich, Richard. *Gertrude Lawrence as Mrs. A.,* New York: Greystone Press, 1954

Alpert, Hollis. *Broadway.* Boston: Arcade–Little Brown, 1991.

Astaire, Fred. *Steps in Time.* London: Heineman, 1959.

Atkinson, Brooks. *Broadway.* New York: Macmillan, 1970.

Banfield, Stephen. *Sondheim's Broadway Musicals.* Ann Arbor: University of Michigan Press, 1995.

Barker, Felix. *The Oliviers.* London: Hamish Hamilton, 1953.

Barrett, Mary Ellin. *Irving Berlin.* New York: Simon and Schuster, 1994.

Bell, Mary Hayley. *Whistle Down the Wind.* New York: E. P. Dutton, 1958.

Bordman, Gerald. *American Musical Revue.* New York: Oxford University Press, 1985.

———. *American Musical Theatre.* New York: Oxford University Press, 1992.

———. *Jerome Kern.* New York: Oxford University Press, 1980.

Bonano, Margaret Wander. *Angela Lansbury.* New York: St. Martin's Press, 1987.

Bowen, Ezra, ed. *This Fabulous Century. 1920–1930.* New York: Time-Life, 1969.

Brahms, Caryl, and Ned Sherrin. *Song by Song.* Bolton: Ross Anderson, 1984.

Briers, Richard. *Coward & Company.* London: Robson Books, 1989.

Brown, Gene. *Show Time.* New York: Macmillan, 1997.

Brown, Peter, with Steven Gaines. *The Love You Make.* New York: McGraw-Hill, 1983.

Burton, Humphrey. *Leonard Bernstein.* New York: Doubleday, 1994.

Citron, Stephen. *The Wordsmiths: Oscar Hammerstein 2nd and Alan Jay Lerner.* New York: Oxford University Press, 1995.

Cochran, Charles. *I Had Almost Forgotten.* London: Hutcheson, 1932.

de Mille, Agnes. *Speak to Me, Dance with Me.* Boston: Little, Brown, 1973.

Edwards, Anne. *Shirley Temple: American Princess.* New York: William Morrow, 1984.

Eells, George. *The Life That Late He Led.* New York: Putnam, 1967.

Engel, Lehman. *The American Musical Theater.* New York: Macmillan, 1975.

Everett, Susan. *London: The Glamour Years, 1919–39.* London: Bison, 1985.

Fordin, Hugh. *Getting to Know Him.* New York: Random House, 1977.

Furia, Philip. *The Poets of Tin Pan Alley.* New York: Oxford University Press, 1992.

Gassner, John. *The Theater in Our Times.* New York: Crown, 1954.

Goldman, William. *The Season.* New York: Harcourt, Brace, 1969.

Gordon, Eric A. *Mark the Music.* New York: St. Martin's Press, 1989.

Gordon, Joanne. *Art Isn't Easy.* New York: Da Capo, 1992.

———, ed. *Stephen Sondheim: A Casebook.* New York: Garland Publishing, 1997.

Gottfried, Martin. *Jed Harris.* Boston: Little Brown, 1984.

———. *Sondheim.* New York: Abrams, 1993.

Gradenwitz, Peter. *Leonard Bernstein.* New York: St. Martin's Press, 1987.

Grafton, David. *Red, Hot and Blue.* Briarcliff Manor, N.Y.: Stein & Day, 1987.

Green, Benny. *A Hymn to Him.* London: Michael Joseph, 1987.

Green, Stanley. *Encyclopedia of the Musical Theatre.* New York: Da Capo, 1984.

———. *Rodgers & Hammerstein Fact Book.* New York: Lynn Farnol Group, 1980.

Hart, Moss. *Act One*. New York: Random House, 1959.

Hawtree, Charles. *The Truth at Last*. London: Butterworth, 1924.

Hirsch, Foster. *Harold Prince and the American Musical Theatre*. New York: Cambridge University Press, 1989.

Holden, Anthony. *Laurence Olivier*. New York: Atheneum, 1988.

Huggett, Richard. *Binkie Beaumont*. London: Hodder & Stoughton, 1989.

Ilson, Carol. *Harold Prince*. New York: Limelight, 1992.

Johnston, Alva. *The Legendary Mizners*. New York: Farrar, Straus & Young, 1953.

Kelly, Kevin. *One Singular Sensation*. New York: Doubleday, 1990.

Kerr, Walter. *Thirty Plays Hath November*. New York: Simon & Schuster, 1969.

Kimball, Robert, ed. *Cole*. New York: Holt, Rinehart & Winston, 1971.

Lahr, John. *Automatic Vaudeville*. New York: Alfred Knopf, 1984.

Laufe, Abe. *Broadway's Greatest Musicals*. New York: Funk and Wagnalls, 1977.

Leiter, Samuel L. *The Great Stage Directors*. New York: Facts on File, 1994.

Lees, Gene. *Singers and the Song*. New York: Oxford University Press, 1987.

Loesser, Susan. *A Most Remarkable Fella*. New York: Donald Fine, 1993.

Logan, Joshua. *Josh*. New York: Dell, 1976.

Mantle, Jonathan. *Fanfare*. London: Michael Joseph, 1989.

Maxwell, Elsa. *The Celebrity Circus*, London: W. H. Allen, 1964.

McKnight, Gerald. *Andrew Lloyd Webber*. New York: St. Martin's Press, 1984.

Meredith, Scott. *George S. Kaufman and His Friends*. New York: Doubleday, 1974.

Morley, Sheridan. *Shooting Stars*. London: Quartet, 1983.

———. *Spread a Little Happiness*. London: Thames & Hudson, 1987.

———. *A Talent to Amuse*. London: Michael Joseph, 1969.

Nichols, Beverley. *The Sweet and Twenties*. London: Weidenfeld & Nicolson, 1958.

Nightingale, Benedict. *Fifth Row Center*. New York: Times Books, 1986.

Nolan, Frederick. *Lorenz Hart*. New York: Oxford University Press, 1994.

Ostrow, Stuart. *A Producer's Broadway Journey*. Westport, Conn.: Praeger, 1999.

Peyser, Joan. *Bernstein*. New York: William Morrow, 1987.

———. *The Memory of All That*. New York: Simon & Schuster, 1992.

Prince, Harold S. *Contradictions*. New York: W. Clement Stone, 1974.

Rockwell, John. *All American Music*. New York: Vintage, 1983.

Rodgers, Richard. *Musical Stages*. New York: Random House, 1975.

Rosenberg, Deena. *Fascinating Rhythm*. New York: Dutton, 1991.

Schwartz, Charles. *Cole Porter*. New York: Dial, 1977.

Secrest, Meryle. *Stephen Sondheim*. New York: Alfred Knopf, 1998.

Suskin, Steven. *Opening Night on Broadway*. New York: Schirmer, 1990.

———. *Show Tunes*. 3rd Ed. New York: Oxford University Press, 2000.

Taylor, Theodore. *Jule*. New York: Random House, 1979.

Teichman, Howard. *George S. Kaufman*. New York: Atheneum, 1972.

Thomas, Bob. *I Got Rhythm! (The Ethel Merman Story)*. New York: Putnam, 1985.

Trewin, J. C. *Theatre Since 1900*. London: Dakers, 1951.

Vargas, Robert, with Baayork Lee, Thommie Walsh. *On the Line*. New York: William Morrow, 1990.

Walsh, Michael. *Andrew Lloyd Webber*. London: Viking-Penguin, 1989.

Webber, Julian Lloyd. *Travels with My Cello*. London: Michael Joseph, 1984.

Wilder, Alec. *American Popular Song: The Great Innovators 1900–1950*. New York: Oxford University Press, 1972.

Wilk Max. *OK, The Story of Oklahoma!* New York: Grove Press, 1993.

Zadan, Craig. *Sondheim & Company*. 2nd Ed. New York: Harper & Row, 1986.

Credits

STEPHEN SONDHEIM

For the following quotations from lyrics and/or music by Stephen Sondheim: All Rights Administered by WB Music Corp. All Rights Reserved. Used by Permission.

From *By George*
"The Reason Why"
Copyright © 1999 by Rilting Music, Inc.

From *The Brass Goddess* (short story)
7-line quotation
Copyright © 1999 by Rilting Music, Inc.

From *Phinney's Rainbow*
"How Do I Know?"
Copyright © 1999 by Rilting Music, Inc.

From *Sweeney Todd*
"The Ballad of Sweeney Todd," "No Place Like London," "Johanna," "The Barber and His Wife," "The Worst Pies in London," "My Friends," "Pirelli's Miracle Elixer"
Copyright © 1978 by Rilting Music, Inc.

From *Pacific Overtures*
"The Advantages of Floating in the Middle of the Sea"
Copyright © 1975 by Rilting Music, Inc.

From *Merrily We Roll Along*
"Our Time," "Good Thing Going," "Opening Doors"
Copyright © 1981 by Rilting Music, Inc.

From *Sunday in the Park with George*
"Sunday in the Park with George," "Sunday," "It's Hot Up Here," "Putting It Together," "Children and Art," "Move On"
Copyright © 1984 by Rilting Music, Inc.

From *Into the Woods*
"Opening—Act One (Part V)," "On the Steps of the Palace," "Opening—Act Two (Part IX)," "Agony," "No One Is Alone"
Copyright © 1987 by Rilting Music, Inc.

From *Assassins*
"Opening (Everybody's Got the Right)," "The Ballad of Guiteau," "How I Saved Roosevelt," "The Ballad of Booth (Part II)," "The Ballad of Booth (Part III)"
Copyright © 1990, 1992 by Rilting Music, Inc.

From *Passion*
"I Read," "I Wish I Could Forget You," "Flashback (Part III)," "Scene 9 (Is This What You Call Love?)," "No One Has Ever Loved Me"
Copyright © 1994 by Rilting Music, Inc.

From *A Little Night Music*
"Send in the Clowns"
Copyright © 1973 by Rilting Music, Inc. (ASCAP)

From *Gypsy*
"Everything's Coming Up Roses"
Words by Stephen Sondheim. Music by Jule Styne.
    Copyright © 1959 by Norbeth Productions, Inc. and Stephen Sondheim.
    Copyright Renewed.
    All Rights Administered by Chappell & Co.

From *Do I Hear a Waltz?*
"What Do We Do? We Fly!"
Music by Richard Rodgers. Lyrics by Stephen Sondheim.
    Copyright © 1965 by Richard Rodgers and Stephen Sondheim.
    Copyright Renewed.
    Williamson Music and Burthen Music Co., Inc., owner of publication and allied rights throughout the world.

ANDREW LLOYD-WEBBER

For the following quotations: Music by Andrew Lloyd-Webber. Lyrics by Tim Rice. International Copyright Secured. All Rights Reserved. Used by Permission.

"Probably on Thursday"
    Copyright © 1967 Peermusic (UK) Limited.
"Kansas Morning"
    Copyright © 1968 Peermusic (UK) Limited.
    All Rights Assigned (1970) to MCA Music Limited.

From *The Likes of Us*
"The Likes Of Us," "Going, Going, Gone"
    Copyright ©1966 Peermusic (UK) Limited.

From *Jesus Christ Superstar*
"Superstar," "Hosanna"
    Copyright © 1970 MCA Music Limited.
From *Evita*
"Requiem for Evita," "A New Argentina," "Lament," "Don't Cry for Me Argentina"
    Copyright © 1976, 1977 Evita Music Limited.
From *Joseph and the Amazing Technicolor Dreamcoat*
"Jacob and Sons," "Poor, Poor Joseph," "Potiphar"
    Copyright © 1969 The Really Useful Group Limited, London.

For the following quotations: Music by Andrew Lloyd-Webber. Lyrics as indicated. International Copyright Secured. All Rights Reserved. Used by Permission.

From *Song and Dance*
"Capped Teeth and Caesar Salad," "Tell Me on a Sunday"
Lyrics by Don Black.
    Copyright © 1979 The Really Useful Group Limited, London, and Dick James Music Limited.

From *Cats*
"Memory"
Text by Trevor Nunn after T.S. Eliot.
    Music copyright © 1981 The Really Useful Group Limited, London.

Text copyright © 1981 Trevor Nunn / Set Copyrights Limited.

From *Starlight Express*
"Poppa's Blues"
Lyrics by Richard Stilgoe.
    Copyright © 1984 The Really Useful Group Limited, London.

From *The Phantom of the Opera*
"Think of Me," "The Music of the Night"
Lyrics by Charles Hart.
Additional lyrics by Richard Stilgoe.

Index

NOTE: Titles in bold refer to films, literary works, plays, and shows; those in italics refer to songs. Figures in italics refer to illustrations.